Macs
ALL-IN-ONE
FOR
DUMMIES®
2ND EDITION

Macs
ALL-IN-ONE
FOR
DUMMIES®
2ND EDITION

by Joe Hutsko

Wiley Publishing, Inc.

Macs All-in-One For Dummies®, 2nd Edition

Published by
Wiley Publishing, Inc.
111 River Street
Hoboken, NJ 07030-5774

www.wiley.com

Copyright © 2010 by Wiley Publishing, Inc., Indianapolis, Indiana

Published by Wiley Publishing, Inc., Indianapolis, Indiana

Published simultaneously in Canada

For general information on our other products and services, please contact our Customer Care Department within the U.S. at 877-762-2974, outside the U.S. at 317-572-3993, or fax 317-572-4002.

For technical support, please visit www.wiley.com/techsupport.

Wiley also publishes its books in a variety of electronic formats. Some content that appears in print may not be available in electronic books.

Library of Congress Control Number: 2009940276

ISBN: 978-0-470-53798-5

Manufactured in the United States of America

10 9 8 7 6 5 4 3 2 1

WILEY

About the Author

Joe Hutsko is the author of *Green Gadgets For Dummies*. Joe lives in Ocean City, New Jersey and blogs about green gadgets for the Green Inc. section of *The New York Times*. For more than two decades, he has written about computers, gadgets, video games, trends, and high-tech movers and shakers for numerous publications and Web sites, including *Macworld, PC World, Fortune, Newsweek, Popular Science, TV Guide, The Washington Post, Wired,* Gamespot, MSNBC, and Salon.com. You can find links to Joe's stories on his tech blog, JOEyGADGET.com.

As a kid, Joe built a shortwave radio, played with electronic project kits, and learned the basics of the BASIC programming language on his first computer, the Commodore Vic 20. In his teens, he picked strawberries to buy his first Apple II computer. Four years after that purchase (in 1984), he wound up working for Apple, where he became the personal technology guru for the company's chairman and CEO. Joe left Apple in 1988 to become a writer and worked on and off for other high-tech companies, including Steve Jobs' one-time NeXT. He authored a number of video game strategy guides, including the bestsellers *Donkey Kong Country Game Secrets: The Unauthorized Edition,* and *Rebel Assault: The Official Insiders Guide.*

Joe's first novel, *The Deal,* was published in 1999, and he recently rereleased a trade paperback edition of it with a new foreword by the author (`tinyurl.com/hutskodeal`).

Dedication

This book is dedicated to three men.

The first two men — Steven P. Jobs and Steve Wozniack — founded Apple, for which millions of other Mac (and iPhone, iPod, and other Apple-created products) users and I are enormously grateful.

The third man is John Sculley, former Apple Chairman and CEO. I worked for John from 1984 to 1988 in a dream job role as his personal technology advisor. Those were great-thinking times John, and I'd work with you again in a New York minute.

Author's Acknowledgments

This (my second *For Dummies*) book wouldn't have my name on its cover if my literary agent, Carole Jelen, hadn't reached out on LinkedIn.com a few summers ago to say hello after we had fallen out of contact since meeting in the 1980s, when I was working at Apple. Thank you, Carole, for pitching me to Wiley acquisition editor Bob Woerner — and thank you, Bob, for saying yes!

Kudos to copy editor Brian Walls for helping me mind my words, grammatically speaking.

Special thanks to Keri Walker of Apple for her always friendly support when it comes to all things Apple products, and to Khyati Shah, for helping me get (and stay) in sync with MobileMe — a many splendored thing!

Super-duper thanks to my good ol' friend Barbara Boyd, for helping me pull off many of the chapters in this book that featured collaborative applications or uses, such as iChat, networking, and a dozen or so others. Thanks, Barbara, for your lifelong friendship, and your "always present" presence — you may live in Rome, but you're never more than a heartbeat away.

Major thanks to every one of my ever-encouraging dear friends, especially Drew Davidson, and to Ric Firmino, David Unruh, David Baron, my cousin Chip McDermott, my brothers Steve and John, and my sister, Janice, and last but never least, my close friend and Monday Night Supper slinging mom, Frances Hutsko.

I'm deeply indebted to eight close friends whose generous support and faith made this book possible (literally!): Susan Godfrey (a.k.a. "E.P."), Lisa Napoli, Linda Williams, Randee Mia Berman, Val Petrosian, Katherine Etzel and Robert Pascale, and my aforementioned mom.

Finally, I'm once again enormously grateful for having the incredibly good fortune of being assigned to project editor Nicole Sholly, for her gently worded yet enormously intelligent guidance, brilliant organization, incisive editing, well-honed instinct, and, above all, tremendous wit and generous sense of humor. Nicole was my editor on *Green Gadgets For Dummies*, and on this mammoth doorstopper of a tome she proved once more to be this author's dream-come-true editor as we worked together to turn the seven minibooks of the first edition of this title into the eight newly updated and revised minibooks you're holding in your hands (or reading on your Kindle). Thank you, Nicole.

Publisher's Acknowledgments

We're proud of this book; please send us your comments at http://dummies.custhelp.com. For other comments, please contact our Customer Care Department within the U.S. at 877-762-2974, outside the U.S. at 317-572-3993, or fax 317-572-4002.

Some of the people who helped bring this book to market include the following:

Acquisitions, Editorial, and Media Development

Project Editor: Nicole Sholly

Executive Editor: Bob Woerner

Copy Editor: Brian Walls

Technical Editor: Dennis Cohen

Editorial Manager: Kevin Kirschner

Editorial Assistant: Amanda Graham

Sr. Editorial Assistant: Cherie Case

Cartoons: Rich Tennant
(www.the5thwave.com)

Composition Services

Project Coordinator: Sheree Montgomery

Layout and Graphics: Carl Byers

Proofreader: Cynthia Fields

Indexer: BIM Indexing & Proofreading Services

Publishing and Editorial for Technology Dummies

    Richard Swadley, Vice President and Executive Group Publisher

    Andy Cummings, Vice President and Publisher

    Mary Bednarek, Executive Acquisitions Director

    Mary C. Corder, Editorial Director

Publishing for Consumer Dummies

    Diane Graves Steele, Vice President and Publisher

Composition Services

    Debbie Stailey, Director of Composition Services

Contents at a Glance

Table of Contents

Book II: Beyond the Basics 161

Introduction

Whether you're a beginner, an intermediate user, or a seasoned computer expert, you can find something in *Macs All-in-One For Dummies,* 2nd Edition, for you. This book is divided into eight minibooks so you can focus on the topics that interest you and skip over the ones that don't. Eventually, you might want more detailed explanations on specific topics than this book can provide — that's when you should look into a more specialized *For Dummies* book. But if you need a quick introduction to get you started on a smorgasbord of topics related to using a Mac, this book can answer your questions, steer you in the right direction, and lead you gently on your way.

About This Book

This book focuses on the basics for all the aspects of using a Mac, from turning it on and using the mouse to connecting your Mac in a network to organizing your digital pictures and videos to create photo albums and home movies with fancy captivating special effects to . . . you get the idea.

This book also shows you how to use and take advantage of Apple's iWork suite, which provides a word processing and desktop publishing program, a presentation program, and a spreadsheet program for calculating formulas and displaying your data as 3D charts. Whether you use a Mac for work, school, or just for fun, you'll find that, with the right software applications, your Mac can meet all your computing needs.

If you're migrating to a Mac from a Windows desktop or notebook PC, this book can show you how to install Windows on your Mac so you can run your favorite Windows programs. By running Windows on a Mac, you can turn your Mac into two computers for the price of one.

If you're new to the Mac, you'll find this book introduces you to all the main features of your Mac. If you're already a Mac user, you'll find information on topics you might not know much about. After reading this book, you'll have the foundation and confidence to move on to more advanced books, or delve deeper into your Mac's bundled applications and others you can buy by experimenting on your own.

Foolish Assumptions

In writing this book, I made a few assumptions about you, dear reader. To make sure we're on the same page, I assume that:

✦ You know something, but not necessarily a whole lot, about computers and you want to find out the basics of using a Mac or doing more with your Mac than you are already.

✦ You have at least a general concept of this wild and crazy thing called the Internet, or more accurately, the phenomena known as the Web.

✦ You'll turn to the introductory chapters if you find yourself scratching your head at such terms as *double-click, drag and drop,* and *Control-click* — or any other terms that sound like things I think you should know but you don't.

✦ You appreciate the speed at which technology-based products like the Mac and the programs you can run on it can change in as little as a few months, with newer, sleeker, faster models and application versions replacing previous versions.

✦ You acknowledge that it's up to you to go on the Web to find updated information about the products described throughout this book.

✦ You know that keeping up with the topic of all things high-tech and Mac (even as a full-time job, as it is for me) still can't make a guy the be-all and end-all Mac Genius of the World. You will, therefore, alert me to cool stuff you discover in your Mac odyssey so that I can consider including it in the next edition of this book.

✦ You're here to have fun, or at least try to have fun, as you dive into The Wonderful World of Mac.

Conventions Used in This Book

To help you navigate this book efficiently, I use a few style conventions:

✦ Terms or words that I *truly* want to emphasize are *italicized* (and defined).

✦ Web site addresses, or URLs, are shown in a special monofont typeface, `like this`.

✦ Numbered steps that you need to follow and characters you need to type are set in **bold**.

✦ *Control-click* means to hold the Control key and click the mouse. If you're using a mouse that has a left and right button, you can right-click instead of Control-click.

What You Don't Have to Read

You don't have to read anything that doesn't pertain to what you're interested in. In fact, you can even skip one or more chapters entirely. I hope you don't skip too many, though, because I think some of the chapters you think you might not be interested in might surprise you and be interesting after all.

That said, if you're absolutely, totally, one-hundred percent new to computers, I suggest you read (or at least scan) the first part, and then move on to the parts you're interested in reading in any order you want.

As for the occasional sidebar you encounter in this book, feel free to ignore them because they contain, for the most part, tangential thoughts, miniature essays, or otherwise forgettable blathering that you're just as likely to forget anyway after you read them. Ditto for any of the text you see alongside the Technical Stuff icon.

How This Book Is Organized

Don't be afraid of this book because of its hefty bulk. You won't necessarily need (or want) to read this whole thing from cover to cover, and that's fine. Think of this book more as a reference along the lines of an encyclopedia or a dictionary than step-by-step operating instructions that require you to read every page.

To help you find just the information you need, this book is divided into eight minibooks where each minibook tackles a specific topic independent of the other minibooks. Any time you have questions, just flip to the minibook that covers that particular topic.

Each minibook introduces a specific topic, and then gives you the basics to doing the focus of that particular minibook. Here's a brief description of what you can find in each minibook:

Book 1: Mac Basics

This minibook explains everything you need to know just to use your Mac, such as how to turn it on and off, how to use the mouse and keyboard, and how to interact with the Mac user interface. Even if you're familiar with using a Mac, you might want to skim through this minibook to pick up tidbits of information you might not know.

Book II: Beyond the Basics

This minibook is the one to read if you want to go beyond the basics and do more with your Mac, such as run Dashboard widgets to keep up on the latest weather, news, or your horoscope with the touch of a button, or back up your Mac with Time Machine so you're important information and programs are always safe and sound.

Book III: Your Mac as Your Entertainment Center

This minibook is all about using your Mac in the most entertaining non-business ways, such as organizing digital photographs, listening to audio files of your favorite songs, and watching movies and videos. In this minibook, you also get a tour of some exciting Mac games, as well as typing tutor programs that can help you increase your words-per-minute rate on your Mac's keyboard.

Book IV: Online Endeavors and Safety

This minibook explains how to connect your Mac to the Internet and what you can do after you're connected. This minibook gives you the basics of using the Safari Web browser, using e-mail with the Mail program, using iChat to conduct video conferences, and taking steps to protect your Mac from online security threats, such as junk e-mail and malicious software known as malware and viruses.

Book V: iLife

Computers are only as useful as the software they can run, so this minibook explains how to use the iLife suite to store and organize digital pictures and digital videos, edit movies and music you create, and output your creations to the Web or to a DVD you can share with family and friends. You also find out how to create your very own Web site!

Book VI: iWork

If you want to write reports, create presentations, or crunch numbers, this minibook has your name written all over it. From using Keynote to turn out crowd-pleasing presentations loaded with charts and videos to using Numbers to crunch numbers every which way to your heart's delight (and your accountant's) to writing the next *Great American Dummies Book* using Pages, this minibook is all about getting down to business — and having a little fun along the way.

Book VII: Address Book, iCal, and Running Windows

This minibook shows you how to store names and addresses with Address Book, track appointments with iCal, and run Windows programs on your Mac. Windows programs? Yes, you heard right — your Mac is an Equal Opportunity Operating System, and running Windows on your Mac is easy thanks to the Boot Camp program that turns your Mac into two computers in one.

Book VIII: Mac Networking

This minibook explains what you need to know to set up a network of Mac computers so you can share hard drives, folders, and printers with other Mac computers. In this minibook, you also discover how to use your Mac's built-in Bluetooth feature to connect to wireless keyboards and mice, and even your smartphone and other Mac and Windows computers, so you can send information over the air between your Mac and other devices and computers. Look, Ma, no wires!

The Appendix

You can modify existing images by taking pictures with a digital camera and then touching up those pictures in a graphics-editing program. You can also create images from scratch (a time-consuming although not terribly difficult task). The Appendix shows you — in a very quick-and-dirty manner — how to do each.

Icons Used in This Book

To help emphasize certain information, this book displays different icons in the page margins.

The Tip icon points out useful nuggets of information that can help you get things done more efficiently or direct you to something helpful that you might not know.

This icon highlights interesting information that isn't necessary to know but can help explain why certain things work the way they do on a Mac. Feel free to skip this information if you're in a hurry, but browse through this information when you have time. You might find out something interesting that can help you use your Mac.

Watch out! This icon highlights something that can go terribly wrong if you're not careful, such as wiping out your important files or messing up your Mac. Make sure you read any Warning information before following any instructions.

This icon points out some useful information that isn't quite as important as a Tip but not as threatening as a Warning. If you ignore this information, you can't hurt your files or your Mac, but you might miss something useful.

Where to Go from Here

If you already know what type of help you need, jump right to that particular minibook and start reading. If you just want to know more about your Mac, feel free to skip around and browse through any minibook that catches your eye.

For starters, you might want to begin with Book I and find out about the basics of using your Mac. This first minibook will likely show you new or different ways to do something and help you fully take control of your Mac.

No matter what your experience is with the Mac, don't be afraid to explore and keep making new discoveries. While you expand your growing knowledge, you'll find the capabilities of your Mac expand right along with you. If you know what you want to do, your Mac can probably help you, and this book can show you how.

Book I

Mac Basics

The 5th Wave   By Rich Tennant

"I'm ordering our new MacBook. Do you want it left-brain or right-brain oriented?"

Contents at a Glance

Chapter 1: Getting to Know Your Mac

In This Chapter

✔ Identifying your Mac model

✔ Understanding Mac processors

✔ Familiarizing yourself with the parts of your Mac

Apple's Macintosh computer — Mac for short — enjoys the enviable reputation of being the easiest computer to use in the world. Additionally, Macs are dependable, durable, and so beautifully designed, they incite techno-lust in gadget geeks like me, and ordinary "Joes" alike. For those doubly good reasons, you probably won't buy a new Mac to replace your old one because you *have* to, but because you *want* to.

Despite the Mac's legendary reputation for being easy to use, you might find the Mac slightly different from other computers you've used before. Taking a few moments to understand the different types of Macs available can help you understand how your Mac works.

Different Macintosh Models

The Macintosh has been around since 1984, and since that time, Apple has produced a wide variety of Mac models. Although you can still find and use older Macs, chances are good that if you buy a newer Mac, it will fall into one of three categories:

✦ **Desktop:** Mac mini or Mac Pro, which require a separate display.

✦ **All-in-one desktop:** iMac, which sandwiches the display and computer into one.

✦ **Notebook:** MacBook, MacBook Air, or MacBook Pro, which have built-in keyboards, trackpads that work like a mouse at the touch of your fingertip, and bright displays; a "clamshell" design lets you close and tote them in your backpack or messenger bag.

Like today's iMac, the original Mac came with a built-in display, a keyboard, and a mouse. The desktop Mac models also come with a keyboard and mouse, but no display. When you buy a Mac desktop, you can plug in a display you already own, or you can buy a new one, such as Apple's LED Cinema Display. This LED display consumes 30 percent less power than conventional LCD displays, and it lights to full brightness when powered on (without needing time to warm up). What's more, the same LED-type display is standard equipment on every MacBook model.

By understanding the particular type of Mac that you have and its capabilities, you'll have a better idea of what your Mac can do. No matter what the capabilities of your Mac are, chances are good that it will work reliably for as long as you own it.

The Mac mini and Mac Pro

The biggest advantage of both the Mac mini and the Mac Pro are that you can choose the type of display to use and place it anywhere you want on your desk as long as you have a cable that can reach. The Mac mini, however, is small enough to hide under your desk, or situate in a corner of your desktop.

The Mac mini is a lower-priced, consumer version designed for people who want an inexpensive Mac for ordinary uses, such as word processing and writing, sending e-mail, browsing the Web, and playing video games. The Mac Pro is a much higher-priced, professional version with multiple drive bays and lots of expandability, as well as greater graphics and processing capabilities because of its advanced graphics processor and use of multiple processors.

The iMac

The all-in-one design of the iMac is an evolutionary extension of the original — 1984-era — Mac design. The iMac combines the computer with a built-in display and speakers. On new and recent iMac models, it's possible to connect external speakers and a second external display if you want.

The advantage of the all-in-one design of the iMac is that you have everything you need in a single unit. The disadvantage is that if one part of your iMac fails (such as the display, or the internal DVD drive), you can't easily replace the failed part.

The MacBook family

The three portable Mac notebook computers, MacBook, MacBook Air, and MacBook Pro, are the most popular Macintosh models. The MacBook and MacBook Air's 13-inch screens are one-size-fits-all, and the MacBook Pro models come in three screen sizes: 13-inch, 15-inch, and 17-inch. All of the MacBook models run on replaceable rechargeable battery packs or external power.

To make the MacBook Air as thin as a magazine, Apple did not include a built-in DVD drive. An optional external DVD drive, or connecting to another computer to use its DVD drive, are how the MacBook Air can access CDs, DVDs, and software programs on discs. The other MacBook models come with built-in DVD drives. If you need to take your Mac everywhere you go, you can choose from the ultralight MacBook Air, or the company's best-selling MacBook, or one of the higher performance MacBook Pro models.

Previous versions of the MacBook were the iBook, and previous versions of the MacBook Pro were the PowerBook.

The main differences in the three Mac notebooks are price and performance. For the lower price of the MacBook, which weighs 4.5 pounds, you get a notebook designed for typical uses, such as word processing, browsing the Internet, and playing 3D video games, albeit on a smaller-screen scale. Weighing in at a scant 3 pounds, the MacBook Air isn't as fast as the MacBook, yet it carries a higher price — being thin and beautiful ain't cheap. For the highest priced MacBook Pro models, you get faster — and at 5.5 and 6.6 pounds, heavier — notebooks, a choice of 13-inch or larger displays, bigger hard drives, and higher performance graphics capabilities designed for professional uses, such as video, audio, and photo-editing.

Although the MacBook, MacBook Air, and MacBook Pro models all have full-size keyboards, none includes the extra numeric keypad found on most external keyboards or on larger Windows notebooks. Instead of the mouse that comes in the box with every desktop Mac (or Windows computer, for that matter), the MacBooks use a built-in trackpad, which responds to your fingertip when you slide it to move the cursor on the screen.

If you find the keyboard or trackpad of your notebook Mac too clumsy to use, you can always plug an external keyboard and mouse into your notebook.

Understanding Mac Processors

If you're going to write the history of the Mac, you'll probably divide it into three eras. The first Macs used processors from the 68000 series, which served Macs well from 1984 to about 1994. Then came the PowerPC era, which lasted from about 1994 to 2005. Now, fast-forward to the present, where Macs use processors made by Intel. If you have an older Mac, it might use a PowerPC or Intel processor. If you just bought a new Mac, it has an Intel processor.

If you're still using a Mac that uses the 68000 processor, you're using an antique 1980s era computer that might be valuable for historical purposes, but it won't be capable of running any of today's software, including the Mac OS X operating system.

The *processor* acts as the brain of your Mac. A computer is only as powerful as the processor inside. Generally, the newer your computer, the newer its processor and the faster it will run.

Apple stopped using PowerPC processors in 2005 and started using Intel processors, which are the same type of processors used in many Windows PCs. Not only were Intel processors less expensive than PowerPC processors, but they were more powerful. As a bonus, using Intel processors also gave the Mac the ability to run the Microsoft Windows operating system (although dyed-in-the-wool Mac loyalists would wryly consider that a drawback — if not outright blasphemy!).

The type of processor in your Mac can determine the application programs (also known as *software*) your Mac can run. The three types of programs available are

✦ PowerPC programs

✦ Universal binaries

✦ Intel programs

Older Mac programs were designed to run only on Mac computers using the PowerPC processor. However, all newer Mac computers that use Intel processors can also run PowerPC programs by using a built-in feature called Rosetta. When you run a PowerPC program on an Intel Mac, Rosetta tricks the program into thinking it's actually running on a PowerPC processor. As a result, all Intel Macs can run nearly all software originally designed for PowerPC Macs.

Most programs now advertise themselves as *universal binaries,* which means they're designed to run on both PowerPC and Intel processors. Before you buy any software, make sure it can run on your computer. If it's a universal binary, it can run equally well on both PowerPC and Intel Macs.

Because Macs are no longer using the PowerPC processor, it's only a matter of time before almost every Mac will be using an Intel processor. That's why some companies are starting to write programs that run only on Intel Macs. If you have a Mac that uses a PowerPC processor, eventually you won't be able to use the latest software, so you'll be forced to switch to an Intel Mac if you want or need that new software.

To identify the type of processor used in your Mac, click the Apple menu in the upper-left corner of the screen and choose About This Mac. An About This Mac window appears, listing your processor as either PowerPC or Intel, as shown in Figure 1-1.

Figure 1-1:
The About
This Mac
window
identifies
the
processor
used in your
Mac.

PowerPC and Intel processors represent a family of related processors. Some of the PowerPC family of processors include the G3, G4, and G5 PowerPC processors where the G3 is the slowest and the G5 the fastest. The Intel family of processors includes the Core Solo, Core Duo, Core 2 Duo, and Xeon, where the Core Solo is the slowest and the Xeon is the fastest. Every processor runs at a specific speed, so a 2.0 gigahertz (GHz) Core 2 Duo processor will be slower than a 2.4 GHz Core 2 Duo processor (refer to Figure 1-1). If understanding processor types and gigahertz confuses you, just remember that the most expensive computer is usually the fastest — except in the case of the MacBook Air, which costs more and runs slower than the lowest price MacBook.

Identifying the Parts of Your Mac

By looking at your Mac, you can tell whether it's an all-in-one design (iMac), a notebook (MacBook, MacBook Air, or MacBook Pro), or a desktop unit that lacks a built-in screen (Mac mini or Mac Pro). However, looking at the outside of your Mac can't tell you the parts used on the inside. To identify the parts and capabilities of your Mac, follow these steps:

1. **Click the Apple menu in the upper-left corner of the screen and choose About This Mac.**

An About This Mac window appears (refer to Figure 1-1).

2. **Click More Info.**

   A System Profiler window appears.

3. **Click the Hardware option in the Contents category pane on the left to view a list of hardware items.**

   If the list of hardware items (such as Bluetooth, Memory, and USB) already appears under the Hardware category, skip this step.

4. **Click a hardware item, such as Memory or Disc Burning.**

   The right pane of the System Profiler window displays the capabilities of your chosen hardware, as shown in Figure 1-2.

   Don't worry if the information displayed in the System Profiler window doesn't make much sense to you right now. The main idea here is to figure out a quick way to find out about the capabilities of your Mac. Pick through the technical details to find the parts that you understand and search the Internet to look up the details you don't understand.

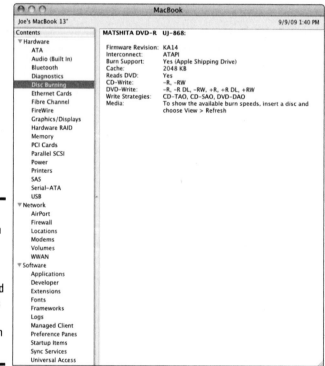

Figure 1-2:
The System Profiler window identifies the type and capabilities of the hardware in your Mac.

5. **When you finish scouting the contents of the System Profiler window, choose System Profiler⇨Quit System Profiler from the menu bar to close the window.**

If you're going to look at anything in the System Profiler window, check out Disc Burning and Graphics/Displays under the Hardware option:

✦ **Disc Burning** tells you all about your DVD/CD–burning hardware, including general info about all the different types of CDs and DVDs your Mac can read and write to, so you'll know exactly which type to buy.

✦ **Graphics/Displays** tells you whether your Mac has a separate graphics card. If you see *shared* in the VRAM category (Video RAM), your Mac doesn't have a separate graphics card and shares the main memory, which means its graphics capabilities will (usually) be slower than a Mac that has a separate graphics card. If you do not see *shared,* the VRAM category simply lists the amount of memory used by the separate graphics card. The more memory, the better your graphics capabilities.

If you have a Mac Pro, you have the option of replacing your graphics card with a better one. If you have any other type of Mac (iMac, MacBook, MacBook Air, MacBook Pro, or Mac mini), your Mac's built-in graphics capabilities cannot be upgraded with a more powerful graphics card.

Chapter 2: Starting Up, Sleeping, and Shutting Down

In This Chapter

✔ **Starting your Mac**

✔ **Putting your Mac in Sleep mode**

✔ **Shutting down a Mac**

*B*efore you can use your Mac, you have to start it up — which makes perfect sense. Now, get ready for the counterintuitive part. After you have your Mac up and running, you can just leave it on. Don't worry about wasting electricity; when not in use, the Mac is smart enough to put itself into a low-energy mode — Sleep mode, to be precise — to burn a minimum of energy.

To adjust the amount of time your Mac sits idle before it goes to sleep, click the Apple menu, choose System Preferences, and then click the Energy Saver icon. To learn more about adjusting your Mac's Energy Saver preferences, check out Book I, Chapter 6.

Now to (kind of) contradict myself. There are times when leaving your Mac on in the wee hours of the morning can actually benefit your Mac's overall performance and usability — sort of the way flossing every night can make for healthier, longer lasting pearly whites. To learn more about exactly what your Mac is up to while you're presumably sleeping, point your Web browser to http://www.osxfaq.com/DailyTips/10-2004/10-04.ws. If, after reading about your Mac's nocturnal habits, you want to make sure yours is awake at the times described in the posting, go to Energy Saver preferences and click the Schedule button to set your Mac to wake at the prescribed hour, as described in the "Adjusting your Mac's Sleep mode and Energy Saver settings" section, later in this chapter. Of course, you'll want to make sure you set your Mac's Energy Saver Schedule setting to put your Mac back to sleep when your Mac is done performing its own version of flossing to minimize unnecessary power consumption and maximize savings on your energy bill.

Turning off your Mac completely when you won't be using it for an extended length of time can extend its useful life, waste less energy, and save you a few bucks on your yearly energy expense to boot — or not to boot, when you think about it.

Shutting down and restarting your Mac can resolve weird situations, such as unresponsive or slow-running programs, because your Mac runs a number of behind-the-scenes file system housekeeping chores every time you start it.

Starting Your Mac

Here's the simple way to start your Mac — the way you'll probably use 99 percent of the time: Press the Power button.

Depending on the type of Mac you have, the power button might be in back (Mac mini and some iMacs), front (Mac Pro and some iMacs), or above the keyboard (on notebook models like the MacBook, MacBook Air, and MacBook Pro).

A few seconds after you press the power button, your Mac chimes to let you know that it's starting. (Techie types say *booting up*, a term derived from the phrase "to lift yourself up by the bootstraps.")

The moment electricity courses through, your Mac's electronic brain immediately looks for instructions embedded inside a special Read-Only Memory (or ROM) chip. While your computer is reading these instructions (also known as *firmware*), it displays a big gray Apple logo on the screen to let you know that the computer is working and hasn't forgotten about you.

The firmware instructions tell the computer to make sure all of its components are working. If some part of your computer (say a memory chip) is defective, your computer will stop. Unless you know something about repairing the physical parts of a Macintosh, this is the time to haul your Mac to the nearest Apple Store or authorized repair shop, or to call Apple Support to arrange shipping your bummed-out Mac directly to Apple for repair (800-275-2273 in the United States).

Sometimes a Mac might refuse to start correctly because of software problems. To fix software problems, check out Book II, Chapter 5, which explains how to perform basic troubleshooting on a Mac.

After your computer determines that all components are working, the last set of instructions on the chip tells the computer, "Now that you know all your parts are working, load an operating system."

When you unpack your Mac and turn it on for the very first time, it asks you to type your name and make up a password to create an account for using your Mac. To guide you through the process of setting up a Mac for the first time, a special program called the Setup Assistant runs, which asks for your time zone, the date, and whether you want to transfer files and programs from another Mac to your newer one. Normally, you need to run through this initial procedure only once, but you also have to perform this procedure if you reinstall your operating system. The most important part of this initial procedure is remembering the password you choose because you'll need it to log in to your account or install new software.

An operating system is the program that controls your computer and is almost always stored on your computer's built-in hard drive (rather than on an external drive). On the Mac, the operating system is named Mac OS X (for Macintosh Operating System number ten) and is followed by a version number, such as 10.6.

Apple code-names each version of OS X. The current version is OS X 10.6 Snow Leopard, which succeeds 10.5 Leopard, which in turn succeeded 10.4 Tiger, which was preceded by 10.3 Panther, and so on.

After the operating system loads and you log in, you can start using your computer to run other programs so you can write a letter or send an e-mail, browse the Web, calculate your taxes, or play a game. (You know, all the things you bought your Mac for in the first place.)

Putting a Mac in Sleep Mode

After you finish using your Mac, you don't have to turn it off and then turn it on when you want to use it again. To save time (and do the "green" thing by conserving energy!), put your Mac into Sleep mode instead. When you put your Mac to sleep, it shuts down almost every power-draining component of your Mac, and draws only a teensy trickle of power so you can instantly wake it up with a touch of the keyboard or click of the mouse. Presto change-o: Your Mac immediately returns to the same state you left it in, without making you wait the minute or more it takes to power on when it's completely shut down.

To put your Mac to sleep, you have a choice of doing it manually or automatically. When you need to be away from your Mac for a short period (such as pouring a second cup of joe), you might want to put your Mac to sleep manually. If you suddenly bolt to the kitchen to tend to a smoking stovetop emergency without putting your Mac to sleep, your Mac can thoughtfully put itself to sleep for you, automatically.

Putting a Mac in Sleep mode manually

To put your Mac to sleep manually, choose one of the following three actions:

+ Choose Sleep.
+ Press the power button (or press Control+Eject) and, when a dialog appears, as shown in Figure 2-1, click the Sleep button (or press the S key on your Mac's keyboard).
+ Press Command+Option+Eject.

Figure 2-1:
If you press the power button, you see a dialog you can use to put your computer in Sleep mode.

> Are you sure you want to shut down your computer now?
>
> Restart   Sleep   Cancel   Shut Down

The Apple menu is located in the upper-left corner of the screen.

To wake a sleeping Mac, click the mouse button or tap any key. To keep from accidentally typing any characters into a currently running program, press a noncharacter key, such as Shift, or one of the arrow keys.

If you have a MacBook, a faster way to put it to sleep is to close its lid. When a MacBook is sleeping, you can safely move it without worrying about jarring the built-in hard disk that spins most of the time your MacBook is "awake" and in use. Open the lid on your sleeping MacBook to wake it up.

Depending on which Mac model you own, you may notice a built-in combination power/sleep indicator light that softly pulses like a firefly when your Mac is in Sleep mode. On my MacBook Air, the power/sleep indicator light is on the front edge below the right wrist rest. On my Mac mini, the indicator light is in the lower-right corner. No such light is anywhere on my iMac, which appears to be totally in the dark when it's asleep.

Adjusting your Mac's Sleep mode and Energy Saver settings

To change your Mac's energy-saving options — such as whether it powers off the hard disk when possible, or how long it waits before entering Sleep mode — you use the Energy Saver Preferences pane.

Because you can't always plan how long you might be away from your Mac, you can make it put itself in Sleep mode after a fixed period — say, ten minutes or so. That way, if your Mac doesn't detect any keyboard or mouse activity within that fixed period, your computer will put itself into Sleep mode automatically.

To make your computer go to sleep automatically, you need to set the *inactivity time* (also known as *idle time*), which defines how long your computer waits before putting itself into Sleep mode. This time can be as short as one minute or as long as three hours. The shorter you define the inactivity period, the sooner your Mac might suddenly go to sleep while you're just staring at the screen.

Optionally, you can specify whether your Mac's display or hard drive (or both) can go to sleep rather than (or before) putting your Mac completely to sleep in Sleep mode. Because the hard drive and the display consume the most power, letting your Mac put at least one or both to sleep can dramatically reduce the amount of power your Mac consumes when it's on and awake.

You can also activate the Energy Saver Schedule option to tell your Mac when to turn itself on or off or enter Sleep mode, based on day and time choices that you set to suit your individual workday, nighttime, and weekend routine.

To adjust your Mac's automatic Sleep mode, whether the display and hard disk can be put to sleep when your Mac is on and still awake, and set a schedule your Mac can follow to automatically wake up and go to sleep, follow these steps:

1. **Click the Apple menu and choose System Preferences.**
2. **Click the Energy Saver icon.**

   The Energy Saver Preferences pane opens.

If you use a MacBook, you see two clickable tabs at the top of the Energy Saver preferences pane: Battery and Power Adapter (see Figure 2-2). Desktop Mac users see two options: Sleep and Options.

If you can't move the sliders or select and deselect the check boxes, the likely reason is that the settings are locked. To unlock the settings so that you can change them, do what it says alongside the tiny lock icon in the lower-left corner: Click the lock to make changes.

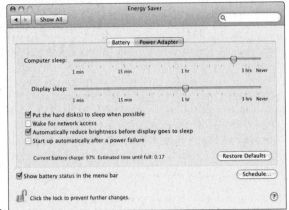

Figure 2-2:
The Energy
Saver
controls
make saving
energy a
cinch.

Depending on which Mac model you use, you might see some but not all of the options in the following list. Don't worry, there's nothing wrong with your Mac if you don't see an option or two — it's not there because your Mac has no use for it.

Here's a description of the Energy Saver options:

✦ **Graphics:** Select this option to adjust the tradeoff between battery life and graphics performance. You need to log out and log in again for the change to take effect.

✦ **Battery, Power Adapter, and UPS:** Clicking one of these tabs chooses which group of options to change. Your computer will use that group of options when it's getting power from that source.

✦ **Computer Sleep:** Moving this slider to the left is the more energy-efficient way to go. Moving to the right is less efficient because it allows a smart device to do nothing other than burn energy for no good reason.

✦ **Display Sleep:** Maybe you take a break and then return to your computer at regular intervals and you don't want to wake your Mac from lots of catnaps several times a day. Fair enough. Set the Computer Sleep slider (see the preceding bullet) a little farther to the right and then drag the Display Sleep slider to the left to snap your Mac to attention in a flash, with only the slightest pause before the screen comes back to life.

✦ **Put the Hard Disks(s) to Sleep When Possible:** Select this option to "snooze" the hard disk whenever it determines that the programs you're running don't need to keep the drive (or drives) spinning. If you regularly perform hard disk intensive tasks, such as editing or watching videos, listening to music using iTunes, or playing 3D games, deselect this option.

✦ **Wake for Ethernet Network Administration Access:** Choose this option if you want other users in your house or workplace to access your Mac's shared resources, such as shared printers or iTunes playlists, even when your computer is in Sleep mode.

✦ **Automatically Reduce the Brightness of the Display Before Display Sleep:** When you select this option, the brightness level on the display drops a few notches before blanking out the screen after the length of time you select in the Display Sleep setting (see previous bullet).

✦ **Start Up Automatically After a Power Failure:** Whether brownouts, blackouts, or black cats knocking out power cords, power failures happen. Use this option to specify how your Mac should react when the lights come on after a power failure. Select the check box if you want your Mac to restart, and deselect it if you prefer to turn it back on yourself after the power is running again.

For the environmentally friendliest choice, deselect this option unless your Mac is pulling duty as a file server or performing some other service that absolutely requires it to be on 24/7.

✦ **Show Battery Status in the Menu Bar:** Selecting this option on your MacBook notebook lets you keep visual tabs on how much battery juice remains when your machine is unplugged from the wall outlet — and how long you need to wait until its battery is fully charged after you plug into a power outlet. To change the information you see, click the Battery Status icon, choose Show, and then choose Icon Only, Time, or Percentage to see your battery's status the way you like it.

✦ **Schedule:** Click the Schedule button to open these scheduling options:

• *Start Up or Wake:* Choose when you want your Mac to greet you on weekdays or weekends, every day, or one day in particular. (The scheduler has no option for folks whose "Friday night" begins on a weekday.) Click the up and down arrows to adjust the time, as shown in Figure 2-3 — or click the time slots and enter your preference directly.

• *Sleep/Restart/Shutdown:* Choose one of these pop-up options if you want your Mac to do as instructed and adjust the time, as described in the preceding bullet, to suit your schedule.

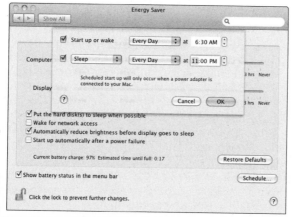

Figure 2-3:
Awaken
your Mac on
a schedule.

Shutting Down Your Mac

If you won't use your Mac for an extended period, you can shut it down to save energy and extend the life of your beloved computer. You have three ways to shut down your Mac:

✦ **Choose ⑩⇨Shut Down** as shown in Figure 2-4. A dialog appears, asking if you're sure that you want to shut down. (Refer to Figure 2-1.) Click Cancel or Shut Down. (If you don't click either option, your Mac will shut down automatically after one minute.)

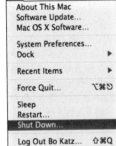

Figure 2-4:
Use this
menu to
turn off your
computer.

Holding the Option key and then choosing ⑩⇨Shut Down bypasses the prompt asking if you're sure that you want to shut down. Yes, Mr. Mac, I'm sure I'm sure, but thank you for your concern.

✦ **Press Control+Eject** (or press the power button) and when a dialog appears (refer to Figure 2-1), click the Shut Down button, or press the Return key.

✦ **Press and hold the power button** to force your Mac to shut down after a few seconds wait (or press and hold ⌘+Control and then press the power button to force your Mac to shut down at once).

This option, a *force shutdown,* forces all running programs to shut down right away. Generally, a force shutdown is your last resort if your Mac appears to have frozen, making it unresponsive. If only a single program is freezing or acting flaky, it's usually better to force quit that single program instead of shutting down your entire computer. (See Book I, Chapter 4 for information about how to force quit a single program.) Performing a force shutdown can cause you to lose any changes you've made to a letter or other file you're working on since the last time you saved it before the lockup. That's why you should use force shutdown only as a last resort.

You can also force shutdown your Mac by pressing the
Control+Option+⌘+Eject keystroke combination.

Restarting a Mac

Sometimes the Mac can start acting sluggish, or programs might fail to run.
When that happens, you can choose ⌘⇨Shut Down or Restart to properly
shut down or restart your Mac then start it again, which essentially clears
your computer's memory and starts it fresh.

To restart your computer, you have three choices:

✦ Press the power button (or press Control+Eject) and, when a dialog
   appears, click the Restart button (refer to Figure 2-1) or press the R key.

✦ Choose ⌘⇨Restart.

✦ Press Control+⌘+Eject.

When you restart your computer, your Mac closes all running programs; you
will have the chance to save any files you're working on. After you choose to
save any files, those programs are closed and then your Mac will shut down
and boot up again.

Chapter 3: Getting Acquainted with the Mac User Interface

In This Chapter

✔ Using the mouse and keyboard

✔ Acquainting yourself with the Mac user interface

✔ Working with icons in the Dock and in the Finder

✔ Getting help

Theoretically, using a computer is simple. In practice, using a computer can cause people to suffer a wide range of emotions from elation to sheer frustration and despair.

The problem with using a computer stems mostly from two causes:

✦ Not knowing what the computer can do

✦ Not knowing how to tell the computer what you want it to do

In the early days of personal computers, this communication gap between users and computers arose mostly from ordinary people trying to use machines designed by engineers for other engineers. If you didn't understand how a computer engineer thinks (or doesn't think), computers seemed nearly impossible to understand.

Fortunately, Apple has solved this problem with the Mac. Instead of designing a computer for other computer engineers, Apple designed a computer for ordinary people. And what do ordinary people want? Here's the short (but definitely important) list:

✦ Reliability

✦ Ease of use

From a technical point of view, what makes the Mac reliable is its operating system, Mac OS X. An operating system is nothing more than a program that makes your computer actually work.

An operating system works in the background. When you use a computer, you don't really notice the operating system, but you do see its *user interface*. The *user interface* is like a clerk at the front desk of a hotel. Instead of talking directly to the housekeeper or the plumber (the operating system), you always talk to the front desk clerk, and the clerk talks to the housekeeper or plumber.

Apple designed a user interface that everyone can understand. Dubbed Aqua, Apple's user interface puts the friendly face on the Mac.

Mastering the Mouse and Keyboard

To control your Mac, you use the mouse (or trackpad on notebook Macs) and the keyboard. Both the mouse (or trackpad) and the keyboard can choose commands, manipulate items on the screen, or create such data as text or pictures.

To modify how your Mac's mouse (or trackpad) and keyboard operate, click the Apple menu in the upper-left corner of the screen and choose System Preferences. Then click the Keyboard icon, or the Mouse icon, or the Trackpad icon, to adjust each accordingly.

To learn how you can make the trackpad built into the latest MacBook notebook models work like a very advanced mouse, check out the nearby sidebar, "Look Ma, no mouse!"

The parts of the mouse

A typical mouse looks like a bar of soap with one or more buttons and a rubber wheel or ball in the middle. The main purpose of the mouse is to move a pointer on the screen, which tells the computer, "See what I'm pointing at right now? That's what I want to select."

Clicking, double-clicking, and dragging with the left mouse button

A mouse typically has one button on the left and one on the right. To select an item on the screen, you move the mouse to point at that item and then press and release (click) the left mouse button.

The Apple Mighty Mouse features right and left mouse buttons, but try as you might, you won't be able to spot them with the naked eye. Mighty Mouse can sense when you press either the left or right side of its smooth surface, thanks to touch-sensitive technology that detects your fingertip gestures just like the MacBook touchpads.

✦ **Clicking (also called single-clicking):** Moving the mouse and pressing the left mouse button or the mouse's single button is the most common activity with a mouse.

✦ **Double-clicking:** If you point at something and click the left mouse button or the mouse's single button twice in rapid succession (that is, you *double-click* it), you can often select an item and open it at the same time.

✦ **Dragging:** Another common activity with the mouse is *dragging*. Dragging means pointing at an item on the screen, holding down the left mouse button or the mouse's single button, moving the mouse, and then releasing the button. Dragging is often used to move items on the screen.

Look Ma, no mouse!

All of Apple's current MacBook models sport cool new trackpads that can do more than most advanced multi-button mice — some of the trackpads even do away with the single button found on earlier MacBook, iBook, and PowerBook notebooks. Thanks to the track-pads' smart sensing abilities, you can pull off a number of mouse-like actions with a single, two, three, or four touch, tap, or gesture of your fingertips (or a combination of both). As the figure illustrates, turning on the MacBook trackpad's fancy ~~foot~~finger-work options gives you the ability to perform a single click by tap-ping the touchpad surface, scroll Web pages by sliding two fingertips up and down, perform a Control-click by tapping the trackpad with two fingertips at the same time, or switch between programs you're running by swiping four finger-prints left or right across the trackpad. Thanks to super-handy features like these, it's safe to bet that the extinction rate of mice will certainly climb as more people buy new MacBooks.

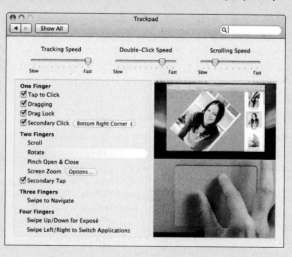

If you know how to point and click, double-click, and point and drag the mouse, you've mastered the basics of controlling your Mac with a mouse.

Scrolling with the scroll wheel or ball

Many mice have a rubber wheel or ball embedded in the middle. By rolling this wheel or ball, you can make items (such as text or a picture) scroll up/down or right/left on the screen. Using the scroll wheel or ball can make your Mac a lot easier to use. Clicking with the right mouse button (or Control-clicking) opens a shortcut menu of commands that can be faster to choose than clicking the menu bar menus at the top of the screen.

Like the scroll wheel or ball, the right mouse button is optional but convenient. Pointing the mouse and pressing the right mouse button is *right-clicking*.

Right-clicking commonly displays a menu of commands (called a contextual or shortcut menu) at the point you clicked to do something with the item that the mouse is currently pointing at. For example, if you point at a misspelled word, right-clicking that misspelled word can display a list of properly spelled words to choose from, as shown in Figure 3-1.

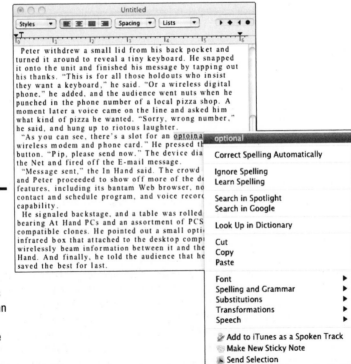

Figure 3-1: Right-clicking typically displays a list of commands that you can choose to manipulate an item.

Some older mice (as well as MacBook notebook models) do not have a right mouse button. To simulate a right-click with a single-button mouse, hold down the Control key and click the mouse button. On MacBooks, hold down the Control key and click the trackpad button, or hold two fingers down on the trackpad and then click the trackpad button.

If you don't like the mouse that came with your Mac, you can always buy a replacement mouse or trackball. Some mice are molded to better fit the shape of your hand, so find a mouse that you like and plug it into the USB port of your Mac, or get a wireless mouse that connects to your Mac using your Mac's Bluetooth wireless connection feature if it has one.

The parts of the keyboard

The primary use of the keyboard is to type information. However, the keyboard can also select items and menu commands — sometimes more quickly than using the mouse. Figure 3-2 shows that the keyboard groups related keys together. The next few sections cover each group of keys in detail.

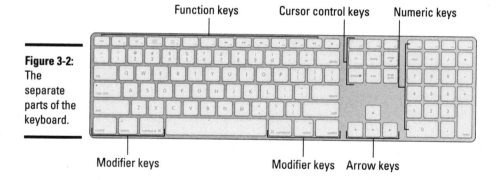

Figure 3-2:
The separate parts of the keyboard.

Special feature and function keys

Depending on your particular keyboard, you might see 12 to 20 function keys running along the top of the keyboard. These function keys are labeled F1 through F12/F19, along with an Escape key — brilliantly abbreviated "Esc" — and an Eject key that looks like a triangle on top of a horizontal line.

By default, every new and recent Mac's function key labels are tiny and shared by larger icons that represent special feature keys that you press to do things like turn down the screen brightness (F1), play or pause music you're listening to in iTunes(F8), or open your Mac's Dashboard Widgets program to check the weather forecast (F4). Although the icons on each of these special feature keys are self-evident, check out Table 3-1 to find out what all of your Mac's special features keys do when you press them.

Table 3-1	Mac Assigned Commands
Function Key	*What It Does*
F1	Decreases display brightness
F2	Increases display brightness
F3	Displays Exposé thumbnail images of all open windows in a single workspace
F4	Displays Dashboard Widgets
F5	Decreases keyboard backlight brightness
F6	Increases keyboard backlight brightness
F7	Video and audio rewind
F8	Video and audio play/pause
F9	Video and audio fast-forward
F10	Mutes sound
F11	Decreases sound volume
F12	Increases sound volume

In actuality, the Mac's program-specific function keys are selected by pressing and holding the Fn key, and then pressing one of the function keys on the upper row of the keyboard. In Microsoft Word, for instance, pressing Fn+F7 tells Word to run the spell checker feature, while pressing Fn+F5 opens the Find and Replace dialog.

In other words, holding down the Fn key tells your Mac, "Ignore the special feature controls assigned to that function key listed in Table 3-1 and just behave like an old-fashioned function key."

To reverse the way the Mac's function keys work when you press them, click ⊄ System Preferences⊅Keyboard icon. Click the Keyboard tab at the top of the window, then check the box next to Use all F1, F2, etc. Keys as Standard Function Keys. When you activate this option, you *must* hold down the Fn key to perform the commands shown in Table 3-1, but you do not need to hold down the Fn key to use program-specific function keys as described above.

Holding the Fn key and pressing the F8 function key (Fn+F8) displays multiple workspaces defined by the Spaces feature (which you find out more about in Book I, Chapter 4).

Holding the Fn key and pressing the F9 through F11 function keys activates a feature on your Mac called Exposé. Pressing Fn+F9 lets you see all the open windows so you can pick the one you want to use. Pressing Fn+F10 shows you all windows that belong to the active program. (You can identify the active program by looking for its name on the left side of the menu bar.) Pressing Fn+F11 shoves all windows out of the way so you can see the Desktop.

Pressing Fn+F12 displays the Dashboard program and its widgets, which are simple miniprograms, such as a calculator, calendar, or a display of your local weather forecast. (You find out more about Dashboard in Book II, Chapter 4.)

Although Fn+F9 and Fn+F12 keys work as I say, you can skip all this hold-down-the-Fn-key business and just press the buttons dedicated to those features and others as listed in Table 3-1.

As for the other keys — F1 through F7 and (possibly) F13 through F19 — holding the Fn key and pressing these fellows can carry out shortcut commands on a program by program basis. For instance, pressing Fn+F7 in Microsoft Word for the Macintosh opens the program's spelling and grammar checker utility.

Originally, function keys existed because some programs assigned commands to different function keys. Unfortunately, every program assigned different commands to identical function keys, which sometimes made function keys more confusing than helpful. You can assign your own commands to different function keys, but just remember that not every Mac will have the same commands assigned to the same function keys. (Not everyone thinks exactly like you, as amazing as that might seem.) To customize which function keys perform which commands, choose ⌘⇨System Preferences⇨Keyboard; then click the Keyboard Shortcuts tab at the top of the window and adjust your Mac's keyboard shortcuts to your heart's content.

Turning to the two other keys grouped with the function keys, here's what you need to know. The Esc key often works as a "You may be excused" command. For example, if a pull-down menu appears on the screen and you want it to go away, press the Esc key. The Eject key ejects a CD or DVD from your Mac.

Typewriter keys

You use the typewriter (also known as the alphanumeric) keys to create *data* — the typing-a-letter-in-a-word-processor stuff or the entering-of-names-and-addresses-into-the-Address-Book-program stuff. When you press a typewriter key, you're telling the Mac what character to type at the cursor position, which often appears as a blinking vertical line on the screen.

You can move the cursor by pointing to and clicking a new location with the mouse or by pressing the arrow keys as explained in the upcoming "Arrow keys" section.

One typewriter key that doesn't type anything is the big Delete key that appears to the right of the +/= key. The Delete key deletes any characters that appear to the left of the cursor. If you hold down the Delete key, your Mac deletes any characters to the left of the cursor until you lift your finger.

Two other typewriter keys that don't type anything are the Tab key and the Return key, which is sometimes labeled Enter on older Mac keyboards or certain external keyboards you can buy to use with your Mac. The Tab key indents text in a word processor, but it can also highlight different text boxes, such as ones in which you type your shipping address on the Web page form of an online bookstore or another merchant.

The Return key moves the cursor to the next line in a word processor, but can also choose a default button (which appears in blue) on the screen. The default button in the Print dialog is labeled Print, and the default button in the Save dialog is labeled Save.

Numeric keys

The numeric keys appear on the right side of the keyboard (if yours has them!) and arrange the numbers 0 through 9 in rows and columns like a typical calculator keypad. The main use for the numeric keys is to make typing numbers faster and easier than using the numeric keys on the top row of the typewriter keys.

On earlier MacBook keyboards, the numeric keys were assigned to a section of keys on the normal typewriter keys. To switch the numeric keys on, you had to press the Num Lock key. To switch the numeric keys off, you had to press the Num Lock key again. Recent and new MacBooks no longer sport these numeric keys.

Arrow keys

The cursor often appears as a vertical blinking line and acts like a placeholder. Wherever the cursor appears, that's where your next character will appear if you press a typewriter key. You can move the cursor with the mouse, or you can move it with the arrow keys.

The up arrow moves the cursor up, the down arrow moves the cursor down, the right arrow moves the cursor right, and the left arrow moves the cursor left. (Could it be any more logical?) Depending on the program you're using, pressing an arrow key might move the cursor in different ways. For example, pressing the right arrow key in a word processor moves the cursor right one character, but pressing that same right arrow key in a spreadsheet might move the cursor to the adjacent cell on the right.

On some Mac keyboards, you might see four additional cursor control keys labeled Home, End, Page Up, and Page Down. Typically, the Page Up key scrolls up one screen, and the Page Down key scrolls down one screen. Many programs ignore the Home and End keys, but some programs let you move the cursor with them. For example, Microsoft Word uses the Home key to move the cursor to the beginning of a line or row and the End key to move the cursor to the end of a line or row.

Just because you might not see the Home, End, Page Up, and Page Down keys on your Mac or MacBook keyboard doesn't mean those command keys aren't there. On the MacBook that I'm using to write this, holding down the Fn key and then pressing the left arrow key acts as the Home key, which moves the cursor to the start of the line I'm on. Pressing Fn+→ jumps the cursor to the end of the current line, Fn+↑ scrolls the chapter up one page, and Fn+↓ scrolls the text down one page. Because seeing is believing, try it on your own Mac keyboard so you can see what I mean — even if you don't see keys bearing those actual labels.

To the left of the End key, you might find a smaller Delete key. Like the bigger Delete key, this smaller Delete key also deletes characters one at a time.

The big Delete key erases characters to the *left* of the cursor. The small Delete key erases characters to the *right* of the cursor.

Modifier keys

Modifier keys are almost never used individually. Instead, modifier keys are usually held down while tapping another key. The four modifier keys are the Function (Fn) keys previously mentioned in a few of the previous sections: Shift, Control (Ctrl), Option, and ⌘ (Command).

If you press the S key in a word processing document, your Mac types the letter "s" on the screen, but if you hold down a modifier key, such as the Command key (⌘), and then press the S key, the S key is modified to behave differently. In this case, holding down the ⌘ key followed by the S key (⌘+S) tells your word processing program to issue the Save command and save whatever you typed or changed since the last time you saved the document.

Most modifier keystrokes involve pressing two keys, such as ⌘+Q (the Quit command), but some modifier keystrokes can involve pressing three or four keys, such as Shift+⌘+3, which saves a snapshot of what you seen on your screen as an image file, which is commonly referred to as a *screenshot.*

The main use for modifier keys is to help you choose commands quickly without fumbling with the mouse. Every program includes dozens of such keystroke shortcuts, but Table 3-2 lists the common keystroke shortcuts that work in most programs.

Table 3-2	Common Keystroke Shortcuts
Command	*Keystroke Shortcut*
Copy	⌘+C
Cut	⌘+X
Paste	⌘+V
Open	⌘+O
New	⌘+N
Print	⌘+P
Quit	⌘+Q
Save	⌘+S
Select All	⌘+A
Undo	⌘+Z

Most Mac programs display their keystroke shortcuts for different commands directly on their pull-down menus, as shown in Figure 3-3.

Figure 3-3: Most pull-down menus list shortcut keystrokes for commonly used commands.

Keystroke shortcuts

Instead of describing the modifier keys to press by name (such as Shift), most keystroke shortcuts displayed on menus use cryptic graphics. Figure 3-4 displays the different symbols that represent shortcut commands.

Figure 3-4:
A keystroke
command
symbol
guide.

⌘	Command
⌫	Delete
⌥	Option
⎋	Esc
⇧	Shift
^	Ctrl

Some people love the keyboard that comes with their Mac, but others feel that it's too soft and squishy, like touching the belly of an animal. If you want a more solid-feeling keyboard that provides tactile feedback (and that good ol' fashioned clickity-clackity sound), check out the Das Keyboard (www. daskeyboard.com).

Getting to Know the Mac User Interface

The Mac user interface acts like a communication pathway between you and the operating system and serves three purposes:

✦ To display all the options that you can choose

✦ To display information

✦ To accept commands

One of the most crucial parts of the Mac user interface is a program called the Finder, which displays files stored on your Mac. You find out more about the Finder later in this chapter.

The menu bar

The menu bar provides a single location where you can find nearly every possible command you might need. Think of the menu bar as a restaurant menu. Any time you want to order another dish, you can look at the menu to see what's available. Likewise, when using a Mac, you always know the menu bar will appear at the top of the screen. The menu bar consists of three parts, as shown in Figure 3-5:

Figure 3-5:
The three
parts of the
menu bar.

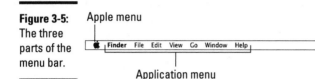

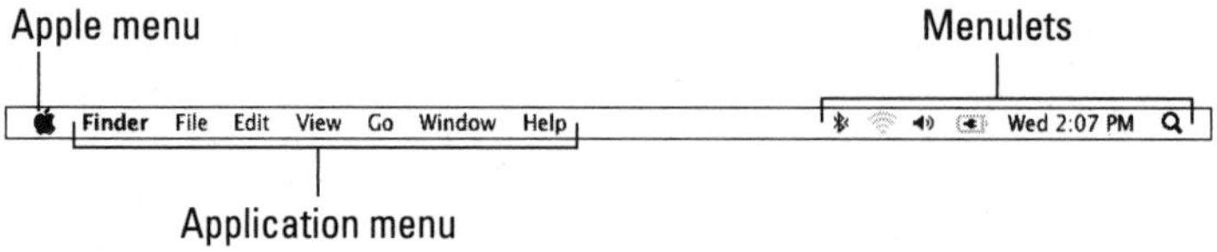

Apple menu   Menulets

Application menu

+ **The Apple menu:** This menu always appears on the menu bar and gives
  you one-click access to commands for controlling or modifying your Mac.

+ **The Application menu:** Here's where you find the name of the active
  program along with several menus that contain commands for controlling that particular program and its data. (If you don't run any additional
  programs, your Mac always runs the Finder program, which you find out
  more about in this chapter.)

+ **Menulets (Icons):** *Menulets* act like miniature menus that perform one or
  more functions for specific programs or system features, such as providing fast access to a troubleshooting utility, adjusting the volume, or displaying the current time. Clicking a menulet displays a small pull-down
  menu or control, as shown in Figure 3-6.

Figure 3-6:
Menulets let
you control
program
or feature
functions of
your Mac.

If you don't want a menulet cluttering up the menu bar, you can typically
remove it by holding down the ⌘ key, moving the pointer over the menulet
you want to remove, dragging (moving) the mouse off the menu bar, and
then releasing the mouse button.

Understanding menu commands

Each menu on the menu bar contains a group of related commands. The File
menu contains commands for opening, saving, and printing files, and the

Edit menu contains commands for copying or deleting selected items. The number and names of different menus depend on the program.

To give a command to your Mac, click a menu title on the menu bar (such as File or Edit) to call up a pull-down menu listing all the commands you can choose. Then click the command you want the computer to follow (File⇨Save, for example).

Working with dialogs

When your Mac needs information from you or wants to present a choice you can make, it typically displays a *dialog* — essentially a box that offers a variety of choices. Some common dialogs appear when you choose the Print, Save, and Open commands.

Dialogs often appear in a condensed version, but you can blow them up into an expanded version, as shown in Figure 3-7. To switch between the expanded and the condensed version of the Save dialog, click the Arrow button.

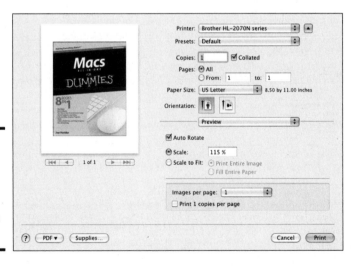

Figure 3-7:
When expanded, the Print dialog offers more options.

Whether expanded or condensed, every dialog displays buttons that either let you cancel the command or complete it. To cancel a command, you have two choices:

+ Click the Cancel button.

+ Press Esc.

To complete a command, you also have two choices:

+ Click the button that represents the command that you want to complete, such as Save or Print.

+ Press Return to choose the default button, which appears in blue.

Viewing data in a window

Every program needs to accept, manipulate, and/or display data, also referred to as information. A word processor lets you type and edit text, an accounting program lets you type and calculate numbers, and a presentation program lets you display text and pictures. To help you work with different types of information (such as text, pictures, audio, and video files), every program displays information inside a rectangular area called a *window,* as shown in Figure 3-8.

In the early days of personal computers, a program treated the entire screen as a window for displaying information. This was fine when computers could run only one program at a time, but nowadays every computer lets you run several programs at the same time. To give each program a chance to display information on the screen, computers can present multiple windows for each program you're running, allowing each window to act like a miniature screen that you can stack on top of other windows.

Dividing a screen into multiple windows offers several advantages:

+ Two or more programs can display information on the screen simultaneously.

+ A single program can open and display information stored in two or more files or display two or more views of the same file.

+ You can copy (or move) data from one window to another. If each window belongs to a different program, this action transfers data from one program to another.

Of course, windows aren't perfect. When a window appears on the screen, it might be too big or too small, hard to find because it's hidden behind another window, or displaying the beginning of a file when you want to see the middle or the end. To control the appearance of a window, most windows provide the built-in controls shown in Figure 3-9. The following sections show you what you can do with these controls.

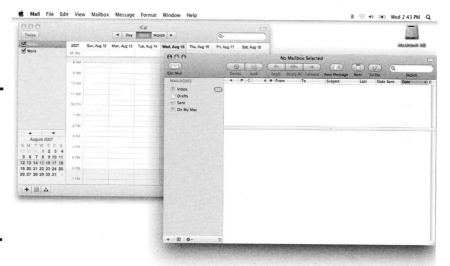

Figure 3-8:
Windows
allow
multiple
programs
to display
information
on the
screen.

Moving a window with the title bar

The title bar of every window serves two purposes:

✦ Identifies the filename that contains the information displayed in the window.

✦ Provides a place to grab when you want to drag (move) the window to a new location on the screen.

If you want to move a window on the screen, you can typically do so by dragging its title bar. Here's how:

1. **Move the pointer over the title bar of the window you want to move.**

2. **Hold down the mouse button and drag the mouse.**

   If you have a two-button mouse, hold down the left mouse button.

   The window moves wherever you drag the mouse.

3. **Release the mouse button when you're happy with the new location of the window.**

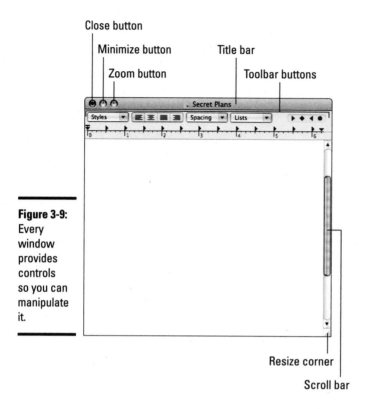

Close button

Minimize button

Zoom button

Title bar

Toolbar buttons

Figure 3-9:
Every
window
provides
controls
so you can
manipulate
it.

Resize corner

Scroll bar

Resizing a window

Sometimes a window might be in the perfect location, but it's too small or too large for what you want to do at that moment. To change the size of a window, follow these steps:

1. **Move the pointer over the resize corner in the bottom-right corner of the window.**

2. **Hold down the mouse button and drag the mouse.**

If you have a two-button mouse, hold down the left mouse button.

The window grows or shrinks while you drag the mouse.

3. **Release the mouse button when you're happy with the new size of the window.**

Closing a window

When you finish viewing or editing any information displayed in a window, you can close the window to keep it from cluttering the screen. To close a window, follow these steps:

1. **Click the Close button (the little red button) of the window you want to close.**

If you haven't saved the information inside the window, such as a letter you're writing with a word processing program, the application displays a dialog that asks whether you want to save it.

2. **In the dialog that appears, click one of the following choices:**

- *Don't Save:* Closes the window and discards any changes you made to the information inside the window.

- *Cancel:* Keeps the window open.

- *Save:* Closes the window but saves the information in a file. If this is the first time you've saved this information, another dialog appears, giving you a chance to name the file and to store the saved information in a specific location on your hard drive.

Computers typically offer two or more ways to accomplish the same task, so you can choose the way you like best. As an alternative to clicking the Close button, you can also click inside the window you want to close and then choose File⇨Close or press ⌘+W.

Minimizing a window

Sometimes you might not want to close a window, but you still want to get it out of the way so it doesn't clutter your screen. In that case, you can *minimize* a window, which tucks the window (displayed as a tiny icon) into the right side of the Dock, as shown in Figure 3-10.

Figure 3-10: Minimized window icons on the Dock.

The Secret Agent Ch01

A minimized window icon on the Dock actually displays the contents of that window. If you squint hard enough (or have a large enough screen), you can see what each minimized window contains.

To minimize a window, choose one of the following:

✦ Click the Minimize button of the window you want to tuck out of the way.

✦ Click the window you want to minimize and choose Window⇨Minimize (or press ⌘+M).

✦ Double-click the window's title bar. (This feature can be turned off, as I explain later in this section.)

To open a minimized window, follow these steps:

1. **Move the mouse over the minimized window on the Dock.**

2. **Click the mouse button.**

Your minimized window pops back onto the screen.

Zooming a window

If a window is too small to display information, you can instantly make it bigger by using the Zoom button — the green button in the upper-left corner most windows. (When you move the mouse over the Zoom button, a plus sign appears inside.)

Zooming a window makes it grow larger, as shown in Figure 3-11. Clicking the zoom button a second time makes the window shrink back to its prior size.

Sometimes when you click the zoom button the window appears to expand only slightly but doesn't fill most of the screen. Other times clicking the zoom button makes a window fill the screen. To adjust how much or how little a window zooms in or out, you can resize the window, as described in the earlier section, "Resizing a window."

Scrolling through a window

No matter how large you make a window, it may still be too small to display the entire contents of the information contained inside. Think of a window as a porthole that lets you peek at part, but not all, of a file's contents. If a window isn't large enough to display all of the information inside it, the window lets you know by displaying vertical or horizontal scroll bars.

Figure 3-11:
The Zoom
button
expands or
shrinks a
window.

You can scroll what's displayed in a window three ways, as shown in
Figure 3-12:

✦ **Click the scroll arrows:** Scrolls the window up/down or right/left. If you
move the mouse over a scroll arrow and hold down the mouse button,
the window continuously scrolls.

✦ **Drag the scroll box:** Scrolls through a window faster.

✦ **Click in the scroll bar:** Scrolls up/down or right/left in large increments
or directly to the spot where you click.

To set how your Mac scrolls when you click the scroll bar, choose ❡⇨System
Preferences⇨Appearance; then click either Jump to the Next Page or Jump
to the Spot That's Clicked to set the Click In the Scroll Bar To option.

Many mice have a built-in scroll wheel in the middle. By rolling this scroll wheel, you can scroll a window's display up or down. The Apple Mighty Mouse has a scroll ball in the middle that lets you roll it to scroll up/down or right/left. On new and recent MacBook models, you can scroll up, down, left, and right (and even in circles!) by dragging two fingers on the trackpad in whatever direction you want to scroll.

 Depending on your Mac model, your Mac's keyboard may have dedicated Page Up and Page Down keys, which you can press to scroll what's displayed up and down. Not seeing Page Up and Page Down keys on your Mac or MacBook keyboard doesn't mean they aren't there. To use your Mac's invisible Page Up and Page Down keys, refer to the subtopic "Arrow keys," in the preceding section "The parts of a keyboard."

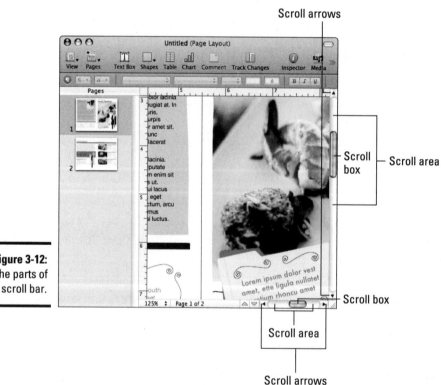

Figure 3-12:
The parts of a scroll bar.

Using the Toolbar button

Some windows display a row of icons at the top of the window, known as a *toolbar*. The purpose of a toolbar is to give you one-click access to commonly used commands, such as saving or printing a file. However, these toolbar icons can also clutter the appearance of a window.

To give you the option of hiding (or viewing) a window's toolbar icons, a window might display a Toolbar button in its upper-right corner, as shown in Figure 3-13, but not all windows have a Toolbar button.

Some programs, such as Microsoft Word, let you Control-click on a toolbar to choose other toolbars you may want to see (or hide open toolbars you don't want to see). Control-clicking on your Mac's Safari Web browser toolbar displays a pop-up menu with the Customize Toolbar command, which you can choose to display a window of toolbar icons you can drag to (or from) the Safari toolbar to make it look the way you want.

Manipulating windows with Exposé

The more windows you open, the more cluttered your screen can appear, much like taking stacks of paper and throwing them all over your desk. To organize your windows, you could move, resize, and minimize each window individually, but that's too tedious and time-consuming. As a faster alternative, you can use a handy feature called Exposé.

Toolbar button

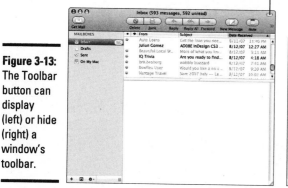
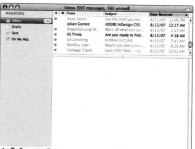

Figure 3-13:
The Toolbar button can display (left) or hide (right) a window's toolbar.

If your Mac's Exposé key doesn't respond when you press it, flip back to the section "Special feature and function keys" to change the way your Mac's keyboard responds to those keys when you press them.

The whole idea behind Exposé is to give you these fast, convenient ways to organize your windows:

✦ Shrinking all windows to the size of thumbnail images so you can see and choose the window you want to use, as shown in Figure 3-14. The Exposé key, dedicated to the F3 key, bears an icon of a minidesktop and windows. Pressing the Exposé key does the shrinking for you. You can also press Fn+F9 to activate Exposé.

✦ Showing only those windows that belong to the active program, as shown in Figure 3-15. Pressing Fn+F10 is the trick here (or pressing Ctrl+F3).

✦ Hiding all windows so you can see what's on the Desktop. Pressing Fn+F11 (or ⌘+F11) pulls out the old invisibility cloak.

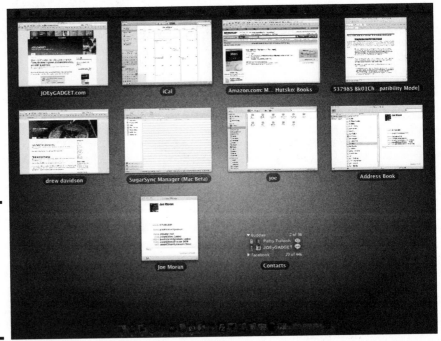

Figure 3-14: Pressing Fn+F9 shrinks all open windows into thumbnails.

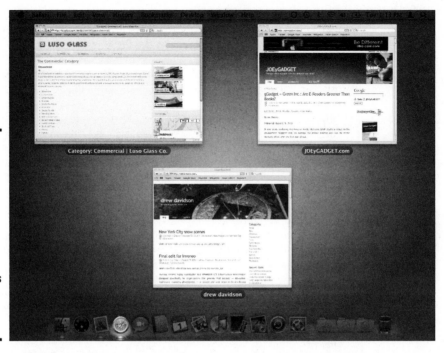

Figure 3-15:
Pressing
Fn+F10
hides all
windows
except for
the active
program
(the name
that appears
in the
Application
menu).

Pressing the Exposé key, Fn+F9, Fn+F10, and Fn+F11 toggles the display. So pressing Fn+F9 initially shrinks all windows as thumbnail images, but pressing Fn+F9 a second time reverts all windows to normal size.

When windows appear as thumbnail images after you press Fn+F9 or Fn+F10, you can move the pointer over the thumbnail image and view the filename that appears in that particular window.

To switch to a window, click the thumbnail image of that window. Exposé immediately displays your chosen window (at full size) on the screen.

Playing with Icons in the Dock and Finder

A Mac shows programs and files as pictures, or *icons*. Program icons are visual depictions of the program, such as the postage stamp icon that represents the Mail program, or the calendar icon that represents the iCal schedule program.

File icons typically contain the filename along with a picture that corresponds to the program that created it. By providing this visual clue, you can see which specific programs created the files.

Icons commonly appear on the Desktop, in the Dock, and inside a Finder window, as shown in Figure 3-16.

The Desktop

The Desktop is always onscreen, although open windows cover up part or all of it. In the old days, placing program and file icons on the desktop for quick access was common, much like placing an important book or day planner in one corner of your desk so you can grab it easily.

Unfortunately, the more icons you store on the Desktop, the more cluttered it appears, making it harder to find anything. Although you can still store program and file icons on the Desktop, storing program and folder icons in the Dock and in folders in the Finder is more common.

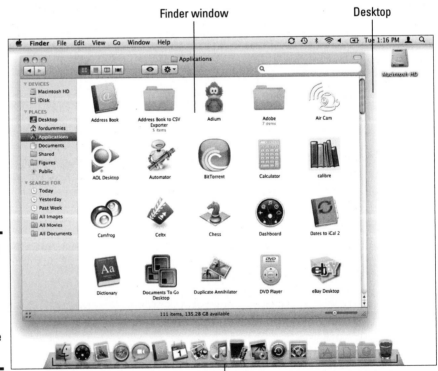

Finder window　　　　Desktop

Figure 3-16:
The three common locations where you can find icons on the Mac.

Dock

The Desktop generally shows an icon that represents your hard drive. If you have any additional storage devices attached to your Mac (such as an external hard drive, a CD or DVD, or a USB flash drive), you typically see icons for those storage devices on your Desktop, too.

You can change what your Mac displays on the Desktop. To do so, click the Finder icon in the Dock, click the Finder menu, and then choose Preferences. In the Finder Preferences window, check, uncheck, or change the different options to suit your style.

The Dock

The Dock is a rectangular strip that contains both program icons and file and folder icons. To help keep your icons organized, the Dock places program icons on the left side of a divider and file icons on the right side, as shown in Figure 3-17.

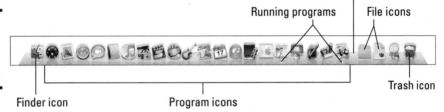

Figure 3-17:
The Dock can hold many icons.

Divider

Running programs   File icons

Trash icon

Finder icon   Program icons

Besides acting as a convenient place to store and find frequently used programs and files, the Dock can also tell you which programs are running by displaying a glowing dot under the icon of each running program. Clicking a running program's Dock icon gives you a quick and easy way of bringing that program and any of its windows to the front of any other program windows.

Moving the Dock

The Dock initially appears at the bottom of the screen, but you can move it to the left or right of the screen. (You can't move the Dock to the top or else it would cover the menu bar.)

To move the Dock to a new location, follow these steps:

1. **Choose ⌘⇨Dock.**

A submenu appears, as shown in Figure 3-18.

Figure 3-18:
The Dock submenu lets you change the position of the Dock on the screen.

2. **Click a new position — Left, Bottom, or Right.**

A check mark appears next to your selection, and the Dock makes its move.

Resizing the Dock

The Dock grows each time you add more program and file icons to it. However, you might want to modify the size of the icons on the Dock so that the Dock as a whole doesn't appear too small or too large. To resize the Dock, follow these steps:

1. **Choose ⬛⇨Dock⇨Dock Preferences.**

The Dock preferences window appears, as shown in Figure 3-19.

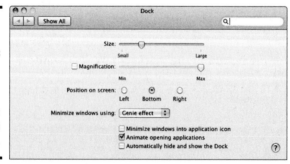

Figure 3-19:
The Dock preferences window lets you control the appearance and position of the Dock.

2. **Drag the Size slider to adjust the size of all the icons on the Dock.**

3. Click the Close button of the Dock preferences window.

The individual icons on the Dock are resized according to your wishes.

Another way to resize the Dock is to move the pointer over the Dock divider, hold down the mouse button, and drag the mouse left or right. (If you have a two-button mouse, hold down the left mouse button.)

Magnifying the Dock

When you shrink the size of the Dock to hold more icons, the icons can appear too small, and it can be hard to see which icon the mouse is pointing at. Fortunately, the name of the program beneath the pointer appears to tell you what program it is. To make Dock icons zoom in size when you move the pointer over them, you can turn on Magnification, as shown in Figure 3-20.

Figure 3-20:
Magni-
fication
makes an
icon on the
Dock easier
to see.

To turn magnification of the Dock on or off, follow these steps:

1. Choose ⬤➪Dock➪Dock Preferences.

The Dock preferences window appears. (Refer to Figure 3-19.)

2. Select (or clear) the Magnification check box.

3. Drag the Magnification slider to adjust the magnification of the Dock.

4. Click the Close button of the Dock preferences window.

For a fast way to turn Magnification on or off, choose ⬤➪Dock➪Turn Magnification On (Off).

Hiding the Dock

The Dock might be convenient, but it can take up precious screen real estate when you view Web pages or work with lengthy word processing documents. To get all the advantages of the Dock without the disadvantage of using extra screen space to display the Dock all the time, you can hide the Dock.

Hiding the Dock means that the Dock tucks itself out of sight, but as soon as you move the mouse near the edge of the screen where the Dock is located (bottom, left, or right), the Dock pops into view.

To hide (or show) the Dock, click the Apple menu and choose Dock⇨Turn Hiding On (Off).

You find out how to customize the icons on the Dock in Book I, Chapter 4.

The Finder

The Finder is a program that lets you find, copy, move, rename, delete, and open files and folders on your Mac. You can run programs directly from the Finder, but the Dock makes finding and running programs much more convenient.

The Finder runs all the time. To switch to the Finder, click the Finder icon in the Dock (the Picasso-like faces icon on the far left of the Dock).

Sometimes when you switch to the Finder, you might not see a Finder window. Clicking the Finder icon a second time in the Dock opens a new Finder window. You can also open a new Finder window by choosing File⇨New Finder Window. You can open as many Finder windows as you want, although it's common just to have one or a few Finder windows open at a time.

The Finder window looks different from the windows of other programs. Because the Finder helps you manage the files stored on your hard drive, a Finder window consists of two panes, as shown in Figure 3-21.

The left pane, called the Sidebar, displays four different categories:

✦ **Devices:** Lists all the storage devices connected to your Mac, such as hard drives, flash drives, and CD/DVD drives.

✦ **Shared:** Lists all shared storage devices connected on a local area network.

Figure 3-21:
The Finder
displays
two panes
to help you
navigate
to different
parts of your
hard drive.

✦ **Places:** Lists the Desktop, Home, Applications, and Documents folders, which are the default folders for storing files, as well as any others you drag to Places so you can access them more quickly.

✦ **Search For:** Lists the programs or files you've stored or modified today, yesterday, or in the past week.

The right pane displays the contents of an item selected in the left pane. If you click the hard drive icon in the left pane, the right pane displays the contents of that hard drive. All programs and files displayed in a Finder window appear as icons with text labels, regardless of which type of view you've chosen to view the Finder window.

You find out how to use the Finder in more detail in Book I, Chapter 6.

Getting Help

Theoretically, the Mac should be so easy and intuitive that you can teach yourself how to use your computer just by looking at the screen. Realistically, the Mac can still be confusing and complicated. Thankfully, your Mac includes a built-in Help feature. Any time you're confused using your Mac, try looking for answers in Mac Help — you just might find the answer you're looking for!

Mac Help offers two types of help. First, it can point out specific menu commands to choose for accomplishing a specific task. For example, if you want to know how to save or print a file, Mac Help will point out the Save or Print command so you'll know which command to choose.

Second, Mac Help can provide brief explanations for how to accomplish a specific task. By skimming through the brief explanations, you can (hopefully) figure out how to do something useful.

Pointing out commands to use

To use Mac Help to point out commands you can use with the Finder or a program you're running, follow these steps:

1. **Click the Help menu at the far right end of the menu bar for any program you're running (or click the Finder icon to switch to the Finder and then click Help).**

   A Search text box appears.

2. **Begin typing a word or phrase.**

   If you want help on working with using printing, for example, type **print**. While you type, a list of possible topics appears, as shown in Figure 3-22.

   Help topics for the program you're running appear first under the Menu Items category, followed by the Help Topics category, which lists topics for the Finder and any other programs stored on your Mac.

3. **Move your pointer over a Menu Items topic.**

   A floating arrow points to the command on a menu to show you how to access your chosen topic for the program you are running, as shown in Figure 3-23.

When accessing the Help feature of specific programs, you see a Help window, as shown in Figure 3-24.

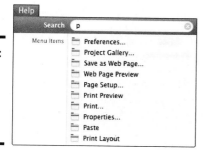

Figure 3-22:
While
you type,
Help lists
possible
topics.

Figure 3-23:
Mac Help
tries to
show you
how to
access a
particular
command.

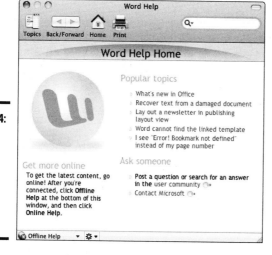

Figure 3-24:
The Help
feature
of many
programs
displays
topics you
can click.

Reading Help topics

To use Mac Help to read brief explanations of different topics, follow these steps:

1. **Click the Finder icon in the Dock.**

2. **Click the Help menu and then choose Mac Help.**

A Mac Help window appears, as shown in Figure 3-25.

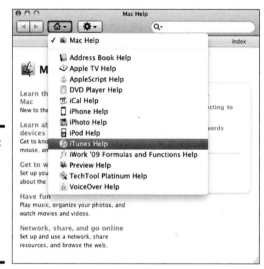

Figure 3-25: The Mac Help window displays topics that you can click.

3. **Click a topic, displayed in blue, or click and hold on the Home icon to display a menu of help choices for applications stored on your Mac.**

Mac Help displays additional information about your chosen topic.

4. **Click the Back (or Forward) button to jump to a previously viewed topic.**

You might also want to click the Home button to return to the original Mac Help window.

5. **Click the Close button to close the Mac Help window.**

Chapter 4: Running, Installing, and Uninstalling Programs

In This Chapter

✔ **Running programs from the Dock**

✔ **Double-clicking icons to start programs**

✔ **Switching between programs**

✔ **Using Spaces**

✔ **Shutting down programs**

✔ **Finding software**

✔ **Installing software**

✔ **Uninstalling software**

*A*fter you power on your Mac and have the OS X operating system up and running, you can run any additional programs, such as a word processor, a video game, a Web browser, or an e-mail program. The number of programs you can load and run simultaneously is limited only by the amount of hard drive space and memory installed inside your Mac.

This chapter explains how to run, install, and uninstall software — also referred to as programs, or applications — for your Mac. Of course, before you install any software, you want to know how to run the programs that come with your Mac. When you're comfortable running your Mac's bundled software, you can then find new programs to install.

Because you have a physical limit on the amount of software you can install on your Mac, you have two choices. One, you can get another hard drive (an external drive or a larger internal drive) so you can keep installing more programs. Two, you can delete some programs that you don't want or need, which makes room for more programs that you do want and need.

Launching a Program

Running a program or application is also referred to as launching a program or application, or starting up a program or application. Very hip Mac users shorten the term by saying they run this app or that app.

To start a program, you can choose any of the four most common methods:

✦ Click a program or document icon in the Dock.

✦ Double-click a program or document icon in the Finder.

✦ Choose a program name from the Apple menu's Recent Items.

✦ Find the program with the Spotlight search feature and then select it to run.

The next few sections take a closer look at each one of these methods.

Two other not-so-obvious but nifty ways to launch programs include attaching a device (such as a digital camera or mobile phone with a camera to automatically launch iPhoto) or inserting a disc (such as a DVD or CD to automatically launch iTunes), and then Control-clicking (or right-clicking, if your mouse has a right button) on a document and choosing Open or Open With from the shortcut menu.

From the Dock

To run a program from the Dock, just click the program icon that you want to run. (What? Were you expecting something difficult?) The Dock contains icons that represent some (but not all) of the programs installed on your Mac. When you turn on your Mac for the first time, you see that the Dock already includes a variety of programs that Apple thinks you might want to use right away. However, you can always add or remove program icons from the Dock (more on that later).

When using programs, you can use the Dock in several ways:

✦ To gain one-click access to your favorite programs.

✦ To see which programs are running.

✦ To switch between different programs quickly.

✦ To see which windows you have minimized. (Minimized windows are tucked out of sight but still open.)

✦ To view a specific program window.

✦ To hide all windows that belong to a specific program.

Your Mac displays a glowing dot underneath the icon of running programs. By glancing at the Dock, you can identify all running programs quickly. (See Figure 4-1.)

Figure 4-1:
The Dock identifies running programs with a glowing dot.

Running programs

Clicking a running program's Dock icon makes it easy to switch between all of the programs you're running at the same time. So, if you want to switch to the iTunes program from the GarageBand program, you just click the iTunes program icon. Doing so immediately displays the iTunes window(s) and displays the iTunes program name in the Application menu on the menu bar at the top of the screen. (Clicking the iTunes program icon brings iTunes to the fore, but the GarageBand program doesn't quit on you; it just moseys to the background, waiting for its turn to step into the limelight again.)

The Dock identifies running programs by displaying a glowing dot underneath the icon of each running program. The Application menu on the menu bar identifies the active program. You can have multiple programs running, but you can have only one active program. The *active program* is the one that is front and center on your screen, ready to accept any data or commands you give.

You can add or remove program icons from the Dock so it contains only the programs you use most often, and you can arrange the icons in the Dock to suit yourself and make starting programs even easier. The following sections give you all you need to know about the relationship between the Dock and its icons.

Adding program icons to the Dock

The Dock includes several programs already installed on your Mac, but if you install more programs, you might want to add those program icons to the Dock as well. One way to add a program icon to the Dock is to click and drag the icon onto the Dock. Here's how that's usually done:

1. **Click the Finder icon in the Dock and then click the Applications folder in the Finder window's sidebar.**

The Finder displays the contents of the Applications folder.

2. **Click the program icon and hold down the mouse button, drag the pointer where you want to place the icon in the Dock, and then release the mouse button.**

Your chosen program icon now has its own place in the Dock.

Make sure you drag program icons in the Dock to the left of the divider, which appears as a gap near the Trash icon. To the left of the divider, you see program icons. To the right of the divider, you can store file or folder icons.

Be careful not to drag the program icon to the Trash bin unless you really want to delete it from your hard disk.

When you drag a program icon to the Dock, you aren't physically moving the program from the Applications folder onto the Dock; you're just creating a link, or *alias,* from the Dock to the actual program (which is still safely stashed in its folder).

You can also add a program icon to the Dock right after you load a program. Remember that the Dock displays the icons of all running programs at all times, but when you exit a program, that program's icon — if it's not one of Apple's Chosen Few and you haven't added it to the Dock — will disappear from the Dock. To keep an icon of a running program in the Dock so it stays there when you quit the program, Control-click the running program's icon in the Dock — or click and hold down on the program icon, and choose Keep in Dock from the shortcut menu, as shown in Figure 4-2. Now when you exit from this program, the program icon remains visible in the Dock.

Figure 4-2: Control-click a program icon in the Dock to display a shortcut menu.

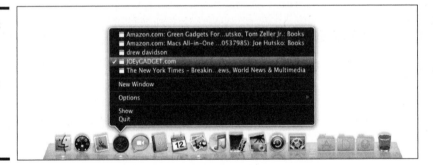

Rearranging program icons in the Dock

After you've placed program icons in the Dock, you might want to rearrange their order. How you rearrange your Dock is up to you! To rearrange program icons in the Dock, click the program icon that you want to move and drag the mouse sideways to where you want to move it; then release the mouse button.

You notice that while you move a program icon, the existing icons move to the side to show you where the icon will appear when you let go of the mouse button. Neat effect, right?

You can rearrange program icons on the Dock how you want, but one icon you cannot move or remove is the Finder icon, which won't budge no matter how hard you try to drag it from its Number One position on the Dock.

Removing program icons from the Dock

If you keep adding program icons to the Dock, eventually, you find that you rarely use some of these programs. Rather than let them clutter your Dock, it's better to get rid of them. You have two ways of removing a program icon from the Dock:

✦ Click the program icon that you want to remove from the Dock and drag it up and away from the Dock; then release the mouse button. Your unwanted program icon disappears in an animated puff of smoke.

✦ Control-click the program icon and choose Remove from Dock from the shortcut menu.

Note: Removing a program icon from the Dock doesn't remove or delete the actual program. To do that, see the "Uninstalling Software" section, later in this chapter.

If you like having a program icon in the Dock but want to make room for other programs, you can store program icons in a folder and then store that folder on the right of the divider in the Dock, thanks to a feature called Stacks. Now to load that program, you can click its folder icon in the Dock and then click the program icon. To find out more about using Stacks to add, remove, and work with folders on the Dock, check out Book I, Chapter 5.

A couple of things you can't do:

✦ You can never remove the Finder and Trash icons from the Dock.

✦ You can't remove a program icon from the Dock if the program is still running.

By double-clicking icons

The Mac represents a file as a graphically descriptive icon with a name. Icons can represent two types of files: programs and documents.

Program files represent software programs that actually do something, such as play a game of chess or send, receive, and organize your e-mail. *Document files* represent data created by software programs, such as a letter created by a word processor, a business report created by a presentation application, or a movie created by a video-editing program.

Program icons are often distinct enough to help you identify the type of program they represent. For example, the iTunes program icon appears as a musical note over a CD, the iPhoto icon appears as a camera over a photograph, and the Mail program icon (for sending and receiving e-mail) appears as a postage stamp.

Document icons often appear with the icon of the program that created them or as thumbnail images of their content, as shown in Figure 4-3. So, if you save a Web page in Safari, your file appears as a page with the Safari icon over it.

Figure 4-3:
Document icons usually display either thumbnail images of their content or the icon of the program that created them.

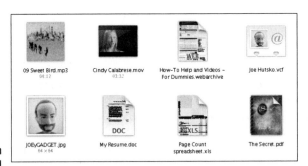

A third type of icon you might see is an *alias* icon, which represents a link to a program icon or a document icon. You find out more about alias icons in the "Working with Alias Icons" section, later in this chapter.

Double-clicking a program icon

Because a program's icon might not appear in the Dock, you have to be able to access icons another way. Luckily, you can find program icons by looking for them using the Finder. (You can find most programs stored in the Applications folder, but the Finder can help you find any programs that are stored in another folder.)

It's actually possible to store a program icon in any folder on your hard drive, but you should always store programs in the Applications folder. That way, if you need to find that program again, you just have to look in the Applications folder instead of trying to remember whether you stored it somewhere else.

To run a program by double-clicking its icon, follow these steps:

1. **Click the Finder icon in the Dock and then click the Applications folder in the Finder window's sidebar to display the programs installed on your Mac.**

2. **Scroll through the Applications folder window until you see the program icon you want and then double-click the icon to run the program (you can also choose File⇨Open, or ⌘+O, or ⌘+↓).**

(You might have to double-click a folder that contains a program icon.)

Your chosen program appears, typically with a blank window, ready for you to do something programmy — such as typing text.

Here are a couple of shortcuts for you to try:

✦ Click your Mac's Desktop and press ⌘+Shift+A to open your Mac's Applications folder.

✦ Typing the first letter of a program file or document you are looking for in any Finder window will instantly jump to and select the first icon that matches the letter you type. For instance, to locate Safari in the Applications folder quickly, press S to jump to and select Safari (or another program icon whose name starts with S that might come before Safari, if one is present).

Double-clicking a document icon

When you double-click a program icon, you start (that is, *run* or *launch*) that particular program. Unfortunately, if you want to use your newly opened program to work on an existing file, you then have to search for and open that file by using the program's File⇨Open command.

As an alternative to running a program and then having to find and open the file you want to work with, the Mac gives you the option of double-clicking the document icon you want to open. When you double-click a document icon, your Mac typically opens the program that created that document and then loads that document in the program window.

Sometimes if you double-click a document icon, an entirely different program loads and displays your file. This can occur if you save your file in a different file format. For example, if you save an iMovie project as a QuickTime file, double-clicking the QuickTime file opens the QuickTime Player instead of iMovie.

Think of double-clicking a document icon as equivalent to the two-step process of first opening a program and then opening the document you want to view or revise.

To double-click a document icon, follow these steps:

1. **Click the Finder icon in the Dock and then click the Documents folder in the sidebar (or double-click the Documents folder icon on the right side of the Finder window) to open the Documents window.**

2. **Scroll through the Documents window until you see the document icon you want and then double-click it.**

   (You might need to double-click one or more folders until you find the document you want.)

   Your Mac loads the program that created the document (if it's not already running) and displays your chosen document in a window. If your Mac can't find the program that created the document, it might load another program, or it might ask you to choose an existing program on your Mac that can open the document.

Here are a couple of other ways you can quickly access your Mac's Documents folder:

✦ Click the Desktop and press ⌘+Shift+D to open your Mac's Documents folder.

✦ Control-click the Documents icon in the Dock and choose "Open Documents" (or click and hold on the Documents icon to see the folders and documents inside it, move the pointer to the one you want to open, and then let go of the mouse button).

Although it's possible to store document icons anywhere on your hard drive, it's a good idea always to store documents inside the Documents folder so you'll know where to start looking first.

From the Apple menu's Recent Items

This one's a no-brainer: Choose ⌘⇨Recent Items and then choose the application you want to run from the list of recently run programs. You can also choose a recently created or viewed document or other file to automatically launch the associated program and load the document or file.

With Spotlight

As an alternative to clicking an application's Dock icon, or locating a program or document by clicking through folders, you can use your Mac's handy Spotlight feature to quickly open programs or documents for you. There are two ways to use Spotlight to run programs and open documents.

To use the Finder to open a program or document with your Mac's Spotlight feature, follow these steps:

1. **Click the Finder icon in the Dock, click in the Search text box and type all or part of a document name (or the contents of a document you want to open), and then press Return.**

   A list of documents matching what you typed appears in the Finder, as shown in Figure 4-4.

2. **Double-click the document you want to open.**

   Your Mac loads a program that displays the contents of your document in a window, ready for you to work with it.

Running, Installing, and Uninstalling Programs

Figure 4-4: The Search text box can help you find any file, including music tracks, pictures, and e-mail messages.

To use the Spotlight menu bar icon to open a program or document with Spotlight, follow these steps:

1. **Click the Spotlight icon in the far right corner of your Mac's menu bar (or press ⌘+spacebar) and begin typing the first few letters of the program name or file (or contents of a file) you're looking for, as shown in Figure 4-5.**

2. **Move the pointer to the program or document you want to open and click the mouse.**

   When you select an application from the Spotlight list of matches, the program will run and a blank document will appear. When you select a document from the list of matches, the program will run and the document you select will appear.

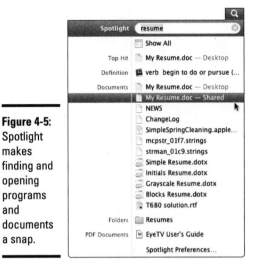

Figure 4-5:
Spotlight
makes
finding and
opening
programs
and
documents
a snap.

Working with Alias Icons

An *alias icon* acts like a link to another icon. Double-clicking an alias icon works identically to double-clicking the actual program or document icon. The biggest advantage of alias icons is that you can move and place alias icons anywhere you want without physically moving (and perhaps losing) a program or document icon.

One way to use alias icons is to create alias icons to your program icons and then store those alias icons in a folder. Now store that folder to the right of the divider in the Dock, and you have easy access to lots of program icons without cluttering the Dock.

You can do the following things with alias icons:

✦ **Create an alias icon:** Click the Finder icon in the Dock, click the icon you want to select, and then choose File➪Make Alias. (You can also Control-click it and choose Make Alias, or press ⌘+L.) A copy of your chosen icon appears in the window with an arrow and *alias* added to its name, as shown in Figure 4-6.

✦ **Move an alias icon:** Because it's pointless to store the original icon and the alias icon in the same location, you should store the alias icon in a new location. To move an alias icon, click it to select it and then drag it to the Desktop or folder you want to move it to.

✦ **Delete an alias icon:** Simply Control-click it and choose Move to Trash, or press ⌘+Delete. Note that deleting an alias icon never deletes the original icon — meaning that if you delete an alias icon that represents a program, you never delete the actual program. The only way to delete a program or document is to delete the original program or document icon.

Alias icon

Figure 4-6:
A tiny arrow
identifies an
alias icon.

You can store alias icons on the Desktop for fast access, or in specific folders to organize documents without physically moving them to a new location. (Essentially, the Dock replaces the need to place alias icons on the Desktop, and Smart Folders duplicate the process of creating and storing alias icons in a folder. You find out how to use Smart Folders in Book I, Chapter 5.)

Switching between Programs

When you run multiple programs, you have multiple windows from different programs cluttering your screen, much like covering a clean tabletop with piles of different papers. To help keep your screen organized, you can switch between different programs (say a word processor and a Web browser) as well as switch to different windows displayed by the same program (such as a word processor displaying a window containing a letter of resignation and a second window containing a resume).

Your Mac offers quite a few different ways to switch between different programs, including using the Dock, using the Application Switcher, clicking a window of a different program, using Exposé, or by hiding programs or entire desktops (which I write about in Book I, Chapter 3).

I discuss the first three ways of switching between running programs in the following list:

✦ **Using the Dock:** Click a program icon in the Dock that has a dot underneath it. That's all there is to it! If you want to switch to a specific document window opened by a certain program, you can switch to that program and that document window at once. Control-click the icon of the program you want to switch to and then click the name of the document you want to open. Easy peasy!

✦ **Using the Application Switcher:** The Application Switcher is a feature that displays icons of all active programs. After you open the Application Switcher, choose the icon of the program you want to use by holding down the ⌘ key and pressing the Tab key repeatedly to move left to right from one running program to the next, as shown in Figure 4-7. When you release the ⌘ key, the chosen program moves to the front of your screen.

Figure 4-7: The Application Switcher displays icons of all currently running programs.

Pressing the Shift key while holding down ⌘ and pressing Tab will move the selection from right to left. You can also press ⌘+Tab and then let go of the Tab key and use the arrow keys to navigate left and right.

If a program has several files open in different windows, the Application Switcher just switches you to that program, but you still have to find the specific window to view.

✦ **Clicking different windows:** A fast, but somewhat clumsier way to switch between programs is to rearrange your windows so you can see two or more windows at one time, as shown in Figure 4-8. To switch to another window, click anywhere inside that window (or press ⌘+`).

Save some mouse clicks by pressing ⌘+` to switch between open windows in a running program!

The Dock or the Application Switcher can switch to a specific program, but if that program has several open windows, you need to take time to search for the specific window you want to use. As a faster alternative, Exposé, shown in Figure 4-9, lets you view thumbnail versions of all your open windows from all running programs. Then all you have to do is click the exact window you want to use. To learn how to use Exposé, check out Book I, Chapter 3.

Figure 4-8:
Arranging windows side by side lets you view and access each one at the click of the mouse.

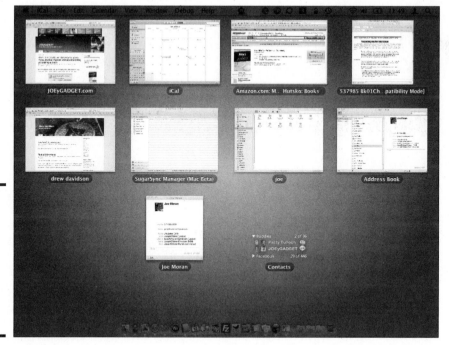

Figure 4-9:
Exposé shows you all open windows so you can choose the one you want.

Quitting Programs

When you shut down a program, you also shut down all document windows that program may have open. However, if you only shut down a document in an open application, the program keeps running.

Closing a document

If you want to stop working with or viewing a specific document but want to keep the program running, you can close just that particular document. You have three different ways to close a document window:

+ Choose File⇨Close.

+ Press ⌘+W.

+ Click the Close button of the document window.

If you try to close a window before saving the file, a dialog appears, asking whether you want to save your file.

Shutting down a program

When you finish using a program, it's a good idea to shut it down to free up your Mac's memory to run other programs. The more programs you have running at the same time on your Mac, the slower your Mac can become, so always shut down programs if you don't need them anymore.

To shut down a program, you have three choices:

+ Choose the menu associated with the application and choose Quit (such as iPhoto⇨Quit iPhoto to shut down the iPhoto program).

+ Press ⌘+Q.

+ Control-click the program icon in the Dock and choose Quit from the shortcut menu that appears.

If you try to shut down a program that displays a window containing a document that you haven't saved yet, a dialog appears, asking whether you want to save your file.

Force-quitting a program

Despite the Mac's reputation for reliability, there's always a chance that a program will crash, freeze, or hang, which are less-than-technical-terms for a program screwing up and not reacting when you click the mouse or press a key. When a program no longer responds to any attempts to work or shut down, you might have to resort to a last-resort procedure known as a *force-quit.*

As the name implies, force-quitting makes a program shut down whether it wants to or not. You can force-quit a program two ways:

✦ **Choose ⬛➪Force Quit (or press ⌘+Option+Esc).** The Force Quit dialog appears, as shown in Figure 4-10. Frozen or crashed programs might appear in the Force Quit dialog with the phrase `(not responding)` next to its name. Just click the program you want to force-quit and click the Force Quit button.

Figure 4-10:
The Force Quit dialog shows you the names of all currently running programs.

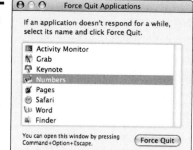

✦ **Control-click a program icon in the Dock and choose Force Quit from the shortcut menu that appears.** If the program hasn't really crashed or if your Mac thinks the program hasn't crashed, you won't see a Force Quit option in this pop-up menu. In that case, you may want to wait a minute or so to give your Mac time to correct the seemingly hung-up program. If after waiting, the program still appears stuck but you don't see the Force Quit option, hold down the Option key, Control-click a program icon in the Dock, and then choose Force Quit.

If you force-quit a program, you will lose any data you changed right before the program suddenly froze or crashed. For instance, if I just performed ⌘+S to save this chapter before writing this sentence, then performed a force-quit, this sentence would be missing the next time I reopened this chapter.

Organizing Multiple Desktops with Spaces

Spaces is a handy feature available since Mac OS X 10.5 Leopard. Essentially, Spaces multiplies your Mac's single display into up to 16 separate "virtual" screens, or Desktops. The main purpose of Spaces is to help organize multiple programs running at the same time. Rather than cram multiple program windows on a single screen (Desktop), Spaces lets you store multiple programs in separate Desktops. One Desktop might contain only Internet programs, such as Safari and Mail, whereas a second Desktop might contain only Microsoft Word and the Mac's built-in Dictionary program.

If one program has multiple windows open, you can store each program window on a separate Desktop. For example, if you have a word processor and open a personal letter and a business letter, you could store the personal letter window on one Desktop and the business letter window on a second Desktop.

Spaces creates multiple Desktops to create the illusion of multiple computer screens. Any configured settings will apply to all Desktops, such as the appearance of the Dock or a screensaver.

After you enable Spaces and define the total number of Desktops to create, you can view all your Desktops as thumbnail images. Then you can open and move windows from one Desktop to another.

Turning on Spaces and creating Desktops

Before you can use Spaces to switch between multiple Desktops, you have to turn on Spaces and create some Desktops. Initially, Spaces creates four Desktops, but you can add up to 16 Desktops if you want. The more Desktops you add the harder it can be to manage them all, so the trick is to pick the number of Desktops you can manage, such as two or three or four. Later, if you find that you need more Desktops, you can add more. Likewise, if you find that you created too many Desktops, you can delete some.

Turn on Spaces and create your desired number of Desktops by following these steps:

1. **Choose ⌘⇨System Preferences and then choose the Exposé & Spaces icon.**

2. **Click the Spaces tab in the top center of the pane (if it isn't selected already) and then select the Enable Spaces check box, as shown in Figure 4-11.**

3. **Click the Plus or Minus icons in the Rows and Columns fields to change the number of Desktops (between 2 and 16).**

The number of rows and columns you create defines how many Desktops you create, and how they're arranged. You might choose, for instance, to create up to 16 Desktops in a single row, or arrange four Desktops in two rows of two columns (see Figure 4-11).

The layout of Desktops matters only when you switch between Desktops by using the Control key in conjunction with the arrow keys. If you arrange 16 Desktops in a row, switching from Desktop 2 to Desktop

14 would require pressing the Control+→ twelve times (or Ctrl+←
four times). However, if you arrange 16 Desktops in four rows and columns, switching from Desktop 2 to desktop 14 would require pressing
Control+↓ three times.

4. **Click the Close button of the System Preferences window.**

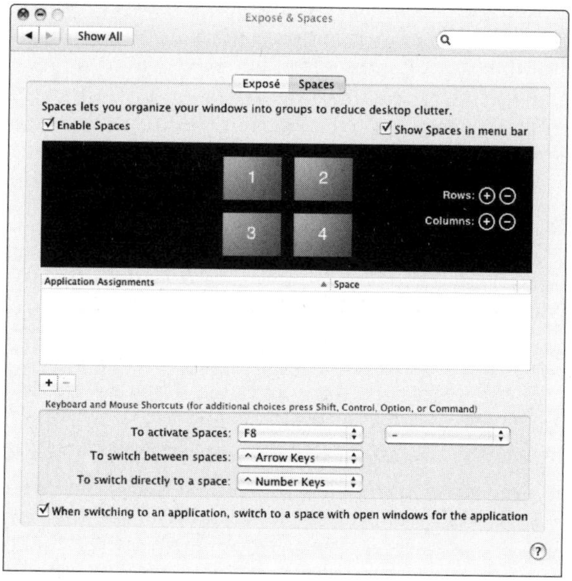

Figure 4-11:
The Spaces
pane lets
you turn
on Spaces
and define
how many
desktops to
create.

Configuring Spaces

When you configure Spaces, you can define the number of Desktops to use
and the shortcut keys to activate Spaces or switch to a specific Desktop.

From the Spaces pane of the Exposé & Spaces pane (refer to Figure 4-11),
you can change the following settings to your liking:

✦ **Using a Spaces menulet:** Select (or clear) the Show Spaces in Menu Bar
check box. Selecting this check box displays a Spaces menulet on the
right side of the menu bar that you click to switch between Desktops.

✦ **Activating Spaces:** Choose a function key from the To Activate Spaces
pop-up menu. The default Spaces function key is Fn+F3. You can hold
down Shift, Control, Option, or Command — or a combination of these
keys — to add additional keys to the Activate Spaces function key you
choose from the pop-up menu.

Note: On most Mac keyboards, you must press the Fn key to activate a function key. Therefore, to use the Activate Spaces function key, you press Fn+F3.

✦ **Switching between Desktops:** Choose a shortcut key from the To Switch between Spaces pop-up menu. The default is the Control+arrow keys combination.

✦ **Switching to a specific Desktop:** Choose a shortcut key from the To Switch Directly to a Space pop-up menu. The default is the Control+number keys combination where the number key you press (1 through 0 for Desktops 1 through 10) identifies the number of the Desktop you want to view. To switch to Desktops beyond number 10, either use the Control+arrow keys shortcut described in the preceding bullet, or click the Spaces menulet on the menu bar to choose those Desktops.

✦ **Switch to a space with open windows:** Click the When Switching to an Application, Switch to a Space with Open Windows for the Application check box to make a Space containing windows for a running application with open document windows come to the front when you click that application's icon.

Moving program windows to different Desktops

When you run a program, it appears in the Space you're working in. So, if you're in Space 1 and you run the Safari Web browser, Safari appears on the Desktop of Space 1. You can switch to another Space to launch another program that appears in that space. Or, you can move a program's window from one Space to another, so the window appears where you want.

You can move program windows to different Desktops by using the Spaces function key or by dragging a program window from one Desktop Space to another Desktop Space. To move a program window to a different Desktop by using the Spaces function key, follow these steps:

1. **Press the Spaces function key (Fn+F3, unless you changed it) and then press Fn+F9.**

Exposé displays every window as a thumbnail within each Desktop image, as shown in Figure 4-12.

2. **Click and drag a program window from one Desktop to a different Desktop, release the mouse button, and then repeat for each program window you want to move to a different Desktop.**

3. **Click the Desktop that you want to use right now.**

Your chosen Desktop expands to fill the screen.

Figure 4-12:
Spaces
displays
thumbnail
images of
all your
separate
Desktops.

To drag a program window from one Desktop Space to another one:

1. **Click and hold down the mouse pointer on the Title bar of the program window you want to move to another Desktop; while still holding down the mouse, drag the program window to the left, right, bottom, or top edge of your Mac's screen and keep holding down until the Spaces switching indicator appears, as shown in Figure 4-13.**

2. **If the adjacent Desktop Space is the one you want to move to, release the mouse button, and begin working with the program window in the Desktop Space you moved to. Otherwise, continue holding down the mouse button and move to the left, right, top, or bottom edge of the screen to move to the next adjacent Desktop Space and repeat until you arrive on the Desktop Space you want to move to.**

Switching Desktops

After you arrange program windows on each Desktop, you can switch to a different Desktop at any time by using one of the following methods:

✦ Press Fn+F3 (or whatever function key you assigned to activate Spaces) and then click the thumbnail of the Desktop you want to switch to.

✦ Click the Spaces menulet on the menu bar and choose a Desktop number from the drop-down menu.

✦ Press the Control+arrow key combination to move left, right, up, and down until you arrive on the Desktop you want to switch to.

✦ Press the Control+number key combination. (To view Desktop 1, for example, press Control+1.) With the Control+number key combination, you can switch to Desktops 1 through 10. To switch to Desktops 11 through 16, use one of the above three methods.

Turning off Spaces

If you want to turn off Spaces, choose ⌘⇨System Preferences⇨Exposé & Spaces, click the Spaces tab, and then deselect the Enable Spaces check box.

When you turn off Spaces, all your program windows return to a single Desktop. If you turn Spaces on again, your Mac remembers the number of Desktops you had before you turned Spaces off. If you restart your Mac while Spaces is displaying multiple Desktops, your Mac shuts down all windows in all Desktops. When your Mac starts up again, all your Desktops are empty.

Figure 4-13: Spaces will switch from the original Desktop to the adjacent Desktop Space.

Acquiring New Software Programs

You can find the more popular Mac programs packaged in pretty boxes that typically contain a single CD/DVD, a thin manual (if any), and a lot of air. Most of these commercial programs are written and sold by big companies, such as Apple, Microsoft, Intuit, and Adobe.

All new Mac programs are designed to run on today's Macs with Intel processors running the Mac OS X operating system. However, they cannot run any software designed for earlier Macs running OS X's predecessor, OS 9, without the help of an additional program (such as SheepShaver, `http://gwenole.beauchesne.info/en/projects/sheepshaver`).

No matter how big your local computer store is, it can offer only a fraction of all available Macintosh programs. For a much greater selection of software, you have to browse for Mac programs on the Web where you can find three types of software: commercial, shareware, and freeware/open source. The following list spells out how they differ:

✦ **Commercial software:** Most companies that sell software through stores also sell the same commercial programs on the Web. Sometimes you can even get a discount if you buy the program directly from the publisher and download it via the Internet.

As a further enticement, many commercial programs on the Web often offer a trial version that you can download and use for a limited amount of time, such as 30 days. After your trial period is over, the program will either stop working or run with many features turned off. If you pay for the software, the publisher will send you a registration key that converts the trial program into a fully functional version. To find trial versions of programs, just visit the Web sites of different software publishers.

✦ **Shareware software:** Usually, shareware programs are limited functionality, time-limited trial versions, or fully functional programs written by individuals or small companies. The idea is for you to try out the program, and if you like it, you're then supposed to pay for it.

✦ **Freeware software:** Freeware programs are typically simple utilities or games, although some commercial companies distribute freeware programs to promote their other products. Sometimes companies offer a freeware version of a program and then sell a more advanced version of that same program. As the name implies, freeware programs are available for you to copy and use at no cost. *Donationware* is a term for a freeware program whose creator welcomes donations to help the developer cover the cost of maintaining and developing new versions of the program.

A variation of freeware programs is *open source.* Like freeware programs, open source programs can be copied and used without paying for them. The main difference is that open source programs let you modify the program yourself if you know the specific programming language that the program is written in.

Table 4-1 lists some popular open source programs and their commercial equivalents.

Besides being free, many open source programs offer additional features that their commercial rivals lack.

For example, the Safari Web browser comes free with every Mac, but many Web sites are designed to work only when viewed through Internet Explorer or Firefox. If you use Safari, it's possible that you won't be able to view some Web sites correctly, so you might want to switch to Firefox (or at least keep Firefox on your hard drive) and if you run across a Web site that Safari can't open, you can view that Web site in Firefox.

You can try tricking Web sites that don't work correctly with Safari into thinking you're running a different Web browser: To do so, turn on Safari's Develop menu, and then click Develop➪User Agent and choose one of the other Web browser choices (such as Internet Explorer or Firefox). To turn on the Develop menu, click Safari➪Preferences to open the Safari Preferences window, and then click the Advanced tab and check the Show Develop Menu in Menu Bar check box.

To find more shareware, freeware, and open source programs for your Mac, visit the following sites:

✦ Open Source Mac (www.opensourcemac.org)

✦ VersionTracker (www.versiontracker.com)

✦ MacShare.com (www.macshare.com)

✦ Pure-Mac (www.pure-mac.com)

✦ MacForge (www.macforge.net)

✦ Tucows (www.tucows.com)

✦ MacUpdate (www.macupdate.com)

Installing Software

The most common place to install software is inside the Applications folder, so you should specify that folder when installing software. Some programs store their program icon inside the Applications folder plain as day, but others hide their program icons within another folder.

Table 4-1	**Popular Open Source Programs and the Commercial Programs They Can Replace**	
Open Source Program	*Purpose*	*Commercial Equivalent*
NeoOffice (www.neooffice.org)	Office suite containing word processing, spreadsheet, presentation, drawing, and database programs	Microsoft Office
OpenOffice.org (www.openoffice.org)	Office suite containing word processing, spreadsheet, presentation, drawing, and database programs	Microsoft Office
AbiWord (www.abisource.com)	Word processor	Microsoft Word
Firefox (www.mozilla.com)	Web browser	Safari
Camino (www.caminobrowser.org)	Web browser	Safari
Thunderbird (www.mozilla.com)	E-mail program	Mail
Tux Paint (www.tuxpaint.org)	Children's painting program	Broderbund Kid Pix
Paintbrush (http://paintbrush.sourceforge.net)	Basic image editing	Adobe Photoshop Elements
Nvu (www.nvu.com)	Web page designing	Adobe Dreamweaver
Audacity (http://audacity.sourceforge.net)	Audio editing	Adobe SoundBooth
ClamXav (www.clamxav.com)	Antivirus scanner	Norton AntiVirus
Buddi (http://buddi.sourceforge.net)	Money management program	Quicken
celtx (www.celtx.com)	Screenplay word processor	Final Draft

A program icon actually represents a folder containing multiple files. Hiding these details from you and letting you treat a folder of files as a single program icon ensures that you can't accidentally delete or move a single crucial file that the entire program needs to work. For the technically curious, you can see the hidden files tucked inside an application by Control-clicking the application icon and choosing Show Package Contents from the shortcut menu. You're free to look around, but I strongly advise that you don't delete, move, modify, or rename any of the files you see because doing so might render the program inoperable.

Installing software from a CD/DVD

Software bought from a store will probably come on a CD/DVD. When you insert the CD/DVD into your Mac, you might see nothing but a single program icon, along with several other files labeled Read Me or Documentation.

Other times, you might insert a CD/DVD and see an icon labeled Install. When you see an Install icon, you need to run this installation program to install the program on your hard drive.

When installing software, your Mac might ask for your password — the one you set up when you created your user account. (For more on user accounts, see Book I, Chapter 6.) Requiring you to enter your password is your Mac's way of attempting to prevent malicious computer viruses or Trojan horse programs from installing themselves without your knowledge.

Requiring your password to install a program also keeps unauthorized people (such as your kids) from installing programs that you might not want on your Mac, or programs you want to approve of before allowing another user to install on your Mac.

Requiring you to enter your password to install a program doesn't guarantee a program you want to install doesn't contain a virus or Trojan horse program. And although most programs you can install on your Mac are scanned for viruses and other nasty threats before they're made available to download or run from a disc, installing an anti-virus protection program and taking additional steps to secure and protect your Mac is your safest bet when it comes to protecting your identity, your privacy, and the integrity of files and information on your Mac's hard drive. I show you ways you can secure and protect your Mac from online threats in Book IV, Chapter 4.

Dragging a program icon off the CD/DVD

If you insert a program's CD/DVD into your computer and just see a program icon, you install the program by dragging the program icon into your Applications folder. To do this, follow these steps:

1. **Insert the software CD/DVD into your Mac.**

    A window appears, showing the contents of the CD/DVD, as shown in Figure 4-14.

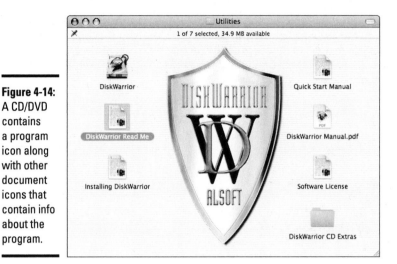

Figure 4-14: A CD/DVD contains a program icon along with other document icons that contain info about the program.

2. **Click the Finder icon in the Dock and then choose File⇨New Finder Window (or press ⌘+N).**

   A second Finder window appears, and is ready to do your bidding.

3. **Move the CD/DVD window and the Finder so they appear side by side.**

4. **Click and drag the program icon displayed in the CD/DVD window to the Applications folder in the Finder Sidebar.**

   Doing so copies the program icon from the CD/DVD to the Applications folder.

Running an installer program

Instead of displaying a program icon, a CD/DVD might display an Install icon, as shown in Figure 4-15. The installer is simply a special program designed to copy a program from the CD/DVD and place it in your Applications folder, as well as other files to other folders on your Mac.

To install software using an installer program on a CD/DVD, follow these steps:

1. **Insert the software CD/DVD into your Mac, and look for an icon labeled Install in the window that appears showing the contents of the CD/DVD.**

   The Install icon typically looks like a cardboard box with its top opened up.

2. **Double-click this Install icon and then click Continue on the dialog that appears asking whether you really want to continue installing.**

3. **Follow the on-screen instructions.**

If you have multiple hard drives, the installation program might ask where to install the program. (Generally, you should choose your Mac's built-in hard drive unless you have a reason to store the program elsewhere.) Right before the program installs, you're asked for your password.

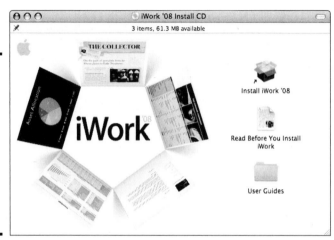

Figure 4-15: A CD/DVD might contain an Install icon that can automatically install a program on your Mac.

Installing software from the Web

Although you can buy software in a box from your local computer store, it's becoming far more common to buy software directly from the Web. Not only does this save the publisher the time and expense of packaging a program in a fancy box and shipping it to a store, but it also gives you the software to use right away.

When you download a program off the Internet, the program usually arrives as a DMG (disc image) file. Safari, Mac OS X's default Web browser, stores all downloaded files in a special Downloads folder in your Home folder (unless you direct it to your Mac's Desktop or another folder of your choosing). The Downloads folder also appears right next to the Trash icon in the Dock. (If you're using a different browser, such as Firefox, you might need to define where it stores downloaded files.)

Distributing software as a DMG file is the most common way to compress files for sending via the Internet. A DMG file essentially copies the contents of an entire folder and smashes it into a single file. You can always identify a DMG file because its icon appears with a hard drive icon, and the name includes the three-letter .dmg extension, as shown in Figure 4-16.

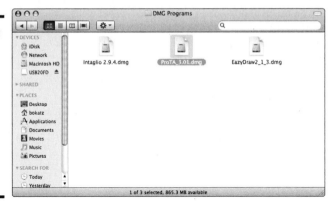

Figure 4-16:
DMG files always use the same icon and include the .dmg extension at the end of the filename.

After you have a DMG file on your Mac, you're set to install the software inside it. Just follow these steps:

1. **Double-click the DMG file that contains the program you want to install on your Mac. (If a License Agreement window appears, click the Agree button.)**

   The DMG file displays a device icon on the Desktop and displays a Finder window that contains the program icon stored inside the DMG file, as shown in Figure 4-17.

2. **Click the Finder icon in the Dock, choose File⇨New Finder Window, and then click and drag the program icon in the DMG Finder window to the Applications folder in the second Finder window.**

   Doing so installs the program in your Applications folder.

3. **Control-click the DMG device icon on the Desktop, and when a short-cut menu appears, choose Eject.**

If a DMG file you double-click reveals a program's installer icon instead of a program icon, double-click the program installer and follow the steps the installer displays.

When you open a DMG file, it creates a device icon, which acts like a separate storage device. This device icon acts like a temporary disk so you can copy files from it. After you install a program from the DMG file, you might want to eject the DMG device icon just to clear it out of the way. (Leaving it on your Desktop won't hurt anything.)

After you install a program on your Mac, you can always find it again by looking in the folder where you stored it, which is usually the Applications folder. At this point, you might want to add the program icon to the Dock or place an alias icon on the Desktop (see the earlier section "Working with Alias Icons").

DMG Finder window

Figure 4-17: Expanding a DMG file displays a program icon that you can drag to the Applications folder.

DMG device icon

 The first time you run a newly installed program, a dialog might pop up (see Figure 4-18), informing you that the program was downloaded from the Internet, and/or you are running the program for the first time. To run the program, click Open. This dialog pops up to as a way of trying to protect you from malicious programs that might try to install and run automatically. If you didn't try to run a program and see this dialog pop up, click Cancel.

Figure 4-18: A dialog alerts you when you're running a program for the first time.

> You are opening the application "AppZapper" for the first time. Are you sure you want to open this application?
>
> "AppZapper" was downloaded today at 2:50 AM from appzapper.com.
>
> (?)   (Show Web Page)   (Cancel)   (Open)

ZIP, SIT, and other strange files

Occasionally, you might run across files with such extensions as ZIP, SIT, .SEA, or RAR. These types of files are all different ways to pack multiple files into a single, compressed file. The Mac can recognize and open ZIP compressed files, but if you need to open other kinds of compressed files, you need to install and use a free program called StuffIt Expander (www.stuffit.com). The StuffIt Expander program can open most kinds of compressed files, even those compressed files originally created on Windows or Linux computers. Your Mac can create ZIP and DMG files (which you find out more about in Chapter 5 of this mini-book), but, if you want to create other types of compressed files, such as SIT or RAR files, you have to get another program, such as the commercial version of the StuffIt program.

Uninstalling Software

If you no longer use or need a program, you can always remove it from your hard drive. By uninstalling a program, you can free up space on your hard drive.

Before uninstalling a program, make sure you don't uninstall a program that you might need after all.

Uninstalling a program can involve three parts:

✦ **Uninstalling the program:** Uninstalling a program, either by dragging it to the Trash or running an accompanying uninstaller program, physically removes the program from your hard drive.

✦ **Deleting program icons/alias icons:** When you delete a program, you don't necessarily delete that program's icon from the Dock or any alias icons that you created from that program icon. To delete a program's alias icon from the Dock, click and drag the alias icon up and away from the Dock; then let go to make the alias icon disappear in a puff of smoke. To delete a program's alias icon from the Desktop or inside a folder, click and drag the alias icon to the Trash; then click Finder➪Empty Trash to delete the alias icon (and any other items you may have dragged into the Trash bin).

✦ **Deleting program settings:** Most programs store user settings in the Library folder, which is located inside your Home folder. When you uninstall a program by dragging it to the Trash, its user settings files — also referred to as *program preferences* — remain on your hard drive. Uninstalling a program using an accompanying uninstaller program sometimes deletes your user settings files automatically, or offers you the option to do so if you wish. Although not necessarily harmful, you might want to delete a program's user settings files off your hard drive to free up space for more programs or documents, and to protect potentially personal information from prying eyes if you are giving away or selling the computer to another person. To delete a program's user settings files from your Mac's hard drive, check out the "Removing user setting files" section, a few pages ahead.

If a program you want to uninstall comes with an uninstaller program, such as this one that comes with Microsoft Office:

Double-click it to uninstall your program rather than dragging it to the Trash. However, the next few sections give you a more detailed look at what's involved when you uninstall a program by dragging it to the Trash.

Uninstalling a program

Uninstalling a Mac program is typically as simple as dragging and dropping its program icon into the Trash.

To uninstall a program, follow these steps:

1. **Make sure the program you want to uninstall isn't running. If it is running, shut it down by choosing the Quit command (⌘+Q) and then clicking the Finder icon in the Dock.**

The Finder appears.

2. **Click the Applications folder in the Finder Sidebar to display the programs installed on your Mac and then click the program icon or folder that you want to uninstall.**

3. **Choose File⇨Move to Trash. (You can also drag the program icon or folder to the Trash icon in the Dock, or press ⌘+Delete to move the program icon or folder to the Trash.)**

In some cases, you might be prompted for your password when you move a program file to the Trash. If so, type in your password, then click OK or press Return.

The Trash icon displays an image showing the Trash filled with crumpled papers.

Before emptying the Trash, make sure you permanently want to delete any other programs or documents you've might have dragged into the Trash. After you empty the Trash, any files contained therein are deleted from your hard drive permanently.

4. **Choose Finder⇨Empty Trash. (You can also Control-click the Trash icon and choose Empty Trash, or press ⌘+Shift+Delete to empty the Trash.)**

Adios, application!

Removing program icons from the Dock and Desktop

After you uninstall a program, it's also wise to remove all Dock or alias icons because those icons will no longer work. To remove a program icon from the Dock, click the program icon that you want to remove, drag the icon up and away from the Dock, and then release the mouse button. Your chosen program disappears in a puff of animated smoke.

If you created multiple alias icons of a program, click the Finder icon to open a new Finder window, click in the Spotlight text box, and then type the name of the program you uninstalled followed by the word *alias,* such as **PowerPoint alias** or **Adium alias**. The Finder will display the location of the specified alias icons, as shown in Figure 4-19. Hold down the ⌘ key, click each alias icon you want to delete, and then press ⌘+Delete to move them to the Trash. *Au revoir!*

Spotlight text box

Figure 4-19:
Spotlight can help you find all alias icons no matter where you stored them.

Removing user setting files

Almost every program creates special user setting files that contain custom settings and preferences for the program, such as the default font used to type text when you use the program or your choice of toolbar icons displayed by the program. When you uninstall a program by dragging it to the Trash, the program's user setting files remain on your computer.

The more unnecessary files you have cluttering your hard drive, the slower your Mac might perform because it needs to keep track of these unused files even though it isn't using them anymore. To keep your Mac in optimum condition, you should delete the user setting files of programs you uninstall from your computer. You can do that manually, or you can buy a program to do it for you automatically. I explain both ways.

Manually removing user setting files

Manually removing user setting files requires deleting individual files or entire folders from your Mac's hard drive. This process isn't difficult, though it can be tedious.

If you feel squeamish about deleting files that you don't understand, don't delete them without an expert's help. If you delete the wrong files, you could mess up the way your Mac works.

Many programs store their user setting files in one or both of two folders: the Application Support folder and the Preferences folder. To find these two folders, click the Finder icon to open your Home folder, and then look inside the Library folder. Look inside both folders and click any icons or folders bearing the name of the program you uninstalled; then drag them to the Trash and choose File⇨Empty Trash (or press ⌘+Shift+Delete).

Automatically removing user setting files

Because manually deleting user setting and preference files might seem scary and intimidating, you might prefer to remove these files automatically. To do this, you need to buy and install a special uninstaller program. When you run an uninstaller program, you tell it which program you want to uninstall, and the uninstaller program identifies all the files used by that program, as shown in Figure 4-20.

Figure 4-20: An uninstaller program, such as AppZapper, can automatically find and delete all files used by a program.

Some popular uninstaller programs include

✦ AppZapper (www.appzapper.com), shown at work in Figure 4-20

✦ Spring Cleaning (http://my.smithmicro.com/mac/spring cleaning)

✦ Uninstaller (http://macmagna.free.fr)

Chapter 5: Working with Files and Folders

In This Chapter

- ✔ Using the Finder
- ✔ Organizing and viewing folders
- ✔ Creating folders
- ✔ Manipulating files and folders
- ✔ Archiving files and folders
- ✔ Searching files
- ✔ Working with Smart Folders
- ✔ Storing stuff on the Dock
- ✔ Burning files and folders to CD/DVD
- ✔ Deleting files and folders

*W*hen you need to organize stuff scattered around the house, one strategy would be to toss everything in the middle of the floor. However, it's probably easier to take a more organized approach by storing off-season clothes in one box, retired gadgets in another box, bills in one file folder (and receipts in another), and new books you want to read on your nightstand.

Computers work in a similar way. Although you could dump everything on the top level of your hard drive, it's more helpful to divide your hard drive in a way that can help you sort and arrange your stuff in an orderly, easy to get to fashion. Instead of boxes or shelves, the Mac uses *folders* (which tech-types such as yours truly also refer to as directories).

A folder lets you store and organize related files. The two most commonly used folders on your hard drive are the Applications folder and the Documents folder. The Applications folder contains programs; the Documents folder contains anything you create and save while using a program, such as a letter created by a word processor.

Folders can contain files or even other folders. The whole purpose of folders is to help keep your files organized so you can find them again.

Using the Finder

The main program for managing drives, files, and folders is the Finder. To access the Finder, click the Finder icon (the smiley face icon on the far left) in the Dock. The Finder is divided into two parts, as shown in Figure 5-1:

✦ A left pane, containing the *Sidebar,* which is where you find a list of connected storage devices as well as commonly used folders.

✦ A right pane, containing the contents of the selected drive or folder. If you switch to List, Column, or Cover Flow view, the right pane also shows a hierarchy of files stored inside folders.

Sidebar   Eject button

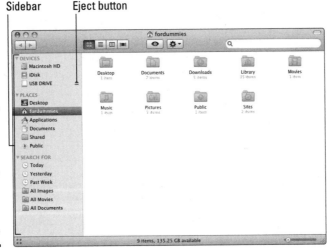

Figure 5-1: The Finder displays the files, folders, and storage devices connected to your Mac.

Understanding devices

The Devices category of the Sidebar lists all removable or nonremovable storage devices you can use for storing and saving files. Nonremovable devices are always connected to your Mac. Every Mac has one nonremovable device, which is the drive that your Mac boots from; typically, it's an internal hard drive, which is named Macintosh HD.

A removable drive is any additional drive that you plug into your Mac, such as an external hard drive. If your desktop Mac has a second hard drive installed, it also appears in the list of devices. You can eject a removable drive when you no longer need to access it or want to take it with you. Ejecting a removable hard drive or USB memory keychain drive removes its icon from the Finder. However, you cannot eject a nonremovable drive. After you eject a removable external hard drive or USB memory keychain drive, you can physically disconnect it.

If you physically try to disconnect a removable drive before you eject it, your Mac might mess up the data on that drive. Always eject removable drives before physically disconnecting them.

Removable devices can be attached and disconnected at any time. Common types of removable devices are external hard drives, USB flash drives, and digital cameras.

To connect a removable device to your Mac, just plug it in with the appropriate FireWire or USB cable.

To remove a removable device from a Mac, follow these steps:

1. **Click the Finder icon in the Dock to open the Finder window and then click the Eject button next to the connected drive you want to remove in the Finder window sidebar.**

If the removable device is a CD/DVD, your Mac ejects it. If the removable device is plugged into a USB (Universal Serial Bus) port or a FireWire port on your Mac, you physically have to disconnect the device.

2. **Wait until the device's icon disappears from the Finder.**

3. **Physically disconnect the device from your Mac.**

Some other ways to choose the Eject command are

✦ Click the device icon on the Desktop and choose File⇨Eject.

✦ Click the device icon and press ⌘+E.

✦ Control-click the device icon and choose Eject from the shortcut menu that appears.

✦ Drag the device icon to Trash on the Dock (it turns into an Eject button); then let go of the mouse.

Understanding folders

All the data you create and save by using a program (such as a word processing document or a photograph you copy from your digital camera to your Mac's hard drive) is stored as a file. Although you can store files on any storage device, the more files you store on a single device, the harder to find the one file you want at any given time.

Folders help you organize and manage files on a storage device in a logical way. You can even store folders inside other folders. Initially, every Mac hard drive contains the following folders:

✦ **Applications:** Contains all the software programs installed on your Mac.

✦ **Library:** Contains data and settings files used by programs installed on your Mac.

✦ **System:** Contains files used by the Mac OS X operating system.

✦ **Users:** Contains any files you create and save, including documents, pictures, music, and movies.

Never delete, rename, or move any files or folders stored in the Library or System folders, or else you might cause your Mac (or at least some programs on your Mac) to stop working. Files in the Library and System folders are used by your Mac to make your computer work. If you delete or rename files in either folder, your Mac might not operate the way it's supposed to, or worse, grind to a halt.

The Users folder contains the Home folder of each account for each person using your Mac, as shown in Figure 5-2. (See Book I, Chapter 6 for more information about creating accounts.) Each Home folder consists of additional folders:

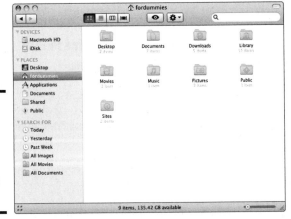

Figure 5-2:
The typical hierarchy of folders dividing your Mac's hard drive.

✦ **Desktop:** Contains any program and document icons that appear on your Mac's Desktop.

✦ **Documents:** Contains any files you create and save using different programs. (You'll probably want to organize this folder by creating multiple folders inside it to keep all your files organized in a logical, easy-to-manage way.)

✦ **Downloads:** Contains any files you've download from the Internet.

✦ **Library:** Contains folders and files used by any programs installed on your Mac. (*Note:* There are two Library folders, one stored on the top level of your hard drive, and one stored inside your Home folder.)

✦ **Movies:** Contains video files created by iMovie and certain other video playing or editing programs, such as Final Cut Express or QuickTime Player.

✦ **Music:** Contains audio files, such as music tracks stored in iTunes, or created by Garage Band or another audio program such as Audacity.

✦ **Pictures:** Contains digital photographs, such as those you import into iPhoto.

✦ **Public:** Provides a folder that you can use to share files with other user accounts on the same Mac, or with other users on a local area network.

✦ **Sites:** Provides a folder for storing any Web pages, such as those created with iWeb.

Every drive (such as your hard drive) can contain multiple folders, and each folder can contain multiple folders. A collection of folders stored inside folders stored inside other folders is a *hierarchy*. It's important to know how to view and navigate through a folder hierarchy (refer to Figure 5-2) to find specific files.

Navigating through the Finder

To access files you've stored on your Mac, you navigate through the different folders and devices by using the Finder. To navigate, you must first choose a connected drive or device and then you can open and exit folders or jump between specific folders. I explain each of these throughout these sections.

Opening a folder

After you choose a device, the Finder displays all the files and folders stored on that device. To open a folder (and move down the folder hierarchy), you have five choices:

✦ Double-click the folder.

✦ Click the folder and choose File⇨Open.

✦ Click the folder and press ⌘+O.

✦ Click the folder and press ⌘+↓.

✦ Control-click the folder and choose Open from the shortcut menu that appears.

Each time you open a folder within a folder, you're essentially moving down the hierarchy of folders stored on that device.

Exiting a folder

After you open a folder, you might want to go back and view the contents of the folder that encloses the current folder. To view the enclosing folder (and move up the folder hierarchy), choose one of the following:

+ Choose Go⇨Enclosing Folder.

+ Press ⌘+↑.

+ Hold down the ⌘ key, click the Finder title bar to display a list of enclosing folders, and then click an enclosing folder.

Click the Finder icon in the Dock, and then choose View⇨Show Path Bar to display the series of folders that lead to a folder you're currently viewing. Double-click on any of the folders in the series to switch to that folder's view.

Jumping to a specific folder

By moving up and down the folder hierarchy on a device, you can view the contents of every file stored on a device. However, you can also jump to a specific folder right away by choosing one of these options:

+ Choose a folder from the Go menu, such as your Mac's Utilities folder, for example, by choosing Go⇨Utilities, or press ⌘+Shift+U. Other folders listed in the Go menu can also be accessed by pressing the appropriate shortcut keys, which appear next to the folder name on the menu.

+ By clicking a folder displayed in the Sidebar.

+ Using the Go⇨Recent Folders command to jump to a recently opened folder. (Using this command sequence displays a submenu of the last ten folders you visited.)

If you display the contents of a folder in List, Column, or Cover Flow views, you can view folder hierarchies directly in the Finder. (You find out more about using the List, Column, and Cover Flow views later in the "Organizing and Viewing a Folder" section.)

Jumping back and forth

While you navigate from one folder to the next, you might suddenly want to return to a folder for a second look. To view a previously viewed folder, you can choose the Back command as follows:

+ Click the Back arrow.

+ Choose Go⇨Back.

+ Press ⌘+[.

A command that lets you jump back to a previously opened folder is not the same thing as the Go⇨Enclosing Folder command. If you opened an external drive and then switched to the Utilities folder on your hard drive, the Back command would return the Finder to the external drive, but the Go⇨ Enclosing Folder command would open the Applications folder.

After you use the Back command at least once, you can choose the Forward command. The Forward command reverses each Back command you choose. To choose the Forward command, pick one of the following:

✦ Click the Forward arrow.

✦ Choose Go⇨Forward.

✦ Press ⌘+].

Organizing and Viewing a Folder

The Finder shows the contents stored on a device, such as a hard drive, which acts like a giant folder. If your Mac's hard drive contains a large number of files and folders, trying to find a particular file or folder can be frustrating. To organize a folder's contents, the Finder can display the contents of a folder in five views (shown in Figure 5-3), which I discuss throughout this section.

To switch to a different view, in the Finder, choose View and then choose As Icons, As Lists, As Columns, or As Cover Flow — or just click one of the view icons shown in Figure 5-3.

Selecting items in the Finder

No matter how you view the contents of a folder, selecting items remains the same. You always have to select an item before you can do anything with it, such as copy or delete it. You can select items three ways:

✦ Select a single item (file or folder) by clicking it.

✦ Select multiple items by holding down the ⌘ key and clicking each item.

✦ Selecting a range of items by clicking and dragging the mouse or by using the Shift key.

The Shift key trick works only in List, Column, or Cover Flow view. Just click the first item you want to select in your particular view, hold down the Shift key, and then click the last item in the range that you want to choose. Your desired range is selected, just like that.

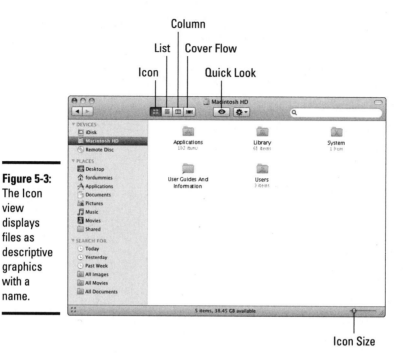

Figure 5-3:
The Icon
view
displays
files as
descriptive
graphics
with a
name.

Using Icon view

Icon view displays all files and folders as icons. To organize files in Icon view, you can manually drag icons around, or you can have your Mac automatically arrange icons based on certain criteria, such as name or date modified.

To arrange icons within Icon view manually, follow these steps:

1. **Move the pointer over an icon you want to move.**

   You can select two or more icons by holding down the ⌘ key and clicking multiple icons.

2. **Click and drag the mouse.**

   Your selected icon(s) move when you move the mouse.

3. **Release the mouse button when you're happy with the new location of your icon(s).**

When you arrange icons manually, they might not align with one another. To fix this problem, make sure no items are selected and then choose View➪ Clean Up Selection to straighten them up.

Click and drag the Icon Size slider (refer to the lower-right corner of Figure 5-3) left or right to decrease or increase the display size of icons in the Finder window.

Manually arranging icons can be cumbersome if you have dozens of icons you want to arrange. As a faster alternative, you can arrange icons automatically in Icon view by following these steps:

1. **Choose View⇨Arrange By.**

A submenu appears, as shown in Figure 5-4.

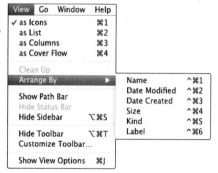

Figure 5-4:
The Arrange
By submenu
lists
different
ways to
organize
your icons.

2. **Choose one of the following options:**

- *Name:* Arranges icons alphabetically.

- *Date Modified:* Arranges the most recently modified items at the top of the window.

- *Date Created:* Arranges the most recently created items at the top of the window.

- *Size:* Arranges the smallest sized files and folders at the top of the window.

- *Kind:* Arranges items alphabetically by file extension, clustering together Microsoft Word files, JPG picture files, and music tracks, for instance.

- *Label:* Arranges icons alphabetically by color. Icons with no color appear near the top of the window followed by icons colored blue, gray, green, orange, purple, red, and yellow.

Using List view

List view displays each item by name, size, date it was last modified, and the kind of item it is, such as a folder or a PDF (Portable Document Format) file. The biggest advantages of List view are that it always displays more items in the same amount of space than the Icon view, and it displays hierarchies of folders as indented items, as shown in Figure 5-5.

Macintosh HD
DEVICES
iDisk
Macintosh HD
Remote Disc
PLACES
Desktop
fordummies
Applications
Documents
Pictures
Music
Movies
Shared
SEARCH FOR
Today
Yesterday
Past Week
All Images
All Movies
All Documents
Name
Date Modified
Size
Kind
Applications Today, 9:40 AM -- Folder
Library May 22, 2009 9:56 AM -- Folder
System May 21, 2009 1:40 PM -- Folder
User Guides And Information Feb 25, 2009 8:15 PM 4 KB Alias
Users May 21, 2009 1:49 PM -- Folder
fordummies May 24, 2009 10:26 AM -- Folder
Desktop Today, 10:55 AM -- Folder
Documents May 11, 2009 12:27 PM -- Folder
About Stacks.pdf Jan 8, 2009 2:13 PM 639 KB Portable Document Format (PDF)
Microsoft User Data May 11, 2009 12:30 PM -- Folder
Downloads Apr 29, 2009 4:37 PM -- Folder
Library May 11, 2009 12:26 PM -- Folder
Movies Apr 29, 2009 4:37 PM -- Folder
Music May 19, 2009 11:12 AM -- Folder
iTunes Today, 11:07 AM -- Folder
Album Artwork May 11, 2009 12:33 PM -- Folder
iTunes Library Jan 13, 2009 3:23 PM 61 KB iTunes Database File
iTunes Library Extras.itdb Jan 13, 2009 3:21 PM 12 KB iTunes Database File
iTunes Library Genius.itdb Jan 13, 2009 3:21 PM 33 KB iTunes Database File
iTunes Music Jan 13, 2009 3:21 PM -- Folder
Pictures Apr 29, 2009 4:37 PM -- Folder
Public Apr 29, 2009 4:37 PM -- Folder
Sites Apr 29, 2009 4:37 PM -- Folder
joe Yesterday, 7:11 AM -- Folder
Shared Today, 10:57 AM -- Folder
25 items, 38.16 GB available

Figure 5-5: List view displays items in rows and folders as hierarchies.

TIP: The List view also makes it easy to select multiple folders at one time by holding down the ⌘ key and clicking once on each folder you want to select. When you're done selecting folders, you can then click and hold on one of the folders and drag them to wherever you want to move them.

TIP: Because List view can display the contents of two or more folders at one time, you can select files from multiple folders. Additionally, if you click a column heading in List view (such as Name or Date Modified), the Finder sorts your items in ascending or descending order.

List view identifies folders by a folder icon and a triangle symbol (which Apple officially refers to as a *disclosure triangle*) pointing to it. Clicking that triangle symbol expands that folder to display its contents — files, more folders, whatever. Clicking the triangle again collapses that folder to hide its contents.

Using Column view

Column view initially displays files and folders in a single column. As with List view, all folders display a triangle next to the folder name. (Okay, okay, in List view, the triangle is just to the left of the folder name, and Column view has the triangle at the far right, but you get to the idea.) Clicking a folder displays the contents of that folder in the column to the right, as shown in Figure 5-6.

Figure 5-6:
Column
view
displays
the folder
contents
in adjacent
columns.

To arrange items in all columns in the Column view, follow these steps:

1. **Choose View⇨Show View Options.**

An Options window appears.

2. **Click the Arrange By pop-up menu (shown in Figure 5-7) and choose
one of the following options:**

- *Name:* Arranges icons alphabetically.

- *Date Modified:* Arranges the most recently modified items at the top
of the window.

- *Date Created:* Arranges the most recently created items at the top of
the window.

- *Size:* Arranges the smallest sized files and folders at the top of the
window.

- *Kind:* Arranges items alphabetically by file type, clustering together
Microsoft Word files, JPG picture files, and music tracks, for instance.

- *Label:* Arranges icons alphabetically by the color label. Icons with no
label appear near the top of the window followed by icons labeled
blue, gray, green, orange, purple, red, and yellow.

3. **(Optional) Use the Text Size pop-up menu to modify the size of text
used for folder labels.**

4. **(Optional) Select one or more of the following check boxes:**

- *Always Open in Column View:* Forces the folder to display its contents in Column view every time you click that folder.

- *Show Icons:* Displays or hides files and folder icons.

- *Show Icon Preview:* Displays or hides thumbnail images of the file contents.

- *Show Preview Column:* Displays a column that lists additional details about a file including its size, kind of file, and when the file was created, modified, and last opened.

5. **Click the Close button of the Show View Options window.**

Figure 5-7: Sort items through the Arrange By pop-up menu.

Using Cover Flow view

Cover Flow view combines List view with the graphic elements of Icon view, as shown in Figure 5-8. Cover Flow originated from jukeboxes that let you pick songs by viewing and flipping through album covers. In the Finder, Cover Flow lets you choose files or folders by flipping through enlarged icons of those files or folders, which can make finding a particular file or folder easier.

Figure 5-8: The Cover Flow view displays both icons and item names.

To scroll through items in the Cover Flow view, you have a number of choices:

✦ Click the left and right scroll arrows on the Cover Flow scroll bar (that appears below the enlarged icon preview images).

✦ Drag the scroll box in the Cover Flow scroll bar.

✦ Click in the scroll area to the left or right of the scroll box on the Cover Flow scroll bar.

✦ Click an icon on either side of the icon preview image that appears in the middle of the Cover Flow view.

✦ Press the up- and down-arrow keys to select a different file or folder in the list portion of the Cover Flow view. Each time you select a different file or folder, the Cover Flow icon for that file or folder appears.

Using Quick Look to view file contents

Quick Look is a nifty feature that enables you to see the contents of a file for many file types without having to run the program you use to create, view, and save it. Just select a file icon and then click the Quick Look view button (or press the spacebar) to display an enlarged preview icon of the selected file, as shown in Figure 5-9. You have three options to close the Quick Look display:

✦ Click the Close button in the upper-left corner.

✦ Press the spacebar.

✦ Press the Escape key.

You can resize the Quick Look display by clicking and dragging the lower-right corner of the Quick Look display or by clicking the Zoom arrows icon (bottom-center of the display), which fills the entire screen with the Quick Look display.

The Quick Look view behaves differently depending on the type of file you're peeking into:

✦ An audio file plays in its entirety so you can hear its contents.

✦ A full-size picture file appears in a window so you can see what the picture looks like.

✦ A movie file plays in its entirety so you can see and hear its contents.

✦ PDF (Portable Document Format) files and HTML files (Web pages) appear in a window so you can scroll through the files and read their contents.

Figure 5-9: Click a file icon and press the spacebar to preview the file's contents with Quick Look.

+ A document file (created by other programs such as spreadsheets and word processors) displays the first screen of its contents along with a listing of its name, size, and date of last modification.

+ A folder appears as a graphic icon listing its name, size, and last modified date.

+ A program file displays its icon along with a name, size, and last modified date.

Creating Folders

In addition to letting you navigate your way through different folders, the Finder also lets you create folders. The main purpose for creating a folder is to organize related files and folders together. You create a folder in the Finder or the Save As dialog. The next sections walk you through each method.

Creating a folder using the Finder menu

You can create a folder anywhere, although the first place you're likely to create a folder is inside the Documents folder to organize your files. You might create multiple folders named Word Processor Files, Spreadsheets, and Databases. Or, you might create multiple folders based on topics, such as 2010 Tax Info, which might contain a mix of word processor, spreadsheet, and database files. The way you organize your folders is up to you.

To create a folder by using the Finder menu, follow these steps:

1. **Click the Finder icon in the Dock.**

   The Finder appears.

2. **In the Sidebar of the Finder, click the Places location, such as Desktop or your Home folder (or click a device, such as an external USB memory keychain, where you want to create a folder).**

3. **Navigate to and open the folder where you want to store your new folder, such as inside the Documents folder.**

4. **Choose File⇨New Folder (or press ⌘+N).**

   An untitled folder icon appears with its name selected.

5. **Type a descriptive name for your folder and then press Return.**

   Your new folder is christened and ready for use.

Creating a folder through the Save As dialog

The Finder isn't the only way to create a new folder. When you save a file for the first time or save an existing file under a new name (using the Save As command), you can also create a new folder to store your file at the same time. To create a folder within the Save As dialog, follow these steps:

1. **Create a new document in any program, such as TextEdit.**

2. **Choose File⇨Save As.**

   A Save As dialog appears, as shown in Figure 5-10

Arrow button

Figure 5-10:
Create a
new folder
while you're
saving a file.

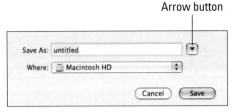

3. **Click the Arrow button to the right of the Save As text box.**

   The Save As dialog expands to display your Mac's storage devices and common folders.

4. **In the Sidebar of the dialog, click the device where you want to create a folder and then open the folder where you want to create a new folder.**

5. **Click the New Folder button.**

   A New Folder dialog appears, as shown in Figure 5-11.

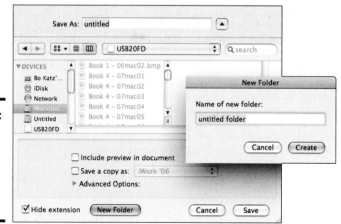

Figure 5-11:
The New
Folder
dialog lets
you pick a
name for
your folder.

6. **Type a name for your folder in the dialog's text box and then click Create.**

A new folder is created in the location you specified.

This name cannot be identical to the name of any existing folder in that location.

7. **In the main window of the Save As dialog, type a name for your document in the Save As text box and then click Save.**

Your new document is stored in your new folder.

Manipulating Files and Folders

After you create a file (by using a program like a word processor) or a folder (by using the Finder or a Save As dialog from a program), you might need to change or edit the name of that file or folder to correct a misspelling or to change the name altogether. Additionally, you might need to move or copy that file or folder to a new location, or delete it altogether.

To make sure you're copying, moving, or changing the correct file, you might want to open it first. However, this can take time, and a faster way to view the contents of a file is to click that file in the Finder window and then click the Quick Look icon (or press the spacebar) to take a peek into the file's contents (refer to Figure 5-9).

Renaming a file or folder

The only limitation on naming a file or folder is that a name can't be longer than 255 characters and the name can't be identical to another file of the same type or a folder in that same location. For example, you can't have two files or folders named Tax Info created by the same program stored in one folder (such as the Documents folder). However, you can have two identically named files stored in different folders.

You can't use certain characters when naming files or folders, such as the colon (:). Additionally, some programs might not let you use the period (.) or slash (/) characters in a filename.

You *can* store identically named files in the same location — as long as a different program created each file. That means you can have a word processor document named My Resume and a spreadsheet file also named My Resume stored in the same folder.

The reason for this is that a file's complete name consists of two parts: a name and a file extension. The name is any arbitrary descriptive name you choose, but the file extension identifies the type of file. A program file actually consists of the .app file extension, a Microsoft Word file consists of the .doc file extension, a Pages file consists of the .pages file extension, and a Keynote file consists of the .key file extension.

Therefore, a My Resume file created by Microsoft Word is actually named My Resume.doc, and the identically named file created by Pages is actually named My Resume.pages.

Not all files may have a file extension. It's possible to save a file without a file extension, although this can make it difficult to determine what type of file it is.

To view a file's extension, click that file and choose File⇨Get Info (or press ⌘+I). An Info window appears and displays the file extension in the Name & Extension text box. To view file extensions in the Finder, deselect the Hide Extension check box, as shown in Figure 5-12.

Folders don't need file extensions, because file extensions identify the contents of a file, and folders can hold a variety of different types of files.

For a fast way to rename a file or folder, follow these steps:

1. **Click a file or folder that you want to rename and then press Return.**

   The file or folder's name appears highlighted.

2. **Type a new name (or use the left- and right-arrow keys and the Delete key to edit the existing name) and then press Return.**

   Your selected file or folder appears with its new name.

Figure 5-12:
You can
selectively
choose to
display file
extensions
of individual
files by
using
the Info
window.

When editing or typing a new name for a file, changing the file extension can confuse your Mac and prevent it from properly opening the file because it can no longer identify which program can open the file.

Copying a file or folder

At any time, you can copy a file or folder and place that duplicate copy in another location. When you copy a folder, you also copy any files and folders stored inside. To copy a file or folder, you can use either menus or the mouse.

Using menus to copy a file or folder

To copy a file or folder by using menus, follow these steps:

1. **Click the Finder icon in the Dock.**

The Finder appears.

2. **Navigate to (and open) the folder that contains the files or folders you want to copy.**

Use the Sidebar and the various other navigation techniques outlined earlier in this chapter to find what you want.

3. **Select one or more files or folders you want to copy and then choose Edit➪Copy (or press ⌘+C).**

4. **Navigate to (and open) the folder where you want to store a copy of the file or folder.**

5. **Choose Edit➪Paste (or press ⌘+V).**

   You have your own cloned file or folder right where you want it.

**Book I
Chapter 5**

**Working with
Files and Folders**

Using the mouse to copy a file or folder

Using the menus to copy a file or folder is simple, but some people find clicking and dragging items with the mouse to be more intuitive. Clicking and dragging works slightly differently, depending on whether you're dragging between two separate devices (such as from a flash drive to a hard drive) or between different folders on the same device.

If you want to use the click-and-drag method to copy a file or folder *from one device to a second device,* follow these steps:

1. **Click the Finder icon in the Dock.**

   The Finder shows its face.

2. **Navigate to (and open) the folder where you want to store your copied files or folders.**

3. **Choose File➪New Finder Window.**

   A second Finder window appears.

4. **In the Sidebar of the new Finder window, click a device.**

   This device must be different from the device you choose in Step 2.

5. **In this second Finder window, navigate to (and open) the folder containing the file or folder you want to copy.**

6. **Using your mouse, click or drag to select one or more files or folders.**

   If you want to drag a file or folder to a new location on the same device, hold down the Option key while dragging the mouse.

7. **Move the pointer over one of your selected items and then click and drag the selected items into the first Finder window and onto the folder that you opened in Step 3.**

   Notice that a green plus sign appears near the pointer while you drag the mouse. The green plus sign means you're copying an item, as shown in Figure 5-13.

8. **Release the mouse button.**

   Your selected files and folders appear as copies in the folder you selected.

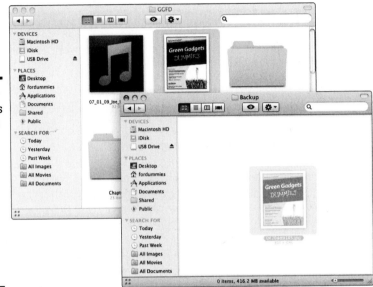

Figure 5-13: A green plus sign always appears near the mouse pointer whenever you're copying items from one device to another.

 Copying (or moving) a file or folder from one device (or folder) to another without having to open two windows, described in the steps below, is easy to accomplish thanks to your Mac's *spring-loaded folders* feature. Drag and hold the file or folder you want to copy (or move) over the icon of the device or folder you want to copy to and wait a moment or two until the folder will spring open. (You can keep springing open folders this way until you reach the one you want.) Let go of the mouse button to copy (or move) the file or folder. To adjust how long it takes for folders to spring open, click the Finder, then choose Finder⇨Preferences and click the General tab, then drag the slider at the bottom of the window to adjust how quickly (or slowly) folders spring open when you hover over them with a selected file or folder.

 If you want to use the click-and-drag method to copy a file or folder from one folder to another folder *on the same device,* you need to use the Option key. If you don't hold down the Option key in Step 4, you move your selected items rather than copy them.

Moving a file or folder

Dragging a file or folder to a new location on the same device (such as from one folder to another on the same hard drive) always moves that file or folder (unless you hold down the Option key, which ensures that the original stays where it is and a copy is created in the new location). On the other hand, dragging a file or folder from one device to another (such as from a USB flash drive to a hard drive) always copies a file or folder — unless you use the ⌘ key, which puts a halt to the cloning business and moves the file or folder to a new location.

Archiving Files and Folders

Files and folders take up space. If you have a bunch of files or folders that you don't use, yet want or need to save (such as old tax information), you can archive those files. *Archiving* grabs a file or folder (or a bunch of files or folders) and compresses them into a single file that takes up less space on your hard disk than the original file or files.

After you archive a group of files, you can delete the original files. If necessary, you can later *unarchive* the archive file to retrieve all the files you packed into it.

You have two common ways to archive files and folders:

✦ **Creating ZIP files:** ZIP files represent the standard archiving file format used on Windows computers. (By the way, ZIP isn't an acronym. It just sounds speedy.)

✦ **Creating DMG files:** DMG files (DMG stands for disc image) are meant for archiving files to be shared only with other Mac users. Generally, if you want to archive files that Windows and Mac users can use, store them in the ZIP file format. If you want to archive files just for other Mac users, you can use the ZIP or DMG file format.

The ZIP file format is faster and creates smaller archives than the DMG file format. However, the DMG file format offers more flexibility by allowing you to access individual files in the archive without having to unzip everything the way you must with a ZIP file. Most people use ZIP archives to store data. The most popular use for DMG files is for storing and distributing software.

Creating a ZIP file

A ZIP file can contain just a single file or folder, or dozens of separate files or folders. To create a ZIP file, follow these steps:

1. **Click the Finder icon in the Dock.**

The Finder comes to the fore.

2. **Navigate to (and open) the folder that contains the file or folder you want to archive.**

3. **Select one or more items you want archive.**

4. **Choose File⇨Compress.**

If you select three items in Step 3, the Compress command displays `Compress 3 items`.

An archive file named `Archive.zip` appears in the folder that contains the items you selected to compress, as shown in Figure 5-14. (You can rename this file to give it a more descriptive name.)

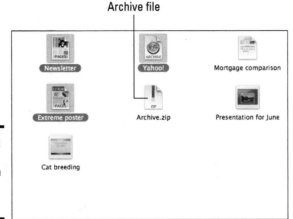

Archive file

Newsletter

Yahoo!

Mortgage comparison

Extreme poster

Archive.zip

Presentation for June

Cat breeding

Figure 5-14:
ZIP files
appear with
a zipper
icon.

REMEMBER

To open a ZIP file, just double-click it. This creates a folder inside the same folder where the ZIP file is stored. Now you can double-click this newly created folder to view the contents that were stored in the ZIP file.

Creating a DMG file

Although ZIP files are handy for storing files, DMG files more often are used to compress and store large items, such as the contents of an entire folder, CD, or hard drive. To create a DMG file, follow these steps:

1. **Click the Finder icon in the Dock.**

The Finder appears.

2. **Move or copy the files you want to store in the DMG file into a single folder.**

3. **Choose Go➪Utilities and double-click the Disk Utility program icon.**

The Disk Utility program loads and displays its window, as shown in Figure 5-15.

4. **Choose File➪New➪Disc Image from Folder.**

The Select Folder to Image dialog appears.

5. **Using the Select Folder to Image dialog, navigate to and then select the folder containing the files you chose in Step 2.**

6. **Click Image.**

A New Image from Folder dialog appears, as shown in Figure 5-16.

New Image icon

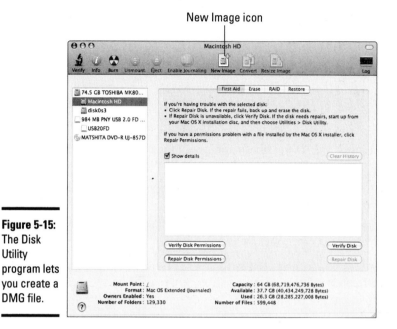

Figure 5-15:
The Disk
Utility
program lets
you create a
DMG file.

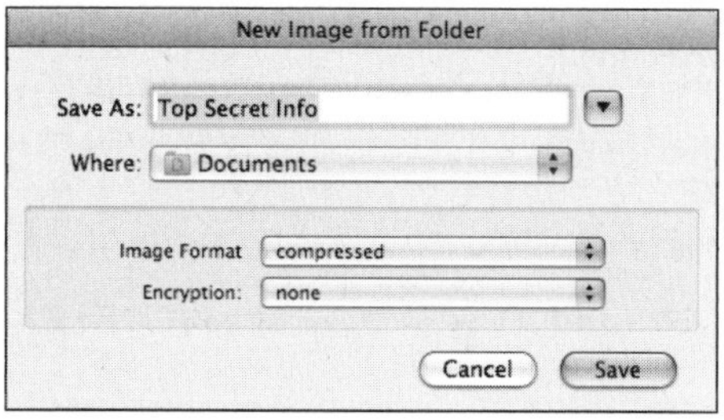

Figure 5-16:
A dialog
appears
where you
can name
and define
the location
of your disk
image file.

7. **Click in the Save As text box and type a name for your disk image file.**

8. **(Optional) Click the Where pop-up menu and choose a folder or device to store your disk image.**

9. **Click the Image Format pop-up menu and choose one of the following:**

   • *Read-Only:* Saves files in the DMG file, but you can never add more files to this DMG file later.

   • *Compressed:* Same as the Read-Only option, except squeezes the size of your DMG file to make it as small as possible.

   • *Read-Write:* Saves files in a DMG file with the option of adding more files to this DMG file later.

- *DVD/CD Master:* Saves files for burning to an audio CD or a video DVD.

- *Hybrid Image (HFS + ISO/UDF):* Saves files in a DMG file designed to be burned to a CD/DVD for use in computers that can recognize Hierarchical File Structure (HFS), ISO 9660 (International Organization for Standardization), or Universal Disk Format (UDF) for storing data on optical media. (Most modern computers can recognize HFS and UDF discs, but older computers might not.) Also saves files in a DMG file designed for transfer over the Internet.

10. **(Optional) Click the Encryption pop-up menu and choose None, 128-bit AES, or 256-bit AES encryption.**

If you choose encryption, you have to define a password that can open the DMG file.

AES stands for Advanced Encryption Standard, which is the latest American government standard algorithm for scrambling data. Choose one of these options if you want to prevent prying eyes from viewing your disk image file's contents (unless you share the password with those you trust).

11. **Click Save.**

Disk Utility displays a progress message while it compresses and stores the files in your chosen folder as a DMG file.

12. **When the disk imaging is complete, choose Disk Utility⇨Quit Disk Utility to exit the program.**

Double-clicking a DMG file displays the contents of that DMG file in the Finder.

Searching Files

No matter how organized you try to be, there's a good chance you might forget where you stored a file. To find your wayward files quickly, you can use the Spotlight feature.

Spotlight lets you type a word or phrase to identify the name of the file you want or a word or phrase stored inside that file. Then Spotlight displays a list of files that matches what you typed. Therefore, if you want to find all the files related to your baseball collection, you could type **baseball** and Spotlight would find all files that contain *baseball* in the filename or in the file itself if it's one your Mac can peer into (such as a Word document, or an Excel spreadsheet.)

Using Spotlight

Spotlight searches for text that matches all or part of a filename and data stored inside of a file. When using Spotlight, search for distinct words. For example, searching for *A* will be relatively useless because so many files use *A* as part of their file name and in most files. However, searching for *ebola* will narrow your search to the files you most likely want.

To use Spotlight, follow these steps:

1. **Click the Finder icon in the Dock.**

The Finder promptly shows up.

2. **Click in the Spotlight text box, as shown in Figure 5-17.**

3. **Type a word or phrase.**

While you type, Spotlight displays the files that match your text.

At this point, you can double-click a file to open it, or you can copy and move it to a new location.

You can change the way your search results appear by choosing View⇨ As Icons, View⇨as List, or View⇨As Cover Flow.

Figure 5-17: The Spotlight text box always appears in the upper-right corner of Finder windows.

TIP

Press ⌘+spacebar to quickly open the Spotlight search feature on your Mac's menu bar, as shown in Figure 5-18.

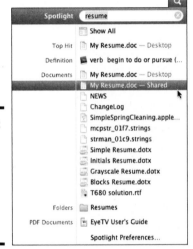

Figure 5-18: Press ⌘+ spacebar to quickly access the Spotlight search feature.

Using Smart Folders

Spotlight can make finding files and folders fast and easy. However, if you find yourself constantly searching for the same types of files repeatedly, you can create a Smart Folder.

A Smart Folder essentially works behind the scenes with Spotlight to keep track of a bunch of files that share one or more common characteristics. For example, you can tell a Smart Folder to store info about only those files that contain *top secret* in the filename or the file; and from now on, you can look in that Smart Folder to access all files and folders that match *top secret* without having to type the words in the Spotlight text box.

Think of Smart Folders as a way to organize your files automatically. Rather than take the time to physically move and organize the files, you can have Smart Folders do the work for you.

REMEMBER

A Smart Folder doesn't physically contain any files or folders. Instead, it contains only links to files or folders. This saves space by not duplicating files.

Creating a Smart Folder with Spotlight

To create a Smart Folder, follow these steps:

1. **Click the Finder icon in the Dock.**

The Finder appears.

2. **Click in the Spotlight text box and type a word or phrase.**

   Spotlight displays a list of files and folders that match your word or phrase.

3. **Click the Save button that appears underneath the Spotlight text box.**

   A Save As dialog appears, as shown in Figure 5-19.

Figure 5-19:
Name your Smart Folder and define where to store it.

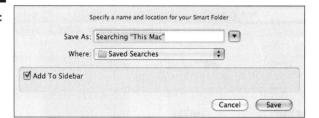

Specify a name and location for your Smart Folder

Save As: Searching "This Mac"

Where: Saved Searches

☑ Add To Sidebar

Cancel   Save

4. **Click in the Save As text box and type a descriptive name for your Smart Folder.**

5. **Choose a location to store your Smart Folder from the Where pop-up menu (or click the down-arrow and navigate to the location where you want to save your Smart Folder).**

6. **(Optional) Select or Deselect the Add To Sidebar check box.**

   Check the box if you want the Smart Folder to appear in the Sidebar in the Searches section near the bottom. Uncheck the box if you don't want to see your Smart Folder in the Sidebar.

7. **Click Save.**

Dance Tunes

   Your Smart Folder appears in your chosen location. Instead of displaying an ordinary folder icon, Smart Folder icons always contain a gear inside a folder.

After you create a Smart Folder, it automatically keeps your list of files and folders up to date at all times. If you create new files or folders that match the text used to define a Smart Folder, that new file or folder name will appear in the Smart Folder automatically. Delete a file, and the Smart Folder deletes its link to that file as well.

Creating a Smart Folder using other criteria

Besides organizing files and folders using Spotlight, Smart Folders can also list files and folders based on dates, sizes, color labels, and other criteria. To create a Smart Folder using these other criteria, follow these steps:

1. **Click the Finder icon in the Dock.**

   The Finder appears.

2. **Choose File⇨New Smart Folder.**

   A New Smart Folder window appears.

3. **Click the plus sign icon that appears to the right of the Save button.**

   The Kind and Any pop-up menus appear.

   Clicking the plus sign icon adds something to the New Smart Folder window — in this case, a new pop-up menu and a couple of check boxes. In other words, it expands the window. After the window expands, the plus sign icon changes to a minus sign icon, which you use to contract the window to its original state.

4. **Click the Kind pop-up menu and choose a criterion, such as Name or Last Opened date.**

5. **Click the Any pop-up menu and choose the type of files you want to find, such as Documents, Movies, or PDF, as shown in Figure 5-20.**

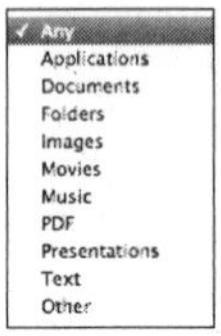

Figure 5-20: Select the types of files to appear in the Smart Folder.

6. **Click the Save button that appears underneath the Spotlight text box.**

   A Save As dialog appears (refer to Figure 5-19).

7. **Click in the Save As text box and type a descriptive name for your Smart Folder.**

8. **Choose a location to store your Smart Folder from the Where pop-up menu.**

9. **(Optional) Select or Deselect the Add To Sidebar check box.**

   Check the box if you want the Smart Folder to appear in the Sidebar in the Searches section near the bottom. Uncheck the box if you don't want to see your Smart Folder in the Sidebar.

10. **Click Save.**

    Your Smart Folder appears in your chosen location. Instead of displaying an ordinary folder icon, Smart Folder icons always contain a gear inside a folder.

Using Smart Folders in the Sidebar

To make searching for files easier, the Finder has already created several Smart Folders in the Sidebar. These Smart Folders are named Today, Yesterday, Past Week, All Images, All Movies, and All Documents, and they can be found under the Search For category, as shown in Figure 5-21.

Figure 5-21:
The Finder window Sidebar contains several Smart Folders you can use right away.

By clicking one of these Smart Folders, you can view certain types of files, such as all files created today (in the Today Smart Folder) or all pictures stored on your hard drive (stored in the All Pictures Smart Folder).

Storing Files and Folders in the Dock

You can always find the files and folders you want by using the Finder. However, you might find that loading the Finder constantly just to access the contents of a particular folder can be tedious. As a faster alternative, you can store pointers to files and folders directly in the Dock.

Storing files in the Dock

If you have a file that you access regularly, consider placing an icon for that file directly in the Dock. That way, the file icon remains visible at all times (as long as the Dock is visible), and gives you one-click access to your frequently used files.

To place a file icon in the Dock, follow these steps:

1. **Click the Finder icon in the Dock and then navigate to the folder containing the file you use frequently.**

2. **Click and drag the file to the Dock into any space to the left of the Trash icon and then release the mouse button.**

   The icons in the Dock slide apart to make room for the icon. To open this file, just click its file icon.

A file icon in the Dock is just a link to your actual file. If you drag the file icon off the Dock, your physical file remains untouched.

Creating Stacks in the Dock

Rather than clutter the Dock with multiple file icons, consider storing a folder in the Dock. A folder icon, when stored in the Dock, is called a *Stack*. After you create a Stack in the Dock, you can view its contents by clicking the Stack.

To store a Stack in the Dock, follow these steps:

1. **Click the Finder icon in the Dock to open a new Finder window and then navigate to a folder you use frequently.**

2. **Click and drag the folder to the Dock into any space to the right of the divider and then release the mouse button.**

   The Dock icons slide apart to make room for your Stack to give your folder a place all its own.

A Stack in the Dock is just a link to your actual folder and files. If you drag the Stack off the Dock, your folder and its file contents remain untouched.

Opening files stored in a Stack

After you place a Stack on the Dock, you can view its contents — and open a file in that Stack — by following these steps:

1. **Click a Stack folder on the Dock.**

   If you have only a few files stored in a Stack, its contents fan out. If you have many files stored in a Stack, its contents appear in a grid.

2. **Click the file you want to open in the fan, grid, or list.**

   Your chosen file opens.

Control-click on a Stack icon to display a shortcut menu of options you can choose to customize the way a Stack folder displays its contents when you click it.

Burning Files and Folders to CD/DVD

A simple way to transfer or back up data is to store it on CDs or DVDs. (A CD can store 650–700 megabytes, whereas a DVD can store 4.7 or 8.5 gigabytes.) After you store data on a CD or DVD, you can easily transfer the data to another computer, including PCs running Windows or Linux.

Two types of CDs and DVDs exist: read-only and rewritable. Read-only discs are labeled CD-R or DVD-R, and you can copy data to them exactly once. Rewritable discs can store and erase data repeatedly. Rewritable discs cost more and they're slower when it comes to burning and reading files to and from them, but they're reusable so they're more useful. The main advantage of read-only CDs is that some older audio CD players can only read read-only CDs, but not rewriteable CDs. Likewise, some older DVD players cannot read rewritable DVDs, but can read read-only DVDs.

The process of copying data to a CD or DVD is *burning a disc*. To burn a disc, you must specify which files or folders you want to burn to the disc.

Because copying or moving all files to a single folder can be cumbersome, you can create a special folder called a Burn Folder. A Burn Folder doesn't store physical copies of your files or folders. Instead, a Burn Folder contains links to the files and folders you want to burn to a CD or DVD. That way, a Burn Folder won't take double the amount of space needed to store your data.

Creating a Burn Folder

To create a Burn Folder, follow these steps:

1. **Click the Finder icon in the Dock to open a new Finder window and then navigate to (and open) the folder where you want to store your Burn Folder.**

2. **Choose File⇨New Burn Folder.**

   Burn Folder

   A Burn Folder appears bearing a circular yellow and black radiation logo.

3. **Drag the files and folders you want to burn to a disc into the Burn Folder.**

Burning the contents of a Burn Folder

After you drag links to your various files and folders into a Burn Folder, you can burn the contents onto as many discs as you want without having to specify each file and folder to burn each time. To burn the contents of a Burn Folder to a disc, follow these steps:

1. **Click the Finder icon in the Dock to open a new Finder window, navigate to (and open) the folder where you stored your Burn Folder, and then double-click it to open it.**

Your Burn Folder opens.

2. **Click the Burn button in the upper-right corner of the Burn Folder's Finder window, or choose File⇨Burn *folder name* to Disc, where *folder name* is the name of the folder you chose to burn.**

A dialog appears, asking you to insert a blank disc.

3. **Insert a blank CD or DVD into your Mac's disc drive.**

Sit back and wait for the burning process to complete. (An alert sound chimes at the end of a burning session.) If you try to burn more data than the CD or DVD can hold, your Mac won't even try to burn your files. In this case, you have to remove some files from the Burn Folder and try again.

4. **When the burning session is over, eject the finished disc by pressing the Eject button on the keyboard, or Control-click the disc icon on the Desktop and choose Eject from the shortcut menu.**

Burn Folders are nice for burning files to a CD or DVD, but if you want more than just basic disc-burning capabilities, consider getting a standalone CD/DVD burning program, such as Toast Titanium (www.roxio.com) or the aptly named, ultra-simple, freebie burning program, Burn (burn-osx.sourceforge.net). Besides duplicating the basic disc-burning features of Burn Folders, Toast Titanium also provides a wealth of features for mixing and editing audio, compressing video, copying entire discs, and burning files on the Blu-ray disc format.

Deleting a File or Folder

To delete a file or folder, you first have to place that item in the Trash. But putting an item in the Trash doesn't immediately delete it. In fact, you can retrieve any number of files or folders you've "thrown away." Nothing is really gone — permanently deleted — until you empty the Trash.

Deleting a folder deletes any files or folders stored inside. Therefore, if you delete a single folder, you might really be deleting 200 other folders containing files you might not have meant to get rid of, so always check the contents of a folder before you delete it, just to make sure it doesn't contain anything important.

To delete a file or folder, follow these steps:

1. **Click the Finder icon in the Dock to open a new Finder window and
then navigate to (and open) the folder that contains the file or folder
you want to delete.**

2. **Select the file or folder (or files and folders) that you want to delete.**

3. **Choose one of the following:**

- Choose File⇨Move to Trash.

- Drag the selected items onto the Trash icon in the Dock.

- Press ⌘+Delete.

- Control-click a selected item and choose Move to Trash from the
shortcut menu that appears.

Retrieving a file or folder from the Trash

When you move items to the Trash, you can retrieve them again as long as
you haven't emptied the Trash since you threw them out. If the Trash icon
in the Dock appears filled with a pile of crumbled up paper, you can still
retrieve files or folders from the Trash. If the Trash icon appears empty,
there are no files or folders there you can retrieve.

To retrieve a file or folder from the Trash, follow these steps:

1. **Click the Trash icon in the Dock.**

A Finder window appears, showing all the files and folders you deleted
since the last time you emptied the Trash.

2. **Select the item (or items) you want to retrieve, drag them onto a
device or folder where you want to store your retrieved items, and
then release the mouse button.**

Emptying the Trash

Every deleted file or folder gets stored in the Trash, where it eats up space
on your hard drive until you empty the Trash. When you're sure that you
won't need items you trashed any more, you can empty the Trash to permanently delete the files and free up additional space on your hard drive.

To empty the Trash, follow these steps:

1. **Click the Finder icon in the Dock (or click the Desktop) and then
choose File⇨Empty Trash.**

A dialog appears, asking whether you're sure that you want to remove
the items in the Trash permanently.

2. **Click OK (or Cancel).**

If you open the Finder and choose Finder⇨Secure Empty Trash, your Mac will write over the deleted files with random data to foil any attempt to recover deleted files later with a special file recovery program. If you want to delete something sensitive that you don't want to risk falling into the wrong hands, choose Finder⇨Secure Empty Trash.

For a faster way of emptying the Trash, Control-click the Trash icon in the Dock and choose Empty Trash from the shortcut menu that appears, or click the Finder icon (or the Desktop) and press ⌘+Shift+Delete.

Chapter 6: Customizing Your Mac and Adjusting Settings

In This Chapter

✔ Changing the Desktop

✔ Customizing the screen saver

✔ Changing the display and appearance

✔ Changing the date and time

✔ Adjusting sounds

✔ Saving energy

✔ Picking a printer

✔ Creating accounts

✔ Making Mac more accessible for people with special needs

✔ Talking to your Mac

Every Mac works the same, but that doesn't mean they all have to look and feel the same. To personalize your Mac, you can change the way it looks and even how it behaves.

If you have trouble with your vision, hearing, or movement, even using a computer as friendly as your Mac can be difficult. Thankfully, every Mac comes with special universal access features that you can turn on and modify.

By customizing your Mac — and adjusting to how it works to make things easier on your eyes, ears, or hands — you can stamp it with your personality and truly turn your Mac into a personal computer that feels like it is working with you and for you, rather than against you.

Changing the Desktop

The Desktop fills the screen in the absence of any program windows. Generally, the Desktop displays a decorative background image, but you can display any image, such as a picture captured with a digital camera or a favorite picture you downloaded from the Internet.

Choosing a built-in Desktop image

Your Mac comes with a variety of images stored and organized into different categories. To choose one of these images as your Desktop image, follow these steps:

1. **Control-click anywhere on the Desktop and choose Change Desktop Background from the shortcut menu that appears.**

The Desktop preferences pane appears, as shown in Figure 6-1.

2. **Click a category, such as Nature or Plants.**

Figure 6-1: Desktop preferences let you choose a different background image.

3. **Click the image that you want to adorn your Desktop and then click the Close button to close the preferences pane.**

The Desktop preferences pane offers other options, which you can see near the bottom of Figure 6-1:

✦ **Change Picture:** Click the pop-up menu to tell your Mac to change the Desktop background picture to another one in the selected category based on a time interval, when you log in to your Mac, or when you wake it from Sleep mode.

✦ **Random:** Randomly changes the Desktop background image.

✦ **Translucent Menu Bar:** Gives your Mac's menu bar a translucent "see through" effect.

Choosing an iPhoto image for the Desktop

If you capture images with a digital camera and store those images in iPhoto, you can choose one of your iPhoto images to appear on your Desktop by following these steps:

1. **Control-click anywhere on the Desktop and choose Change Desktop Background from the shortcut menu.**

   The Desktop preferences pane appears (refer to Figure 6-1).

2. **Click the disclosure triangle that appears to the left iPhoto in the left column, click an iPhoto category, such as Photos, and then click the image you want to display as your new Desktop background.**

   Your chosen iPhoto image appears on the Desktop as the background image, and a new pop-up menu appears above your iPhoto images.

3. **Click the pop-up menu above your iPhoto images to choose:**

   - *Fill Screen:* Expands the image to fill the screen but might cut off edges, depending on the dimensions of the original image.

   - *Fit to Screen:* Expands the image to fill most of the screen, but might leave edges uncovered depending on the dimensions of the original image; click the menu to the right of this option to choose the color of the border that may surround the image.

   - *Stretch to Fill Screen:* Stretches a picture to fill the entire screen, which might distort the image similar to the way a carnival mirror can.

   - *Center:* Places the image in the middle of the screen at its original size, and might leave edges uncovered depending on the image's dimensions; click the menu to the right of this option to choose the color of the border that may surround the image.

   - *Tile:* Duplicates the image in rows and columns to fill the screen.

4. **Click the Close button of the System Preferences window.**

Choosing your own image for the Desktop

You might have images stored on your hard drive that you have not imported into iPhoto. To display non-iPhoto images on the Desktop background, follow these steps:

1. **Control-click anywhere on the Desktop and choose Change Desktop Background from the shortcut menu to open the Desktop preferences pane (refer to Figure 6-1).**

2. **Click the triangle symbol that appears to the left of Folders in the left column.**

You have two options:

- Click the Pictures folder to display any pictures you've stored in your Pictures folder. Any images stored in separate folders inside the Pictures folder will not be visible.

- Click the Add (+) button in the lower-left corner and use the dialog that appears to navigate to the folder that contains the image you want to use.

3. **Click the image that you want to use for the Desktop background and then click the Close button to close the preferences pane.**

Customizing the Screen Saver

A screen saver is an animated image that appears on the screen after a fixed period when your Mac doesn't detect any keyboard or mouse activity. When selecting a screen saver, you can choose an image to display and the amount of time to wait before the screen saver starts.

Screen savers were important in the old days when most monitors used cathode-ray tubes (CRTs). If a CRT monitor displayed the same static image for long periods, such images eventually *burned in,* or became physically etched into the glass. (Look at the screens of old arcade video games to see these "ghost" images.) If you have a liquid-crystal display (LCD) monitor — standard for modern computers — this won't happen, so screen savers are mostly for decorative purposes today.

For an eco-friendlier alternative to using the screen saver, check out the Energy Saver setting described in the "Saving Energy" section of this chapter.

To choose a screen saver, follow these steps:

1. **Choose ⌘⇨System Preferences from the Finder menu and then click the Desktop & Screen Saver icon.**

   The Desktop & Screen Saver preferences pane appears.

2. **Click the Screen Saver tab to display the Screen Saver preferences pane, as shown in Figure 6-2, and then click one of the screen savers listed in the Apple or Pictures category in the left column.**

   The preview pane shows you what your screen saver will look like. (If you select the Use Random Screen Saver check box, your Mac will pick a different screen saver image every time the screen saver starts. After your randomly chosen screen saver starts, that same animated image appears until you press a key to turn off the screen saver.)

   Under the Pictures category, you can choose the Pictures folder, an iPhoto album, or the Choose Folder option, which lets you pick any folder on your hard drive to locate an image to use.

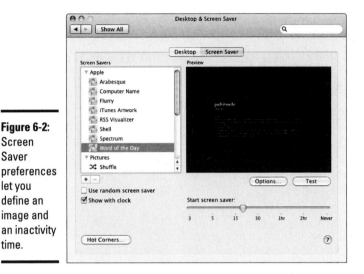

Figure 6-2:
Screen
Saver
preferences
let you
define an
image and
an inactivity
time.

3. **Drag the Start Screen Saver slider to specify an amount of time to wait before your screen saver starts.**

   A short amount of time can mean the screen saver starts while you're reading a Web page or document, so you might have to experiment a bit to find the best time for you.

4. **(Optional) Select the Show with Clock check box to display the time with your screen saver.**

5. **(Optional) Click Options.**

   A dialog appears that gives you additional choices for modifying the way your screen saver appears, such as changing the speed that the screen saver image moves.

6. **(Optional) Click Test to preview the way your Screen Saver will look when it turns itself on.**

   Moving the mouse or tapping a key gets you out of test mode.

7. **(Optional) Enable Hot Corners.**

   a. *Click the Hot Corners button (refer to Figure 6-2).*

   b. *Click one (or each) of the four pop-up menus and choose a command that your Mac will carry out when you move your pointer to the specified corner, as shown in Figure 6-3.*

      Two common uses for a hot corner are to turn on the screen saver, or to put your Mac's display to sleep to save energy.

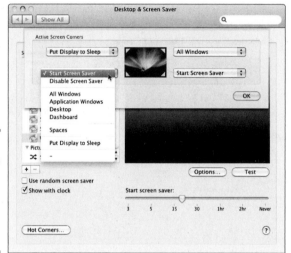

Figure 6-3:
Each pop-up menu defines a function for a hot corner.

You can define multiple hot corners to do the same task, such as defining the two top corners to start the screen saver and the two bottom corners to put the display to sleep.

   c. Click the OK button to close the Hot Corner dialog.

8. Click the Close button in the Desktop & Screen Saver preferences pane.

In the early days of the Mac, one of the most popular screen savers displayed pieces of toast and winged chrome toasters flying across the screen. To relive these good old days, download a flying toaster screensaver from Uneasy Silence (http://uneasysilence.com/toast).

Changing the Display and Appearance

Because you'll be staring at your Mac's screen every time you use it, you might want to modify the way the screen displays information. Some changes you can make include changing the Desktop size (resolution), or selecting another color scheme of your various menus, windows, and dialogs. The next sections show you how.

Changing the screen resolution

The display defines the screen resolution, measured in *pixels* — the dots that make up an image. The higher the display resolution, the more pixels you have and the sharper the image — but everything on your screen might appear smaller.

Selecting your Mac display's highest resolution generally puts your Mac's best face forward, so to speak, when it comes to making everything look sharp and correct on your screen.

To change the screen resolution, follow these steps:

1. **Choose ⚫⇨System Preferences and then click the Displays icon to open the Display preferences pane, as shown in Figure 6-4.**

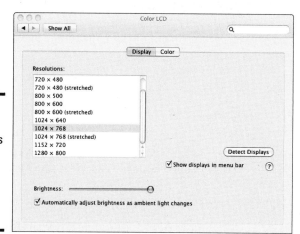

Figure 6-4:
Display preferences let you choose a different screen resolution.

2. **Click the Display tab (if it isn't already chosen), and then choose a screen resolution from the Resolutions list.**

   Your Mac immediately changes the resolution so you can see how it looks. If you don't like the resolution, try again until you find one that's easy on your eyes.

3. **(Optional) Click the Color tab, click the Calibrate button, and then follow the steps that display to tweak the way your Mac displays colors; click the Done button when you reach the final step to return to the Display preferences pane.**

4. **Click the Close button in the System Preferences window when you're happy with the screen resolution.**

Changing the color of the user interface

Another way to change the appearance of the screen is to modify the colors used in windows, menus, and dialogs. To change the color of these user interface items, follow these steps:

1. Choose ⚫⇨System Preferences and click the Appearance icon to open the Appearance preferences pane, as shown in Figure 6-5.

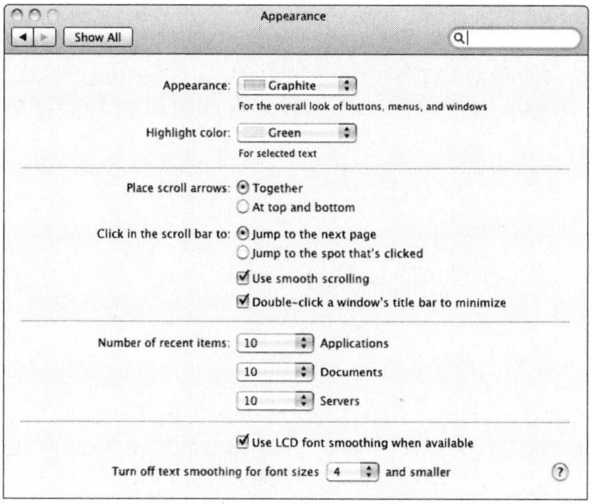

Figure 6-5:
Appearance preferences let you modify colors.

2. Use the Appearance and Highlight Color pop-up menus to choose your color variations.

   The Appearance pop-up menu defines the colors that normally show up on windows, buttons, and so on, whereas the Highlight Color pop-up menu defines the color of items that you select.

3. Click the Close button to close the Appearance preferences pane.

Changing the Date and Time

Keeping track of time might seem trivial, but knowing the right time is important so your Mac can determine when you created or modified a particular file and keep track of appointments you've made through programs, such as iCal.

Of course, keeping track of time is useless if you don't set the right time to begin with. To set the proper date and time, follow these steps:

1. Choose ⚫⇨System Preferences and then click the Date & Time icon to open the Date & Time preferences pane, as shown in Figure 6-6.

2. Select (or deselect) the Set Date & Time Automatically check box. If you select this check box, click the drop-down list to choose a location.

   This feature works only if you're connected to the Internet. If you aren't connected to the Internet, click the calendar to pick a date and click the clock to pick a time.

Figure 6-6:
Date & Time preferences let you set the clock in your Mac.

3. (Optional) If you didn't select the Set Date & Time Automatically check box in Step 2, click the Time Zone tab at the top of the window and then click near your home city on the map.

You can also click in the Closest City field and then begin typing the name of the city nearest you, or click the drop-down list and select the city nearest you, as shown in Figure 6-7.

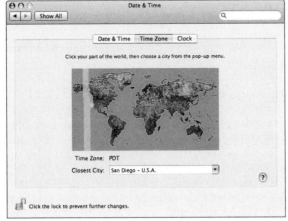

Figure 6-7:
The Time Zone pane lets you pick the closest city in your time zone.

4. Click the Clock tab and then select (or deselect) the Show Date and Time in Menu Bar check box, as shown in Figure 6-8.

If selected, this displays the time in the right side of the menu bar. After you make your selection, you can check the other options to change the appearance of the clock, such as choosing between a digital or analog clock, and choosing whether to show the day of the week.

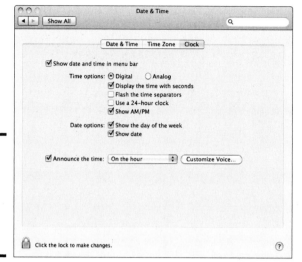

Figure 6-8:
The Clock
pane lets
you pick
the type of
clock you
want.

5. **Select (or deselect) the Announce the Time check box if you want
   your Mac to recite the time using a synthesized voice every hour, half
   hour, or quarter hour.**

   The associated pop-up menu lets you specify when announcements are
   made; the Customize Voice button is what you click to choose what kind
   of voice is used, and how quickly and loudly it utters the time.

6. **Click the Close button to close the Date & Time preferences pane.**

Adjusting Sounds

Every Mac can play sound through speakers (built-in or external) or headphones, from making the simplest beeping noise to playing audio CDs like
a stereo. Three primary ways to modify the sound on your Mac involve
volume, balance, and input/output devices.

Volume simply means how loud your Mac plays sound by default. Many
programs, such as iTunes, also let you adjust the volume, so you can set the
default system volume and then adjust the volume within each program,
relative to the system volume, as well.

Balance defines how sound plays through the right and left stereo speakers. By adjusting the balance, you can make sound louder coming from one
speaker and weaker coming from the other.

Depending on your equipment, it's possible to have multiple input and
output devices — speakers and headphones as two distinct output devices,
for example. By defining which input and output device to use, you can
define which one to use all the time.

To modify the way your Mac accepts and plays sound, follow these steps:

1. **Choose ⌘⇨System Preferences and then click the Sound icon to open the Sound preferences pane, as shown in Figure 6-9.**

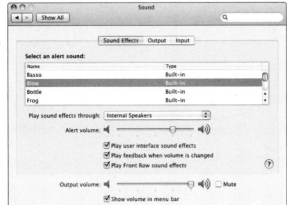

Figure 6-9:
Sound
Effects
preferences
let you
define
which
sound to
use as an
alert.

2. **Click the Sound Effects tab if it isn't already selected and then choose the sound your Mac will play when it needs your attention, such as when you're quitting a program without saving a document.**

3. **(Optional) Click the Play Sound Effects Through pop-up menu to choose whether your Mac plays sounds through its built-in Internal Speakers or through another set of speakers you might have connected to your Mac.**

4. **(Optional) Drag the Alert Volume slider to the desired location to set how loudly (or softly) your Mac will play the alert when it needs to get your attention.**

5. **(Optional) Select (or deselect) any of the following three check boxes:**

   - *Play User Interface Sound Effects:* Lets you hear such sounds as the crinkling of paper when you empty the Trash or a whooshing sound if you remove an icon from the Dock.

   - *Play Feedback When Volume Is Changed:* Beeps to match the sound level while you increase or decrease the volume.

   - *Play Front Row Sound Effects:* Plays sound effects when you're using the Front Row program. (See Book III, Chapter 4 for more information about using Front Row.)

6. **(Optional) Drag the Output Volume slider.**

   Output volume defines how loud (or soft) your Mac plays any type of audio, from alert beeps to audio CDs.

7. **Click the Output tab to display the Output preferences pane, as shown in Figure 6-10.**

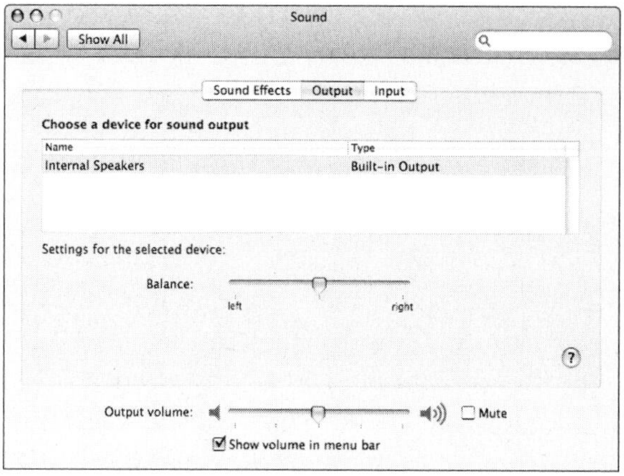

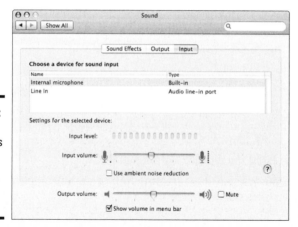

Figure 6-10: Output preferences let you define how to play sound.

8. **Click the output device you want to use if you have another output option connected to your Mac, such as headphones or external speakers.**

9. **(Optional) Drag the Balance slider to adjust the balance.**

10. **(Optional) Select (or deselect) the Show Volume in Menu Bar check box, which, when selected, lets you see and adjust your Mac's volume with the menulet in the menu bar.**

11. **Click the Input tab to open the Input preferences pane, as shown in Figure 6-11, and then click the input device you want your Mac to use to receive sound, such as the built-in microphone, or the Line In port, which you can plug a TV or stereo into to record sound.**

Figure 6-11: Input preferences let you define how to record sound.

12. **(Optional) Drag the Input Volume slider to adjust the default input volume.**

13. **(Optional) Select (or deselect) the Use Ambient Noise Reduction check box to eliminate background noise if someone having a voice or video chat with iChat complains they can't hear you clearly.**

14. **Click the Close button to close the Sound preferences pane when you finish making adjustments.**

Saving Energy

To change your Mac's energy-saving options — such as whether it powers off the hard disk when possible, or how long it waits before turning off the display or entering Sleep mode — you use the Energy Saver preferences pane.

To open the Energy Saver preferences pane, choose &⇨System Preferences and then click the Energy Saver icon. The Energy Saver preferences pane, shown in Figure 6-12, opens. If you use a MacBook, you see two clickable tabs, Battery and Power Adapter, at the top of the pane. Desktop Mac users see two options: Sleep and Options. (To close the pane, simply click the Close button in the upper-left corner.)

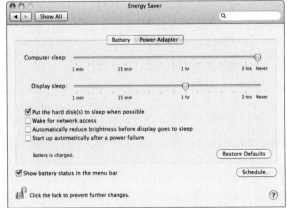

Figure 6-12: Energy Saver preferences make saving energy a cinch.

Starting from the top, here's a description of your Mac's Energy Saver options:

✦ **Computer Sleep:** Moving this slider to the left is the greener way to go. Moving to the right is less efficient because it allows a smart device to do nothing other than burn energy for no good reason.

✦ **Display Sleep:** Maybe you take a break and then return to your computer at regular intervals but you don't want to wake your Mac from lots of catnaps several times a day. Fair enough. Set the Computer Sleep slider (see the preceding bullet) a little farther to the right and then drag the Display Sleep slider to the left to snap your Mac to attention in a flash, with only the slightest pause before the screen comes back to life.

✦ **Put the Hard Disks(s) to Sleep When Possible:** Select this option to "snooze" the hard disk whenever it determines that the programs you're running don't need to keep the drive (or drives) spinning. If you regularly perform hard disk intensive tasks, such as edit videos or play 3D games, deselect this option.

✦ **Wake for Ethernet Network Administration Access:** Choose this option if you want other users in your house or workplace to be able to access your Mac's shared resources, such as shared printers or iTunes music playlists, even when your computer is in Sleep mode.

✦ **Automatically Reduce the Brightness of the Display Before Display Sleep:** When you select this option, the brightness level on the display drops a few notches before blanking out the screen after the length of time you select in the Display Sleep setting (see previous bullet).

✦ **Start Up Automatically After a Power Failure:** Whether by brownouts, blackouts, or black cats knocking out power cords, power failures happen. Use this option to specify how your Mac should react when the lights come on after a power failure. Select the check box if you want your Mac to restart, and deselect it if you prefer to turn it back on when the power is running again.

✦ **Show Battery Status in the Menu Bar:** Selecting this option on your MacBook lets you keep visual tabs on how much battery juice remains when your machine is unplugged from the wall outlet — and how long you need to wait until its battery is fully charged after you plug into a power outlet. To change the information you see, click the Battery Status icon, click Show, and then choose Icon Only, Time, or Percentage to see your battery's status the way you like it.

✦ **Schedule:** Click the Schedule button to open these scheduling options:

  • *Start Up or Wake:* Choose when you want your Mac to greet you on weekdays or weekends, every day, or one day in particular.

    Click the up and down arrows to adjust the time, as shown in Figure 6-13 — or just click the time slots and enter your preference directly.

  • *Sleep/Restart/Shutdown:* Choose one of these pop-up options if you want your Mac to do as instructed to suit your schedule at a time you set, as described in the preceding bullet.

Figure 6-13: Awaken and put your Mac to sleep on a schedule.

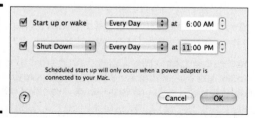

☑ Start up or wake   Every Day   at   6:00 AM

☑ Shut Down   Every Day   at   11:00 PM

Scheduled start up will only occur when a power adapter is connected to your Mac.

Cancel   OK

Choosing a Printer

Out of the box, your Mac comes with a number of special files called *printer drivers,* which tell your Mac how to communicate with a number of popular brands of printer models. When you buy a new printer, it often comes with a CD that contains a printer driver that you can install to unlock special features that the Mac's built-in drivers might not take advantage of.

Check the support section of the printer manufacturer's Web site to see whether a newer version of the printer installation software has become available. After you run the installer, you can check the Web site every now and then to see whether an even newer version (than the one you've installed) is available.

Making your Mac work with your printer involves a two-step process. First, you must physically connect your printer to your Mac, usually with a USB cable or network connection.

More and more new printer models come with built-in wireless connection options such as Bluetooth and Wi-Fi, which means no more tangled cables between your Mac and your printer.

Second, you must install the proper printer driver on your Mac (if you don't want to use the built-in driver that comes with your Mac, or if your Mac doesn't have a driver for it). After you connect your printer to your Mac and install or select the correct printer driver, you can then print documents and control your printer's options.

You can download printer drivers (and drivers for other types of hardware, such as scanners and pressure-sensitive tablets) directly from Apple's Web site (www.apple.com/downloads/macosx/drivers) or from the printer manufacturer's Web site.

After you physically connect a printer to your Mac and install its printer driver, you might need to take one additional step and tell your Mac that this particular printer is connected. To get your Mac to recognize a connected printer, follow these steps:

1. **Choose ⌘⇨System Preferences and then click the Print & Fax icon to open the Print & Fax preferences pane.**

2. **Click the Add (+) button, as shown in Figure 6-14.**

 Note: Your Mac might list local printers (printers directly attached to your Mac) as well as printers linked to your Mac via a network.

3. **Click a printer name in the Printers list and then click the Default Printer pop-up menu to choose the new printer (or another) your Mac's programs will always print to (unless you specify otherwise).**

4. **Click the Close button to close the Print & Fax preferences pane.**

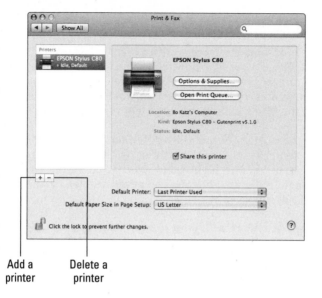

Figure 6-14:
The Print
& Fax
preferences
pane lets
you add
or delete
printers.

Add a
printer

Delete a
printer

If you replace your printer with another one, your Mac might still try to use the printer you're no longer using anyway. To prevent this, click the printer as described above but click the minus sign to delete the printer.

Creating Separate Accounts

Rather than buy separate Mac computers for everyone in your household, you can do the next best thing by creating a separate user account for each person using the Mac. Accounts essentially give a Mac multiple personalities to suit each person using the Mac. If you create three accounts on your Mac, each account can have its own personality based on each user's preference, such as their favorite screen saver and desktop background image, preferred system sound and energy savings settings, and a separate Home folder for saving and organizing files and folders without affecting any other accounts. By using accounts, each person can engage with the Mac as though they're the only person using it.

Types of accounts

When you turn on your Mac for the very first time, a set of automatic setup steps run to create a user account consisting of a username and password. Multiple people can share this single account, but doing so increases the risk of someone deleting an important file that belongs to somebody else.

Sharing the same account also means everyone can see everyone else's files and folders. In other words, nothing saved on the Mac's hard drive is private. As such, it's a better bet to set up multiple accounts on the Mac for multiple users.

You can create four types of accounts:

✦ **Administrator:** Gives the user access to create, modify, and delete accounts. You should limit the number of Administrator accounts you have to perhaps one or two (one for each parent in a household). Note that when you turn on your Mac for the first time, the type of account that is created is an Administrator account.

✦ **Standard:** Gives the user access to their individual account's files and folders, but doesn't let the user create, modify, or delete any additional accounts.

✦ **Managed with Parental Controls:** Gives the user restricted access to the computer based on the parental controls defined by an Administrator account.

✦ **Guest:** Gives the user access but doesn't let the user modify the Mac's settings or save any files to the hard disk.

This section looks at how to create accounts in general, but Book IV, Chapter 4 specifically explains how to create and manage Guest and Managed with Parental Controls accounts.

The number one reason to have only one Administrator account is to protect yourself. If you create two or more Administrator accounts, anyone using those other Administrator accounts has full power to erase your Administrator account along with all your important files. If you have the only Administrator account, no one else can delete your account or files.

Creating an account

Before you create an account, you need to decide the type of account to create and come up with the account's username and password. To create an account, follow these steps:

1. **Choose **⌘⇨System Preferences and then click the Accounts icon to open the Accounts preferences pane, as shown in Figure 6-15.**

2. **Click the Lock in the bottom-left corner to gain the ability to create accounts, type your password into the dialog that appears, and then click OK.**

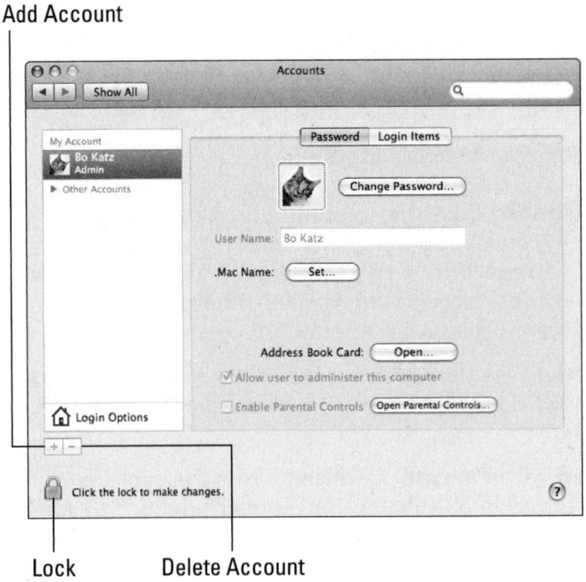

Add Account

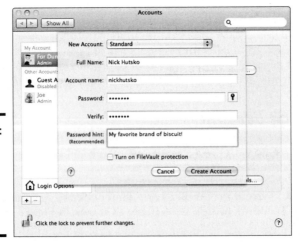

Figure 6-15:
The
Accounts
preferences
pane shows
you the
accounts on
your Mac.

Lock   Delete Account

3. Click the Add Account (+) button to open the New Account dialog, as shown in Figure 6-16.

Figure 6-16:
The New
Account
dialog lets
you define
your new
account.

4. Choose an account type from the New Account pop-up menu.

Standard is a good choice if you don't want the new user to have the ability to delete your Administrator account (or any other user account).

5. **Type the name of the person who'll be using the account into the Full Name text field and press Tab.**

6. **(Optional) Click the Short Name text box and modify the short name for the account if you don't like the one your Mac automatically created after you pressed Tab in the previous step.**

7. **Click the Password text box, type a password for this account, click the Verify field, and then retype the password to confirm your choice.**

8. **(Optional) Click the Password Hint text box and type a descriptive phrase you think will help the new user remember the password if it's forgotten.**

9. **(Optional) Select the Turn On FileVault Protection check box to have your Mac protect the user's personal files and folders by encrypting the user's Home folder and all of the files and folders the user stores inside it.**

   To learn more about how you can use FileVault to secure your Mac against prying eyes and other security threats, check out Book II, Chapter 2.

10. **Click the Create Account button.**

   You return to the Accounts preferences pane, which now displays the name of your new account. A dialog appears, asking whether you want to turn Automatic Login on or off. With multiple accounts, your Mac doesn't know which account to log in to unless you specify an account.)

11. **Choose how to log in.**

   Click Keep Automatic Login if you want to log in automatically to your Administrator account at startup. Alternatively, you can choose a different account to log in to from the Automatic Login pop-up menu. Click Turn Off Automatic Login if you want to choose which account to use each time you turn on your Mac.

12. **Click the Close button of the System Preferences window.**

Switching between accounts

The Mac offers several ways to switch between accounts. The most straightforward way is to log out of one account and then log in to a different account. A faster and more convenient way is to use Fast User Switching, which essentially lets you switch accounts without having to log out of one account first.

To log out of an account, simply choose ⌘⇨Log Out (or press ⌘+Shift+Q). After you log out, the login window appears, listing the names and user icons of all accounts. At this time, you can click a different account name to log in to that account.

Before you can log out, you must close any files and shut down any running programs. If you use Fast User Switching, you won't have to bother with any of that, because Fast User Switching gives the illusion of putting the currently active account in "suspended animation" mode while your Mac opens another account.

Enabling Fast User Switching

Before you can use Fast User Switching, you have to turn on this feature. Log in as Administrator and then follow these steps:

1. **Choose ➪System Preferences and click the Accounts icon to open the Accounts preferences pane (refer to Figure 6-15).**

2. **Click the Lock icon (if it is locked) in the lower-left corner of the Accounts window to allow you to edit your accounts, type your password into the dialog that appears, and then click OK.**

3. **Click the Login Options icon near the bottom-left corner of the Accounts window to display the Login Options pane, as shown in Figure 6-17.**

Figure 6-17: Login Options is where you can turn on Fast User Switching.

4. **Select the Show Fast User Switching Menu As check box, click the pop-up menu, and then choose how you want to display the Fast User Switching Menu: Name, Short Name, or Icon.**

These options display what appears on the menulet. Name displays full account names, Short Name displays abbreviated account names, and

Icon displays a generic icon that takes up the least amount of space in the menu bar.

5. **Click the Close button to close the Accounts preferences pane.**

Changing accounts with Fast User Switching

When you enable Fast User Switching, the Fast User Switching menulet appears in the right side of the menu bar, as shown in Figure 6-18. The menulet displays the names of accounts you can choose.

Figure 6-18:
The Fast
User
Switching
menulet.

To switch to a different account at any time, follow these steps:

1. **Click the Fast User Switching menulet on the right side of the menu bar and then click the account name you want to use.**

2. **Type the account password in the dialog that appears and then press Return.**

   Your Mac switches you to your chosen account.

Deleting an account

After you create one or more accounts, you might want to delete them. When you delete an account, your Mac gives you the option of retaining the account's Home folder, which might contain important files. To delete an account, follow these steps:

1. **Make sure the account you want to delete is logged out and you are logged in to your Administrator account.**

2. **Choose ☀️⇨System Preferences and then click the Accounts icon to open the Accounts preferences pane (refer to Figure 6-15).**

3. **Click the Lock icon in the bottom-left corner of the Accounts preferences pane to allow you to edit your accounts, type your password into the dialog that appears, and then click OK.**

4. **Select the account you want to delete in the accounts list and then click the Delete Account (-) button in the lower-left corner of the Accounts preferences pane.**

   A dialog appears, asking whether you really want to delete this account and presents options to save the Home folder of the account, as shown in Figure 6-19.

   - *Save the Home Folder in a Disk Image:* Saves the home folder and its contents in a compressed disk image (DMG) file. This keeps the files compressed, so they take up less space on the hard drive than if you choose the next option (which does not compress the files contained in the Home folder). Choosing this option is like stuffing stuff in an attic to get it out of sight, but still keeping it around in case you need it later.

   - *Do Not Change the Home Folder:* Keeps the Home folder and its contents exactly as they are before you delete the account, so you can browse through the files contained within the folder at any time.

   - *Delete the Home Folder:* Wipes out any files the user might have created in the account.

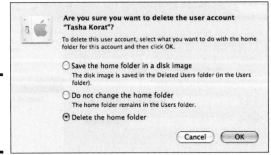

Figure 6-19:
Do you
really want
to delete?

> Are you sure you want to delete the user account "Tasha Korat"?
>
> To delete this user account, select what you want to do with the home folder for this account and then click OK.
>
> ○ Save the home folder in a disk image
>   The disk image is saved in the Deleted Users folder (in the Users folder).
>
> ○ Do not change the home folder
>   The home folder remains in the Users folder.
>
> ◉ Delete the home folder
>
> (Cancel)   (OK)

5. **Select a radio button and then click OK.**

   Your Mac deletes the specified account.

Using Your Mac's Accessibility Features

Right out of the box, every Mac behaves exactly the same. This can be a good thing because it means you can use any Mac anywhere and expect it to work the same — whether the Mac is in New Jersey or Norway.

Unfortunately, not everyone has perfect eyesight, hearing, or eye-hand coordination. If you have trouble with your vision, hearing, or ability to use the keyboard or mouse (or both), using a computer can be difficult. That's why every Mac comes with special universal access features that you can turn on and modify. These universal access features fall under four categories — seeing, hearing, keyboard, and mouse and trackpad — all of which I discuss in some detail on the following pages.

Mitigating vision limitations

To help the visually impaired, every Mac includes a VoiceOver feature, which essentially lets your Mac read text, e-mail, and even descriptions of the screen in a computer-generated voice. For partially sighted users, the Mac can magnify images on the screen or change the contrast of the screen to make it easier to read. To modify the vision assistance features of your Mac, follow these steps:

1. **Choose ⌘⇨System Preferences and then click the Universal Access icon to open the Universal Access preferences pane, as shown in Figure 6-20.**

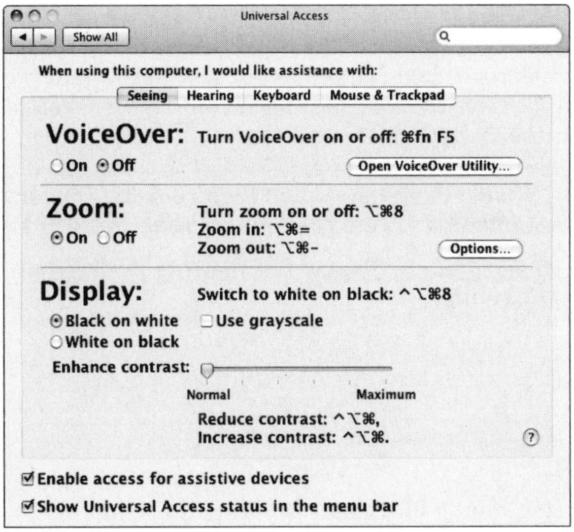

Figure 6-20:
The Seeing preferences pane displays options for making the Mac easier to use for the visually impaired.

2. **Click the Seeing tab and then select the options you want to activate, which include:**

- *VoiceOver:* Allows your Mac to describe what's on the screen and assist you in using the Macintosh menus. Click the Open VoiceOver Utility button to customize such options as how fast your Mac speaks and whether it speaks with a male or female synthesized voice.

- *Zoom:* Allows you to magnify the screen around the cursor by pressing Option+⌘+= (equal sign) or return to normal by pressing Option+⌘+– (minus sign).

- *Display:* Choose either the Black on White (the default option) or White on Black (which gives a photographic negative effect) radio button.

  Check the Use Grayscale option if you want to make your Mac's screen have the look and feel of a black and white photograph. Drag the Enhance Contrast slider to increase/decrease the screen contrast.

- *Enable Access for Assistive Devices:* Check this option to allow external devices (such as unique keyboards or mice) to use AppleScript to control the Mac user interface.

- *Show Universal Access Status in the Menu Bar:* If selected, this option displays a Universal Access menulet on the menu bar, allowing you to turn Universal Access features on or off.

3. **Click the Close button or press ⌘+Q to close the Universal Access Preferences pane.**

Compensating for hearing limitations

To adjust for hearing impairments, you can increase the volume for your various system alerts or you can have your Mac flash the screen to catch your attention. To have the Mac flash the screen rather than make a beeping noise, follow these steps:

1. **Choose ⟹System Preferences and then click the Universal Access icon to open the Universal Access preferences pane (refer to Figure 6-20).**

2. **Click the Hearing tab to display the Hearing preferences pane, as shown in Figure 6-21.**

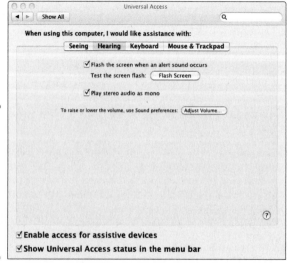

Figure 6-21:
The Hearing preferences pane gives you the option to set a flashing screen to alert you.

3. **Select the Flash the Screen When an Alert Sound Occurs check box.**

4. **Click Play Stereo Audio as Mono to remove the stereo effect from music or other stereo-enabled sounds your Mac plays.**

5. **(Optional) Click the Adjust Volume button to open the Sound Preferences dialog, where you can adjust the system volume to suit your hearing needs.**

6. **Click the Close button or press ⌘+Q to close the Universal Access Preferences pane.**

Easing keyboard limitations

If you have physical limitations using the keyboard, the Mac offers two solutions: the Sticky Keys feature and the Slow Keys feature. Sticky Keys can help you use keystroke shortcuts, such as ⌘+P (Print), which usually require pressing two or more keys at the same time. By turning on Sticky Keys, you can use keystroke shortcuts by pressing one key at a time. The first key you press, such as the ⌘ key, "sticks" in place and waits until you press a second key to complete the keystroke shortcut.

The Slow Keys feature slows the reaction time of the Mac every time you press a key. Normally when you press a key, the Mac accepts it right away, but Slow Keys can force a Mac to wait a long time before accepting the typed key. That way, your Mac will ignore any accidental taps on the keyboard and patiently wait until you hold down a key for a designated period before it accepts it as valid.

To turn on Sticky Keys or Slow Keys, follow these steps:

1. **Choose ⌘⇨System Preferences and then click the Universal Access icon to open the Universal Access preferences pane (refer to Figure 6-20).**

2. **Click the Keyboard tab to display the Keyboard preferences pane, as shown in Figure 6-22.**

3. **Click the On radio button to turn on Sticky Keys and then click any additional options you want to activate, including:**

   • *Press the Shift key Five Times to Turn Sticky Keys On or Off:* Lets you turn the Sticky Keys feature on or off with the keyboard.

   • *Beep When a Modifier Key Is Set:* Alerts you when you've pressed a so-called "modifier" key — a key such as Option or ⌘ — which is used in combination with another key to modify how that key works.

   • *Display Pressed Keys On Screen:* When activated, any modifier keys you press (such as the ⌘ or Option key) display onscreen in the upper-right corner of the screen, so you can verify that you've pressed the right key.

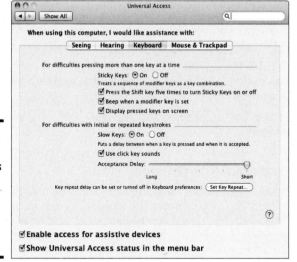

Figure 6-22:
Keyboard
preferences
let you
adjust the
behavior
of the
keyboard.

4. **Click the On radio button to turn on Slow Keys and then choose or adjust additional options you want to activate, including:**

   • *Use Click Key Sounds:* This option causes your Mac to make a clicking sound every time you press a key to give you audible feedback.

   • *Acceptance Delay:* Dragging this slider to the left lengthens the time it takes your Mac to recognize when you press and hold down a key; dragging the slider to the right shortens the time your Mac waits to recognize when you press and hold down a key.

   • *Set Key Repeat:* Click this button to turn on, turn off, and adjust how slowly (or quickly) your Mac repeats a key when you hold it down.

5. **Click the Close button or press ⌘+Q to close the Universal Access preferences pane.**

Dealing with mouse limitations

If you have physical limitations using the mouse, you can turn on the Mouse & Trackpad feature, which lets you control the mouse through the numeric keys, as shown in Table 6-1.

Table 6-1	Mouse Key Commands
Numeric Key	*What It Does*
9	Moves the pointer diagonally up to the right
8	Moves the pointer straight up

Numeric Key	What It Does
7	Moves the pointer diagonally up to the left
6	Moves the pointer to the right
5	"Clicks" the mouse button
4	Moves the pointer to the left
3	Moves the pointer diagonally down to the right
2	Moves the pointer down
1	Moves the pointer diagonally down to the left
0	"Right-clicks" the right mouse button

The Mouse Keys feature is really designed for keyboards that have a separate numeric keypad. If you're using a laptop or other keyboard that doesn't have a separate numeric keypad, the numeric keys might be embedded in the regular typewriter keys. To control the mouse, you have to turn on the Number Lock key to use the numeric keys to move the mouse. Then you have to press the Number Lock key again to use the keys for typing ordinary letters.

Unfortunately, new MacBook and desktop Mac compact keyboards (without dedicated numeric keypads) do not have Number Lock keys and corresponding numeric key overlays on their keyboards. If your Mac or MacBook keyboard doesn't have a Number Lock key, you might want to consider buying an optional external numeric keypad, such as the one sold by Logitech (www.logitech.com) shown in Figure 6-23.

Figure 6-23:
An external numeric keypad lets a MacBook play the numbers.

With an external numeric keypad, you can easily control your Mac's pointer using the Mouse Keys feature. The Mouse Keys feature can replace the mouse altogether or just provide you with another way to move the mouse. No matter how you plan to move the mouse, you might still have trouble finding it on the screen. Fortunately, you can enlarge the size of the pointer to make it easy to spot and use.

To turn on the Mouse Keys feature or change the size of the pointer, follow these steps:

1. **Choose ⌘⇨System Preferences and then click the Universal Access icon to open the Universal Access preferences pane (refer to Figure 6-20).**

2. **Click the Mouse (or Mouse & Trackpad, on MacBooks) tab and then click the On radio button to turn on the Mouse Keys feature, as shown in Figure 6-24.**

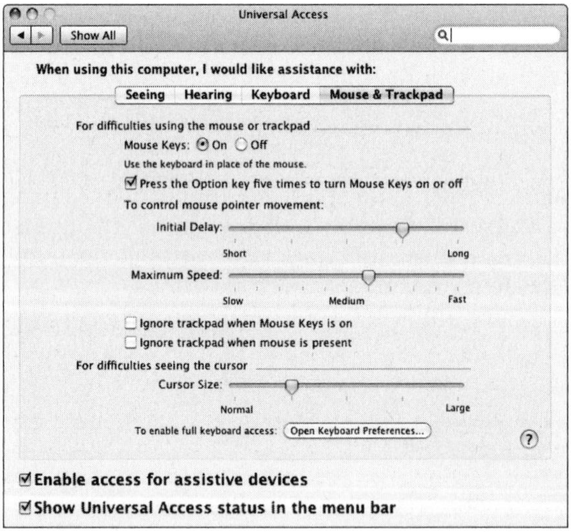

Figure 6-24: The Mouse & Trackpad pane lets you adjust the size of the pointer and determine whether to control the mouse with the keyboard.

3. **Choose or adjust any other Mouse Keys options you want to activate, including:**

   • *Press the Option Key Five Times to Turn Mouse Keys On or Off:* Lets you turn the Mouse Keys feature on or off from the keyboard.

   • *Initial Delay:* Drag the slider to define how long the Mac waits before moving the pointer with the numeric key. A short value means the Mac might immediately move the pointer as soon as you press a number key. A long value means you must hold down a numeric key for a longer period before it starts moving the pointer.

- *Maximum Speed:* Drag the slider to adjust how fast the Mouse Keys feature moves the pointer with the keyboard.

- *Ignore Trackpad When Mouse Keys Is On:* Checking this option prevents your MacBook trackpad from detecting your fingertips and misinterpreting those touchy moments as mouse commands.

- *Cursor Size:* Drag the slider to adjust the size of the pointer on the screen. Enlarging the size of the pointer can make it easier to spot and use.

4. **Click the Close button or press ⌘+Q to close the Universal Access preferences pane.**

Using Voice Recognition and Speech

Your Mac offers both voice recognition and speech capabilities. The voice recognition feature lets you control your Mac using spoken commands, and the speech capability lets your Mac read text or beep to alert you when something happens, such as a dialog popping up on the screen.

Even if you don't have an impairment, your Mac's voice recognition and speech capabilities can be useful for controlling your Mac, or listening to text you've written to catch typos or other errors you might miss by only reading what you've written rather than hearing it aloud.

Setting up voice recognition

To use the Mac's built-in voice recognition software, you have to define its settings and then assign specific types of commands to your voice. Defining the voice recognition settings means choosing how to turn on voice recognition and how your Mac will acknowledge it received your voice commands correctly. For example, your Mac may wait until you press the Esc key or speak a certain word before it starts listening to voice commands. When it understands your command, it can beep.

To define the voice recognition settings, follow these steps:

1. **Choose ⌘⇨System Preferences and then click the Speech icon to open the Speech preferences pane.**

2. **Click the Speech Recognition tab, as shown in Figure 6-25, and then click the On radio button to turn on the Speakable Items feature.**

3. **Choose an appropriate device for accepting your spoken commands from the Microphone pop-up menu.**

   Internal Microphone would be an obvious choice here unless you happen to have an external microphone connected to your Mac.

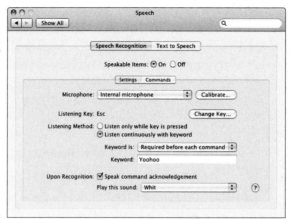

Figure 6-25:
Speech
Recognition
preferences
let you
define how
your Mac
recognizes
spoken
commands.

4. **Click Calibrate to open the Microphone Calibration dialog, as shown in Figure 6-26.**

5. **Recite the phrases displayed in the Microphone Calibration dialog and if necessary, adjust the slider until your Mac recognizes your spoken commands.**

   Each command phrase in the listing blinks when your Mac successfully recognizes your phrasing of the command.

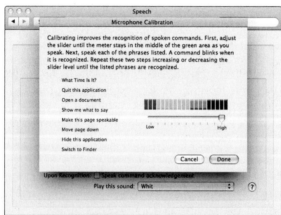

Figure 6-26:
The
Microphone
Calibration
dialog lets
you train
your Mac to
recognize
your voice.

6. **When all phrases are recognized by your Mac, click Done to return to the Speech Recognition preferences pane.**

7. **Click the Change Key button if you want to choose a key other than Esc (as shown in Figure 6-27), which, when you press it, tells your Mac to begin listening for your spoken commands.**

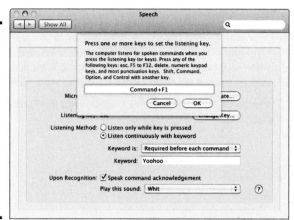

Figure 6-27: The Speech Recognition feature lets you define a listening key to alert your Mac when you'll start giving spoken commands.

8. **Press a key (such as ` or one of your Mac keyboard function keys) and then click OK to return to the Speech Recognition dialog.**

9. **Select one of the following radio buttons in the Listening Method category:**

   - *Listen Only while Key Is Pressed:* Your Mac accepts only spoken commands as long as you hold down the Escape key, or a different listening key you defined in Step 8. If you choose this radio button, go to Step 12.

   - *Listen Continuously with Keyword:* Your Mac waits to hear a spoken keyword (such as "Computer" or "Yoohoo!") before accepting additional spoken commands. If you choose this radio button, go to Step 10.

10. **Click the Keyword Is pop-up menu and choose one of the following:**

    - *Optional before Commands:* Your Mac listens for spoken commands all the time. This can make it easier to give spoken commands, but it also means your Mac might misinterpret the radio or background conversations as commands.

    - *Required before Each Command:* You must speak the keyword before your Mac will accept spoken commands.

    - *Required 15 Seconds after Last Command:* You must repeat the keyword within 15 seconds after each command.

    - *Required 30 Seconds after Last Command:* Same as the preceding option except the Mac waits up to 30 seconds for the next spoken commands.

11. **Click the Keyword text box and type your keyword if you don't want to use the default keyword (Computer) to speak to your Mac.**

12. (Optional) Make choices in the Upon Recognition area.

If you want your Mac to use the voice Whit to confirm commands it successfully recognizes, select the Speak Command Acknowledgement check box. If you prefer to hear an alert sound instead of Whit's voice, click the Play This Sound pop-up menu and choose the alert sound you want.

13. Click the Commands tab to open the Commands preferences pane, as shown in Figure 6-28.

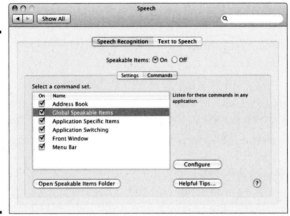

Figure 6-28: Speech Recognition feature's Commands options let you assign different actions to voice commands.

14. Select the check boxes for one or more of the following command sets:

- *Address Book:* Listens for names stored in your Address Book.

- *Global Speakable Items:* Listens for common commands applicable to any situation, such as asking your Mac, "What time is it?" or "Tell me a joke" — and that's no joke!

Click the Open Speakable Items Folder to open a Finder window containing file icons of all the commands you can say to your Mac, as shown in Figure 6-29.

- *Application Specific Items:* Listens for commands specific to each application. A word processor might have a Format menu, but an audio-editing program might not.

- *Application Switching:* Listens for commands to switch between, start, or quit programs.

- *Front Window:* Listens for the commands to control specific items in the displayed window, such as telling your Mac to click a button or check box.

- *Menu Bar:* Listens for commands to display pull-down menus and choose a command.

Figure 6-29:
The
Speakable
Items Folder
contains
file icons of
commands
your Mac
can
recognize.

15. Click the Close button or press ⌘+Q to close the Speech preferences pane.

If you find the Mac's built-in voice recognition features inadequate for your special needs, consider buying a different program that lets you control your Mac with your voice. Two popular voice-recognition programs for the Mac are iListen (www.macspeech.com) and IBM ViaVoice (www.nuance.com/viavoice).

Setting up speech capabilities

Your Mac has a collection of different computer-synthesized voices that can read text to you or alert you when something occurs, such as when you try to quit a program without saving a document. To define the speech capabilities of your Mac, follow these steps:

1. Choose ⇨System Preferences and then click the Speech icon to open the Speech preferences pane.

2. Click the Text to Speech tab to open the Text to Speech preferences pane, as shown in Figure 6-30.

3. Click the System Voice pop-up menu and choose the voice you want to hear when your Mac speaks to you.

My personal favorite is Victoria.

4. Drag the Speaking Rate slider to a desired speed and then click Play to hear your chosen synthesized voice at the specified speaking rate.

Drag the Speaking Rate slider to the left to slow how quickly your Mac speaks; drag the Speaking Rate slider to the right to make your Mac speak more quickly.

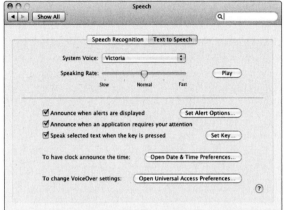

Figure 6-30:
Text to Speech preferences let you define the synthesized voice characteristics of your Mac.

5. **Click the check boxes for any of the following additional Text to Speech options you want to enable:**

   • *Announce When Alerts Are Displayed:* Makes your Mac speak when it needs your attention. It might utter a message saying you don't have enough room on your hard drive to save a file, for instance.

   • *Set Alert Options*: When you select Announce When Alerts Are Displayed, click this button to open a dialog and define how your Mac should speak an alert, as shown in Figure 6-31. Make any changes you want in the Set Alert Options dialog and then click OK to return to the Text to Speech preferences pane.

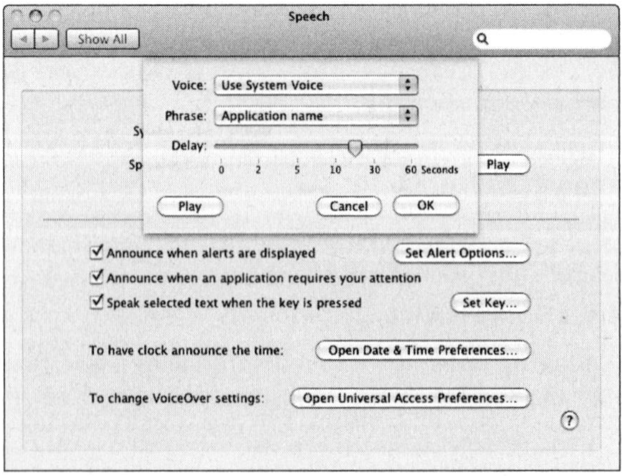

Figure 6-31:
You can customize which voice and phrase to speak along with a delay time.

- *Announce When an Application Requires Your Attention*: Makes your Mac speak when a specific program needs additional information from you, such as when you try to close a file without saving it first.

- *Speak Selected Text When the Key Is Pressed:* Opens a dialog, as shown in Figure 6-32, allowing you to press a key combination (such as ⌘+F1) to tell your Mac when to start reading any text you select. Press a keystroke combination and then click OK to return to the Text to Speech preferences pane.

Figure 6-32:
You can define a keystroke combination to tell the Mac when to start speaking selected text.

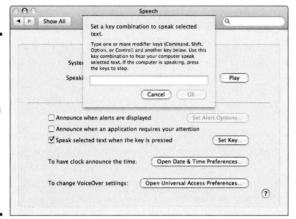

6. **Click the Close button or press ⌘+Q to close the Speech preferences pane.**

Clicking with other mouse and keyboard options

To find different types of keyboards and mice designed to make controlling your computer even more comfortable, search for *"ergonomic input devices"* using your favorite search engine, such as google.com, yahoo.com, or bing.com. Search results will contain a list of product reviews and Web sites selling everything from left-handed keyboards and mice to foot pedals and keyboards designed to type letters by pressing multiple keys like piano chords. For a little extra money, you can buy the perfect keyboard and mouse that can make your Mac more comfortable for you to use.

Book II

Beyond the Basics

The 5th Wave   By Rich Tennant

THE TRAGEDY OF POORLY WRITTEN
SLINKY DOCUMENTATION.

Contents at a Glance

Chapter 1: Doing More with Dashboard Widgets

*M*any programs have so many features crammed into them that succeeding versions get more bloated and harder to use. If you only want to perform a simple task, such as adding a few numbers together or printing an envelope, you probably don't need to load a full-blown spreadsheet or word processing program. Instead, you're better off using a much simpler program specifically designed to solve a single task.

That's the idea behind Dashboard. Dashboard provides you with quick access to a collection of small, simple-task programs called *widgets*. Some typical widgets display a calendar, weather forecasts for your city, a calculator, stock market quotes, and movie times for your neighborhood movie theaters.

Widgets are designed to simplify your life, and Dashboard is the program that helps you display, manage, and hide widgets. By using Dashboard, you can be more productive without having to learn an entirely new program to do so.

Getting to Know Your Dashboard Widgets

To view your widgets, open Dashboard by pressing the Dashboard key on your new or recent Mac or MacBook's keyboard — it's the fifth key from the left in the upper row, sharing space with the F4 function key. You can also press Fn+F12 on your new, recent, and older Macs alike, including models that don't have dedicated special function keys for Dashboard, Exposé, and other nifty, one-touch Mac controls and features. If you prefer the mouse, you can click the Dashboard icon on the Dock. When you finish using a widget, you close it (and the Dashboard) the same way: by pressing the Dashboard key or Fn+F12, or by clicking the mouse pointer on your Mac's Desktop.

While most MacBook keyboards have a Function (Fn) key, other Mac keyboards don't always have the Fn key. If your Mac's keyboard doesn't have a Fn key, you can just press whatever function key I tell you to press and ignore my mention of Fn key whenever you encounter it.

As soon as you open Dashboard, several widgets pop into view, as shown in Figure 1-1. The default widgets that appear are the calendar, clock, calculator, and weather widgets.

The calendar widget lets you view dates for different months and years. The clock widget displays the time in a big clock, which can be easier to read than the tiny time display in the right end of the menu bar. The calculator widget acts like a typical four-function calculator, and the weather widget offers forecasts for a city of your choosing.

If you don't like the position of your widgets on the screen, you can always move them to a new location. To move a widget, click it and drag it to its new position. After you use a widget, you can hide Dashboard, and all its widgets are out of sight once more.

Many widgets, including the weather widget, rely on an Internet connection. If you aren't connected to the Internet when you display such a widget, the widget can't display the latest information.

Figure 1-1:
Dashboard displays widgets that appear over any other programs you're running.

Customizing a widget

Some widgets always appear the same way, such as the calculator widget. Other widgets let you customize them to change their appearance or the type of data they display. To customize a widget, follow these steps:

1. **Press the Dashboard key to open Dashboard and display all your widgets (or press Fn+F12 if your Mac's keyboard doesn't have a dedicated Dashboard key).**

2. **Hover the mouse on the widget you want to customize and then click the Information button, as shown in Figure 1-2.**

   The *i* button (the Information button) appears only for widgets you can customize, such as the weather widget.

Figure 1-2:
An Informa-
tion button
lets you
know you
can custom-
ize a widget.

Information button

3. **Click any check boxes the widget may provide to display additional information, type the new information you want the widget to display, and then click Done.**

   In this case, type the city and state or zip code of a city whose weather forecast you want to keep track of, as shown in Figure 1-3, and check the Include Lows in 6-Day Forecast if you want to see that information as well.

Figure 1-3:
A widget
with an
Information
button
displays
options you
can modify.

Displaying and then clicking a widget changes or expands the information that appears. For instance, clicking the weather widget shows or hides the six-day forecast, and clicking the day/date display of the calendar widget toggles the month-at-a-glance and upcoming appointments displays. Click other widgets to discover whether they offer other additional displays.

Customizing the Dashboard shortcut key

By default, new and recent Macs use the Dashboard special function key (which it shares with F4) to open and close Dashboard. Mac keyboards with the Function key (Fn) can also display the Dashboard when you press Fn+F12. If you want to change this (or any other shortcut key, for that matter — click a different shortcut in Step 3 if desired), you can do so by following these steps:

1. **Choose ⬤⇨System Preference, and then click the Keyboard icon to open the Keyboard preferences pane.**

2. **Click the Keyboard Shortcuts tab, and then click Dashboard & Dock in the left column, as shown in Figure 1-4.**

3. **Double-click the Dashboard shortcut in the right column — the default is F12 — to highlight it, then hold down the Fn key and press the function key you want to assign to Dashboard.**

   You can also assign one or more modifier keys and keyboard keys to the Dashboard feature. For instance, if you press ⌘+Control+D in this step, that key combination then replaces the Dashboard feature's default key assignment of Fn+F12.

4. **Click the Close button or press ⌘+Q to close the Keyboard preferences pane.**

Figure 1-4:
The list of Keyboard Shortcuts shows which keys are assigned to specific tasks.

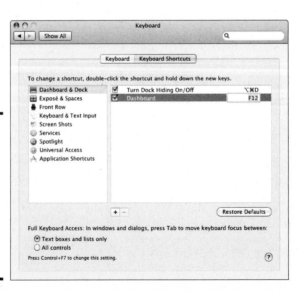

Adding and Removing Widgets

When you open Dashboard, you see several widgets, even if you actually want to use just one widget. In case you don't want to see a particular widget, you can remove it from Dashboard. (Don't worry; you can always put it back on Dashboard again.) Conversely, you can also add more widgets to your Dashboard.

Removing a widget from Dashboard

When you remove a widget from Dashboard, you don't physically delete the widget. Instead, you just tuck the widget into storage where you can retrieve it later. To remove a widget from Dashboard, follow these steps:

1. **Press the Dashboard key or Fn+F12 to open Dashboard and display all your widgets.**

2. **Click the plus sign button that appears inside a circle in the bottom-left corner of the screen to display Close buttons in the upper-left corner of every widget, as shown in Figure 1-5.**

If you hover the pointer on the widget you want to remove and hold down the Option key, a Close button appears in the upper-right corner of just that one widget (and you don't have to click the circled plus sign icon).

**Book II
Chapter 1**

Doing More with
Dashboard Widgets

Close buttons

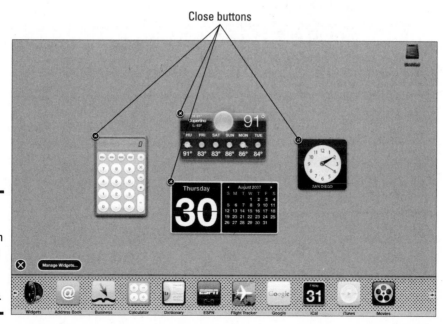

Figure 1-5:
Click the
Close button
to remove a
widget you
no longer
want to see.

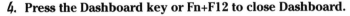

3. **Click the Close button of the widget you want to remove to make it disappear from the screen.**

4. **Press the Dashboard key or Fn+F12 to close Dashboard.**

Clicking anywhere on the screen except on another widget is another way to close Dashboard.

Displaying more widgets in Dashboard

When you open Dashboard, you see only a handful of all the widgets in the Dashboard's library of widgets that come with every Mac. In addition to these, you can download additional widgets from the Web.

Table 1-1 lists all of Dashboard's available widgets that you can choose to display every time you open Dashboard, some of which are shown in Figure 1-6. (***Note:*** Apple may have changed the lineup since I wrote this, so keep in mind that your mileage may vary.)

Table 1-1	Dashboard's Library of Widgets
Widget	*What It Does*
Address Book	Lets you search for names stored in your Address Book
Business	Displays a Yellow Pages directory for looking up business names and phone numbers
Calculator	Displays a four-function calculator
Dictionary	Displays a dictionary and thesaurus for looking up words
ESPN	Displays sports news and scores
Flight Tracker	Tracks airline flights
Google	Displays a text box to send a query to Google and display the results in Safari (or your preferred Web browser)
iCal	Displays a calendar and any appointments stored within iCal
iTunes	Lets you Pause, Play, Rewind, or Fast Forward a song currently playing in iTunes
Movies	Displays which movies are playing at which times at a certain ZIP code
People	Displays a White Pages directory that lets you search for a person's name and address to find his or her telephone number
Ski Report	Displays the temperature and snow depth at your favorite ski resort

Widget	What It Does
Stickies	Displays color-coded windows for jotting down notes
Stocks	Displays stock quotes
Tile Game	Displays a picture tile game in which you slide tiles to recreate a picture
Translation	Translates words from one language to another, such as Japanese to French
Unit Converter	Converts measurement units, such as inches to centimeters
Weather	Displays a weather forecast for your area
Web Clip	Displays parts of a Web page that you've clipped from Safari (see Book IV, Chapter 1 for more information about creating Web Clips)
World Clock	Displays the current time

**Book II
Chapter 1**

**Doing More with
Dashboard Widgets**

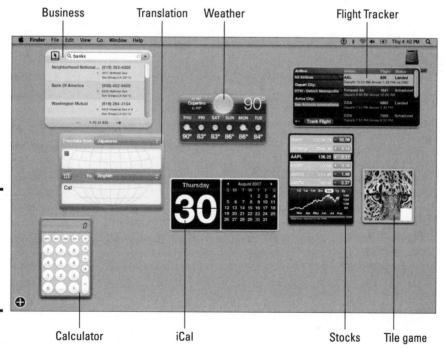

Figure 1-6:
Dashboard widgets can display a wide variety of information.

So you wanna be a widget star?

If you have an idea for a cool widget, you can try creating one yourself by using the free Dashcode program. (You might need to retrieve Dashcode from your Mac OS X 10.6 installation disc, or you can download Dashcode from Apple's Web site at `www.apple.com/` `macosx/developer`.) Dashcode provides templates to help you create a widget. Who knows? With a little bit of creativity and a little help from Dashcode, you could create the next widget that appears on Apple's Web site one day.

To display a hidden Dashboard widget, follow these steps:

1. **Press the Dashboard key or Fn+F12 to open Dashboard, and then click the plus sign that appears inside a circle in the bottom-left corner of the screen to display a list of widgets (refer to Figure 1-1).**

2. **Click a widget that you want to display in Dashboard, such as ESPN or Stocks, to make it appear on the screen.**

   Click the left or right arrows on either side of the widget list to scroll through all the widgets your Mac has to offer.

3. **Move the cursor to the widget, click and drag the widget to wherever you want it to appear on your screen, and then release the mouse button.**

4. **Press the Dashboard key or Fn+F12 to close Dashboard.**

   All your widgets disappear. The next time you open Dashboard, your newly added widgets appear on the screen.

You can have multiple instances of the same widget opened at the same time. For instance, to track the weather in two or more cities, you can just repeat Step 2 in the above for each additional instance of the Weather you want to display.

To create your own widgets from a section of a Web page you're viewing with Safari, choose File➪Open in Dashboard and then drag the selection box to the section you want to turn into a Dashboard widget, as I explain in more detail in Book IV, Chapter 1.

Finding New Widgets

Dashboard comes with a library of widgets, but people are always creating more, which you can browse and download by visiting Apple's Web site. To find the latest widgets, follow these steps:

1. **Visit Apple's Web site (www.apple.com/downloads/dashboard) using your favorite browser (such as Safari) to access the widget download page, as shown in Figure 1-7.**

Figure 1-7:
Apple's
Web site
organizes
widgets by
category.

2. **Click a category, such as Business, Food, or Games, to display a list of the category's widgets in the middle pane.**

3. **Click a widget in the middle pane to display details about the widget in the third pane and then click the Download button if you decide to add the widget to your Mac's library of Dashboard widgets.**

   Your Mac downloads the chosen widget to the Downloads folder and displays a dialog, asking whether you want to install your newly down-loaded widget in Dashboard, as shown in Figure 1-8.

Figure 1-8:
You can
install your
new widget
right away.

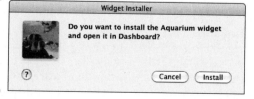

4. **Click the Install button to give your Mac permission to open Dashboard and install the new widget; then click the widget and drag it to where you want it to appear on your screen.**

If Safari doesn't ask whether you want to install the widget, as shown in Figure 1-8, you might need to activate the Open "Safe" Files after Downloading option in Safari's preferences window, as shown in Figure 1-9. To do so, choose Safari➪Preferences (click the General preferences icon if it isn't already selected) and then check the box next to Open "Safe" Files after Downloading. Click the Close button to close the Safari preferences window.

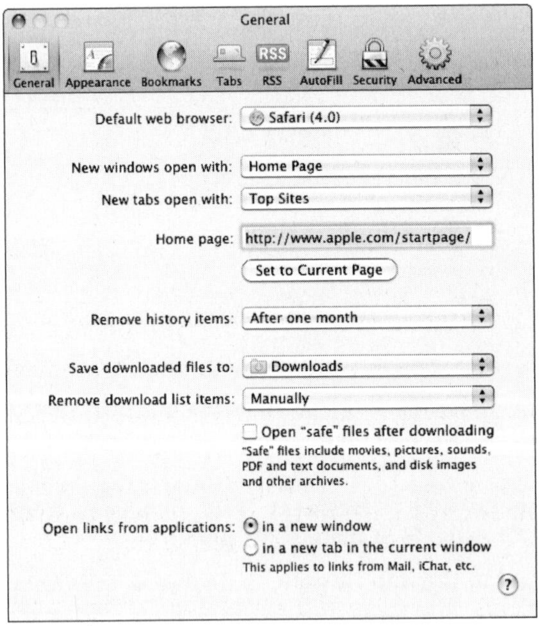

Figure 1-9:
Check Open "Safe" Files after Down- loading in Safari's preferences window to install widgets you download.

	General

General Appearance Bookmarks Tabs RSS AutoFill Security Advanced

Default web browser: Safari (4.0)

New windows open with: Home Page
New tabs open with: Top Sites

Home page: http://www.apple.com/startpage/
Set to Current Page

Remove history items: After one month

Save downloaded files to: Downloads
Remove download list items: Manually

☐ Open "safe" files after downloading
"Safe" files include movies, pictures, sounds, PDF and text documents, and disk images and other archives.

Open links from applications: ● in a new window
○ in a new tab in the current window
This applies to links from Mail, iChat, etc.

Disabling and Deleting Widgets from Dashboard

If you keep installing new widgets, eventually your list of available widgets can get crowded and overwhelming. To reduce the number of available wid- gets, you can disable or delete them.

Disabling a widget hides it from view but keeps it stored on your hard drive in case you change your mind and decide to display it after all. Deleting a widget physically removes it from your hard drive.

Disabling a widget

To disable a widget and temporarily remove it from view, follow these steps:

1. **Press the Dashboard key (or Fn+F12) to open Dashboard and then click the plus sign that appears in a circle in the bottom-left corner of the screen to display a list of installed widgets.**

2. **Click the Manage Widgets button in the lower-left corner to open a list of installed widgets, as shown in Figure 1-10.**

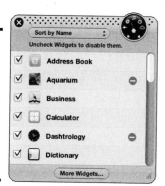

Figure 1-10:
A window lists all installed widgets with a check box next to each one.

3. **Uncheck the check box in front of any widgets you want to disable.**

   If its check box is deselected, the widget is disabled and isn't available for display through Dashboard.

4. **Click the Close button of the Manage Widgets window and then press the Dashboard button (or Fn+F12) or click anywhere on the screen (except over a widget) to close the Dashboard.**

To re-enable a widget you disabled, repeat these same steps *except* click any unchecked widgets to enable them again so they reappear in the row of available dashboard widgets you can display when you activate Dashboard.

Deleting a widget

You can delete any widgets that you install (see the "Finding New Widgets" section, earlier in this chapter, for more about downloading additional widgets). To delete a widget, follow these steps:

1. **Press the Dashboard key or Fn+F12 to open Dashboard and then click the plus sign that appears in a circle in the bottom-left corner of the screen to display a list of installed widgets.**

2. **Click the Manage Widgets button in the lower-left corner to open a list of installed widgets (refer to Figure 4-10) and then click the minus sign that appears to the right of the widget you want to delete.**

   A dialog appears, asking whether you really want to move the widget to the Trash, as shown in Figure 1-11.

Figure 1-11: A dialog appears when you try to delete a widget.

3. **Click OK to delete the widget and then click the Close button of the Manage Widgets window.**

4. **Press the Dashboard key (or Fn+F12) or click anywhere on the screen (except over a widget) to close the Dashboard.**

Peeking at Other Widget Programs

In addition to using your Mac's Dashboard feature to display widgets, two other free programs work like Dashboard: Yahoo! Widgets and Google Desktop (which prefers to use the term *gadgets* to refer to what Yahoo and Apple call widgets).

As Figure 1-12 shows, Yahoo! Widgets and Google Desktop can display bite-size bits of information similar to the Mac Dashboard.

You can download Yahoo! Widgets by steering your Web browser to widgets.yahoo.com; Google Desktop can be downloaded by visiting desktop.google.com.

Figure 1-12:
Yahoo!
Widgets
(top) and
Google
Desktop's
gadgets
(bottom)
offer
Dashboard-
like displays.

Chapter 2: Protecting Your Data with Time Machine and Other Programs

In This Chapter

✔ **Understanding backup options**

✔ **Using Time Machine**

✔ **Working with data-recovery programs**

✔ **Encrypting your data**

*B*acking up data is something that many people routinely ignore, like changing the oil in their car on a regular basis. The only time most people think about backing up their data is after they've already lost something important, such as a business presentation, or a folder full of close-to-the-heart family photos. Of course, by that time, it's already too late.

Backing up your data might not sound as exciting as playing video games or browsing the Web, but it should be a part of your everyday routine. If you can't risk losing your data, you can't risk not taking the time to back it up.

Understanding Different Backup Options

The simplest and most obvious solution for backing up your data is to make duplicate copies of every important file. Although this seems simple in theory, you must make sure to copy your files periodically, such as at the end of every day. If you forget to copy your files, your backup copies could become woefully outdated, which can make them nearly useless.

Another issue with backing up data concerns storing and retrieving it. If you store duplicates of your important files on your hard drive, you have to make sure you don't accidentally use those backup files instead of the original files (and then accidentally copy the obsolete original files over the backup copies that are actually more current). Additionally, if you experience a hardware problem with your hard drive and it stops working, you lose both your original files and your backup files.

To back up your files, consider using more than one method, because the more backup copies you have of your critical files, the more likely it is that you'll never lose your data no matter what might happen to your Mac.

To reduce the amount of storage space needed to store copies of your files, you can archive and compress your files into a ZIP or DMG file. (See Book I, Chapter 5 for more information about creating ZIP and DMG files.)

Using your hard drive

The simplest way to back up your files is to create and store duplicate copies of the files in a backup folder on your Mac's hard drive. This method has the advantage of not requiring that you buy any new equipment. The huge disadvantage of this option is that if your Mac's hard drive fails, you might lose both your original data and any backup files you have stored.

Another problem is that the more data you need to back up, the more space both your original and backup files will gobble up, until eventually, you might run out of room on your hard drive. For these reasons, using your hard drive to store backup copies of files is suitable for backing up a handful of files, but it's both impractical and risky for backing up large amounts of data.

Backing up to CDs/DVDs

Every Mac can write to CDs, and most Macs can write to DVDs. As a result, storing backups on CDs or DVDs is a popular option because CDs and DVDs are easy to store and are durable. The biggest drawback of CDs and DVDs is their limited storage capacities. CDs can store up to 700MB of data, and DVDs can store 4.7GB of data, with the newest *dual-layer* DVDs capable of storing up to 8.5GB of data.

A dual-layer disc employs a second physical layer within the disc, which the drive accesses by shining its laser through the disc's first, semitransparent layer.

If you need to back up only word processor or spreadsheet files, a single CD should be sufficient. However, music, video, and digital photographs take up more space, which means that you might need to use several CDs or DVDs to back up all your files of those types.

DVDs can store much more data than CDs, but even they can be limited when you're backing up hard drives that contain several gigabytes worth of files. The more discs you need to back up your files completely, the harder to keep track of all the discs.

Storing data on multiple discs can be slow and tedious, which means you might not back up your data as often as you should. Eventually, this means your backup files are too out of date to be useful, which defeats the purpose of backing up your data.

Fitting your most crucial files on a CD or DVD can be a simple and fast backup option. But if your data frequently exceeds the storage limits of a single CD or DVD, using multiple discs can be cumbersome, and you should probably rely on another backup method.

Storing backups on USB flash drives

The low-cost and high-storage capacities of USB flash drives make them an attractive alternative to using CDs for backing up your most crucial files. USB flash drives offer ease of use because you can plug them into any open USB port in a Mac and move them to another Mac. Many USB flash drives have built-in keyrings. Carrying one in your pocket or purse is not only convenient, but also assures that your data is always safe and on your person should something happen to your Mac's hard drive at home or in the office, where your backup drive's original files are stored.

The biggest drawback of USB flash drives is their limited storage capacities, which typically range from 1GB to 32GB or sometimes more. While USB flash drives in those capacity ranges can usually cost between $5 and $100, a whopping 128GB model sold Amazon (www.amazon.com) costs around $400. Whatever the capacity, USB flash drives are especially convenient for carrying your most critical files but not necessarily for backing up all your important files. In contrast to the hassles of writing (or *burning*) data to a CD or DVD, saving files to a USB flash drive is speedier and as simple as saving a file to a backup folder on your hard drive.

If you lose your USB flash drive, anyone who finds it can open and view your files. If the idea of strangers peeking at your files gives you the heebie-jeebies, consider buying a special USB flash drive that offers encryption to protect your files from anyone who doesn't have your password.

Backing up with external hard drives

To prevent the loss of all your data if your hard drive should suddenly bite the dust, you can use external hard drives that connect to your Mac's USB or FireWire port with a cable that's typically included with the hard drive.

Both USB (Universal Serial Bus) and FireWire ports connect peripherals to a computer. USB ports commonly connect a mouse, printer, or digital camera, and FireWire ports often connect video camcorders or other computers. FireWire ports and USB 2.0 ports transfer data at roughly the same speed, so one isn't necessarily better than the other. The MacBook Air and a few earlier-model MacBooks lack a FireWire port, so if you're in the market for a new Mac, and your digital camera or video camcorder can only connect using a FireWire cable, make sure the Mac model you're considering offers a FireWire port.

The main advantage of external hard drives is that copying large files is much faster and more convenient than copying the same files to CD/DVD discs, and they offer more capacity than USB drives. Additionally, external hard drives are easy to unplug from one Mac and plug into another Mac. Because of their low cost, fast copying speed, and ease of moving and plugging into any Mac, external hard drives are the most popular choice for backing up files.

Perhaps the biggest drawback of external hard drives is that they can't protect against a catastrophe near your computer, such as a fire burning down your house or a flood soaking your computer desk and office. If a disaster wipes out the entire area around your computer, your external hard drive might be wiped out in the catastrophe as well.

You can treat an external hard drive as just another place to copy your files, but for greater convenience, you should use a special backup program. Backup programs can be set to run according to a schedule (for example, to back up your files every night at 6:00 p.m.)

If the files haven't changed since the last time you backed them up, the backup program saves time by skipping over those files rather than copying the same files to the external hard drive again.

To retrieve files, you could just copy the files from your external hard drive back to your original hard drive, but be careful! If you changed a file on your original hard drive, copying the backup copy can wipe out the most recent changes and restore an old file to your hard drive, which probably isn't what you want.

To keep you from accidentally wiping out new files with older versions of that same file, backup programs always compare the time and date a file was last modified to make sure you always have copies of the latest file. To try a free backup program for use with an external hard drive, grab a copy of SilverKeeper (www.lacie.com/silverkeeper), PsyncX (http://psyncx.sourceforge.net), Carbon Copy Cloner (www.bombich.com), or SuperDuper (www.shirt-pocket.com).

Storing backups off-site

Backing up your Mac's important files to an off-site storage service virtually guarantees that you'll never lose your data.

Many low-cost (and even free) off-site storage options are available for Mac users. One simple way to create off-site storage is to open a free e-mail account, such as Google Gmail (www.gmail.com), and e-mail yourself your important files. Now you can always retrieve your important files from anywhere in the world that offers Internet access.

Many companies sell off-site storage space for a monthly fee. However, to entice you to try their services, they often provide a limited amount of free space that you can use for an unlimited period at no cost whatsoever. To get your free off-site storage space, sign up with one or more of the following off-site data backup sites:

+ **SugarSync** (`www.sugarsync.com`): Free 2GB of storage space
+ **Syncplicity** (`www.syncplicity.com`): Free 2GB of storage space
+ **MediaMax** (`www.mediamax.com`): Free 25GB of storage space
+ **Mozy** (`http://mozy.com`): Free 2GB of storage space
+ **ElephantDrive** (`www.elephantdrive.com`): Free 1GB of storage space

Apple's MobileMe service, which costs $99 a year, can automatically synchronize your Mac's Address Book contacts, iCal calendar events, Safari bookmarks, as well as backup files and folders between multiple Macs or between your Mac and your iPhone, iPod touch music and media player, or Windows PC you might also use. MobileMe (`www.me.com`) also provides you with an iDisk online backup storage space that you can access from the Finder just like a hard drive; however, copying files to and from your iDisk is slower than copying to a locally connected drive.

Blasting into the Past with Time Machine

One problem with traditional backup programs is that they store the latest or last two or three previous versions of your files. Normally, this is exactly what you want, but what if you want to see an earlier version of a short story you began working on two weeks ago? Unless you kept a copy of your backups you made two weeks ago, trying to find files created on certain dates in the past is nearly impossible.

Fortunately, that type of problem is trivial for your Mac's backup program, Time Machine. Unlike traditional backup programs that copy and store the latest or last one or two versions of files, Time Machine takes snapshots of your Mac hard drive so that you can view its exact condition from two hours ago, two weeks ago, two months ago, or farther back. *Note:* The external hard drive you use to back up your Mac with Time Machine should have oodles of storage space. The bigger the hard drive, the farther back in time you can go to recover old files and information.

By viewing the exact condition of what your Mac hard drive looked like in the past, you can see exactly what your files looked like at that time. After you find a specific file version from the past, you can easily restore it to the present with a click of the mouse.

Setting up Time Machine

To use Time Machine, you need to connect an external hard drive to your Mac with a USB or FireWire cable, or have an additional hard drive installed in one of the additional drive bays inside your Mac Pro desktop computer.

To set up Time Machine to back up the data on your Mac's primary hard drive to an external hard drive, follow these steps:

1. **Connect the external hard drive to your Mac.**

When you plug in a new hard drive, the Time Machine backup feature typically starts automatically and asks if you want to use the hard drive to back up your Mac, as shown in Figure 2-1.

Figure 2-1:
Time Machine thoughtfully offers to back up your Mac when you plug in an external hard drive.

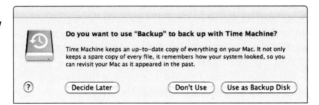

If Time Machine automatically runs and prompts you as described, skip to Step 4. If Time Machine does not prompt you, continue to the next step.

2. **Choose ⌘⇨System Preferences and then click the Time Machine icon to open the Time Machine preferences pane, as shown in Figure 2-2.**

Figure 2-2:
To set up Time Machine, you need to turn it on and choose an external drive to use.

Note: If the lock icon in the lower-left corner of the Time Machine preferences pane is bolted, click it, enter your password when prompted, and then click OK.

3. **Click the On button.**

   A dialog appears, listing all available external hard drives you can use, as shown in Figure 2-3.

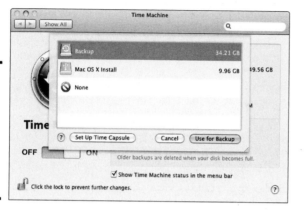

Figure 2-3: You must choose an external hard drive to use with Time Machine.

**Book II
Chapter 2**

Protecting Your Data
with Time Machine
and Other Programs

4. **Select an external hard drive and click the Use for Backup button.**

   The Time Machine pane appears again, listing your chosen external hard drive, as shown in Figure 2-4, and after a short amount of time the Time Machine program begins backing up your Mac's data to the external hard drive you selected.

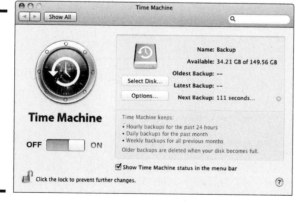

Figure 2-4: The Time Machine pane can show how much free space remains on your external hard drive.

To find how frequently Time Machine backs up and manages your Mac's data, see the nearby sidebar, "How Time Machine does its backup thing."

How Time Machine does its backup thing

The first time you turn on and begin using Time Machine, it backs up your Mac's entire hard drive — which can take a long time if your Mac's hard drive contains lots of programs and data. One thing you can do is start the Time Machine backup before going to bed, so when you wake the next morning your Mac will be completely (or almost completely) backed up.

After its initial backup of your Mac's hard drive, Time Machine automatically performs an incremental backup of any data changed on your

Mac's hard drive (providing the backup drive is attached) every hour. Time Machine saves hourly backups for the past 24 hours, daily backups for the past month, and weekly backups for everything older than a month. Time Machine skips backing up files you created and then deleted before the next hourly backup.

When your external backup hard drive starts running out of free space for more backups, Time Machine deletes the oldest files it finds in order to make room for the newer ones.

5. **(Optional) Click Show Time Machine Status on the Menu Bar if it isn't already checked.**

With this option checked, the Time Machine icon on the menu bar animates with a twirling arrow whenever Time Machine is backing up your Mac's data. Clicking the Time Machine icon at any time (see Figure 2-5) is how you can keep tabs on the status of an active backup, start or stop a backup, and choose the Enter Time Machine command to run the Time Machine recovery program, as described in the upcoming section "Retrieving files and folders."

Figure 2-5: Access your Mac's backup options from the menu bar.

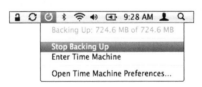

6. **Click the Close button to close the Time Machine preferences pane.**

Skipping files you don't want to back up

To save space, you can identify certain files and folders you're not concerned about losing that you want Time Machine to ignore. For example, you might not want to back up your Applications folder if you already have all your programs stored on separate installation discs. Or you might choose to skip backing up TV episodes your Mac recorded using the EyeTV program (sold separately; www.eyetv.com) because you always record the same episodes on the TiVo or other Digital Video Recorder (DVR) in the family room, so there's no use wasting all of that precious space on your Mac's backup drive.

To tell Time Machine which files or folders to skip, follow these steps:

1. **Choose ⬛⇨System Preferences and then click the Time Machine icon to open the Time Machine preferences pane (refer to Figure 2-4).**

2. **Click Options to open the Exclude These Items from Backups dialog, as shown in Figure 2-6.**

Figure 2-6: Click the plus sign (+) to open a dialog for choosing files you don't want to backup.

3. **Click the plus sign (+) and then navigate to the file or folder you want Time Machine to ignore, as shown in Figure 2-7.**

Figure 2-7: Select the hard drive, folder, or files you want Time Machine to ignore.

You can select multiple drives, files, and folders by holding down the ⌘ key and then clicking what you want Time Machine to ignore.

4. **Click the Exclude button.**

   The Exclude These Items from Backups dialog appears again (refer to Figure 2-6).

5. **Select or deselect these additional optional Time Machine features if you want:**

   • *Backup While on Battery Power:* Allows Time Machine to back up your MacBook when it's running on battery power. Turning this option on will drain your MacBook's battery faster than if you turn this option off.

   • *Notify After Old Backups Are Deleted:* Time Machine displays a dialog requesting your approval before it deletes any old backup files.

6. **Click the Done button and then click the Close button to close the Time Machine preferences pane.**

Retrieving files and folders

After you configure Time Machine to back up your Mac, you can use the Time Machine recovery program to retrieve old files or information you deleted or changed after Time Machine backed them up. The two ways to use the Time Machine recovery program to recover files, folders, or other pieces of information, such as address cards, e-mail messages, or iCal calendar items, are as follows:

✦ By running an application and then clicking the Time Machine icon in the Dock, or choosing the Enter Time Machine command from the Time Machine icon on the menu bar.

✦ By clicking the Finder icon in the Dock to open a new Finder window and then clicking the Time Machine icon in the Dock, or choosing the Enter Time Machine command from the Time Machine icon on the menu bar.

Time Machine consists of two components:

✦ The Time Machine preferences pane (described earlier in this section) that you use to turn the Time Machine backup feature on or off, or to adjust its settings.

✦ The Time Machine restore program you use to recover files you deleted or changed from earlier backups. You run the restore program by clicking the Time Machine icon in the Dock, or by choosing the Enter Time Machine command from the Time Machine icon on the menu bar.

Recovering data from within an application

To use Time Machine to retrieve a specific piece of information from within a program (such as an address card from your Mac's Address Book, which I use in this example), follow these steps:

1. **Click the Address Book icon in the Dock to launch Address Book.**

The Address Book program opens and displays the Address Book window, which lists all your contacts.

2. **Click the Time Machine icon in the Dock (or click the Time Machine icon on the menu bar and choose Enter Time Machine) to run the Time Machine recovery program.**

If the Time Machine icon doesn't appear in the Dock or the menu bar, you have to double-click the Time Machine icon in the Applications folder.

Your Mac's screen will appear to literally space out while it launches the Time Machine restore program into another dimension known as The Time Machine Zone, as shown in Figure 2-8.

Figure 2-8:
The Time
Machine
recovery
program
displays
a far-out
view of your
Address
Book.

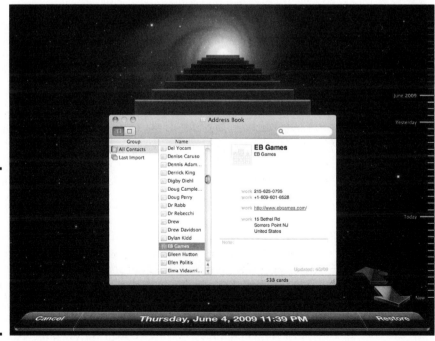

3. **Choose one of the following ways to select a contact card (or cards) that you want to restore from a past backup:**

    •   *Click the Backward and Forward Arrow buttons near the bottom-right corner of the screen.* Click the Backward button to move the Address Book window backward in time to earlier Time Machine backups. Click the Forward button to move forward to more recent Time Machine backups.

    •   *Click an Address Book window in the stack of windows behind the frontmost Address Book window.* You can click the Address Book window directly behind the front Address Book window, or one behind it stretching farther back in time. Each time you click an Address Book window in the stack, Time Machine moves it to the front of the screen.

    •   *Move the pointer to the Time Machine timeline along the right edge of the screen.* The timeline bars expand to display a specific date. To choose a specific date, click it.

4. **When you locate the contact card you want to retrieve, click it, click the Restore button in the lower-right corner, and then proceed to Step 6.**

    To select more than one contact card, hold down the ⌘ key and click each additional contact you want to recover.

5. **If the contact you want to restore is nowhere to be found in the Address Book windows — or if you change your mind and don't want to recover a backed up contact — click the Cancel button in the lower-left corner (or press the Escape key).**

    Time Machine closes and returns you to the present.

6. **The Time Machine Address Book window zooms forward and then closes, returning you to the Address Book program window, which now includes the recovered contact card (or cards).**

    That's it — you've been saved!

You can perform these same steps to recover data that you typically create and use within a particular program, such as iPhoto pictures, iTunes music, movies and other audio files, and iCal calendar events.

Retrieving files and/or folders using the Finder

To use the Finder window to retrieve files, folders, or a combination of both with the Time Machine recovery program, follow these steps:

1. **Click the Time Machine icon in the Dock (or click the Time Machine icon on the menu bar and choose Enter Time Machine) to run the Time Machine recovery program, as shown in Figure 2-9.**

If the Time Machine icon doesn't appear in the Dock or menu bar, you have to double-click the Time Machine icon in the Applications folder.

2. **Choose one of the following ways to locate the file or folder you want to recover using the Finder window from the past:**

   • *Click the Backward and Forward Arrow buttons near the bottom-right corner of the screen.* Click the Backward button to move the Finder window backward in time to previous Time Machine backups. Click the Forward button to work your way forward to more recent Time Machine backups.

   • *Click a Finder window behind the frontmost Finder window.* Each time you click a Finder window, Time Machine moves it forward to the front of the screen.

   • *Move the pointer to the Time Machine timeline along the right edge of the screen.* The timeline bars expand to display a specific date. To choose a specific date, click it.

To take a peek at the contents of a particular document, picture, audio track, or other file, click it and then press the Spacebar to open the Quick Look view (see Figure 2-10), which gives you a speedy way to view the contents of your selected file to make sure it's the one you really want to recover.

Figure 2-9:
Use Time Machine's Finder window to choose files or folders you want to recover.

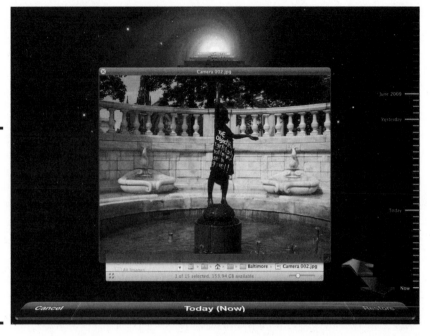

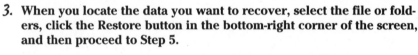

Figure 2-10:
Select a file icon and then press the Spacebar to preview the file's contents with the Quick Look view.

3. **When you locate the data you want to recover, select the file or folders, click the Restore button in the bottom-right corner of the screen, and then proceed to Step 5.**

   To select more than one file or folder, hold down the ⌘ key and click each additional item you want to recover.

4. **If the data you want to recover is nowhere to be found in the Finder windows — or if you change your mind and don't want to recover backup data — click the Cancel button in the bottom-left corner (or press the Escape key).**

   The Time Machine recovery program closes and you return to the present.

5. **The Time Machine Finder window zooms forward and then closes, safely returning you to a Finder window that now includes your recovered file or folder.**

   Consider yourself saved!

Working with Data-Recovery Programs

Suppose you're a well-protected Mac user who backs up your data regularly. You're completely safe, right, and you never have to worry about losing files you can't retrieve? Not exactly. Here are three situations where backup programs can't help you, and you might need to rely on special data-recovery programs instead.

Data-recovery programs work by taking advantage of the way computers store and organize files by physically placing them in certain areas, known as *sectors,* on your Mac's internal hard drive (or removable storage device). To learn more about the nitty-gritty of how hard disks manage files, check out the nearby sidebar, "Hard drive: A tale of control, corruption, and redemption."

You can lose files in these ways in which your backups can't help you:

✦ **Accidentally deleted from the hard drive:** The most common way to lose a file is by accidentally deleting it. If you try to recover your lost file through a backup program, such as Time Machine, you might be shocked to find that your backup program can recover only your file from the previous hour or older, but not in the span of time between Time Machine backups. So if you spent the last 45 minutes changing a file and accidentally deleted it before Time Machine was able to run its next automatic backup, you're out of luck as far as recovering the changes you made in the last 45 minutes.

Hard drive: A tale of control, corruption, and redemption

To keep track of where each file is stored, your Mac maintains a directory that tells the computer the names of every file and the exact physical location where each file is stored. When different programs, such as word processors or spreadsheets, need to find and open a file, these programs depend on the Mac OS X operating system to keep track of this directory so they know where to find a file.

When you delete a file, the computer simply removes that file's name from the directory. However, your file still physically exists on the disk surface, but the computer can't find it again. Therefore, data-recovery programs ignore the directory listing of a disk and search for a file by examining every part of the entire storage device to find your missing files.

If you didn't add any files since you last deleted the file you want to retrieve, a data-recovery program will likely retrieve your entire file again. If you saved and modified files since you last deleted a particular file, there's a good chance any new or modified files might have written over the area that contains your deleted file. In this case, your chances of recovering the entire file intact drops rapidly over time.

If a hardware failure corrupts a file, all or part of your file might be wiped out for good. However, in many cases, a hardware failure won't physically destroy all or part of a file. Instead, a hardware failure might physically scramble a file, much like throwing a pile of clothes all over the room. In this case, the file still physically exists, but the directory of the disk won't know where all the parts of the file have been scattered. So, to the computer, your files have effectively disappeared.

A data-recovery program can piece together scattered files by examining the physical surface of a disk, gathering up file fragments, and putting them back together again like Humpty Dumpty. Depending on how badly corrupted a file might be, collecting file fragments and putting them back together can recover an entire file or just part of a file, but sometimes recovering part of a file can be better than losing the whole file.

✦ **Hardware failure:** Another way to lose a file is through a hardware failure, such as your hard drive mangling portions of its disk surface or corrupting a file because a power outage knocked out your Mac without properly shutting it down first, thereby wrecking any open files that you were working on or that were stored. Such a failure can go unnoticed because the hard drive still works. As a result, your backup program copies and saves these mangled versions of your file. The moment you discover your file is corrupted, you also find that your backup program has been diligently copying and saving the same corrupted version of your file.

✦ **Deleted from removable media:** You might lose data by deleting it from removable media, such as a USB flash drive or digital camera flash memory card (such as a Compact Flash or Secure Digital card). Most likely, your backup programs protect only your hard drive files, not any removable storage devices, which means you could take twenty price-less pictures of your dog doing midair back-flip Frisbee catches, only to delete all those pictures by mistake (and tanking your dog's chances at YouTube stardom). Because your backup program might never have saved those files, you can't recover what was never saved.

Even if you format and erase your entire hard drive, your files may still physically remain on the hard drive, making it possible to recover those files.

Some popular data-recovery programs include:

✦ **Disk Warrior (www.alsoft.com/DiskWarrior; $99):** Builds a new replacement directory using data recovered from the original directory, thereby recovering files, folders, and documents that you thought were gone forever.

✦ **FileSalvage (www.subrosasoft.com; $90):** FileSalvage retrieves deleted and corrupted files from your Mac's hard drive.

✦ **Stellar Phoenix Macintosh and Stellar Phoenix Photo Recovery (www.stellarinfo.com; $99):** Stellar Phoenix Macintosh retrieves deleted and corrupted files. Stellar Phoenix Photo Recovery recovers deleted files from flash memory cards.

✦ **Klix (www.joesoft.com; $30):** Specialized program for recovering lost digital images stored on flash memory cards, such as Secure Digital or Compact Flash cards.

✦ **Data Rescue II (www.prosofteng.com; $100):** This program recovers and retrieves data from a hard drive your Mac can no longer access because of a hard disk failure.

✦ **Mac Data Recovery (www.datarecoverymac.com; $145):** This program specializes in recovering files from corrupted or reformatted hard drives.

The art of computer forensics

Most anything you store on your Mac can be recovered, given enough time and money. When most people lose data, they're thankful when a data-recovery program can retrieve their files. However, in the criminal world, people may want to delete files so that nobody can ever find them again to hide evidence. To retrieve such deleted files, law enforcement agencies rely on something called computer forensics.

The basic idea behind computer forensics is to make an exact copy of a hard drive and then try to piece together the deleted files on that copy of the original hard drive. Some criminals have

lit hard drives on fire, poured acid on them, and sliced them apart with a buzz saw — and law enforcement agencies can still manage to read and recover the files from the slivers of hard drive fragments that contain the magnetic traces of the original files.

The good news is that if you can't recover a file yourself by using a data-recovery program, you can often hire a professional service that can recover your data for you — but that data better be really important to you, because the cost of data recovery services like those offered by DriveSavers (`www.drivesaversdata recovery.com`) is very expensive.

Encrypting Data with FileVault

Sometimes your biggest threat isn't from hardware failure or accidentally deleting your data, but from the prying eyes of others who want to peek at your data. To protect your data, you can take one or more of the following steps:

✦ Physically lock your Mac behind closed doors (armed guards optional).

✦ Make sure everyone using your Mac has his or her own separate account (see Book I, Chapter 6 for more information about creating accounts).

✦ Encrypt your files by using the Mac's built-in encryption program called FileVault.

Encryption physically scrambles your files so that even if people can access your files, they can't open or edit them unless they know the correct password. When you use FileVault, your Mac encrypts your entire home folder that contains your folders, including Documents, Music, and Pictures.

FileVault uses an encryption algorithm called Advanced Encryption Standard (AES), which is the latest American government standard for scrambling data that even national governments with supercomputers can't crack.

Setting up FileVault

FileVault scrambles your files so that only your password (or the system's Master Password) can unlock the files so you — or someone you trust and give the password to — can read them. When you type in a password, you can access your files and use them normally, but as soon as you close a file, FileVault scrambles it once more. FileVault works in the background so that you never even see it working.

FileVault uses your *login* password to encrypt your data. For added safety, FileVault prompts you to create a second password, a *master* password that can decrypt any encrypted files for all user accounts and the files for each account that you have stored on your Mac. If you forget your login password and your master password, your data will be encrypted forever with no hope of unscrambling and retrieving it again.

To turn on FileVault, follow these steps:

1. **Choose ⇨System Preferences and then click the Security icon to open the Security preferences pane.**

   The Security preferences pane appears.

2. **Click the FileVault tab to open the FileVault preferences pane, as shown in Figure 2-11.**

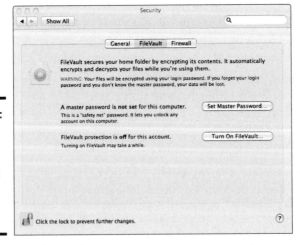

Figure 2-11: The FileVault pane lets you turn on FileVault and set a password.

Note: If the lock in the lower-left corner of the FileVault preferences pane is locked, click it, enter your password when prompted, and then click OK.

3. **Click the Set Master Password button. In the dialog that appears (see Figure 2-12), fill in the Master Password, Verify, and Hint fields, and then click OK.**

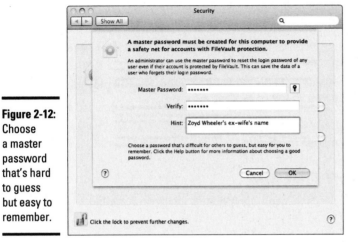

Figure 2-12:
Choose
a master
password
that's hard
to guess
but easy to
remember.

Book II
Chapter 2

Protecting Your Data
with Time Machine
and Other Programs

4. **On the FileVault tab, click the Turn On FileVault button, enter your login password when prompted, and then click OK.**

   A warning dialog appears, telling you how FileVault can prevent Time Machine from retrieving your old files again, as shown in Figure 2-13.

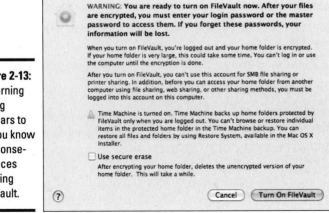

Figure 2-13:
A warning
dialog
appears to
let you know
the conse-
quences
of using
FileVault.

5. **(Optional) Click the Use Secure Erase check box if, after encrypting your Home folder, you want FileVault to delete the previous unencrypted version of your Home folder that it duplicated and encrypted.**

    Choosing this option carries the warning that it can take a long time to delete the unencrypted Home folder completely.

6. **Click the Turn On FileVault button.**

    A window appears to let you know that FileVault is encrypting your home folder. (Be patient. This can take a while.)

7. **When FileVault finishes encrypting, your Mac displays a dialog prompting you to log in to your account.**

When FileVault is turned on, your Mac might run slower because it needs to decrypt and encrypt files while you open and close them.

Turning off FileVault

In case you turned FileVault on and later change your mind, you can always turn FileVault off by following these steps:

1. **Choose ⇨System Preferences and then click the Security icon to open the Security preferences pane.**

    The Security preferences pane appears.

2. **Click the FileVault tab to open the FileVault preferences pane, (refer to Figure 2-11).**

    Note that when FileVault is turned on, the Turn Off FileVault button appears.

3. **(Optional) Click Change if you want to change your master password.**

4. **Click the Turn Off File Vault button, enter your login password, and then press OK.**

    A dialog appears, informing you that you are about to turn off FileVault.

5. **Click the Turn Off FileVault button.**

You're now free to roam about the cabin — or whatever your surroundings — until FileVault finishes decrypting your Mac's Home folder and the files contained within.

Chapter 3: Syncing Your Mobile Phone or PDA with iSync

In This Chapter

✓ Connecting your mobile phone or PDA to Mac

✓ Synchronizing your contacts and calendar data

✓ Considering other mobile phone syncing solutions

Many people I know laboriously type contact names, phone numbers, and other information into their mobile phones one thumb-numbing keystroke at a time. Such a waste of time and energy when they could simply connect their mobile phone (or PDA) to their Mac and transfer their Address Book contacts, iCal calendar events and other information in a matter of minutes using iSync, which comes preloaded on every Mac. What's more, anytime you add, change, or delete information on your Mac or on your mobile device, you can run iSync again so that the two sides are always on the same proverbial page, so to speak.

Connecting a Mobile Phone or PDA to a Mac

Many people store names and contact information on their mobile phones or personal digital assistant (PDA) handheld devices. However, such mobile, handheld devices create two main problems. First, if you already store names, contact information, and appointments using iCal and Address Book on your Mac, you probably don't want to retype this information into your mobile device. Second, if you lose your mobile phone or PDA, you could wind up losing all of your important contact information.

To prevent both of these problems, your Mac comes with a program called iSync. By using iSync, you can connect and transfer data between your Mac and many handheld devices, such as a mobile phone or PDA. Now you can type a name on your mobile phone's contacts program, type an appointment on your Mac using iCal, and then run iSync to bring all this information together by updating your contact information and schedule on both your mobile phone and your Mac.

Besides sharing contact information and appointments between your Mac and a handheld device, iSync also lets you transfer files from your Mac to your handheld device. If you need to read some important documents, transfer them from your Mac to your mobile phone or PDA so you can read them in an airport terminal, while waiting in line at the supermarket, or any time you're away from your Mac.

The iSync program can work with a wide variety of mobile phones and Palm PDAs. For a complete list of devices compatible with iSync, visit Apple's Web site (`http://support.apple.com/kb/HT2824`). If you have a Windows Mobile, a BlackBerry, Palm Pre, or an older Palm OS device, you can buy a program called Missing Sync for your particular device from Mark/Space (`www.markspace.com`), which will allow you to synchronize your data with a Mac.

I don't tell you about synchronizing an iPhone or an iPod Touch with iSync in this section because you synchronize your iPhone with your Mac using iTunes (or Apple's MobileMe service). You can also use iTunes to copy your calendar and contacts to your iPod, but you cannot add, edit, or delete those contacts or calendar items from your iPod and then synchronize those changes to your Mac.

The three basic steps for using iSync are

1. Add your handheld device to your Mac's iSync Devices list.

This links the handheld device to your Mac. The idea here is to keep your handheld device from trying to synchronize with multiple Macs, which could prevent contact information and appointments from synchronizing correctly. You need to add a handheld device to your Mac only once.

2. Connect the handheld device with your Mac.

Handheld devices connect through either a USB cable or Bluetooth wireless connection.

3. Decide what to transfer or synchronize between your Mac and the handheld device.

You can specify whether to synchronize and transfer names and contact information, appointments, or files, such as word processor or spreadsheet files.

Adding a handheld device to your Mac

Before you can use iSync to synchronize data between your Mac and your handheld device, you need to add the handheld device to iSync.

If you have a handheld device that connects using Bluetooth or a USB cable, open iSync and choose Devices⇨Add Device (or press ⌘+N), as shown in Figure 3-1.

Figure 3-1:
The Devices menu in iSync provides commands for adding a handheld device to your Mac.

In case you want to synchronize your handheld device with another computer, you must first remove the device from the iSync Devices list on your Mac by following these steps:

1. **Run the iSync program by double-clicking the iSync icon in the Applications folder.**

2. **In the iSync window, click the icon for the handheld device that you want to remove.**

3. **Choose Devices⇨Remove Device.**

Synchronizing a handheld device with your Mac

After you add a handheld device to the iSync Devices list so your Mac can recognize it, you can synchronize and transfer data between your Mac and a handheld device by following these steps:

1. **Connect your handheld device (mobile phone or PDA) to your Mac.**

   If you have a Bluetooth handheld device, just place it near your Mac. To read about how to make a connection between your Bluetooth-enabled handheld device and your Mac (which is referred to as *pairing*), turn to Book VIII, Chapter 3.

2. **Run iSync.**

   The iSync window appears, displaying an icon for your handheld device, as shown in Figure 3-2.

Figure 3-2:
The iSync window displays icons of all your handheld devices.

3. **Click the icon of the handheld device that you want to synchronize.**

   The iSync window expands to display additional options, as shown in Figure 3-3.

Figure 3-3:
The iSync window displays synchronization options for your chosen handheld device.

4. **Choose your options for synchronizing data and click the Sync Devices icon or choose Devices⇨Sync Devices.**

Your iSync setup experience might vary. Some devices, such as my spare Nokia 6620 mobile phone that I keep in a drawer in case my Palm Pre or iPhone stops working, require additional steps to make them work with iSync. When I first added my Nokia 6620 as a device to iSync, a dialog popped up, informing me that I had to install a small iSync client program on the Nokia to allow the phone to communicate with iSync. iSync transferred the Nokia program to the mobile phone over Bluetooth, and the Nokia prompted me to install the program. When installed, iSync recognized the Nokia 6620 and when I clicked the Sync button in iSync, my Mac's Address Book contacts and iCal events transferred from the big computer to the little one.

Resetting a handheld device with your Mac

Synchronizing your handheld device with your Mac can keep your crucial contact and appointment information stored in two locations. However, sometimes the data on your handheld device might get hopelessly outdated if you don't use it for a long time, or it can become scrambled if someone accidentally uses (plays with) your handheld device.

If this happens, the only accurate information might be on your Mac, so you can reset your handheld device, essentially wiping the handheld device clean and replacing it with the data on your Mac instead. To reset your handheld device, follow these steps:

1. **Connect your handheld device (mobile phone or PDA) to your Mac.**

   If you have a Bluetooth handheld device, just place it near your Mac. To read about how to make a connection between your Bluetooth-enabled handheld device and your Mac (which is referred to as *pairing*), turn to Book VIII, Chapter 3.

2. **Run iSync.**

   The iSync window appears, displaying an icon for your handheld device (refer to Figure 3-2).

3. **Click the icon of the handheld device that you want to reset.**

   Resetting wipes out all data stored on your handheld device, so make sure you don't need any of this data.

4. **Choose Devices⇨Reset Device (or Reset All Devices to reset all handheld devices added to your Mac).**

Considering other Mobile Device Sync Solutions

Point your Web browser to the Web site `macncell.com` to learn about the latest news and programs you can buy (or download free) to keep your Mac and mobile phone in sync.

Other products for keeping your Mac in sync with your mobile phone include:

✦ **MobileMe (`www.me.com`):** Apple's $99-per-year Internet-based sync and backup service for keeping your iPhone and iPod touch in sync with single or multiple Macs and Windows PCs. MobileMe can also keep those Windows in Macs in sync with each other even if you don't have an iPhone or iPod touch. What's more, MobileMe lets you access your e-mail, contacts, calendar items, and files you can back up to your very own MobileMe iDisk from any computer that's connected to the Internet, be it your other Mac in the family room, or a Windows PC in an Internet cafe halfway around the world. Who says we can't all get along?

✦ **SugarSync (www.sugarsync.com):** Offers 2GB of free Internet-based storage for keeping your music, video, documents, and other files in sync between your Mac or Windows PC and your iPhone, BlackBerry or Windows Mobile mobile phone or PDA; monthly and yearly subscription plans are available for 30GB to 250GB of online storage space.

✦ **PocketMac: (www.pocketmac.com):** Sells Mac contact, calendar, and other data sync programs that work with more than fifty mobile phones and PDAs.

✦ **Missing Sync for Mac (www.markspace.com):** Offers a wide range of Missing Sync for Mac versions for keeping your Mac in sync with numerous mobile devices, including:

• *Palm Pre:* Synchronizes contacts and calendars automatically and wirelessly via WiFi, and enables transfer and sync of music, ringtones, photos, files, and videos fast with a USB cable.

• *Palm:* Synchronizes contacts, calendars, notes, and more between Mac and several Palm models, including Treo and Centro smartphones.

• *BlackBerry:* Synchronizes contacts, calendar, music, notes and files wirelessly via Bluetooth and automatically whenever your BlackBerry is within range of your Mac. Works with many BlackBerry models, including Bold, Storm, and Curve.

• *iPhone:* Enables two-way syncing between iPhone or iPod touch and a Mac for notes, tasks, and files over WiFi; can also do tasks in iCal or Entourage, notes in Bare Bones Yojimbo or Entourage, and sync folders of files.

• *Windows Mobile:* Synchronizes contacts, calendars, tasks, and other information with hundreds of smartphones running the Windows Mobile platform, including HTC Touch, Samsung Omnia, Sony Ericsson Xperia, and Palm Treo.

• *Symbian OS:* Synchronizes contacts, calendars and more via Bluetooth with a number of mobile phone models by Nokia, Samsung, and Sony Ericsson. Proximity Sync feature automatically synchronizes when your phone nears your Mac.

• *Nokia:* Synchronizes archive and backup contacts, calendars and other information for Nokia smartphone models, such as the N95 and E71.

• *HTC Touch:* Synchronizes contacts, calendars, videos, and more for HTC Touch, Touch Pro, and Diamond smartphone models.

• *Sony PSP:* Backs up games and transfers video, iPhoto pictures, and iTunes music from your Mac to your PSP, as well as to Safari Web pages and bookmarks.

Chapter 4: Automating Your Mac

In This Chapter

- ✔ Getting to know Automator
- ✔ Understanding actions
- ✔ Exploring sample Automator workflows
- ✔ Creating Automator programs

C omputers are supposed to make your life easier, but sometimes they complicate life unnecessarily. Many times, you might need to perform a repetitive task, such as renaming a batch of digital photographs every time you copy them from your digital camera. Although such a task is trivial, it's also tedious and time-consuming to rename each photograph's file.

Fortunately, your Mac can carry some of these burdens for you through a feature called Automator. With Automator, you can program your Mac to perform specific tasks that you don't want to do yourself.

Getting Automator to Take Action for You

Automator lets you choose from a library of predefined tasks, called *actions*, which tell specific programs on your Mac what to do. By stringing these actions together, you can create simple *workflows* that act like miniprograms that can, for example, retrieve a Web page and read the text aloud, or rename groups of files automatically.

Automator organizes its library of actions into these categories:

- ✦ **Calendar:** Adds, deletes, or retrieves items from iCal.
- ✦ **Contacts:** Finds and retrieves names from the Address Book.
- ✦ **Files & Folder:** Manipulates items within the Finder.
- ✦ **Fonts:** Adds, retrieves, and deletes fonts from the Font Book.
- ✦ **Internet:** Retrieves Web pages from the Internet using Safari.
- ✦ **Mail:** Finds and retrieves messages from Mail.
- ✦ **Movies:** Plays, converts, or retrieves images using iDVD, DVD Player, and QuickTime Player.
- ✦ **Music:** Manipulates songs in iTunes and on an iPod.
- ✦ **PDF:** Renames, searches, converts, and retrieves data from PDF files.

✦ **Photos:** Manipulates digital photographs.

✦ **Presentations:** Plays and displays slides in a Keynote presentation.

✦ **Text:** Manipulates text within the TextEdit program.

✦ **Utilities:** Provides a variety of tasks for burning CDs/DVDs and running or quitting programs. Also contains the Watch Me Do task, which lets you record mouse and keyboard actions.

Most actions need to accept input. For example, if you create an action that retrieves a Web page from the Web, its input would be a specific Web site address, such as www.JOEyGADGET.com. You can also make an action more flexible, such as by having it ask you for input or retrieve input from another action.

After an action receives input, it does something with that input, such as renaming files a certain way or running a program. Many actions also create some form of output, which can be used as another action's input. Figure 4-1 shows two simple actions. The first action, Get Specified Text, retrieves a chunk of text. The second action, Speak Text, uses a computer-synthesized voice to read the text.

Actions link via compatible input and output. That is, an action that produces text as output can link to another action that accepts text as input. However, an action that produces text as output can't link to an action that accepts a PDF file as input. The output from one action must always be compatible with the input of another action if the two are to cooperate. If the output and input of two actions aren't compatible, Automator won't display the connecting input and output links between actions.

When using Automator, you need to understand the Automator user interface. The left pane displays Automator's library of actions, organized by categories that reflect applications on your Mac, including the Finder. By clicking an application's library, the middle pane lists specific actions stored in that library.

Clicking an action displays a brief description in the bottom-left corner of the Automator window. The right pane is where you drag and drop actions to link them and form a complete Automator workflow.

Understanding Actions

To create a workflow, you need to link actions together. However, even though Automator provides many different types of actions, not every action can link together. To help you understand the variety of actions available, actions typically work with one of four types of objects:

✦ Files and folders

✦ Music (audio) files

✦ Digital photographs

✦ Text

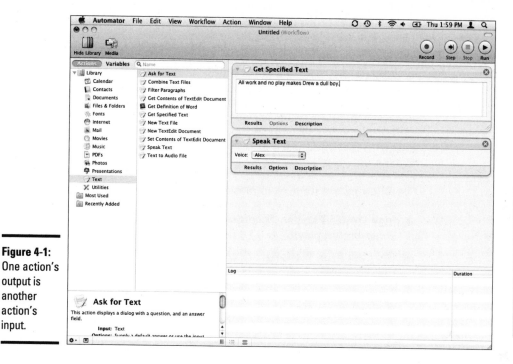

Figure 4-1:
One action's
output is
another
action's
input.

To work on different objects, such as text or digital photographs, each type
of action automates a specific program on your Mac, such as the Finder,
iTunes, iPhoto, Safari, iCal, or TextEdit program.

Actions either retrieve data or process the data retrieved by another action
or sometimes nothing at all (such as with the action Pause). Actions can
retrieve data by prompting you for input or having you make a choice when
the workflow runs. This method gives the workflow the flexibility to work
with different types of data, but it adds the inconvenience of not running
completely without user intervention.

A second way actions can retrieve data is by having you specify exactly
what type of data the action should use, such as a specific file. This method
lets your workflow run without any intervention from you, but you lose the
flexibility of working with different data unless you modify the action within
Automator.

Some examples of actions that retrieve data are as follows:

✦ **Find Sources in iTunes:** Lets you define which songs or playlists to use
and then outputs the song or playlist.

✦ **Get Specified URLs:** Retrieves a Web page from a specific URL, such
as www.dummies.com or www.whitehouse.gov, and outputs the
Web page.

✦ **Ask for Text:** Displays a dialog so the user can enter text information and outputs this text information.

✦ **Get Specified Finder Items:** Retrieves the name of a file or folder and outputs the name of a file or folder.

Actions that retrieve data usually then pass that data to another action that processes that data. Some actions that process data then create output for another action to use. Other actions simply accept input and then do something with that input, such as playing a specific song in iTunes or rotating a digital photograph.

The following are some examples of actions that process data:

✦ **Play iTunes Playlist:** Accepts a playlist name and starts playing the songs in that playlist.

✦ **Get Text from Webpage:** Accepts a Web page, retrieves the text from that Web page, and outputs this text.

✦ **Speak Text:** Accepts text and reads this text aloud in a computer-synthesized voice.

✦ **Rename Finder Items:** Accepts the name of a file or folder and changes that name.

Eventually, every workflow needs to end with an action that does something to data. In the preceding list, the Get Text from Webpage action accepts a Web page as input and sends the text of that Web page out as output. You can't end a workflow with this particular action because it doesn't do anything useful that you can see or hear. However, you can retrieve text from the first Web page on the New York Times Web site and link the Get Text from Webpage action to the Speak Text action, which reads all text from the New York Times Web page, as shown in Figure 4-2.

Creating a workflow

The first step to creating a workflow is to pick an action that retrieves data. To help you get started, you can have Automator create an initial action by choosing a *template* for your workflow, by following these steps:

1. **Double-click the Automator icon in the Applications folder to load Automator. (If Automator is already running, choose File⇨New.)**

A dialog appears, letting you choose the type of data you want to manipulate, such as folders, music, photos, or text, as shown in Figure 4-3.

Figure 4-2:
An action that processes data can output that data to an action that actually does something with that data.

2. **Click a template icon, such as Workflow, and then click the Choose button to open the Automator program window, as shown in Figure 4-4.**

Figure 4-3:
Automator provides a variety of starting points for creating a workflow.

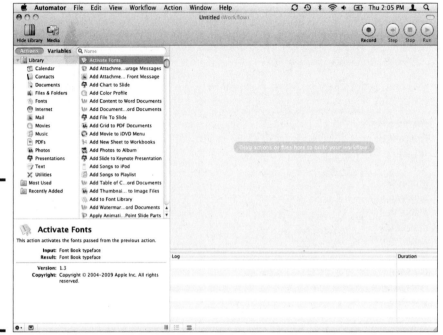

Figure 4-4:
The
Automator
program
window
is what
you use
to create
workflows.

Adding, rearranging, and deleting actions

After you select an action that starts your workflow by retrieving data, you need one or more actions that process that data. To add an action to a workflow, follow these steps:

1. **Click a library category in the Actions Library (left pane) of the Automator window, which contains the action you want to choose.**

   (If you need an action that works with Text, click the Text library. If you need an action that involves the Internet, click the Internet library.) A list of actions, stored in your chosen library, appears in the right column of the left pane of the Automator window.

2. **Drag and drop an action from the right column of the Actions library to the workflow area (right pane) of the Automator window (or double-click the action to add it to the end of the workflow).**

In case you place an action in the wrong location, you can move an action to a new location by dragging it with the mouse or clicking the action and choosing Action⇨Move Up (or Move Down).

To delete an action, click its Close button in the upper-right corner of the action's tile in the workflow. If you delete an action by mistake, press ⌘+Z or choose Edit⇨Undo.

Running and testing a workflow

After you arrange multiple actions into a workflow, you can test your workflow to make sure it works the way you want. To run a workflow, you have two choices:

◆ Click the Run button or choose Workflow⇨Run.

◆ Choose Workflow⇨Step.

When you run a workflow, Automator runs through every step in your workflow. If you choose Workflow⇨Step, Automator runs one action at a time. Click the Step button or choose Workflow⇨Step to run each additional action.

The main reason for using the Step command is to verify that each action is doing exactly what you want at each step of your workflow. If an action can't run for some reason, Automator displays an error message, as shown in Figure 4-5.

**Book II
Chapter 4**

Automating
Your Mac

Figure 4-5:
An error
message
appears if
an action
can't run
because
it's not
receiving
the proper
input.

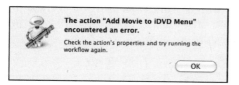

The action "Add Movie to iDVD Menu" encountered an error.

Check the action's properties and try running the workflow again.

OK

To fix problems with your workflow, you might need to delete the faulty action and replace it with another one, or you might need to add another action that outputs the proper data that the other action can accept as input.

Saving a workflow

For any file in any program you work on, remember this: Save early and save often! To save a workflow, follow these steps:

1. Choose File⇨Save to open the Save As dialog.

2. In the Save As text box, type a descriptive name for your file.

3. Choose the Where pop-up menu, choose a folder where you want to store your file, and then click the Save button.

Opening a saved workflow

After you save a workflow, you can open it by following these steps:

1. **Double-click the Automator icon in the Applications folder to load Automator if it's not already open.**

2. **Click the Open an Existing Workflow button. (You can also choose File⇨Open to open an existing workflow.)**

   An Open dialog appears.

3. **Click the workflow file you want to open and then click Open.**

Creating Example Workflows

Trying to piece together actions to create a workflow can get frustrating if you don't know how different actions might work. To create your own workflows easily, study the following examples that manipulate text, digital photographs, and files.

As you can see by browsing through Automator's libraries, dozens of other types of actions involve different types of programs, such as iCal or Address Book. Experiment with creating workflows using different actions to discover more ways to control your Mac than you ever thought were possible.

Playing with text

The following workflow consists of three actions, as shown in Figure 4-6:

✦ **Get Specified URLs:** Asks for a URL (such as `www.cnn.com`) and retrieves the Web page from that site.

✦ **Get Text from Articles:** Retrieves the text of RSS feeds.

✦ **New TextEdit Document:** Displays the text of the RSS feeds in a TextEdit document that you can read or print.

RSS feeds are summarized headings and text that describe new content on a Web page. By reviewing RSS feeds from a Web site, you can decide whether you want to visit that Web site to read the complete article.

To create this workflow, follow these steps:

1. **Double-click the Automator icon in the Applications folder to load Automator.**

   A dialog appears (refer to Figure 4-1).

2. **Click the Workflow template icon and then click Choose.**

   The Automator window appears.

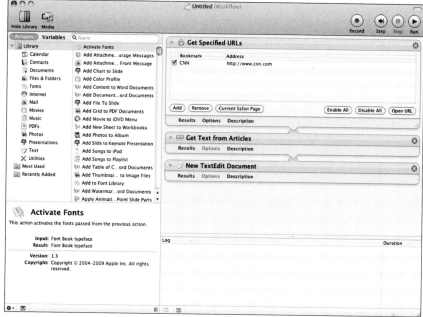

Figure 4-6:
Three
actions that
retrieve RSS
feeds from
a Web page
and display
them in a
TextEdit
document.

3. **Click the Internet library in the left pane of the Automator window.**

4. **Drag and drop the Get Specified URLs action to the Automator window's right pane.**

   The Get Specified URLs action appears.

5. **Double-click Apple under the Bookmark heading to highlight Apple, and then type** CNN **(or the name of any Web site that offers RSS feeds) under the Bookmark category to replace Apple with CNN.**

6. **Double-click the** http://www.apple.com **address to highlight the entire URL address, then type** http://www.cnn.com **(or the Web site you entered in the prior step) under the Address column and press Return.**

   This replaces http://www.apple.com with http://www.cnn.com, as shown in Figure 4-7.

7. **Drag and drop the Get Text from Articles action from the right column of the Actions library pane to beneath the Get Specified URLs action in the workflow area.**

   The Get Text from Articles action appears directly underneath the Get Specified URLs action and connects the two actions together.

8. **Click the Text library in the left pane of the Automator window.**

9. **Drag and drop the New TextEdit Document action to beneath the Get Text from Articles action in the right pane.**

All three actions appear connected in the workflow.

10. **Click the Run button or choose Workflow➪Run.**

A TextEdit document appears, containing the text from the RSS feeds taken from the CNN Web site, as shown in Figure 4-8.

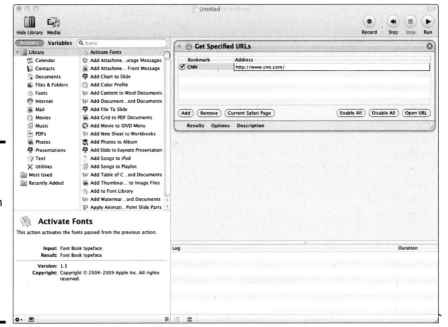

Figure 4-7:
The Get Specified URLs action lets you define a specific Web site that contains RSS feeds.

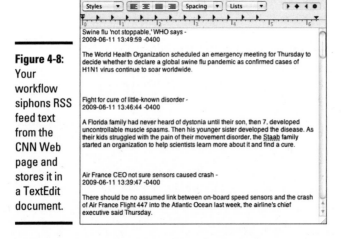

Figure 4-8:
Your workflow siphons RSS feed text from the CNN Web page and stores it in a TextEdit document.

11. **Choose TextEdit⇨Quit TextEdit.**

A dialog appears, asking whether you want to save the TextEdit document containing the CNN story text.

12. **Click Save (or Don't Save).**

If you click Save, you need to give the CNN text document a descriptive name.

Playing with digital photography

The following workflow consists of three actions, as shown in Figure 4-9:

✦ **Take Video Snapshot:** Captures and saves your picture using the built-in iSight camera.

If your Mac doesn't have a built-in iSight camera, you can also plug in a USB webcam or a video camcorder through a FireWire cable.

✦ **Flip Images:** Flips an image horizontally or vertically.

✦ **Open Images in Preview:** Displays your flipped image in a window.

Book II
Chapter 4

Automating
Your Mac

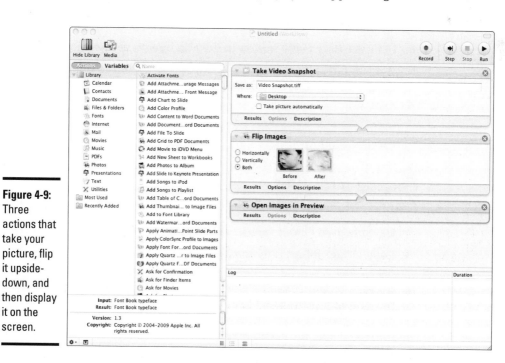

Figure 4-9:
Three actions that take your picture, flip it upside-down, and then display it on the screen.

Here are the steps to build the workflow:

1. **Double-click the Automator icon in the Applications folder to load Automator.**

   A dialog appears (refer to Figure 4-1).

2. **Select the Workflow template icon and then click the Choose button.**

   The Automator window appears.

3. **Click the Photos library in the Actions Library.**

4. **Drag and drop the Take Video Snapshot action to the workflow area.**

   The Take Video Snapshot action appears in the right pane.

5. **Click the Take Picture Automatically box.**

6. **Drag and drop the Flip Images action to beneath the Take Video Snapshot action in the workflow area.**

   A dialog appears, asking whether you want to make copies of your pictures before flipping them.

7. **Click Don't Add.**

   The Flip Images action appears beneath the Take Video Snapshot action.

8. **Click the Both radio button in the Flip Images action.**

9. **Drag and drop the Open Image in Preview action to beneath the Flip Images action in the workflow area.**

10. **Click the Run button.**

    Your workflow takes your picture and displays the flipped picture in a Preview window.

Playing with files

The following workflow consists of three actions, as shown in Figure 4-10:

✦ **Get Specified Finder Items:** Selects a file or folder on your hard drive.

✦ **Copy Finder Items:** Copies a file or folder to an existing folder on your hard drive.

✦ **Rename Finder Items:** Lets you specify how to rename a file by using the date or time to help identify it.

These steps create the example workflow:

1. **Double-click the Automator icon in the Applications folder to load Automator (refer to Figure 4-1).**

Figure 4-10:
Three
actions that
take a file,
copy the
file to the
Desktop,
and then
rename
that copy of
the file.

2. **Select the Workflow template icon and then click the Choose button.**

   The Automator window appears.

3. **Click the Files & Folders library in the Actions Library (left pane).**

4. **Drag and drop the Get Specified Finder Items to the workflow area (right pane).**

   The Get Specified Finder Items action appears in the right pane.

5. **Click the Add button in the bottom-left corner of the Get Specified Finder Items action panel to bring up the Open dialog.**

6. **Choose a document from your Mac's Documents folder and then click the Add button.**

   The document file you selected appears in the Get Specified Finder Items action.

7. **Drag and drop the Copy Finder Items action to beneath the Get Specified Finder Items action in the workflow area.**

   The Copy Finder Items action appears beneath the Get Specified Finder Items action.

8. **Drag and drop the Rename Finder Items action underneath the Copy Finder Items action in the workflow area.**

   The Rename Finder Items action appears below the Copy Finder Items action in the right pane with a variety of pop-up menu choices, as shown in Figure 4-11.

9. **Click the Run button.**

   Automator copies the file you chose in Step 6 to your Mac's Desktop bearing a new name.

Making your Mac imitate you with the Watch Me Do action

Most actions represent specific tasks that various programs can do, such as setting an event (appointment) in iCal or playing a song in iTunes. To give you greater flexibility with your tasks, Automator also includes a Watch Me Do action that's stored in the Utilities library.

Figure 4-11:
The Rename Finder Items action displays pop-up menus for defining how to name a file.

The Watch Me Do action records your mouse or keyboard commands (or both) as a series of actions until you stop recording your commands. You can then run the resultant workflow to repeat the same mouse or keyboard commands without needing to touch the mouse or keyboard. For example, if you record your mouse double-clicking the Calculator program, then your keyboard typing **1 + 1 =** and then stop recording, The Watch Me Do action will repeat these commands every time you run the workflow.

To record mouse or keyboard commands in a Watch Me Do action, follow these steps:

1. **Click the Record button or choose Workflow⇨Record.**

Your Mac's Desktop appears along with an Automator Recording window, as shown in Figure 4-12.

Figure 4-12: The Automator Recording window lets you know that it's recording mouse and keyboard activity.

2. **Click the Finder icon in the Dock to open a new Finder window and then click Applications in the Finder window sidebar to display the contents of the Applications folder.**

3. **Double-click the Calculator icon to launch the Calculator.**

4. **Type** 1 + 1 =.

5. **Click the Stop button on the Automator Recording window to stop recording your keyboard and mouse actions.**

The Automator window appears with an action in the right pane listing the mouse and keyboard commands you recorded in a Watch Me Do action, as shown in Figure 4-13.

6. Switch to and close the Calculator program and the Applications folder by clicking the Close button for each one.

7. Switch to the Automator window and then choose Workflow⇨Run to see the Watch Me Do action replay your recorded mouse and keystroke commands.

Figure 4-13:
The Watch Me Do action contains a list of your recorded mouse and keyboard commands.

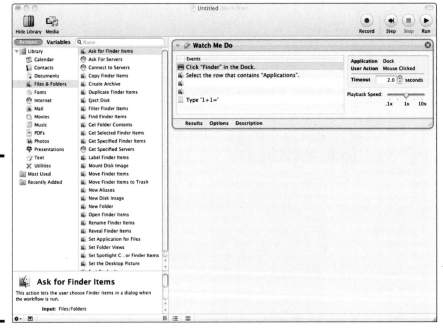

Chapter 5: Maintenance and Troubleshooting

In This Chapter

✔ Fixing startup troubles

✔ Taking care of program freezes and hang-ups

✔ Unjamming jammed CDs/DVDs

✔ Troubleshooting disk problems and repairs

✔ Performing routine maintenance

*N*o matter how well designed and well built a Mac is, it's still a machine, and all machines are liable to break down through no fault of your own. Many times, you can fix minor problems with a little bit of knowledge and willingness to poke and prod around your Mac. If your Mac isn't working correctly, you can check obvious things first, like making sure it's plugged in and that any connecting cables to your Mac are plugged in and secure. However, sometimes your Mac might be in more serious trouble than you can fix, so don't be afraid to take your Mac into your friendly neighborhood computer repair store (one that specializes in repairing Macs, of course).

Only open your Mac if you know what you're doing. If you open the case and start fiddling around with its electronic insides, you might damage your Mac — and invalidate your Mac's warranty.

Handling Startup Troubles

Sometimes you might press the power button to turn on your Mac and nothing seems to happen. Other times, you might press the power button and see the usual Apple logo on the screen, and then nothing happens from that point on.

Before you rush your Mac to the emergency room of Mac repairs, do some simple troubleshooting yourself. At the very least, be sure to back up your important files — before you have any troubles — so you won't lose them if you wind up sending your Mac to the repair shop.

Booting up in Safe Mode

If you turn on your Mac and you can't see the familiar Desktop, menu bar, and Dock, don't panic. The first thing to do is try to boot up your Mac in what's called *Safe Mode,* a boot sequence that loads the bare minimum of the Mac OS X operating system, just enough to get your computer running.

Many startup problems occur when nonessential programs, such as appointment reminders, automatically load at login time and wind up interfering with other startup programs, preventing your Mac from booting up correctly. Other startup programs load before you see the login screen or the Desktop (if you've set your Mac to automatically bypass the login window and go directly to the Desktop when it starts up). Booting up in Safe Mode cuts all the nonessential pre- and post-login programs out of the loop, so that only your core programs load. A successful boot in Safe Mode at least tells you that your Mac's core system hasn't been compromised.

By booting up your Mac in Safe Mode, you can remove any programs you recently installed, turn off any startup options you may have activated, and then restart to see whether that fixes the boot-up problems. If you remove recently installed programs and deactivate startup options and problems persist, copy any important files from your hard drive to a backup drive to protect your crucial data in case the hard drive is starting to fail (see Book II, Chapter 2).

To boot up in Safe Mode, turn on your Mac, then immediately hold down the Shift key until the Apple logo appears on the screen, indicating that your Mac is booting up.

Your Mac comes with a free utility program called Disk Utility, which can repair minor problems. Third-party utility programs, such as DiskWarrior (`www.alsoft.com`), are designed to repair major problems that Disk Utility can't fix.

If the problem isn't because of other programs trying to load when you turn on your Mac, you might have a more serious problem with your hard drive. A minor problem might involve scrambled data on your hard drive that you might be able to repair with a special utility diagnostic program, such as DiskWarrior (`www.alsoft.com`). A more serious problem could be physical damage to your hard drive. In that case, the only solution might be to replace the hard drive, and then restore your most recent Time Machine backup to the new hard drive so you're back in business again as though nothing (or almost nothing) went kaput in the first place.

To learn how to use Time Machine to back up your Mac's hard drive, check out Book II, Chapter 2.

Booting from a CD/DVD

If you can't boot up from your hard drive, even in Safe Mode, and any utility program you run can't fix the problem, you might have to boot from a CD or DVD. Use either the original Mac OS X Install disc that came with your Mac (or the disc containing a newer version of Mac OS X that you used to upgrade your Mac's operating system) or a technical troubleshooting utility CD/DVD.

Every Mac comes with a DVD that contains the entire Mac OS X operating system. The purpose of this DVD is to let you run the Disk Utility program's Repair Disk feature on your Mac's primary hard drive, or to reinstall the operating system and return your Mac to its original condition when you first brought your computer home. You might want to reinstall the operating system for two reasons:

✦ Your computer is so hopelessly fouled up it might be easier to wipe out everything and start from scratch rather than try to rescue the hard drive.

✦ You plan on selling or giving your Mac away, and you want to wipe out your data and return the Mac to its original condition so someone else can personalize the Mac for himself.

Wiping out your hard drive and reinstalling the operating system from scratch will also wipe out any important files stored on your hard drive, so make sure you're willing to accept this before reinstalling the operating system off a DVD. Ideally, you should have all your important files backed up on a separate external drive, such as an external hard drive or a CD/DVD, before wiping out your hard drive completely.

To learn how to back up your Mac's hard drive using the Time Machine backup program that comes with every Mac, turn to Book II, Chapter 2.

The second type of CD/DVD you can boot from is a troubleshooting disc. Apple provides the free Disk Utility program on the original installation DVD that came with your Mac. However, you can buy a troubleshooting CD/DVD, such as DriveGenius (www.prosofteng.com), TechTool Pro (www.micromat.com), or DiskWarrior (www.alsoft.com). By running any of these programs directly from the CD/DVD, you can attempt to repair or resurrect any hard drive that fails to boot up on its own. Sometimes these troubleshooting CDs/DVDs can repair a hard drive, and sometimes they can't. If you have important files trapped on your hard drive, this option might be your only hope of retrieving your files to back them up before sending or taking your Mac to a repair service to repair or replace your Mac's hard drive.

The type of CD/DVD you use depends on what you want to do. Start by booting up your Mac with the Mac OS X Install disc that came with your Mac and running the Disk Utility program. If that doesn't work, try booting up with one of the technical troubleshooting CDs/DVDs described in the preceding paragraph to fix your hard drive. If you can't fix your hard drive, you might have to resort to the more drastic step of wiping out your hard drive and reinstalling everything from the original Mac OS X CD/DVD.

No matter which CD/DVD you use, you still need to use it to boot your Mac instead of letting your Mac attempt to boot from its own hard drive. Here's how:

1. **Turn on your Mac.**

2. **Insert a CD/DVD into your Mac, and wait for your Mac to boot up to the Desktop if it can.**

    If your Mac gets stuck and cannot boot up to the Desktop, insert the CD/DVD while your Mac is still on, then hold down the Power button for 5 seconds until your Mac turns off, then turn it on again and skip to Step 4.

3. **Choose ⇨Restart.**

4. **After your Mac has shut down the Desktop and the screen goes blank, hold down the C key while your Mac restarts until you see the Apple logo, at which point you can release the C key.**

    This command tells your Mac to boot from the CD/DVD instead of the hard drive.

5. **If you booted from a troubleshooting disc you purchased, follow the instructions on the screen.**

6. **If you booted from your Mac's original OS X Install disc (or a newer OS X Install disc you purchased to upgrade your Mac), follow the steps in the "Running Disk Utility from DVD" section, later in this chapter, to attempt to repair your Mac's hard drive.**

7. **If after trying Steps 5 or 6 you were unable to repair your Mac's hard drive and your only choice is to reinstall your Mac's operating system, follow the prompts displayed by the Mac OS X Restore CD/DVD to restore your Mac's hard drive.**

Booting from another Mac through a FireWire cable

An alternative to booting up from a CD or DVD, you can also boot up from another Mac connected to your computer through a FireWire cable. A FireWire cable simply plugs into the FireWire ports of each Mac, connecting the two Macs together (providing, that is, your Mac has a FireWire port; some models don't).

After connecting two Macs through a FireWire cable, you boot up the working Mac normally and boot up the other Mac in FireWire Target Mode. This makes the second Mac's hard drive appear as an external hard drive when viewed through the working Mac's Finder.

By doing this, you can run a Disk Utility on the Target Mode Mac's hard drive as described in the previous section, or you can run another hard drive utility program (such as Tech Tools Pro, DriveGenius, or DiskWarrior) on the working Mac to rescue the hard drive of the defective Mac. This is much like jump-starting a car's dead battery by using a second car with a good battery.

To boot up from a second Mac connected by a FireWire cable, follow these steps:

Book II
Chapter 5

1. **Connect the second Mac to your Mac using a FireWire cable.**

2. **Turn on the working Mac.**

3. **Turn on the Mac that's having startup troubles and hold down the T key.**

   When the defective Mac's hard drive appears as an external drive on the working Mac, you can copy your important files from the hard drive or run a utility program to fix the hard drive on the defective Mac. After copying files or repairing the hard drive, you need to disconnect the FireWire cable and restart both Macs.

Shutting Down Frozen or Hung-Up Programs

Programs that always run perfectly might suddenly stop working for no apparent reasons, and no matter which keys you press or where you click the mouse, nothing happens. Sometimes you might see a spinning cursor (affectionately referred to as the "spinning beach ball of death"), which stays onscreen and refuses to go away until you take steps to unlock the frozen program.

Sometimes being patient and waiting a few minutes results in the hung-up program resolving whatever was ailing it as though nothing was wrong in the first place. More often, however, the spinning cursor keeps spinning in an oh-so-annoying fashion. To end the torment, you need to *force-quit* the frozen or hung-up program — basically, you shut the program down so that the rest of your Mac can get back to work. To force-quit a program, choose one of the following methods:

✦ Right-click the program's icon on the Dock and choose Force Quit from the menu that appears. (If Force Quit doesn't appear on the shortcut menu, hold down the Option key and Control-click the program icon in the Dock again.)

Maintenance and
Troubleshooting

✦ Choose ⬤➪Force Quit to display the Force Quit Applications dialog, as shown in Figure 5-1. Then select the name of the hung-up program and click the Force Quit button.

✦ Press Option+⌘+Esc to display the Force Quit Applications dialog (see Figure 6-1). Then select the name of the hung-up program and click the Force Quit button.

✦ Load the Activity Monitor program (located inside the Utilities folder in the Applications folder), select the process name, as shown in Figure 5-2, and then choose View➪Quit Process. A Quit Process dialog appears. Click Force Quit.

Figure 5-1:
The Force Quit Applications dialog lets you choose a program to force-quit.

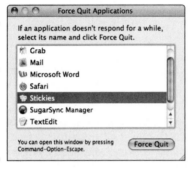

Figure 5-2:
The Activity Monitor lets you choose a process name to force-quit.

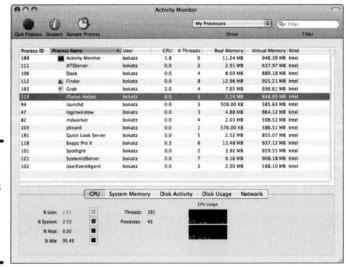

Besides using the methods in the preceding list, you can also use the Terminal program to force-quit a program. Just follow these steps:

1. **Load the Terminal program (located in the Utilities folder inside the Applications folder).**

The Terminal window appears, as shown in Figure 5-3.

Figure 5-3:
The Terminal window lets you control your Mac by typing commands.

2. **Type** top **and press Return.**

The Terminal window displays a list of all programs currently running, as shown in Figure 5-4.

```
000              Terminal — top — 80×24
Processes: 56 total, 2 running, 1 stuck, 53 sleeping... 213 threads    13:01:27
Load Avg: 0.27, 0.21, 0.09   CPU usage: 1.44% user, 1.44% sys, 97.12% idle
SharedLibs: num =   1, resident =   48M code, 5652K data, 7944K linkedit.
MemRegions: num = 5072, resident = 144M + 153M private, 123M shared.
PhysMem: 228M wired, 302M active, 4228K inactive, 533M used, 485M free.
VM: 9425M + 140M   28244(0) pageins, 0(0) pageouts

PID  COMMAND     %CPU   TIME     #TH #PRTS #MREGS RPRVT  RSHRD  RSIZE  VSIZE
315  top         3.6%   0:00.87   1   18    29    488K   196K   976K   74M
303  bash        0.0%   0:00.01   1   14    19    264K   180K   888K   74M
302  login       0.0%   0:00.01   1   16    55    240K   224K   716K   75M
301  Terminal    0.8%   0:00.54   3   94-   141   1812K  7148K  6528K  398M
296  AppleSpell  0.0%   0:00.03   1   37    27    536K   2960K  1448K  86M
295  cupsd       0.0%   0:00.06   2   30    35    660K   224K   1600K  75M
293  Keynote     0.0%   0:03.94   6   114   457   51M    17M    79M    527M
292  Pages       0.0%   0:03.11   8   109   380   13M    13M    45M    487M
291  Calculator  0.0%   0:00.64   1   74    167   2300K  6424K  6884K  398M
290  Grab        0.5%   0:11.72   8   173+  273   9584K+ 19M+   18M+   439M+
275  mdworker    0.0%   0:00.27   4   69    45    756K   2600K  2240K  88M
146  CrossOver   0.0%   0:00.04   1   52    43    496K   1648K  2316K  341M
145  ocspd       0.0%   0:00.02   1   18    21    432K   180K   976K   74M
144  iTunesHelp  0.0%   0:00.04   1   49    40    420K   292K   2000K  331M
137  ATSServer   0.0%   0:00.92   2   93    112   1220K  3188K  4264K  112M
136  Finder      0.0%   0:10.43   6   148   214   4980K  18M    15M    417M
```

Figure 5-4:
The Terminal window displays information about every running program.

3. **Under the COMMAND column, look for the name of the program you want to force-quit.**

Sometimes only an abbreviated form of the complete program name appears, rather than the full name.

4. **In the PID (Process ID) column, find the number that appears to the left of the program name; write this PID number down.**

5. **Type** q.

   The Terminal window removes the list of running programs and waits for your next command, as shown in Figure 5-5.

6. **Type** kill ### **and press Return, where** ### **is the PID number of the program you wrote down from Step 4.**

   This force-quits your chosen program.

   If you can't kill a program using the normal `kill ###` command, try `kill -9 ###`, where ### represents the PID number of the program you want to kill. This `-9` option can usually kill programs that the ordinary kill command can't.

7. **Choose Terminal⇨Quit Terminal.**

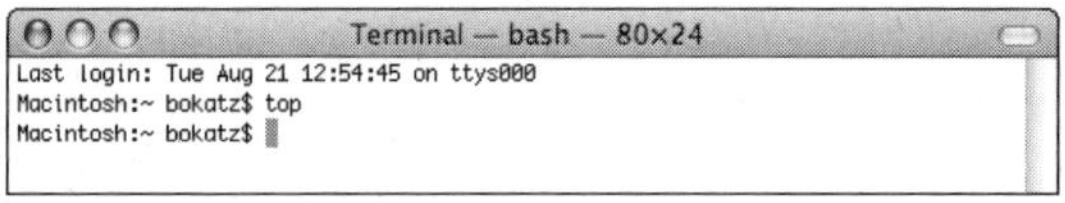

Figure 5-5:
The Terminal window waits for your next command.

```
000                Terminal — bash — 80×24
Last login: Tue Aug 21 12:54:45 on ttys000
Macintosh:~ bokatz$ top
Macintosh:~ bokatz$ ▌
```

Removing Jammed CDs/DVDs

If a CD/DVD gets jammed in your Mac's CD/DVD drive, you can try one (or more) of the following methods to eject the stuck disc:

✦ Press the Eject key on your keyboard.

✦ Drag the CD/DVD icon on the Desktop to the Trash icon in the Dock. (The trash icon turns into an Eject icon, to let you know your Mac wants to eject the disc but does not intend to delete the information on the disc.)

✦ Choose ⌘⇨Restart, and hold down the mouse or trackpad button while your Mac boots up.

✦ Click the Eject button next to the CD/DVD icon in the Sidebar of a Finder window (click the Mac-faced Finder icon in the Dock to open a new Finder window).

✦ Click the Eject button next to the CD/DVD icon in iTunes.

✦ Choose Controls⇨Eject DVD from inside the DVD Player program.

✦ Load the Disk Utility program (located in the Utilities folder inside the Applications folder), click the CD/DVD icon, and click the Eject icon.

✦ Click to select the CD/DVD icon on the Desktop and choose File⇨Eject from the main menu.

✦ Click to select the CD/DVD icon on the Desktop and press ⌘+E.

✦ Control-click the CD/DVD icon on the Desktop and choose Eject from the menu that appears.

Although it might be tempting, don't jam tweezers, a flathead screwdriver, or any other object inside your CD/DVD drive to pry out a jammed disc. Not only can this scratch the disc surface, but also it can physically damage the CD/DVD drive.

Prevention is the best medicine, so I include here a few pointers on how to avoid getting discs jammed in the drive in the first place:

✦ Do not use mini CDs/DVDs in slot-loading drives.

✦ Be careful of using hand-applied labels on discs you put in the drive. These can easily jam or make the disc too thick to eject properly.

✦ If your Mac's disc drive is repeatedly acting strange or not working properly when you try to play a music CD or watch a DVD, it's possible your disc drive is on its last leg and it might need repairs. Stop using the drive and take or send your Mac to Apple or an authorized service provider for a checkup.

Repairing and Maintaining Hard Drives

Hard drives can fail in for a number of reasons. In some cases, the data could be scrambled on the hard drive, confusing your Mac and making it impossible to read data from it. If data is scrambled, you can often reorganize your data (using a disk utility program) to get your hard drive back in working condition.

Another reason hard disks can fail is if the surface of your hard drive becomes damaged. If this occurs, your only option is to copy critical files from the damaged hard drive (if possible) and replace it with a new one. If you run a disk utility program and it fails to repair any problems on your hard drive, this might be a sign that your hard drive surface is physically damaged.

The Disk Utility program that comes free with every Mac — tucked away in the Utilities folder inside the Applications folder — can examine your hard drive. However, to fix any problems it might find, you have to boot your Mac from a different hard drive or from the Mac OS X Install DVD that came with your Mac.

In the following sections, I show you the tools for figuring out which problem you have and what to do to fix it.

Verifying a disk

If you suspect that your hard drive might be scrambled or physically damaged, you can run the Disk Utility program to verify your suspicions. When using Disk Utility, select a device and choose one of the following:

✦ **Verify Disk:** Checks to make sure all the files on that device are neatly organized.

✦ **Verify Disk Permissions:** Checks to make sure relevant files, installed with each program, maintain the permissions originally assigned. (Permissions apply only to your startup disk.)

The Disk Utility program can verify and repair all types of storage devices (except optical discs like CDs and DVDs), including hard drives, flash drives, and other types of removable storage media, such as compact flash cards.

To verify a disk, follow these steps:

1. **Load the Disk Utility program (stored inside the Utilities folder in the Applications folder).**

   The Disk Utility window appears.

2. **Click the device (hard drive, flash drive, and so on) that you want to verify in the left pane of the Disk Utility window. (See Figure 5-6.)**

3. **Make sure the First Aid pane is visible. (If not, click the First Aid tab to call it up.)**

4. **Click the Verify Disk button.**

   The Disk Utility program examines your chosen device. If Disk Utility can't verify that a device is working, you see a message informing you that First Aid feature of Disk Utility has failed, as shown in Figure 5-7.

5. **Click OK and then click the Repair Disk button.**

   You can do this step only with a non-startup disk — to repair your Mac's startup disk, skip ahead to the next set of steps.

   Disk Utility tries to fix your device. If it succeeds, you see a message informing you that the device is repaired.

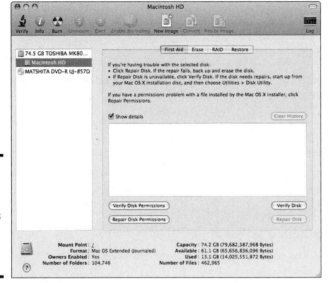

Figure 5-6:
The Disk Utility window lets you pick a drive to examine.

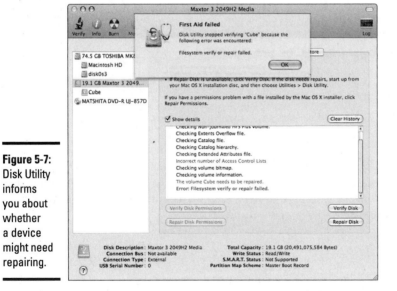

Figure 5-7:
Disk Utility informs you about whether a device might need repairing.

You can verify your hard drive to identify any problems, but you cannot repair your startup hard drive using the copy of Disk Utility stored on your startup hard drive. To repair your startup hard drive, you need to follow these steps:

1. **Insert your Mac OS X Install disc that came with your Mac if you're still running that version of Mac OS X.**

   If you've since upgraded your Mac to a newer version of Mac OS X, insert the newer Mac OS X Install disc.

   The Mac OS X installation disc contains the Disk Utility program to help you troubleshoot your startup hard drive.

2. **Restart your Mac by choosing ⇨Restart.**

   The Restart dialog appears.

3. **Click Restart to restart your Mac.**

4. **Hold down the C key while your Mac restarts.**

   You can release the C key when your Mac boots up and you see the Apple logo appear on the screen.

   This boots your Mac from the Mac OS X Install disc. Your Mac starts its Mac OS X installation program and displays a list of languages to choose.

   Booting and running off your install disc can be slow, so be patient.

5. **Select the language you want to use and click the arrow button in the bottom-right corner of the window.**

   An OS X Installer Welcome window appears.

6. **Click the Utilities menu and choose Disk Utility.**

   The Disk Utility window appears.

7. **Click the Macintosh HD startup drive (or whatever your Mac's primary hard drive is named if you renamed it) in the left pane of the Disk Utility window.**

8. **Make sure the First Aid pane is visible. (If not, click the First Aid tab to call it up.)**

9. **Click the Repair Disk button.**

   The Repair feature of Disk Utility does what it can to fix any problems on your hard drive and informs you of its success — or failure.

10. **Choose Disk Utility⇨Quit Disk Utility.**

   The Mac OS X Installer Welcome window appears again.

11. **Click the Mac OS X Installer menu, choose Quit Mac OS X Installer, and then click the Restart button to restart your Mac.**

12. **Hold down the Eject button while your Mac restarts to eject the Mac OS X Install disc.**

   If your Mac starts up normally and presents you with the Desktop, then Disk Utility managed to repair your Mac's hard drive successfully. Phew, crisis averted!

Verifying disk permissions

Disk permissions apply to your startup disk and define what each program's files are allowed to access and which users have access to which files. If permissions aren't correct, your files could become scrambled, which can cause your Mac to act erratically or prevent a program from launching.

Unlike repairing a hard drive, you can verify and fix disk permissions without having to boot up from a separate hard drive or CD/DVD.

To verify disk permissions, follow these steps:

1. **Load the Disk Utility program (stored inside the Utilities folder in the Applications folder).**

   The Disk Utility window appears.

2. **Click your Macintosh HD (or whatever you renamed your Mac's hard drive if you changed the name) in the left pane of the Disk Utility window.**

3. **Make sure the window is on the First Aid pane. (If not, click the First Aid tab to call it up.)**

4. **Click Verify Disk Permissions.**

   If Disk Utility finds any problems, it displays a message to let you know. Otherwise, it displays a message to let you know all permissions are okay, as shown in Figure 5-8.

5. **Click Repair Disk Permissions.**

   Disk Utility displays any messages concerning permission problems it found and repaired.

6. **Choose Disk Utility⇨Quit Disk Utility.**

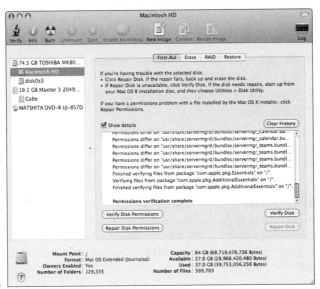

Figure 5-8:
The Disk
Utility
program
checks
to make
sure the
permissions
for program
files haven't
changed
since
they were
installed.

Preventative Maintenance

Your Mac has daily, weekly, and monthly maintenance tasks that it runs
periodically early in the morning if you leave your Mac on at night. However,
if your Mac is asleep during this time, it won't run these maintenance tasks.
You can wake yourself up before dawn every day and wake your Mac so it
can run its maintenance tasks, or you can force your Mac to run its daily,
weekly, and monthly maintenance tasks.

To automate running your Mac preventative maintenance programs, consider
getting a free program called MainMenu (http://www.santasw.com/).

To force your Mac to run its maintenance tasks, follow these steps:

1. **Load the Terminal program (located in the Utilities folder inside the
   Applications folder).**

   The Terminal window appears (refer to Figure 5-3).

2. **Type** sudo periodic daily **and then press Return.**

   The Terminal window asks for your password.

To make your Mac run weekly or monthly maintenance tasks, type **sudo periodic weekly** or **sudo periodic monthly**, respectively. Weekly and monthly tasks can take a long time to run. You'll know when a maintenance task is done when you see the cryptic-looking prompt (like *mycomputer$*) reappear.

3. **Type your password and then press Return.**

   Wait until you see the Terminal prompt (like *mycomputer$*) reappear, as shown in Figure 5-9.

4. **Choose Terminal⇨Quit Terminal.**

Figure 5-9:
When the Terminal prompt appears, the Mac's maintenance tasks are finished.

Book III

Your Mac as Your Entertainment Center

The 5th Wave   By Rich Tennant

"You ever notice how much more streaming media there is than there used to be?"

Contents at a Glance

Chapter 1: Tuning In to Music, Audio, and iTunes

In This Chapter

✔ Understanding audio file formats

✔ Playing audio files with iTunes

✔ Burning audio files to disc

*L*ugging around a case full of CDs (or even vinyl records or audio tapes) is cumbersome and bulky; which is why (since the advent of the original iPod) most people store music as digital audio files. Not only are digital audio files much easier to store and copy, storing individual songs as digital audio files means you need to carry only the songs you want to hear.

Besides storing music, audio files can also contain spoken-words content, such as speeches, interviews, magazine and newspaper articles, and radio shows. Many audio files that contain interviews or entire radio shows are called *podcasts* because they're commonly played on iPods.

Understanding Audio File Compression Formats

Audio files offer tremendous advantages in storage and audio quality compared to previous forms of audio storage. However, dozens of different audio file compression types — the underlying conversion technology used to save audio as digital files — are out there. Therefore, to hear different audio files, you might need to use different programs. This would be like having to buy two separate radios where one radio receives only AM stations and the second radio receives only FM stations.

Different types of audio file compression formats exist because each file format offers certain advantages. The three most popular types of audio file compression schemes used for saving audio as digital files are lossless, lossless compression, and lossy compression.

Any audio file format can play on your Mac as long as you install the right software.

Lossless audio files

The highest-quality audio files are called *lossless* because they never lose any audio data. As a result, lossless audio files offer the highest-quality sound, but they also create the largest file sizes.

The two most popular lossless audio file formats are WAV (Waveform audio format) and AIFF (Audio Interchange File Format). WAV files typically end with the `.wav` file extension; whereas AIFF files typically end with the `.aiff` or `.aif` file extension.

Compressed lossless audio files

Lossless audio files take up large amounts of space, so compressed lossless audio files are designed to squeeze audio data into a smaller file size. Three popular compressed lossless audio file formats are FLAC (Free Lossless Audio Codec), Shorten, and Apple Lossless. FLAC files typically end with the `.flac` file extension, Shorten files typically end with the `.shn` file extension, and Apple Lossless files typically end with the `.m4a` file extension.

You can play Apple Lossless files in iTunes, but not FLAC or Shorten audio files. To play FLAC files, grab a free copy of SongBird (`www.songbirdnest.com`) or VLC Media Player (`www.videolan.org/vlc`). To play Shorten files, use Audion (`www.panic.com/audion`).

Compressed lossy audio files

A lossy audio file compresses audio files by stripping certain audio data to shrink the file size, much like pulling unnecessary clothing from a suitcase to lighten the load. The greater the audio quality, the more audio data the file needs to retain and the bigger the file. The smaller the file, the less audio data the file can hold, and the lower the audio quality. As a result, most audio file formats strive for an optimal balance between audio quality and file size.

The amount of data an audio file format retains is measured in kilobits per second (Kbps). The higher the kilobits, the more data stored and the higher the audio quality. Table 1-1 shows approximate kilobit values and the audio quality they produce.

Table 1-1	Audio Quality Comparisons
Bit Rate (Kilobits per Second)	*Audio Quality*
32 Kbps	AM radio quality
96 Kbps	FM radio quality
128–160 Kbps	Good quality, but differences from the original audio source can be noticeable

Bit Rate (Kilobits per Second)	Audio Quality
192 Kbps	Medium quality, slight differences from the original audio source can be heard
224–320 Kbps	High quality, little loss of audio quality from the original source

The most popular compressed lossy audio file formats are MP3 (MPEG-1 Audio Layer 3), AAC (Advanced Audio Coding), and WMA (Windows Media Audio). MP3 audio files are the most popular because the MP3 audio file standard was one of the first compression file formats that could compress audio files to a smaller size and retain much of their audio quality. You can recognize MP3 audio files by their .mp3 file extension.

Because the MP3 audio file format is copyrighted, programmers have created a free equivalent audio file format called Ogg Vorbis, which uses the .ogg file extension. Ogg Vorbis offers slightly higher audio quality and slightly greater compression ratios.

Another alternative to MP3 files is the AAC audio file format. Similar to Ogg Vorbis, AAC audio files offer greater audio quality and smaller file compression than equivalent MP3 files. Unlike the Ogg Vorbis format, the AAC format offers a digital rights management (DRM) feature that allows copy protection. AAC files typically end with the .aac or .m4a file extension (if it does not have DRM) or the .m4p file extension (if it does have DRM).

To play Ogg Vorbis files, you can use VLC Media Player, which you can download free at www.videolan.org/vlc.

Streaming audio

Except for sound effects or mobile phone ringtones, most audio files are 2 to 4 megabytes in size. Before you can play such an audio file, you must first copy the entire file to your Mac. Normally, this isn't a problem except if you want to listen to audio right away, such as a live radio broadcast on a radio station's Web site, or a recording of a speech given by the President of the United States on a news Web site. These kinds of audio files are called *streaming audio*.

Two features distinguish streaming audio from ordinary audio files. First, streaming audio plays while it's being downloaded — or streamed — to your Mac. Second, streaming audio is not typically saved to your hard drive.

The iTunes program (included with every Mac) can play streaming audio. Some other popular (and free) programs for listening to streaming audio include Audion (www.panic.com/audion), RealPlayer (www.real.com), and AOL Radio (http://music.aol.com/radioguide/bb).

Playing Audio with iTunes

You can buy audio files of your favorite songs from such services as the iTunes Store or from Amazon.com. Perhaps the most popular way to get audio files is by importing (also known as *ripping*) songs from an audio CD and storing them as audio files on your hard drive.

When you have an audio file, you need a special program that can play that audio file. To play the three most common audio files (MP3, AAC, and AIFF) on your Mac, you can use iTunes. The iTunes program is a combination audio and video player, audio file converter, and disc-burning program. Using the iTunes disc-burning feature, you can copy your favorite audio files to a CD that you can play in your home CD player or on the CD player in your car.

You don't have to use iTunes to play audio CDs and digital audio files on your Mac. You can always use another audio player on your Mac (such as RealPlayer, which you can get free at www.real.com, VLC Media Player at www.videolan.org/vlc, or Audion at www.panic.com/audion). Other audio players can be especially useful if you want to play oddball audio formats like Ogg Vorbis or FLAC, but in most cases, you'll probably find that iTunes works just fine.

Listening to CDs

You probably have audio CDs of your favorite albums, but rather than play them in a CD player, you can play them in your Mac by using iTunes. Much like a CD player, iTunes can play audio tracks on a CD in order or randomly. Even better, iTunes lets you selectively choose which audio tracks you want to hear. To play an audio CD in iTunes, follow these steps:

1. **Click the iTunes icon in the Dock to launch iTunes if it isn't already running (or double-click the iTunes icon in the Applications folder).**

2. **Insert an audio CD into your Mac.**

A dialog appears, asking whether you want to import all audio tracks on the CD into iTunes. I discuss this process in the next section. For now, proceed to Step 3.

3. **Click No.**

If you're connected to the Internet, iTunes searches an Internet Website called GraceNotes for information about the CD you inserted, based on multiple criteria, including the number and length of tracks on the CD. If GraceNotes finds a match for your CD, iTunes displays that information, which can include the album name and artist, track titles, and, if available, the album's cover artwork, as shown in Figure 1-1.

4. **Click the Play button or press the spacebar to start playing your selected audio tracks.**

The Play button turns into a Pause button (which you can click to pause the track you're listening to).

Figure 1-1:
You can see all the audio tracks on your CD by name and track length.

Here are some tricks you can use to enhance your CD-listening experience:

✦ **Volume slider:** Drag the volume slider to adjust the sound.

✦ **Selective play:** Deselect the check boxes of any audio tracks you don't want to hear.

✦ **Random play:** Choose Controls➪Shuffle to play your audio tracks in random order. Choosing the Shuffle command again turns off random play. You can keep toggling this command off and on until you see a random order that you like.

✦ **Repeat-selection play:** Choose Controls➪Repeat➪All to play the selected audio tracks continuously on the CD. (Choose Controls➪Repeat Off to turn off the repeat play feature.)

If you select an audio track and then choose Controls➪Repeat One, you can play a single audio track over and over.

✦ **Adjust play:** Click one of the following buttons:

  • *Pause:* Temporarily stops playing audio. You can also press the spacebar to toggle the Play and Pause button.

  • *Previous:* Starts playing the selected audio track from the beginning. Clicking the Previous button a second time starts playing the previous audio track from the beginning.

  • *Next:* Skips the selected audio track and starts playing the next audio track.

When you're listening to an audio CD, you can eject it by choosing Controls➪ Eject Disc (or by clicking the Eject Disc icon to the right of the CD icon).

Importing a CD's audio tracks into iTunes

Having to insert a CD into your Mac every time you want to hear a few songs can be cumbersome, which is why you might find it easier to store your favorite songs as digital audio files instead.

The process of converting audio tracks on a CD into digital audio files is known as *ripping*.

To convert an audio disc into digital files, follow these steps:

1. **Click the iTunes icon in the Dock to launch iTunes if it isn't already running (or double-click the iTunes icon in the Applications folder).**

2. **Insert an audio CD into your Mac.**

A dialog appears, asking if you want to import all audio tracks on the CD into iTunes, as shown in Figure 1-2.

Figure 1-2:
When you insert a CD, iTunes offers to copy its contents to your Mac's hard drive.

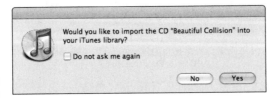

Would you like to import the CD "Beautiful Collision" into your iTunes library?

☐ Do not ask me again

No   Yes

3. **Click Yes if you want to convert every audio track into a digital audio file.**

The iTunes program copies and converts all of the CD's audio tracks into digital audio files and saves them to your Mac's hard drive in the Music folder. Skip to Step 5.

4. **If you want to choose which files to select, click No, and uncheck the check boxes of the tracks you don't want to import.**

Check marks should appear in the check boxes of the audio tracks you want to import.

5. **Click the Import CD button in the lower-right corner of the iTunes window.**

   iTunes imports your CD's audio tracks into the iTunes library one at a time until all tracks have been copied to your Mac's hard drive.

6. **When iTunes finishes importing your CD's audio tracks, eject the CD by choosing Controls⇨Eject Disc (or by clicking the Eject Disc icon to the right of the CD icon).**

Adjusting CD importing options and other settings

Choosing how iTunes should respond when you insert a CD, what type of audio file format it uses to import your CD audio tracks, and which Library categories you want to display in the left-hand column of the iTunes program window are all options you can adjust by accessing the iTunes Preferences dialog. To open the iTunes's Preferences dialog and adjust the program's settings, follow these steps:

1. **Choose iTunes⇨Preferences.**

   The iTunes Preferences window appears.

2. **Click the General icon (if it isn't already selected) to display the General settings pane, as shown in Figure 1-3.**

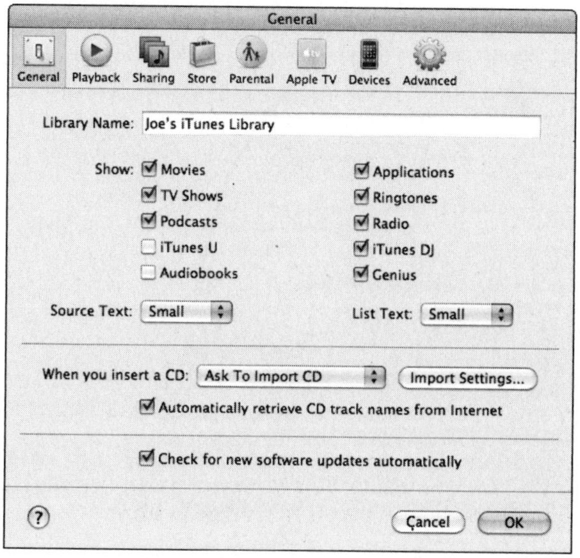

**Book III
Chapter 1**

Tuning In to Music, Audio, and iTunes

Figure 1-3:
The iTunes
Preferences
dialog lets
you tailor
iTunes to
your liking.

3. **(Optional) To specify what you want to happen whenever you insert an audio CD into your Mac, click the When You Insert a CD pop-up menu and choose one of the following:**

   • *Show CD:* Displays a list of audio tracks.

   • *Begin Playing:* Displays a list of audio tracks and starts playing the first track.

   • *Ask to Import CD:* Displays a dialog, asking whether you want to import all audio tracks from the CD (this is the default setting).

   • *Import CD:* Automatically converts all audio tracks into digital files.

   • *Import CD and Eject:* Automatically converts all audio tracks into digital files and ejects the CD when it finishes without playing any tracks.

4. **(Optional) Click Automatically Retrieve CD Track Names from Internet if you want iTunes to identify audio tracks by their song titles. If this option isn't selected, each audio track will have a generic name like Track 1.**

5. **(Optional) To specify the file format and audio quality of the audio files iTunes will create when importing CD audio tracks, click the Import Settings button.**

   The Import Settings preferences pane, shown in Figure 1-4, opens.

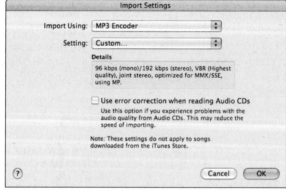

Figure 1-4:
Use the Import Settings preferences to choose audio file format and quality.

a. *Click the Import Using pop-up menu and choose one of the following:*

   AAC Encoder: Stores audio tracks as AAC files.

   AIFF Encoder: Stores audio tracks as AIFF files.

Apple Lossless Encoder: Stores audio tracks as a losslessly compressed .m4a file.

MP3 Encoder: Stores audio tracks as MP3 files.

WAV Encoder: Stores audio tracks as WAV files.

b. *Click the Setting pop-up menu and choose the audio quality for your files.*

The higher the audio quality, the larger the file size.

c. *(Optional) Select the Use Error Correction When Reading Audio CDs check box to increase the chances that iTunes can retrieve and convert audio tracks from a damaged or scratched CD.*

d. *Click the OK button to close the Import Settings preferences pane and return to the General preferences pane.*

6. **(Optional) Click Check for New Software Updates Automatically to allow iTunes to check periodically for newer versions of the iTunes program.**

7. **(Optional) Click the other iTunes preferences icons in the iTunes Preferences dialog toolbar to explore any other options you might want to select, deselect, or adjust.**

8. **Click OK to close the iTunes Preferences dialog.**

You return to the main iTunes program window.

Importing digital audio files

Besides ripping audio tracks from a CD and storing them on your Mac, you might also get digital audio files through the Internet or handed to you on a flash drive or external hard drive. Before you can play any digital audio files in iTunes, you must first import those files, which essentially copies them into the iTunes folder inside your Music folder.

To import audio files into iTunes, follow these steps:

1. **Click the iTunes icon in the Dock to run iTunes if it isn't already running (or double-click the iTunes icon in the Applications folder).**

2. **Choose File⇨Add to Library to open the Add to Library dialog, as shown in Figure 1-5.**

3. **Navigate to the folder, audio file, or files you want to import into iTunes, click your selections, and then click the Choose button.**

iTunes imports the folder, audio file, or files into your Music folder.

Figure 1-5:
The Add
to Library
dialog lets
you copy an
audio file
from other
sources or
places on
your hard
drive.

Sorting your digital audio files

After you store some digital audio files in iTunes, you can sort through them to find the audio files you want. The iTunes program offers three ways to display your audio files:

✦ **List view:** Displays audio files alphabetically by category, such as name, album, artist, or genre. Optionally, you can choose View⇨Show Artwork Column to display an album's cover artwork alongside listed audio files.

✦ **Grid view:** Displays album cover artwork of audio files grouped alphabetically by album name.

✦ **Cover Flow view:** Displays album covers as 3-D images in upper pane and album details in lower pane.

To customize the way your List view displays your iTunes music collection, choose View⇨Column Browser and then check or uncheck any columns you want to see in the List view. Choose On Top or On Left to choose how the columns you've selected appear — above the music tracks pane, or to the left of the music tracks pane (see Figure 1-6).

Displaying audio files in List view

The List view is best suited for when you want to see as many names of your audio files as possible. In the List view, you can view your audio files alphabetically sorted by different categories, such as Artist or Album. To see the List view, follow these steps:

1. **In iTunes, choose View⇨As List (or click the List View icon) to display the List view, as shown in Figure 1-6.**

Figure 1-6:
The List view lets you arrange your audio files alphabetically by categories, such as Name or Artist.

2. **Click a category heading, such as Name or Artist.**

   When you click a category heading, iTunes sorts your entire audio library alphabetically in ascending order based on that category. If you click the same category again, iTunes sorts your audio files alphabetically in descending order.

   Optionally, you can choose View⇨Show Artwork Column to display an album's cover artwork alongside listed audio files.

   The List view makes it easy to find audio files for a particular artist.

Displaying audio files in Grid view

The Grid view visually groups songs by album cover artwork. If cover artwork is not available for an album, the Grid view displays a musical note icon. If you find the List view too boring because it displays only text, try the Grid view instead. To see the Grid view, follow these steps:

1. **In iTunes, choose View⇨As Grid (or click the Grid View icon) to display the Grid view, as shown in Figure 1-7.**

2. **Click the Albums, Artists, Genres, or Composers buttons to sort the Grid view based on those categories.**

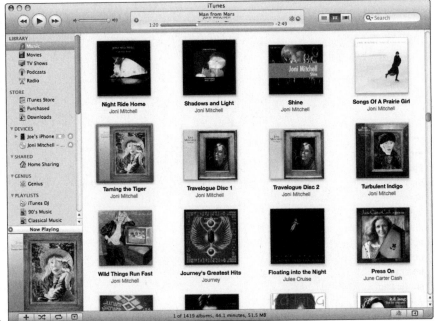

Figure 1-7:
The Grid view organizes songs alphabetically by album cover artwork.

Displaying audio files in Cover Flow view

Another way to sort through your audio file collection is with the Cover Flow view, which mimics the appearance of displaying album covers in a jukebox, where you can flip through different album covers to find the songs you want to play. Like the Grid view, the Cover Flow view lets you browse through your favorite songs sorted by album cover artwork.

To download album cover artwork, you need an iTunes account. If you have an iTunes account, choose Store➪Sign In to sign in to your iTunes account. To create an iTunes account, choose Store➪Create Account. Creating an account won't cost you anything, but you will need to enter a credit card number in case you decide to buy anything from the iTunes online store.

To see the Cover Flow view, follow these steps:

1. **In iTunes, choose View➪Cover Flow View (or click the Cover Flow View icon) to display the Cover Flow view, as shown in Figure 1-8.**

2. **Click an album cover to see the songs associated with that album.**

   Optionally, you can click the Full Screen icon located next to the right-hand scrollbar arrow to make the Cover Flow view fill the entire screen.

Figure 1-8:
The Cover Flow view lets you flip through album covers to find the songs you want.

Playing digital audio files

After you import one or more audio files into iTunes, you can view your list of audio files within the iTunes window, as outlined in the previous section. To play one or more digital files, follow these steps:

1. **Choose a view for displaying your audio file collection, such as List, Grid, or Cover Flow view.**

   Check marks appear in the check boxes of selected songs.

2. **Select the check boxes of the audio tracks you want to hear and deselect the check boxes of audio tracks you don't want to hear.**

   To deselect all audio tracks so you don't have to listen to them, hold down the ⌘ key and select a check box. To reselect all audio tracks, repeat the process.

3. **Click the Play button or press the spacebar to start playing your selected audio tracks.**

   The Play button turns into a Pause button.

Searching for a song

To help you find a song, you can search by typing some or all of its name, album, artist, and so on. To search for a song, follow these steps:

1. **Click the Search field in the upper-right corner of the iTunes window and type part of the song, album, or other item that you want to find.**

Each time you type a letter in the Search field, iTunes narrows the list of available songs in your music collection, as shown in Figure 1-9.

2. **Click the Close button of the Search field when you find the song you want.**

Using an iTunes Playlist

Rather than go through the hassle of selecting the same group of songs over and over, you can select a group of songs once and store that list as a *playlist.* When you want to hear the group of songs, just select the playlist rather than each song.

Figure 1-9: Typing in the Search field helps you find a particular song in your music collection.

You can create two types of playlists: an ordinary playlist or a Smart Playlist. An ordinary playlist is a list of favorite songs you select to include in that playlist. A Smart Playlist lets you define rules for which songs to include, such as only songs recorded by a specific artist. While your audio file collection grows, a Smart Playlist can automatically include any new songs by that specific artist or by whatever other criteria you define for the particular Smart Playlist.

When you create an ordinary playlist or a Smart Playlist, those playlists appear in the source pane of the iTunes window. By default, iTunes already includes several Smart Playlists, including Recently Added, Recently Played, and Top 25 Most Played.

Creating a playlist

The simplest playlist to create is one that contains specific songs, such as a favorite album, a group of songs you want to listen to when you go for a run or workout, or perhaps every song by a particular artist. To create a playlist of particular songs you want to group, follow these steps:

1. **In iTunes, hold down the ⌘ key and click each song you want to store in your playlist.**

2. **Choose File⇨New Playlist from Selection.**

   An untitled playlist appears in the source pane of iTunes under the Playlists category, and your chosen songs appear in the right pane.

3. **Type a name for your playlist and press Return.**

You can always edit a playlist name by double-clicking the name in the source pane.

Adding songs to a playlist

After you create a playlist, you can add or remove songs to that playlist at any time. To add a song to a playlist, click a song you want to add and drag it to the playlist in the source pane of the iTunes window. The song you added appears in the playlist.

Putting a song in a playlist doesn't physically move the song from the folder it's stored in on your Mac's hard drive.

Deleting songs from a playlist

To delete a song from a playlist, follow these steps:

1. **In iTunes, click the playlist that contains the songs you want to delete to display the songs in your chosen playlist.**

2. **Click a song to delete and then press the Delete key.**

   A dialog appears, asking whether you really want to remove the song from your playlist.

3. **Click Remove.**

Deleting a song from a playlist doesn't delete the song from your iTunes library.

To delete a song from your music collection, click Music under the Library category in the source pane of the iTunes window, click a song you want to delete, and then press the Delete key. When a dialog appears, asking whether you want to delete the song from your Library, click Remove. When a second dialog appears, click Move to Trash if you want to delete the song track from your Mac's hard drive. Click Keep File if you want to keep the song track on your Mac's hard drive but no longer display it in your iTunes music library.

Creating a Smart Playlist

Manually adding and removing songs from a playlist can get tedious, especially if you regularly add new songs to your iTunes audio collection. Instead of placing specific songs in a playlist, a Smart Playlist lets you define specific criteria for what types of songs to store in that playlist, such as songs recorded earlier than 1990 or songs under a particular genre, such as Blues, Country, Hard Rock, or Folk. To create and use a Smart Playlist, you tag songs, define rules to determine which songs to include, and finally, edit existing playlists.

Tagging songs

To sort your song collection accurately into Smart Playlists, you can tag individual songs with descriptive information. Most songs stored as digital audio files already have some information stored in specific tags, such as the artist or album name. However, you might still want to edit or add new tags to help Smart Playlists sort your song collection.

To edit or add tags to a song, follow these steps:

1. **In iTunes, click a song that you want to tag and then choose File⇨Get Info (or press ⌘+I) to display the song track's information.**

2. **Click the Info tab to display text boxes where you can type in or change the song track's associated information, as shown in Figure 1-10.**

3. **Click a text field and edit or type new information.**

4. **In the same Info pane, click the Genre pop-up menu to add or change the song's genre.**

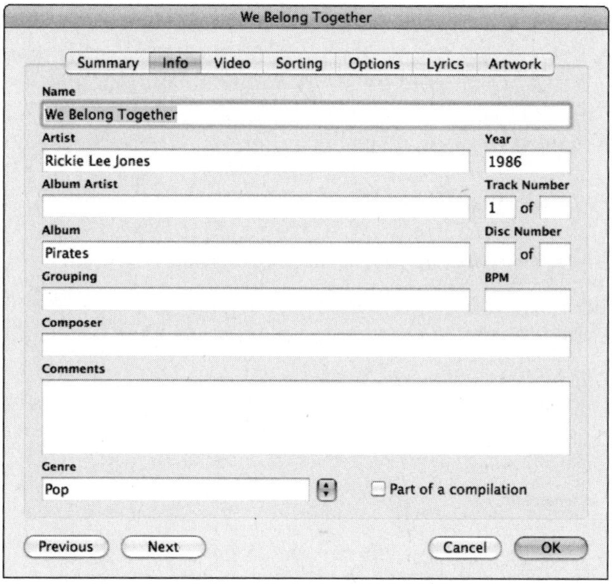

Figure 1-10:
The Info pane lets you edit or type new labels to identify a song.

5. **Click the song track's other tabs, such as Sorting or Options, as shown in Figure 1-11, to make additional adjustments to your selected audio file.**

6. **When you finish tagging the song track, click the OK button to close the dialog and return to the main iTunes window.**

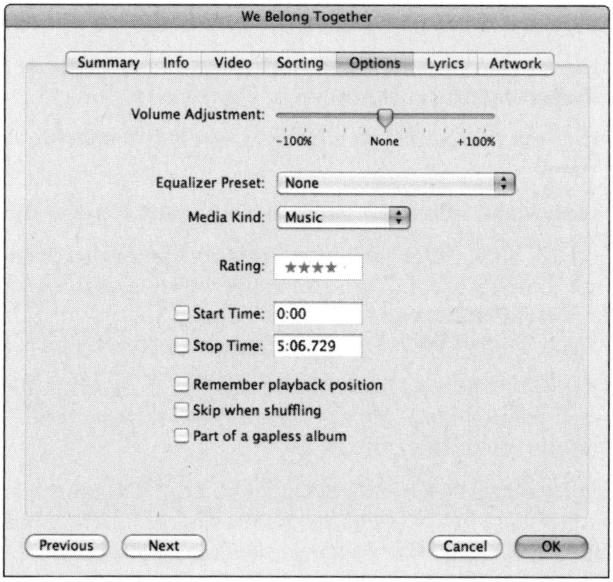

Figure 1-11:
The Options pane lets you adjust volume, choose an equalizer setting, and rate audio files with one to five stars.

Defining a Smart Playlist rule

Smart Playlists use tags to sort and organize your song collection. You can use existing tags that are created for songs automatically (such as Artist and Album) as well as tags that you add to your songs to define the type of songs you want that Smart Playlist to store. A specific criterion for choosing a song is a *rule*.

To create a Smart Playlist, follow these steps:

1. **In iTunes, choose File⇨New Smart Playlist.**

A Smart Playlist dialog appears, prompting you to define a rule for specifying which songs to store in the playlist, as shown in Figure 1-12.

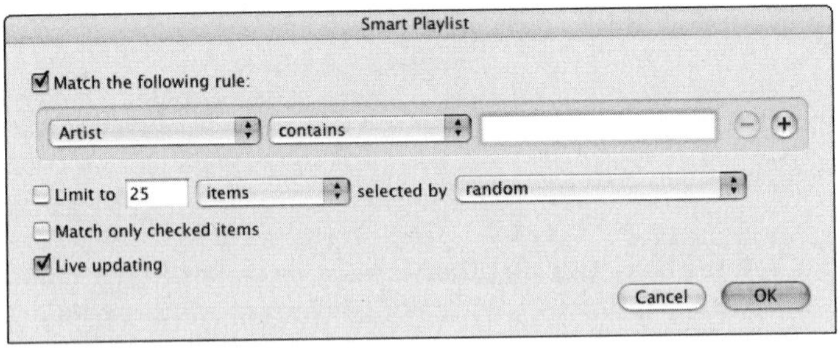

Figure 1-12:
The Smart Playlist dialog lets you define a rule for automatically choosing certain songs.

2. **Click the first pop-up menu on the left and choose a category, such as Artist or Date Added, for deciding which songs the Smart Playlist will automatically choose, as shown in Figure 1-13.**

3. **Click the second pop-up menu in the middle and choose how to use your chosen category, as shown in Figure 1-14.**

4. **Click the text box and type a criteria, such as a specific date or an artist name.**

5. **(Optional) Make other selections in the Smart Playlist dialog:**

- *Limit To:* Select this option and enter a number to define the maximum number of (choose one) songs/file size/minutes/hours/items the Smart Playlist can hold; then choose an option (that suits your desired Smart Playlist criteria) in the Selected By pop-up menu.

- *Match Only Checked Items:* If you want to store only songs that both match your criteria and are selected with checkmarks in the iTunes window, select this option.

- *Live Updating:* Select this option if you don't want the Smart Playlist to update its list of songs automatically each time you add or remove a song from your iTunes song collection library.

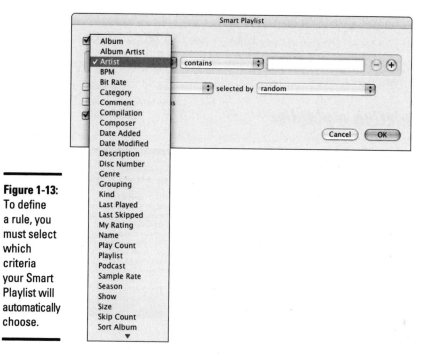

Figure 1-13:
To define
a rule, you
must select
which
criteria
your Smart
Playlist will
automatically
choose.

6. **Click the OK button to create and add your Smart Playlist to the list of
playlists in the source pane of the iTunes program window.**

Figure 1-14:
The second
pop-up
menu
defines how
to use your
chosen
category.

Editing a Smart Playlist

After you create a Smart Playlist, you might want to modify the way it works,
such as adding more rules or editing any existing rules. To edit a Smart
Playlist, follow these steps:

1. **In iTunes, select the Smart Playlist that you want to edit in the source
pane of the iTunes window.**

2. **Choose File⇨Edit Smart Playlist.**

   The Smart Playlist dialog appears (refer to Figure 1-12).

3. **Make any changes to your Smart Playlist rule and click the OK button when you finish.**

Deleting a playlist

After you create a playlist or a Smart Playlist, you might want to delete that list later. To delete a playlist, follow these steps:

1. **In iTunes, click a playlist that you want to delete in the source pane of the iTunes window and then press the Delete key.**

   A dialog appears, asking whether you really want to delete your playlist.

   Deleting a playlist doesn't physically delete the audio files from your iTunes library.

2. **Click the Delete button.**

Burning an Audio CD

After you add your favorite songs to your iTunes music library, you can copy music tracks to a custom CD (often called a *mix CD* or just a *mix*) that you can play in your car or home stereo. To burn an audio CD, you first create a playlist and then instruct iTunes to copy all the songs in the playlist to an audio CD.

CDs can hold approximately 70–80 minutes of audio. More stereos can recognize and play CD-Rs although newer stereos can recognize and play CD-RWs as well. (CD-Rs let you write to them only once; whereas CD-RWs allow you to erase and reuse them.)

To burn a disc using a playlist, follow these steps:

1. **Click the Playlist you want to burn to CD.**

2. **(Optional) Deselect the check boxes of any songs you don't want to burn to the CD.**

3. **(Optional) Arrange the songs in the order you want them to play on the CD.**

   To arrange songs in a playlist, click in the first column (that displays the number of each song) and then drag a song up or down to a new position.

4. **Click the Burn Disc button in the bottom right corner of the iTunes program window.**

A Burn Settings dialog appears with different radio buttons for choosing the type of CD you want to burn, such as Audio CD, MP3 CD, or Data CD or DVD, as shown in Figure 1-15.

Figure 1-15:
Choose the type of CD you want to burn.

5. **Select a Disc Format radio button (Audio CD, MP3 CD, or Data CD or DVD).**

6. **(Optional) Click the Preferred Speed pop-up menu and choose a disc burning speed, such as Maximum Possible or 24x.**

If the CDs you burn on your Mac don't play correctly on other CD players, choose a slower burning speed. Otherwise, use the Maximum Possible option.

If you choose Audio CD, consider these additional options:

- (Optional) Click the Gap between Songs pop-up menu and choose none or 1 to 5 seconds of silence between each song track.

- (Optional) Select the Use Sound Check check box to instruct iTunes to ensure that all the song tracks play from the CD at the same volume level.

- (Optional) Select the Include CD Text check box to display information about the CD on CD player models that offer a CD text information feature.

7. **Click the Burn button.**

8. **When prompted, insert a blank CD-R or CD-RW into your Mac.**

The top of the iTunes window displays the progress of your disc burning. If you're burning more than one or two songs, you now have enough time to go get a cup of coffee, tea, or another beverage of your choosing.

**Book III
Chapter 1**

Tuning In to Music, Audio, and iTunes

Chapter 2: Importing, Viewing, and Organizing Photos

In This Chapter

✔ **Understanding digital photography**

✔ **Transferring pictures to your Mac**

✔ **Capturing pictures**

✔ **Finding image-editing programs**

More people are taking pictures than ever before with digital cameras and mobile phones. Both gadgets let you capture a picture, see it right away, and then decide whether you want to keep it. Even better, after you capture a picture, you can edit it to make it look better than the subject or scene did in real life. You can even alter a digital image with an image-editing program. You can use iPhoto, which is part of the iLife suite, for image editing, but many other programs are available, and I discuss them briefly here.

Understanding Digital Photography

Instead of using film, digital photography captures images on memory storage devices. Not only does this make storing digital photographs easy on your Mac, you can also make identical copies of your pictures at any time without losing the quality of your images. When using a digital camera or mobile phone equipped with a camera, it's helpful to understand how digital cameras and mobile phones store images so you can transfer them to your Mac.

Megapixels

Digital photographs capture images as a collection of tiny dots called *pixels*. A single picture consists of hundreds, thousands, or (more commonly) millions of pixels. The greater the number of pixels used to create a picture, the sharper the overall image. To help you understand the capabilities of different digital cameras and mobile phones, manufacturers identify the gadgets by how many millions of pixels they can capture in each picture. This total number of pixels, called the *resolution*, ranges from as little as less than one megapixel (MP) to 16 megapixels or more. Figure 2-1 shows how pixels create an image.

Figure 2-1:
Every digital image consists of hundreds, thousands, or millions of pixels.

The higher the megapixels of a digital camera, the sharper the image resolution. A picture captured with a 2-megapixel camera may not look as sharp as that same image captured with an 8-megapixel camera, especially if you enlarge it.

Flash memory cards

Every time you snap a digital picture, your camera or mobile phone needs to save that picture somewhere. Some digital cameras and mobile phones (such as the Palm Pre and Apple iPhone) come with built-in memory, which can temporarily store any digital images that you capture. However, to store large numbers of pictures, most digital cameras and some mobile phones can also store pictures on removable storage devices called *flash memory cards.*

Okay, in no particular order, here are a few things to keep in mind about flash memory cards:

✦ **Reuse:** The biggest advantage of flash memory cards over film is that you can erase and reuse flash memory cards. You can take as many pictures as the flash memory card can hold, copy your pictures to your Mac's hard drive, and then erase the pictures from the flash memory card so you can use it again.

✦ **Resolution versus storage:** The number of pictures you can store on flash memory cards depends on the resolution of the pictures you take. If you capture pictures at a high resolution, you can store far fewer pictures than if you capture those same pictures at a lower resolution.

✦ **Storage and speed measurement:** Flash memory cards are often measured in terms of their storage size and speed. The amount of storage a flash memory card can hold is measured in megabytes (MB) and gigabytes (GB), such as 512MB or 2GB. The greater the storage capability of a flash memory card, the higher the cost.

The speed of flash memory cards is often described as minimum read and write speeds, measured in megabytes per second (MB/sec) such as 10MB/sec. The higher the write speed of a flash memory card, the faster you can capture and store pictures. Sometimes the speed of a flash memory card might also be described as a number — 60x, for example — which tells you the flash memory card is 60 times faster than the original flash memory cards.

✦ **Image recovery:** If you ever accidentally erase a picture from a flash memory card, don't panic (and don't store any more pictures on that flash memory card). If you buy a special file-recovery program, such as MediaRECOVER (www.mediarecover.com) or Digital Picture Recovery (www.dtidata.com), you can often retrieve deleted pictures from any type of flash memory card. However, if you delete a picture and then store more pictures on the flash memory card, the new pictures will likely wipe out any traces of your deleted pictures, making it impossible to retrieve the deleted pictures ever again.

Many different types of flash memory cards exist because each design is meant to set the "standard" for flash memory cards. Unfortunately, every flash memory card has its limitations, so companies keep coming up with newer designs to overcome these limitations. Because so many "standards" exist, the result is that there is no standard. The following are the most popular flash memory cards:

✦ **Compact Flash Type I (CFI) and Compact Flash Type II (CFII):** Introduced in 1994, CompactFlash cards were one of the first flash memory cards available and one of the largest. There are two types of CompactFlash cards: Type I (3.3 mm thick), or CFI; and Type II (5.0 mm thick), or CFII.

Because of the thickness differences, make sure you use the right CompactFlash cards for your digital camera and card reader. A digital camera and card reader that can use a CFII card can also use a CFI card, but the reverse isn't true.

✦ **Secure Digital (SD) and Plus Secure Digital (Plus SD):** SD cards are much smaller than CompactFlash cards and offer built-in encryption to prevent storing copyright-infringing materials, such as illegal songs, although this encryption feature is rarely used. Because of their small size, Secure Digital cards are slowly evolving into the standard for digital photography. Even smaller versions of Secure Digital cards include Mini and Micro SD cards, which are often the type of flash memory card used in mobile phones.

✦ **Memory Stick (MS), Memory Stick Pro (MS Pro), Memory Stick Duo (MS Duo), Memory Stick Pro Duo (MS Pro Duo), and Memory Stick Micro (MS Micro):** The Memory Stick format was developed by Sony, which means that only Sony devices (digital cameras, video camcorders, and PlayStations) use Memory Sticks for storing digital images. The original Memory Stick could store a maximum of only 128MB of data, so Sony created the Memory Stick Pro, which can hold up to 32GB of data. The Memory Stick Duo and Memory Stick Pro Duo look like an original Memory Stick cut in half.

Despite Sony's backing, the Memory Stick format has never gained popularity with other manufacturers. If you buy a Sony camera, you'll probably be stuck with using Memory Sticks, although some of the latest Sony cameras now use Secure Digital cards instead.

✦ **xD Picture Cards (xD):** Olympus and Fuji invented the xD Picture Cards to provide yet another standard. Because xD Picture Cards are fairly recent, far fewer cameras use them — with the exception, of course, of Olympus cameras and some Fuji cameras. An xD Picture Card is often more expensive than other flash memory cards, making them less attractive.

Digital image file formats

When you take pictures, your digital camera stores those pictures in a specific graphics file format. The three most common file formats for storing digital photographs are

✦ **JPEG (Joint Photo Experts Group):** JPEG is the most common file format because it is recognized by most computers and offers the ability to compress images to shrink the overall file size. (*Compressing* a JPEG file means decreasing the number of colors used in an image, which shrinks the file size but lowers the visual quality.)

✦ **TIFF (Tagged Image File Format):** If picture quality is more important than file size, save your pictures as TIFF files. You can still compress TIFF files slightly, but TIFF files always retain all colors. As a result, a compressed TIFF file is usually larger than an equivalent compressed JPEG file.

✦ **RAW (which doesn't stand for anything!):** RAW files offer greater visual quality; however, there is no single RAW file format standard. As a result, every digital camera manufacturer offers its own RAW file format.

The biggest advantage is that RAW files allow for greater manipulation. As a result, professional photographers often use RAW files for greater control over manipulating their images. The biggest disadvantage is that RAW images take up a large amount of storage space and take longer for a digital camera to store them, which means you can't capture images in rapid succession as you can with JPEG files or ordinary film cameras.

Ultimately, there is no single "best" file format. If a digital camera lets you save images in different file formats, experiment to see which one you like best. You might prefer one type of file format, such as JPEG, for ordinary use but prefer RAW for capturing images in special situations that don't require capturing images quickly, such as taking pictures of a landscape.

Transferring Digital Images to the Mac

To transfer pictures from a digital camera to your Mac, you have two choices. First, you can connect your digital camera to your Mac by using a USB cable. Second, you can pop the flash memory card out of your digital camera and plug it into a card reader, such as the Kingston model shown in Figure 2-2, that's plugged into your Mac. At the time this edition was written, Apple introduced new MacBook Pro notebook computers with built-in SD card readers. So, unless you have one of these MacBook Pros, you have to buy the card reader separately if you want to copy pictures to your Mac that way.

Figure 2-2: A USB memory card reader allows your Mac to access memory cards.

No matter which method you use, your Mac then treats all the images stored on your digital camera's flash memory card as just another external drive that you can copy pictures from to your Mac's hard drive (such as into the Pictures folder).

When you connect a digital camera or a mobile phone to your Mac, it can automatically load a program to retrieve those images. Two programs included with your Mac that you can use to retrieve digital snapshots automatically are iPhoto and Image Capture.

If you organize pictures in iPhoto, choose it as your default application to retrieve pictures from a digital camera. If you use a different program to organize your pictures, such as Adobe Photoshop, you can make that program your default application. If you use more than one program to organize your pictures, you can make Image Capture your default application and then run the program you want to work with your imported pictures on a program-by-program basis.

Defining a default program for retrieving photos

If you need to transfer digital images from a camera to your Mac on a regular basis, you can define a default program to use for retrieving these images by following these steps:

1. **Double-click the Image Capture icon in the Applications folder.**

   The Image Capture window appears.

2. **Connect your camera or smartphone to your Mac's USB or FireWire port with the appropriate cable.**

   Your connected camera or smartphone will appear under the Devices group in the left pane, as shown in Figure 2-3.

Figure 2-3:
Your camera or smartphone appears in the left pane under the Devices group.

You can also define a default application by running iPhoto and choosing iPhoto➪Preferences.

3. **Click the Connecting This [*your device name here*] Opens pop-up menu in the bottom-left corner and then choose iPhoto or Image Capture.**

   You can choose another program listed on the pop-up menu, or click Other to choose a program in your Mac's Applications folder that isn't listed in the pop-up menu so it can automatically run when you connect your camera to your Mac.

4. **Choose the following options if you want to:**

- *Share Camera (or whatever your device is named):* Allows others on your Mac's network to view and import pictures from your connected camera or smartphone.

- *Delete after Import:* Copies your photos from your connected device to your Mac's hard drive and then deletes the pictures from your camera or smartphone, freeing memory on the device so you can take more pictures.

- *Location:* Click the pop-up menu to the left of the Import button to choose where you want Image Capture to save your imported pictures.

5. **Choose File⇨Quit to exit the Image Capture program.**

Retrieving photos using iPhoto

If you defined iPhoto as the default program to run when you connect a digital camera to your Mac, follow these steps:

1. **Connect your digital camera or smartphone to your Mac with the appropriate cable (or plug your memory card into your memory card reader).**

iPhoto automatically launches (if it isn't already running) and displays your camera or smartphone pictures in the right pane, as shown in Figure 2-4.

Book III
Chapter 2

Importing, Viewing, and Organizing Photos

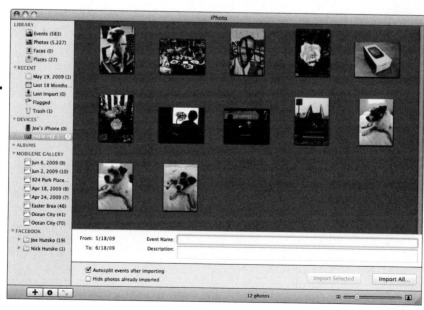

Figure 2-4:
iPhoto displays the photos stored on your camera or smartphone (or memory card) when you plug it into your Mac.

2. **(Optional) Before importing your pictures, you can adjust or choose the following options in the lower area of the iPhoto window:**

   - *Event Name:* Click the text field and type a name for the batch of photos you're importing, such as My Wedding Day, or Summer Vacation.

   - *Description:* Click the text field and type a description that can include details of the batch of photos you're importing, such as the names, places, and things captured in your pictures.

   - *Autosplit Events after Importing:* Select this check box to make iPhoto automatically create separate event folders for pictures you're importing based on the date you snapped the photos.

   - *Hide Photos Already Imported:* Select this check box to make iPhoto ignore (therefore, not display) any photos you chose not to delete from your camera or smartphone after previously importing those photos.

3. **(Optional) Click and drag the slider in the bottom-right corner of the iPhoto window left or right to increase or decrease the size of your picture icons.**

4. **Click a picture that you want to transfer and then click Import Selected.**

   If you click Import All, iPhoto retrieves all pictures stored on your camera or smartphone.

   To select multiple images, hold down the ⌘ key and click each picture you want to import.

5. **When iPhoto finishes importing your pictures, a dialog appears asking if you want to keep or delete the photos from your camera or smartphone.**

6. **If you want to delete the pictures from your device to make room so you can take more photos, click the Delete Photos button. Otherwise, click the Keep Photos button to leave the pictures on your camera or smartphone.**

7. **Choose iPhoto⇨Quit iPhoto to exit iPhoto.**

Retrieving photos using Image Capture

If you define Image Capture as the default program to run when you connected a digital camera to your Mac, follow these steps:

1. **Connect your digital camera or smartphone to your Mac with the appropriate cable.**

   The Image Capture window appears, displaying your camera or smartphone pictures in the right pane (refer to Figure 2-3).

   You can also use the Image Capture program to capture and copy images from a scanner.

2. **(Optional) Before importing your pictures, you can click the icons below the right pane of the Image Capture window, as shown in Figure 2-5, to:**

   - *Switch between List view and Icon view*

   - *Rotate a selected picture left*

   - *Rotate a selected picture right*

   - *Delete a selected picture*

   - *Choose the location where you want Image Capture to save your imported photos (click the pop-up menu)*

Figure 2-5:
Click the icons to do things to a selected photo before you import it.

3. **(Optional) Click and drag the slider in the bottom-right corner of the Image Capture window left or right to increase or decrease the size of your picture icons.**

4. **Click a picture that you want to transfer and click Import, or click Import All to retrieve all pictures stored on your camera or smartphone.**

   To select multiple images, hold down the ⌘ key and click each picture you want to import.

5. **Image Capture marks each picture with a check mark after it copies each one to the location selected in the pop-up menu to the left of the Import button, as shown in Figure 2-6.**

6. **Choose Image Capture⇨Quit Image Capture.**

If you didn't select the Delete after Import check box, you have to erase the pictures from your flash memory card after you import them to your Mac so the memory card has space to store more snapshots.

Figure 2-6: Checkmarks indicate the photo's Image Capture copied to your Mac.

Retrieving photos using a USB memory card reader

A second way to transfer digital images is to use a separate device called a card reader (refer to Figure 2-2) which plugs into your Mac's USB port — unless, that is, you have a newer model MacBook Pro that comes with a card reader already built-in.

To access a memory card with your Mac, you remove the memory card from your camera or smartphone and then plug it into the card reader connected to your Mac. Your Mac displays the flash memory card icon on the Desktop and its contents in a Finder window the same way it displays an external hard drive, as shown in Figure 2-7.

Figure 2-7: A USB memory card reader displays external memory cards on your Mac's desktop.

Never yank a flash memory card out of a card reader because doing so might cause your Mac to scramble the data on the memory card. Before physically removing a flash memory card from a card reader, choose one of the following ways to remove a flash memory card safely from your Mac:

✦ Drag the flash memory card icon to the Trash icon in the Dock to eject it.

✦ Click the flash memory icon and choose File➪Eject.

✦ Click the flash memory icon and press ⌘+E.

✦ Control-click the flash memory icon and choose Eject from the shortcut menu that appears.

✦ Click the Eject button that appears to the right of the flash memory icon in the Sidebar of the Finder window.

Capturing Pictures from Other Sources

If you don't have a separate digital camera, you might have a built-in digital camera in your Macintosh. This built-in camera, called iSight, is standard equipment on all newer MacBook and iMac models. You can also find a built-in iSight camera on Apple's LED Cinema Display external monitor that can connect to your Mac desktop computer, or act as a second display for your MacBook computer. To capture pictures using this built-in camera, the simplest method is to use the Photo Booth program located in your Mac's Applications folder.

If you're the type who doesn't like taking pictures, you might prefer to save pictures you like on Web sites you visit. By copying pictures from Web sites, you can find images that you wouldn't normally capture yourself, such as images of fighting in the Middle East or pictures of mountain climbers scaling Mount Everest.

Pictures stored on Web sites are usually copyrighted, so you cannot legally capture those pictures and reuse them for commercial purposes.

Capturing pictures with Photo Booth

If your Mac comes with an iSight camera built-in, you can capture pictures of yourself (or whoever or whatever is stationed in front of your Mac), by using the Photo Booth program. Pictures you snap with Photo Booth save as JPEG files in a Photo Booth folder tucked inside your Pictures folder.

You can plug in an optional external Webcam, such as one of the models sold by Logitech (www.logitech.com) or Microsoft (www.microsoft.com/hardware), or plug in certain camcorders, to capture pictures with Photo Booth. You can also use one of these optional external choices to conduct live, two-way video chats with friends and family, as I write about in Book IV, Chapter 3.

**Book III
Chapter 2**

Importing, Viewing, and Organizing Photos

To capture pictures with Photo Booth, follow these steps:

1. **Double-click the Photo Booth icon, which you can find in the Applications folder.**

   The Photo Booth window appears, displaying the image seen through the iSight camera, as shown in Figure 2-8.

Figure 2-8: Photo Booth lets you capture pictures using your Mac's built-in iSight camera.

If you click the Effects button, you can capture a picture using visual effects (such as fish-eye) or in front of a background (such as the Eiffel Tower).

2. **Click the camera icon in the middle of the iSight window (or press ⌘+T).**

   Photo Booth counts down from 3 (in seconds) before capturing your picture. Each captured picture appears at the bottom of the Photo Booth window.

If you hold down the Option key when you click the camera icon (or press ⌘+T), Photo Booth snaps your picture right away without going through the three-second countdown.

3. **When you finish snapping pictures, choose Photo Booth⇨Quit Photo Booth or press ⌘+Q to exit Photo Booth.**

Photo Booth stores its pictures in a Photo Booth folder inside the Pictures folder.

You can delete pictures you take with Photo Booth three ways:

✦ Run Photo Booth as described in the previous steps (refer to Figure 2-8), click a photo icon in the lower pane that you want to delete, and then press the Delete key.

✦ To delete all your Photo Booth photos at one time, choose Edit⇨Delete All Photos and then click the OK button to confirm your choice.

✦ Open the Photo Booth folder (Pictures⇨Photo Booth), click a photo icon you want to delete, drag it to the Trash, and then choose File⇨Empty Trash. (To select more than one picture, hold down the ⌘ key and then click each photo you want to delete.)

When you choose the Delete All Photos command, you remove all pictures stored in the Photo Booth folder inside the Pictures folder.

Capturing pictures from Web sites

By browsing through different Web sites, you can find a variety of images that you might want to use for personal use, such as adding them to an album in your iPhoto library of a movie star or public servant whose career you follow.

To save images from a Web page, follow these steps:

1. **Load your favorite Web browser, such as Safari (Applications⇨Safari).**

2. **Browse to a Web page and Control-click a picture you want.**

Doing so opens a shortcut menu, as shown in Figure 2-9.

Generally, because of copyright rules, don't copy pictures from Web sites and reuse those pictures on a commercial Web site.

3. **Choose one of the following commands from the shortcut menu:**

• *Save Image to "Downloads":* Saves the picture in the Downloads folder, stored inside your Home folder.

• *Save Image As:* Lets you choose a name for your picture and a folder where you want to save the picture.

• *Add Image to iPhoto Library:* Saves the image in your iPhoto photo library.

• *Copy Image:* Copies the image to the Mac's invisible clipboard so you can paste it into another document, such as an e-mail message or a letter to your mom.

The Save Image As option is the only one that lets you choose your own descriptive name for an image and specify the save location. All the other options save an image using that image's original filename, which might be something cryptic like `wild_things_LJ-0187.jpg`, although you can always rename the file later if you want.

Clicking and dragging a Web image to your Mac's Desktop (or to a Finder window) is one way to quickly capture pictures from Web sites.

Getting Acquainted with Digital Image Editing

One advantage that digital photographs have over traditional film is that you can easily edit and modify digital photographs using your Mac. By controlling an image right down to the appearance of individual pixels, digital editing gives you the power to enhance pictures, remove unwanted portions and unpleasant effects, such as "red-eye," or create your own imaginary images from your fantasies and dreams.

Editing a picture is typically a two-step process. First, you must select which part of the picture you want to change. Second, you have to select how to change it, such as by deleting it or coloring it.

To edit a photograph digitally, you can use the iPhoto program that comes with your Mac, which I write about in Book V, Chapter 1.

You can also try another digital-editing program, such as one of the following:

✦ **Picasa (`picassa.google.com`):** Free image editing and management program for organizing your photos, turning photos into movies, collages, and slideshows, and uploading images to Picasa Web Albums to share with friends and family.

✦ **Photoshop or Photoshop Elements (`www.adobe.com`):** Photoshop ($699) is the most popular (and expensive) program used by graphics artists and designers to manipulate images. A much cheaper and simpler version is Photoshop Elements ($89.99), which offers the most commonly used features of Photoshop.

✦ **Pixelmator (`www.pixelmator.com`):** Like Photoshop, Pixelmator ($59) offers layer-based image editing at a fraction of Photoshop's cost. You can quickly create layers from your photos, other pictures, or even your iSight camera.

✦ **Aperture 2 (`www.apple.com/aperture`):** Aperture ($199) is Apple's professional-level image editing and management program that offers advanced image processing, a streamlined interface, faster performance, and standout Mac integration.

✦ **GraphicConverter (`www.lemkesoft.com`):** Dubbed by the press as the "Swiss penknife" of Mac image-editing programs, GraphicConverter ($34.95) offers all-round image editing with ease of use, a wide range of functions, stability, and reliability.

Chapter 3: Watching Videos and Movies on Your Mac

In This Chapter

✔ **Understanding movie formats**

✔ **Understanding digital movie formats**

✔ **Playing a digital video file**

✔ **Playing a VCD**

✔ **Playing a DVD**

*L*ooking to unwind after a busy day of work? Feel free to kick back, relax, and cozy up to a movie on your Mac. Not only can your Mac act as a DVD player, but your Mac can also bookmark and store your favorite scenes so you can easily rewatch your favorite parts of a movie.

Although many full-length movies appear on DVD, many shorter movies and videos are stored entirely as digital video files. Whether a movie is stored on DVD or as a digital video file, your Mac can play it at your convenience.

Understanding Video Disc Formats

The most common video disc format is DVD (Digital Video Disc). However, DVDs aren't the only video disc format. An earlier video disc format is VCD (Video Compact Disc), which essentially stores video files on ordinary CDs. VCDs typically offer lower video quality (comparable to videotape) than DVDs and offer much less storage capability than DVDs. Another popular format is DiVX, which more and more DVD players can play.

Although DVDs are the video disc standard for most of the world, two competing standards — HD DVD (High-Definition Digital Versatile Disc) and Blu-ray — battled it out to become the next hi-def digital disc dominator. The war between these two competing formats lasted for about a year, with Blu-ray emerging victorious, leaving buyers of HD DVDs with players and discs that are now (technically speaking) a thing of the past.

HD DVD can store roughly three times as much data as ordinary DVDs (15GB for HD DVD versus 4.7GB for DVDs). Because HD DVDs are similar to ordinary DVDs, HD DVDs cost nearly the same to produce.

The main advantage of Blu-ray discs is that they can store much more data than even HD DVDs (25GB for a Blu-ray disc versus 15GB for an HD DVD). However, Blu-ray discs are also much more expensive to produce.

The Mac can play DVDs and VCDs out of the box, but if you want to watch video stored on HD DVDs or Blu-ray discs, you need to buy a special HD DVD or Blu-ray disc drive and a program to use it.

Understanding Digital Video Formats

Video discs are popular for storing and distributing videos, but with high-speed Internet connections and lower hard drive storage costs, storing full-length movies as a single digital video file has become both popular and practical. The biggest problem with digital video is the wide variety of digital video formats available. To play a digital video file, you need a video player program that accepts the type of video file you have. The following is a list of digital video file types and the programs that you can use to play them:

✦ **QuickTime (.mov):** Playable by the QuickTime Player that comes with every Mac.

✦ **Audio/Video Interleaved (.avi):** An older video file format introduced by Microsoft in 1992, although still commonly used today.

✦ **Windows Media Video (.wmv):** Playable on a Mac if you first install the Flip4Mac program (www.flip4mac.com), which allows the QuickTime Player to open and play Windows Media Video files.

✦ **DivX (.divx):** A high-quality video format known for storing DVD-quality video images in a digital video file format. DivX files can play on a Mac with the free DivX player (www.divx.com) or the free VLC media player (www.videolan.org).

Because DivX is a proprietary video file format, programmers have created a similar open source equivalent called Xvid (www.xvid.org).

✦ **Flash video (.flv):** A video file format commonly used on Web sites, such as news sites that offer video (CNN and Reuters) and YouTube, MySpace, and Yahoo! Video. You can play flash videos by using the free Adobe Flash player (www.adobe.com).

✦ **RealVideo (.rm):** A video file format often used for streaming video. You can play RealVideo files by using the free Real Player program (www.real.com).

✦ **Moving Picture Expert Group (MPEG) (.mpg):** A video file format that consists of different versions, including:

• *MPEG-1:* Used for storing video on VCDs.

• *MPEG-2:* Broadcast-quality video used for storing video on SVCDs, DVDs, HD TV, HD DVDs, and Blu-ray discs.

- *MPEG-3:* Originally designed for HD TV but now rarely used.
- *MPEG-4:* For storing video on HD DVD and Blu-ray discs.

You can view MPEG videos with the QuickTime Player, the free VLC media player (www.videolan.org), or the commercial MacVCD player (www.mireth.com).

The QuickTime Player can't play MPEG videos if the audio is stored as AC3 (Dolby Digital) files.

Most video players are free because the companies developing and promoting a specific video file format want as many people as possible to use (and rely on) their particular video file format. Then these companies can make money by selling programs that create and store video in their specific file format.

You can download and install a free Mac video enabler (known as a *codec*) called Perian (www.perian.org) that can give QuickTime the ability to play lots of video file types it can't normally play without such an add-in.

Playing a Digital Video File

Playing a digital video file is as simple as double-clicking that file, which opens the appropriate video player on your Mac and displays your video file on the screen. If you find a video file on a Web site, you can usually click the video file directly on the Web page to see it play within your browser.

Occasionally, you might find a video file format that you can't play on your Mac. In this case, you have two choices:

✦ Download and install a video player for that particular video file format.

✦ Convert the video file into a format that your Mac can play.

Sometimes it might be simpler just to download and install (yet another) free video player to watch video encoded in a different video file format. However, downloading and installing multiple video players can be annoying, so you might prefer to convert digital file formats instead. To convert digital video files, you need a special digital video file format conversion program.

To convert non-copy-protected (and most copy protected) DVD videos to a digital video file, such as an AVI or MPEG, you can use a free program called HandBrake (http://handbrake.fr). In case you need to convert one digital video file format into another one (such as converting a DivX file into a QuickTime file), grab a copy of the oddly named ffmpegX (www.ffmpegx.com) or MPEG StreamClip (www.squared5.com).

By converting digital video files, you can store all your videos in a single file format, such as QuickTime, to avoid having to download and install half a dozen video players just to watch your collection of video files.

Playing a DVD

The most common video disc format is the DVD format. To play DVDs, just insert your DVD into your Mac. DVD Player loads and displays your DVD's main menu, as shown in Figure 3-1.

Figure 3-1: When DVD Player starts, it displays the inserted DVD's main menu.

Click the menu options to select them (or use your Mac's arrow keys to move through the DVD's menu options and then press the Return key or spacebar to select them), such as Play Movie, or Special Features.

If you just want to watch a DVD from start to finish, you don't have to read the rest of this chapter. However, if you want to use some of the special features of DVD Player, keep reading.

Understanding full screen mode and window mode

One of the simplest ways to customize your video is to switch between full screen mode and window mode. In full screen mode, the video fills your entire computer screen. In window mode, the video fills only part of your computer screen while giving you access to the rest of your Mac Desktop, such as the Dock and other program windows, as shown in Figure 3-2.

Figure 3-2:
DVD Player can shrink a video inside a window on your Desktop.

Exiting and returning to full screen mode

The first time you insert a DVD into your Mac, DVD Player displays your video in full screen mode. To exit full screen mode, choose one of the following:

✦ Press Esc.

✦ Press ⌘+F.

✦ Click the Exit Full Screen button on the Controller, as shown in Figure 3-3.

In full screen mode, you can view the DVD Player menu bar by moving the pointer to the top of the screen. You can also view the DVD Controller in full screen mode by moving the pointer to the bottom of the screen.

Previous chapter   Closed Captioning

DVD Menu controls   Fast Forward   Eject Disc

DVD menu   Play/Pause   Exit Full Screen

Figure 3-3:
The Controller appears at the bottom of the screen.

Title menu   Playback   Stop   Player settings

Rewind   Next chapter

Viewing a video in a window

When you exit full screen mode, your video appears in a window with the Controller displayed underneath the DVD window. (Refer to Figure 3-2.) By choosing the View menu, you can display a video in the following window sizes:

+ Half Size

+ Actual Size

+ Double Size

+ Fit to Screen

+ Enter Full Screen

When viewing a video in a window, the Controller takes on a different *skin* (the display appearance), as shown in Figure 3-4.

Although the Controller in both full screen and window mode allows you to control a DVD, each Controller offers slightly different features. You can access some features in both full screen and window mode, but many features are available only in one mode or the other.

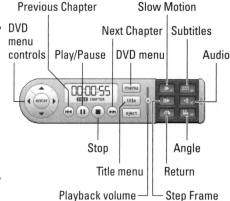

Previous Chapter   Slow Motion

DVD menu controls   Next Chapter | Subtitles

Play/Pause | DVD menu   Audio

Figure 3-4: The Controller appears in new garb when underneath a video window.

Stop   Angle

Title menu | Return

Playback volume — └ Step Frame

TIP

To avoid letting any other window cover up part of your video window, choose View⇨Viewer Above Other Apps. To turn off this feature, choose the same command again.

Viewing the DVD and Title menus

Most DVDs include an initial menu that lets you choose what to watch, such as the feature presentation or trivia clips. Some DVDs also offer a Title menu that lets you pick different episodes, such as a DVD containing multiple episodes from a single TV show season. Some DVDs offer both an initial menu and a Title menu. To jump to the initial DVD or Title menu (and note that not all DVDs have one), try clicking the Menu button (DVD menu) or the Title button on the Controller.

If you want to start the DVD from the very beginning, follow these steps:

1. In full screen mode, move the pointer to the top of the screen to display the DVD Player menu bar.

2. Choose Go⇨Beginning of Disc.

Your DVD starts playing from the beginning.

Skipping through a video

Sometimes you might want to skip over or replay part of a video. To skip backward or forward through a video, follow these steps:

1. Switch to full screen mode and then click the Pause button.

2. Click one of the following buttons on the Controller:

- *Rewind:* Reverses the video a few frames and starts playing normally again

- *Fast Forward:* Jumps the video ahead a few frames and starts playing normally again

Hold down the ⌘ key and press the left or right arrow keys to move backward or forward. Press the arrow key again while still holding down the ⌘ key to increase the rewind or fast forward speed incrementally by 2X, 4X, 8X, 16X, or 32X with each press of the arrow key. To stop rewinding or fast-forwarding and resume playing the video at normal speed, press the Play button or press the spacebar.

When you click the Rewind or Fast Forward buttons, the video jumps back (or ahead) only a few frames. If you want to keep rewinding or fast-forwarding continuously, follow these steps:

1. Switch to window mode and choose Controls⇨Scan Forward (or Scan Backwards).

Your video continuously rewinds or fast-forwards.

2. Click the Play button on the Controller or press the spacebar to play the video at its normal speed.

Hold down the ⌘ key and tap the left or right arrow keys to move continually backwards or forwards. (You can let go of the ⌘ key.) Hold down the ⌘ key again and tap the arrow key again to increase the rewind or fast forward speed incrementally by 2X, 4X, 8X, 16X, or 32X with each press of the arrow key. To stop rewinding or fast-forwarding and play the video at normal speed, click the Play button or press the spacebar.

You can also drag the slider at the bottom of the Controller (in full screen mode) to rewind or fast-forward a video.

Viewing frames in steps and slow motion

If you want to study a particular part of a video, the DVD Player lets you view individual frames one at a time or view your video in slow motion. To view individual frames, follow these steps:

1. **In window mode, click the Step Frame button on the Controller.**

   Each time you click the Step Frame button, the video advances one frame.

2. **Click the Play button on the Controller, or press the spacebar to play the video at normal speed.**

Stepping through a video one frame at a time can be tedious, so an easier way to step through a video is in slow motion. To view your video in slow motion, follow these steps:

1. **Switch to window mode and then click the Slow Motion button on the Controller or choose Controls⇨Slow Motion.**

2. **Click the Play button on the Controller, or press the spacebar to play the video at normal speed.**

Skipping by chapters

Most DVD videos are divided into segments called *chapters,* which are usually listed somewhere on or inside the DVD case. If you want to view a favorite scene, just jump to the chapter that contains your favorite scene.

To move between chapters, choose one of the following:

+ In full screen mode, move your pointer to the top of the screen and then click the thumbnail image of the chapter you want to skip to.

+ Click the Previous Chapter or Next Chapter button on the Controller.

+ Press the left-arrow (previous) or right-arrow (next) key while the video is playing.

Placing bookmarks in a video

Sometimes your favorite parts of a movie don't correlate exactly to chapter sections on a DVD. In case you want to be able to jump to a specific part of a video, you can create a bookmark.

DVD Player saves your bookmarks on your Mac's hard drive, so if you pop the DVD out and back in again, your bookmarks are still preserved.

Creating a bookmark

To create a bookmark, follow these steps:

1. **Click the Pause button (or press the spacebar) to pause the video at the spot where you want to place a bookmark.**

2. **In full screen mode, move the pointer to the top of the screen to display the DVD Player menu bar and then press ⌘+= to open the new bookmark dialog, as shown in Figure 3-5.**

3. **Enter a descriptive name for your bookmark in the text field and then click Add.**

Figure 3-5: The bookmark dialog lets you choose a descriptive name for your bookmark.

If you select the Make Default Bookmark check box, you can jump to this bookmark in window mode by choosing Go⇨Default Bookmark.

Jumping to a bookmark

After you create at least one bookmark, you can jump to that bookmark by following these steps:

1. **In full screen mode, move the pointer to the top of the screen to display the DVD Player menu bar and then choose Go⇨Bookmarks.**

   A pop-up menu appears, listing all your saved bookmarks.

2. **Click the bookmark name you want to jump to.**

You can also click the bookmarks icon near the top of the window (between Chapters and Video Clips) and then click the bookmark you want to jump to.

Deleting a bookmark

After you create at least one bookmark, you can delete a bookmark by following these steps:

1. **In full screen mode, move the pointer to the top of the screen to display the DVD Player menu bar and then choose Window⟶Bookmarks.**

A Bookmarks window appears, as shown in Figure 3-6.

Figure 3-6: The Bookmarks window shows you all your bookmarks.

— Remove Bookmark

— Add Bookmark

2. **Click to select the bookmark you want to delete and then click the Remove bookmark button (minus sign).**

A dialog appears, asking whether you're sure that you want to delete your chosen bookmark.

3. **Click OK (or Cancel) and then click the Close button to close the Bookmarks window.**

Creating video clips

A bookmark can mark the spot where you want to start viewing a video, but you can also create a video clip with a start and an end that you determine.

That way, you can define a specific part of a video to watch again or show to others.

Creating a video clip

To create a video clip, follow these steps:

1. **Click the Pause button on the Controller (or press the spacebar) to pause the video at the point where you want to create the beginning of a video clip.**

2. **In full screen mode, move the pointer to the top of the screen to display the DVD Player menu bar and then choose Controls⇨New Video Clip (or press ⌘+–).**

   A New Video Clip dialog appears, as shown in Figure 3-7.

Set Start

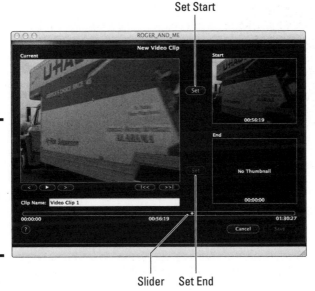

Figure 3-7: The New Video Clip dialog lets you choose a name for your video clip.

Slider   Set End

3. **Click the Clip Name text box and then type a descriptive name for your video clip.**

4. **Click the Set button to the left of the Start video box to define the starting point you chose in Step 1.**

5. **Drag the slider until you see the frame you want to use as the ending point of your video clip.**

6. **Click the Set button to the left of the End video box to define the ending point you chose in Step 6.**

The Start box displays the frame that starts the beginning of your video clip, and the End box displays the frame that defines the end of your video clip.

7. **Click the Save button to save your video clip and close the New Video Clip window.**

Your video clip isn't saved on your hard drive; the start and ending position information are saved. To view a saved video clip, the DVD you played to create the video clip must be inserted in your Mac's DVD drive.

Viewing a video clip

To view a video clip, be sure your DVD is back in your Mac and then follow these steps:

1. **In full screen mode, move the pointer to the top of the screen to display the DVD Player menu bar and then choose Go⇨Video Clips.**

A submenu appears, listing all the video clips you've created.

2. **Select the name of the video clip you want to watch (or click the Video Clips icon in the upper window and click the one you want).**

If you want to exit from your video clip, choose Go⇨Video Clips⇨Exit Clip Mode.

Deleting a video clip

To delete a video clip, follow these steps:

1. **In full screen mode, move the pointer to the top of the screen to display the DVD Player menu bar and then choose Window⇨Video Clips.**

A Video Clips window appears, as shown in Figure 3-8.

2. **Click to select the video clip you want to delete and then click the Remove Selected Video Clip button (minus sign).**

A dialog appears, asking whether you're sure that you want to delete your chosen video clip.

3. **Click OK (or Cancel) and then click the Close button of the Video Clips window.**

Figure 3-8:
The Video Clip window lets you delete any saved video clips.

└ Remove Selected Video Clip

└ Add Video Clip

Viewing closed captioning

Many DVDs (but not all) include closed captioning and subtitles. Closed captioning displays written dialogue onscreen in the same language that's being spoken — English, for example — whereas subtitles give you a choice of reading dialogue onscreen in a language other than what's being spoken, such as French and Spanish.

To turn on closed captioning, choose one of the following:

✦ In window mode, choose Features⇨Closed Captioning⇨Turn On.

✦ In full screen mode, click the Closed Captioning button on the Controller and choose Turn On Closed Captioning.

To view subtitles in different languages, choose one of the following:

✦ In window mode, choose Features⇨Subtitles and then choose a language, such as French or Spanish.

✦ In full screen mode, click the Closed Captioning button on the Controller and choose a language under the Subtitles category.

Viewing different camera angles

Some DVDs, such as those containing video of concerts, offer a choice of multiple camera angles. This gives you a chance to view a DVD and, at a certain spot, switch from looking at the drummer to the lead guitarist.

To switch to a different camera angle, choose one of the following methods:

+ In window mode, click the Angle button on the Controller and then choose an angle. (If the DVD you're watching doesn't offer optional angles, the video will continue playing without changing the way it looks.)

+ In window mode, choose Features➪Angle and then choose an angle.

+ In full screen mode, click the Streams/Closed Captioning button on the Controller and then choose an angle under the Angle category.

Choosing different audio tracks

Sometimes a DVD might offer multiple audio tracks, such as a default audio track and alternative audio tracks of foreign languages. To switch to different audio tracks, choose one of the following:

+ In window mode, click the Audio button on the Controller and then choose an audio track. (If the DVD you're watching has only one audio track, the audio will continue playing without changing how you're hearing the audio.)

+ In window mode, choose Features➪Audio and then choose an audio track.

+ In full screen mode, click the Streams/Closed Captioning button on the Controller and then choose an audio track under the Audio Streams category.

Customizing DVD Player

Normally, you can pop a DVD into your Mac and watch it play right away. However, you might want to take some time to customize DVD Player to change how it plays.

Parental controls

If you don't want your children watching certain DVDs, you can turn on DVD Player's parental controls. These parental controls are designed either to block certain types of DVDs from playing or to prevent certain objectionable scenes from appearing while allowing the rest of the movie to be seen.

Because of the extra expense involved in adding parental control features to a DVD, many DVDs don't support parental controls. If you turn on parental controls, it's entirely possible to watch an inappropriate DVD on your Mac if the DVD isn't programmed to implement the parental control features.

To turn on (or off) parental controls, follow these steps:

1. **In full screen mode, move the pointer to the top of the screen to display the DVD Player menu bar and then choose Features➪ Enable Parental Controls.**

   A dialog appears, asking for your password.

2. **Type your password and then click OK.**

To disable parental controls choose Features➪Disable Parental Controls.

Defining DVD Player preferences

DVD Player offers six categories for modifying how to play DVDs:

+ **General:** Defines how DVD Player behaves when running, such as whether to start in full screen mode.

+ **Disc Setup:** Allows you to change the language used to display audio, subtitles, and DVD menus.

+ **Full Screen:** Defines how other program windows behave when you watch a DVD video in full screen mode.

+ **Windows:** Defines how to display closed captioning in a window.

+ **Previously Viewed:** Defines how to handle a DVD that was ejected and inserted back into your Mac, such as whether to start playing the DVD at the beginning or at the last scene viewed before you ejected the DVD.

+ **High Definition:** Defines how to play high-definition DVDs that were burned to a DVD using the optional program DVD Studio Pro.

To change DVD Player's preferences settings, follow these steps:

1. **In full screen mode, move the pointer to the top of the screen to display the DVD Player menu bar and then choose DVD Player — Preferences.**

   A Preferences dialog appears, as shown in Figure 3-9.

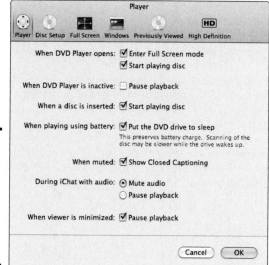

Figure 3-9:
Player
preferences
let you
customize
different
features of
DVD Player.

2. **Click an icon, such as Player or Full Screen, and change any options.**

   Some of these options let you mute sound in case you receive an iChat invitation or define colors for displaying closed captioning so it's easier to read on the screen. Feel free to experiment with different options to see which ones are most useful.

3. **Click OK (or Cancel) to close the DVD Player preferences dialog.**

Chapter 4: Using a Mac Remote to Control Programs and Using Front Row for Music, Movies, and Photos

In This Chapter

✔ **Using the Apple Remote**

✔ **Accessing Front Row**

✔ **Playing movies and videos**

✔ **Playing music and podcasts**

✔ **Viewing pictures**

*I*f you want to watch videos, play music, or browse through digital photographs, you could load QuickTime Player, iTunes, and iPhoto and search for the videos, audio files, or pictures you want to hear or see. However, this can be something of a juggling act, especially if you want to play music and browse through your photograph collection at the same time.

To give you another way to access your video, audio, and digital images, your Mac comes with a program called Front Row. The whole purpose of Front Row is to integrate the features of the QuickTime Player, iTunes, the DVD Player, and iPhoto to make it easy for you to access your media without having to load a bunch of programs.

Although new Macs don't come with an Apple Remote control, some earlier model Macs do, and you can also buy one for your Mac (www.apple.com) if your Mac has an Infrared port. With the Apple Remote control, you control Front Row from your easy chair. You can also use the Apple Remote to control many of your Mac's other programs, including Keynote, iTunes, and iPhoto.

If your Mac doesn't have a built-in Infrared port, you can buy an external Infrared receiver called Mira (twistedmelon.com/mira) that plugs into your Mac's USB port and gives it the same remote-control-friendly capabilities as a Mac with a built-in Infrared port.

Using the Apple Remote

The easiest way to control Front Row is by using the Apple Remote, although you can also control Front Row by using your Mac's keyboard (in case you don't have an Apple Remote). The Apple Remote provides the following controls, as shown in Figure 4-1:

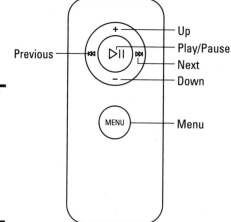

Figure 4-1:
The Apple Remote provides standard remote control features.

+ **Up:** Moves the highlighting up one option.

+ **Down:** Moves the highlighting down one option.

+ **Next:** Fast-forwards a media file or selects the next item.

+ **Previous:** Rewinds a media file or selects the previous item.

+ **Play/Pause:** Toggles between playing and pausing a media file. Also used to select a highlighted option.

+ **Menu:** Displays the main Front Row menu. Also used to go back to a previous menu.

For your Mac to pick up the Apple Remote's Infrared (IR) signal, your Mac must be in "line of sight" range when you point it at your Mac and press the remote control's buttons.

Although the Apple Remote can control the Front Row program, it can also control your Mac and other programs, such as Keynote, which can be handy if you want to control it from a distance when you're using your Mac to give a presentation.

Pairing an Apple Remote with a Mac

If you have two or more Mac computers, an iPod, or an Apple TV unit in the same room, your Apple Remote can accidentally control multiple devices instead of only the one you want to control. To make sure your Apple Remote works with only a particular Mac, you can pair the Apple Remote with that specific Mac.

To pair an Apple Remote to a specific Mac, follow these steps:

1. **Hold the Apple Remote 4 to 6 inches away from the Infrared (IR) port on the Mac you want to control and then press the Menu and Next buttons at the same time.**

2. **When a paired-remote icon appears a few seconds later, release the Menu and Next buttons.**

Your Apple Remote is now paired to work only with that specific Mac.

To unpair an Apple Remote from a specific Mac, follow these steps:

1. **Choose ⌘⟹System Preferences on the Mac that you want to unpair from an Apple Remote to open the System Preferences window.**

2. **Click the Security icon to open your Mac's Security preferences pane and then click the General tab (if it isn't already selected) to display the General options, as shown in Figure 4-2.**

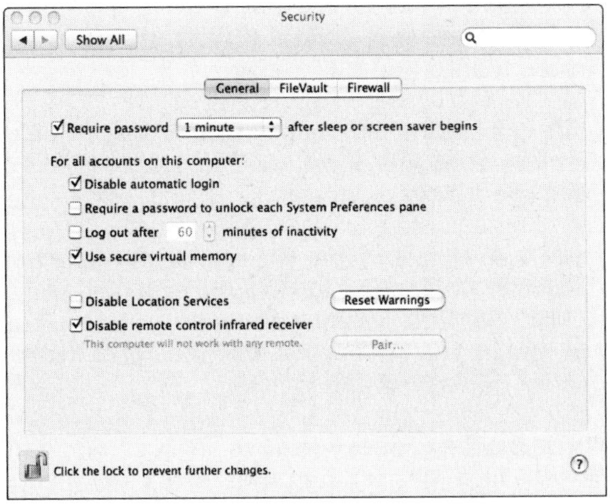

Figure 4-2:
The General
options of
the Security
preferences
pane let
you unpair
an Apple
Remote.

3. **Deselect the Disable Remote Control Infrared Receiver check box to let your Mac work with any Apple Remote.**

Making a Mac go to sleep

To make your Mac go to sleep by using the Apple Remote, hold down the Play/Pause button until a sleeping Apple Remote icon appears on the screen and then release the Play/Pause button.

To wake up a sleeping Mac with the Apple Remote, just tap any button on the Apple Remote.

Booting up a Mac

If you've divided your hard drive into partitions and installed two different operating systems (such as using Boot Camp to run Windows), you can use the Apple Remote to help you choose which partition and operating system to use by following these steps:

1. **Hold down the Menu button on the Apple Remote and turn on (or restart) your Mac.**

   The hard drive icons that appear list all the startup partitions you can choose.

2. **Press the Previous and Next buttons to select a hard drive and then press the Play/Pause button to start your Mac with the selected hard drive.**

Controlling applications

You can use the Apple Remote to control several popular programs, including Keynote, iTunes, iPhoto, and DVD Player.

The Apple Remote can control different programs, but it won't let you switch, open, or close programs. If you want to do this from a distance, use a wireless keyboard and mouse.

The Apple Remote is so simple to use, you can usually figure out how it works with a particular program by loading the program, pointing the Apple Remote at your Mac, and then pressing its couple of buttons to see what they do. Some programs you can control with the Apple Remote, and tips on how you can control these programs include

+ **Keynote:** Press the Play/Pause button to begin viewing a presentation. To view the next (or previous) slide, press the Next (or Previous) button. Press the Menu button to display thumbnails of your slides. Holding down the Menu button exits your presentation and returns you to the main Keynote screen.

+ **iTunes:** Choose a playlist (or choose your entire music collection) and then press the Play/Pause button to start listening to your selection. Press the Previous button to restart the playing track from the beginning. Press the Previous button twice in rapid succession to start playing the previous audio track. Jump to the next song by pressing the Next button. The Up and Down buttons control the volume level.

+ **iPhoto:** Select an album that contains the pictures you want to see and then press the Play/Pause button. To view the previous (or next) photograph, press the Previous (or Next) button. Exit from your slideshow by holding down the Menu button.

+ **DVD Player:** To start playing a DVD, press the Play/Pause button. Choose an option from the DVD menus by pressing the Previous and Next buttons and select an option by pressing the Play/Pause button. Use the Up and Down buttons to adjust the volume.

Using Front Row

You can easily control separate programs, such as iTunes and DVD Player, with the Apple Remote, but you must manually switch between your Mac's different media-playing programs to listen to music, watch a movie, or look at your photographs. To overcome the hassle of working with multiple programs, Front Row provides a simple, consistent user interface for accessing all your media files whether they're stored in your Music, Movies, or Pictures folder.

Before using Front Row, you need to store your favorite songs, podcasts, and music videos in iTunes; your favorite pictures in iPhoto; and your favorite movies in your Movies folder. Alternatively, you can have a CD or DVD in your Mac.

The really great thing about Front Row is that after you learn how to control its simple menus, choosing, viewing, or listening to your content works pretty much the same across the board — be it watching a home video or Hollywood blockbuster movie you rent with iTunes, enjoying a photo slideshow of your family vacation, or listening to a podcast you subscribe to or new album you ripped to your Mac's hard drive.

Starting Front Row

To start Front Row, choose one of the following:

+ Press the Menu button on the Apple Remote.

  If you have a program running that can accept commands from the Apple Remote, such as Keynote, pressing the Menu button might control that program instead of starting Front Row.

+ Double-click the Front Row icon in the Applications folder.

+ Press ⌘+Esc.

Each time you start Front Row, the Front Row menu appears, as shown in Figure 4-3.

**Book III
Chapter 4**

Using a Mac
Remote and Using
Front Row

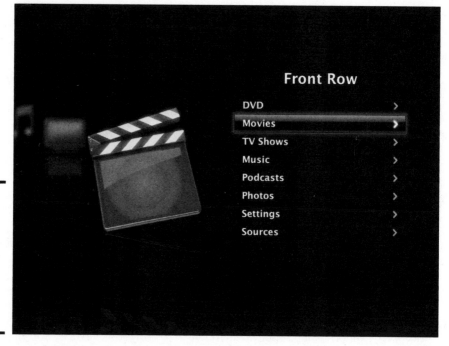

Figure 4-3:
The Front Row menu gives you access to movies, music, and pictures on your Mac.

The DVD option appears only if you have a DVD inserted in your Mac.

The following list highlights ways to navigate through the Front Row menu:

✦ **Highlighting an option in Front Row:** To highlight an option on the Front Row menu, press the Up and Down buttons on the Apple Remote or press the up- and down-arrow keys on the keyboard.

✦ **Selecting an option in Front Row:** After you highlight an option on a Front Row menu, you can select that option by pressing the Play/Pause button on the Apple Remote or by pressing Return on the keyboard.

You find out more about different options in Front Row later in this chapter.

✦ **Exiting a Front Row submenu:** To exit from a Front Row submenu and see the previous menu, press the Menu button on the Apple remote or press Esc on the keyboard.

If you keep pressing the Menu button on the Apple Remote or keep pressing Esc on the keyboard, you'll eventually exit from the main Front Row menu altogether and exit Front Row in the process.

In all of the following step-by-step sections, I assume you're already running Front Row and you know how to navigate the different screens and options with an Apple Remote control or your Mac's keyboard, as I describe in the previous "Using Front Row" section.

Playing Movies and Videos

Front Row can play DVDs or digital video files you copied to your Mac's hard drive, and music videos, TV shows, and full-length motion pictures that you purchased from the iTunes Store. The four Front Row menu options that allow you to watch movies and videos are

✦ **DVD:** Plays a movie from the DVD you insert into your Mac's DVD drive.

✦ **Movies:** Plays digital video files, such as digital video you shot with your camcorder and copied to your Mac's hard drive, or digital video you downloaded from the iTunes Store or from some other place on the Internet.

✦ **TV Shows:** Plays TV show segments and entire shows you downloaded from the iTunes Store or obtained from another source.

✦ **Music:** Plays music videos you downloaded from the iTunes Store or acquired from other sources.

Playing a DVD

To play a DVD in Front Row, insert a DVD into your Mac, and when the DVD menu appears, choose one of the following options:

✦ **Resume Playing:** Starts playing from the last part of the DVD that you watched before ejecting the disc or quitting Front Row.

✦ **Start from Beginning:** Starts playing the DVD from the very beginning, including the usual FBI notice warning about copyright infringement.

✦ **Eject Disk:** Ejects the DVD.

✦ **DVD Menu:** Displays the DVD's menus.

Playing movies, TV shows, music videos, and other videos

You can play video content with Front Row by selecting one of Front Row's main menu categories, scrolling through that category's list of content items, and then selecting the one you want to watch.

Here I describe the options and choices that appear when you select each of the different kinds of videos you can play with Front Row, and how to play them.

Movies

Selecting Movies displays the following choices, as shown in Figure 4-4:

+ **iTunes Top Movies:** Displays trailers of the most popular movies purchased from the iTunes Store.

+ **Theatrical Trailers:** Displays trailers of the latest movies currently in theaters.

+ **Movies Folder:** Displays digital video files stored in your Movies folder.

+ **iTunes Movies:** Lists movies you added to your Mac with iTunes that are stored in the Movies folder of your Mac's iTunes Music folder (typically in your Mac's Home folder⇨Music⇨iTunes⇨Movies).

If you select iTunes Top Movies or Theatrical Trailers, you see another menu listing your options, similar to the menu shown in Figure 4-5. If you select Movies Folder, you see a list of all digital video files stored in your Movies folder.

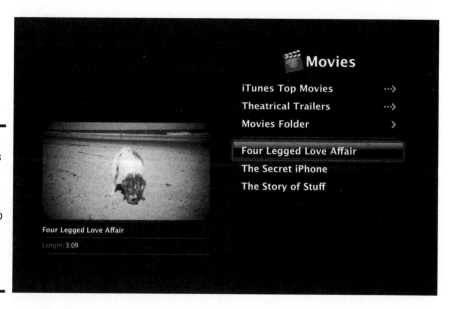

Figure 4-4: The Movies menu lets you view trailers or digital video files stored on your Mac's hard drive.

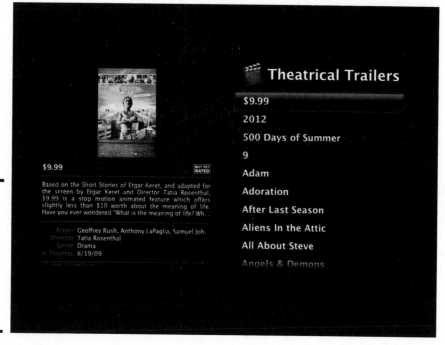

Figure 4-5:
The
Theatrical
Trailers
menu lets
you choose
a specific
trailer to
watch.

TV Shows

Selecting TV Shows displays a list of TV shows, as shown in Figure 4-6, that you can watch by selecting one with your Apple Remote or Mac keyboard.

The iTunes Top TV Episodes option lets you view teasers of the latest shows, and the Date and Show tabs let you rearrange how to view your list of shows, either by the date they were recorded or by their name. If you select iTunes Top TV Episodes, you have to select a specific episode to watch.

Music videos

Selecting Music displays all your Front Row music-listening options, including iTunes Top Music Videos or Music Videos, as shown in Figure 4-7. To watch a music video, select either iTunes Top Music Videos or Music Videos, scroll through the list of music videos, and then select the one you want to watch.

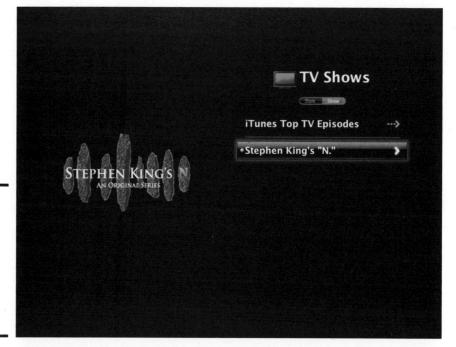

Figure 4-6:
The TV Shows menu lets you view TV show episodes stored on your Mac.

Figure 4-7:
The Music menu lets you view music videos stored on your Mac or view teasers of music videos on iTunes.

Playing Music and Other Audio

Front Row can play CDs, audio files downloaded from the iTunes Store, such as songs, podcasts, and audiobooks, and audio ripped from CDs or copied from another source to your Mac's hard disk. The following four Front Row menu options allow you to play audio files:

✦ **Audio CD:** Plays music stored on a CD.

✦ **Music:** Plays digital music files you downloaded from iTunes, or audio tracks you copied to your Mac's hard drive.

✦ **Podcasts:** Plays digital audio files that contain interviews, reported stories, or other journalistic special features, or recordings of radio shows.

✦ **Audiobooks:** Plays spoken audio recordings of books.

Playing an audio CD

To play an audio CD in Front Row, insert the audio CD into your Mac, select the Music option to display the Music menu and your audio CD, select your audio CD to display a list of songs (as shown in Figure 4-8), and then select the first song you want to hear.

Book III
Chapter 4

Using a Mac
Remote and Using
Front Row

Figure 4-8:
The Music menu displays the cover artwork and name of your audio CD.

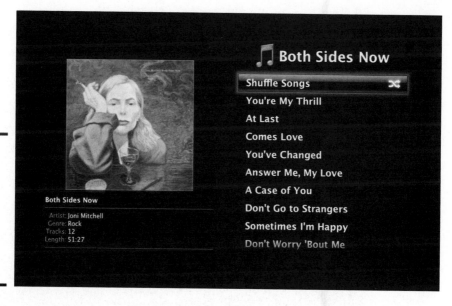

If you choose Shuffle Songs, Front Row randomly chooses the first song and starts playing it, and plays the remaining songs in random order.

Playing digital audio files

You can play audio content with Front Row by selecting one of Front Row's main menu audio categories, scrolling through that category's content items, and then selecting the audio item you want to listen to. Here I describe the options and choices that appear when you select to play either music or podcasts with Front Row, and how to play them.

Music

Choosing Music displays the Music menu, including the name of any CD you might have inserted in your Mac's drive, such as a music or audiobook CD, or songs in your iTunes library, as shown in Figure 4-9:

✦ **Shuffle Songs:** Randomly mixes all the songs stored in iTunes.

✦ **Music Videos:** Lists all music videos you have stored in iTunes.

✦ **Playlists:** Lists all the playlists you've created in iTunes.

✦ **Artists:** Lists all the recording artists' names.

✦ **Albums:** Lists all albums that have at least one song you've stored in iTunes.

✦ **Songs:** Lists all songs alphabetically that you've stored in iTunes.

✦ **Genres:** Lists all song genres, such as Country or Rock.

✦ **Composers:** Lists all composers so you can pick the songs they've written.

✦ **Audiobooks:** Lists all audiobooks stored in iTunes.

Figure 4-9: The Music menu displays a variety of ways to play your iTunes music.

Selecting any of these choices other than Shuffle Songs opens another menu listing the audio tracks contained within the category. Scroll through the lists to view your audio tracks and then select the one you want to listen to.

Podcasts

Podcasts are recorded interviews, radio shows, or other kinds of informational and episodic audio or video recordings that you can download with iTunes and listen to at your convenience.

Choosing Podcasts from the Front Row main menu (refer to Figure 4-3) displays the Podcasts menu. Scroll through your list of podcasts and then select the one you want to listen to or watch.

Playing audiobooks

Audiobooks are spoken recordings of books, which can be convenient to hear while you're exercising, dining, or commuting. After you download or rip an audiobook from a CD and store it in iTunes, you can hear the audiobook through Front Row by selecting Music Menu⇨Audiobook and then selecting the audiobook you want to listen to.

Understanding Apple TV

Front Row turns your Mac screen into an entertainment center, but what if you have a 52-inch high-definition TV in your living room? Rather than use Front Row to watch a DVD on your MacBook's comparatively miniscule 13-inch screen, you might want to play that DVD on your 52-inch big-screen TV. In that case, you can ignore your Mac completely and buy a separate DVD player connected to your big-screen TV. Or you can use your Mac's video-out port and a special adapter (that you may have to buy separately) to connect your Mac to one of your HDTV's video-in ports with a special video cable (that you also may have to buy separately). Or you can skip the separate DVD player and cable clutter and get Apple TV to control DVDs, downloaded movies, music and audio, and picture slideshows with your Apple Remote.

Apple TV is a component that physically connects to your TV with audio and video cables. After you connect Apple TV to your TV screen, Apple TV wirelessly (or through cables if you prefer) connects to your Mac (or PC) to transfer movies, TV shows, music, and photos from your computer to the Apple TV unit. Apple TV then broadcasts those media on your big-screen TV and plays the sound through your TV's speakers or a surround-sound system if you have one connected to your home entertainment system. Essentially, Apple TV acts like a wired or wireless connection between your Mac and your big-screen TV for playing movies, TV show episodes, and music that you downloaded from iTunes or copied to your Mac's hard drive from CDs, DVDs, and other sources, such as your digital camera or camcorder.

Viewing Pictures

Front Row can display an ongoing slideshow of pictures you saved on your Mac's hard drive with iPhoto. Viewing your iPhoto library with Front Row can be a convenient way to show photo albums during a party or family gathering.

To view your iPhoto pictures in Front Row, select the Photos from the Front Row main menu (refer to Figure 4-3) and then select an album, such as Photos or Last 12 Months, to watch the slideshow.

Chapter 5: Having Fun with a Mac

In This Chapter

✔ **Learning a foreign language**

✔ **Learning to play music**

✔ **Teaching yourself to type**

✔ **Expanding your mind**

✔ **Managing your hobby**

✔ **Playing video games**

Work, work, work. At the end of the day, why not fire up your Mac and escape from the workaday world with a favorite video game? Your Mac is great for helping you get stuff done — and it's equally talented at showing you a good time without breaking any laws to do it. There are loads of ways you can have fun with your Mac. You can start with several free games that can turn your Mac into a chess, checkers, or tic-tac-toe opponent. If you get tired of these games, you can always buy more from a vast array of video games to choose from.

Games can double as effective learning tools, too. With the right programs, you can turn your Mac into an inspiring math, grammar, or science tutor, or a motivating foreign language or music teacher. Or, rather than pick up a new skill, you can use your Mac to help with your current hobbies. Although Macs might not help you skydive or do the Mambo, your Mac can run unique programs covering everything from needlepoint to gardening to collecting and trading baseball cards. Read on to explore some ideas for enjoying your free time (or ways to take a break and goof off at work when the boss isn't looking).

¿No Hablas Español? Then Get Crackin'!

Perhaps you've always wanted to learn another language but don't have the time to take a class. Good news: With your Mac, you can learn a new language on your own schedule without having to step foot outside your own front door.

The best way to learn any foreign language is to immerse yourself in listening, speaking, and reading it. Your Mac can't literally put you on the streets of, say, Osaka, Japan, but it can act as a friendly guide and tutor while exposing you to the voices of native speakers. You can even speak into your Mac's built-in microphone and have your pronunciation analyzed (a great way to hone your accent before anyone hears you and questions which language you're trying to speak). Whether you're learning a foreign language in school, for fun, or for business, you can use programs on your Mac to practice speaking, reading, and writing a foreign language.

For free language lessons, visit the BBC site at `www.bbc.co.uk/languages` to find introductory vocabulary lessons, pronunciation audio files, and videos in a variety of languages. (See Figure 5-1.) These introductory lessons won't make you fluent in a new language, but they can teach you the basics.

Another useful (and free) language Web site is UniLang (`http://home.unilang.org`), which is a community-run site that provides free resources to anyone interested in learning practically any language, including Lithuanian, Afrikaans, and Gaelic. Some of its many language resources include children's stories, phrasebooks, and vocabulary lists so that you can make your own flash cards.

Figure 5-1:
The BBC Web site offers a variety of free video and audio files to teach different languages.

Free language lessons can get you started, but for more advanced language lessons, you'll want to consider buying a language course. Here are some choices, for your consideration:

✦ **Berlitz (www.berlitzbooks.com):** Provides audio courses focused on helping travelers master useful phrases that they'll likely need when they travel overseas, such as "May we have the check, please?" or "Do you speak Portuguese?"

✦ **Pimsleur (www.pimsleurapproach.com):** Named after its creator, Dr. Paul Pimsleur, the Pimsleur method focuses on teaching foreign languages primarily by listening to the most commonly used words in each language. Besides emphasizing listening, the Pimsleur method also encourages responding by gradually piecing together the grammar of a language through constant repetition and practice. Pimsleur's principle is that anyone can learn a new language in the same way that infants learn to speak, which is by listening and then attempting to speak back to their parents (until they're old enough to start arguing with their parents).

✦ **Transparent Language (www.transparent.com):** Offers free language articles (so that you can practice reading), free language games, and free introductory language lessons to teach you how to recognize and speak basic vocabulary so you can communicate with people in other countries without resorting to hand signals.

✦ **Rosetta Stone (www.rosettastone.com):** One of the most acclaimed language courses, Rosetta Stone emphasizes listening, reading, writing, and speaking another language. By focusing on four different elements of learning any language, Rosetta Stone is the closest you can get to immersing yourself in another country. Figure 5-2 shows different phrases on the screen that you can choose in response to hearing a question in a foreign language. By turning learning into a game, you can pick up a new language while having fun in the process.

✦ **Unforgettable Languages (www.unforgettablelanguages.com):** If you have trouble remembering foreign words, you might try this course, which teaches foreign words by relating them to another word. For example, to help you remember the Mandarin word for tree (*shu*, pronounced like "shoe"), you're told to think of a shoe in a tree. By using such vivid word associations, this course can make memorizing vocabulary words fun.

✦ **Power-Glide (www.power-glide.com):** These courses make learning a new language interactive through videos, stories, and games. By reinforcing language concepts in multiple ways, Power-Glide helps make learning and remembering a foreign language as effortless as possible.

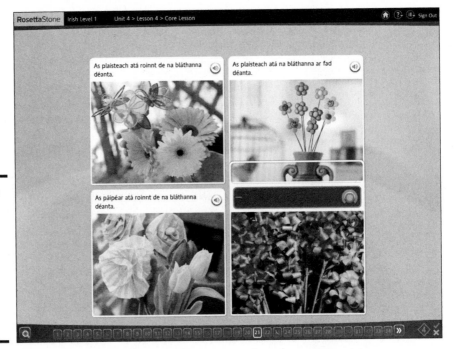

Figure 5-2: Rosetta Stone immerses you into a new language through various exercises.

Tooting Your Own Horn

Learning to play an instrument is much like learning a foreign language. You can't just read about it; you have to hear and try it yourself, listening and correcting as you go along. The good news is that with the right program you can turn your Mac into an interactive music teacher.

To learn how to read music and chords, check out Practica Musica (www.ars-nova.com), shown in Figure 5-3, which can help train your ear to recognize different notes while practicing writing your own music at the same time.

Figure 5-3: Practica Musica teaches how to read music "by ear."

After you understand how music works and how to read it, you might be anxious to start making music of your own. If you want to learn to play the guitar, buy GuitarVision (`www2.guitarvision.com`), which works with iTunes to help you learn the exact chords, notes, and finger positioning to play many of your favorite songs stored in iTunes.

Or, you might try learning to tickle the ivories with PianoWizard (`www.pianowizard.com`), which uses video games to help you play your favorite songs, in genres from classical to pop. If you're a teenager, you can play and hear your favorite music while annoying your parents at the same time.

If you're into the idea of playing more than one instrument as a one-man- or one-woman-band, you'll want to check out the guitar, drums, piano, or violin tutorial programs for your Mac produced by eMedia (`www.emediamusic.com`).

If you don't want to spend any money, why not mosey on over to the musically inclined GarageBand program that comes with your Mac or can be purchased separately as part of Apple's iLife creative suite of programs?

With GarageBand, you can learn to play piano and guitar, record your tunes, and mix them to produce the perfect song. Think of GarageBand as your Mac's all-in-one production studio, music teacher, and recording engineer that's ready, willing, and able to help you write and record your music.

To learn more about using GarageBand to express yourself, musically speaking, check out Book V, Chapter 4.

Getting Touchy-Feely with Your Keyboard

No more poking along on the computer keyboard with your index fingers. You *know* people are looking at you funny. Even your Jack Russell Terrier types better than you do. To finally start getting the hang of your keyboard, check out one of the most popular typing tutorials, Mavis Beacon Teaches Typing (available from `www.broderbund.com`), which has been used in schools and employment agencies for years. This program combines typing lessons with arcade games to make learning fun. (Now if bosses would only use arcade games to make working in an office fun, we'd be all set.)

Another popular typing program is Ten Thumbs Typing Tutorial (`www.tenthumbstypingtutor.com`), shown in Figure 5-4. In addition to providing the usual drills and games to teach typing, the program also works with iTunes by letting you type lyrics from your favorite songs. For greater flexibility, practice typing lyrics from different types of songs, or else if you only type lyrics from rap music, you might get really good at typing four-letter words and nothing else.

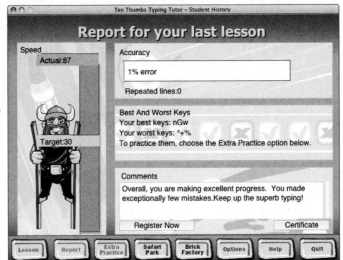

Figure 5-4:
Ten Thumbs
Typing
Tutorial
uses
colorful
graphics to
make typing
fun.

For a free typing tutorial, grab a copy of Letter Invaders (www.fooledya. com/games/letters), which is based on the ancient arcade game Space Invaders. With this typing tutorial, letters fall from above, and you have to type them correctly to destroy them. You can even learn something about programming while you're becoming a real typist by downloading the source code so that you can see exactly how the program works. (You can even modify and improve it yourself, if you already know what you're doing.)

Taking Your Grey Matter to the Gym

The brain is like a muscle. (The only difference is that it's not as easy for guys to attract women on the beach by showing off their brains.) The more you use it, the stronger it gets, so to help keep your brain strong, visit Custom Solutions of Maryland (www.customsolutionsofmaryland. 50megs.com) and browse through the site's various free programs, such as:

✦ **Auto Flash:** Create and display flash cards for any subject.

✦ **Brain Tease:** Unravel brainteasers to keep your mind sharp and active.

✦ **eBook Library:** Read electronic books to practice and learn speed-reading.

✦ **Math Practice:** Play simple games with algebra and Roman numerals.

✦ **Mimic:** Practice memory skills using music.

✦ **SAT Vocab Prep:** Learn new words to increase your vocabulary.

✦ **Speak N Spell:** Practice your spelling.

✦ **TickerType:** Learn to type.

To find all sorts of educational software for you or your children, go shopping on the Web at Academic Superstore (www.academicsuperstore.com). With so many different ways to keep yourself amused while learning, you'll never have an excuse for not learning something new today.

Playing Hooky with Your Hobby

Most folks have a hobby that they'd rather be doing instead of work. Although hobbies can be fun, they often have tedious or repetitive actions that can suck up your time and make you feel like you're at a job. To keep such necessary, mind-numbing actions from stopping you from fully enjoying your hobby, load the right program and let your Mac help you speed up and simplify your hobby more than ever.

If you enjoy scrapbooking, that is, combining photographs, memorabilia, and journaling into a book to keep track of your memories, you might want to digitize the whole process. Grab your favorite digital photographs and place them in a digital scrapbook using iScrapbook 2 (available at www.chronosnet.com) or iRemember (www.macscrapbook.com). Best of all, both programs can import pictures from iPhoto so you can take advantage of all the photos you've gathered and organized into your existing iPhoto photo library.

Not only can digital scrapbooks store your memories, but also they allow you to share them with others in ways that physical scrapbooks cannot. You can e-mail them or print them after embellishing them with fancy borders and graphics.

Naturally, the people who might want to share your memories are your relatives. To help you keep track of your relatives and your family tree, you can use MacFamilyTree 5 (available at www.onlymac.de), Family 2.3 (www.saltatory.com), or Reunion 9 (http://leisterpro.com). By making it easy to track family names, photographs, birthdates, and locations, you can track your relatives wherever they go (and avoid them if necessary).

If you enjoy working with needlepoint, you might want to create your own designs with Stitch Painter (www.cochenille.com). Coin collectors might want to grab a copy of Numismatist's Notebook (available at www.tabberer.com/sandyknoll), and comic book collectors might want a copy of ComicBookLover (www.bitcartel.com). If you're the outdoor type who enjoys gardening, try using PlanGarden (www.plangarden.com) to choose the best plants for your area.

Want to design your dream house or need to remodel your current house? You can draw your own plans by using Interiors (www.microspot.com). To help pay for your new house or remodeling project, try Lotto Sorcerer (www.satoripublishing.com/LS) to help you win your state's lottery. Lotto Sorcerer predicts the numbers most likely to appear based on it being impossible to create truly random numbers, so some numbers will always have a slightly greater chance of being picked than others.

No matter what your hobby or interests are, likely a program can help you enjoy your hobby even more.

Bring On the Games!

Historians might someday chronicle the computer's role in increasing business productivity and communication, but everyone really knows that the computer's greatest contribution to society has been to help people play games. Four popular types of video games are

+ Computerized versions of traditional board games like chess and backgammon

+ Strategy games that emphasize planning and thinking

+ Arcade games that emphasize eye-hand coordination

+ Multiplayer, online virtual worlds

Some games combine multiple elements, such as a multiplayer game that emphasizes arcade-style play, or a multiplayer game that lets people play bridge or poker online.

Some video games can be educational, such as teaching you how to manage a business, whereas other video games can be nostalgic, such as ancient arcade video games like Pac-Man or Space Invaders. Still other video games can provide an emotional outlet so you can blast away aliens, terrorists, and other fictional computer-generated characters to vent your frustration on them rather than on a living creature within your reach. If you just want to play video games, you can turn your Mac into a great entertainment center.

Playing strategically

Strategy games are typically based on their complicated board game counterparts. Unlike arcade-style games where reflexes determine your success, strategy games rely on planning and thinking to win. Aspyr (www.aspyr. com) provides several popular strategy games.

Aspyr also sells Sid Meier's Civilization game, which lets you control an entire civilization. Using trade, politics, and outright war, you can expand your civilization at the expense of others and try to take over the world without having to be elected to political office to do it.

If you ever dreamed about running your own TV station, play TV Station Manager (available from Winter Wolves at www.winterwolves.com), where you control the programming of an independent TV station and do whatever you can to boost ratings. If you think there's too much garbage on TV these days, see whether you can make your TV station profitable by offering quality entertainment. Like most real TV stations, you might find that trashy TV shows really are more profitable in the long run.

The same company, Winter Wolves, also provides Soccer Manager and Boxing Manager. In Soccer Manager, you manage a soccer team and choose different players to build the most successful soccer team. In Boxing Manager, you pick a boxer and manage him through fights. Manage your boxer effectively, and he can work his way up to the championship. Manage him poorly, and he'll wind up flat on his back on the canvas.

Sports Interactive Games (www.sigames.com) offers Out of the Park Baseball Manager and NHL Eastside Hockey Manager, where you can pretend to manage a professional sports team and guide them to victory. See if you can win a baseball championship without any of your players relying on banned performance-enhancing drugs. Take your hockey team to the top while trying to keep the front teeth of all your players intact. The challenges can be endless.

One popular series of strategy games is the Tycoon series, such as Roller Coaster Tycoon (where you design and manage an amusement park) and Zoo Tycoon (where you design and manage a zoo). These Tycoon games let you fantasize about how you could make your local zoo or amusement park more exciting and profitable if only given the chance. Add a death-defying roller coaster to your amusement park and see how sales of milkshakes from a nearby concession stand might go down. Add an exotic animal to your zoo and see how much additional revenue you can generate without exploiting the animal in the process.

If the idea of being a manager sounds too tame for you, consider destroying entire civilizations at the touch of a button with DefCon (www.ambrosiasw.com), a game in which you play the role of a general in control of a nuclear arsenal. (See Figure 5-5.) Launch nuclear missiles at your enemies and see how much faster you can destroy the planet by using atomic weapons rather than diplomacy.

In case you'd rather save the planet than destroy it (which pretty much rules out any chance you might have for becoming a dictator), play Global Warning (available at www.midoritech.com). By playing the game, you can see how your actions can help save the planet both in the make-believe world inside your Mac and in the real world outside your window.

Rather than play a strategy game that you've never heard of, you might prefer playing a game that you already know how to play. If you like Stratego, buy WebStratego (www.metaforge.net), which lets you play against people from all over the world by way of the World Wide Web. If you like playing Risk, try taking over the world with a computer version called Lux Delux (http://sillysoft.net).

**Book III
Chapter 5**

**Having Fun
with a Mac**

Figure 5-5:
DefCon lets you conquer the world by deploying thermo-nuclear weapons.

One of the more unique strategy games is Bridge Construction Set (www. garagegames.com), where you attempt to design a bridge that can hold up a train. Design the bridge correctly, and the train crosses safely. Design the bridge poorly, and the train crashes into the river below. By teaching you how to build a bridge, this game indirectly teaches physics at the same time.

Video game accessories

You can play most games by using the keyboard and the mouse. However, arcade-style video games can be much clumsier to play. Trying to fly an F-16 jet fighter simulator with the keyboard can seem unnatural and confusing, so that's why many companies sell special game-playing accessories, such as joysticks, steering wheels, and even special mice designed to put more controls at your fingertips than a traditional mouse.

If you want to play a flight simulator or a first-person shooter game, you'll probably want a joystick. If you want to play a racing simulator, you'll probably want a steering wheel and pedals. If playing realistic games is important

to you and you're in the market for a new Mac, consider buying Apple's top-of-the line Mac Pro desktop, which boasts the most powerful graphics processor available among Apple's lineup of Mac computer models.

Some popular companies that make game-playing accessories include TrustMaster (www.thrustmaster.com), CH Products (www.chproducts.com), and Logitech (www.logitech.com). With the right joystick or steering wheel, you can immerse yourself in your favorite driving or flying simulation game and leave the real world behind (until, of course, someone from the real world reminds you to pay your electricity bill).

Head on down to the arcade Long before video games appeared in coin-operated arcades, people used to play pinball. Although pinball machines have faded into obscurity, that doesn't mean you can't still play them on your Mac. (It's just that tilting your Mac won't help boost your score any.)

For an electronic version of a pinball game, visit LittleWing Pinball (www.littlewingpinball.com). These pinball games let you shake, rattle and roll a virtual pinball machine to achieve the ultimate title of a self-proclaimed Pinball Wizard.

Pinball machines may be ancient history for today's generation of gamers. Instead, they might prefer arcade games that originated with Pong, Space Invaders, Asteroids, and Pac-Man. The goal of these games was simple: Use your reflexes to stay alive as long as possible in order to rack up the highest score possible.

For a free Pac-Man clone, download a copy of Pac the Man X (www.mcsebi.com). If you remember playing Frogger, trying to navigate a frog across a busy highway without being squished, you can relive your childhood by playing the Christmas Super Frog (www.koingosw.com), which is like Frogger but with a Christmas theme. If you remember trying to save cities from nuclear missiles with Missile Command, you can download a free Missile Command clone (http://iskub.sippan.se/missile) and see whether you still have what it takes to protect the world from a nuclear Armageddon.

Growing beyond the primitive two-dimensional graphics of the early arcade games, the latest computer arcade games employ ultra-sharp and often life-like three-dimensional graphics for use in first-person shooter games and sports simulations.

First-person shooter games typically give you the view of a soldier running through a maze or rough terrain, blasting away targets and trying to avoid being shot in return. For a free first-person shooter game, grab a copy of AssaultCube (http://assault.cubers.net), which lets you play with others to roam around buildings and gun each other down (virtually speaking, of course).

For a contemporary first-person shooter game, check out the highly decorated Call of Duty 4: Modern Warfare (www.aspyr.com), which plunges you into the midst of intense, up-to-the-minute action to see whether you can survive. If you'd rather play a flight simulator and dogfight other planes, buy a copy of OSX Skyfighters 1945 (www.donsgames.com) and strap yourself into the virtual cockpit of a P-51, Fw-190, Hellcat, or Japanese Zero and see if you can become an ace.

If the idea of killing even virtual enemies makes you squeamish, try to win a battle of wits and skill by playing a sports simulation game instead. Take a swing at GL Golf (`http://nuclearnova.com`) to practice your putting and golf strokes on days it's raining outside when hitting the real golf course isn't in the cards. If playing 18 holes sounds too exhausting, conquer a miniature golf course by playing Wacky Mini Golf (`www.danlabgames.com`), complete with those pesky windmills blocking the putting green. If you think that your game is good enough to play with the pros, take on Tiger Woods in Tiger Woods PGA Tour (`www.aspyr.com`) and see whether your golf skills match up with the masters.

In case golf doesn't get your adrenaline pumping, jump into a race car and run your opponents off the track in Jammin' Racer (`www.danlabgames.com`). For a more realistic racing simulation, grab a free copy of VDrift (`http://vdrift.net`), which lets you simulate racing on tracks in Detroit, Le Mans, Monaco, and Barcelona, as shown in Figure 5-6. If the idea of playing a motocross simulation gets your motor revving, download a free copy of X-Moto (`http://xmoto.sourceforge.net`) and take out your road rage on animated opponents.

Figure 5-6: VDrift lets you drive a race car through the world's toughest courses.

To play football without being whupped on the playing field, try PlayMaker Football (`http://playmaker.com`). To play table tennis and test your meanest serve against virtual opponents, try Table Tennis Pro (`www.grassgames.com`). For a snowboarding simulation, check out Slope Rider (`www.monteboyd.com`) — but if you'd rather control a penguin sliding down a snow-covered slope, try the free Tux Racer (`http://tuxracer.sourceforge.net`) game instead.

Writing your own games

If you enjoy playing games, perhaps you dream of creating your own games. Although writing your own game might seem scary, you can get a lot of help by buying various tools to make game creation easier.

To create simple games, check out the GameMaker (`http://www.macgame creator.com`), which allows you to create adventure games with graphics, buttons, and text.

To create simple 2D graphics, such as card games or board games, consider purchasing Revolution Media (`www.runrev.com`). If you want to develop more sophisticated games, you'll have to learn a programming language, such as C++.

Although you can create an entire game from scratch by using any programming language, such as C++, even the professionals don't do that. To speed up game development, the professionals use a game engine, which contains programming code modules for animating objects on the screen. By using a game engine, programmers can focus on writing the commands to make their game work rather than spending time reinventing the wheel when it comes to displaying and manipulating graphics on the screen.

Some popular game engines include the Torque Game Engine (`www.garagegames. com`), Unity Game Engine (`www.unity3d. com`), and the PTK Game Engine (`http:// www.phelios.com/ptk`). By combining these game engines with the C++ programming language, you can create games the same way professional developers do.

No matter what type of game you want, you can typically find one that runs on your Mac. If you want to play a game that runs only on Windows, install a copy of Windows on your Mac by using Boot Camp (see Book VII, Chapter 3) and turn your Mac into a game-playing PC. By adding the capability to play games designed for Windows, you instantly open your Mac to a wider variety of available games — which means your only limitation is finding the time to play all the games you want.

Playing multiplayer, online role-playing games

After a while, playing even the most exciting game by yourself can get boring, which is why many people prefer playing games online and competing against others. Such an online experience can give people a sense of community, even if you never actually meet in person because the people you're playing with live halfway around the world. One of the most popular online role-playing games is the World of Warcraft (`www.worldof warcraft.com`), a fantasy virtual world that lets you create an animated character called an *avatar* and roam around bartering, negotiating, and attacking other players or mythical creatures with a sword or a magic spell. With tens of millions of players worldwide, no session of World of Warcraft is ever the same.

Although some people like fantasy worlds, others prefer science fiction scenarios. If you'd rather use a laser blaster than a sword to conquer universes instead of castles, consider EVE Online (www.eve-online.com). Play EVE Online and you can roam through outer space, shoot at spaceships, trade with other planets, and negotiate with aliens (who might not be any more bizarre than the people you normally associate with at work). Who knows, you just may wind up taking over a galaxy while mere mortals on this planet remain ignorant of your true accomplishments and abilities.

If battling for victory in a virtual world of fantasy or science fiction doesn't appeal to you, you might prefer Second Life (www.secondlife.com), which puts you inside a virtual world similar to the real world. The only difference is that inside this virtual world, you can experiment with different ways of living that you might never do in real life, like playing different genders or acting aggressive (if you're normally shy) or making yourself ugly (if you're normally attractive). Second Life also offers a special Teen Life area so teenagers can explore the virtual world within a safe environment with other teenagers. (Now you just have to worry about the danger of meeting other teenagers.) In both Second Life and Teen Life, you create a character (an avatar) and roam around interacting with others. You can buy virtual land or outfits, start and operate a business, fly in the air over gorgeously rendered terrain and seascapes, or just meet new people without the fear of real-life rejection.

To stay up-to-date on all the latest Mac games, news, reviews and roundups, pay a visit to these two Web sites dedicated to Mac games:

✦ Mac Games and More (www.macgamesandmore.com)

✦ Inside Mac Games (www.insidemacgames.com)

With so many games available for your Mac, you need never be bored again.

Book IV

Online Endeavors and Safety

The 5th Wave   By Rich Tennant

"My spam filter checks the recipient address, http links, and any writing that panders to postmodern English romanticism with conceits to 20th-century graphic narrative."

Contents at a Glance

Chapter 1: Connecting to the Internet and Browsing the Web

In This Chapter

✔ Setting up an Internet connection

✔ Browsing Web sites

✔ Searching a Web page

✔ Saving Web pages

✔ Viewing and playing multimedia files

✔ Downloading files

You can use a computer all by itself, but to get the most out of your Mac, you need an Internet connection. The Internet can also open a whole new world for you by letting you browse and read news on the Web, watch movies, listen to radio stations, find and download new applications, update versions of your existing programs, and shop online. For most people, an Internet connection is no longer an option but a necessity.

Setting Up an Internet Connection

From a technical point of view, to connect to the Internet, your Mac must connect to another computer, run by a company called an Internet Service Provider (ISP); it's through the ISP that your Mac actually connects to the Internet.

To connect your Mac to an ISP, you have three options:

✦ Ethernet (also called high-speed broadband)

✦ Wireless (also called WiFi high-speed broadband)

✦ Dialup access

Ethernet connection

A broadband Ethernet connection is the fastest way to connect to the Internet. The two most common broadband connections are through cable modems or DSL (Digital Subscriber Line) modems.

Your Mac can connect to a cable modem or DSL modem with an Ethernet cable, which plugs into the Ethernet port with a plug that looks like a wider version of a telephone plug. After you connect your Mac to a cable or DSL modem, you can usually start using the Internet right away.

Your Mac can also connect to your broadband modem wirelessly if the model you buy (or rent from your cable or phone provider) has a built-in WiFi radio, which your Mac's built-in AirPort WiFi feature can access.

When you connect your Mac to a broadband modem using your Mac's Ethernet port, your Mac can recognize the Internet connection right away through the Dynamic Host Configuration Protocol (DHCP). DHCP means that your Mac automatically figures out the proper settings to connect to the Internet without you having to type a bunch of cryptic numbers and fiddle with confusing technical standards.

For more information about setting up a network and sharing a single Internet connection with multiple computers, see Book VIII, Chapter 1.

Wireless (Wi-Fi) access

Wireless broadband access is popular because it allows you to connect to the Internet without stringing cables across the room to trip over. Every new and recent Mac comes with a built-in wireless capability called AirPort, but if your older Mac doesn't have this, you can buy a special wireless receiver that plugs into your Mac so that it can connect to your home's WiFi network.

If your Mac is so old that it doesn't have a built-in wireless receiver, check out the AfterTheMac wireless adapter (www.afterthemac.com) that plugs into a USB port.

After you have wireless access capability in your Mac, you need to connect to a wireless network in your home, or out of the house at another location if you're using a MacBook that you can take wherever you go. Public libraries and many coffee houses offer free wireless Internet access. You can set up your own wireless network at home or work by using a wireless router (which I discuss next) that lets several computers and other WiFi-cable gadgets (like video game consoles and iPhones) share a single Internet connection.

Choosing a wireless router

A *wireless router* connects to your cable or DSL modem and broadcasts radio signals to connect your Mac wirelessly to the Internet. Some cable and DSL modems come with built-in WiFi transmitters, which means one device does the job of two if you choose to use a separate WiFi router to connect to your cable or DSL modem.

Apple sells three wireless router models:

✦ **AirPort Express:** Small and ideal for small homes, apartments, and dorm rooms.

✦ **AirPort Extreme:** Ideal for homes; 4 Ethernet ports to connect to Macs in the same room with an Ethernet cable; a built-in USB port lets you connect a printer or hard drive to share wirelessly with other people in your house or workplace.

✦ **Time Capsule:** Same features as AirPort Extreme but also includes a built-in hard drive for wirelessly backing up one or more Macs that connect to it.

Apple's WiFi routers are nice, but you can buy any brand of wireless router to connect to your DSL or cable modem and create a home WiFi network. The brand name of your wireless router is less important than the speed offered by the router, which is determined by the wireless standard the router uses. A *wireless standard* simply defines the wireless signal used to connect to the Internet. Table 1-1 lists the different wireless standards.

Table 1-1   Wireless Standards and Speeds of Different Routers

Wireless Standard	Speed	Indoor Range
802.11a	Up to 54 Mbps	30 meters (98 feet)
802.11b	Up to 11 Mbps	35 meters (114 feet)
802.11g	Up to 54 Mbps	35 meters (114 feet)
802.11n	Up to 248 Mbps	70 meters (229 feet)

The upload/download speed of wireless standards is measured in megabits per second (Mbps) although this maximum speed is rarely achieved in normal use. The speed and range of a wireless Internet connection also degrade with distance or if obstacles, such as walls or heavy furniture, stand between the WiFi router and your Mac.

To connect to a wireless network, you need to make sure your router and your Mac's built-in wireless radio (or an external one you buy and connect to your Mac) use the same wireless standard. All new and recent Macs connect to WiFi routers that use one or up to all four types of the wireless network standards.

REMEMBER

The 802.11g wireless standard is the most popular wireless standard, but the newer 802.11n standard is becoming more popular because it offers greater range and higher speeds. Most routers are compatible with multiple standards, such as 802.11a, 802.11b, and 802.11g. The newer routers also include compatibility with the 802.11n standard.

Connecting to a WiFi network

If your Mac has wireless capability, you can connect to a wireless network (such as at a cafe or a WiFi network in your home) by following these steps:

1. **Click the AirPort icon in the right corner of the menu bar to open a pull-down menu displaying a list of any WiFi networks within range of your Mac and then select the network name you want to connect to, as shown in Figure 1-1.**

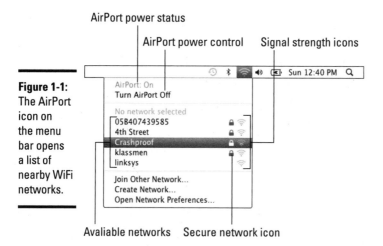

AirPort power status

AirPort power control   Signal strength icons

Figure 1-1:
The AirPort icon on the menu bar opens a list of nearby WiFi networks.

Avaliable networks   Secure network icon

Note: If you see AirPort: Off AirPort when you click the AirPort icon on the menu bar, choose Turn AirPort On and then click the AirPort menu icon again to display a list of any nearby wireless networks (refer to Figure 1-1).

If you don't see the AirPort icon on the menu bar, click and choose System Preferences, click the Network icon, and then click the Show AirPort Status in Menu Bar check box.

The signal strength icon next to a WiFi network name shows how strongly you're receiving that network router's wireless signal (stronger signal strength means faster, more reliable connections).

A lock icon to the left of the network's signal strength indicates a *secured* (also known as *encrypted*) wireless network that is protected by a password. You must know what password to enter when prompted if you try to connect to a secured network.

2. **If a dialog appears indicating the network you selected requires a password to connect to it, as shown in Figure 1-2, type the password and then click OK.**

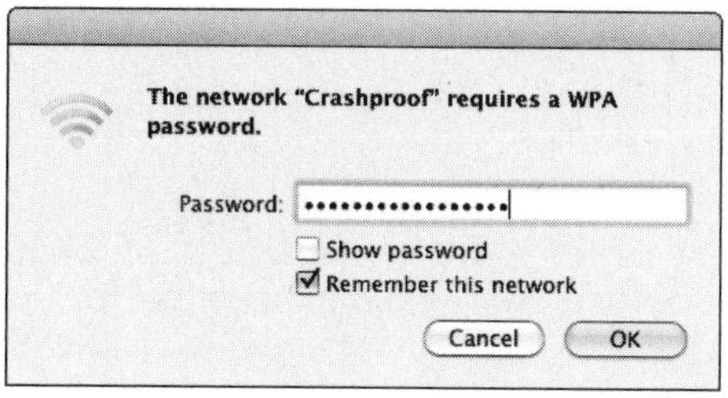

Figure 1-2:
Secure WiFi
networks
require a
password to
connect to
them.

> The network "Crashproof" requires a WPA password.
>
> Password: ●●●●●●●●●●●●●●●
>
> ☐ Show password
> ☑ Remember this network
>
> (Cancel) (OK)

3. **(Optional) Check the following options on the password dialog prompt if you want to:**

    • *Show Password:* Displays actual characters you type rather than dots that hide your password in case anyone is looking over your shoulder.

    • *Remember This Network:* Remembers you connected to the selected network and automatically connects to it whenever you're within range of its signal. (If you've chosen to remember more than one wireless network, AirPort always connects to the one with the strongest signal first.)

4. **The AirPort icon on the menu bar shows black bars to indicate the strength of the WiFi network signal your Mac is connected to — as with mobile phone reception and gold, more bars are better.**

    You're now free to choose any activity that requires an Internet connection, such as running Safari to browse the news on the New York Times Web site (www.nytimes.com), or launching iChat to partake in a text chat with a friend who's also connected to the Internet and signed in to their particular chat program.

When you connect to a wireless network that doesn't require you to enter a password, your Mac essentially broadcasts any information you type (such as credit card numbers or passwords) through the airwaves. Although the likelihood of anyone actually monitoring what you're typing is small, tech-savvy engineers or hackers can "sniff" wireless signals to monitor or collect information flowing through the airwaves. When you connect to a public WiFi network, assume that a stranger is peeking at your data. Then only type data that you're comfortable giving away to others. Connecting to a secured network that requires you to type a password to connect to it can lessen the likelihood that anyone is monitoring or collecting what you're typing.

**Book IV
Chapter 1**

**Connecting to
the Internet and
Browsing the Web**

Dialup access

Dialup access involves using a telephone and a telephone modem, which lets you connect to an ISP and the Internet. Because telephone lines were designed for voice communication, dialup connections are terribly slow at transferring computer data. With the advent of super-speedy DSL or cable broadband Internet access, dialup access is almost obsolete — so old-fashioned that Apple no longer bothers to include built-in dialup modems in Macs.

A *modem* is a device that enables your Mac to connect to the Internet. If a cable TV provider provides your broadband Internet connection, you need a cable modem. If your broadband Internet connection is the DSL type coming into your house through your home's telephone line, you need a DSL modem. If neither DSL nor cable broadband is available where you live, or if you haven't jumped on the high-speed bandwagon for reasons all your own, you can still connect to the Internet over your ordinary phone line with a slowpoke, dialup data modem. Each type of modem works only with its specific type of Internet connection, which means you can't substitute a telephone modem for a cable modem and expect it to work.

To use dialup access, you need a modem, which plugs into an ordinary telephone line. Because new and recent Macs don't come with a dialup modem, you have to buy a USB external modem from Apple (`www.apple.com/store`) or another company. If you have an older Mac, you might have a built-in modem. Just peek at your Mac's lineup of connection ports and look for a plug for a telephone jack, which looks almost identical to an Ethernet port but slightly smaller.

Dialup access is the slowest way to connect to the Internet. If you have a choice, use an Ethernet or wireless connection because you can view Web sites much faster. Dialup access will work, but it's like riding a tricycle down a freeway: You'll eventually get to your destination, but it will take a long time.

To connect to the Internet through a telephone line, you need to know your ISP's telephone number, the account name your ISP gave you, and the account's password. The telephone number connects you to the ISP's computers, but you can't get access to the Internet unless you also have a valid account and password. After the ISP computer verifies that you A) have a valid account and B) know the right password, you can access the Internet.

To configure your Mac to use your telephone line to connect to the Internet, follow these steps:

1. **Choose System Preferences and then click the Network icon to open the Network preferences pane.**

2. **Click the Modem icon in the left pane to open the Modem preferences pane.**

3. **Type the account name, password, and telephone number your ISP gave you to connect to their computer network into the appropriate fields and then click Apply.**

4. **Click the Connect button if you want to connect to the Internet now, or click the Close button to close the Network preferences pane if you want to connect later.**

You can connect to the Internet using your dialup modem at any time by repeating Steps 1 and 2 and then clicking the Connect button to make the connection.

Browsing Web Sites

After you connect to the Internet (through your Mac's Ethernet or AirPort wireless broadband connections, or using a dialup modem), you can run a Web browser program to browse Web sites that interest you. The most popular browser for the Mac is the one that comes with it: Safari. Besides Safari, you can download and run another Web browser, such as Firefox (www.mozilla.com), Google Chrome (www.google.com/chrome), Camino (caminobrowser.org), OmniWeb (www.omnigroup.com), or Opera (www.opera.com).

Setting Safari's home page

Every time you run Safari, it automatically loads a start page, which is the first Web page that you'll always see. The default start page in Safari is the Apple Web site, but you can change your Mac's home page to whatever you want — even a blank page, if that's what you prefer.

Throughout this chapter, all step-by-step instructions are given for Safari. Just keep in mind that other browsers (Firefox, Chrome, Camino, and so on) work in similar ways.

To define a home page in Safari, follow these steps:

1. **Click the Safari icon in the Dock to run Safari and display the home page window.**

2. **Choose Safari⇨Preferences to open the General preferences pane; then type a Web site address, such as www.nytimes.com, as shown in Figure 1-3, in the Home Page field.**

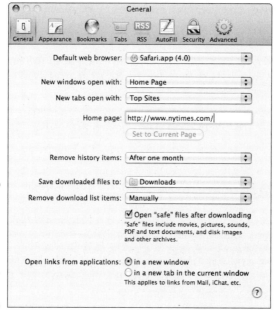

Figure 1-3:
Safari's
General
preferences
let you
change your
home page.

If you click the Set to Current Page button, you can make the currently displayed Web page your new home page without having to type the Web page's address. To use this feature, visit your favorite Web site immediately after Step 1. Then when you click the Set to Current Page button, the current Web site address instantly fills in the Home Page field as if you typed it yourself.

3. **Click the Close button to close the Safari preferences pane.**

Visiting a Web site

Although the first Web site you see will generally be your home page, you probably don't want to stare at your home page all the time. To visit another Web site, you use the Web site's *address* (also known as a *URL*, which stands for Uniform Resource Locator).

Most Web site addresses, such as `http://www.dummies.com`, consist of several parts:

✦ `http://www`: Identifies the address as part of the World Wide Web that uses the HyperText Transfer Protocol (http).

Some Web sites omit the `www` portion of the name. Other Web sites use something else like `mobile`. Just keep in mind that `www` is common, but not always necessary for many Web site addresses.

✦ **The domain name of the Web site (dummies):** Most Web site names are abbreviations or smashed-together names of the Web site, such as whitehouse for the White House's Web site.

✦ **A three-letter identifying extension, such as .com:** The extension identifies the type of Web site, as shown in Table 1-2.

Table 1-2	Common Extensions Used in Web Site Addresses	
Three-Letter Extension	*Type of Web Site*	*Examples*
.com	Often a commercial Web site, but can be another type of Web site	www.apple.com
.gov	Government Web site	www.nasa.gov
.edu	School Web site	www.mit.edu
.net	Network, sometimes used as an alternative to the .com extension	www.earthlink.net
.org	A nonprofit organization Web site	www.redcross.org
.mil	Military Web site	www.army.mil

Many Web sites in other countries end with a two-letter country address, such as .uk for the United Kingdom, .ca for Canada, and .fr for France.

When visiting different Web pages on a site, you might see additional text that identifies a specific Web page, such as www.dummies.com/how-to/computers-software.html or www.apple.com/iphone.

To visit a Web site by typing its Web site address, follow these steps:

1. **Click the Safari icon in the Dock to run Safari.**

2. **Click the address bar and type an address (such as www.dummies.com), as shown in Figure 1-4, and then press Return.**

Safari displays the Web site corresponding to the address you typed.

3. **(Optional) Click the Navigation buttons if you want to:**

• *Go Back:* Takes you to the previous Web page; click again to go back another page, and so on, until you wind up on the first page you viewed when you launched Safari.

Book IV Chapter 1

Connecting to the Internet and Browsing the Web

- *Go Forward:* Moves you forward to a page you backed away from; click again to advance to the next page you backed away from, and so on, until you wind up on the last page you visited before you clicked the Back button.

- *Reload/Stop:* Clicking the little arrowed-circle icon on the right side of the address bar reloads the current Web page and displays any new information that changed since you arrived on the Web page (such as breaking news on the New York Times home page, for instance). When Safari is loading or reloading a Web page, the arrowed-circle turns into an X icon. Clicking the X icon stops Safari from loading or reloading the Web page (for example, when you're trying to log in to your banking site but nothing appears on the screen when you click the Web site's login or sign-in button).

Bookmarks bar

Back

Forward

Top Sites view

Reload/Stop

Search text box

Figure 1-4: Type an address in the address bar to go to another Web site.

If you type a Web site address and see an error message, it might mean one of a few things: You typed the Web site address wrong, your Internet connection isn't working, or the Web site is temporarily (or permanently) unavailable.

Searching for Web sites

Typing a Web site address can get tedious, and sometimes you don't even know what Web site you want. That is, you know what kind of information you want, just not where to find it.

One way to find a Web site that can contain information of interest to you is to use a *search engine,* which is a behind-the-scenes technology used by special Web sites that can look for other Web sites and the information they contain based on a word or phrase you enter.

Because search engines are so convenient, Safari (and most other browsers) offers a built-in search engine text box in its upper-right corner. By typing a word or phrase that describes the kind of Web site or information you want, the search engine can find a list of related Web search results (referred to as *hits* or *links*), that you can click to go to a Web site page containing more information about what you're trying to find.

Safari uses the Google search engine. Other browsers, such as Firefox, let you choose a different search engine to use.

To search for a Web site that might contain information that you're looking for, follow these steps:

1. **Click the Safari icon in the Dock to run Safari.**

2. **Click the Search text box (refer to Figure 1-4), enter a word or phrase, and then press Return.**

    The Safari window displays a Web page of Web links Google found based on contents that match or relate to the word or phrase you typed, as shown in Figure 1-5.

3. **Click the Web site you want to visit.**

If you mistype a word or phrase, the search engine might offer suggestions for the correct spelling and look for Web sites that contain that misspelled word or phrase, which probably won't be the Web site you really want to see.

**Book IV
Chapter 1**

Connecting to
the Internet and
Browsing the Web

Figure 1-5:
Words or
phrases you
search for
appear as
Web links in
a new Web
page.

Every time you type a word or phrase in the Search text box, Safari (and most other browsers) saves the last ten words or phrases you searched. If you want to search for that same word or phrase later, just click the downward-pointing arrow that appears in the left side of the Search text box to display a pull-down menu. Then click the word or phrase you want to search for again.

Returning to Web site search results with SnapBack

If you search for Web sites and find yourself wandering down a number of blind alleys because the Web pages you navigate to aren't what you're looking for, the SnapBack feature can catapult you to where you began before losing your Web-footed way.

To try out the SnapBack feature, follow these steps:

1. **Click the Search field, type a word or phrase that describes a Web site you want to find, and then press Return.**

The Safari window displays a Web page of Web links Google found based on contents that match or relate to the word or phrase you typed (refer to Figure 1-5).

2. **Click the Web site you want to visit to display its Web page in the Safari window.**

3. **Click any link on the Web page to navigate to another Web page.**

   The new Web page opens in the Safari window and an orange left-pointing SnapBack icon appears in the far right of the Search text box, as shown in Figure 1-6.

4. **Click the SnapBack button to return to the Web page displaying your initial search results.**

   The SnapBack icon disappears from the Search field. Welcome back!

Figure 1-6:
Click the
SnapBack
icon to
return to
your search
results.

The SnapBack icon

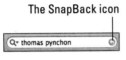

Searching previously viewed Web sites

If you visit a Web site and find it interesting, you might want to visit it again later. Fortunately, Safari stores a list of your previously visited Web sites in its History menu for up to one year.

To view a list of the Web sites you visited, follow these steps:

1. **In Safari, click History on the menu bar.**

   A pull-down menu appears, displaying the most recent Web sites you've visited. Additionally, the History menu lists the past week's dates so you can view Web sites that you visited several days ago, as shown in Figure 1-7.

2. **Choose a Web site to have Safari display your selected site.**

You can define how long Safari stores your previously visited Web sites by following these steps:

1. **Choose Safari➪Preferences to open the preferences window to open the General preferences pane.**

2. **Click the Remove History Items pop-up menu and then choose an option, such as After One Month or After One Day, as shown in Figure 1-8.**

Figure 1-7:
The History
menu lets
you revisit
previously
viewed Web
sites.

3. **Click the Close button to close the Safari preferences pane.**

Although the History menu only displays the past seven days, you can choose History⇨Show All History to view a list of all the Web sites you've visited in the period specified by the Remove History Items pop-up menu in the General preferences pane.

You might want to choose a shorter period in the Remove History Items pop-up menu if you share your Mac with others or if you're using a friend's Mac and you don't necessarily want to leave a trail of Web sites you've recently visited.

Protecting your Web history privacy with Private Browsing

You can erase your Web browsing history at any time by choosing History⇨Clear History.

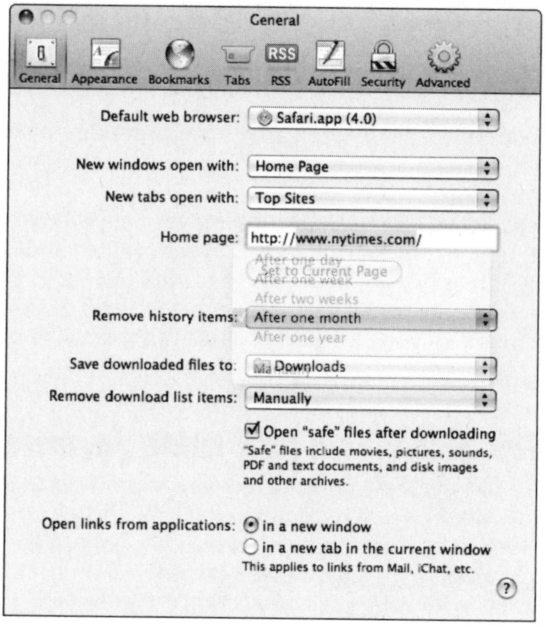

Figure 1-8:
Define how long Safari keeps track of Web sites you visit.

A more secure way to prevent others from seeing which Web sites you've recently visited is to turn on Safari's Private Browsing feature by choosing Safari⊅Private Browsing. When you choose Private Browsing, the dialog shown in Figure 1-9 appears, asking whether you're sure you want to turn on Private Browsing.

Figure 1-9:
Choose the Private Browsing option to cover your Web browsing tracks.

In a nutshell, turning on the Private Browsing keeps your Web browsing history usage private by:

✦ Not tracking which Web sites you visited

✦ Removing any files that you downloaded from the Downloads window
(Window⟶Downloads)

✦ Not saving names or passwords that you entered on Web sites

✦ Not saving search words or terms that you entered in the Google
search box

In other words, the Private Browsing feature gives Safari a case of amnesia
when you turn it on, making Safari mind its own business until you turn off
Private Browsing. When Private Browsing is turned off, Safari goes back to
thoughtfully keeping track of the Web sites you visit and terms you type into
the Google search box so you can easily return to those sites or searches
again later.

Using the Top Sites view to display favorite sites

While you browse the Web and go from one site to another to another,
behind the scenes Safari pays attention to which Web sites you visit most.
By tracking the Web sites you visit most frequently, Safari can display a
selection of Top Sites that you can browse through to return to what Safari
deems to be your favorite Web sites, as shown in Figure 1-10.

Top Sites view icon

Figure 1-10:
The Top
Sites view
displays
thumbnail
images of
your favorite
Web sites.

Click to access display options.

To display the Top Sites view of Web sites you've visited, that Safari believes are your favorite Web sites, follow these steps:

1. **In the Safari window, click the Top Sites icon in the Bookmarks bar to open the Top Sites display window (refer to Figure 1-10).**

2. **Click a Top Sites thumbnail image of a Web site you want to visit.**

3. **(Optional) Click the Edit button in the lower-left corner to turn on the Top Site display's view options, as shown in Figure 1-11:**

   • *Thumbnail Size:* Click the Small, Medium, or Large buttons in the lower-right corner to change the size of the Top Sites thumbnail images to display 24, 12, or 6 thumbnail images, respectively.

   • *Exclude Web site:* To exclude a Top Sites selection that Safari deemed a favorite, click the X in the upper-left corner of that Top Sites' thumbnail image.

   • *Permanent Web site:* To unmark a Top Sites selection as a permanent top site, click the blue pushpin icon next to the X in the upper-left corner of the Top Sites' thumbnail image. The pushpin icon turns black to indicate the Web site is no longer a permanent top site. Click a black pushpin icon to reverse the action so that the page stays in the Top Sites display and isn't replaced by a Web site you might visit more frequently.

Figure 1-11:
The Top Sites display view options let you add or remove Top Sites choices.

- *New Web site:* To add a new Web site to the Top Sites display window, type a Web site address in the address bar of the site that you want to add, click the tiny icon to the left of the address, and then drag and drop it into the Top Sites display window where you want it to appear. ***Note:*** You can drag a link from another source directly into the Top Sites display window, such as a Web site link in an e-mail message, or from another open Safari Web page window.

- *Rearrange Thumbnails:* To rearrange the order in which your Top Sites thumbnail images appear, click a top site and drag and drop it to the location where you want it to appear, as shown in Figure 1-12.

- *Done:* Click the Done button in the lower-left corner to close the Top Sites display view options and return to the main Top Sites display window.

4. **(Optional) Click the Search History field in the lower-left corner of the Top Sites display window to switch to the Top Sites search view and then choose from these options:**

- *Search Box:* Begin typing a word or phrase in the Search box to search for frequently viewed Web sites that match your search criteria.

- *Scroll Bar:* Drag the Scroll button beneath the search view left or right to flip through your Top Sites favorite Web sites, as shown in Figure 1-13.

Figure 1-12: Drag and drop Top Sites thumbnails to rearrange how they appear in the window.

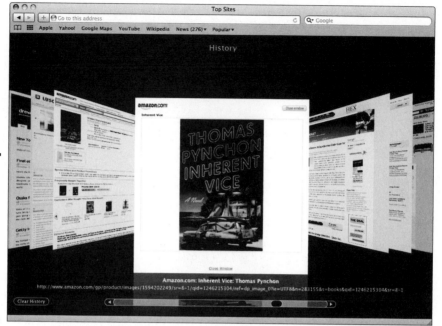

Figure 1-13:
Use the Top Sites search view to browse through Web sites you previously visited.

- *Clear History:* Click Clear History in the lower-left corner to clear your Top Sites history; a dialog appears asking whether you're sure you want to clear Safari's history of previously visited Web sites. Before clicking the Clear button, you can mark the Also Reset Top Sites check box if you want to erase Safari's memory of Web sites it deems favorites. Click the Clear button to clear the history of previously visited Web sites.

- *Close Search View:* Click the tiny X button on the right side of the Search box to close the Top Sites search view and return to the main Top Sites display window.

5. **To exit the Top Sites display window, type a Web address in the address bar and press Return to go to that Web site.**

    You can also click a bookmark button beneath the address bar to close the Top Sites view and go to that bookmarked Web site, which I show you how to do in the next section.

Using bookmarks

Bookmarks let you store and organize your favorite Web sites into groups, such as news sites, book review sites, or gadgets sites. By organizing your favorite Web sites into groups, you can quickly find them again. You can save and view bookmarks in either the Bookmarks menu or the Bookmarks bar, as shown in Figure 1-14:

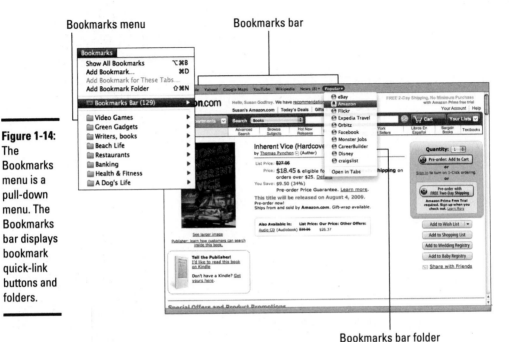

Figure 1-14:
The Bookmarks menu is a pull-down menu. The Bookmarks bar displays bookmark quick-link buttons and folders.

Storing bookmarks on the Bookmarks menu tucks them out of sight. The drawback is that you must click the Bookmarks menu to find your bookmarks.

Storing bookmarks on the Bookmarks bar keeps bookmarks buttons for Web sites you visit often visible and within easy access at all times. The drawback is that the Bookmarks bar can display only a limited number of bookmark buttons that link to your favorite Web sites.

Generally, use the Bookmarks bar for one-click access to your favorite Web sites and use the Bookmarks menu to store Web sites that you don't access as often.

One way to cram more bookmarks onto the Bookmarks bar is to create a folder based on a particular category on the Bookmarks bar, which you can fill with more bookmarks related to that particular category (refer to Figure 1-14). Clicking a Bookmarks bar folder opens a list of all the bookmarks saved in that bookmark folder. For instance, you can create a Lunch Joints folder on the

Bookmarks bar and then bookmark the Web sites of nearby restaurants you frequent for lunch inside the folder. Today's lunch specials are now only two clicks away.

Bookmarks behave the same whether they appear on the Bookmarks menu or on the Bookmarks bar.

By default, Safari comes with several bookmarks already placed on the Bookmarks bar. If you've saved bookmarks on both the Bookmarks menu and Bookmarks bar (see the next subtopic, "Adding bookmarks"), you can choose bookmarks from either location (refer to Figure 1-14).

To choose a bookmark on the Bookmarks bar, do either of the following:

✦ Click a bookmark on the Bookmarks bar to view your chosen Web page.

✦ Click a bookmark folder on the Bookmarks bar to view a pull-down menu of additional bookmarks or folders. Then click the bookmark you want to view.

To choose a bookmark on the Bookmarks menu, click the Bookmarks menu and do either of the following:

✦ Click a bookmark on the Bookmarks menu to view your chosen Web page.

✦ Click a bookmark folder on the Bookmarks menu to view a submenu of additional bookmarks or folders. Then click the bookmark you want to view.

Adding bookmarks

To bookmark a Web site address in either the menu or the bar, follow these steps:

1. **In Safari, visit a Web site that you want to store as a bookmark.**

2. **Choose Bookmark⇨Add Bookmark (or click the plus sign button that appears to the left of the address bar) to open the dialog shown in Figure 1-15.**

By default, the Name text box displays the current Web page's title — which is typically the main Web site's name.

3. **(Optional) Type a new name for the bookmark if you don't want to keep the default name.**

**Book IV
Chapter 1**

Connecting to
the Internet and
Browsing the Web

Figure 1-15:
Safari
names
a new
bookmark
based on
the Web
site, or you
can give it a
new name.

4. **Click the Location pop-up menu and choose a location for storing your bookmark.**

   You can choose the Bookmarks bar, Bookmarks menu, or a specific folder stored on the Bookmarks bar or Bookmarks menu. (You discover how to create a bookmark folder in the later "Storing bookmarks in a folder" section of this chapter.)

5. **Click the Add button.**

Deleting bookmarks

After you start saving bookmarks of your favorite Web sites, you might find that you have too many bookmarks that you don't use any more. To delete a bookmark, follow these steps:

1. **In Safari, choose Bookmarks⇨Show All Bookmarks.**

   Safari displays a window divided into three panes, as shown in Figure 1-16. The left pane displays a list of bookmark folders. (Safari treats the Bookmarks bar and Bookmarks menu as folders.) The right panes display the contents of the currently selected bookmark folder or individual bookmark, displaying a Cover Flow thumbnail view in the upper-right pane, and a list of bookmark folders and individual bookmarks in the lower-right pane.

2. **Click the folder in the left pane that contains the bookmark you want to delete.**

   The right panes display the contents of your chosen bookmark folder, which might include bookmarks and additional folders that contain other bookmarks (refer to Figure 1-16).

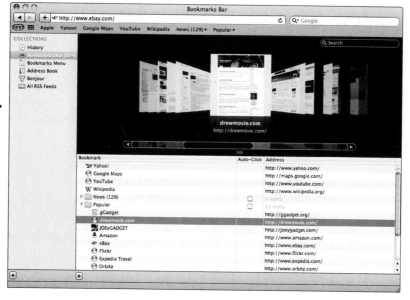

Figure 1-16:
The
Show All
Bookmarks
window
displays
your
bookmarks
and
bookmark
folders.

3. **(Optional) Click the triangle that appears to the left of any folder displayed in the lower-right pane to display the bookmarks and any other folders in that particular folder.**

   You might need to repeat this step several times to find the bookmark you want.

4. **Click the bookmark name that you want to delete and then press the Delete key.**

   Your chosen bookmark disappears.

   You can also Control-click a bookmark and, when a pop-up menu appears, choose Delete, or choose Edit⇨Delete.

   To restore a bookmark you mistakenly deleted, press ⌘+Z or choose Edit⇨Undo Remove Bookmark.

5. **Choose Bookmarks⇨Hide All Bookmarks (or press Option+⌘+B).**

Moving bookmarks and bookmark folders

Your browser saves your bookmarks and bookmark folders in the order you create them. However, chances are you want to rearrange your bookmarks or bookmark folders and put them in a more logical order. You can move a bookmark and bookmark folder by following these steps:

1. **Choose Bookmarks⇨Show All Bookmarks to display your saved book-marks (refer to Figure 1-16).**

2. **Click the folder in the left pane that contains the bookmark or book-mark folder you want to move.**

   The right panes display the contents of your chosen bookmark folder.

3. **(Optional) Click the triangle that appears to the left of any folder that appears in the lower-right pane to display the contents of the folder.**

   You might need to repeat this step several times to find the bookmark you want.

4. **Drag and drop the bookmark or bookmark folder you want to move onto a folder in the left or right pane.**

   Safari moves your chosen bookmark to its new location.

5. **Choose Bookmarks⇨Hide All Bookmarks (or press Option+⌘+B).**

Storing bookmarks in folders

After you save many bookmarks, you might find that they start to clutter the Bookmarks menu or Bookmarks bar. To organize your bookmarks, you can store related bookmarks in folders. To create a bookmark folder, follow these steps:

1. **In Safari, choose Bookmarks⇨Show All Bookmarks to display your saved bookmarks.**

2. **Click Bookmarks Bar or Bookmarks Menu in the left pane to choose a location to store your folder.**

3. **(Optional) Click the triangle that appears to the left of a folder that appears in the lower-right pane to display the contents of the folder.**

4. **Click any bookmark or a specific bookmark folder in the right pane.**

   When you create a bookmark folder, it appears inside the same folder that holds the bookmark or folder you click in this step.

5. **Choose Bookmarks⇨Add Bookmark Folder, or click the plus sign button in the bottom corner of the left or right pane, depending on where you'll store your new folder.**

   An untitled bookmark folder appears.

6. **Type a descriptive name for your bookmark folder in the text field and then press Return.**

7. **Choose Bookmarks⇨Hide All Bookmarks (or press Option+⌘+B).**

After you create a bookmark folder, you can copy or move existing book-marks into that folder, or move the folder into another folder.

Importing and exporting bookmarks

After you collect and organize bookmarks, you might become dependent on your bookmarks to help you navigate the Web. Fortunately, if you ever want to switch browsers, you can export bookmarks from one browser and import them into another browser.

To export bookmarks from Safari, follow these steps:

1. **In Safari, choose File➪Export Bookmarks to open the Export Bookmarks dialog, as shown in Figure 1-17.**

Figure 1-17:
You can give your exported bookmarks a descriptive name and choose a location to store them.

Export Bookmarks

Save As: Safari Bookmarks.html

Where: Downloads

Cancel   Save

2. **(Optional) Type a descriptive name for your bookmarks if you don't want to keep the default, Safari Bookmarks.**

3. **Click the Where pop-up menu to choose where you want to store your exported bookmarks file.**

If you click the Arrow button that appears to the right of the Save As text box, a window appears displaying all the drives and folders that you can choose to store your bookmarks.

4. **Click Save.**

After you export bookmarks from one browser, it's usually a snap to import them into a second browser. To import bookmarks into Safari, follow these steps:

1. **In Safari, choose File➪Import Bookmarks to open the Import Bookmarks dialog (shown in Figure 1-18) and navigate to the folder where the exported bookmarks file is stored.**

**Book IV
Chapter 1**

**Connecting to
the Internet and
Browsing the Web**

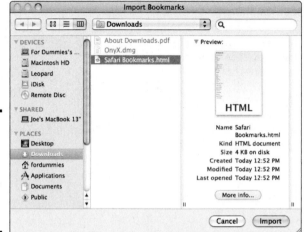

Figure 1-18:
Safari can
import
bookmarks
that another
browser
exported.

2. **Click the bookmark file you want to use and click the Import button.**

   Your imported bookmarks appear in an Imported folder that includes the date you imported the folder. At this point, you can move this folder or its contents to the Bookmarks bar or Bookmarks menu to organize them (see the previous section, "Moving bookmarks and bookmark folders).

Using tabbed browsing

One problem with browsing Web sites is that you might want to keep track of more than one Web site while browsing a second, third, or fourth site. Although you could open two separate browser windows, Safari and most other browsers offer a handy *tabbed browsing* feature. Essentially, tabbed browsing lets you easily jump around among multiple Web pages in a single window — all you have to do is click the tab associated with the Web page. (See Figure 1-19.)

Creating new tabs

When you load Safari, you see a single Web page displayed. To create a tab, follow these steps:

1. **Choose File⇨New Tab (or press ⌘+T) to open a new tabbed window.**

2. **Click a bookmark (or type a Web site address into the address bar and then press Return) to display your chosen Web page in your new tab.**

Figure 1-19:
Tabbed browsing lets you juggle multiple Web pages inside a single window.

Managing tabs

When you open three, four, or fifteen tabbed windows, you can do things such as rearrange the way they are ordered, close tabs, and save a group of tabs as a bookmark that you can reopen all at once with a single click of your mouse, just to name a few.

Some cool things you can try doing with tabbed windows include:

✦ Add a new tab by clicking the plus sign at the far right of the Tab bar (or pressing ⌘+T).

✦ Switch from tab to tab by pressing ⌘+Shift+→ or ⌘+Shift+←.

✦ Close a tab by moving your mouse over the tab and then clicking the Close icon that appears (or press ⌘+W). You can also Control-click a tab and then choose Close Tab, or Close Other Tabs.

✦ Rearrange the order of your tabs by dragging and dropping a tab to the left or right of another tab.

✦ Move a tab to a new window by dragging it below the Tab bar and then letting go of your mouse button, or by Control-clicking a tab and then choosing Move Tab to New Window.

✦ Save your collection of every currently loaded tabbed window as a bookmark by Control-clicking any tab and then choosing Add Bookmark for These Tabs.

✦ Merge a bunch of open Web page windows into a single Web page with tabs for each of the windows by choosing Windows➪Merge All Windows.

✦ View tabs that get shoved off the row of visible tabs when you've opened too many tabs to display them all by clicking the double right-pointing arrows on the rightmost tab, as shown in Figure 1-20.

Figure 1-20: Crowded-out tabs appear when you click the double arrows on the rightmost tab.

Capturing Web Clips

Rather than view an entire Web page, you might really care about only a certain part of a Web page that's frequently updated, such as status updates on such social networking sites as Twitter or Facebook, traffic reports on local highways, or breaking news. Fortunately, Safari lets you copy part of a Web page and store it as a Dashboard widget called a *Web Clip*.

Dashboard widgets are programs that perform a single task and pop up whenever you press the Dashboard key (also labeled F4 on recent and new Mac keyboards) or press Fn+F12. You find out more about Dashboard widgets in Book II, Chapter 1.

Creating a Web Clip

To create a Web Clip, follow these steps:

1. **In Safari, go to the Web page you're interested in and then choose File⇨Open in Dashboard.**

The Web page darkens and highlights a portion of the currently displayed Web page.

2. **Move your pointer over the part of the Web page that you want to view as a Dashboard widget and then click the mouse to create a selection box, as shown in Figure 1-21.**

3. **(Optional) Click one of the selection box handles surrounding the selection box and then drag your mouse to make the box bigger or smaller around the section of information you want to capture.**

4. **Click the Add button in the upper-right corner to save your Web Clip as a Dashboard widget.**

Dashboard automatically opens and displays your newly created Web Clip widget, as shown in Figure 1-22.

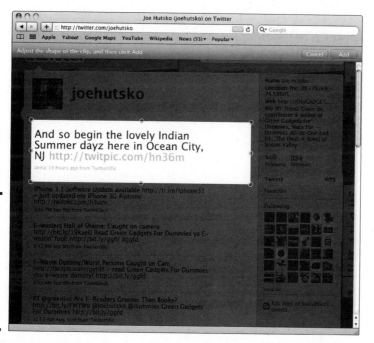

Figure 1-21:
Click a section of a Web page to turn it into a Dashboard Web Clip.

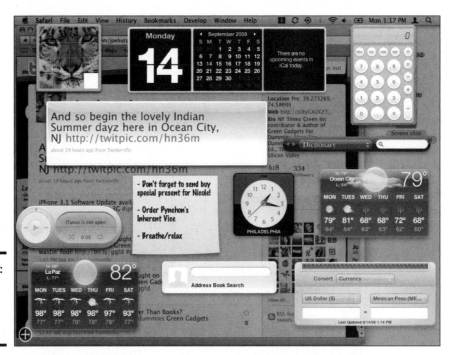

Figure 1-22:
Web Clips
appear as
Dashboard
widgets.

To delete a Web Clip, Click the Dashboard icon in the Dock (or press Fn+F12 to display your Dashboard widgets), hold down the Option key, move your pointer over the widget you want to delete, and then click the Close button that appears in the upper-left corner. Adios, Web Clip.

Search for text on a Web page

One quick way to skim a Web page is to search for specific words or phrases to find what you're looking for. A more focused approach is to search for specific text, which you can do by using Safari's Find feature.

The Find feature not only finds multiple instances of a word or phrase, but also highlights them on the Web page to make them easier to see. To search for text on a Web page, follow these steps:

1. **In Safari, go to a Web page that you want to search.**

2. **Choose Edit➪Find➪Find (or press ⌘+F).**

A Find bar (with text box) appears at the top of the Web page, ready for you to type your word or phrase.

3. **Type a word or phrase in the Find bar's text box.**

   The Find bar lists how many matches it finds in the currently displayed Web page and Safari highlights each match and selects the first instance, as shown in Figure 1-23.

Figure 1-23: Safari highlights each match in a box.

4. **Click the Next (or Previous) button to view the next (or previous) instance of the searched term.**

   If Safari can't find another match, it simply starts highlighting the previous words or phrases.

5. **Click the Done button in the Find bar when you finish searching through the text (or press Escape).**

Saving and Sharing Web Pages

When you come upon a Web page containing a story or a recipe that you want to share with friends, you can save, print, or e-mail the Web page to your friends so they can have a look at what you find so interesting.

**Book IV
Chapter 1**

**Connecting to
the Internet and
Browsing the Web**

Saving a Web page as a file

When you save a Web page as a file, you store the complete text and graphics of that Web page as a file on your Mac's hard drive. Safari gives you two ways to save a Web page:

✦ **As a Web Archive:** A Web archive is meant for viewing a Web page only in the Safari browser. Saving a Web page as an HTML source file lets you view and edit that file in any browser or Web page authoring program — which is helpful if you want to figure out how someone designed that particular Web page.

✦ **As an HTML Source File (called Page Source):** If you view a Web page saved as Page Source, you won't see any of the graphics, but you will see text references to the graphics and each one's associated URL address.

HTML stands for *HyperText Markup Language,* which is a special language used to design the layout of all Web pages.

To save a Web page as a file, follow these steps:

1. **In Safari, find the Web page that you want to save and then choose File⇨Save As to open the Save As dialog, as shown in Figure 1-24.**

Figure 1-24:
The Save As
dialog lets
you choose
where and
how to save
a file.

2. **(Optional) Type a new descriptive name in the Export As field if you don't want to keep the one Safari automatically fills in for you.**

3. **Click the Where pop-up menu and then choose where you want to store your file on your Mac's hard drive.**

If you click the Expand (downward-pointing arrow) button to the right of the Export As field, the Save As dialog expands to let you choose more folders to store your file.

4. **Click the Format pop-up menu, choose Web Archive or Page Source, and then click Save.**

After you save a file as a Web Archive or a Page Source, you can view it by double-clicking the file icon in the folder where you saved the Web Archive or Page Source file.

Only Safari can view a Web Archive file, but any browser can view a Page Source file.

Printing a Web page

Rather than save a Web page as a file, you might just want to print it instead. To print a Web page, follow these steps:

1. **In Safari, find the Web page you want to print and choose File⇨Print to open the Print dialog.**

2. **Click the Printer pop-up menu and then choose the printer to use.**

   If you click the PDF button, you can save your Web page as a PDF file. If you click the Expand button (downward-pointing arrow) to the right of the Printer pop-up menu, the Print dialog expands to let you select which pages to print and other print-related options.

3. **Click Print.**

Sending a Web page by e-mail

After saving a Web page as a separate file, you can then attach that file to an e-mail message to send it to a friend. An easier way to send a Web page to one or more people is to send the Web page in an e-mail message, as shown in Figure 1-25. (You can also just send a link to the Web page rather than the entire Web page itself.)

The main advantage of sending a Web page link is that it doesn't take as much space as sending the actual Web page.

To send a Web page (or just a link to a Web page) in an e-mail message, follow these steps:

1. **In Safari, click the File menu and then choose one of these options:**

   • *Mail Contents of This Page:* To send the entire Web page in an e-mail message.

   • *Mail Link to This Page:* To send a link to the Web page that the recipient can click to open the Web page with his or her Web browser.

   The Mail program loads and opens a new e-mail message containing your Web page or your Web page link, depending on which command you select.

2. **In the To: field that's automatically selected, type the e-mail address (or addresses) of the person that you want to send the Web page to and then click the Send button.**

   The Mail program sends your e-mail message.

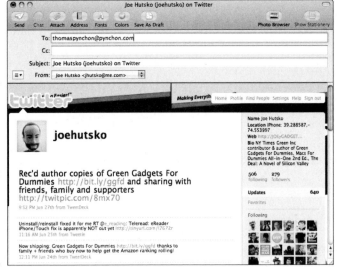

Figure 1-25:
Sending a
Web page
as an e-mail
message
displays that
Web page
directly
in the
message
text box.

If you send a link to a Web page and that Web page or Web site is changed or is no longer available, anyone who clicks the link will see an error message instead of the Web page you wanted him or her to see.

Viewing and Playing Multimedia Files

The most basic Web pages consist of mainly text and sometimes graphics. However, most Web sites offer robust content beyond simple words and pictures, including content stored as video, audio, and other types of common files, such as PDF (Portable Document Format) files. Although your Mac includes many programs for viewing and listening to video, audio, and PDF files, you might still need additional software to view some Web sites.

Watching video

Many news sites offer videos that require Windows Media Player or RealPlayer.

To download the necessary program so you can play Windows Media video content, go to www.microsoft.com/mac/products/flip4mac. mspx. Microsoft actually gives you two choices. First, you can download the Windows Media Player for the Mac. However, Microsoft has stopped developing this program, so as a second choice, Microsoft offers a free program called Flip4Mac.

Some Web sites won't work unless you're using Microsoft Windows. In this case, you might need to run Windows on your Mac with one of the programs described in Book VII, Chapter 3.

The Flip4Mac program allows the QuickTime Player that comes with your Mac to play most video files designed to run with the Windows Media Player.

Besides downloading and installing the Flip4Mac program, you should also download and install the RealPlayer program (www.real.com). After you have both Flip4Mac and RealPlayer installed, you should be able to watch videos on most every Web site you visit.

Listening to streaming audio

Many Web sites offer audio that you can listen to, such as live interviews or radio shows. Such audio is often stored as *streaming audio,* which means your computer downloads a temporary audio file and begins playing it almost instantly but doesn't actually save the radio program as a file on your hard drive.

Sometimes you can listen to streaming audio through the iTunes program, sometimes you need a copy of Windows Media Player (or Flip4Mac), and sometimes you need a copy of RealPlayer.

Viewing PDF files

Some Web sites offer downloadable documents, booklets, brochures, eBook editions of *New York Times* best-selling non-fiction and fiction titles, and user guides as a PDF (Portable Document Format) file, which is a special file format for storing the layout of text and graphics so they appear exactly the same on different computers. If a Web site offers a PDF file as a link you can click to open, you can view and scroll through it directly within Safari.

You can save a PDF document you're viewing to look at it later by clicking the document displayed in the Safari Web browser window and then choosing File⇨Save As. If you double-click a PDF file icon, you can view the contents of that PDF file by using the Preview program included with every Mac.

You can also view PDF files by using the Adobe Reader program — a free download from Adobe (www.adobe.com) — which offers the basic features of the Preview program plus extra features for opening and viewing PDF documents. If you have problems printing certain PDF files with the Preview program, try printing them with the Adobe Reader program instead.

Downloading Files

Part of the Web's appeal is that you can find interesting content — music tracks, or free demos of programs you can try before you buy, for example — that you can download and install on your own computer. (When you copy a file from the Web and store it on your computer, that's *downloading*. When you copy a file from your computer to a Web site — such as your electronic tax forms that you file electronically on the IRS's Web site — that's *uploading*.)

Only download a file if you trust the source. If you visit an unknown Web site, that unknown Web site might be trying to trick you into downloading a file that could do harmful things to your Mac, such as delete files, spy on your activities, or even bombard you with unwanted ads, so be careful. To learn about ways you can protect your Mac (and yourself) from potentially dangerous Internet threats, take a look at Book IV, Chapter 4.

To download a file, click a link or button on a Web site that offers downloadable content, such as MacUpdate (www.macupdate.com), or Apple's Downloads Web page (www.apple.com/downloads). When you find a file you want to download, follow these steps:

1. **Click the Download link or button to begin downloading the file you want to save on your Mac's hard drive.**

The Downloads window appears, showing the name of the file you're downloading and approximately how much time remains until the download completes, as shown in Figure 1-26.

Figure 1-26:
The Downloads window shows you how much longer you'll need to wait to finish downloading a file.

2. **When the file has completely downloaded, double-click the file icon in the Downloads window to open the file.**

If you downloaded a program, that program might start running or installing itself on your Mac, so follow the onscreen instructions.

If you click the magnifying glass icon to the right of a file displayed in the Downloads window, Safari opens a Finder window and displays the contents of the folder where your downloaded file is saved.

The Downloads window keeps track of every file you download. You can open the Downloads window at any time by choosing Window➪Downloads. To clear the list of files you've downloaded from Downloads window, click the Clear button in the lower-left corner of the Downloads window.

Chapter 2: Sending and Receiving E-Mail

In This Chapter

✔ Configuring an e-mail account

✔ Writing e-mail

✔ Receiving and reading e-mail

✔ Organizing e-mail

✔ Cleaning up junk e-mail

*S*ending and receiving e-mail is one of the most popular uses for the Internet. E-mail is fast, (almost always) free, and accessible to anyone with a computer and an Internet connection.

To send and receive e-mail, you first have to set up an e-mail account. The three types of e-mail accounts you can set up are POP (Post Office Protocol), IMAP (Internet Message Access Protocol), and Exchange.

A POP e-mail account usually transfers (moves) e-mail from the POP server computer to your computer. An IMAP or Exchange e-mail account stores e-mail on its server, which allows multiple individuals to access their e-mail accounts simultaneously. Most individuals have POP accounts, whereas many corporations have IMAP or Exchange accounts.

Setting Up an E-Mail Account

When you have an e-mail account, you often have two choices for reading and writing messages:

✦ Through a Web browser, such as Safari or Firefox

✦ Through an e-mail program, such as the Mac's free Mail program

You don't have to choose between the methods because you can use both — an e-mail program on your Mac, and a Web browser on your Mac or on another computer, such as at your friend's house, or in an Internet cafe — to access one or more of your e-mail accounts.

Accessing an e-mail account through a Web browser is simple because you don't need to know how to use another program, and you don't have to worry about knowing the technical details of your e-mail account. The drawback is that you need Internet access every time you want to read or respond to messages.

Accessing an e-mail account through an e-mail program lets you download messages so you can read or respond to them even if you aren't connected to the Internet. (Of course, you won't be able to send or receive any messages until you connect to the Internet again.) The drawback of using an e-mail program is that you must configure it to work with your e-mail account.

You can use dozens of e-mail programs, but the most popular one is the free Mail program that comes with your Mac. If you don't like Mail, you can download and install a free e-mail program, such as Thunderbird (`www.mozilla.com`), or buy an e-mail program, such as Eudora (`www.eudora.com`), or Microsoft Entourage (`www.microsoft.com/mac`), which is part of the Office 2008 for Mac suite of productivity applications.

If you plan to access your e-mail account only through a browser, such as Safari, you can skip this entire chapter because this chapter explains how to use Mail.

Gathering your e-mail account information

To make an e-mail program work with your e-mail account, you need to gather the following information:

✦ **Your username (also called an account name):** Typically a descriptive name (such as nickyhutsko) or a collection of numbers and symbols (such as nickyhutsko09). Your username plus the name of your Internet Service Provider (ISP) defines your complete e-mail address, such as `nickyhutsko@gmail.com`.

✦ **Your password:** Any phrase that you choose to access your account. If someone sets up an e-mail account for you, he or she might have already assigned a password that you can always change later.

✦ **Your e-mail account's incoming server name:** The mail server name of the computer that contains your e-mail message is usually a combination of POP or IMAP and your e-mail account company, such as `pop.acme.com` or `imap.gmail.com`.

✦ **Your e-mail account's outgoing server name:** The name of the outgoing mail server that sends your messages to other people. The outgoing server name is usually a combination of SMTP (Simple Mail Transfer Protocol) and the name of the company that provides your e-mail account, such as `smtp.gmail.com` or `smtp.acme.com`.

If you don't know your account name, password, incoming server name, or outgoing server name, ask the company that runs your e-mail account. If for some reason you're unable to find the information, chances are you might still be able to set up your e-mail account on your Mac thanks to the Mail program's ability to detect the most popular e-mail account settings, such as those for Gmail or Yahoo!.

If you subscribe to Apple's MobileMe service and typed your MobileMe account name and password when you completed the Welcome setup process, Mail is already configured to access your MobileMe e-mail account.

Configuring your e-mail account

After you collect the technical information needed to access your e-mail account, you need to configure Mail to work with your e-mail account by following these steps:

1. **Click the Mail icon in the Dock to open the Welcome to Mail dialog.**

The Welcome to Mail dialog prompts you to enter your name, e-mail address, and password, as shown in Figure 2-1.

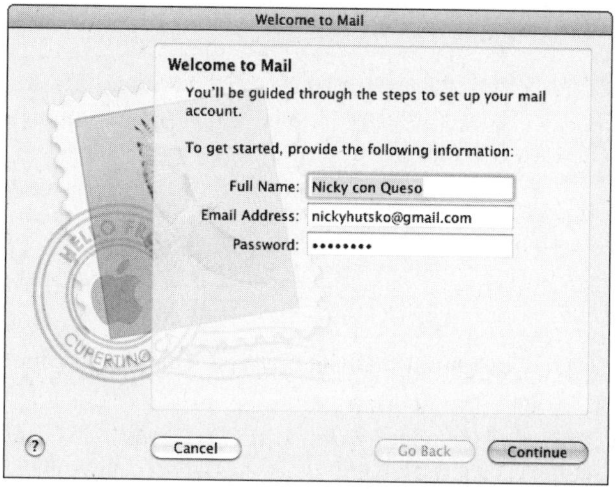

Figure 2-1:
The New
Account
dialog
asks for
your name,
e-mail
address,
and
password.

> **Welcome to Mail**
>
> **Welcome to Mail**
>
> You'll be guided through the steps to set up your mail account.
>
> To get started, provide the following information:
>
> Full Name: Nicky con Queso
> Email Address: nickyhutsko@gmail.com
> Password: •••••••
>
> Cancel   Go Back   Continue

2. **Enter your full name, e-mail address, and password in the text boxes and then click Continue.**

Your full name is any name you want to associate with your messages. If you type "Nickycito con Queso" in the Full Name text box, all your messages will include "From: Nickycito con Queso." Your e-mail address includes your username plus ISP name, such as `nickyhutsko@gmail. net`. Your password might be case-sensitive, so type it exactly.

Mail connects to your email account and attempts to fill in your e-mail account settings automatically.

a. If Mail succeeds in detecting your e-mail account's settings, Mail closes the setup dialog and displays your Inbox and you can skip the rest of these steps. (Read the rest of these steps if you want to learn about additional settings that you can adjust to gain greater control over how Mail handles your e-mail.)

b. If mail doesn't automatically detect your e-mail account settings, continue following these steps to configure Mail to work with your e-mail account.

3. **Click Continue.**

An Incoming Mail Server dialog appears, as shown in Figure 2-2.

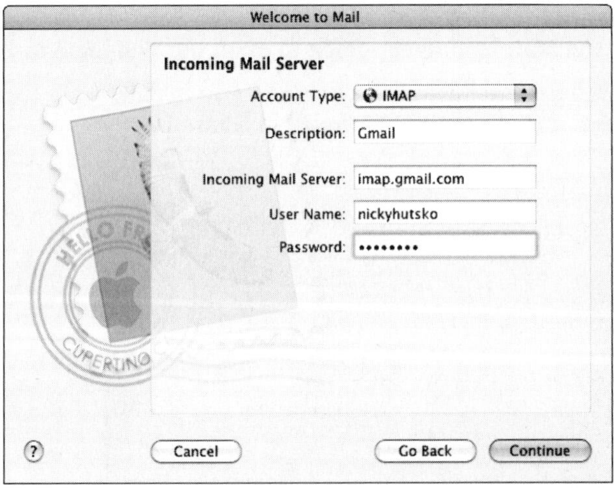

Figure 2-2:
The
Incoming
Mail Server
dialog lets
you specify
where to
retrieve
your e-mail.

4. **Choose your incoming mail server type from the Account Type pop-up menu.**

Your choices here include POP, IMAP, Exchange 2007, Exchange IMAP, and, if you typed in a @mac.com or @me.com e-mail address, MobileMe.

5. **(Optional) Click the Description text box and type a description of your account.**

This description is for your benefit only, so feel free to type anything you want. Because you can configure Mail to access two or more e-mail accounts, you might want to identify an account as a Work account or a Gmail account.

6. **Click the Incoming Mail Server text box and type the name of your server.**

   If you don't know this name, you'll have to ask your ISP or e-mail account provider.

7. **Click the User Name text box and type your username.**

   Depending on your e-mail account provider, your username may be a standalone word or combination of letters and numbers, such as "nickyhutsko", or it may also include the e-mail account provider's Internet domain, such as `nickyhutsko@gmail.com` or `nickyhutsko@earthlink.net`.

8. **Click the Password text box and type your password.**

   Your password appears onscreen as a series of dots to keep anyone peeking over your shoulder from seeing your password.

9. **Click Continue to display the Outgoing Mail Server dialog, as shown in Figure 2-3.**

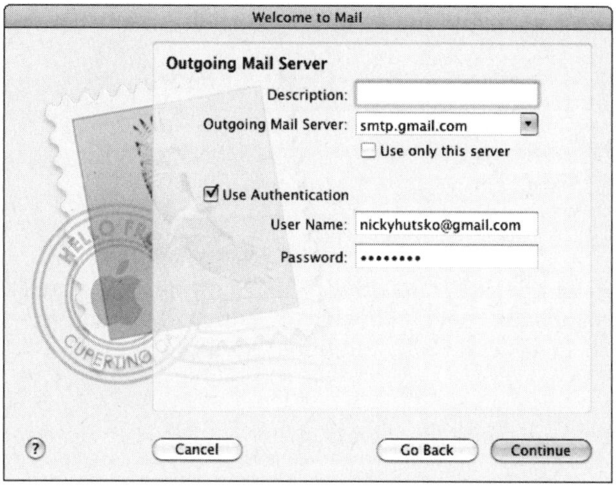

Figure 2-3:
The Outgoing Mail Server asks for the name of the server to send your e-mail through to the rest of the Internet.

Book IV
Chapter 2

Sending and Receiving E-Mail

10. **(Optional) Click the Description text box and type a description of your account.**

    This description is for your benefit only, so feel free to type anything you want. If you type in the technical support number of your ISP as the outgoing mail server, you'll know whom to call if you're having trouble.

11. **Click the Outgoing Mail Server text box and type the name of your outgoing mail server.**

    If you don't know this name, you'll have to contact your ISP or e-mail account provider.

12. **Click the User Name text box and type your username.**

13. **Click the Password text box and type your password.**

14. **Click Continue.**

The Account Summary dialog appears as shown in Figure 2-4.

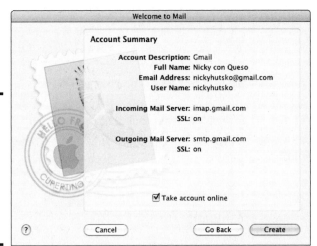

Figure 2-4: The Account Summary dialog shows your e-mail account settings.

15. **Click Create.**

The Mail window appears.

You can configure Mail to retrieve e-mail from multiple e-mail accounts. To add more e-mail accounts, choose File⇨Add Account and repeat the preceding steps to add one or more additional e-mail accounts.

Writing E-Mails

After you configure Mail, you can start writing and sending e-mail to anyone with an e-mail address. In this section, I describe the three ways to write and send an e-mail:

✦ Create a new message from scratch.

✦ Reply to a message you received from someone else.

✦ Forward a message you received from someone else.

Creating a new e-mail

When you write a message to someone for the first time, you have to create a new message by following these steps:

1. **In Mail, choose File➪New Message (or click the New Message button) to open a New Message window.**

2. **Click the To text box and type an e-mail address, or just begin typing someone's name you have stored in Address Book to automatically fill in that person's e-mail address.**

   You can type multiple e-mail addresses in the To text box by separating them with a comma, such as `steve@apple.com, bill@microsoft.com`.

3. **Click the Subject text box and type a brief description of your message for your recipient.**

4. **Click the Message text box and type your message.**

5. **Click the Send button.**

Replying to a message

You'll often find yourself responding to messages others send to you. When you reply to a message, your reply can contain the text that you originally received so the recipient can better understand the context of your reply.

To reply to a message, you need to receive a message first. To receive messages, just click the Get Mail button. You find out more about receiving messages later in this chapter.

To reply to a message, follow these steps:

1. **In Mail, click the Inbox icon under the Mailboxes category in the left pane of the Mail window.**

   The top-right pane lists all the messages stored in your Inbox folder.

2. **Click to select a message in the Inbox that you want to reply to.**

3. **Choose Message➪Reply (or click the Reply button, or press ⌘+R).**

   A new Message window appears with the e-mail address of your recipient, the subject already entered, and the text of the message so that the other person can understand the context of your reply.

   If you're replying to a message that was sent to you and several other people, you can reply to everyone who received the same message by choosing Message➪Reply All (or by clicking the Reply All button, or by pressing ⌘+Shift+R).

4. **Click the Message text box and type a message.**

5. **Click Send.**

Forwarding a message

Sometimes you might receive a message and want to send that message to someone else. When you *forward* (send a copy of) a message, that message appears directly in the Message text box, as shown in Figure 2-5.

Figure 2-5:
A forwarded message appears directly in the Message text box.

To forward a message, follow these steps:

1. **In Mail, click the Inbox icon under the Mailboxes category in the left pane of the Mail window.**

    The right pane lists all the messages stored in your Inbox folder.

2. **In the Inbox, click to select a message that you want to forward.**

3. **Click the Forward button at the top of the Mail window.**

4. **Click the To text box and type an e-mail address.**

5. **Click Send.**

Sending a file attachment

When you send an e-mail, you're sending text. However, sometimes you might want to send pictures, word processor documents, or videos and links to Websites you think others may want to visit. Anyone receiving your message and file attachment can then save the file attachment and open it later. Because so many people need to share Microsoft Word files or digital photographs, file attachments are a popular way to share files with others.

Your e-mail account may have a maximum file size limit you can send, such as 10MB. If you have a file larger than the maximum limit, you might have to send your files through a free, separate file-delivery service, such as YouSendIt (www.yousendit.com), SendThisFile (www.sendthisfile.com), or BigUpload (www.bigupload.com).

To attach a file to a message, follow these steps:

1. **In Mail, open a new Message window as described in one of the preceding sections.**

   You can open a new Message window to create a new message, reply to an existing message, or forward an existing message.

2. **Choose File⇨Attach File (or click the Attach button).**

   A dialog appears.

3. **Navigate through the folders to get to the file you want to send and then click it.**

   To select multiple files, hold down the ⌘ key and click each file you want to send. To select a range of files, hold down the Shift key and click the first and last files you want to send.

4. **Click Choose File.**

5. **Click Send.**

Sending a message to multiple recipients

If you want to send the same message to several people, you can type multiple e-mail addresses, separated by a comma, in one or more of the following fields:

✦ **To:** The To field is where you type e-mail addresses of people who you want to read — and possibly reply to — your message.

✦ **Carbon copy (Cc):** The Cc field is where you type e-mail addresses of people who you want to keep informed, but who don't necessarily need to write a reply.

✦ **Blind carbon copy (Bcc):** The Bcc field sends a copy of your message to e-mail address that you type here, but those e-mail addresses will not be visible in the message to the recipients you enter in the To: and Cc: fields.

When sending out a particularly important message, many people type the recipient's e-mail address in the To field and their own e-mail address in the Cc: or Bcc: fields. This way they can verify that their message was sent correctly.

When someone receives an e-mail message, he or she can read all the e-mail addresses stored in the To and Carbon copy fields. If you don't want anyone else to know who received your message, use Blind carbon copy. (It's possible to use both Carbon copy and Blind carbon copy in the same message.)

Whenever you write a message, the To field is always visible because you need to send your message to at least one e-mail address. However, Mail can hide and display both the Carbon copy and Blind carbon copy fields because you don't always want or need them in every message you write.

To send multiple copies of the same message as Carbon copy or Blind carbon copy, follow these steps:

1. **In Mail, open a new Message window as described in one of the preceding sections.**

   You can open a new Message window to create a new message, reply to an existing message, or forward an existing message.

2. **(Optional) Choose View⇨Cc Address Field if the Cc field isn't visible.**

   A check mark means the Cc text box appears in the new Message window.

3. **(Optional) Choose View⇨Bcc Address Field if the Bcc field isn't visible.**

   A check mark means the Bcc text box appears in the new Message window.

4. **Click the Cc and/or Bcc text box and type an e-mail address.**

   You can type multiple e-mail addresses in the To, Cc, and Bcc text boxes by separating each e-mail address with a comma, such as `john@yahoo. com, bill@microsoft.com`.

5. **Click Send.**

Using e-mail stationery

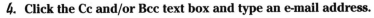

E-mail stationery consists of graphic designs and formatted text that you can edit. By using stationery, you can create e-mail messages that look more interesting than plain text. Keep in mind, however, that all of those pretty accents increase the size of any e-mail messages you create using stationery.

Picking a stationery design

To use the Mail program's Stationery feature to create a new message, follow these steps:

1. **In Mail, choose File⇨New Message (or click the New Message icon) to open a New Message window.**

2. **Click the Show Stationery button.**

A list of stationery categories (Birthday, Photos, and so on) appears in the upper-left pane and a list of stationery designs appears in the upper-middle of the New Message window, as shown in Figure 2-6.

3. **Click a Stationery category, such as Sentiments or Birthday.**

Each time you click a different category, the Mail window displays a list of stationery designs in that category.

4. **Click the stationery design that you want to use.**

Your chosen stationery appears in the main section of the New Message window.

5. **Click any text and edit or type new text.**

Modifying photographs in a stationery design

After you choose a stationery design, you can edit the text and replace it with your own message. If the stationery displays a photograph, you can replace the photograph with another picture stored in iPhoto or somewhere else on your hard drive.

To add your own pictures to a stationery design, follow these steps:

1. **Make sure Mail displays a stationery design that includes one or more pictures, as shown in top part of Figure 2-7.**

2. **Do one of the following actions:**

- Call up the Finder by clicking the Finder icon in the Dock. (You might need to move the Finder and Mail windows so they appear side by side.)

- Click the Photo Browser icon. The Photo Browser window appears, containing all the photographs you've stored in iPhoto.

3. **In either the Finder or the Photo Browser, navigate to the folder that contains a photograph that you want to use in your stationery.**

Show/Hide Stationery button

Figure 2-6:
Stationery
lets you
choose from
predesigned
templates
for different
types of
e-mail
messages.

4. **Click and drag your chosen photograph onto the picture in your stationery design.**

5. **Release the mouse button.**

   Your chosen picture now appears in your stationery, as shown in the lower part of Figure 2-7.

6. **Click the Close button of the Finder or Photo Browser window.**

Spelling and grammar checking

Although e-mail is considered less formal than other forms of communication, such as letters or a Last Will and Testament, you probably don't want your e-mail message riddled with spelling errors and typos that can make you look like, well, a dummy. That's why Mail provides a spelling and grammar checker.

Figure 2-7:
Click and
drag to
replace
stationery
pictures
with your
own images.

To use the built-in spelling and grammar checker, you need to configure it to
define whether you want it to check while you type or wait until you finish
typing.

Configuring the spelling and grammar checker

By default, Mail has its spell checker turned on to check misspellings while you type. When Mail finds a misspelled word, it underlines the word in red so you can Control-click on the underlined word and then choose another word from the shortcut menu of best guesses. Or, you can choose Learn Spelling from the shortcut menu to add the word to your Mac's list of correctly spelled words if your Mac doesn't already have it in its own list of spell checker words. If you find the red underline feature annoying or want to turn on the grammar checker, too, you need to configure the spelling and grammar checker. If you're happy with the way the spell checker works, you don't have to configure the spelling and grammar checker at all.

To configure the spelling and grammar checker, follow these steps:

1. **Open a new Message window as described earlier in this chapter, then click in the Message text box and enter some text or an actual e-mail message you want to send.**

   You can open a new Message window to create a new message, reply to an existing message, or forward an existing message.

2. **Choose Edit⇨Spelling and Grammar⇨Check Spelling and then choose one of the following from the submenu, as shown in Figure 2-8:**

   - *While Typing:* Underlines possible misspellings and grammar problems while you write.

   - *Before Sending:* Spelling and grammar checking of your message before it's sent.

   - *Never:* Doesn't perform spelling and grammar checking.

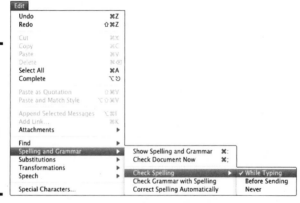

Figure 2-8:
The Check Spelling menu provides spelling and grammar checking options.

3. (Optional) Choose Edit⇨Spelling and Grammar⇨Check Grammar with Spelling if you want to have Mail flag potential grammatical errors.

4. (Optional) Choose Edit⇨Spelling and Grammar⇨Correct Spelling Automatically if you want Mail to automatically correct words it deems incorrect.

Checking spelling and grammar

If you have spell checking turned on while you type, the spell checker will underline suspected misspelled words in red to help you find potential problems easily. If you want to spell check and grammar check your entire message, follow these steps:

1. **Open a new Message window as described earlier in this chapter.**

You can open a new Message window to create a new message, reply to an existing message, or forward an existing message.

2. **Choose Edit⇨Spelling and Grammar⇨Show Spelling and Grammar.**

The spelling and grammar checker does it thing, with a Spelling and Grammar dialog appearing each time Mail finds a potentially misspelled word, as shown in Figure 2-9.

Figure 2-9: The Spelling and Grammar dialog suggests possible correct spellings.

3. **Click one of the following buttons:**

   - *Change:* Changes the misspelled word with the spelling that you choose from the list box on the left.

   - *Find Next:* Finds the next occurrence of the same misspelled word.

   - *Ignore:* Tells Mail that the word is correct.

   - *Learn:* Adds the word to the dictionary.

   - *Define:* Launches Mac's Dictionary program and looks up and displays the word's definition in the Dictionary's main window.

   - *Guess:* Offers best-guess word choices.

4. **Click Send.**

The spelling and grammar checker can't catch all possible errors (words like *to* and *two*, or *fiend* and *friend* can slip past because the words are spelled correctly), so make sure you proofread your message after you finish spelling and grammar checking your message.

Receiving and Reading E-Mail

To receive e-mail, your e-mail program must contact your incoming mail server and download the messages to your Mac. Then you can either check for new mail manually or have Mail check for new mail automatically.

Retrieving e-mail

To check and retrieve e-mail manually in Mail, choose Mailbox⇨Get New Mail (or click the Get Mail icon). The number of new messages appears next to the Inbox icon, and in a red circle on the Mail icon in the Dock.

Checking for new e-mail manually can get tedious, so you can configure Mail to check for new mail automatically at fixed intervals of time, such as every 5 or 15 minutes. To configure Mail to check for new messages automatically, follow these steps:

1. **In Mail, choose Mail⇨Preferences to open the Mail preferences window.**

2. **Click the General icon to display the General pane, as shown in Figure 2-10.**

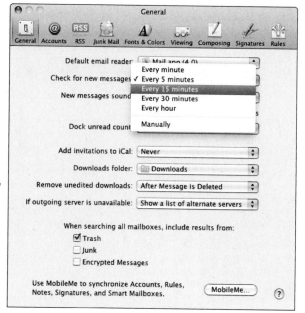

Figure 2-10:
The General pane lets you define how often to check for new e-mail.

3. **From the Check for New Messages pop-up menu, choose an option to determine how often to check for new messages.**

   You can check every minute, every 5 minutes, every 15 minutes, every 30 minutes, or every hour.

4. **(Optional) Choose a sound to play when you receive new messages from the New Messages Sound pop-up menu.**

   You can also choose None in case any sound bothers you.

5. **Click the Close button of the Mail preferences window.**

Mail can check for new messages only if you leave Mail running. If you quit Mail, it can't check for new messages periodically.

Reading e-mail

After you start receiving e-mail, you can start reading your messages. When you receive a new message, Mail flags it with a dot in the Message Status column, as shown in Figure 2-11.

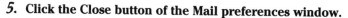

Message status column

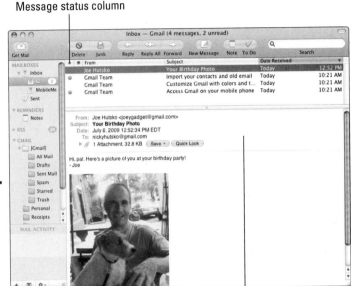

Figure 2-11:
Mail shows
you which
messages
you haven't
read yet.

Preview pane

To read a message, follow these steps:

1. **In Mail, click the Inbox icon in the left pane.**

A list of messages stored in the Inbox appears.

2. **Do one of the following:**

- Click a message and read the message in the Preview pane.
- Double-click a message to display and read a message in a separate window.

The advantage of the Preview pane is that you can scan your messages quickly by clicking each one without having to open a separate window. The advantage of reading a message in a separate window is that you can resize that window and see more of the message without having to scroll as often as you would if you were reading that same message in the Preview pane.

Viewing and saving file attachments

When you receive a message that has a file attachment, Mail identifies how many attachments there are and displays a Save button and a Quick Look button, as shown in Figure 2-12.

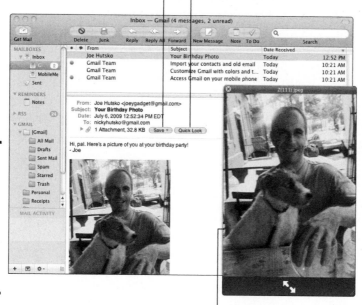

The Save button

The Quick Look button

The Quick Look window

Figure 2-12:
A Save button appears whenever a message includes a file attachment.

To save a file attachment, follow these steps:

1. **In Mail, click the Inbox icon in the left pane.**

A list of messages stored in the Inbox appears.

2. **Click a message in the right pane.**

If the message has a file attachment, the number of attachments, the amount of space they take up, the Save button, and the Quick Look button all appear in the message headers that list who sent the message, the date sent, and the message subject.

If the attachment is a picture or video clip, the image or clip will appear in the body of the e-mail message (refer to Figure 2-11).

3. **(Optional) Click the Quick Look button (refer to Figure 2-12).**

A window appears, displaying the contents of your file attachment (or playing the file if it's a music or video file). Click the Close box of the Quick Look window when you finish looking at its contents.

**Book IV
Chapter 2**

**Sending and
Receiving E-Mail**

4. **Click the Save button, or click and hold down on the Save button to display a list of attachments, and then choose either Save All to save all attachments, or choose an individual attachment to save it but not the others if the e-mail message contains more than one attachment.**

You can also just click and drag attachments from the message body to the Desktop or a Finder window. To do so, hold down the Command key to select more than one attachment; then click and drag any one of the selected attachments to the Desktop or a Finder window.

Mail saves your attachments into the Downloads folder stored inside your Home folder. (You may also access the Downloads folder in the Dock, to the left of the Trash icon.)

Storing e-mail addresses

Typing an e-mail address every time you want to send a message can get tedious — if you can even remember the address. Fortunately, Mail lets you store names and e-mail addresses in the Address Book. Then you can just click that person's name to send a message without typing that person's entire e-mail address.

Adding an e-mail address to the Address Book

When you receive an e-mail from someone you like, you can store that person's e-mail address in the Address Book by following these steps:

1. **In Mail, click the Inbox icon in the left pane.**

   A list of messages appears in the top-right pane.

2. **Click to select a message sent by someone whose e-mail address you want to save.**

3. **Choose Message⇨Add Sender to Address Book.**

   Although nothing appears to happen, your chosen e-mail address is now stored in the Address Book.

To view your list of stored names and e-mail addresses, you can open the Address Book by choosing Window⇨Address Panel.

Retrieving an e-mail address from the Address Book

When you create a new message, you can retrieve an e-mail address from your Address Book. To retrieve an e-mail address, follow these steps:

1. **In Mail, choose File⇨New Message (or click the New Message icon).**

   A New Message window appears.

2. **Click the Address button (or choose Window⇨Address Panel).**

   The Addresses window appears, as shown in Figure 2-13.

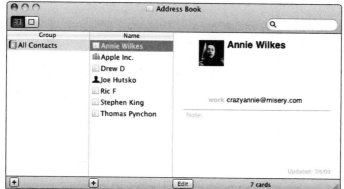

Figure 2-13:
The Addresses window lets you pick an e-mail address.

3. **Click to select the name of the person you want to send a message to.**

4. **Click the To button.**

   Your chosen e-mail address appears in the To text box. (If you click the Cc or Bcc buttons, you can add an e-mail address to the Cc or Bcc text boxes, respectively.)

5. **Click the Close button of the Addresses window.**

Deleting a name and e-mail address from the Address Book

After you store names and e-mail addresses in your Address Book, you might want to delete some of them one day. To delete an e-mail address in the Address Book, follow these steps:

1. **Click the Address Book icon in the Dock (or double-click the Address Book icon in the Applications folder).**

   The Address Book window appears.

2. **Click the name you want to delete and then press the Delete key.**

   A dialog appears asking whether you're sure that you want to delete the address card.

3. **Click Delete.**

   The Address Book deletes your chosen name.

   If you accidentally delete a name, you can retrieve it right away by choosing Edit⇨Undo Delete Record.

4. **To quit Address Book, choose Address Book⇨Quit Address Book or press ⌘+Q.**

Book IV
Chapter 2

Sending and
Receiving E-Mail

Deleting messages

After you read a message, you can either leave it in your Inbox or delete it. Generally, it's a good idea to delete messages you won't need again, such as an invitation to somebody's birthday party back in the summer of 2008. By deleting unnecessary messages, you can keep your Inbox organized and uncluttered — and if you're using an IMAP or Exchange account, free up space on the mail server where your e-mail messages are stored.

To delete a message, follow these steps:

1. **In Mail, click the Inbox icon in the left pane.**

   A list of messages stored in the Inbox appears.

2. **Click the message you want to delete.**

   To select multiple messages, hold down the ⌘ key and click additional messages. To select a range of messages, hold down the Shift key, click the first message to delete, click the last message to delete, and then release the Shift key.

3. **Choose Edit➪Delete (or click the Delete button).**

Deleting a message doesn't immediately erase it, but stores it in the Trash folder. If you don't "empty the trash," you still have the chance to retrieve deleted messages, as outlined in the next section.

Retrieving messages from the Trash folder

Each time you delete a message, Mail stores the deleted messages in the Trash folder. If you think you deleted a message by mistake, you can retrieve it by following these steps:

1. **In Mail, click the Trash folder.**

   A list of deleted messages appears.

2. **Click the message you want to retrieve.**

3. **Choose Message➪Move To➪Inbox.**

You can set up Mail to automatically move deleted messages to the trash and permanently erase those trashed messages after a month, a week, a day, or upon quitting Mail. To configure this option, choose Mail➪Preferences, click the Accounts tab, click a mail account in the Accounts column, and then click Mailbox Behaviors and adjust the settings for Trash to suit your e-mail housekeeping style.

Emptying the Trash folder

Messages stored in the Trash folder continue to take up space, so you should periodically empty the Trash folder by following these steps:

1. **In Mail, choose Mailbox➪Erase Deleted Messages.**

A submenu appears, listing all the e-mail accounts in Mail.

2. **Choose either In All Accounts (to erase all deleted messages) or the name of a specific e-mail account (to erase messages only from that particular account).**

Organizing E-Mail

To help you manage and organize your e-mail messages, Mail lets you search and sort your messages. Searching lets you find specific text stored in a particular message. Sorting lets you arrange your messages in folders so one folder might contain personal messages and a second folder might contain business messages.

Searching through e-mail

To manage your e-mail effectively, you need to be able to search for one message (or more) you want to find and view. To search through your e-mail for the names of senders or text in a message, follow these steps:

1. **In Mail, click the Spotlight text box in the upper-right corner.**

2. **Type a word, phrase, or partial phrase that you want to find.**

When you type, Mail displays a list of messages that match the text you're typing, as shown in Figure 2-14.

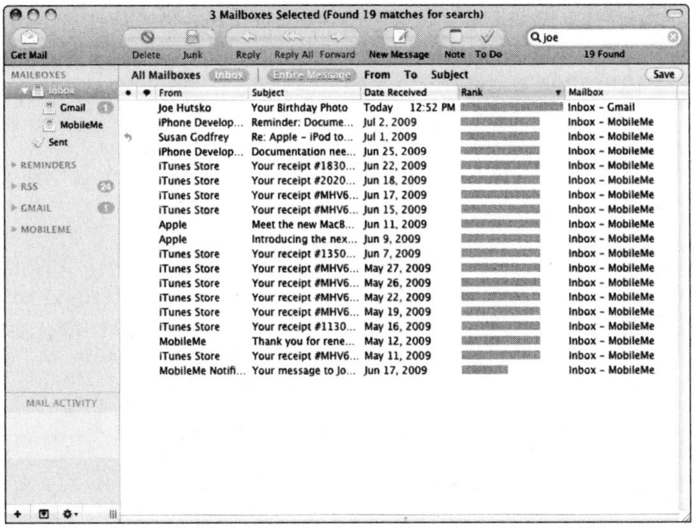

Figure 2-14: While you type in the Spotlight text box, Mail displays a list of messages that match your text.

3. **(Optional) Click the buttons above the right pane to narrow your search.**

    Your options are to search through All Mailboxes or the Inbox, or to search only the To, From, or Subject fields, or the Entire Message.

4. **(Optional) Click the Save button in the upper-right corner to open a Smart Mailbox window, type in a name for your new Smart Mailbox search, choose any options you want to customize your search, and then click OK to save your Smart Mailbox search.**

5. **Click a message to read it.**

Sorting e-mail

You can sort e-mail in ascending or descending order based on different categories, such as alphabetically by the sender, chronologically by date sent, or alphabetically by subject.

The easiest way to sort your e-mail is by clicking a column heading, such as From or Subject.

To sort your e-mail, you can also follow these steps:

1. **In Mail, choose View⇨Sort By.**

    A submenu appears, as shown in Figure 2-15.

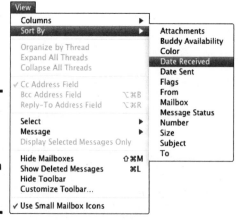

Figure 2-15: Mail lets you sort your e-mail messages in a variety of ways.

2. **Choose a criteria to sort, such as by Date Sent or Subject.**

    Mail then sorts the e-mail according to your whims.

Organizing e-mail with mailbox folders

When you receive e-mail, all of your messages are dumped in the Inbox. After a while, you might have so many messages stored there that trying to find related messages can be nearly impossible.

To fix this problem, you can create separate folders for organizing your different e-mails. After you create a folder, you can group related messages together so you can quickly find them later.

One common type of e-mail to organize is junk e-mail, which you can route automatically to the Trash folder, as I write in the upcoming "Dealing with junk e-mail" section.

Creating a mailbox folder

To create a mailbox folder, follow these steps:

1. **In Mail, choose Mailbox⇨New Mailbox.**

A New Mailbox dialog appears, as shown in Figure 2-16.

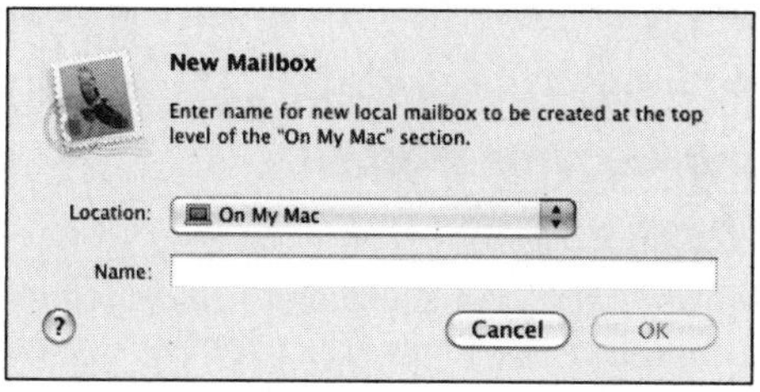

Figure 2-16:
The New Mailbox dialog lets you choose a name for your mailbox folder.

> **New Mailbox**
>
> Enter name for new local mailbox to be created at the top level of the "On My Mac" section.
>
> Location: [On My Mac ‡]
>
> Name: [   ]
>
> (?)   (Cancel) (OK)

2. **In the Name text box, type a descriptive name for your mailbox folder and then click OK.**

Your mailbox folder appears in the left pane of the Mail window.

Storing messages in a mailbox folder

When you create a mailbox folder, it's completely empty. To store messages in a mailbox folder, you must manually drag those messages to the mailbox folder. Dragging physically moves your message from the Inbox folder to your mailbox folder.

Book IV
Chapter 2

Sending and
Receiving E-Mail

To move a message to a mailbox folder, follow these steps:

1. **In Mail, click the Inbox icon in the left pane to view your e-mail messages.**

2. **Click a message and drag it to the mailbox folder you want to move it to, then release the mouse.**

   Your selected message now appears in the mailbox folder.

   If you hold down the ⌘ key while clicking a message, you can select multiple messages. If you hold down the Shift key, you can click one message and then click another message to select those two messages and every message in between.

Deleting a mailbox folder

You can delete a mailbox folder by following these steps:

1. **In Mail, click the mailbox folder you want to delete.**

2. **Choose Mailbox⇨Delete.**

   A dialog box appears, asking whether you're sure that you want to delete your folder.

   When you delete a mailbox folder, you delete all messages stored inside.

3. **Click Delete.**

Automatically organizing e-mail with smart mailboxes

Mailbox folders can help organize your messages, but you must manually drag messages into those folders. To make this process automatic, you can use *smart mailboxes*.

A smart mailbox differs from an ordinary mailbox in two ways:

✦ A smart mailbox lets you define the type of messages you want to store automatically; that way, Mail sorts your messages without any additional work from you.

✦ A smart mailbox doesn't physically contain a message but only a link to the actual message, which is still stored in the Inbox folder (or any folder that you move it to). Because smart mailboxes don't physically move messages, it's possible for a single message to have links stored in multiple smart mailboxes.

Creating a smart mailbox

To create a smart mailbox, you need to define a name for your smart mailbox along with the criteria for the types of messages to store in your smart mailbox. To create a smart mailbox, follow these steps:

1. **In Mail, choose Mailbox⇨New Smart Mailbox.**

A Smart Mailbox dialog appears, as shown in Figure 2-17.

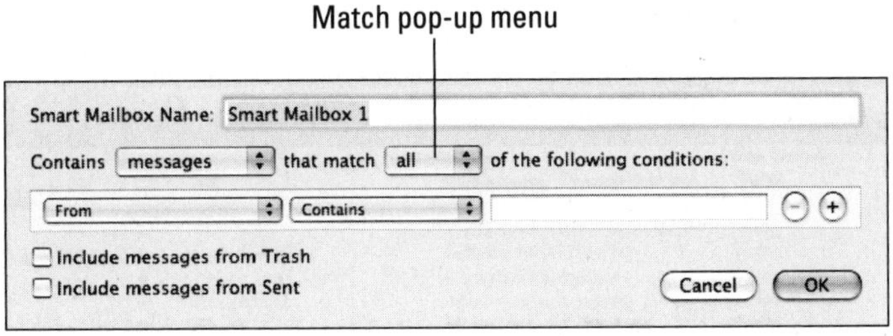

Match pop-up menu

Figure 2-17:
The Smart
Mailbox
dialog lets
you define
the types of
messages to
automatically
store.

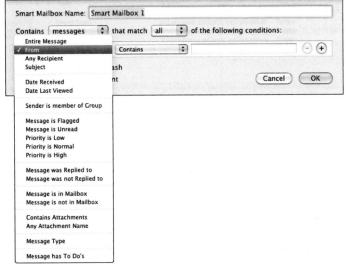

2. **Click the Smart Mailbox Name text box and type a descriptive name for your smart mailbox.**

3. **Click the Match pop-up menu and choose All (of the Following Conditions) or Any (of the Following Conditions).**

4. **Click the first criteria pop-up menu and choose an option, such as From or Date Received, as shown in Figure 2-18.**

Figure 2-18:
The first
pop-up
menu lets
you choose
criteria for
the type of
messages to
include.

5. **Click the second criteria pop-up menu and choose how to apply your first criteria, such as Contains or Ends with, as shown in Figure 2-19.**

Figure 2-19:
The second
pop-up
menu lets
you choose
how to
apply your
chosen
criteria.

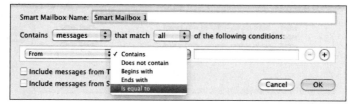

6. **Click the criteria text box and type a word or phrase that you want to use for your criteria.**

7. **(Optional) Click the Add Rule icon (Plus Sign button) and repeat Steps 5 through 7.**

8. **Click OK.**

Your smart mailbox appears in the left pane of the Mail window. If any messages match your defined criteria, you can click your smart mailbox icon to see a list of messages.

The messages stored in a smart mailbox are just links to the actual messages stored in your Inbox folder.

Deleting a smart mailbox

Deleting a smart mailbox doesn't physically delete any messages because a smart mailbox only contains links to existing messages. To delete a smart mailbox, follow these steps:

1. **In Mail, click the smart mailbox folder you want to delete.**

2. **Choose Mailbox⇨Delete.**

A dialog appears, asking whether you're sure that you want to delete your smart mailbox.

3. **Click Delete (or Cancel).**

Automatically organizing e-mail with rules

Smart mailboxes provide links to e-mail messages that physically remain in your Inbox folder. However, you might want to physically move a message from the Inbox folder to another folder automatically, which you can do by defining rules.

The basic idea behind rules is to pick criteria for selecting messages, such
as all messages from specific e-mail addresses or subject lines that contain
certain phrases, and route them automatically into a folder.

To create a rule, follow these steps:

1. **Choose Mail⇨Preferences to open the Mail preferences window.**

2. **Click the Rules icon.**

The Rules window appears, as shown in Figure 2-20.

Figure 2-20:
The Rules
window
shows you
all the rules
you've
created
and lets you
create new
ones.

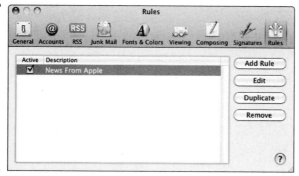

If you click an existing rule (such as the preconfigured News From Apple
rule shown in Figure 2-20) and click Edit, you can modify an existing rule.

3. **Click Add Rule.**

The Rules window displays pop-up menus for defining a rule, as shown
in Figure 2-21.

Figure 2-21:
Clicking
different
pop-up
menus lets
you define
a rule for
routing your
messages.

4. **Click the Description text box and type a description of what your rule does.**

5. **Click one or more pop-up menus to define how your rule works, such as what to look for or which folder to move the message to, as shown in Figure 2-22.**

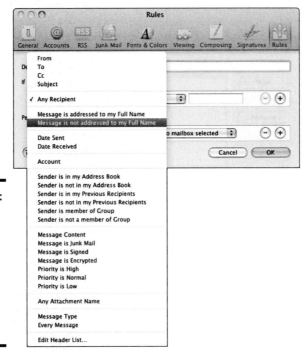

Figure 2-22:
Pop-up
menus
provide
different
options for
selecting
messages
to sort by
your rule.

6. **(Optional) Click the Plus Sign button to define another sorting criterion for your rule and repeat Steps 5 and 6 as often as necessary.**

7. **Click OK when you finish defining your rule.**

A dialog appears, asking whether you want to apply your new rule to your messages.

8. **Click Apply.**

9. **Click the Close button of the Rules window.**

Mail now displays your messages sorted into folders according to your defined rules.

Dealing with Junk E-Mail

As soon as you get an e-mail address, you're going to start receiving junk e-mail (or *spam*), and there's nothing you can do to stop it. However, Mail gives you tools for handling the inevitable flow of junk e-mail so you can keep your e-mail account from getting overwhelmed. Two ways to manage your junk e-mail are by bouncing junk e-mail back to the sender or by filtering junk e-mail into a special junk folder.

Most junk e-mail messages are advertisements trying to sell you various products, but some junk e-mail messages are actually scams to trick you into visiting bogus Web sites that ask for your credit card number. This form of spam is called *phishing*. Other times, junk e-mail might contain an attachment masquerading as a free program that secretly contains a computer virus. Or, a junk e-mail might try to trick you into clicking a Web link that downloads and installs a computer virus on your Mac. By filtering out such malicious junk e-mail, you can minimize potential threats that can jeopardize your Mac's integrity or your personal information.

Bouncing junk e-mail

When spammers send e-mail, the majority of their messages are sent to nonexistent e-mail addresses. When this occurs, the mail server computer *bounces* the message back to the sender so the sender knows that the e-mail address is invalid. Then the spammer knows not to waste time sending that nonexistent e-mail address any more messages.

Fortunately, you can take advantage of this feature by bouncing unwanted messages back to the sender. When you bounce a message back to the sender, this bounced message makes it appear as though your e-mail address is invalid (when it really isn't). Then the spammer might remove your e-mail address from the mailing list, so you'll receive less junk e-mail.

That's the theory, anyway. In real life, this can work if the spammer sent e-mail from a valid e-mail address. If the spammer sent junk e-mail through another computer (such as one hijacked without the owner's knowledge), bouncing e-mail will never reach the spammer, and your e-mail address will continue to receive junk e-mail.

Although not perfect, bouncing junk e-mail back to its sender might help reduce the amount of junk e-mail in your Inbox. To bounce a message, follow these steps:

1. **In Mail, click the Inbox icon in the left pane.**

A list of messages appears in the right pane.

2. **Click a message that you consider junk.**

3. **Choose Message⇨Bounce.**

    A dialog appears, letting you know that bouncing messages works only if your unwanted message came from a valid e-mail address.

4. **Click the Bounce button (or click Cancel).**

Bouncing e-mail is more effective when you know the sender's e-mail address is valid, such as bouncing messages sent to you from a former partner or a person who keeps harassing you because you gave their book a negative review.

Filtering junk e-mail

More effective than bouncing is *filtering*. Filtering means that Mail examines the content of messages and tries to determine whether the message is junk. To improve accuracy, Mail allows you to train it by letting you manually identify junk e-mail that its existing rules didn't catch.

After a few weeks of watching you identify junk e-mail, the Mail program's filters will eventually recognize common junk e-mail so it can route it automatically to a special junk folder. By doing this, Mail can keep your Inbox free from most junk e-mail so you can focus on reading the messages that matter to you.

To train Mail to recognize junk e-mail, follow these steps:

1. **In Mail, click the Inbox icon in the left pane.**

    A list of messages appears in the right pane.

2. **Click a message that you consider junk.**

3. **Click the Junk icon.**

    This tells the Mail program's filters what you consider junk e-mail.

4. **Click the Delete icon at the top of the Mail window.**

    This deletes your chosen message and "trains" Mail to recognize similar messages as junk.

Many Web-based e-mail providers — including Google Gmail, Yahoo! Mail, and Microsoft Hotmail — have special programs running on their e-mail servers that try to sniff out junk e-mail before it has a chance to land in your Inbox. Sometimes legitimate e-mail messages can wind up in the junk or spam folders those service providers provide for catching potential junk e-mail. Log in to your Web-based e-mail account from time to time to check whether messages you wanted to receive might have been flagged as junk e-mail, click those messages, and then click the Not Junk or Not Spam button or option to tell the e-mail service provider's junk e-mail sniffing program the sender of the message is "safe."

Although Mail's built-in junk e-mail filters can strip away most junk e-mail, consider getting a special junk e-mail filter as well. These e-mail filters strip out most junk e-mail better than Mail can do, but the Mail program's filters might later catch any junk e-mail that slips past these separate filters, which essentially doubles your defenses against junk e-mail. Some popular e-mail filters are SpamSieve (`http://c-command.com`), Purify (`www.hendricom.com`), and Personal Antispam (`www.intego.com`). Spam filters cost money and take time to configure, but if your e-mail account is overrun by junk e-mail, a separate junk e-mail filter might be your only solution short of getting a new e-mail account.

Chapter 3: Instant Messaging and Video Chatting with iChat

In This Chapter

✔ **Setting up an account**

✔ **Finding people to chat with**

✔ **Chatting via text, audio, and video**

✔ **Sharing pictures, files, and screens with iChat Theater**

✔ **Taking a look at other chat programs**

The idea behind instant messaging is that you can communicate with someone over the Internet using text, audio, or even video — and it's all free. (Well, it's sort of free, when you ignore the fact that you're paying your broadband Internet provider a pretty penny every month so you can access the Internet.)

Now you can swap messages with your friends, chat in real time across the planet, and even see each other through live video windows while you speak. Instant messaging offers another way for you to communicate with anyone in the world using an Internet connection and your Mac.

By using your Mac's iChat program you can conduct basic text chat messages with others instantly. And iChat also makes integrating live video, audio, and sharing files with others you connect to practically as easy as chatting over the telephone.

Setting Up an iChat Account

If you have an existing instant messaging chat account with one of the following services, you're ready to set up iChat and start chatting in a matter of minutes. If you don't have a chat account, you need to set up an account with at least one of the following services:

✦ **MobileMe:** Formerly known as .Mac, you can create a free 60-day trial MobileMe account ($99 per year). If you later decide to cancel, you can still use your MobileMe account name free with iChat. Former .Mac trial users and subscribers who stuck with the service when it changed to MobileMe can also use their *yourname*@mac.com account name with iChat. You can sign up for MobileMe at www.apple.com/mobileme.

Can't we all just get along?

You can only use some of iChat's livelier features, like video chatting and screen sharing, when you connect to friends using the same kind of account as you. That means Mac.com and MobileMe account users can send text messages and video chat with one another and with AIM users, but they cannot conduct video chats with Google Talk or Jabber users.

On the other hand, Google Talk accounts act as Jabber accounts, and Jabber accounts act as Google Talk accounts. That is, Google Talk and Jabber account holders running iChat get along to take advantage of iChat's audio and video chat, and screen sharing features, in addition to text chat.

To get the most from using iChat with friends, you want to sign in with an account that matches the ones your friends are using. If your friends use Google Talk to sign in to iChat and you use MobileMe, you might want to create a Google Gmail account and add your Google Talk account to iChat so you can audio chat and video chat with your friends who sign in with a Google Talk account name.

To add additional account names to iChat, check out the nearby sidebar, "Managing multiple chat personalities and options."

 ✦ **Mac.com:** If you don't want to bother signing up for the MobileMe trial offer, you can still get a free iChat account name that ends with @mac.com. I explain how to do this in Step 3 of the step-by-step directions following these bullets.

 ✦ **AOL Instant Messenger (AIM):** Available free at www.aim.com, existing AIM account users and new users are warmly welcome to use their account name with iChat.

 ✦ **Google Talk:** Got a Google Gmail account? If so, you automatically have a Google Talk account, which lets you send and receive text messages or conduct video conferences with other Gmail account holders from your Gmail Web page (gmail.google.com). Having a Google Gmail account also means you can use it to set up iChat to send and receive text messages and connect with other Gmail account buddies with iChat's audio and video chat, and screen-sharing feature. Google Talk user names end with @gmail.com.

 ✦ **Jabber:** The original IM service based on XMPP, the open standard for instant messaging, you can create a Jabber account by visiting register.jabber.org or one of the other public XMPP services, and then use your Jabber account, which ends with @jabber.org, to log in and start chatting.

To understand which chat accounts can communicate with which other chat accounts, check out the nearby sidebar, "Can't we all just get along?"

After you create a chat account, you can set up an iChat account by following these steps:

1. **Click the iChat icon in the Dock to launch iChat.**

An iChat welcome window appears.

2. **Click Continue.**

The Account Setup window appears, ready to receive your account type, name, and password information, as shown in Figure 3-1.

Figure 3-1:
The iChat window prompts you for your account information.

3. **Click the Account Type pop-up menu and choose your account type.**

Your choices here include MobileMe, Mac.com, AIM, Jabber, and Google Talk accounts.

If you don't have one of these accounts, choose AIM, MobileMe or Mac.com in the Account Type pop-up menu, and then click the Get an iChat Account button to launch Safari and take you to the service's Web site and new account sign-up form, which you can fill out to create your own chat account name.

4. **Type your account username in the first text box.**

The name to the left of the text box changes depending on which account type you select in Step 3. In Figure 3-1, the name reads Screen Name.

5. **Type your password in the Password text box.**

6. Click Continue to take you to a third iChat window informing you that you've successfully set up your iChat account and then click Done to close the iChat window.

7. The iChat Buddy List window appears and iChat automatically logs in to your account.

If you sign in using an existing instant messaging account, the iChat Buddy List window displays a list of any buddies who are online when you are.

If you sign in to iChat using an existing chat account, you can go about your merry way and communicate with the friends, family, and coworkers you previously added whenever they're online and you want to get in touch with them (or vice versa).

If you're brand new to instant messaging, setting up a chat account is only half the process to using iChat. Your next step is to contact your friends and other contacts you want to chat with to exchange instant messaging account names. Think of account names as telephone numbers; you can't call a friend without first knowing her phone number, and similarly, you can't chat with someone if you don't know her account name.

Managing multiple chat personalities and options

If you have more than one chat account, iChat allows you to add, switch between, and juggle two or more chat accounts at the same time.

To add, change, or delete additional chat accounts, choose iChat⇨Preferences to open the iChat preferences window shown here and then click the Accounts tab.

Things you can do with the iChat Accounts preferences pane include:

✔ Click the Add (+) button to add a new chat account to iChat; then follow the steps in the "Setting Up an iChat Account" section.

✔ Click a chat account listed in the Accounts column and click the Delete (-) button to delete a chat account you no longer want to use with iChat.

✔ Click a chat account in the Accounts column and click the Account Information tab to select, deselect, or change the following options:

✔ *Enable This Account:* When selected, makes the chat account available to sign in to and then displays a buddy list for the account.

✔ *Log In Automatically When iChat Opens:* When selected, signs in to the chat account and displays the account's buddy list when you launch iChat.

✔ *Allow Multiple Logins for This Account:* When selected, lets you sign in to your AIM chat account with iChat, for instance, and sign in to your AIM chat account on AOL's AIM Web site (www.aim.com) at the same time. When deselected, iChat (or the AIM Web site) detects the chat account is

signed in on another location and offers you the option to sign off in one location or keep both signed in at the same time.

✔ *Description, Screen Name, and Password:* Click these fields to change the name of the chat account, the screen name, or the password. (**Note:** You must sign out of your chat account before you can change what's in this trio of fields.)

✔ *Add New Buddies I Chat with to "Recent Buddies":* When selected, iChat updates your buddy list with any buddies you chat with who aren't already added.

✔ Click Configure AIM Mobile Forwarding (AIM, Mac.com, and MobileMe accounts only) to launch your Web browser and open the AIM Mobile Forwarding Web page where you can type your mobile phone number to enable it to receive SMS text messages when someone sends you a text chat message and you're not signed in to iChat.

✔ Click the Security tab to enable or disable various privacy and security settings, which I describe in more detail in the section "Accepting (or blocking) chat invitations with privacy levels," later in this chapter.

If you're not brand new to instant messaging, but the instant messaging account you use isn't one that works with iChat, you can install and run other chat programs to send and receive instant messages and conduct voice and video chats with your buddies who use other chat accounts and chat programs. To learn more about the most popular chat accounts and programs, check out the "Taking a look at other chat programs" section at the end of this chapter.

If, like me, you have more than one chat account, you can add your additional chat accounts to iChat so you can sign in and display a buddy list for each of your chat accounts. To add, manage, or delete more than one iChat chat account, check out the nearby sidebar, "Managing multiple chat personalities and options."

**Book IV
Chapter 3**

Instant Messaging and Video Chatting with iChat

Storing names in a buddy list

A *buddy list* lets you store the account names of your friends. Stored names automatically appear in your iChat buddy lists whenever your friends log in to their particular chat program (which can be a program other than iChat, such as AOL Instant Messenger for Mac or Windows, or even a mobile chat program running on a smartphone).

To add a name to your buddy list, follow these steps:

1. **Click the iChat icon in the Dock to launch iChat.**

   If you don't see a Buddy List window, click the Window menu and then select the account name you use to sign in to iChat. If you added more than one chat account, choose the account name with the buddy list you want to display. Repeat the same step to display buddy lists for any other chat accounts you added to work with iChat.

2. **Choose Buddies⇨Add Buddy, or click the Add (+) button in the lower-left corner of the iChat Buddy List window and select Add Buddy from the pop-up menu.**

   A dialog appears, as shown in Figure 3-2.

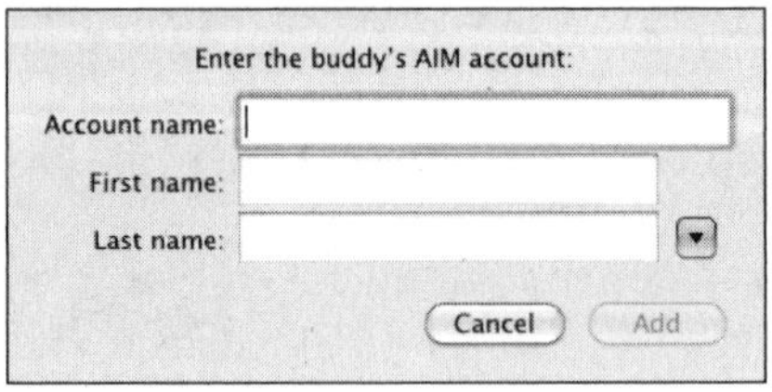

Figure 3-2:
To add a contact to your buddy list, type their chat account name or e-mail address.

Enter the buddy's AIM account:

Account name:

First name:

Last name:

Cancel   Add

3. **Fill in your buddy's chat account name and real name.**

   You have two ways to do this:

   * *Type your buddy's account name and real name in the three text boxes shown in Figure 3-2.* Depending on the chat account your buddy has, the account name might be a single word or an e-mail address.

   Filling in your buddy's first and last name is for your convenience only. If you don't know someone's first or last name, or if you prefer to see his chat account name rather than his real name in your buddy list, just leave the name fields blank.

- *Add contacts from your Address Book.* Click the down-arrow button next to the Last Name field (refer to Figure 3-2) to expand the Add Buddy dialog and show your Mac's Address Book contacts. Use the search field or click the scroll arrows — both are visible in Figure 3-3 — to locate your buddy's contact card and then click your buddy's name to select him or her.

Your buddy's account name, first name, and last name automatically fill in the related fields of the Add Buddy dialog.

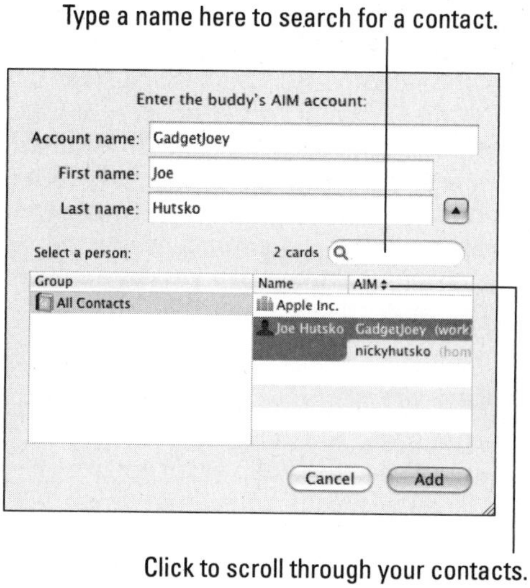

Type a name here to search for a contact.

Figure 3-3:
Clicking on a buddy's contact card automatically fills in the blanks.

Click to scroll through your contacts.

4. **(Optional) Click the column heading to the right of the Name column (named AIM in Figure 3-3) to open a pop-up menu that lets you choose between displaying contact chat names or e-mail addresses.**

5. **(Optional) Click the Add to Group pop-up menu (which only appears if more than one group is available), and then choose the group category where you want to store your friend's name, such as Buddies, Family, or Co-Workers.**

    You can change which group your buddy appears in at any time.

6. **Click the Add button.**

    Your new buddy appears in your buddy list.

If you don't see your newly added buddy (or buddies you previously added) in your buddy list, chances are you might have inadvertently chosen an iChat option to hide offline buddies from your buddy list. To show offline buddies in your buddy list, choose View➪Show Offline Buddies. Conversely, if you only want your buddies to appear in the iChat Buddy List window when they're online, choose View➪Show Offline Buddies.

The names of buddies who are online when you're online appear as normal text with an accompanying generic chat icon or a custom icon of your buddy's choosing (if he uses a custom icon with his chat program). The names of buddies who are offline when you're online appear dimmed on your iChat buddy list.

Organizing a buddy list

When you add a name to your buddy list, you have to store it within an existing group, such as Buddies, Family, or Co-Workers. If you want, you can always move or copy a buddy's chat account name to a different group or even create completely new groups, such as a group of people involved in a specific project. For instance, a community recycling team that you organize in a group named WeCyclers, or new acquaintances you met at that Jack Russell Terriers for National Office conference you recently attended, all of whom you can organize in a buddy list group called JRT4NO.

Moving a name to another group

The first time you add a chat name to your buddy list, you might have unintentionally put the name in your Family group when you really want the name in the Co-Workers group. To move a name to another group, follow these steps:

1. **Double-click the iChat icon in the Applications folder to launch iChat.**

   If you don't see a buddy list window, click the Window menu and then choose the account name you use to sign in to iChat.

2. **Click the triangle to the left of a group name in the buddy list window to reveal all the names stored within that group.**

3. **Click and drag a name to a new group name and then let go of the mouse button to make the name appear in the new group.**

   If you hold down the Option key when you drag a name to another group, you create a duplicate copy of the name rather than move it from one group to the other.

Creating a new group

iChat includes Buddies, Co-Workers, and Family groups, but you might want to create new groups of your own. To create a group, follow these steps:

1. **Click the Add (+) button in the bottom-left corner of the Buddy List window to open a pop-up menu and then select Add Group, as shown in Figure 3-4.**

Figure 3-4: The Add button lets you add a new group (or a new buddy).

A dialog appears, asking for a group name.

2. **Type a descriptive name for your group in the Enter Group Name text box and then click the Add button.**

Your new group appears in the buddy list, ready for you to copy or move names into your newly created group.

You can rename a group by Control-clicking the group name and choosing Rename Group from the shortcut menu that appears.

Sorting names in a buddy list

To customize the appearance of your buddy lists, you can sort the names by first or last name alphabetically, by availability, or manually.

To sort names in your buddy list, follow these steps:

1. Choose View➪Sort Buddies to open a submenu, as shown in Figure 3-5.

Figure 3-5:
The Sort
Buddies
submenu
lets you
rearrange
your buddy
list.

2. Choose one of the following:

• *By Availability:* Groups all buddies who are online and available for chatting when you are.

• *By First Name:* Sorts names alphabetically by first name.

• *By Last Name:* Sorts names alphabetically by last name.

• *Manually:* Lets you drag names to sort them any which way you want.

Shortening names in a buddy list

iChat can display names as full names (Joe Hutsko), as shortened names (Joe), or by nicknames (GadgetJoey). For friends, it might be fun to display names based on nicknames, but for business use, you might prefer to stick with full or shortened names.

To define how names should appear in your buddy list, follow these steps:

1. Choose View➪Buddy Names to open a submenu.

2. Choose one of the following:

• Show Full Names

• Show Short Names

• Show Handles

Deleting names and groups in a buddy list

Eventually, you might want to prune names from your buddy lists to make it easier to keep track of people you actually chat with on a regular basis.

To delete a name from your buddy list, follow these steps:

1. **In the iChat Buddy List window, click the triangle next to a group to display the names in that group.**

2. **Click the name you want to delete.**

3. **Choose Buddies⇨Remove Buddy (or press the Delete key).**

   A dialog appears, asking whether you really want to delete the name.

4. **Click the Delete button (or Cancel if you suddenly change your mind before giving your buddy the axe).**

Rather than delete names one by one, you can also delete a group and all names stored in that group. To delete a group from your buddy list, follow these steps:

1. **In the iChat Buddy List window, Control-click a group that you want to delete to open a shortcut menu.**

2. **Choose Delete Group from the shortcut menu.**

   A dialog opens asking whether you really want to delete this group and all names in the group.

3. **Click Delete (or Cancel).**

iChat requires at least one buddy list group to exist in order to operate. If you delete all but one buddy list group, you cannot delete the remaining group. If you don't like the name of the necessary group you're stuck with, Control-click the group name, choose Rename Group, and then type a name that you can live with for your one and only group.

Chatting with Others

After you store your friends in your buddy lists and give your account name to others to store in their buddy lists, you're ready to start chatting. Of course, before you can chat, you have to find someone who wants to chat.

You can chat with someone in five ways:

✦ **Text:** You type messages back and forth to each other.

✦ **Audio:** You can talk to and hear the other person, much like a telephone.

✦ **Video:** You can talk to, hear, and see the other person in a live video window.

✦ **Screen Sharing:** You can talk to and hear the other person while you take over her screen, mouse, and keyboard to fill your screen as though you're sitting in front of her computer. Likewise, your chat partner can take over your screen and control your keyboard or mouse as if she were sitting in front of your computer.

Screen sharing can be especially handy for helping family members or friends solve a problem with their Mac. If you can't easily travel to the person in need, use screen sharing. I show you how in the "Sharing files, photos, and screens with buddies" section, later in this chapter.

✦ **iChat Theater:** You can talk and hear each other while you share a file (or files), such as a document, a Keynote presentation, or photos in your iPhoto library. The files you want to share appear on your chatting partner's screen. Likewise, if your chatting partner is sharing photos (or other files) with you, you see them on your screen.

Anyone on your buddy list can use text chatting because it requires only an Internet connection and a keyboard.

To participate in audio chatting, each person needs a microphone and speakers or headphones. Most Macs come with a built-in microphone, but you might want an external microphone, such as one built into a headset, to capture your voice (and hear the other person's side of the conversation) more clearly.

Participating in a video chat with a buddy (or up to ten buddies in a multi-person video chat) requires a video camera, such as the iSight video camera built-in to all new and recent Macs. If your Mac is an older model without a video camera (or if you want to connect a different kind of video camera to your Mac that has a built-in iSight video camera), you can buy and connect an external video camera, such as one of the models offered by Microsoft (`microsoft.com/hardware`), Creative Labs (`www.creative.com`), or Logitech (`logitech.com`).

If your Internet connection is too slow, iChat might refuse to let you start an audio or video chat.

Initiating a text chat

To begin a text chat (or any kind of chat) with someone, you must first make sure the person is online and available when you are online. The easiest way to find someone to chat with is to look at your buddy list. All names displayed in the Offline group are people unavailable. All names displayed in other groups, such as Family or Co-Workers, are connected to the Internet and might be available for chatting.

Someone being connected to the Internet doesn't necessarily mean that he's in front of his computer and/or wants to chat. So if you find your instant messages are falling on deaf ears (or fingertips) and the person is not bothering to reply to your messages or chat requests, chances are the buddy you're trying to chat with has gone fishing or is otherwise away from their computer.

Starting a text chat

To initiate a chat with someone listed in your buddy list, follow these steps:

1. **In the Buddy List window, double-click the name of a buddy who is online (or click the Text Chat button at the bottom of the buddy list window) to open a new chat window, as shown in Figure 3-6.**

Figure 3-6:
The chat window lets you type a message in the bottom text box.

2. **Type a message in the text box at the bottom of the chat window and press Return to send your message.**

The recipient of your message will see your message, as shown in Figure 3-7. The recipient can choose to Block, Decline, or Accept your invitation. (I talk more about blocking and accepting invitations in the section "Making Yourself Available (or Not) for Chatting," later in this chapter.) If the recipient accepts your invitation to chat, you can start typing messages back and forth to one another. You type in the lower text box, and your dialog with the other person appears in the main text box.

**Book IV
Chapter 3**

Instant Messaging
and Video Chatting
with iChat

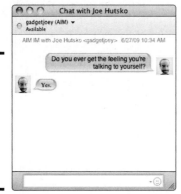

Figure 3-7:
Your
invitation
to chat
appears
on the
recipient's
screen.

Starting a group text chat

Instead of chatting with a single person, you might want to chat with multiple people at the same time. To create a group text chat, follow these steps:

1. **Hold down the ⌘ key, click each online buddy's name in the Buddy List window who you want to invite to your group chat, and then press the Return key (or click the Text Chat button at the bottom of the Buddy List window).**

    A chat window appears (refer to Figure 3-7).

2. **Type a message that you want everyone in the group to see and then press Return on your keyboard.**

Initiating an audio chat

To initiate an audio chat, everyone needs a microphone and speakers, which are standard equipment on every Mac and on most Windows PCs (if that's what the person or people you want to chat with are using). You can initiate an audio chat by following these steps:

1. **Click the name of your online buddy in the Buddy List window and then click the Audio Chat button at the bottom of the buddy list window (or choose Buddies⇨Invite to Audio Chat).**

    A message appears, informing you that your audio chat invitation is sent and that iChat is waiting for a reply, as shown in Figure 3-8.

    If this feature is dimmed, you don't have a microphone on your Mac or you don't have a fast enough Internet connection to support audio chatting.

Figure 3-8:
A message
informs you
when you're
sending an
audio chat
invitation.

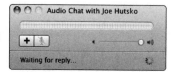

2. **When a buddy you invited to an audio chat clicks the Accept button, your audio chat begins and you can both start talking as though you were speaking over a telephone.**

You might need to drag the volume slider to adjust the sound level. If you click the plus sign button, you can invite another person into your chat. If you click the mute button, you can mute your microphone during the audio chat in case you need to shout at your dog to stop barking at the cat, or whatever else you want to say but don't want your audio chat partner to hear.

Initiating a video chat

To initiate a video chat, everyone's Mac needs a microphone and a video camera. Most Macs have a built-in iSight video camera, but for Macs without a built-in iSight camera, you have two options:

✦ Plug a digital video camcorder into your Mac's FireWire port (if your Mac model has a FireWire port; some don't).

✦ Buy a USB video camera from Logitech (www.logitech.com), Creative Labs (www.creative.com), or Microsoft (www.microsoft.com/hardware) and plug it into your Mac.

After everyone (up to ten people) has a video camera connected to their Macs along with a fast Internet connection (a minimum of 100 Kbps), you can participate in a video chat.

Possibly, your Mac has a camera and a fast Internet connection, but someone you want to connect with in a video chat does not. In that case, you might be limited to using an audio or text chat instead.

You can initiate a video chat by following these steps:

1. **Click your online buddy's name in the buddy list window and then click the Video Chat icon to the right of your buddy's name to send a**

**Book IV
Chapter 3**

Instant Messaging
and Video Chatting
with iChat

video chat invitation (or click the Video Chat icon at the bottom of the buddy list window, or choose Buddies➪Invite to Video Chat).

Your invitation is sent, and a video chat window appears, showing how you will look to the other person you want to video chat with, as shown in Figure 3-9.

If you don't see a Video Chat icon next to your buddy's name in the buddy list window, your buddy does not have a video camera built-in or connected to their computer. If you see a Video Chat icon next to your buddy's name but it is dimmed, your buddy is currently in a video chat with another buddy or group of buddies.

Figure 3-9:
A preview window appears so you can see how you will look to others.

2. **When your buddy accepts your invitation, your buddy's live video fills the video chat window and a small window showing your live video appears in a corner of the window, as shown in Figure 3-10.**

Figure 3-10:
A video chat lets you see and speak to another person.

Add | Zoom

Mute

You can click and hold on your live video chat window and drag it to any corner in your buddy's live video window.

3. **(Optional) Click the Effects button in the bottom-left corner of the video chat window.**

Doing so opens a window showing several different visual effects you can choose to change the way your live video appears on your buddy's screen, as shown in Figure 3-11.

Figure 3-11:
You can pick a unique visual effect to spice up your appearance.

4. **(Optional) Click a visual effect to select it and then click the Close button to close the visual effects window.**

5. **(Optional) Use the three buttons centered beneath the main video chat window if you want to:**

   • *Add*: Click the plus sign button to invite one or more additional buddies to join the video chat, or start and stop iChat Theater (see the "Using iChat Theater to share files, photos, and screens" section).

   • *Mute:* Click the mute button to stop your microphone from sending sound to your buddy on the other end of the video chat.

   • *Zoom:* Click the zoom button (double arrows) to make the video chat window fill your Mac's entire screen. Press the Escape key to close the full-screen view and return to the window view.

Using iChat Theater to share files, photos, and screens

Some fun things you can try with a selected online buddy (or buddies) include sharing a file (such as a document or picture), sharing an album or your entire iPhoto images collection, and sharing your screen. If you choose to share your screen, you let your buddy control it as though it were her screen (or vice versa, if a buddy shares her screen with you).

To share files, photos, and screens with iChat, click an online buddy in your buddy list and then choose

✦ **File⇨Share a File with iChat Theater:** Locate and select a file you want to share in the file window that opens, click the Share button, follow the iChat Theater prompts, and then click the Video Chat icon next to your buddy's name in the buddy list window to initiate the iChat Theater connection.

✦ **File⇨Share iPhoto with iChat Theater:** Select an album name (or the Photos icon to share your entire iPhoto library) in the iPhoto window that opens, click the Share button, follow the iChat Theater prompts, and then click the Video Chat icon next to your buddy's name in the buddy list window to show off your selected photos. Click the control buttons in the iPhoto control window that appears to move forward and backward through your photos, as shown in Figure 3-12, or to pause or quit sharing your photos with your buddy.

Figure 3-12: Show off your iPhoto collection with the iChat Theater feature.

✦ **Buddies⇨Share My Screen or Buddies⇨Ask to Share Screen:** Choosing Share My Screen fills your buddy's screen with your screen, as though he's seated in front of your Mac, which he can now control with his mouse and keyboard. Choosing Ask to Share Screen fills your screen with your friend's screen as though you're seated in front of his Mac and controlling it with your keyboard and mouse (assuming they grant you permission to possess their Mac's body, virtually speaking of course).

To end any of the above sharing sessions, press Control+Escape.

Making Yourself Available (or Not) for Chatting

As soon as you connect to the Internet, your Mac broadcasts your availability to all the friends in your buddy lists. The moment someone wants to chat with you, you'll see a window.

Chat invitations can be fun to receive, but sometimes they can be distracting if you're trying to get work done and don't want to stop what you're doing to chat with someone. One thing you can do is change the status description others see next to your name in their own buddy lists.

Changing your status description to Away or something that indicates you're not in a chatting mode can discourage others from sending you chat invitations until they see that you've set your status to Available again.

Changing your status

To let others know that you're busy, you can change your status message to indicate you're out to lunch, on the phone, or revising a big book and not really in the mood to chat with others unless it's about something important. (Otherwise, you might as well just exit iChat altogether.)

Although you change your status to indicate you are away or unavailable to chat, you can still receive chat messages and invitations your buddies send if they choose to disregard your status message. Therefore, you'll still need to click Accept or Decline for each invitation you receive.

Alternately, you can change your status to make yourself *invisible,* which means you don't appear in your friends' Buddy List windows. However, you still see your friends in your Buddy List window (unless they choose to make themselves invisible, in which case neither of you can see the other).

To change the status friends see about you in their buddy list, click the arrow button beneath your name in the Buddy List window to open the My Status menu. (Alternatively, you can choose iChat⇨My Status to open the My Status menu.) Choose a status line, as shown in Figure 3-13, and your chosen status now appears in your friends' buddy lists.

You can also choose a status that lets your buddies know you are available and what you are doing, such as surfing the Web or reading e-mail. If you choose Current iTunes Song, people can see the name of the song you're listening to. If you choose Custom Available, you can type your own message that others will see. Choosing Custom Away lets you type your own away message.

Book IV
Chapter 3

Instant Messaging
and Video Chatting
with iChat

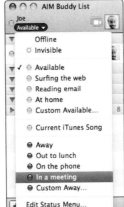

Figure 3-13:
The My Status menu provides a variety of statuses you can display.

Becoming invisible

Another way to avoid receiving chat invitations is to make yourself invisible to your buddies. Being invisible lets you see who on your buddy lists might be available to chat, but when other people see your name on their buddy lists, your name appears as though you are offline.

To make yourself invisible in iChat, click the arrow beneath your name in the buddy list window to open the My Status menu and then choose Invisible.

To make yourself visible again, open the My Status menu and choose a status that indicates you are online and available or away, such as Available or On the Phone.

If you want to leave iChat running but sign out so that you are truly offline and unavailable, open the My Status menu beneath your name in the buddy list window and choose Offline.

As an alternative to taking time to click Decline on every chat invitation you receive, iChat offers several ways to decline invitations automatically.

Accepting (or blocking) chat invitations with privacy levels

Rather than block invitations from everyone, you might want to accept chat invitations from some people but block them from others. For example, your editor might be harassing you so you want to block that person, but someone close to you, such as a family member or good friend, might need to reach you so you want that person to get through at any time.

To set your privacy level, follow these steps:

1. **Choose iChat⇨Preferences to open the iChat preferences window.**

2. **Click the Accounts icon to open the Accounts preferences pane.**

3. **If you added more than one chat account, click the account whose privacy level you want to change and then click the Security tab.**

You see the Security pane, as shown in Figure 3-14, showing these options:

- *Allow Anyone:* Allows anyone to send you a chat invitation, close friends or complete strangers alike.

- *Allow People in My Buddy List:* Allows only people in your buddy lists to contact you.

- *Allow Specific People:* Allows you to create a list of specific people who have permission to contact you. Click the Edit List button to open the Allow Specific People window; then click the plus sign and type in the name of the person you want to allow to contact you.

- *Block Everyone:* Stops all chat invitations from friends, family, co-workers, and everyone else in the world.

- *Block Specific People:* Allows you to create a list of specific people you always want to keep from contacting you. Click the Edit List button to open the Block Specific People window; then click the plus sign and type in the name of the person you want to block from contacting you.

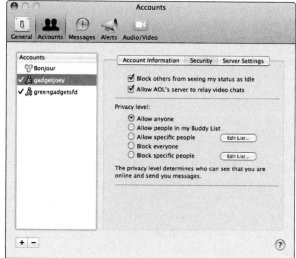

Figure 3-14:
The Security pane lets you choose a privacy level.

**Book IV
Chapter 3**

Instant Messaging and Video Chatting with iChat

4. **In the Privacy Level section, click the radio button that corresponds to the privacy level you want to use.**

   For general privacy, you might want to choose the Allow People in My Buddy List option.

   Note: If you select the Allow Specific People or Block Specific People radio buttons, you need to click the Edit List button and then type the exact account names of the people you want to allow or block.

5. **Click the Close button to close the iChat preferences window.**

Taking a Look at Other Chat Programs

Although your Mac comes with iChat, you might need to use other chat programs to connect with your friends, family, and coworkers. For example, some of your friends might use Windows PCs, and others might use a Mac but have a chat account that doesn't work with iChat, such as Yahoo! or MSN Messenger.

Here's a list of a few chat programs you can check out to make your Mac more fluent when it comes to chatting with more people and more text, audio, and video chat accounts and programs:

✦ **AOL Instant Messenger (www.aim.com):** AOL's chat program has one thing iChat does not: Annoying advertisements that play in a portion of your Buddy List window whenever you're running AIM. Because iChat lets you connect to fellow AIM buddies, you don't need to bother with downloading, installing, and running AIM — but you can encourage your friends who use Windows PCs to use it so you can connect with them using iChat on your Mac.

✦ **Microsoft Messenger (www.microsoft.com/mac):** Popular on Windows PCs and also available for Mac, people using Microsoft Messenger's chat program typically sign in with an e-mail address that ends with @hotmail.com, @live.com, or @msn.com, and acts as the user's chat account sign-in name. You can also use any other existing e-mail address to create a Windows Live ID that you can then use to sign in to Microsoft Messenger.

   If you use Microsoft Hotmail or sign in to an Xbox LIVE account when you play your Xbox 360, you already have a Windows Live ID that you can use to sign in to Microsoft Messenger for Mac. Microsoft Messenger for Mac lets you connect with buddies to send and receive text messages, share files and photos, and conduct audio and video chats.

✦ **Yahoo! Messenger (`messenger.yahoo.com`):** Popular on Macs and Windows PCs alike, Yahoo! Messenger can connect you with other buddies who have a free @yahoo.com e-mail address so you can send and receive text messages, share files and photos, and conduct audio and video chats.

✦ **Skype (`www.skype.com`):** Like the programs in the above list, Skype offers you free text and audio and video chat with friends who also have a Skype account. Skype can also make audio chat calls to someone's real telephone number — but using that feature will cost you. Fortunately, Skype's monthly rates are reasonable for unlimited calls to

  • Landlines and cellphones in the United States and Canada for $2.95 per month

  • Landlines in a particular country of your choosing, such as Mexico, Italy, or Japan, for $5.95 per month

  • Landlines to over 40 countries for $12.95 per month

✦ **Google Gmail Video (`google.com/gmail`):** Got a free @gmail.com e-mail account? Bet you don't know you can use it to conduct audio and video chats with other Gmail users via your Gmail Web-based Inbox page. To use the audio and video chat feature, sign in to your Gmail account, click the Settings link at the top of the Web page, click the Chat link on the Settings Web page, and then follow the directions to download and install the voice and video chat program that enables your Mac to take advantage of the feature.

✦ **Adium (`www.adiumx.com`):** Adium (shown in Figure 3-15) is a free chat program that lets you set up multiple chat accounts, some of which include:

  • AIM

  • Jabber

  • MSN Messenger

  • Yahoo! Messenger

  • MobileMe

  • Google Talk

  • Facebook

  • Twitter

  • MySpace

  • LiveJournal

  • ICQ

Figure 3-15:
Adium
unifies all
your chat
account
buddy lists
under one
roof.

With a huge library of user-generated add-ons that lets you change the way Adium looks and works, Adium is my favorite all-around, all-in-one chat program except for one thing: You can't use it to conduct audio or video chats. Adium's developer does state however that they understand audio and video chatting are high-demand features and that a future release of the program might offer those features.

✦ **Digsby (www.digsby.com):** Like Adium, Digsby can consolidate a gaggle of chat accounts into one nice, neat buddy list. Unlike Adium however, Digsby does allow you to partake in audio and video chats, sort of. Unlike the way iChat, MSN Messenger, Skype, Yahoo! Messenger, and AIM open a separate live video window or full-screen display when you conduct a video chat, Digsby handles video chats by launching your Web browser and displaying your video chat on a Web page.

Chapter 4: Protecting Your Mac against Threats

In This Chapter

✔ Locking your Mac

✔ Setting up user accounts

✔ Using parental controls

*W*ith the worldwide connectivity of the Internet, everyone is vulnerable to everything, including malicious software (known as *malware*) and malicious people with above average computer skills (known as *hackers*). Although threats over the Internet attract the most attention, your Mac is also vulnerable from mundane threats, such as thieves who might want to steal your computer.

No matter how much you know about computers, you can always become a victim if you're not careful. Therefore, this chapter looks at the different ways to protect your Mac from both physical and cyber threats.

Locking Down Your Mac

Most people lock their car and house doors when they're away, and your Mac should be no exception. To protect your Mac physically, you can get a security cable that wraps around an immovable object (like that heavy rolltop desk you have in the den) and then attaches to your Mac. You can attach it by using glue, by threading it through a handle or hole in your Macintosh case, or by connecting it to a security slot built into your Mac. (The security slot is a tiny slot that a security cable plugs into. You might have to peek around the back or side of your Mac to find this security slot.)

Some companies that sell security cables are

✦ **Kensington** (http://us.kensington.com)

✦ **Targus** (www.targus.com)

✦ **Belkin** (www.belkin.com)

Security cables can be cut. The main purpose of a security cable is to deter a thief who isn't carrying a pair of bolt cutters.

After protecting your Mac physically, you have two other ways to lock down your Mac and keep other people out: by using a password, to stop intruders from sneaking into your computer if you step away from your desk, and by using a software or hardware firewall, or both, to stop intruders from sneaking into your computer over the Internet.

Anyone with enough time, determination, and skill can defeat passwords and firewalls. Security can only discourage and delay an intruder, but nothing can ever guarantee to stop one.

Using passwords

Before you can ever use your Mac, you must configure it by creating an account name and password. If you're the only person using your Mac, you'll probably have just one account. If you disable automatic login, your password can keep others from using your Mac without your knowledge.

As a rule, your password should be difficult for someone to guess but easy for you to remember. Unfortunately, that often means people use simple passwords. To make your password difficult to guess but easy to remember, you should create a password that uses a combination of letters and numbers, such as "OCHSco'10alum" (which sounds out the phrase, "Ocean City High School class of 2010 Alumnus").

Two popular ways to create passwords include taking the first letters of the words in a phrase that you'll never forget or using a name of a dearly departed pet (or a combination of both). By picking a memorable phrase or lyric, such as "I'm walkin' on sunshine" and turning it into a nonsensical combination of letters, paired with the name of your long-gone pet hermit crab, Louise (IwosLouise), you'll easily remember your password, but others won't easily guess it. Presumably, nobody would ever know the lyrics of a song you like or the name of a dog, cat, goldfish, or yes, hermit crab, you had when you were ten years old. Pairing these two things that are unique to you makes for a password that's easy for you to remember but hard for someone to guess.

Changing your password

For additional security, you should change your password periodically. To change your password, follow these steps:

1. **Choose ⌘⇨System Preferences.**

   The System Preferences window appears.

2. **Click the Accounts icon to open the Accounts preferences pane, as shown in Figure 4-1.**

   If the lock icon in the lower-left corner of the preferences window is locked, you must unlock it to make changes to your Mac's user account details.

Click the lock icon, type your password in the dialog that appears, and then press Return to unlock your Mac's user account details.

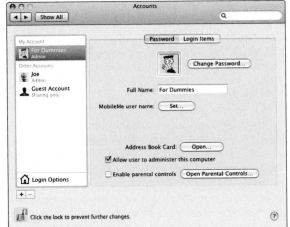

Figure 4-1: Accounts preferences let you change your user account details.

3. **Click your account name under My Account in the left pane (or another account name under Other Accounts that you want to modify).**

   If you haven't created any additional accounts, you see only your own account listed.

4. **Click the Change Password button.**

   A dialog appears, displaying text boxes for typing your old password and then typing a new password twice to verify that you typed your new password correctly, as shown in Figure 4-2.

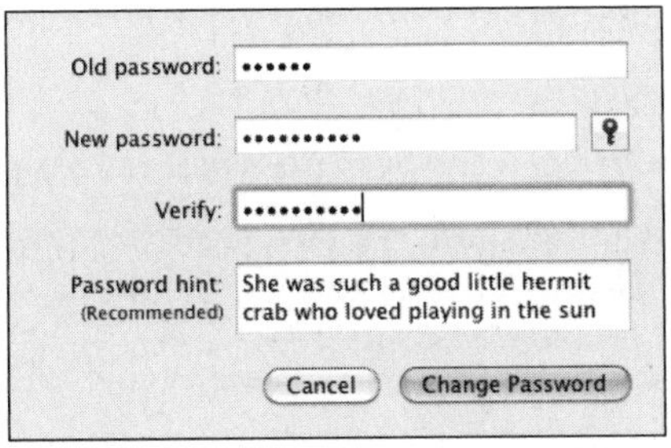

Figure 4-2: The Password dialog lets you change your password.

5. **Enter your current password in the Old Password text box.**

6. **Enter your new password in the New Password text box.**

7. **Enter your new password in the Verify text box.**

8. **Enter a descriptive phrase into the Password Hint text box.**

   Adding a hint can help you remember your password, but it can also give an intruder a hint on what your password might be.

9. **Click Change Password.**

   The password dialog disappears.

10. **Click the Close button to close the Accounts preferences window.**

Applying password protection

Normally, you need your password to log in to your account, install new software, or make certain changes to your Mac's settings. That means anyone can use your Mac if you walk away and don't log out.

If you leave your Mac without logging out, your Mac will either go to sleep or display a screen saver. At this time, anyone could tap the keyboard and have full access to your Mac. To avoid this problem, you can password-protect your Mac when waking up from sleep or after displaying a screen saver.

For further protection, you can also password-protect your Mac from allowing an unauthorized person to make any changes to your Mac's various System Preferences. By applying password protection to different parts of your Mac, you can increase the chances that you'll be the only one to control your computer.

If you're the only person who has physical access to your Mac, you won't have to worry about password protection, but if your Mac is in an area where others can access it easily, password protection can be one extra step in keeping your Mac private.

To password-protect different parts of your Mac, follow these steps:

1. **Choose ⌘⇨System Preferences.**

   The System Preferences window appears.

2. **Click the Security icon to open the Security preferences pane.**

   If the lock icon in the lower-left corner of the preferences window is locked, you must unlock it to make changes to your Mac's user account details. Click the lock icon, type your password in the dialog that appears, and then press Return to unlock your Mac's user account details.

3. **Click the General tab.**

   The General preferences pane appears, as shown in Figure 4-3.

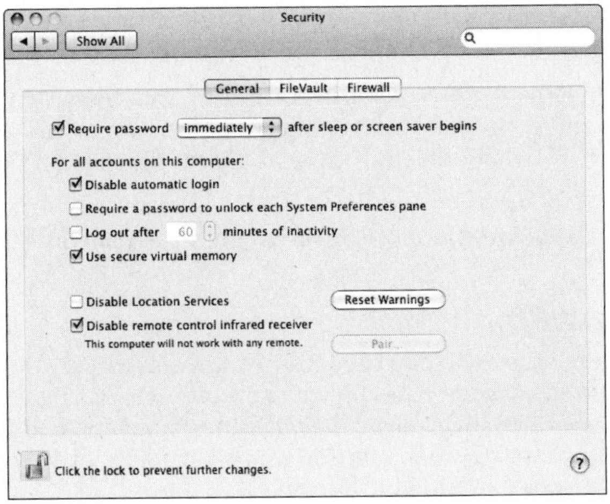

Figure 4-3:
General
Security
preferences
let you
choose
different
ways to
password-
protect your
computer.

4. (Optional) Select (or deselect) the **Require Password** *<immediately>* after Sleep or Screen Saver Begins check box.

5. (Optional) Select (or deselect) the **Disable Automatic Login** check box.

If this check mark is deselected, your Mac won't ask for a password before logging in to your account.

6. (Optional) Select (or deselect) the **Require a Password to Unlock Each System Preferences Pane** check box.

If this check box is selected, nobody can modify a number of your Mac's System Preferences (such as the one you're adjusting right now!) without the proper password.

7. (Optional) Select (or deselect) the **Log Out after ___ Minutes of Inactivity** check box.

If selected, this option logs off your account after a fixed period so anyone trying to access your computer will need your password to log in to and access your account.

Three additional check boxes are available:

- *Use Secure Virtual Memory:* Selecting this option means that your Mac will encrypt the temporary data that almost every program stores on your hard drive while the program is running. If you don't use secure virtual memory, other highly tech-savvy people might be able to read this temporary data that can remain on your hard drive even after you turn off your computer.

- *Disable Location Services:* Disabling this option prevents your Mac from revealing your time zone or other location-related information to a technically adept person who might try to tap into your Mac via the Internet.

- *Disable Remote Control Infrared Receiver:* Disabling this option simply keeps someone from controlling your Mac with an infrared remote control. (This option won't appear if your Mac doesn't have an infra-red receiver.)

8. **Click the Close button of the Security preferences window.**

Using firewalls

When you connect your Mac to the Internet, you essentially open a door to your Mac that allows a highly technical person (such as a hacker) situated anywhere in the world to access your computer, copy or modify your files, or erase all your data. To keep out unwanted intruders, every computer needs a special program called a *firewall.*

A firewall simply blocks access to your computer while still allowing you access to the Internet so you can browse Web sites or send and receive e-mail. Every Mac comes with a *software* firewall that can protect you whenever your Mac connects to the Internet.

Many people use a special device, called a *router,* to connect to the Internet. A router lets multiple computers use a single Internet connection, such as a high-speed broadband cable or DSL Internet connection. Routers include built-in *hardware* firewalls, and using one in combination with your Mac's *software* firewall can provide your Mac with twice the protection of using only one of these types of firewall options. To learn more about how to configure your own router's firewall settings, refer to the router's user guide or look for more information in the support section of the router manufacturer's Web site.

Configuring a firewall

Although the default setting for your Mac's firewall should be adequate for most people, you might want to configure your firewall to block additional Internet features for added security. For example, most people will likely need to access e-mail and Web pages, but if you never transfer files using FTP (File Transfer Protocol), you can safely block this service.

Don't configure your firewall unless you're sure you know what you're doing. Otherwise, you might weaken the firewall or lock programs from accessing the Internet and not know how to repair those problems.

To configure your Mac's firewall, follow these steps:

1. Choose **System Preferences to open the System Preferences pane.

2. Click the Security icon to open the Security preferences pane.

If the lock icon in the lower-left corner of the preferences window is locked, you must unlock it to make changes to your Mac's user account details. Click the lock icon, type your password in the dialog that appears, and then press Return to unlock your Mac's user account details.

3. Click the Firewall tab.

The Firewall preferences pane appears, as shown in Figure 4-4.

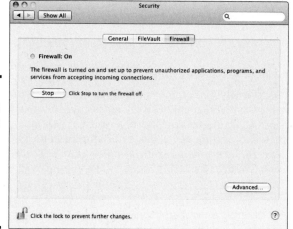

Figure 4-4:
The Firewall preferences pane displays your options for configuring the firewall.

4. Click the Start button to turn on your Mac's firewall if it isn't already turned on.

5. Click the Advanced button to display the firewall's advanced preferences, as shown in Figure 4-5.

The dialog that appears offers three check boxes.

In the center list box you might see one or more sharing services you turned on using the Sharing preferences pane (**System Preferences▷ Sharing).

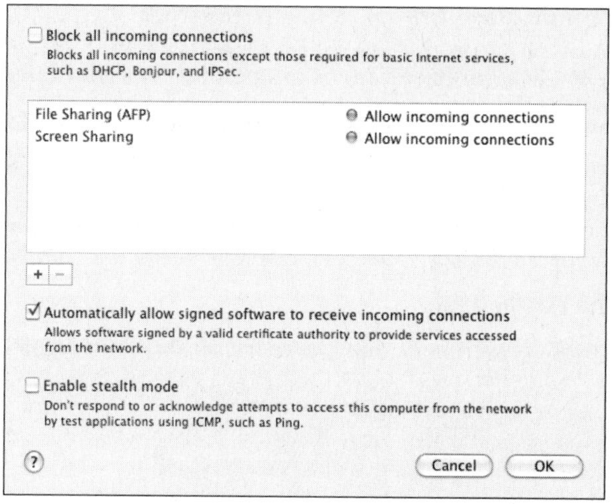

Figure 4-5:
The
Advanced
preferences
pane offers
additional
firewall
security
options.

6. **Select (or deselect) the following check boxes:**

   • *Block All Incoming Communications:* Allows only essential communications for basic Internet and Web access, and blocks sharing services, such as iTunes music sharing, or iChat screen sharing. When you check this option, any services or applications listed in the pane disappear, replaced with a static warning that indicates all sharing services are being blocked.

   • *Automatically Allow Signed Software to Receive Incoming Connections:* Allows typical commercial applications like Microsoft Word to check for software updates, for Safari to access the Web, and for e-mail to allow you to send and receive e-mail messages.

   • *Enable Stealth Mode:* Makes the firewall refuse to respond to any outside attempts to contact it and gather information based on its responses.

7. **Continue to Step 8 if you want to make additional adjustments to your Mac's firewall feature; otherwise skip to Step 12.**

8. **(Optional) Click the Add (+) button to add applications that you want to allow or block from communicating over the Internet.**

   A dialog appears, listing the contents of the Applications folder.

9. **Click a program that you want to allow to access the Internet.**

10. **Click Add.**

    Your chosen program appears under the Applications category.

11. **(Optional) Click the pop-up button to the right of an application in the applications list and choose Allow Incoming Communications or Block Incoming Communications.**

12. **(Optional) To remove a program from the applications list, click the program name to select it and then click the Delete (–) button below the program list.**

13. **Click the Close button of the Security preferences window.**

Buying a firewall

Although the built-in Mac firewall blocks incoming connections well, it allows all outgoing connections. Allowing all outgoing connections means a malicious program you might inadvertently download could communicate via the Internet without your knowledge. To prevent this problem, you need a firewall that can block both incoming and outgoing connections.

Dealing with nasty malware and RATs

There are two big threats that exploit personal computers that aren't protected by properly configured firewall preferences or properly configured router firewall settings. The first of these threats, *malware*, consists of programs that sneak on to your computer and then secretly connect to the Internet to do merely annoying (and offensive) things like retrieve pornographic ads that appear all over your screen, or do more serious things like infect your computer with a virus that can erase your personal data. Or, they can keep track of every keystroke you type on your computer, which in turn is transmitted to a snooping program on a malicious person's computer so they can find out things like your credit card numbers and usernames and passwords.

A second type of program that requires an outgoing Internet connection is a *RAT* (Remote Access Trojan). Malicious hackers often trick people into downloading and installing a RAT on their computer. When installed, a RAT can connect to the Internet and allow the malicious

hacker to completely control the computer remotely over the Internet, including deleting or copying files, conducting attacks through this computer, or sending junk e-mail (spam) through this computer.

Although computer malware and RATs written and released by hackers typically target PCs running Windows, security experts agree it's only a matter of time before the same digital nastiness begins infecting Macs. To guard against potential viruses, spyware, and RATs, your Mac displays a dialog that alerts you when you run a program for the first time. This feature can alert you if a virus, spyware, or a RAT tries to infect a Mac, but for further protection, consider purchasing a router with built-in firewall features, or installing an antivirus and antimalware program such as ClamXav (www.clamxav.com), which is free, or buying a commercial protection suite such as those offered by Intego (www.intego.com) and Symantec (www.symantec.com).

You should use only one software firewall at a time, although it's possible to use one software firewall and a hardware firewall built into your router. If you use two or more software firewall programs, they may interfere with each other and cause your Mac to stop working correctly.

If you want a more robust firewall than the one that comes with the Mac (and the added security of antivirus and antimalware protection), consider one of the following:

✦ **ClamXav** (free; `www.clamxav.com`)

✦ **Intego NetBarrier or Internet Security Barrier** ($50 - $100; `www.intego.com`)

✦ **Norton Internet Security** ($80; `www.symantec.com`)

One problem with a firewall is that, in the normal scheme of things, you never really know how well it's working. To help you measure the effectiveness of your firewall, visit one of the following sites that will probe and test your computer, looking for the exact same vulnerabilities that hackers will look for.

✦ **Audit My PC** (`www.auditmypc.com`)

✦ **HackerWatch** (`www.hackerwatch.org/probe`)

✦ **Shields Up!** (`www.grc.com`)

✦ **Symantec Security Check** (`http://security.symantec.com`)

Because each firewall-testing Web site might test for different features, testing your Mac with two or more of these sites can help ensure that your Mac is as secure as possible. Figure 4-6 shows the results of a Symantec Security Check test of the Mac's built-in firewall feature.

Figure 4-6: Your Mac's built-in firewall does a decent job at keeping intruders out of your Mac.

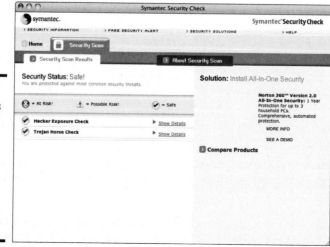

Creating Multiple Accounts

Every Mac has at least one account that allows you to use your computer. However, if multiple people need to use your Mac, you probably don't want to share the same account, which can be like trying to share the same pair of pants.

One problem with sharing the same account is that one person might change the screen saver or delete a program that someone else might want. To avoid people interfering with each other, you can divide your Mac into multiple accounts.

Essentially, multiple accounts give your Mac a split personality. Each account lets each person customize the same Mac while shielding other users from these changes. Therefore, one account can display pink daffodils on the screen, and a second account can display pictures of Mt. Rushmore.

To access any account, you need to log in to that account. To exit an account, you need to log out.

Not only do separate accounts keep multiple users from accessing each other's files, but creating multiple accounts also gives you the ability to restrict what other accounts can do. That means you can block Internet access from an account, limit Internet access to specific times, or limit Internet access to specific Web sites. (It's great for parents, of course, which is why such limits are referred to as *parental controls.*)

To protect your files and settings, you should create a separate account for each person who uses your Mac. You can create four types of accounts:

+ **Administrator:** Gives the user access to create, modify, and delete accounts. Typically, you have only one Administrator account; however, another user you trust implicitly, such as your partner or spouse, might also have an Administrator account.

+ **Standard:** Gives the user access to the computer and allows them to install programs or change their account settings, but doesn't let the user create, modify, or delete accounts or change any locked System Preferences settings.

+ **Managed with Parental Controls:** Gives the user restricted access to the computer based on the parental controls defined by an Administrator account.

+ **Guest:** Gives the user access, but any Web site history the user generates by visiting Web sites, or any files the user saves on the hard drive, are deleted when the guest account user logs off.

The only difference between the Administrator and Standard accounts is that the Standard account cannot create, modify, or delete other accounts

**Book IV
Chapter 4**

Protecting Your
Mac against
Threats

or change any locked System Preferences settings. Otherwise, a Standard account gives users unrestricted freedom to do anything they want on the Mac.

The Managed with Parental Controls and Guest accounts restrict access to what users can do on your Mac. The main difference is any files a Guest user downloads to the Mac's hard disk won't be saved once the Guest user logs out.

Creating a Parental Controls user account

If you want users to be able to save files but you still want to restrict their access to the Internet or certain programs, you want to create a Managed with Parental Controls account. To do so, follow these steps:

1. **Choose System Preferences.**

   The System Preferences window appears.

2. **Click the Accounts icon to open the Accounts preferences pane (refer to Figure 4-1).**

   If the lock icon in the lower-left corner of the preferences window is locked, you must unlock it to make changes to your Mac's user account details. Click the lock icon, type your password in the dialog that appears, and then press Return to unlock your Mac's user account details.

3. **Click the Add (+) button in the lower-left corner (above the lock icon).**

   An Accounts dialog appears, as shown in Figure 4-7.

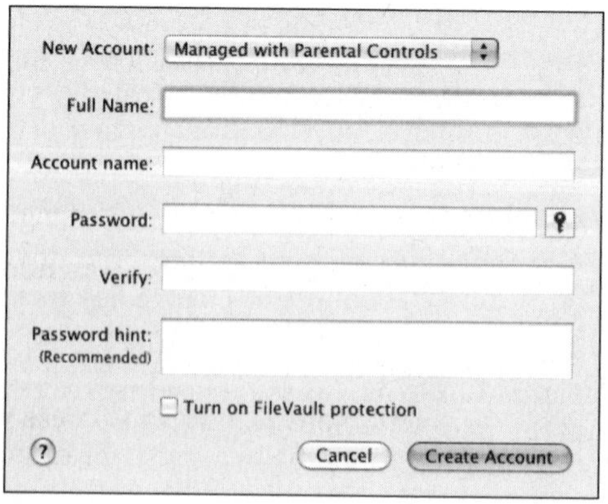

Figure 4-7:
The
Accounts
dialog lets
you define
your new
account.

New Account:	Managed with Parental Controls
Full Name:	
Account name:	
Password:	
Verify:	
Password hint: (Recommended)	

☐ Turn on FileVault protection

⑦   Cancel   Create Account

4. **Choose Managed with Parental Controls from the New Account pop-up menu.**

   Instead of choosing Managed with Parental Controls, you can choose Administrator or Standard to create an Administrator or Standard account if you want to create one of those user account types.

5. **Enter the name of the person who'll be using the account into the Full Name text box.**

6. **(Optional) Click the Account Name text box and edit the short name that your Mac automatically creates.**

7. **Enter a password for this account into the Password text box.**

   If you click the key to the right of the password text box, your Mac will generate a random password that may be more difficult to guess than your doggie's name, but also harder to remember.

8. **Re-enter the password you choose in Step 7 into the Verify text box.**

9. **(Optional) In the Password Hint text box, enter a descriptive phrase to help remind you of your password.**

10. **(Optional) Select the Turn On FileVault Protection check box to encrypt files the user stores in their Home folder.**

    If you allow users to encrypt files, they can hide the contents of their files from anyone — even folks with an Administrator account.

    Keep in mind that turning on FileVault can make your Mac slower because it takes time to encrypt and decrypt your data.

    If you turn on FileVault and the user forgets their password, they won't be able to access their files, but you (or another user with Admin-level account access) can use the FileVault's Master Password feature to retrieve the user's files and reset their password with one they'll hopefully remember next time they log in.

11. **Click the Create Account button.**

    The Accounts preferences pane displays the name of your new account.

12. **Click the Close button of the Accounts preferences window.**

Creating a Guest account

A Guest account is handy if you want multiple users to access your Mac. (If you have a Mac in a public lobby for anyone to use, for example, you use a Guest account.)

You can create only one Guest account because multiple users will access the same Guest account. To create a Guest account, follow these steps:

1. **Choose ⌘⇨System Preferences.**

   The System Preferences window appears.

2. **Click the Accounts icon to open the Accounts preferences pane (refer to Figure 4-1).**

   If the lock icon in the lower-left corner of the preferences window is locked, you must unlock it to make changes to your Mac's user account details. Click the lock icon, type your password in the dialog that appears, and then press Return to unlock your Mac's user account details.

3. **Click the Guest Account icon that appears in the list box on the left, as shown in Figure 4-8.**

Figure 4-8:
When you create a Guest account, you can define additional options for how the Guest account works.

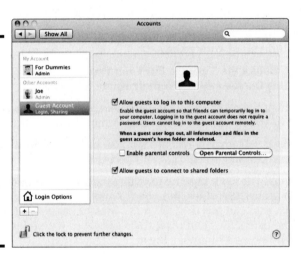

4. **(Optional) Click the Open Parental Controls button if you want to specify which programs guests can use (or not use) and whether they can access the Web.**

   I write about adjusting these settings in the next section, "Defining parental controls."

5. **Select the Allow Guests to Log In to This Computer check box, which allows anyone to use your Mac's Guest account without a password.**

6. **(Optional) Select or deselect the Allow Guests to Connect to Shared Folders check box.**

    If this option is selected, a Guest account can read files created by other accounts and stored in a special shared folder or the other users' Public folder.

7. **Click the Close button of the Accounts preferences window.**

Defining parental controls

You can apply parental controls only to a Guest account or a Managed with Parental Controls account. After you create a Guest account or at least one Managed with Parental Controls account, you can apply parental controls to those accounts.

You can place several types of restrictions on an account:

✦ **System:** Limits which programs the account can run.

✦ **Content:** Limits which Web sites the account can access.

✦ **Mail & iChat:** Limits the account to sending and receiving e-mail and instant messages from a fixed list of approved people.

✦ **Time Limits:** Prevents accessing the account at certain times or on certain days.

✦ **Simple Finder:** Creates a Finder that's easier for novice Mac users to work with.

✦ **Administer Printers:** Prevents modifications to the printers connected to the Macintosh.

✦ **Burn CDs and DVDs:** Prevents saving data to a CD or DVD.

✦ **Password:** Prevents changing the account password.

✦ **Dock:** Prevents modifying the Dock.

To apply parental controls to an account, follow these steps:

1. **Choose ⌘⇨System Preferences.**

    The System Preferences window appears.

2. **Click the Parental Controls icon to open the Parental Controls preferences pane, as shown in Figure 4-9.**

Figure 4-9:
Parental
Controls
preferences
let you
define
restrictions
for an
account.

If the lock icon in the lower-left corner of the preferences window is
locked, you must unlock it to make changes to your Mac's user account
details. Click the lock icon, type your password in the dialog that
appears, and then press Return to unlock your Mac's user account
details.

3. **Click the account icon in the left list to which you want to apply
parental controls.**

4. **Click the System tab (if it isn't already selected).**

   The System preferences pane appears.

5. **(Optional) Select the Use Simple Finder check box.**

   This creates a Finder that's easier for novice Mac users to work with.

6. **Select the Only Allow Selected Applications check box.**

7. **Click the gray triangle to the left of each application category to
display a list of programs for the selected category and then select
or deselect the programs you want to allow or disable the user from
accessing.**

   Selecting or deselecting the check box for an entire application category,
   such as iLife, Internet, or Utilities, gives you a single-click way to allow
   user access to all or none of the programs in that selected category.

8. **(Optional) Select or deselect the following four check boxes:**

- Can Administer Printers
- Can Burn CDs and DVDs
- Can Change Password
- Can Modify the Dock

9. **Click the Content tab to open the Content preferences pane, as shown in Figure 4-10.**

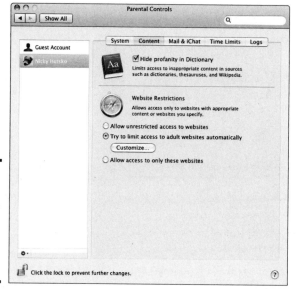

Figure 4-10: Content preferences let you restrict what users can see.

10. **(Optional) Select the Hide Profanity in Dictionary check box.**

11. **Select one of the following radio buttons under the Website Restrictions section:**

- *Allow Unrestricted Access to Websites:* Choosing this option allows Guest account users to access any Web site they want to visit.
- *Try to Limit Access to Adult Websites Automatically:* If you select this option, you can click the Customize button so that you can type the Web sites the account can always access and the Web sites that the account can never access.

Book IV Chapter 4

Protecting Your Mac against Threats

In both cases, you must type the address to allow or block, such as `www.nytimes.com` or `www.playboy.com`. Although the Try to Limit Access to Adult Websites Automatically option can attempt to automatically block most adult Web sites, you will need to enter additional addresses for particular Web sites that slip past the adult Web site filter.

- *Allow Access to Only These Websites:* If you select this option, you can then specify which Web sites the user account can access by clicking the "+" plus-sign button and adding Web sites you permit Guest users to visit. You can also remove Web sites you no longer want guest users to access by clicking on the Web site in the list of allowed Web sites, and then clicking the "-" minus-sign to remove the Web site.

12. **Click the Mail & iChat tab.**

The Mail & iChat preferences pane appears, as shown in Figure 4-11.

Figure 4-11: Mail & iChat preferences lets you restrict who the user can contact.

13. **Select the Limit Mail and/or Limit iChat check boxes.**

These features let you define which e-mail or iChat addresses the account can access.

14. **Click the Add (+) button.**

A dialog appears, as shown in Figure 4-12.

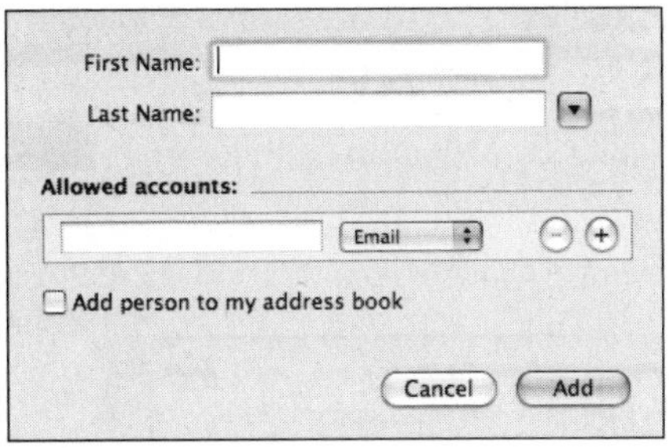

Figure 4-12:
You can specify the name and e-mail or instant messaging addresses of approved people.

First Name:
Last Name:
Allowed accounts:
Email
☐ Add person to my address book
Cancel   Add

15. **Enter the first and last name of a person that you approve of into the First Name and Last Name text boxes.**

16. **Enter an e-mail or instant messaging address of the approved person into the Allowed Accounts text box.**

The iChat program can connect with anyone who has an AIM (AOL Instant Messenger), MobileMe, Mac.com, Google Gmail, or Jabber instant messaging chat account.

17. **Choose the account type (Email, AIM, or Jabber, for example) from the Allowed Accounts pop-up menu.**

If you click the Add Person to My Address Book check box, the instant messaging address and name of the approved person will be added as a contact to your Address Book program.

18. **(Optional) Click the Add (+) button and repeat Steps 15 through 17 to specify another person and the associated e-mail or instant messaging chat account address.**

19. **Click Add.**

20. **Click the Time Limits tab (refer to Figure 4-11) to open the Time Limits preferences pane, as shown in Figure 4-13.**

21. **(Optional) Select the Limit Computer Use To check box under the Weekday Time Limits category and drag the slider to specify how much time the account can use your Mac.**

22. **(Optional) Select the Limit Computer Use To check box under the Weekend Time Limits category and drag the slider to specify how much time the account can use your Mac.**

Book IV
Chapter 4

Protecting Your Mac against Threats

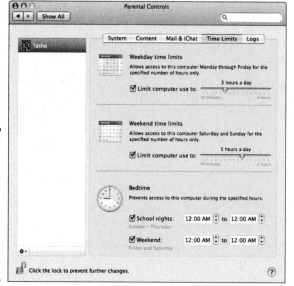

Figure 4-13:
Time Limits
preferences
let you
specify
certain days
or times the
account can
be used.

23. **(Optional) Select the School Nights and Weekend check boxes under the Bedtime category and select the start and end times of when you don't want the account to use your Mac, such as between 9:00 p.m. and 9:00 a.m.**

The School Nights option defines Sunday – Thursday. The Weekend option defines Friday and Saturday, however this option pays no mind to holidays, school vacations, snow days, and other potential nonschool night calendar dates.

24. **Click the Close button of the Parental Controls preferences window.**

Monitoring a parental control managed account

After you create a Managed with Parental Controls account, you can view what that user has been doing on your Mac by reviewing the log files. The log files keep track of all the Web sites the user visited and tried to visit (blocked by the Mac parental controls), the programs the user ran, and the people the user contacted through iChat or e-mail. To view these log files, follow these steps:

1. **Choose ⌘⇨System Preferences.**

The System Preferences window appears.

2. **Click the Parental Controls icon to open the Parental Controls preferences pane (refer to Figure 4-9).**

If the lock icon in the lower-left corner of the preferences window is locked, you must unlock it to make changes to your Mac's user account details. Click the lock icon, type your password in the dialog that appears, and then press Return to unlock your Mac's user account details.

3. **Click the account icon in the list on the left whose log files you want to examine.**

4. **Click the Logs tab to open the Logs preferences pane, as shown in Figure 4-14.**

Figure 4-14:
Logs preferences let you investigate what the user does on your Mac.

5. **Choose a period from the Show Activity For pop-up menu, such as viewing everything the user did in the past week or month.**

6. **Choose Website or Date from the Group By pop-up menu.**

7. **Click Websites Visited, Websites Blocked, Applications, or iChat in the Log Collections list box to review the selected log.**

Figure 4-14 displays the Websites Visited list. Figure 4-15 shows the Websites Blocked list, providing you all the sites the user tried (and failed) to access. If you peek at the Applications or iChat lists, you can see the programs that ran on the account or the iChat addresses the account contacted.

Figure 4-15: In the Logs preferences pane, the Websites Blocked list shows you which Web sites a user was unable to visit.

Not all blocked Web sites are necessarily pornographic. Sometimes a blocked Web site could just be a blocked pop-up ad from an acceptable site.

8. **Click the Close button of the Parental Controls preferences window.**

Book V

iLife

The 5th Wave   By Rich Tennant

"Why can't you just bring your iPod like everyone else?"

Contents at a Glance

Chapter 1: Viewing and Organizing Photos with iPhoto

In This Chapter

✔ **Importing pictures into iPhoto**

✔ **Organizing Events**

✔ **Organizing pictures**

✔ **Organizing with Faces and Places**

✔ **Editing pictures**

✔ **Sharing pictures with others**

Think of iPhoto as a place where you can dump all your digital photographs so you can browse them again later. In iPhoto, all your pictures are stored in a Library. The Library provides five ways to organize your pictures:

✦ **Events** typically contain pictures captured on the same day.

✦ **Albums** typically contain pictures grouped by a common theme, such as pictures of your commitment ceremony or vacation.

✦ **Faces** organizes your Library based on faces of individuals that you *tag* with a name and, over time, iPhoto tries to identify faces in new pictures you import and automatically tag them with the name of the person (or persons) in the pictures.

✦ **Places** automatically tags and organizes your pictures based on where you snapped them with your GPS-capable camera or mobile phone, like the Nikon Coolpix 6000 camera or the iPhone 3G S smartphone, which both have built-in Global Positioning System (GPS) receivers. You can also tag pictures with location information on an individual or group basis.

✦ **Folders** hold and organize multiple albums. You can create a folder called Animals, for instance, and then store albums, such as Goats, Monkeys, Terriers, and Hermit Crabs, inside your Animals folder.

After importing your pictures, iPhoto lets you edit your pictures to modify colors, fix photos containing people afflicted by that vexing "red-eye" condition, or clip out unwanted portions. When your pictures look perfect, you can print them on your printer or through a printing service (which can actually cost less money than what you might spend on ink cartridges and glossy photo paper!). You can also share pictures in your iPhoto Library with others via e-mail, or by posting them to Web sites, such as MobileMe, Facebook, or Flickr. From start to finish, iPhoto can take care of organizing your pictures so you can focus on taking even more pictures.

Importing Pictures

Before you can organize your pictures, you need to import them into iPhoto. The import process saves photos in series of folders based on certain criteria that makes it possible for iPhoto to keep track of everything. If you have pictures stored in other folders on your hard drive, on other storage devices (such as CDs or DVDs), or trapped inside a digital camera, the first step is to copy those pictures into iPhoto.

To copy pictures into iPhoto — or, to use the accepted lingo, to *import* pictures into iPhoto — follow these steps:

1. **Insert or connect the storage device — thumb drive, digital camera, CD, whatever — that contains the pictures you want to import into iPhoto.**

   If your pictures are already stored in a folder on your hard drive, skip this step.

2. **Click the iPhoto icon in the Dock (or double-click the iPhoto icon in the Applications folder) to open iPhoto.**

3. **(Optional) If you're running iPhoto for the first time, two dialogs will appear, as shown in Figures 1-1 and 1-2, asking:**

   • *Do you want to use iPhoto when you connect your digital camera?:* Click Yes if you want iPhoto to automatically open whenever you plug in your digital camera or camera-enabled smartphone. Click No if you don't want iPhoto to automatically open or click Decide Later if you'd rather make this momentous decision another time.

   • *Look up Photo Locations:* Click Yes if you want iPhoto to automatically tag location information when it imports photos you snap with your GPS-capable camera or smartphone.

4. **Choose File⇨Import to Library.**

   An Import Photos dialog appears, as shown in Figure 1-3.

5. **Click the drive or folder in the sidebar that contains the pictures you want to import.**

Figure 1-1:
iPhoto offers to open automatically whenever you connect your camera.

Figure 1-2:
iPhone can automatically tag photos snapped with GPS-capable phones with location information.

Figure 1-3:
The Import Photos dialog lets you choose the device and folder that contains pictures.

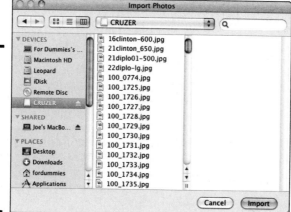

6. Choose one of the following:

- *To import every picture file displayed on a drive or in a selected folder:* Proceed to Step 7.

- *To import individual files from a drive or folder:* Click the picture file in the middle column that you want to import, or click a folder in the middle column that contains the pictures you want to import and then click the picture file that you want to import in the right column.

To select multiple pictures, hold down the ⌘ key and click each picture you want to import. To select a range of pictures, click the first picture you want to import, hold down the Shift key, and then click the last picture to highlight all the pictures in between.

7. Click Import.

iPhoto imports your pictures and organizes them into an Event, or several Events if the picture files you import are tagged with information about them, and/or if you import the contents of two or more separate folders.

A fast way to import pictures into iPhoto is to drag and drop those pictures to the iPhoto icon in the Dock, or to the Photos category under Library in the iPhoto sidebar.

Organizing Events in the Library

The iPhoto Library can store literally thousands of pictures, which can soon become as disorganized as dumping a decade's worth of photographs in a box and then wondering why you can never find a specific picture easily.

Just as most people organize pictures in albums, boxes, or bags, iPhoto can organize groups of pictures in one place. In iPhoto, a group of related pictures is an *Event*.

Two other ways you can organize and view pictures is by using the Faces feature, which sorts pictures by the faces of people in your pictures, and the Places feature, which sorts pictures based on the location where you capture them. Both of these other ways of organizing and viewing pictures in your iPhoto Library are covered in later sections of this chapter.

The main purpose of Events is to group related pictures together. One Event might contain pictures you capture during your stay on a UFO, and a second Event might hold pictures of your new puppy's first visit to the beach. After you group related pictures in an Event, you quickly can find pictures you want to look at again or share with others.

Creating an Event

When you import pictures, iPhoto automatically organizes them as Events, based on the day the picture was captured. Organizing Events by day can automatically sort pictures into one Event (the first day of your vacation when you visited London) and a second Event (the second day of your vacation when you visited Paris, and so on).

You can also create an Event manually by choosing Events➪Create Events.

Browsing through an Event

An Event can represent a single picture you capture on a particular day, but more likely, an Event represents several pictures. To view thumbnail previews of all the pictures stored in an Event, hover the pointer over the Event icon, and then slowly move the pointer left or right (or press the left and right arrow keys) to step through a thumbnail preview of each picture contained in the Event.

When you position the pointer over an Event, iPhoto displays the date of the event and the number of pictures it contains, as shown in Figure 1-4.

Figure 1-4:
Hovering
the pointer
on an Event
reveals its
date and
number of
pictures.

If you'd rather see individual thumbnails of all the pictures stored in a single Event, double-click the Event to display them, as shown in Figure 1-5.

Click the All Events button or press the Escape key to return to the iPhoto window.

Naming an Event

To make finding pictures easier, you can give each Event a descriptive name so you have a rough idea what type of pictures are stored in that Event without having to browse through them. To give your Event a descriptive name, follow these steps:

Figure 1-5:
Double-
clicking
an Event
expands all
the pictures
in the iPhoto
window.

1. Click the Events category under Library in the left pane (the sidebar) of the iPhoto window.

iPhoto displays all your Events in the right pane. If you haven't named your Events, each Event may display the date when you captured those pictures as its name.

2. Click the Event name, which appears directly under the Event picture.

A yellow box highlights the Event and a text box appears along with the number of pictures stored in that Event, as shown in Figure 1-6.

3. Type a new, descriptive name for your Event and then press Return.

Merging Events

You might have pictures stored as separate Events, but you might later decide that the pictures in both Events really should be grouped in a single Event. In this case, you can merge two Events into a single Event by following these steps:

1. Click the Events category under Library in the iPhoto sidebar.

iPhoto displays all your Events in the right pane.

2. **Move the pointer over an Event you want to move or merge into another Event.**

3. **Click and drag the Event to the Event you want to merge it with, as shown in Figure 1-7.**

    The pointer turns into an arrow with a green plus sign.

4. **Release the mouse button when the pointer appears over an Event.**

    A dialog appears, asking whether you want to merge the two Events.

5. **Click Merge.**

    Your two Events now appear as a single Event.

Figure 1-6: Clicking the event text box lets you type a new name or rename an existing event.

Splitting an Event

Sometimes an Event might contain too many pictures. In this case, you might want to store pictures in separate Events. To split an Event, follow these steps:

1. **Click the Events category under Library in the iPhoto sidebar.**

    iPhoto displays all your Events in the right pane.

2. **Double-click an Event you want to split.**

Figure 1-7:
A green plus sign appears under the pointer to identify when two Events merge.

The pictures in your Event appear in the iPhoto window (refer to Figure 1-5).

3. **Hold down the ⌘ key and click each picture you want to add to your new separate Event.**

   A yellow border highlights each chosen picture.

4. **Choose Events⇨Split Event.**

   Your chosen pictures now appear in a separate Event.

5. **Click the All Events button or press Escape.**

   Your original and newly split Events appear highlighted with a yellow border.

Moving pictures from one Event to another

If a picture appears in one Event but you think it should appear in a different Event, you can always move that picture. To move a picture from one Event to another, follow these steps:

1. **Click the Events category under Library in the iPhoto sidebar.**

iPhoto displays all your Events in the right pane.

2. **Click the Event that contains the picture you want to move.**

3. **Hold down the ⌘ key and then click the second Event to which you want to move a picture.**

Yellow borders appear around both Events.

4. **Double-click one of the highlighted Events.**

The iPhoto window splits in half, with pictures of the two Events stacked on top of each other, as shown in Figure 1-8.

5. **Click and drag the picture you want to move to the area containing the pictures of the second Event.**

6. **Release the mouse button.**

Your chosen picture now appears in the other Event.

7. **Click the All Events button (or press Escape) to see all your Events again.**

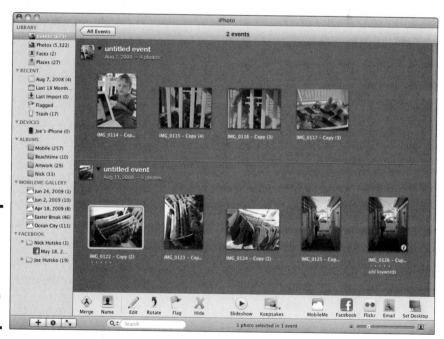

Figure 1-8: Dragging lets you move a picture from one Event to another.

Sorting Events

The more Events you create to store your pictures, the harder it to find what you need. To help keep you organized, iPhoto lets you sort your Events by different criteria:

+ **Date:** Lets you sort Events by time.

+ **Title:** Lets you sort Events by title.

+ **Manually:** Lets you sort Events by clicking and dragging them.

You can also sort pictures by rating and keywords, but you must first give a picture a rating or keyword, which you find out about later in this chapter.

Sorting by date or title

Sorting by date makes it easy to find pictures based on the time you remember capturing those pictures. Sorting by title is helpful after you give all Events a descriptive title and want to find a picture stored under a specific Event title.

To sort Events by date or title within the iPhoto window, follow these steps:

1. **Click the Events category under Library in the iPhoto sidebar.**

iPhoto displays all your Events in the right pane.

2. **Choose View⇨Sort Events.**

A submenu appears with a check mark next to the way you have your Events sorted, as shown in Figure 1-9.

3. **Choose By Date, By Title, Manually, and Ascending or Descending.**

Your Events sort by the criteria you choose.

Figure 1-9:
The Sort Events submenu lists the different ways to sort Events.

If you choose Ascending or Descending, iPhoto sorts your Events based on the sorting method that appears with a check mark in the Sort Events submenu.

Sorting manually

Another way to sort Events is by clicking and dragging them within the iPhoto window. This gives you the freedom to arrange pictures in Events based on your preferences, regardless of date or titles. For example, you might put all your family Events near the top of the iPhoto window, which makes it easy to find pictures of different family members if you're putting together a newsletter for a family reunion.

To sort Events manually within the iPhoto window, follow these steps:

1. **Click the Events category under Library in the iPhoto sidebar.**

iPhoto displays all your Events in the right pane.

2. **Click and drag an Event you want to move to its new location.**

When you move an Event between two other Events, the other Events slide out of the way to make room.

3. **Release the mouse button when you're happy with the new position of the Event.**

Organizing Pictures

After you store pictures in separate Events, you might want to view and organize individual pictures stored in an Event.

Viewing pictures stored in a single Event

If you want to view pictures in only one Event, follow these steps:

1. **Click the Events category under Library in the iPhoto sidebar.**

iPhoto displays all your Events in the right pane.

2. **Double-click an Event.**

All your pictures in that Event appear in the iPhoto window, as shown in Figure 1-10.

3. **Click the All Events button in the upper-left corner of the iPhoto window (or press Escape) to view all your Events again.**

Figure 1-10:
Double-
clicking
an Event
displays all
the pictures
in that
Event.

Viewing pictures stored in all Events

Rather than view pictures stored in a single Event, you might want to view all your pictures in separate Events at the same time. To view pictures in all Events, follow these steps:

1. **Click the Photos category under Library in the iPhoto sidebar.**

   iPhoto displays all your pictures. If you've hidden any photos from view (by choosing Photos⇨Hide Photos), you can view those hidden photos by choosing View⇨Hidden Photos and making sure a check mark appears to the left of Hidden Photos.

2. **Choose View⇨Event Titles so a check mark appears to the left of Event Titles.**

   Note: If a check mark already appears to the left of Event Titles, skip this step.

   Displaying Event Titles lets you see how your pictures are organized into different Events, as shown in Figure 1-11.

3. **Click the triangle to the left of the Event title to display or hide pictures in an Event.**

   This step works only if a check mark appears to the left of Event Titles on the View menu.

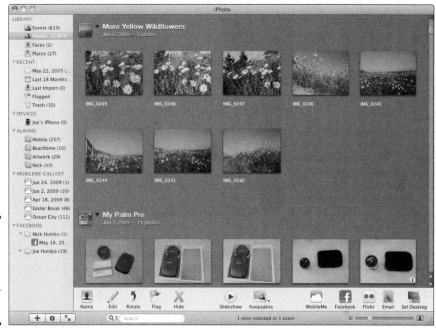

Figure 1-11:
The Photos
category
lets you
view all your
pictures.

Click the Slideshow icon beneath your pictures or events to display the Slideshow options dialog, choose a slideshow theme shown in Figure 1-12, and then click Play to begin the (slide) show!

Naming pictures

Every digital camera stores pictures with generic filenames, such as DSC_846. Fortunately, you can replace these generic titles with more descriptive names.

In iPhoto, you can give descriptive names to your Events and descriptive names to individual pictures as well. So an Event might be named "Spring Break," and pictures stored in that Event might be named "Day 1: Arrival," "Day 2: Imbibing," and "Day 3: Recovering."

To name individual pictures stored in an Event, follow these steps:

1. **Choose one of the methods mentioned earlier (in the section "Viewing pictures in a single Event" or "Viewing pictures stored in all Events") to view your pictures.**

Figure 1-12:
Choose
a theme
and then
click Play
to enjoy a
slideshow.

2. **Choose View⇨Titles.**

   Note: If a check mark already appears to the left of Titles, skip this step.

   Titles appear underneath every picture.

3. **Click the title that you want to change.**

   A text box appears, as shown in Figure 1-13.

4. **Type a new name for your picture or use the arrow and Delete keys to edit the existing name.**

5. **Press Return.**

After you name all pictures in an Event, you can sort them by choosing View⇨Sort Photos⇨By Title. Then you can choose View⇨Sort Photos⇨Ascending (or Descending) to sort by titles in ascending or descending order.

Figure 1-13:
Descriptive titles can help you find pictures easier.

Rating pictures

Some pictures are better than others, so another way to sort and organize pictures is by rating them from zero to five stars. To rate pictures, follow these steps:

1. **Choose one of the methods mentioned earlier (in the section "Viewing pictures in a single Event" or "Viewing pictures stored in all Events") to view your pictures.**

2. **Choose View⇨Rating.**

   Note: If a check mark already appears to the left of Rating, skip this step.

   Titles appear underneath every picture.

3. **Click to select the picture you want to rate.**

   A row of five dots appears beneath your selected picture.

4. **Click the first, second, third, fourth, or fifth dot to mark the picture with that number of stars, as shown in Figure 1-14.**

Figure 1-14:
You can rate each picture with zero to five stars.

You have other ways to rate pictures:

✦ Choose Photos⇨My Rating and then choose the number of stars you want to rate the picture with from the submenu.

✦ Control-click a picture and choose the My Rating submenu to pick a star rating.

✦ Click a picture and press ⌘+0 through ⌘+5 to rate a picture from zero to five stars.

After you rate some or all of your pictures in an Event, you can sort them by choosing View⇨Sort Photos⇨By Rating. To change whether to sort by ascending or descending rating, choose View⇨Sort Photos⇨Ascending (or Descending).

Adding keywords to a picture

A *keyword* helps you organize pictures based on categories, such as Cityscapes, Nature, or All in the Family. By placing keywords on pictures, you can quickly find all your favorite outdoor photos or family pictures.

To add a keyword to a picture, follow these steps:

1. **Choose one of the methods mentioned earlier (in the section "Viewing pictures in a single Event" or "Viewing pictures stored in all Events") to view your pictures.**

2. **Click a picture that you want to label with a keyword.**

If you hold down the ⌘ key, you can click two or more pictures to assign the same keyword to all of them.

3. **Choose Window⇨Show Keywords.**

A Keywords window appears, which displays several common keywords that iPhoto provides for you, as shown in Figure 1-15.

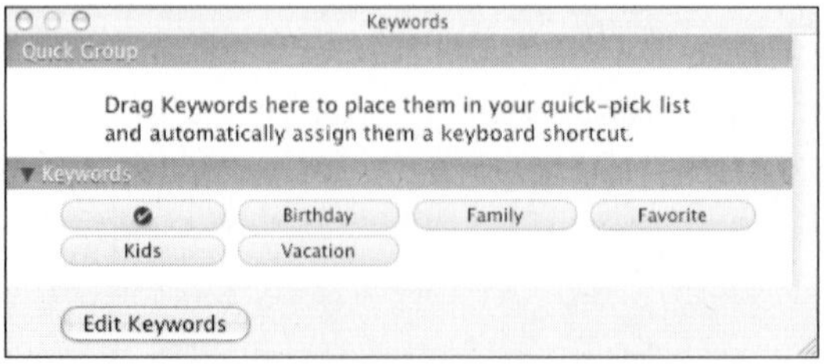

Figure 1-15:
The Keywords window displays a list of keywords you can use.

	Keywords
Quick Group	

Drag Keywords here to place them in your quick-pick list and automatically assign them a keyboard shortcut.

▼ Keywords

✅	Birthday	Family	Favorite
Kids	Vacation		

(Edit Keywords)

To add your own keywords to the Keywords window, click the Edit Keywords button. When the Edit Keywords dialog appears, click the plus sign button to type your own keywords into the Keywords window. (You can also click a keyword and then click the minus sign button to remove a keyword from the Keyword window.)

If you click the Shortcut button, you can assign a key to represent a keyword. That way you can choose View⇨Keywords to display a keywords text box underneath each picture, click that text box, and then press your shortcut key to add a keyword to that picture quickly.

4. **Click a keyword.**

   Your chosen keyword appears underneath the picture you select.

   If you click the same keyword in the keyword window, iPhoto removes the keyword from your chosen picture.

After you add keywords to pictures in an Event, you can sort them by choosing View⇨Sort Photos⇨By Keyword. Then you can sort alphabetically by keyword by choosing View⇨Sort Photos⇨Ascending (or Descending).

Storing pictures in albums and folders

Sorting and organizing pictures into Events can be cumbersome. For example, you might have dozens of birthday pictures stored in separate Events. Although you can store all these birthday pictures in the same Event, you might also want to keep them grouped with other pictures in separate Events that represent different years.

To keep pictures stored in separate Events while grouping them at the same time, you can create an *album*. An album groups related pictures without removing them from the Events they're stored in.

Creating albums and organizing pictures manually

To create an album and store pictures in it, follow these steps:

1. **Choose File⇨New Album.**

   A dialog appears, as shown in Figure 1-16.

   For another way to create an album, click the plus sign button in the bottom-left corner of the iPhoto window. When a dialog appears, click the Album button, type a name for your album, and then click Create.

2. **Type a descriptive name for your album and then click Create.**

   Your album name appears under the Albums category in the iPhoto sidebar.

3. **Choose one of the methods mentioned earlier (in the section "Viewing pictures in a single Event" or "Viewing pictures stored in all Events") to view your pictures.**

4. **Click and drag a picture you want to add to your album to the album folder in the iPhoto sidebar.**

   You can select multiple pictures by holding down the ⌘ key and clicking each picture you want to add to an album.

5. **Release the mouse button to copy your picture to the album.**

6. **Repeat Steps 4 and 5 for each additional picture you want to copy to the album.**

   Now, if you click the album name in the iPhoto sidebar, you can see all the pictures in that album.

Any changes you make to a picture stored in an album automatically appear in the same picture stored in an Event (and vice versa).

The preceding steps create an empty album, which you can then fill up with pictures. If you want to select pictures to store in an album first, follow these steps:

1. **Select one or more pictures that you want to store in an album.**

2. **Choose File⇨New Album from Selection.**

   A dialog appears, asking for a name for your album.

3. **Type a descriptive name for your album and then click Create.**

Creating albums and organizing pictures automatically

If manually dragging pictures in and out of albums is too tedious, you can set up a Smart Album from within iPhoto that will store pictures automatically.

To create a Smart Album that can store pictures automatically, follow these steps:

1. **Choose File➪New Smart Album (or press Option and click the Plus "+" icon in the lower left corner of the iPhoto window).**

A dialog appears, asking for a name for your Smart Album.

2. **Type a descriptive name for your album in the Smart Album Name text box.**

3. **Click the first pop-up menu and then choose a criterion, such as Keyword or Rating, as shown in Figure 1-17.**

4. **Click the second and third pop-up menus to refine the criterion you choose in Step 3, such as choosing only pictures with a rating of four stars or with the Birthday keyword.**

5. **(Optional) Click the plus sign button to define another criterion and repeat Steps 3 and 4.**

6. **Click OK.**

Your Smart Album now stores pictures based on your chosen criteria.

TIP

If you create too many albums, you can organize them into folders by choosing File➪New Folder and dragging each album into that folder.

Figure 1-17: You must define the type of pictures you want the Smart Album to store automatically.

Deleting pictures, albums, and folders

Many times, you'll import pictures into iPhoto and decide that the picture isn't worth saving after all. To keep your iPhoto Library from becoming too cluttered, you can delete the pictures you don't need.

Besides deleting individual pictures, you can also delete albums and folders that contain pictures you don't want. When you delete an album or folder (which contains albums), you don't physically delete the pictures; you just delete the folder or album that contains the pictures. The original pictures are still stored in the iPhoto Library.

To delete a picture, album, or folder, click the picture, album, or folder you want to delete and then press the Delete key (or drag it to the Trash icon in the iPhoto sidebar).

Press ⌘+Z or choose Edit⇨Undo Delete if you want to recover your deleted items right away.

Choosing and Organizing Pictures with Faces and Places

Two more ways to organize and view pictures in your iPhoto Library are to use the Faces and Places features.

The Faces feature lets you add names to the faces of people in your pictures and, over time, iPhoto automatically recognizes and labels the faces of people in new pictures you import into your iPhoto Library.

The Places feature automatically tags and sorts pictures you import that contain GPS information that your GPS-capable smartphone or camera adds to pictures when you snap the pictures with the GPS-tagging feature (referred to as *geotagging*) turned on.

You can use the Places feature even if you don't have a GPS-capable smartphone or camera by selecting and then tagging individual pictures, or a group of pictures, with information that you type about the location where you captured the pictures.

Using Faces to organize pictures

You can organize pictures in your iPhoto Library based on the faces of people in the pictures.

To organize pictures using the Faces feature, follow these steps:

1. **Choose one of the methods mentioned earlier (in the section "Viewing pictures in a single Event" or "Viewing pictures stored in all Events") to view your pictures.**

2. **Click a picture with a person (or persons) in it that you want to identify with a name.**

3. **Click the Name icon in the lower-left corner.**

   iPhoto zooms in to the picture to fill the window.

4. **Click the Add Missing Face button in the lower-left corner.**

   iPhoto displays a selection box in the center of the picture, as shown in Figure 1-18.

Figure 1-18: Move or resize the selection box to frame a face in a picture.

5. **Move the selection box to the center of the face you want to name and then click and drag a corner to make the selection box larger or smaller around your subject's face.**

6. **Click the Click to Name caption box beneath the selection box and then type the name of the face you want to identify.**

   Any names in your Address Book that match what you're typing will appear while you type the letters of the name you want to give the subject in the picture.

7. **(Optional) If more than one person appears in the picture, click the Add Missing Face Button and then repeat Steps 5 and 6 to name the additional person (or persons) in the picture.**

8. **Click Done.**

To view pictures organized by faces in your iPhoto Library, click the Faces category under Library in the iPhoto sidebar to display the snapshots of the people iPhoto has organized by face, as shown in Figure 1-19. Double-click the person's group of pictures to see all your pictures of that person. Click the All Faces button in the upper-left corner to return to the Faces view.

Assigning and correcting faces in pictures

After you identify some pictures by using the Faces feature, iPhoto automatically detects and recognizes faces in other photos in your iPhoto Library and in new photos that you import. iPhoto uses face detection to attempt to match faces that look like the same person from picture to picture. iPhoto also suggests possible matches of people it attempts to recognize that you can confirm with a few clicks of your mouse.

Figure 1-19:
The Faces view groups pictures in your iPhoto Library based on a person (or doggy's!) face.

To display a list of pictures iPhoto finds with a person's face it thinks it recognizes, follow these steps:

1. **Click the Faces category under Library in the iPhoto sidebar.**

2. **Double-click a person's snapshot.**

   iPhoto displays all the pictures you identified or confirmed of the person in the upper-half of the display. In the bottom-half of the display, iPhoto displays thumbnails of pictures it thinks the same person appears in.

3. **Click the Confirm Name button in the lower-left corner.**

   iPhoto displays a confirm button beneath every thumbnail in the bottom-half of the window.

4. **To confirm or decline a person's name in pictures iPhoto thinks the person appears in, do one of the following:**

   Confirm: Click the Confirm button beneath each thumbnail to confirm the person is whom iPhoto suggests and to add the person's name to the picture. The person's name is highlighted in green beneath the thumbnail.

   Reject: Click the Confirm button beneath each thumbnail that doesn't contain the person who iPhoto suggests and then click it a second time. *Not* followed by the person's name is highlighted in red beneath the thumbnail, as shown in Figure 1-20.

Figure 1-20:
Confirm
or reject
people
iPhoto
thinks it
recognizes.

Organizing pictures with Places

You can view pictures in your iPhoto Library based on the locations where you snapped the pictures.

If your camera or smartphone has a GPS feature you've turned on, pictures you import into your iPhoto Library will automatically contain information about the location where you captured the pictures.

Viewing pictures organized by places

You can view pictures organized by the places where the pictures were captured by clicking pushpins on a map of the world, or by clicking a display listing pictures by country, region, state, and city.

To view pictures organized by the Places feature in your iPhoto Library, follow these steps:

1. **Click the Places category under Library in the iPhoto sidebar.**

iPhoto displays a map of the world with red pushpins that indicate locations where your pictures were captured. Moving the mouse pointer to a pushpin displays the name of the location where you captured the pictures, as shown in Figure 1-21.

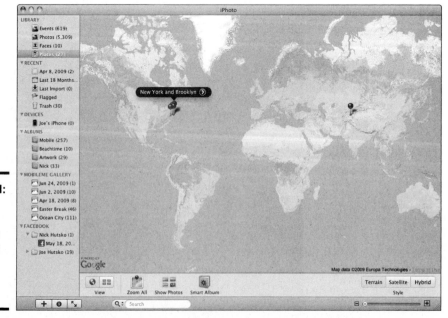

Figure 1-21:
Pushpins represent the places where you captured your pictures.

2. **To view the pictures for a location, move the mouse pointer to a push-pin to display the location name and then click the arrow to the right of the location name.**

iPhoto displays the pictures you captured (or manually tagged, as described in the next section) at the selected location.

To return to the Map View, click the Map View button in the lower-left corner.

3. **(Optional) From the World Map view, you can do these additional things:**

Zoom In/Out: Click and drag the slider button in the lower-right corner to zoom in and out of the World Map view. If you're using a mouse with a scroll wheel, you can zoom in and out on the map by rolling the scroll wheel forward and backward. If you're using a new or recent MacBook, you can zoom in and out on the map by pinching two fingertips together and apart.

Terrain, Satellite, Hybrid view: Click one of these three buttons to change the World Map view. Terrain shows a topographic view. Satellite displays an eye-in-the-sky view based on actual satellite imagery. Hybrid combines both the Terrain and Satellite views into a single view, as shown in Figure 1-22.

List view: Click the List view icon to the right of the Map View icon in the lower-left corner to see a list with four columns displaying the country, state, city, and address or landmark location for pictures you captured or manually identified by location, as shown in Figure 1-23.

Figure 1-22:
The Hybrid view combines topographic and satellite depictions of the world map.

Figure 1-23:
The List view organizes your pictures by country, state, city, and address or landmark location.

Manually identifying locations for pictures

If your camera or smartphone doesn't have a GPS feature that automatically adds a location to pictures you capture, you can still add location information to pictures in your iPhoto collection by selecting and typing location names for your pictures.

To add location names to pictures in your iPhoto Library so you can view them with the Places feature, follow these steps:

1. **Choose one of the methods mentioned earlier (in the section "Viewing pictures in a single Event" or "Viewing pictures stored in all Events") to view your pictures.**

2. **Click a picture that you want to identify by location.**

If you hold down the ⌘ key, you can click two or more pictures to assign the same location to all of them.

3. **Click File⇨Get Info (or press ⌘+I) to display an information window for the selected picture (or pictures), as shown in Figure 1-24.**

4. **Click the name to the right of the location check box, type or edit the name of the location where the picture was captured, and then press Return.**

While you type, a list beneath the location name appears with suggestions of locations that might match the location you want to assign to the picture.

Figure 1-24:
The Get Info window lets you add or change a picture's location information.

5. **(Optional) You can add or edit the following information for the picture (or pictures) by using the following check boxes:**

   Title: Edit or type a title for the selected picture.

   Rating: Click the dots to choose the number of stars you want to give the picture (from one to five stars).

   Description: Edit or type a descriptive word or words to describe the picture so you can search for it when you want to find it again.

6. **Click Done to close the Get Info window and return to the pictures display.**

To view pictures organized by Faces in your iPhoto library, click the Faces category under Library in the iPhoto sidebar, then double-click the snapshot of the person whose pictures you want to look at.

Editing Pictures

Besides organizing your pictures, iPhoto lets you edit them. Such editing can be as simple as rotating or cropping a picture, or it can be as intricate as removing red-eye from a photograph or modifying colors.

If you need more detailed or sophisticated editing, consider buying an image-managing program, such as Adobe Photoshop Elements (www.adobe.com) or GraphicConverter (www.lemkesoft.com).

Rotating a picture

Sometimes pictures appear sideways when you import them into iPhoto. To rotate a picture so you can see it right-side up, follow these steps:

1. **Choose one of the methods mentioned earlier (in the section "Viewing pictures in a single Event" or "Viewing pictures stored in all Events") to view your pictures.**

2. **Click a picture and then click the Edit button in the lower-left corner (or just double-click the picture).**

   iPhoto displays your selected photo in the center pane and buttons for several editing tools appear beneath the picture, as shown in Figure 1-25.

3. **Click the Rotate button until you're happy with the new position of your picture.**

   If you hold down the Option key and click the Rotate button, you can rotate a picture in the opposite direction.

Figure 1-25: The editing tools appear at the bottom of the iPhoto window.

Cropping a picture

Cropping a picture lets you select only the part of the picture you want to keep. To crop a picture, follow these steps:

1. **Choose one of the methods mentioned earlier (in the section "Viewing pictures in a single Event" or "Viewing pictures stored in all Events") to view your pictures.**

2. **Click a picture and then click the Edit button in the lower-left corner (or just double-click the picture).**

   Editing buttons appear at the bottom of the iPhoto window (refer to Figure 1-25).

3. **Click the Crop button.**

   A white box appears on your picture, as shown in Figure 1-26.

4. **Click and drag an edge or corner of the white box to reshape the box.**

   If you select the Constrain check box, you can pick a specific size option for your picture, such as square or 4 x 3.

5. **Click the Apply button.**

   Your cropped picture appears.

6. **Click the Done button.**

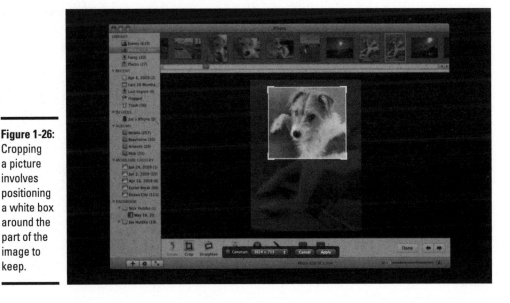

Figure 1-26: Cropping a picture involves positioning a white box around the part of the image to keep.

Straightening a picture

Sometimes a picture might appear slightly cockeyed, so iPhoto lets you straighten an image by following these steps:

1. **Choose one of the methods mentioned earlier (in the section "Viewing pictures in a single Event" or "Viewing pictures stored in all Events") to view your pictures.**

2. **Click a picture and then click the Edit button in the lower-left corner (or just double-click the picture).**

Editing buttons appear at the bottom of the iPhoto window (refer to Figure 1-25).

3. **Click the Straighten button.**

A yellow grid appears over your image along with a slider, as shown in Figure 1-27.

4. **Move the pointer to the slider, hold down the mouse button, and drag the mouse left or right to straighten the image.**

If you click the Decrease/Increase angle of photo icons that appear on opposite ends of the slider, you can adjust the angle of your picture by 0.1 of a degree.

5. **Click the Done button.**

Figure 1-27:
Dragging the slider lets you tilt an image.

Fixing a picture

Not every picture looks perfect, so iPhoto gives you three tools to try to fix an image:

+ **Enhance:** Fixes brightness and contrast problems.

+ **Red-eye:** Removes red-eye caused by flash photography.

+ **Retouch:** Lets you drag the mouse to remove wrinkles, scars, and minor blemishes.

To fix a picture, follow these steps:

1. **Choose one of the methods mentioned earlier (in the section "Viewing pictures in a single Event" or "Viewing pictures stored in all Events") to view your pictures.**

2. **Click a picture and then click the Edit button in the lower-left corner (or just double-click the picture).**

   Editing buttons appear at the bottom of the iPhoto window (refer to Figure 1-25).

3. **Click the Enhance button.**

   Your picture changes appearance by appearing brighter and easier to see details.

4. **If necessary, click the Red-Eye button and then click each red-eye in the picture.**

   The red color in a person's eye is replaced with a darker, more natural color.

5. **If necessary, click the Retouch button, move the pointer to the part of the picture you want to modify, and then click and drag to erase an area and replace it with colors from the surrounding area.**

6. **Click Done.**

Adding visual effects to a picture

Just for fun, you can add visual effects to your pictures, such as making them look like faded pictures taken decades ago or placing them inside a circle with blurred edges. To add effects to a picture, follow these steps:

1. **Choose one of the methods mentioned earlier (in the section "Viewing pictures in a single Event" or "Viewing pictures stored in all Events") to view your pictures.**

2. **Click a picture and then click the Edit button in the lower-left corner (or just double-click the picture).**

   Editing buttons appear at the bottom of the iPhoto window (refer to Figure 1-25).

3. **Click the Effects button.**

   An Effects window appears, as shown in Figure 1-28.

4. **Click an effect.**

   Note: You can click multiple effects.

5. **Click the Done button.**

Controlling colors in a picture

In case you need advanced editing features, iPhoto lets you adjust contrast, saturation, tint, exposure, and other parts of a picture by following these steps:

1. **Choose one of the methods mentioned earlier (in the section "Viewing pictures in a single Event" or "Viewing pictures stored in all Events") to view your pictures.**

2. **Click a picture and then click the Edit button in the lower-left corner (or just double-click the picture).**

   Editing buttons appear at the bottom of the iPhoto window (refer to Figure 1-25).

3. **Click the Adjust button.**

   An Adjust window appears, as shown in Figure 1-29.

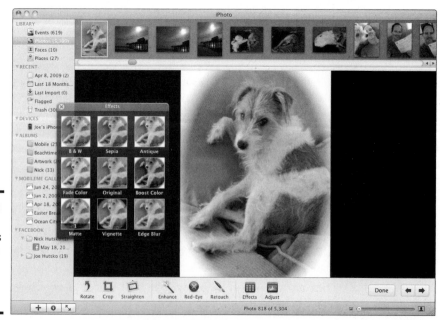

Figure 1-28: The Effects window lets you choose a way to modify your picture.

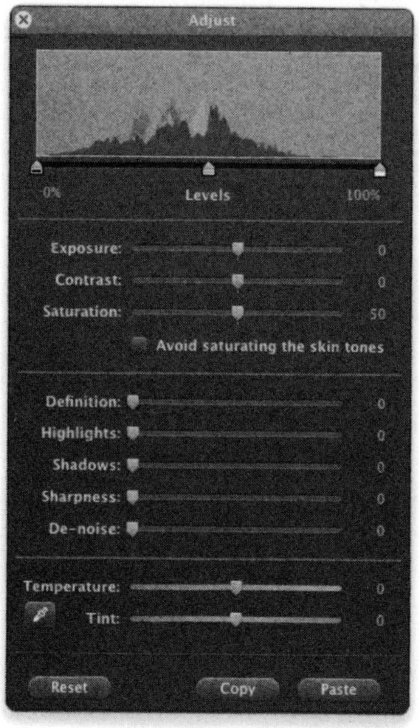

Figure 1-29:
The Adjust
window
provides
multiple
ways to
modify the
colors in a
picture.

4. **Adjust any of the following settings:**

   - *Exposure:* Lightens or darkens a picture.

   - *Contrast:* Alters the differences between light and dark areas.

   - *Saturation:* Alters the intensity of colors in a picture.

   - *Definition:* Reduces haze and improves clarity without adding too much contrast.

   - *Highlights:* Increases detail in a picture by lightening or darkening areas.

   - *Shadows:* Lightens or darkens shadow areas of a picture.

   - *Sharpness:* Adjusts the focus of a picture.

   - *De-noise:* Alters the graininess of a picture.

   - *Temperature:* Alters colors by making them dimmer (colder) or brighter (hotter).

   - *Tint:* Adjusts the red/green colors in a picture.

5. **(Optional) Check the Avoid Saturating the Skin Tones check box if you want to try to make skin coloration look more natural.**

Your image changes as you adjust any of these settings.

If you decide that your original picture looked better without any adjusted settings, click the Reset button.

6. (Optional) Click the Copy button to copy your adjusted settings so you can use the same settings to adjust another photo, which you can open and then click Paste to apply the adjusted settings.

7. Click the Done button (refer to Figure 1-28).

Sharing Pictures

There's no point in taking pictures if you don't share them with others. To help you publicize your pictures to the world, you can print them, post them on a Web page, e-mail them to others, or burn them to a CD/DVD. For an added fee, you can print your pictures as books, calendars, or greeting cards.

Printing pictures

You can print individual pictures or groups of pictures on your home printer by following these steps:

1. Choose one of the methods mentioned earlier (in the section "Viewing pictures in a single Event" or "Viewing pictures stored in all Events") to view your pictures.

2. Hold down the ⌘ key and click all the pictures you want to print.

3. Click the Print button or choose File⇨Print.

A Print dialog appears, as shown in Figure 1-30.

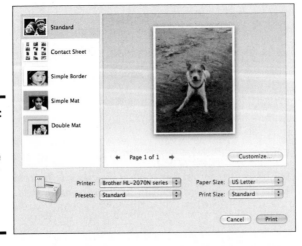

Figure 1-30: The Print dialog lets you choose different ways to print your pictures.

4. **Click one of the following print styles:**

   - *Standard:* Prints pictures to fill the entire page.
   - *Contact Sheet:* Prints thumbnail images of multiple pictures on a single page.
   - *Simple Border:* Prints one picture per page with a plain border around the edge.
   - *Simple Mat:* Prints one picture per page with a tinted border around the edge.
   - *Double Mat:* Prints one picture per page with two borders around the edges.

5. **Choose the following pop-up menu options:**

   - *Printer:* Defines which printer to use (if you have more than one printer).
   - *Paper Size:* Defines what size paper to use.
   - *Presets:* Provides predefined printing settings.
   - *Print Size:* Defines the size to print each picture, such as 3 x 5 or 8 x 10.

6. **Click the Print button.**

You can click the Order Prints button in the bottom-right corner of the iPhoto window to have your pictures sent to Kodak for printing (for a fee, of course). You can also click the Book, Calendar, or Card button to create photo books, calendars, or greeting cards from your pictures.

E-mailing pictures

If you want to share pictures with family members or friends who have an e-mail address, you can e-mail pictures using the Mail program. If you use a different e-mail program, such as America Online or Entourage, you can configure iPhoto to work with your e-mail program by following these steps:

1. **Choose iPhoto⇨Preferences.**

   A Preferences window appears.

2. **Click the General button.**

3. **Click the Email Photos Using pop-up menu and choose your e-mail program or service.**

4. **Click the Close button of the Preferences window.**

After you configure your e-mail program to work with iPhoto, you can send a picture by following these steps:

1. **Choose one of the methods mentioned earlier (in the section "Viewing pictures in a single Event" or "Viewing pictures stored in all Events") to view your pictures.**

2. **Hold down the ⌘ key and then click the picture you want to send.**

3. **Click the Email button or choose Share⇨Email.**

   A Mail Photo dialog appears, letting you choose a size for your picture, as shown in Figure 1-31.

Figure 1-31:
The Mail Photo dialog lets you choose how to e-mail pictures.

4. **Choose any options in the Mail Photo dialog.**

   • *Size:* Lets you define how big (or small) you want your picture to appear in the e-mail message.

   • *Titles:* Includes the picture's title.

   • *Descriptions:* Includes any comments you might have added to the picture.

   • *Location Information:* Includes information about where the picture was captured.

5. **Click Compose Message.**

   iPhoto automatically launches the Mail program (if it isn't already running) and creates a new e-mail message containing your selected picture and any of the optional information you may have selected in Step 4.

6. **Type any additional message, enter an e-mail address, and then click Send.**

Saving pictures to a CD/DVD

If you want to give someone a copy of your pictures, you can store them on CD/DVD so they can pop the CD/DVD into their own computer. To save pictures on CD/DVD, follow these steps:

1. **Choose one of the methods mentioned earlier (in the section "Viewing pictures in a single Event" or "Viewing pictures stored in all Events") to view your pictures.**

2. **Hold down the ⌘ key and then click all the pictures you want to save.**

3. **Choose Share⇨Burn.**

A dialog appears, prompting you to insert a blank CD/DVD into your Mac.

4. **Insert a blank CD/DVD and then click OK.**

Your photos burn to your CD/DVD.

Some older Mac models and the MacBook Air don't come with built-in DVD burner, so your only option is to use a friend's Mac with a DVD drive that can burn DVDs, or buy an external DVD drive. Either way, make sure your Mac can use the type of disc you want to save your pictures on.

Using pictures in iWeb and iDVD

After you store pictures in iPhoto, you can import them directly into iDVD (to burn them to a DVD, complete with fancy menus and music) or into iWeb (to place on Web pages). To transfer pictures from iPhoto to iDVD or iWeb, follow these steps:

1. **Choose one of the methods mentioned earlier (in the section "Viewing pictures in a single Event" or "Viewing pictures stored in all Events") to view your pictures.**

2. **Hold down the ⌘ key and then click all the pictures you want to use.**

3. **Choose one of the following:**

- Share⇨Send to iWeb⇨Photo Page (or Blog). This loads iWeb and creates a photo album page displaying all your chosen pictures.

- Share⇨Send to iDVD. This loads the iDVD program and your chosen photographs so you can arrange them in the order you want.

If you have a MobileMe, Facebook, or Flickr account, you can post your pictures to your personal photo gallery page by clicking Share and then choosing the service where you want your pictures to appear.

Ordering books, calendars, and cards

For a fee, you can have your favorite iPhoto pictures printed as books, calendars, or greeting cards. To choose to print your pictures on a book, calendar, or greeting card, follow these steps:

1. **Choose one of the methods mentioned earlier (in the section "Viewing pictures in a single Event" or "Viewing pictures stored in all Events") to view your pictures.**

2. **Hold down the ⌘ key and then click all the pictures you want to use.**

3. **Click the Keepsakes button at the bottom of the iPhoto window and then choose Book, Calendar, or Card from the pop-up menu.**

A dialog appears, asking that you choose a particular style — a Picture Book or Picture Calendar, for example — as shown in Figure 1-32.

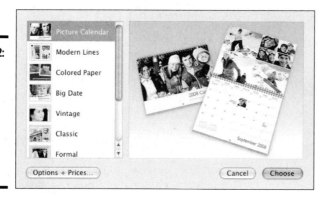

Figure 1-32: You can choose a specific style of book, calendar, or card to create.

4. **Click a style and then click Choose.**

Depending on the type of project you want to create (a book, calendar, or card), you might need to pick additional options.

If you click the Options and Prices button, Safari launches and then takes you to a page on Apple's Web site that lists the formats, options, and prices for the different kinds of keepsakes you can buy.

Eventually, the iPhoto window displays a blank book, calendar, or card for you to drag your pictures to and then design them, as shown in Figure 1-33.

5. **Click the Buy button when you finish designing your project.**

Prices for books and calendars typically cost $10 to $30, and greeting cards cost $2 each. Your order goes directly to Apple, although Kodak does the actual printing.

Figure 1-33: To design a project, drag the pictures you select.

Chapter 2: Making Movies with iMovie

In This Chapter

✔ Discovering how iMovie works

✔ Importing and storing video

✔ Creating a video project

✔ Browsing and organizing video

✔ Adding titles, transitions, and sound

✔ Saving videos

*I*f you have a digital video camcorder, a digital camera, or smartphone that captures video, you can create home movies. To make your home movies fancier and — almost — professional, settle into your Director's chair and get rolling with iMovie. With iMovie, you can turn your home movies into a polished product that you can upload to video-sharing sites (such as YouTube), play on video iPods, or just view on your Mac. You can also transfer them to a DVD to give to your great-aunt Helen who doesn't have a computer but does have a DVD player hooked up to her television. Any digital home movie you might have, iMovie can improve with the help of your skill and creativity.

How iMovie Works

The iMovie program consists of an Event Library and a Project Library. The Event Library appears in the bottom-left corner of the iMovie window and is where you store videos. When you want to work your magic and come up with a film project, you choose parts of any video you have stored in the Event Library and copy these parts (known as *clips*) into the Project Library, which appears in the upper-left corner of the iMovie window.

The basic steps for using iMovie are

1. Import, store, and organize video in the Event Library.

2. Copy video footage from the Event Library to a project in the Project Library.

3. Edit your video clips in the Project pane.

4. Save your video as a digital video file for viewing on other computers, on DVD, or over the Internet.

For the ultimate guide to making movies and burning them to DVDs, check out fellow For Dummies authors Dennis R. Cohen and Michael E. Cohen's *iMovie '09 & iDVD '09 For Dummies* (Wiley).

Importing a Video into the Event Library

The Event Library holds all your videos, acting as your personal film vault. By storing videos in the Event Library, you can selectively choose footage from old videos to use in any new projects.

To store video in the Event Library, you must import a video from one of three sources:

✦ A digital video source, for example a digital video camera or smartphone capable of capturing video

✦ A project created and saved using an earlier version of iMovie

✦ A digital video file stored on your hard drive

Importing from a digital video camera

To *import* (that is, to copy) a movie to your hard drive that you've captured with a digital video camera, follow these steps:

1. **Connect your digital video camera to your Mac with a USB cable.**

The appropriate cable usually comes with the camera.

2. **Double-click the iMovie icon inside the Applications folder or click the iMovie icon in the Dock to load iMovie.**

The Import dialog appears, displaying all the clips recorded on your device.

3. **Choose File⇨Import from Camera if the Import dialog doesn't open and then choose the device you want from the Camera pop-up menu at the bottom.**

4. **Select the clips you want to import.**

• Set the Automatic/Manual switch to Automatic to import all the clips and then click the Import All button.

• Set the Automatic/Manual switch to Manual to import some of the clips. Deselect the clips you don't want to import and then click the Import Checked button.

The Import dialog shown in Figure 2-1 appears, giving you a choice of disks where you can save your video.

5. **From the Save To pop-up menu, choose where to store your video.**

   Video files can be large so you may want to store them on an external hard drive.

Figure 2-1:
The Import dialog lets you choose where you want to save your video file.

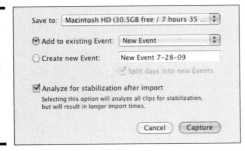

Save to: [Macintosh HD (30.5GB free / 7 hours 35 ... ⬦]

◉ Add to existing Event: [New Event ⬦]

○ Create new Event: [New Event 7-28-09]

☑ Split days into new Events

☑ Analyze for stabilization after import

Selecting this option will analyze all clips for stabilization, but will result in longer import times.

(Cancel) (Capture)

6. **Choose how to organize your video by selecting one of the following:**

   • *Add to Existing Event:* Stores the video as part of an existing event in the Event library.

   • *Create New Event:* Stores the video as a new event in the Event library. The default name for the Event will be the date, but you can always type a more descriptive name.

7. **Select or deselect the Split Days into New Events check box.**

   Many video camcorders time-stamp any video footage you capture, so this option divides a video into parts where each part represents all video footage shot on the same day.

8. **Select Analyze for Stabilization after Import if you want iMovie to attempt to detect and smooth any shaky parts.**

   You analyze only one time but analyzing is time consuming so you might want to do this when you're going to be away from your computer or overnight. You can also analyze your video later.

9. **Click the Capture button.**

   When iMovie is finished importing your file, the Import window appears.

10. **Click Done.**

    Your imported video appears as thumbnail images in the lower pane (the Event pane) of the iMovie window, as shown in Figure 2-2. After you import a video, your original video footage remains on your video camcorder, so you might want to go back and erase it.

Figure 2-2:
iMovie automatically separates a video into scenes.

If you have a digital video camera that records to DV or HDV tape, and which has a FireWire port, you can connect it to your Mac using your Mac's FireWire port (if your Mac has one; most Mac's do!). Follow the preceding steps. The only difference is when you set the Automatic/Manual switch. Automatic rewinds the whole tape and imports the entire video; Manual lets you rewind, fast-forward, and import the parts you want. Either way, the video plays while it's importing so the import takes as long as the video takes to watch.

iMovie divides a video into separate scenes where each scene displays the first frame of a video clip. By browsing through these thumbnail images of scenes, you can see which scene is likely to contain the video footage you want to use.

Importing a digital video file

If you have digital video files stored in QuickTime, MPEG-4, or digital video (DV) lying around on your hard drive, you can import them into iMovie. To import a digital video file, follow these steps:

1. **Choose File⇨Import Movies.**

An Open dialog appears, as shown in Figure 2-3. You might need to navigate through drives and folders to find the file you want to import.

Figure 2-3:
The Open
dialog lets
you import
digital video
files.

2. **Select the digital video file you want to import.**

3. **Click the Save To pop-up menu and choose a drive to store your video.**

4. **Select one of the following radio buttons:**

   • *Add to Existing Event:* Stores the video as part of an existing event in
     the Event Library.

   • *Create New Event:* Stores the video as a new event in the iMovie
     Event Library.

5. **Choose how you want to optimize high definition video in the
   Optimize Video pop-up menu.**

   The Large option reduces the frame size of the HD video to 960 x 540
   pixels, whereas the Full option displays the frame size at the complete
   1,920 x 1,080 pixels.

6. **Select the Copy Files or Move Files radio button.**

   The Copy Files option leaves your original file and creates a duplicate
   file to store in iMovie. The Move Files option physically transfers your
   chosen video file and moves it into iMovie.

7. **Click Import.**

   Your imported movie appears as thumbnail images in the iMovie
   window.

Organizing the Event Library

The more videos you store, the more crowded the Event Library becomes, and the harder it is to find what you want. When you store a new video in the Event Library, iMovie gives you the option of creating an event folder, which identifies the date you imported the video file into iMovie.

Organizing videos in the Event Library by date can be helpful, but you might prefer identifying Events by descriptive name. To rename an Event, follow these steps:

1. **Double-click an Event in the Event Library pane in the bottom-left corner of the iMovie window. (Choose Window⇨Show Event Library if the Event Library is not visible.)**

   Your chosen Event name appears highlighted.

2. **Type a descriptive name for your Event.**

Storing video in different Event folders can help you find the video you want. If you want to edit video of your family vacation, just click the Event folder for that day or span of days to display your video.

The Event Library displays each video file as a series of thumbnail images. To define how to divide a video into multiple thumbnail images, drag the slider in the bottom-right corner of the iMovie window. Dragging this slider to the left divides your video into more thumbnail images, whereas dragging this slider to the right divides your video into fewer thumbnail images. The number on the right of the slider indicates the duration of the clip from a half a second up to 30 seconds or All, which means no divisions.

Instead of forcing you to browse through your entire video to find the one part you need, iMovie lets you jump straight to a scene that contains the footage you want to use. You do this by dragging the mouse pointer over the thumbnail images of the clips. After you find the video footage to edit, copy that video footage into your project by clicking and dragging it with the mouse.

Working with Projects

The Event Library contains your raw, unedited video, and the Project Library contains the copies of your video that you can modify. The Project Library appears in the upper-left corner of the iMovie window, by default. The Project Library lists your projects by title and displays a film-strip next to each project title so you can preview your video. To view (or hide) the Project Library, choose Window⇨Show/Hide Project Library.

Projects contain one or more video clips from movies stored in the Event Library. In the Project Library, you can rearrange, trim, and delete video clips to create your movie. This is where you can also add titles or sound effects to your edited video. If you accidentally erase or mess up a video in the Project Library, just retrieve the original footage from the Event Library and start over. You can copy and store the same video footage in two or more projects.

Creating an iMovie project

To create a project, follow these steps:

1. **Choose File⇨New Project.**

   The New Project dialog appears, as shown in Figure 2-4.

2. **Enter a descriptive name for your project in the Project Name text box.**

3. **Choose Standard, iPhone, or Widescreen from the Aspect Ratio pop-up menu.**

   The aspect ratio optimizes your video project for displaying on different devices. If you want to view your video on a TV set, choose Standard or Widescreen. If you want to view your video on a mobile phone, choose the smaller iPhone aspect ratio.

4. **Choose a theme if you want iMovie to apply transitions and titles to your project; choose None if you want to do the work yourself.**

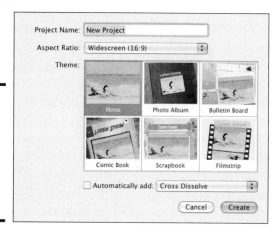

Figure 2-4:
Choose a name, aspect ratio, and theme for your video project.

5. (Optional) To automatically add a particular transition effect to your movie, click the Automatically Add check box, then click the pop-up menu and choose the transition effect you want.

6. Click the Create button.

A Drag Media Here to Create a New Project pane appears in the Project section of the iMovie window, as shown in Figure 2-5.

The stage is set for your cinematic masterpiece.

Selecting video clips

Whether you want to create a new project or edit an existing one, you need to add video clips from the Event Library and place them in a project stored in the Project Library.

Before you can select a video clip to store in a project, you need to see exactly what part of a video to clip. To help you find any part of a video, iMovie displays an entire video as a series of images that appear like individual frames of a filmstrip. To find a specific part of a video, you can skim through a video. When you find the part of a video to use, just click and drag it into a project.

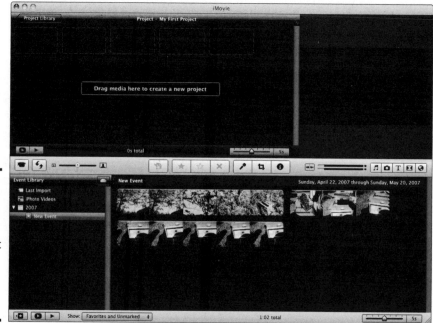

Figure 2-5:
The Drag Media Here to Create a New Project pane is where you arrange video clips.

Skimming a video

Skimming a video lets you see the contents of a video file just by moving the mouse over the video images. To view a video by skimming, follow these steps:

1. **Move the pointer over any of the thumbnail images of a video file displayed in the Event Library section of the iMovie window.**

   A red vertical line appears over the thumbnail image, as shown in Figure 2-6.

2. **Move the mouse left and right to watch your video in the upper-right corner of the iMovie window.**

   The faster you move the mouse, the faster the video plays. Moving the mouse to the left plays the video backward. Moving the mouse to the right plays the video forward.

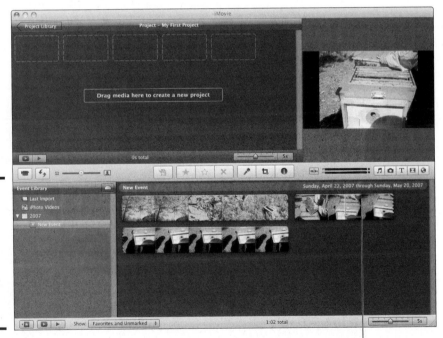

Figure 2-6:
A red vertical line shows you the position of the current image in a video file.

Red vertical line

Selecting a video clip

After you see the part of a video you want to use, you need to select the video clip by following these steps:

1. **In the Event Library, move the pointer to the beginning of the part of the video that you want to use.**

2. **Click and drag to the right.**

   A yellow rectangle appears to define the size of your clip, as shown in Figure 2-7. Drag the handles to define the exact frame to start and end your video clip.

3. **Release the mouse button when you're happy with the portion of the video that your clip contains.**

After you select a video clip, you can view it by choosing one of the following:

✦ Move the mouse over the left selection handle until the pointer turns into a two-way pointing arrow. Then double-click to view your video clip in the Preview pane in the upper-right corner of the iMovie window.

✦ Control-click the video clip and then choose Play Selection from the menu that appears.

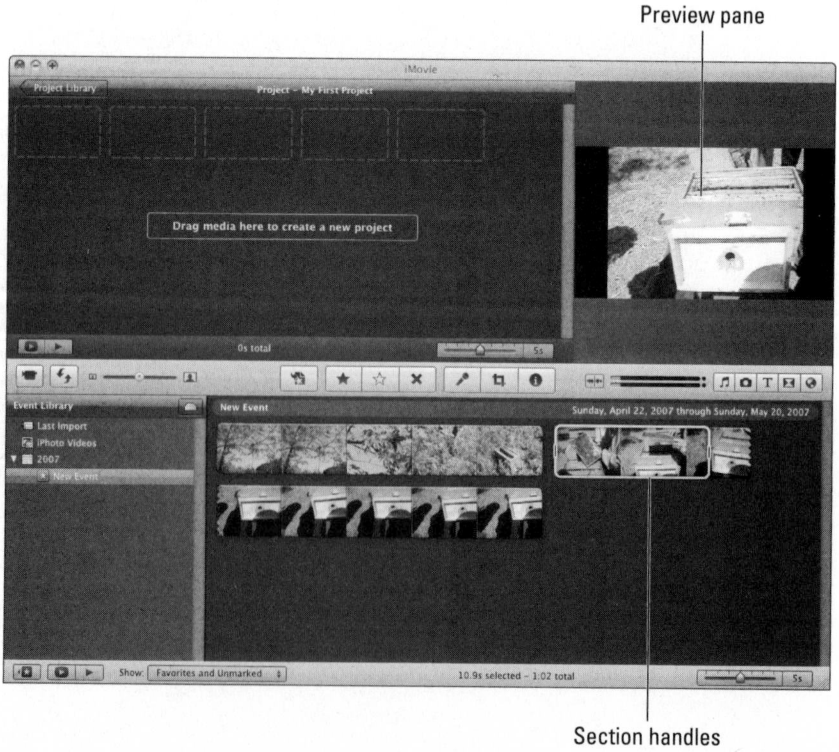

Preview pane

Figure 2-7: A yellow rectangle defines the size of a video clip.

Section handles

Placing a video clip in a project

After selecting a video clip, you can place it in a project. To place a video clip in a project, follow these steps:

1. **Click the project in the Project Library list.**

2. **Click the Edit Project button above the list.**

Thumbnail images of any video clips already stored in the project appear.

Note: If you haven't added any video clips to a project, you see a Drag Media Here to Create a New Project message, along with dotted rectangles (refer to Figure 2-5).

3. **Move the pointer inside the yellow rectangle of the video clip you selected.**

The pointer turns into a hand icon.

4. **Click and drag the selected video clip to one of the dotted rectangles in the Project pane and then release the mouse button, as shown in Figure 2-8.**

Your selected video clip appears as a thumbnail image in the Project Library section of the iMovie window.

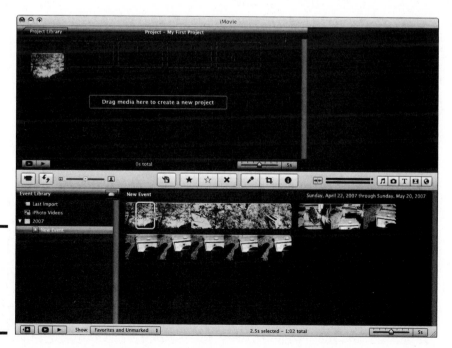

Figure 2-8: Dragging a video clip lets you add it to a project.

To edit a project, click the project in the Project Library list and then click the Edit Project button above the list. To return to the Project Library, click the Project Library button.

Deleting video clips

In case you store a video clip in a project and then decide you don't need that video clip, you can delete it from that project.

Deleting a video clip from a project does not delete the video clip from the Event Library.

To delete a video clip from a project, follow these steps:

1. **Click a project in the Project Library list and then click the Edit Project button.**

   The Project pane displays all the video clips stored in the selected project.

2. **In the Project pane, click the video clip that you want to delete.**

3. **Choose Edit⇨Delete Selection (or press Delete).**

Deleting a project

When you finish a project or decide you don't want it anymore, you can delete an entire project.

When you delete a project, you also delete any video clips stored inside that project. However, the original videos (from which you copied clips to add to the project) remain in the Event Library.

To delete a project, follow these steps:

1. **Click the project you want to delete in the Project Library list.**

2. **Choose File⇨Move Project to Trash.**

If you accidentally delete a project, you can retrieve it by pressing ⌘+Z or choosing Edit⇨Undo Delete Project.

Printing a project

Each project displays thumbnail images of one or more video clips. If you want to review the order and images of the video clips stored in a project, you can print these images on paper. Obviously, this printout of your project thumbnails can't show you the moving images of your video, but it can show you the organization of your video clips.

To print the thumbnail images of video clips stored in a project, follow these steps:

1. **Click a project in the Project Library list.**

2. **Choose File➪Print Project.**

   A Print dialog appears.

3. **(Optional) Drag the slider in the bottom-right corner of the iMovie window to define how many thumbnail images to display.**

   If you drag the slider to the right, you display fewer thumbnail images. Drag the slider to the left, and you display more thumbnail images.

4. **Click the Preview button to see how your project will appear on paper, as shown in Figure 2-9.**

5. **Click Print.**

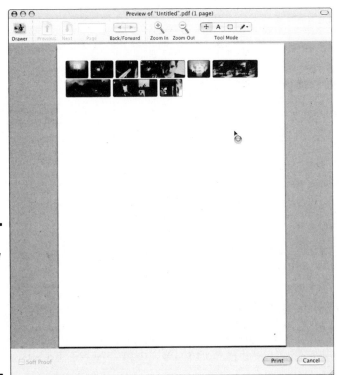

Figure 2-9:
The preview shows you how your printed video clip images will appear on paper.

Organizing the Project Library

You can divide the Project Library into different folders where one folder might contain your family vacation video, and a second folder might contain the footage you captured of a UFO you spotted hovering over a mesa in New Mexico. To create a folder, follow these steps:

1. **In the Project pane, click the Project Library button.**

   The Project Library list appears.

2. **Choose File⇨New Folder.**

   Type the name you want for the folder in the dialog that appears.

3. **Click Create.**

   The folder appears in the Project Library.

4. **Click and drag the projects to the folder.**

Editing Video Clips in a Project

After you place one or more video clips in a project, you usually want to edit those video clips to put them in the best order, trim unnecessary footage, and add titles and audio to spice up your entire video.

Rearranging the order of video clips

A project plays video clips in sequence, but you might want to change the order of your video clips. To rearrange the order of your video clips in a project, follow these steps:

1. **Click a project in the Project Library list.**

2. **Click the Edit Project button at the top of the pane.**

   The Project pane opens.

3. **Click the video clip you want to move and keep the pointer over the clip.**

   The pointer turns into a hand icon.

4. **Click and drag the selected video clip behind another video clip.**

   Vertical lines appear to show you where your video clip will appear.

5. **Release the mouse button.**

   Your video clip now appears in its new location.

Adjusting the size of a video clip

Sometimes a video clip contains a little too much extra footage that you need to trim. Other times, you might have trimmed a video clip a little too much and need to add more footage. In either case, you can fix this problem and change the size of your video clip by following these steps:

1. **Click a project in the Project Library list and then click the Edit Project button.**

2. **Move the pointer over a video clip and then click the lower-left corner of the clip.**

   A gear icon appears.

3. **Click the gear icon and then choose Clip Trimmer from the pop-up menu, as shown in Figure 2-10.**

   A Clip Trimmer pane appears at the bottom of the window. It displays a rectangle that contains the size of your video clip, along with dimmed thumbnail images of the original video that you used to copy the video clip. (See Figure 2-10.)

4. **Move the pointer over the left or right side of the rectangle that defines the size of your video clip.**

   The pointer turns into a two-way pointing arrow.

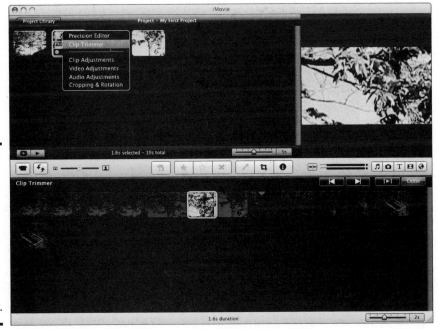

Figure 2-10:
Moving the
pointer over
a video clip
displays a
gear icon
and opens
a pop-up
menu for
adjusting
your project.

5. **Click and drag a handle to increase or decrease the size of your video clip.**

6. **Click the Play button to view your edited video clip.**

7. **Click Done when you're happy with the images stored in your video clip.**

Adding titles

Many times, you might want to add titles to your video, such as at the beginning or end. (Beginning titles can display the video's name and purpose, and the ending titles can list the credits of the people who put the video together.)

Titles can appear by themselves or be superimposed over part of your video. To create titles for a project, follow these steps:

1. **Click a project in the Project Library list.**

2. **Click the Titles button on the iMovie toolbar or choose Window⇨Titles.**

   A list of title styles appears in the Titles browser, as shown in Figure 2-11.

3. **Click and drag a title from the Titles browser to a video clip or in between two clips.**

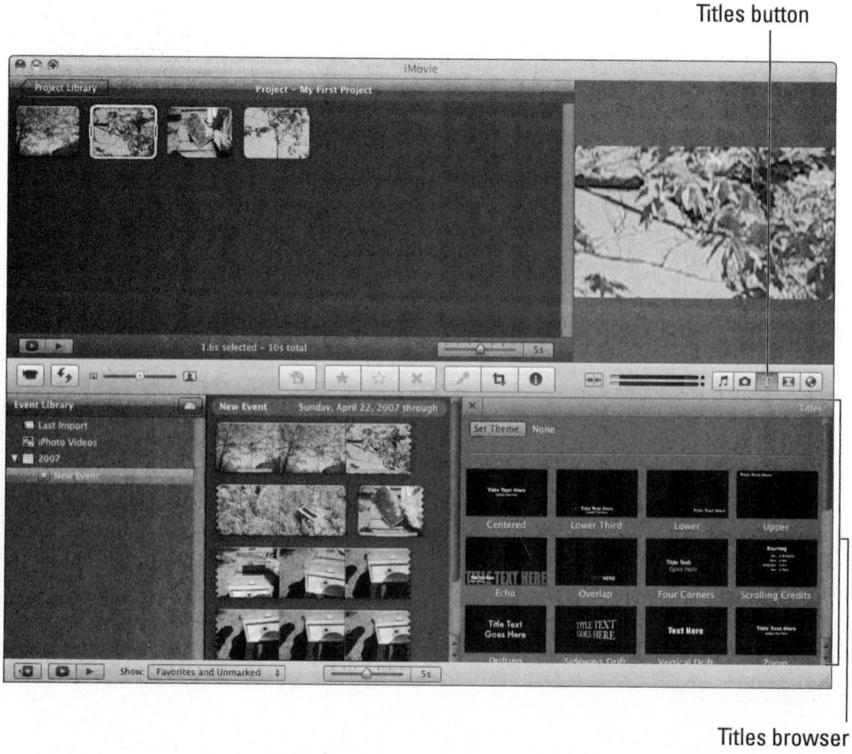

Titles button

Figure 2-11: The Titles button shows (or hides) title styles you can use.

Titles browser

4. **Release the mouse button.**

If you release the mouse button over a video clip, your title appears superimposed over the video image, as shown in Figure 2-12. If you release the mouse button in between video clips, your title appears as a separate video clip between those two video clips.

5. **Click the blue title balloon that appears over a video clip.**

Your chosen title format appears in the Preview pane.

6. **Double-click the text you want to edit and then type new text, or use the arrow and Delete keys to edit the existing title.**

7. **Click the Show Fonts button to display a Fonts window that lets you choose a different color, font size, and typeface for your text.**

8. **Click the Play button to preview how your titles appear.**

9. **Click Done.**

10. **Click the Titles button to hide the list of available title styles from view.**

All titles appear as blue title balloons in the Project pane.

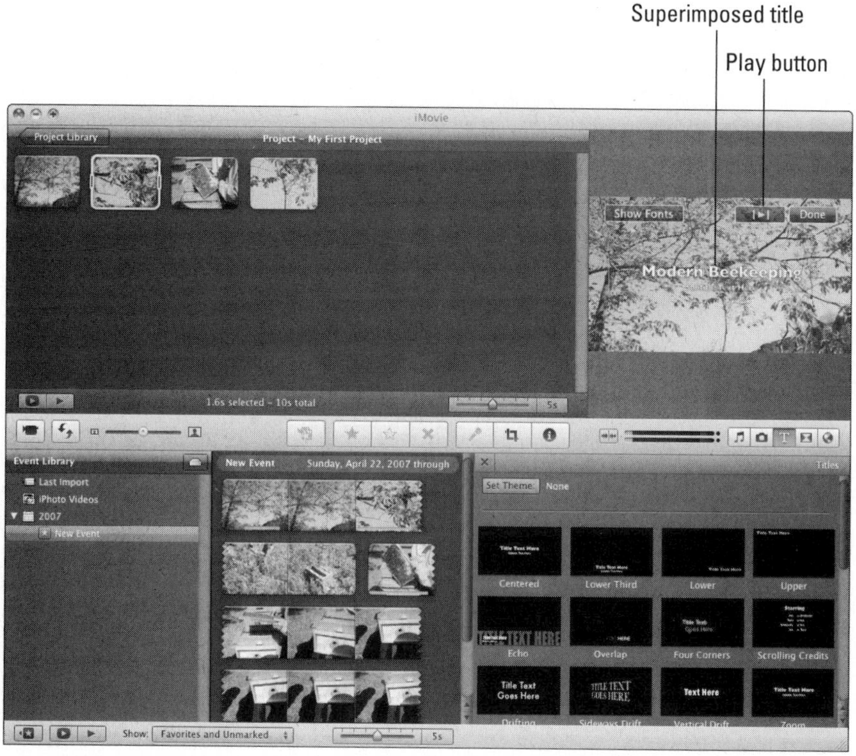

Superimposed title

Play button

Figure 2-12:
Titles can appear as separate clips or superimposed over existing video clips.

To delete a title, click the title balloon and press Delete, or choose Edit➪ Delete Selection.

Adding transitions

Normally, when you place video clips in a project, those video clips play one after another. Rather than abruptly cutting from one video clip to another, you can add transitions that appear in between video clips. To add a transition, follow these steps:

1. Click a project in the Project Library list and then click the Edit Project button.

Thumbnail images of your selected project appear in the Project pane.

2. Click the Transitions button on the iMovie toolbar or choose Window➪ Transitions.

A list of transitions appears in the Transitions browser, as shown in Figure 2-13.

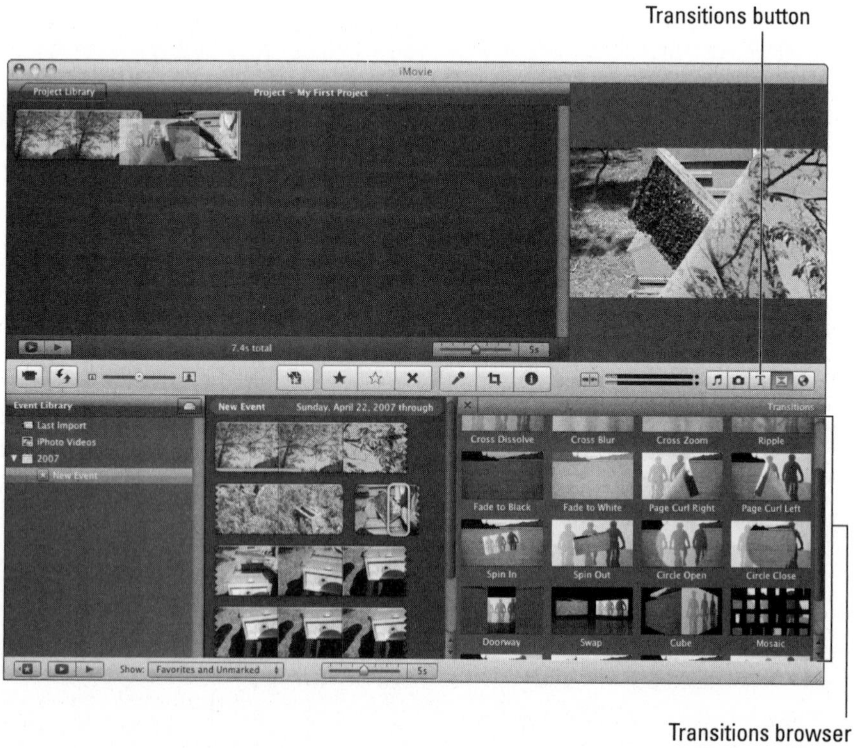

Transitions button

Figure 2-13: Transitions let you create unique visual effects in between video clips.

Transitions browser

3. **Click and drag a transition in the Transitions browser between two video clips in the Project pane.**

   Some different types of transitions include Cube (which spins a cube on the screen where a different video clip appears on each side of the cube) and Page Curl (which peels away one video clip like a piece of paper).

4. **Release the mouse button when a vertical line appears between two video clips.**

5. **Move the pointer over the transition.**

   Move the pointer to the right, and the transition plays forward. To move the transition backward, move the pointer to the left.

6. **Click the Transitions button to hide the list of available transitions.**

If you choose a theme when you create your new project, the title and transition choices are those associated with the theme.

Adding audio files

To spice up your video, you can add audio files that play background music or sound effects to match what appears on your video — a car honking, say, or maybe a telephone ringing. To add an audio file to a project, follow these steps:

1. **Click a project in the Project Library list and then click the Edit Project button.**

2. **Click the Music and Sound Effects button on the iMovie toolbar.**

   A list of audio files appears in the Music and Sound Effects browser, as shown in Figure 2-14.

3. **In the Music and Sound Effects browser, click an audio file library to use, such as iTunes, GarageBand, or iLife Sound Effects.**

   A list of audio files appears.

4. **Click and drag an audio file to a video clip in the Project pane.**

   A red vertical line appears over the video clip to show you where the audio file will start playing.

5. **Release the mouse button.**

6. **Click the Music and Sound Effects button to hide the list of available audio files.**

Music and Sound Effects button

Figure 2-14:
Audio files
can add
music or
sound
effects to
your videos.

Music and Sound Effects browser

Saving a Video

The point of organizing video clips in a project is to create a polished video. With iMovie, you can save your project to view on a computer, in iTunes, on an iPod or iPhone, or even on YouTube. You can save the same video project to different formats in case you need to view your video on your Mac but also want to post a copy on YouTube for other people to enjoy.

If you create an interesting video that you might want to add to other programs, such as a presentation program, you can save a video in the Media Browser to use in other programs.

Saving a project as a digital video file

You might want to save your iMovie project as a digital video file so you can burn it to DVD later (using iDVD) or give a copy to someone who wants to view it on their computer. When you save a project as a digital video file, you can save it as an MPEG-4 or a QuickTime file.

To save a project as an MPEG-4 digital video file, follow these steps:

1. **Click a project in the Project Library list.**

2. **Choose Share⇨Export Movie.**

   The Export Movie dialog appears, as shown in Figure 2-15.

Figure 2-15:
The Export
Movie
dialog
lets you
choose the
resolution
for playing
on different
devices.

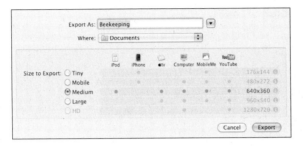

3. **Choose the location to save your project from the Where pop-up menu.**

   You can expand the menu by clicking the disclosure triangle to the right of the Export As field.

4. **Select a Size to Export radio button (such as Medium or Tiny) and then click Export.**

   The sizes define the frame size. Smaller frame sizes are designed for viewing on smaller screens, such as an iPhone screen, whereas larger frame sizes are designed for viewing on bigger screens, such as a computer or TV.

For those of you who are interested in the technical details about what's going on behind the scenes when you export a video, here's the skinny: iMovie saves as MPEG-4 by default (using the H.264 codec for a type 10 encoding). According to Dennis R. Cohen, this book's illustrious (and industrious) technical editor (and fellow Dummies author), the way iMovie saves a video file you export is "a tactical tradeoff Apple makes to conserve space while forsaking as little video/audio quality as possible in the process" (a bit of behind-the-scenes information). Additionally, the way iMovie saves a file you export results in "an extra lossy compression any time another format is desired." Dennis's advice: "Going to iDVD gets best quality results when the DV Stream codec is employed."

Saving (and removing) a video for iTunes

If you create a particularly interesting video and store it on your hard drive, you might later have trouble finding it. To fix this problem, save your videos in your iTunes library. This way you can quickly find and play videos later.

To save a project that you can play in iTunes, follow these steps:

1. **Click a project in the Project Library list.**

2. **Choose Share⇨iTunes.**

   The Publish to iTunes dialog appears, as shown in Figure 2-16.

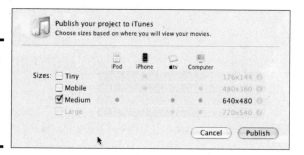

Figure 2-16: Choose the resolution for playing on different devices.

3. **Select or deselect one or more check boxes (such as Medium or Tiny) and then click Publish.**

   The sizes define the frame size of your video. Smaller sizes make your video look best on small screens, such as on mobile phones. Larger sizes make your video look best on larger screens, such as on a TV set. Your movie now appears in your iTunes library on your hard drive.

After you save a movie to iTunes, you can remove it by choosing Share⇨ Remove from iTunes.

Saving (and removing) a project for YouTube

One way to show off your movie is by uploading it to the Web so others can watch it online or download it and watch it whenever they want. The most well-know (and well-trafficked!) video-sharing site is YouTube.

YouTube limits video files you upload to a maximum file size of 100MB and a maximum time length of 10 minutes, whichever comes first.

When you capture an interesting video, you can save your project to YouTube. After setting up a YouTube account (www.youtube.com), you can upload a video from iMovie to YouTube by following these steps:

1. **Click a project in the Project Library list.**

2. **Choose Share⇨YouTube.**

The YouTube dialog appears, as shown in Figure 2-17.

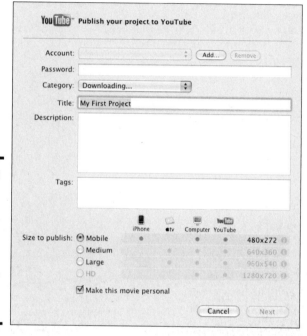

Figure 2-17:
Choose an account, category, and resolution size to upload your video to the Web.

3. **Click the Account and Category pop-up menus and choose an option. Enter your password.**

4. **Enter information to identify your video in the Title, Description, and Tags text boxes.**

The information you type to identify your video can help others find it on YouTube when they want to see videos that offer comedy, dogs, or other categories.

5. **Select one of the Size to Publish radio buttons and then click Next.**

Choose Mobile if you want to create a video frame size of 480 x 272 pixels, which is designed for viewing on small screens, such as an iPhone. Choose Medium or Large if you want to create a video frame size for viewing on an ordinary TV or computer screen. After you click Next, a dialog appears, warning about copyright infringement.

6. **Click the Publish button.**

Presto! You're an Internet Video Superstar!

After you save a movie to YouTube, you can remove it by choosing Share⇨ Remove from YouTube.

Saving (and removing) a project in the Media Browser

If you store your movie in the Media Browser, you can access and insert that movie into any program that uses the Media Browser, such as the iWork suite, many iLife programs (such as iDVD and iWeb), and non-Apple software, such as Toast (www.roxio.com).

To save a movie in the Media Browser, follow these steps:

1. **Click a project in the Project Library list.**

2. **Choose Share⇨Media Browser.**

   The Media Browser dialog appears, as shown in Figure 2-18.

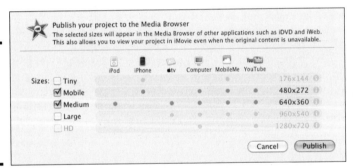

Figure 2-18: The Media Browser dialog lets you choose different resolutions.

3. **Select or clear one or more Sizes check boxes, such as Tiny or Medium.**

   The sizes define the frame size, and the dots identify the type of devices that your video can play on.

4. **Click the Publish button.**

After you save a movie to the Media Browser, you can remove it by choosing Share⇨Remove from Media Browser.

Chapter 3: Burning DVDs with iDVD

In This Chapter

- ✔ Burning a DVD from a video camcorder
- ✔ Creating a DVD with the Magic iDVD option
- ✔ Working with iDVD projects

*I*f you simply want to share digital photographs and movies with others, you could burn your pictures and movies as separate files onto a DVD. Friends and family could see your pictures or movies, but they'd have to search through the DVD's folders to find each individual file. Although this method works, it makes looking at pictures and movies about as tedious as browsing a hard drive to find word processor or spreadsheet documents.

To make DVDs useful for both storing and presenting digital pictures and movies, use the iDVD program. iDVD lets you create photo slideshows or movies complete with menus and graphics that can play on almost any recent or new DVD player. If you ever dreamed of creating your own Hollywood-style DVDs to present your home movies or digital photographs, iDVD can help you achieve your dreams.

To create a DVD, iDVD gives you three choices:

- ✦ **OneStep DVD:** Transfers a video directly from a digital video camcorder or movie file to a DVD.

- ✦ **Magic iDVD:** Provides a variety of DVD templates that you can modify for creating menus to organize the content of digital photographs and movies stored on the DVD.

- ✦ **A DVD project:** Lets you create custom DVD menus and graphics for storing and presenting digital photographs and movies.

 To burn DVDs using iDVD, you need a Mac with a DVD drive that can write to DVD discs. If your Mac's DVD drive can't write to DVDs, you can purchase an external DVD drive that's capable of burning DVD discs, or you can transfer your iDVD project to another Mac to create your DVD.

For the ultimate guide to making movies and burning them to DVDs, check out fellow For Dummies authors Dennis R. Cohen and Michael E. Cohen's *iMovie '09 & iDVD '09 For Dummies* (Wiley).

Burning a Video Straight to DVD

The OneStep DVD option lets you burn a video from your FireWire-enabled video camcorder, or from a movie file on your hard drive, to a recordable DVD in your Mac. When you insert your finished DVD into a DVD player, your video starts playing immediately, with no DVD menus.

Although USB-enabled camcorders, digital cameras, and smartphones don't work directly with OneStep DVD, you can still use video captured from those devices by copying the captured video files to iPhoto, and then choosing those files when you select the files you want to use to create your OneStep DVD.

To burn a video from your video-capturing device to a DVD with the OneStep DVD option, follow these steps:

1. **Click the iDVD icon in the Dock (or double-click the iDVD icon in the Applications folder).**

   The iDVD opening window appears, as shown in Figure 3-1.

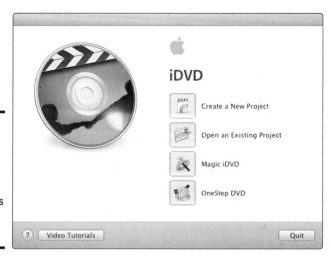

Figure 3-1:
The iDVD opening window displays your options for creating a DVD.

2. **Click OneStep DVD.**

   An alert appears, prompting you to connect your video camcorder to your Mac and insert a recordable DVD.

3. **Connect your video camcorder to your Mac using a FireWire cable.**

4. **Insert a recordable DVD in your Mac and then click the OK button.**

   iDVD rewinds the tape and starts importing the video, displaying a progress dialog.

   You can cancel the process at any desired endpoint before the entire video file is imported by clicking the Stop button in the progress dialog.

   A dialog appears to let you know the DVD has finished burning.

5. **Click Done.**

   The DVD remains in your Mac so you can either view it using the DVD Player or eject it.

To burn a DVD from a movie file on your hard drive, follow these steps:

1. **Choose File⇨OneStep DVD from Movie.**

2. **Select your movie file from the dialog that appears.**

3. **Click Import.**

4. **Insert a recordable DVD in your Mac.**

   A dialog appears to let you know the DVD has finished burning.

5. **Click Done.**

Creating a DVD with the Magic iDVD Option

The Magic iDVD option provides predesigned templates that you can customize to create DVD menus. To choose the Magic iDVD option, follow these steps:

1. **Click the iDVD icon in the Dock (or double-click the iDVD icon in the Applications folder).**

   The iDVD opening window appears (refer to Figure 3-1).

2. **Click Magic iDVD.**

   The Magic iDVD window appears, as shown in Figure 3-2.

3. **Type a descriptive name for your DVD in the DVD Title text box.**

Themes browser

Figure 3-2:
The Magic
iDVD
window
lets you
choose the
template,
pictures,
and video
files to
include on
your DVD.

Drop wells   Play

4. **Choose a theme, such as Vintage Vinyl or Sunflower, from the Themes browser.**

   Each theme offers a different appearance for your DVD menus. Each theme name describes its appearance, so Sunflower displays a big sunflower and Vintage Vinyl displays an old turntable and vinyl record.

5. **In the right pane of the Magic iDVD window — the Media pane — click the Movies tab.**

   A list of movies stored in your Movies folder appears.

6. **Click and drag a movie that you want to add to your DVD onto the Drop Movies Here drop well.**

   To select multiple movies, hold down the ⌘ key and click each movie you want to add to your DVD.

   If you click a movie and click the Play button, you can see a thumbnail image of your movie.

7. **In the Media pane, click the Photos tab.**

   A list of photos stored in iPhoto appears.

8. **Click and drag a picture that you want to add to your DVD onto the Drop Photos Here drop well.**

To select multiple pictures, hold down the ⌘ key and click each picture you want to add to your DVD.

Each drop well represents a separate slideshow. Generally, you want to put several pictures in the same drop well to create a slideshow of multiple pictures. Underneath each drop well, iDVD lists the number of slides currently stored.

9. **In the Media pane, click the Audio tab.**

A list of audio files stored in iTunes and GarageBand appears.

10. **Click and drag an audio file that you want to play during a photo slideshow onto the Drop Photos Here drop well.**

Pictures that include audio appear with an audio icon over them, as shown in Figure 3-3.

Keep in mind that if you add a 3-minute audio file over a slideshow (drop well) that contains three slides, each slide will appear for 1 minute until the entire audio file finishes playing. If you add a 3-minute audio file to a slideshow of 30 slides, each slide will appear for 0.1 minutes. So the more slides (pictures) you add, the faster the images pop up and disappear while the audio file plays.

Figure 3-3:
An audio icon identifies pictures that include an audio file.

Audio icons

11. **Click the Preview icon in the lower-left corner.**

An iDVD Preview window appears with a controller (which mimics a typical remote control) so you can take your DVD through its paces to make sure it works the way you want, as shown in Figure 3-4.

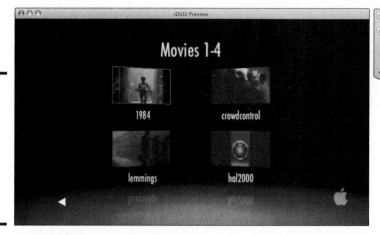

Figure 3-4: The iDVD Preview window shows you how your DVD will look when played.

12. **Click Exit on the controller on the screen.**

The Magic iDVD window appears again.

13. **Select one of the following:**

- *Create Project:* Lets you save your DVD design to modify it later.

- *Burn:* Burns your music, pictures, and movies using your chosen DVD theme. If you choose this option, you'll need to insert a recordable DVD in your Mac.

Working with iDVD Projects

For maximum flexibility, you can design your own DVD menus and add graphics to give your DVD a polished, professional look. When you create your own DVD project, you can save it and edit it later.

The following list explains the different parts of an iDVD project:

✦ **Title menu:** Displays a list of the DVD contents, such as movies or slideshows.

✦ **Slideshows:** Displays a slideshow of digital photographs.

✦ **Movies:** Displays a movie.

✦ **Text:** Displays text — useful for providing instructions or descriptions about the DVD.

✦ **Submenus:** Displays another menu where you can offer additional slideshows or movies.

✦ **Opening content:** Displays a photo or movie that appears as soon as someone inserts the DVD into a DVD player. In many commercial DVDs, the opening content is usually an FBI warning about copyright infringement.

Not every iDVD project uses all the preceding parts. At the very least, an iDVD project needs a title menu and one slideshow or movie.

To create a DVD project, follow these steps:

1. **Click the iDVD icon in the Dock (or double-click the iDVD icon in the Applications folder).**

2. **Click Create a New Project.**

   A Create Project dialog appears, as shown in Figure 3-5.

   If you already created a project and want to edit it, all you need to do is click Open an Existing Project (not shown in the figure).

Figure 3-5: The Create Project dialog lets you define a name and aspect ratio for your DVD.

3. **Enter a descriptive name for your project into the Save As text box and then choose where you want to save your project from the Where pop-up menu.**

4. **Next to Aspect Ratio, click the Standard (for ordinary TV screens) or Widescreen (for widescreen TVs) radio button.**

   Choosing Standard optimizes your DVD project for an ordinary TV set, although it will still play on a widescreen with borders on either side in order to maintain the video's proper resolution and aspect ratio (this is called *pillar-boxing*). Likewise, choosing Widescreen lets a DVD project play on an ordinary TV set with black borders at the top and bottom (called *letter-boxing*), but it will have a lower resolution than that seen on a widescreen TV.

5. **Click Create.**

   An iDVD project window appears with the Themes browser in the right pane, as shown in Figure 3-6.

6. **Scroll through the Themes browser to find one you like.**

   Each theme offers a different appearance for your DVD menus. Click the triangle to the left of the theme to see how it will apply to the Main, Chapters, and Extras menus of your DVD. (Clicking the arrow again compresses the selection.)

   When you click a theme, a preview of the theme appears in the iDVD window (refer to Figure 3-6). Depending on the theme you choose, you might see Drop Zones where you can place pictures or video.

7. **Double-click the title in the iDVD Project pane and then type the title of your movie or slideshow, as shown in Figure 3-7.**

   You can choose the font type and size from the menus that appear. If you click a different theme, your title remains.

8. **Choose File⇨Save.**

   It's a good idea to save your project every so often while you're working on your project.

   After saving your iDVD project, you can quit iDVD or continue with the next sections to add pictures to your title menus, and to add movies and slideshows to your project.

Figure 3-6: The iDVD project window opens with the Themes browser in the right pane.

Figure 3-7:
Type the
title of your
movie or
slideshow
in the iDVD
Project
pane.

Adding photos to the title menu

Some themes just display a colorful graphic background but others provide
placeholders for adding your own pictures to customize the theme further.
To use your own pictures as a background, follow these steps:

1. **Open the iDVD project you want to add pictures to.**

   You can open a previously saved project by choosing File➪Open or
   Open an Existing Project when iDVD first loads.

2. **Click the Media button in the bottom-right corner of the iDVD project
   window.**

   The Media pane opens showing Audio, Photos, and Movies tabs on the
   right side of the iDVD window.

3. **Click the Photos button.**

   A list of photos stored in iPhoto appears, which you can add to your
   title menu.

4. **Click the Edit Drop Zones button (the dotted square with the arrow at
   the bottom).**

   A list of Drop Zones appears, as shown in Figure 3-8.

Photos button

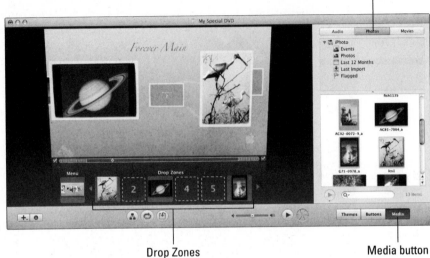

Figure 3-8:
You can
drag and
drop photos
to customize
a DVD
menu.

Drop Zones

Media button

5. **Click and drag a photo to a Drop Zone and then release the mouse button.**

   Your chosen picture now appears as part of the DVD theme.

6. **Repeat Step 6 for any additional photographs you need to add to another Drop Zone.**

7. **Choose File⇨Save.**

   After saving your iDVD project, you can quit iDVD or continue working on your project.

Adding options to the title menu

After you define a theme and possibly add some photos for your title menu, you can add viewer options. The four types of options you can display on the title menu are

✦ Slideshow menus

✦ Movie menus

✦ Text

✦ Submenus

Creating a Slideshow

When a viewer selects a slideshow menu option, the DVD displays one or more digital photographs. To add a slideshow option to the title menu, you need to create a menu that allows viewers to choose your slideshow. Then you need to create the slideshow by following these steps:

1. **Choose Project⊃Add Slideshow (or press ⌘+L).**

   A My Slideshow button appears on your title menu, as shown in Figure 3-9.

Figure 3-9: A slideshow menu option appears as a generic My Slideshow button.

2. **Click the My Slideshow button.**

   The My Slideshow text appears highlighted and displays Font, Style, and Font Size pop-up menus.

3. **Type descriptive text for your slideshow button.**

4. **(Optional) Click the Font, Style, or Font Size pop-up menus to choose how to format your text.**

5. **Double-click your slideshow button.**

   The iDVD project window displays a Drag Images Here box. Now you can start building the slideshow.

6. **Click and drag a photograph displayed in the right pane to the Drag Images Here box and then release the mouse button.**

   To select multiple pictures, hold down the ⌘ key and then click each picture you want to select. A slideshow can hold up to 99 pictures.

   Your chosen pictures appear in the Slideshow window, numbered to show you the order in which your pictures will appear, as shown in Figure 3-10.

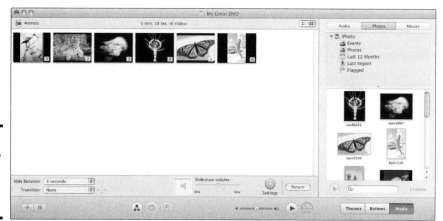

Figure 3-10:
A slideshow
consists
of multiple
pictures.

7. **(Optional) Click the Slide Duration pop-up menu and choose how long a slide stays onscreen, such as 1 or 10 seconds.**

8. **(Optional) Click the Transition pop-up menu and choose a transition to display between slides, such as Dissolve or Twirl.**

9. **(Optional) Click the Audio button, click and drag an audio file from the listing in the right pane onto the Audio drop well (it looks like an iTunes music track icon to the left of the Slideshow volume slider), and then release the mouse button.**

10. **(Optional) If you add an audio file to a slideshow, click the Slide Duration pop-up menu and choose how long you want the audio file to play, such as 10 seconds.**

If you add an audio file to a slideshow, the slide duration defaults to the Fit To Audio option, which means that your pictures appear until the audio file finishes playing.

11. **Click the Return button.**

Your DVD title menu appears again.

12. **Choose File⇨Save.**

You need to create a different slideshow menu option for each slideshow you want to include on your DVD.

Creating a Movie menu option

When a viewer selects a Movie menu option, the DVD plays a movie. To create a Movie menu option on the title menu, follow these steps:

1. **Choose Project⇨Add Movie.**

An Add Movie Here button appears, as shown in Figure 3-11.

Figure 3-11:
An Add
Movie Here
button
provides
a link to a
movie.

2. **Click the Media button to open the Media pane and then choose Movie.**

   The movie files stored on your Mac appear.

3. **Click and drag the movie file of the movie you want on your DVD to the Add Movie Here button.**

   Your movie begins playing in the space where you put it.

4. **Choose File➪Save.**

For a faster way to create Movie menu buttons, click and drag a movie shown in the Media pane anywhere onto your title menu and then release the mouse button to create a button that will play your chosen movie.

Creating text

Sometimes you might want to add text on a title menu to provide additional descriptions or instructions. To add text on the title menu, follow these steps:

1. **Choose Project➪Add Text (or choose ⌘+K).**

   A Click to Edit text box appears.

2. **Click the Click to Edit text box.**

   Font, Style, and Font Size pop-up menus appear, as shown in Figure 3-12.

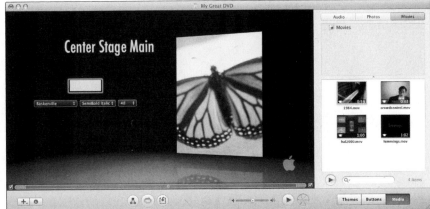

Figure 3-12:
A Click to
Edit text
box lets you
type text
that appears
on the title
menu.

3. **Type descriptive text for your slideshow button.**

4. **(Optional) Click the Font, Style, or Font Size pop-up menus to choose how to format your text.**

5. **Choose File➪Save.**

Creating a submenu

If you have too many options on the title menu, the title menu can look cluttered. To fix this, you might need to create a submenu on your title menu and then place additional Slideshow or Movie options on this submenu. To create a submenu, follow these steps:

1. **Choose Project➪Add Submenu.**

   A My Submenu button appears.

2. **Click the My Submenu button.**

   Font, Style, and Font Size pop-up menus appear.

3. **Type descriptive text for your submenu button.**

4. **(Optional) Click the Font, Style, or Font Size pop-up menus to choose how to format your text.**

5. **Double-click the submenu button.**

   The iDVD window displays a new menu where you can add slideshows, movies, text, or even additional submenus.

6. **Choose Project⇨Add Title Menu Button.**

The Title Menu button lets viewers jump back to the title menu from your submenu. At this point, you need to add a Slideshow or Movie menu option on your submenu. Follow the steps outlined in the previous pages for the title menu.

7. **(Optional) If the theme you choose has additional menu options, such as Extras or Chapters, use them for your submenu.**

Choose the menu option you want from the Themes browser; the submenu changes to that option and keeps the titles, slideshows, or movies you've added.

Moving and deleting buttons

After you create a Slideshow, Movie, Submenu, or Text button on a menu, you can move or delete it. To move a button, follow these steps:

1. **Click the button you want to move.**

The text inside your button appears highlighted.

2. **Click and drag your selected button to its new location and then release the mouse button.**

Rather than move a button, you might want to delete it. To delete a button, follow these steps:

1. **Click the button you want to delete.**

The text inside your button appears highlighted.

2. **Choose Edit⇨Delete.**

Your button disappears in an animated puff of smoke.

Defining opening content for your DVD

You can display a picture or a movie, the *opening content,* as soon as someone inserts your DVD into a DVD player. This opening content appears before the title menu appears. To define a picture or movie to display as the opening content, follow these steps:

1. **Choose View⇨Show Map (or click the Show the DVD Map icon, which looks like a miniature organization chart with a box connected to two other boxes).**

The iDVD window displays a blank content box that displays the message Drag Content Here to Automatically Play When the Disc Is Inserted, as shown in Figure 3-13.

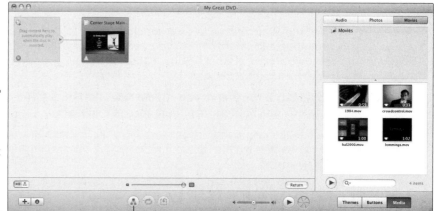

Figure 3-13:
The map
view of your
iDVD project
displays
the blank
content box.

Show Map icon

2. **Click the Photos or Movies button in the Media pane to display your iPhoto pictures or the movies stored in your Movies folder.**

3. **Click and drag a picture or movie to the blank content box.**

4. **Release the mouse button.**

The Show Map command can be particularly useful so that you can see the layout of your entire iDVD project.

Saving your iDVD project

After you design your DVD project, you can save your entire project in one of three ways:

✦ As a DVD

✦ As a disc image (.img) file

✦ As files stored in a VIDEO_TS folder

Burning to a DVD

When you save your iDVD project to a DVD, you create a DVD that you can give to anyone to play on any DVD player. To burn an iDVD project to a DVD, follow these steps:

1. **Insert a blank DVD into your Mac.**

2. **Choose File⇨Burn DVD.**

Saving to a disc image

As an alternative to saving an iDVD project to a DVD, you can also save an iDVD project to a disc image. A *disc image* is a single file that contains the entire contents of a drive or folder. By storing an iDVD project as a disc image, you can transfer a single (large) file to someone over the Internet; if you're on a network, you can copy the file to another computer for storing or burning to a DVD. Then that person can open that disc image to retrieve the entire contents of your iDVD project and burn the disc image contents to a DVD.

To save your iDVD project to a disc image, follow these steps:

1. **Choose File⇨Save as Disc Image.**

   A Save Disc Image As dialog appears.

2. **Type a descriptive name for your disc image in the Save As text box.**

3. **Choose a location to store your disc image from the Where pop-up menu.**

4. **Click Save.**

Saving to a VIDEO_TS folder

You can also save your entire iDVD project inside a VIDEO_TS folder, which essentially lets you store the contents of your iDVD project as separate files stored in a folder. By storing a DVD in a folder, you can play your DVD directly off the hard drive.

To save your iDVD project to a folder, follow these steps:

1. **Choose File⇨Save as VIDEO_TS Folder.**

   A Save VIDEO_TS Folder As dialog appears.

2. **Type a descriptive name for your folder in the Save As text box.**

3. **Choose a location to store your folder from the Where pop-up menu.**

4. **Click Save.**

When you save an iDVD project as a VIDEO_TS folder, you can open and play the contents of that VIDEO_TS folder by using the DVD Player program in the Applications folder of any Mac. If you later decide to burn the contents of a VIDEO_TS folder to a DVD, make sure you burn the DVD in UDF format to create a DVD that can play in other DVD players.

Chapter 4: Making Music with GarageBand

In This Chapter

✔ Recording your music

✔ Playing instruments with Magic GarageBand

✔ Learning to play an instrument

✔ Using Loops

✔ Saving your music

✔ Saving ringtones

✔ Recording your podcasts

GarageBand lets you record, play, alter, and arrange all kinds of sounds to create your own music. GarageBand provides accompanying instruments (such as drums, keyboards, and guitars) that you can use to accompany and complement recordings of your own music. Additionally, you can use these virtual instruments on their own to create new music, turning your Mac into a full-fledged band where you control the sound of each instrument, arrange the separate audio tracks, and smash them together to create your own hit songs. If you don't know how to play an instrument, GarageBand offers guitar and piano lessons to get you started.

Although designed for recording, modifying, and playing music, GarageBand can record, modify, and save audio files in a number of audio file formats. If you're not interested in making music, you can use GarageBand to clean up a recorded speech and save it as a podcast that you can distribute to the rest of the world.

Whether you want to record and arrange music or record speech, the main tasks for using GarageBand are

✦ Recording audio

✦ Arranging and modifying audio

✦ Saving the finished audio file

Whatever your needs, GarageBand can satisfy your artistic side or your serious side, or just give you another way to amuse yourself with your Mac.

Recording Audio

Because GarageBand works with audio, the first task is to record audio into GarageBand by using your Mac's built-in microphone, an external microphone, or audio input (such as a keyboard or guitar plugged directly into your Mac).

If you don't have a real instrument, GarageBand provides a variety of software instruments, which are basically musical instruments, such as pianos, guitars, and drums, that you can play and control through your Mac. All you have to do is specify the notes to play and the tempo and the software instruments let you hear your music played by the instruments you choose.

Apple sells additional Jam Packs, which provide additional software instruments, such as ethnic instruments, vocalists, or symphony orchestras.

Recording audio through Magic GarageBand

Magic GarageBand is great for creating background music quickly and easily. For example, if you're creating a Keynote presentation to present to cowboys, you might want country music playing in the background. Rather than hunt down a country song, just fire up Magic GarageBand, pick the Country genre, modify the song by choosing different instruments, and you git yourself an instant country song without even knowing how to play an instrument. Wee-haw!

Each genre in Magic GarageBand only plays one stock song that you can modify. If you want a country song, Magic GarageBand creates the same country song. It's up to you to customize this song to make it different. If you want to create your own country song, you'll have to create a new music project rather than use Magic GarageBand.

To create a Magic GarageBand, follow these steps:

1. **Double-click the GarageBand icon in the Applications folder (or click the GarageBand icon in the Dock).**

   The GarageBand chooser opens, as shown in Figure 4-1.

2. **Click Magic GarageBand from the sidebar on the left.**

   Magic GarageBand shows different genre icons, such as Rock, Jazz, or Funk, as shown in Figure 4-2.

   Move the pointer over a genre icon to make the Preview button appear (refer to Figure 4-2), and then click the Preview button to hear a snippet or entire song played in your chosen genre. (Click the Preview radio button again to stop the song.)

Figure 4-1:
The GarageBand chooser lets you choose the type of project to create.

Figure 4-2:
The Magic GarageBand icons provide different music genres.

3. **Click a genre, such as Blues or Country and then click Choose (or just double-click on the genre you want to choose).**

   The Magic GarageBand window displays a stage and instruments, as shown in Figure 4-3.

4. **Click an instrument on the stage.**

   The bottom of the Magic GarageBand window displays all available variations of that instrument.

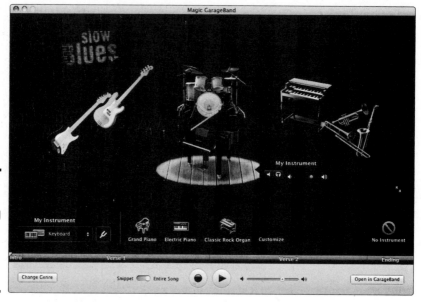

Figure 4-3:
Magic
GarageBand
displays
all the
instruments
of the band.

5. **Click the instrument variant you want in the bottom of the Magic GarageBand window.**

   Your chosen instrument variant appears on the stage.

6. **Click the Play button to hear how the song or snippet sounds with your new instruments.**

   Essentially, Magic GarageBand plays one stock song that you can modify by choosing the types of instruments to play.

7. **Repeat Steps 6 through 8 for any additional instruments you want to change.**

8. **Click Open in GarageBand when you're happy with the instruments in your band.**

   GarageBand displays a window that contains all your instruments arranged in separate tracks, as shown in Figure 4-4. At this point, you can modify the song.

Creating music with software instruments

Magic GarageBand can be handy for creating an instant song from a specific genre, but GarageBand also lets you specify notes so that GarageBand's software instruments can play your music.

Figure 4-4:
The Project window displays separate controllers for all of your instruments.

Software instruments give you a chance to create music starting with one instrumental track and gradually layering other tracks until you've defined the parts for an entire band. To use software instruments, you need to specify the instrument you want to use, such as a baby grand piano or a steel string acoustic guitar. Then define the notes you want that instrument to play by using a virtual keyboard to click or press the notes.

To create a software instrument, follow these steps:

1. **Double-click the GarageBand icon in the Applications folder (or click the GarageBand icon in the Dock).**

The GarageBand chooser opens. (Refer to Figure 4-1.)

2. **Choose File⇨New (or double-click New Project in the sidebar).**

Ignore the instrument icons for now; I get to those a little later.

A New Project dialog appears, as shown in Figure 4-5.

3. **Enter a descriptive name for your project in the Save As text box and then choose a location for storing your project from the pop-up menu — the GarageBand folder (inside your Music folder) is the default location.**

4. **(Optional) Change the Tempo, Time, BPM (beats per minute), and Key options.**

You can always change these options later.

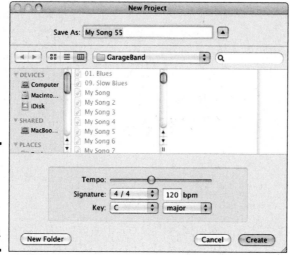

Figure 4-5:
The New
Project
dialog lets
you define
your project.

5. **Click Create.**

   A window appears, displaying a virtual keyboard and a single audio track for a grand piano, as shown in Figure 4-6.

6. **To change the instrument for your single track, choose Track⇨Show Track Info, or click the View/Hide Track Info button ("i") in the bottom-right corner of the GarageBand window.**

   The Track Info pane appears, as shown in Figure 4-7.

7. **Click an instrument category (such as Strings or Bass) and then click the specific instrument to use (such as Trance Bass or Electric Piano).**

8. **Click the virtual keyboard to hear how your chosen instrument sounds.**

9. **(Optional) Click the Musical Typing button on the virtual keyboard, or choose Windows⇨Musical Typing.**

   The Musical Typing keyboard appears, as shown in Figure 4-8. The Musical Typing keyboard allows you to press keys on your Mac keyboard to play certain notes, which you might find more convenient than using your mouse to click keys on the virtual keyboard.

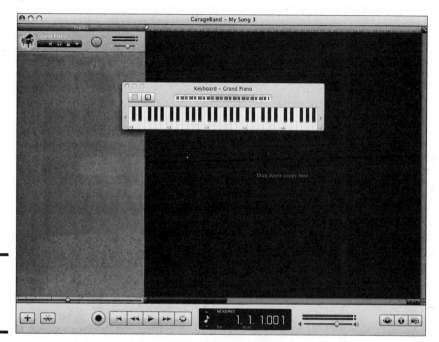

Figure 4-6:
Time to
tickle the
ivories.

Figure 4-7:
The Track
Info pane
displays
a list of
different
instruments
you can
choose.

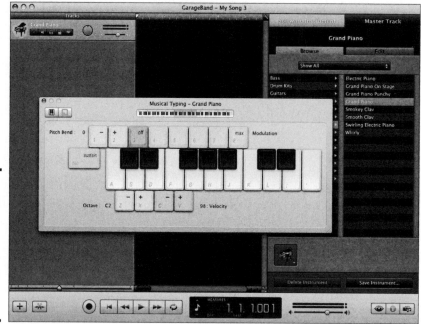

Figure 4-8:
The Musical
Typing
keyboard
lets you
use the
keyboard as
a musical
instrument.

10. **Click the Record button (the red dot inside a black circle at the bottom
    of the GarageBand window) and then click the virtual keyboard or type
    on the Musical Typing keyboard to record the notes you play.**

11. **Click the Record button again to stop recording.**

12. **Click the Go to Beginning button (the line and triangle icon to the
    right of the Record button) to return to the beginning of your record-
    ing, and then click Play to hear the notes you recorded.**

In case you want to add another software instrument, follow these steps:

1. **Click the plus sign button in the lower-left corner of the GarageBand
    window or choose Track⇨New Track.**

    A dialog appears, asking whether you want to create a real or software
    instrument or electric guitar track.

2. **Click the Software Instrument radio button and then click Create.**

    The new instrument track appears in the GarageBand window.

3. **Choose Track⇨Show Track Info to display the Track Info pane.**

   If this window already appears, skip this step.

4. **Click the Software Instrument button.**

   A list of instrument types appears, such as Organs, Guitars, and Drum Kits.

5. **Click an instrument type.**

   The right column displays specific types of instruments.

6. **Click a specific instrument in the right column, such as Electric Piano.**

   Your newly added instrument track will now play using your chosen instrument.

Playing with a real instrument

The easiest way to play music is with a real instrument connected to your Mac's USB port. By playing with a real instrument, you can record yourself, alter the sound, and even save your recording so you can play along with your own recording. To record a real instrument connected to your Mac, follow these steps:

1. **Double-click the GarageBand icon in the Applications folder (or click the GarageBand icon in the Dock) to open the GarageBand chooser window.**

2. **Double-click the Electric Guitar, Voice, or Acoustic Instrument icon, whichever is closest to the instrument you want to use.**

   A New Project from Template dialog appears.

3. **Enter a descriptive name for your project in the Save As text box and then choose a location for storing your project from the pop-up menu.**

4. **Click Create.**

   A window appears displaying tracks associated with your chosen instrument alongside the Track Info pane, as shown in Figure 4-9.

5. **(Optional) If you chose Voice, specify Male or Female and then choose an effect, such as Epic Diva or Male Rock, in the Track Info pane.**

Figure 4-9:
The Track Info pane lets you define the type of instrument you're using.

6. **(Optional) If you chose Acoustic Instrument, click a specific instrument type in the list on the right of the Track Info pane, such as Classic Rock or Metal.**

    The instrument you choose in this step defines how GarageBand plays your real instrument. For example, if you have a keyboard hooked up to your Mac, you can use this step to make your keyboard sound like horns, drums, or guitars.

7. **Click the Input Source pop-up menu and choose how your instrument is connected to your Mac (such as through a USB port or other type of connection).**

8. **Click the Monitor pop-up menu and define whether you want to hear audio through the speakers.**

    To prevent feedback, choose On with Feedback Protection. If you still experience feedback, you might want to choose Off.

9. **Drag the Recording Level slider to set the recording level, or click the Automatic Level Control check box to let GarageBand set the level.**

    Lowering the recording level can reduce feedback. If you select the Automatic Level Control check box, the Monitor option is disabled.

10. **Click the Record button on your track and start playing away.**

    When you finish playing, click the Record button again.

11. **(Optional) If you want to add more instruments, choose Track⇨New Track or click the Add Track button (the plus sign) in the lower-left corner.**

A dialog opens asking if you want to use a Software Instrument, a Real Instrument, or an Electric Guitar, as shown in Figure 4-10.

12. **Choose Real Instrument, click Create, and then repeat Steps 7 through 10.**

Figure 4-10:
Choose
between
a real
instrument,
a software
instrument,
or an
electric
guitar.

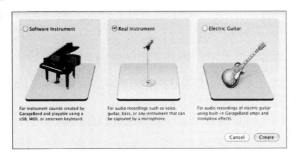

Learning to play with a real instrument

You can learn piano or guitar basics with GarageBand music lessons. GarageBand provides 18 free lessons for learning piano and guitar.

Your first two free lessons are preloaded in GarageBand, and the remaining 16 free lessons can be downloaded by clicking the Lesson Store in the GarageBand chooser window, then clicking the Basic Lessons tab and clicking on each additional lesson you want to download. Additionally, you can click the Artist Lessons tab and download optional lessons priced at $4.99 each, brought to you by distinguished musicians including Sting, Norah Jones, John Fogerty, and Sarah McLachlan.

You can follow the lesson with your freestanding piano or guitar or with a keyboard or guitar hooked up to your Mac. To take a music lesson, follow these steps:

1. **Double-click the GarageBand icon in the Applications folder or click the GarageBand icon in the Dock.**

The GarageBand chooser appears.

2. **Click Learn to Play in the sidebar on the left.**

3. **Double-click Piano Lesson 1 or Guitar Lesson 1.**

A window opens with an instruction video and a keyboard or guitar, and the lesson begins, as shown in Figure 4-11.

Using Loops

Say you want to add a song to your Web page or an intro to your podcast but don't want to play Twinkle Twinkle Little Star with the S-S F-F H-H G combination on your keyboard nor do you have a Fender Stratocaster for an attention-grabbing riff. To easily create your own little ditty, you can use the Loops that come with GarageBand. You choose the instruments and the style effects and then combine the two into short jingles or even full-length songs.

To create a song using Loops, follow these steps:

1. **Double-click the GarageBand icon in the Applications folder (or click the GarageBand icon in the Dock).**

2. **Double-click Loops from the GarageBand chooser.**

3. **Enter a descriptive name for your project in the Save As text box and then choose a location for storing your project from the pop-up menu.**

Figure 4-11:
The piano or guitar lesson opens with an instruction video and instrument.

Recording Audio **535**

4. **Click Create.**

   The Loops browser opens.

5. **Choose the style you want from the first column, such as Urban or Cinematic.**

6. **Choose the instrument you want to use from the second column.**

7. **Choose the adjectives that describe the type of music you want from the third and fourth column.**

   The audio files that meet your criteria display, showing the name, the tempo, and the key of the selection.

8. **Click the file names to hear samples of the songs listed.**

9. **When you find one you like, click and drag the file to the Tracks pane on the left of the window, as shown in Figure 4-12.**

10. **To add other music clips and create a song with multiple instruments, click Reset and then repeat Steps 5 through 9.**

11. **Click the Play button to hear your composition.**

Figure 4-12:
The Loops browser lets you create songs using prerecorded instruments.

Editing Audio

To record audio, click the Record button and start playing. GarageBand includes a metronome (Control⟹Metronome) that you can toggle on and off. If you want to play along with previously recorded tracks, choose Control⟹ Count In so you know when to start playing.

Splitting a track

When you first record an instrument, GarageBand saves it as a single, long track. To make it easier to edit this track, you can split a track into parts that you can modify individually, save and reuse, delete, or rearrange in a new position.

To split a track, follow these steps:

1. **Click to select a track that you want to split.**

   GarageBand highlights your chosen instrument.

2. **Drag the slider (which displays a vertical red line) to where you want to split the track.**

   If you can't find the slider, click the Go to Beginning button to move the slider to the beginning of your track.

3. **Choose Edit⟹Split or press ⌘+T.**

   GarageBand splits your track, as shown in Figure 4-13.

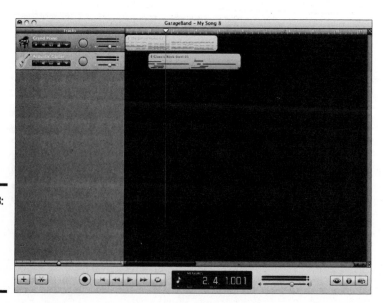

Figure 4-13: Splitting a track can make it easier to edit.

Joining a track

If you split a track, you can always join the parts again later. To join two adjacent parts of a track, follow these steps:

1. **Click the first part of the track that you want to join.**

2. **Hold down the Shift key and then click the second part of the track you want to join.**

3. **Choose Edit⇨Join or press ⌘+J.**

    GarageBand connects the two parts.

Moving tracks

After you record two or more tracks, you might want to adjust how each track plays relative to one another. For example, you can make one track play before or after a second track to create interesting audio effects. To move tracks, follow these steps:

1. **Click the track that you want to move.**

    GarageBand highlights your selected instrument track.

    For more flexibility, split a track into multiple parts so that you can move each part separately.

2. **Click and drag the track to the left or right to adjust the relative positions of the two tracks.**

3. **Release the left mouse button when you're happy with the new arrangement of the track.**

    Figure 4-14 shows a before and after appearance of different tracks rearranged to start and end at different times.

Modifying the key and tempo

You can move tracks and/or regions in a GarageBand song to radically change how a song sounds, but you can also change the key or tempo to introduce a slight (or maybe even a major) change. Changing the key can modify how a song sounds, whereas changing the tempo speeds or slows a song without making the song sound high-pitched or running down.

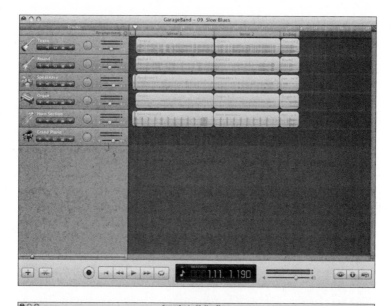

Figure 4-14:
Moving
tracks can
adjust how
they play in
relation to
one another.

To change the time, key, and tempo, you use the LCD (liquid crystal display) feature at the bottom of the GarageBand window. By choosing different LCD display modes, you can modify the key and tempo of your tracks.

To change both the key and tempo, follow these steps:

1. **Click the pop-up menu in the LCD and choose Project.**

   The LCD displays the current key and tempo of your track.

2. **Click the Go to Beginning button and then click Play to hear your song.**

   By playing your song, you can adjust the key and tempo and hear your changes in real time as they occur.

3. **Click the Key pop-up menu and choose a key, such as F or G, as shown in Figure 4-15.**

4. **Click the Tempo pop-up menu.**

   A vertical slider appears.

5. **Drag the vertical slider up or down to speed or slow the tempo of your song.**

Figure 4-15: The Key pop-up menu from the LCD Mode menu lets you change the key that your song plays in.

Saving Music

After you finish arranging and modifying your song, you can choose File↪ Save to save your GarageBand project (so you can edit it later). However, if you want to share your creation with others, the most common ways you can save your audio file so you can share it with others are

✦ As a song or ringtone in the iTunes library

✦ As a song stored anywhere on your hard disk

✦ On a CD

I provide the steps for sharing your song by saving it as a song or ringtone in iTunes, and to a disk or CD, in the following sections.

Saving a song in iTunes

If you create a song that you want to save and play later, you can store that song in iTunes by following these steps:

1. **Choose Share↪Send Song to iTunes.**

   A dialog appears, as shown in Figure 4-16.

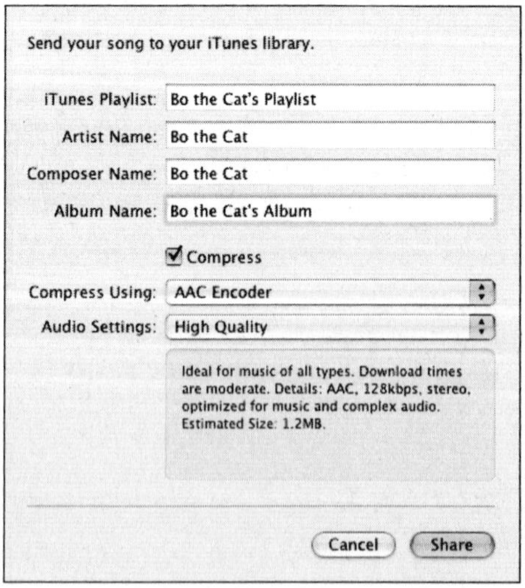

Figure 4-16: GarageBand lets you choose a playlist, artist name, and audio setting for your song.

Send your song to your iTunes library.

iTunes Playlist:	Bo the Cat's Playlist
Artist Name:	Bo the Cat
Composer Name:	Bo the Cat
Album Name:	Bo the Cat's Album

☑ Compress

Compress Using:	AAC Encoder
Audio Settings:	High Quality

Ideal for music of all types. Download times are moderate. Details: AAC, 128kbps, stereo, optimized for music and complex audio. Estimated Size: 1.2MB.

Cancel   Share

2. **Click the iTunes Playlist, Artist Name, Composer Name, and Album Name text boxes and enter any information you want to store.**

   By default, GarageBand uses your name in each text box.

3. **Make sure the Compress check box is checked and then choose either AAC or MP3 Encoder from the Compress Using pop-up menu.**

   The Compress option compresses your audio file as small as possible while retaining audio quality. If, however, you plan to compile a collection of songs that you want to burn to a CD, deselect the Compress check box so that your compilation is saved at the highest quality sound level, which provides the best listening experience when you play the CD with a CD player or on a computer.

4. **Choose either Good, High, or Higher Quality from the Audio Settings pop-up menu.**

5. **Click Share.**

   Your song appears in your iTunes library.

Saving a song as a ringtone

Any of the songs you create can be used as ringtones for your iPhone. Just follow these steps:

1. **Choose Share⇨Send Ringtone to iTunes.**

2. **GarageBand automatically converts your song and opens the iTunes application.**

3. **Your song appears in the Ringtones library on iTunes, ready to be synched to your iPhone.**

Ringtones can't be more than 40 seconds. If your selection is too long, a dialog asks whether you want to adjust it. Click Adjust, and then drag your selection left or right so the start and end points for your selection include the segment you want to hear as a ringtone on your iPhone.

Saving a song to disk

If you don't want to store your song in iTunes, you can save your song as a separate audio file that you can store anywhere, such as on an external hard disk or a USB flash drive. To save your song as an audio file, follow these steps:

1. **Choose Share⇨Export Song to Disk.**

   A dialog appears.

2. **Make sure the Compress check box is selected and then choose either AAC or MP3 Encoder from the Compress Using pop-up menu.**

   The Compress option compresses your audio file as small as possible while retaining audio quality. If, however, you plan to compile a collection of songs that you want to burn to a CD, deselect the Compress check box so that your compilation is saved at the highest quality sound level, which provides the best listening experience when you play the CD with a CD player or on a computer.

3. **Click the Audio Settings pop-up menu and choose Good, High, or Higher Quality.**

4. **Click Export.**

   An Export to Disk dialog appears.

5. **Enter a name for your audio file in the Save As text box.**

6. **Choose a location for storing your project from the Where pop-up menu.**

7. **Click Save.**

Burning a song to CD

If you create a song that you want to share with others, you can burn it to a CD and then give the CD away. To burn a song to a CD, follow these steps:

1. **Choose Share⇨Burn Song to CD.**

   A dialog appears, telling you that it's waiting for a blank CD.

2. **Insert a blank CD into your Mac and then click Burn.**

Recording Podcasts

Podcasts are recorded audio files that contain speech, such as interviews, radio talk show broadcasts, or just monologues of a single person talking about anything. If you store your podcast on a Web site, anyone in the world can download and listen to your podcast.

To customize your podcasts, GarageBand lets you add other audio, picture, or video files using the Media Browser, which appears in the upper-right corner of the GarageBand window.

Recording speech

The most important part about a podcast is recording spoken words, either through the internal microphone in your Mac, an external microphone plugged into your Mac, or even a recording of an iChat audio conversation using a program, such as Conference Recorder (www.ecamm.com), Audio Hijack Pro (www.rogueamoeba.com), or WireTap Studio (http://www.AmbrosiaSW.com).

To record a podcast, follow these steps:

1. **Load GarageBand.**

The GarageBand chooser opens (refer to Figure 4-1).

2. **Click New Project in the sidebar on the left and then double-click the Podcast icon from the chooser.**

A New Project from Template dialog appears.

3. **Enter a descriptive name for your podcast in the Save As text box.**

4. **Choose a location for storing your project from the Where pop-up menu.**

5. **Click Create.**

The GarageBand window appears, as shown in Figure 4-17.

6. **Click the Male Voice or Female Voice track, click the Record button, and start speaking.**

Choosing a male or female voice track makes GarageBand optimize recording for males or females. If you already captured audio and stored it in iTunes or GarageBand, click the Audio button in the Media Browser pane, click GarageBand or iTunes, and then drag an audio file to the Male Voice or Female Voice track.

Figure 4-17:
The GarageBand window displays male and female voice tracks along with a jingles track.

7. **Click the Record button and start talking.**

8. **Click the Stop button when you finish talking.**

Refer to the earlier section, "Editing Audio," for instructions on editing your podcast audio file.

Adding jingles and audio effects

After recording you or someone else speaking, you might want to add music or sound effects to enhance your podcast. For example, you could have introductory music that fades when you start speaking.

To prevent any background jingles or audio effects from drowning out the spoken portion of your audio, GarageBand offers Ducking, a feature that reduces the background music volume level to 15-percent when the Male Voice or Female Voice track starts playing. To turn Ducking on or off, choose Control⇨Ducking.

To add audio effects, follow these steps:

1. **Choose Control⇨Show Loop Browser or click the View/Hide Loop Browser button in the lower-right corner of the GarageBand window (it's the button with the icon that looks like an eye).**

   The Loop Browser appears, as shown in Figure 4-18.

Figure 4-18: The Loop Browser provides categories of music, jingles, and sound effects.

2. **Click an Effects category, such as Jingles or Sound Effects.**

3. **Click and drag an audio effect to the Jingles track.**

4. **Release the mouse button.**

Adding pictures

Although podcasts are heard, you can add pictures to your podcast that represent your entire recording or individual parts of your podcast.

Adding pictures to a podcast is only useful when listening to your podcast on a device that can also display pictures, such as an iPod Classic, iPod Touch, or iPod nano.

To add pictures to a podcast, follow these steps:

1. **Choose Control⇨Show Editor or click the View/Hide Track Editor button — the one sporting a pair of scissors — near the bottom-left corner of the GarageBand window.**

   The Track Editor pane appears at the bottom of the GarageBand window.

2. **Choose Control⇨Show Media Browser.**

   The Media Browser pane appears, as shown in Figure 4-19.

Figure 4-19:
The Media Browser pane lists all pictures stored in iPhoto; the Track Editor pane displays blank areas for adding pictures.

3. **Click the Photos button in the Media Browser.**

4. **Click and drag a picture from the Media Browser to either the Episode Artwork box or the Artwork column in the Track Editor pane and then release the mouse button.**

   The Episode Artwork box is where you can place a picture to represent your entire podcast. The Artwork column is where you can place a picture to represent separate chapters (parts) of your podcast. You can have only one picture in the Episode Artwork box, but you can have multiple pictures in the Artwork column.

5. **(Optional) For each picture you place in the Artwork column, click the Time column and define when you want each picture to appear during your podcast.**

As great as podcasts are, I'm suddenly reminded of that late '70s song "Video Killed the Radio Star" by The Buggles. On that note (sorry, I couldn't resist), keep in mind you can use iMovie to create lively videos featuring you as the star of the show while you sing along to music you create with GarageBand — which you can also post on YouTube so others can enjoy your talents. I show you how to use iMovie in Book V, Chapter 2.

When you finish editing your spoken audio and adding sound effects and pictures, you're ready to share your podcast with the world. Sharing a podcast is identical to sharing an audio file in iTunes, on your hard disk, or on a CD. For information about saving a podcast in different ways, refer to the previous section, "Saving Music."

Chapter 5: Building Web Sites with iWeb

In This Chapter

- ✔ Understanding the parts of a Web page
- ✔ Creating Web sites
- ✔ Designing Web pages
- ✔ Understanding Web host services
- ✔ Publishing Web pages

Almost everyone has a Web site these days. Some people use Web sites to publicize their businesses, and others use Web sites as their sole means of reaching customers, such as online sellers of books, food, or pet products. Some people run Web sites focusing on their favorite hobbies, such as gardening or Star Trek trivia. No matter what your interests and needs, setting up a Web site can be fun, rewarding, and perhaps profitable.

Although creating Web pages isn't difficult, it's not as straightforward as you might hope. That's why Apple created iWeb, a special program designed to make creating Web pages easy, fun, and fast. With iWeb, you can create professional-looking Web pages in minutes instead of days.

The Parts of a Web Page

A Web site is made of Web pages. Think of a Web page as an endless sheet of paper that you can stretch in all directions to make it as large or as small as you want. On this sheet, you can position text, pictures, graphics, movies, songs, and even programs for others to access. To help guide people around your Web pages, you add navigational aids called *hyperlinks,* also commonly called *links.* By clicking a link, people can jump from one Web page to another or from one location on a page to another location on that (or a different) Web page. Figure 5-1 shows the typical parts of a Web page.

Graphics

Figure 5-1:
A Web page
consists
of text,
graphics,
and other
media.

Hyperlinks   Text   Navigation

The purpose of text

Text generally serves two purposes. First, text provides content on a Web page, such as a news story or a step-by-step description for how to bake a cake. Second, text is often used to create hyperlinks to other Web pages or to entirely different Web sites.

To make text easy to find and read, you can add color, change the fonts and font sizes, or display text in different styles, such as bold and italics. Some Web pages might contain lots of text (such as a news site like The New York Times (www.nytimes.com), whereas others might contain a minimal amount of text, such as a Web site displaying photographs with text simply listing the photograph's name or topic.

The purpose of graphics

Graphics can serve a purely decorative function, such as a company logo displayed in the corner of the Web page. Graphics can also be used as content and as hyperlinks.

As content, graphics provide information, such as photographs on a news site or pictures of your family on a personal site. Instead of showing pictures, some graphics can display decorative text in ways that ordinary text cannot produce. For example, a Web site for a plant nursery might have its name displayed in text or graphics.

It's impossible to search for text stored as a graphic image. That's why many Web sites list an e-mail address as a graphic image; if they list that e-mail address as text, another computer can scan the Web site for text that contains an e-mail address to send junk e-mail.

Finally, graphics, like text, are often used to create hyperlinks, such as menus that offer options for displaying different Web pages. Such graphic hyperlinks often provide you with a more colorful way to present hyperlinks than plain text, such as appearing as buttons or pull-down menus.

Putting together a Web page

To create a Web page with other programs, you have to learn the cryptic language that creates Web pages, known as HTML (*Hyper*Text *Markup Language*). Because learning the HTML language just to create a Web page might be intimidating, iWeb simplifies this task by creating HTML code for you "behind the scenes." All you have to do is arrange objects (text and graphics) on a Web page.

Although you *could* create a Web page starting with a blank page, it's far easier to create a Web page by modifying a predesigned one. With iWeb, you can choose from a variety of predesigned Web page templates, which already contain background graphics, text, and pictures that you can customize.

Creating a Web Site with iWeb

Every Web site contains one or more Web pages. To design a Web site, you need to decide how many Web pages you need, the purpose for each Web page, and the overall appearance you want to use for each Web page.

The number of Web pages you need can vary depending on the Web site's purpose. If you're putting together an online store to sell food, books, or pet supplies, you might need dozens (or even hundreds) of separate Web pages to display all your products. You can always add and delete Web pages when you need to.

After you know (approximately) how many Web pages you need, and what you want each Web page to offer, the next step is to pick a theme, which defines the overall appearance of each Web page, such as a background color or decorative graphic along the borders.

Picking a theme

A theme provides a consistent appearance for every Web page that makes up your Web site. One part of your Web site might list products for sale, so you might use one theme for product listings. Another part of your Web site might list company news so those Web pages might use a different theme. Themes simply help visually organize similar information.

To pick a theme for your Web pages, follow these steps:

1. **Click the iWeb icon in the Dock (or double-click the iWeb icon in the Applications folder.)**

A dialog appears, listing different themes in the Theme list on the left and displaying the appearance of specific types of Web pages on the right, as shown in Figure 5-2.

2. **Click a theme in the Theme list.**

Each time you click a different theme, the Web pages in the right pane show you how that new theme displays each type of Web page — Welcome page, About Me page, Photos page, whatever.

If you click the pop-up menu in the upper-left corner of the iWeb dialog, you can choose to see all themes or only those used with specific versions of iWeb, such as version 3.0, 2.0, 1.1, or 1.0.

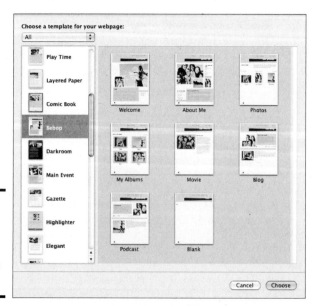

Figure 5-2:
Each iWeb theme displays Web pages differently.

3. **Click one of the following types of Web pages in the right pane:**

- *Welcome:* Introduces your Web site. The Welcome page is typically the first Web page visitors see when they visit a specific site, such as `www.dummies.com`.

- *About Me:* Describes yourself or your company.

- *Photos:* Displays digital pictures, such as those stored in iPhoto, for everyone to see.

- *My Albums:* Displays groups of different photo categories for people to browse.

- *Movie:* Displays a digital video that people can watch directly in your Web page.

- *Blog:* Provides space for typing your thoughts about different topics.

- *Podcast:* Displays lists of audio recordings (podcasts) that others can hear directly off your Web page.

- *Blank:* Provides a Web page that incorporates a specific theme so you can add anything you want to it.

4. **Click Choose.**

The Web page that appears in the iWeb window is decked out in your chosen theme, as shown in Figure 5-3. You may see pictures of strange people and gibberish text. This is placeholder graphics and text, which you have to replace, which I explained in the "Designing a Web Page" section, later in this chapter.

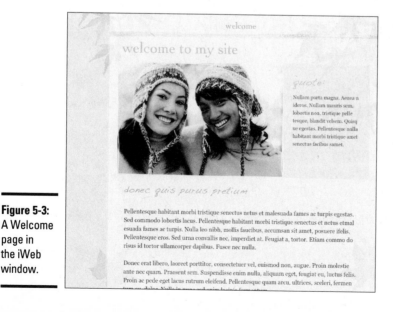

Figure 5-3:
A Welcome
page in
the iWeb
window.

Adding new pages

Because Web sites typically contain more than one Web page, you often need to add more Web pages to your Web site. To add a Web page, follow these steps:

1. **Click the Add Page icon at the bottom of the iWeb window or choose File⇨New Page (or press ⌘+N).**

The list of available Web page templates appears with your current theme highlighted (refer to Figure 5-2).

2. **Select a new page you want to add, such as Podcast or My Albums, and then click Choose.**

Your new Web page appears in the iWeb window.

Deleting Web pages

If you add too many Web pages or suddenly find you don't need a Web page after all, you can delete that Web page. To delete a Web page, follow these steps:

1. **Click the Web page that you want to delete in the sidebar of the iWeb window.**

2. **Choose Edit⇨Delete Page.**

Your chosen Web page disappears, along with any text or graphics you stored on that Web page.

If you accidentally delete a Web page, press ⌘+Z or choose Edit⇨Undo to retrieve the deleted Web page.

Designing a Web Page

With the exception of the Blank Web page template, every iWeb template displays a Web page filled with placeholder text and graphic images that you can then replace with your own text and pictures.

Replacing placeholder text

Placeholder text gives you an idea of what the text might look like on the Web page. To change placeholder text, follow these steps:

1. **In the sidebar of the iWeb window, click the Web page that you want to modify.**

Your chosen Web page appears in the right pane of the iWeb window.

2. **Double-click the text you want to edit or replace.**

   Your chosen text appears highlighted.

3. **Type new text or press the arrow and Delete keys to edit the existing text.**

TIP

Instead of typing new text, you can always copy text from another program and paste it over the placeholder text.

Replacing placeholder graphics

Placeholder graphics give you some idea how a picture would work in a particular area of your page. To replace placeholder graphics with graphics of your own, follow these steps:

1. **In the sidebar of the iWeb window, click the Web page you want to modify.**

   Your chosen Web page appears in the right pane of the iWeb window.

2. **Click the Show Media icon that appears at the bottom of the iWeb window or choose View⇨Show Media.**

   A Media Browser appears.

3. **Click the Photos button.**

   Your iPhoto library appears in the Media Browser, as shown in Figure 5-4.

Figure 5-4:
The Media Browser displays all your iPhoto pictures.

4. **Click and drag a picture you want to use to the placeholder graphic image you want to replace.**

5. **Release the mouse button.**

Your iPhoto picture now appears on your Web page.

6. **Choose View⇨Hide Media to close the Media Browser, or click the Hide Media button (it turns into the Show Media button).**

Changing the Web page theme

You might modify a Web page with text and graphics and suddenly realize that you don't like the theme you chose. To change a Web page's theme while leaving your content (text and graphics you've added) unchanged, follow these steps:

1. **In the sidebar of the iWeb window, click the Web page you want to modify.**

Your chosen Web page appears in the right pane of the iWeb window.

2. **Click the Theme icon (fourth from left) that appears at the bottom of the iWeb window.**

A pop-up menu of themes appears, as shown in Figure 5-5.

Figure 5-5: Choose a new theme by clicking the Theme icon.

3. **Click a new theme.**

   Your Web page changes to match your chosen theme.

Customizing the Parts of a Web Page

Making an iWeb template your own by replacing placeholder text and graphics certainly makes creating Web pages easy, but eventually, you'll come across a template that doesn't have the text and graphics positioned exactly where you want them. To customize a Web page further, you need to know how to add, move, resize, delete, and arrange text and graphics on a Web page. You can modify existing objects or create new objects for storing text and graphics.

Moving an object

To move text or graphics to another part of your Web page, follow these steps:

1. **Move the pointer over the text or graphics you want to move.**
2. **Click and drag the text or graphics to a new location.**
3. **Release the mouse button.**

   The text or graphics stays put in its new location.

Resizing an object

To resize text or graphics to make it bigger or smaller, follow these steps:

1. **Click to select the text or graphics you want to resize.**

   Handles appear around your chosen object, as shown in Figure 5-6.
2. **Move the pointer over a handle until the pointer turns into a two-way pointing arrow and then click and drag the handle to change the size of your object.**
3. **Release the mouse button when you're happy with the new size of the text or graphic object.**

Rearranging an object

If you move or resize an object, it might cover another object, as shown in Figure 5-7. To fix this problem, you might need to rearrange which object appears over another one.

Selection handles

Figure 5-6:
Handles
appear
when you
select an
object.

Think of each object (text or graphic) as a sheet of paper that can lie on or slide under another object.

To rearrange which object appears on top of another one, follow these steps:

1. **Click to select the text or graphics that you want to place over (or under) another object.**

   Handles appear around your selected object.

2. **Choose one of the following:**

   - *Arrange⇨Bring Forward:* Moves the selected object over one object that might be overlapping it. If multiple objects cover your selected object, you might not see any difference.

   - *Arrange⇨Bring to Front:* Moves the selected object on top of all overlapping objects.

   - *Arrange⇨Send Backward:* Moves the selected object underneath one object that it may be covering.

   - *Arrange⇨Send to Back:* Moves the selected object underneath all other overlapping objects.

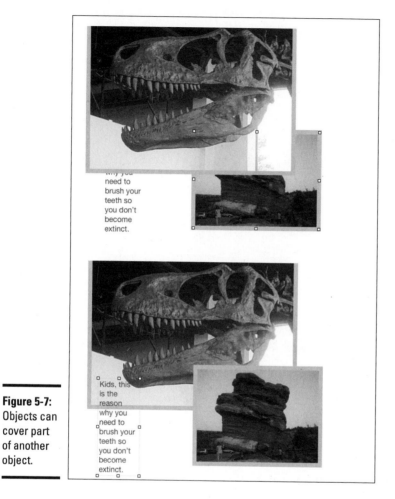

Figure 5-7:
Objects can
cover part
of another
object.

Deleting objects

To delete one or more objects, follow these steps:

1. **Click to select the text or graphics that you want to delete.**

   To select multiple objects, hold down the Shift key and click each object
   you want to delete.

2. **Press Delete or choose Edit⇨Delete.**

If you delete an object by mistake, press ⌘+Z or choose Edit⇨Undo.

Working with text

Text always appears on a Web page inside a text box, which you can move and resize on a Web page. If you create a Web page from a template, it will likely have a text box on the page that you can fill with your own text. If you create a blank Web page, or need more room to display text, you may need to create a text box.

Creating a text box

To create a text box, follow these steps:

1. **Click the Text Box icon at the bottom of the iWeb window or choose Insert⇨Text Box.**

   A blinking cursor appears in the middle of your Web page.

2. **Type your text.**

   If you have any existing objects on the Web page, the text box might appear over an existing object. When you type, you might have a hard time seeing your text, so press ⌘+A to see your text.

3. **Click anywhere on the Web page away from your newly created text box.**

4. **Click your newly created text box to display handles around it.**

5. **Click and drag to move and/or resize the text box.**

Formatting text

After you type text inside a text box, you can format it by following these steps:

1. **Double-click the text box that contains the text you want to modify.**

2. **Select the text you want to modify; alternatively, press ⌘+A (or choose Edit⇨Select All) to select all the text in the text box.**

3. **Choose Format⇨Font.**

   A submenu of options appears, as shown in Figure 5-8.

4. **Choose an option from the Font submenu, such as Bold or Show Fonts.**

   If you click the Fonts icon in the bottom-right corner of the iWeb window, a Fonts dialog appears, letting you pick a font to use.

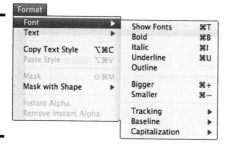

Figure 5-8:
The Font submenu displays different ways to format text.

Creating a text hyperlink

Besides making text look pretty inside a text box, you might also want to turn text into a *hyperlink* — the highlighted or underlined link that can jump a reader to another Web page or Web site. To create a hyperlink, follow these steps:

1. **Double-click the text box that contains the text you want to turn into a hyperlink.**

2. **Select the text you want to turn into a hyperlink.**

3. **Choose Insert⇨Hyperlink to open the Hyperlink submenu, then select one of the following to display a Link pane similar to the one shown in Figure 5-9:**

- *Webpage:* Links to a specific Web site, such as www.dummies.com.

- *Email Message:* Links to an e-mail address, such as JollyOldSaint Nick@gmail.com.

- *File:* Links to a file, such as a PDF or text file, which others can download from your Web page.

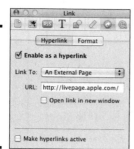

Figure 5-9:
The Link pane lets you customize your hyperlink.

4. **Choose the options in the Link pane.**

The options displayed in the Link pane will look different depending on the option you choose in Step 4. For example, if you choose Webpage, you need to type the Web site address to link to, such as www. dummies.com. If you choose Email Message, you need to specify the e-mail address, such as MrsClaus@yahoo.com.

5. **Click the Close button of the Link pane.**

Working with graphics

You can add and place digital photographs, simple graphic shapes like arrows, or even videos anywhere on a Web page. If you create a Web page from a template, the template will likely provide placeholder graphics for you to add your own pictures. However, if you want to add more pictures, or if you started with a blank Web page, you can add more graphics to any Web page.

Graphics can take time to transfer over the Internet, so the more graphics you place on a Web page — and the larger the graphic images you use — the longer the Web page takes to load and display in someone's Web browser. Don't be afraid to use graphics, but don't go overboard.

Adding a picture or movie to a Web page

Follow these steps to add either a picture or a movie to a Web page:

1. **Click the Show Media icon at the bottom of the iWeb window.**

The Media Browser appears.

2. **Click the Photos or Movies tab, depending on which you want to add.**

A list of pictures and movies stored on your Mac's hard drive appears.

3. **Navigate to the picture or movie you want, then click and drag the movie or picture to your Web page and release the mouse button.**

Your chosen picture (or movie) appears on your Web page. (You might need to move or resize the picture.)

4. **Select View⇨Hide Media to close the Media Browser.**

To insert pictures and movies, choose Insert⇨Choose to open a file-browsing dialog, navigate to the file you want, click it, and then click the Insert button (or just double-click the file to insert it).

Adding a widget to a Web page

You might want to add a widget to your Web page; for example, a Google map that shows your store location or a countdown for an event that you'll be hosting. To add a widget to a Web page, follow these steps:

1. **Click the Show Media icon at the bottom of the iWeb window.**

The Media Browser appears.

2. **Click the Widgets tab.**

A list of widgets appears in the Media Browser.

3. **Click and drag a widget from the Media Browser to your Web page.**

4. **Release the mouse button.**

Your chosen widget appears on your Web page. (You might need to move or resize the widget or specify some information, such as an expiration date or URL address, to make the widget function.)

5. **Choose View⇨Hide Media to close the Media Browser or click the Hide Media icon.**

Publishing Your Web Pages

After you create one or more Web pages, they're trapped on your computer until you upload them to the Internet where others can visit your Web pages with their Web browser. To publish your Web pages on the Internet, you typically need to transfer your Web page files to a Web site hosting service. This transfer is called *uploading.* If you're wondering what kind of hosting service you need, here's a quick rundown.

Types of Web site hosts

A Web site host is a bunch of computers with lots of humongous hard disks, called a *server,* connected to a really, really high-speed Internet connection (a T1 or T3 line). The main reason you need to store your Web pages on a server is that the fast T1 or T3 line allows thousands of people to view your Web site simultaneously. A typical home Internet connection isn't fast enough to support (the potential hordes of) people who visit your Web site at the same time.

Some popular Web site hosting options are

✦ Free advertiser-sponsored Web site hosts

✦ Free ISP (Internet Service Provider) Web site hosts

✦ Fee-based Web site hosts

Free advertiser-sponsored Web site hosts

Many companies offer free Web hosting in exchange for displaying banner or pop-up ads all over your Web pages. If someone wants to visit your Web site, he or she might have to wade through some advertisements first.

The main problem with these types of hosts is that you can't control what type of advertisements might appear on your Web site. If you create a Web site encouraging people to support the prevention of cruelty to animals, for instance, the Web site host might stick advertisements for fur coats or exotic animal foodstuffs all over your Web pages, and you can do nothing about it. Talk about sending the wrong signal!

Another drawback of free advertiser-sponsored Web site hosts is that the specific Web site address is never anything as simple as www.joehutsko. com. Instead, free Web site hosts force you to use a Web site address that includes the Web site host name. So if you host your Web pages on a free site called Tripod or Geocities, your Web site's address might look like this:

```
http://joehutsko.tripod.com
```

or this:

```
http://blogger.joehutsko.com/
```

Unintuitive Web site addresses like these work just like the simpler, descriptive www.joehutsko.com, but they're hard to remember and even harder to type correctly. Telling someone to visit www.joe.com (or simply joehutsko. com) is easy; telling someone to visit http://blogger.joehutsko.com is clumsy to say or write.

By using a free Web hosting service, you can gain experience with designing and uploading your site. You can also see whether you have the stamina to maintain a Web site. Many people rush to create a Web site, furiously update it for the first week, and then gradually lose interest, eventually abandoning their site. You can use a free Web hosting service as a trial before spending money for a fee-based Web hosting service.

Not all free Web hosting services are equal. The amount of storage space and number of ads that appear on your Web pages differs from one to the next, so compare these services until you find one that you like best.

Free ISP Web site hosts

When you pay for Internet service from an Internet Service Provider (ISP), your ISP might throw in free Web site hosting — not all ISP's offer free Web site hosting, some charge a fee, others don't offer it at all. Free ISP Web site hosting services don't put advertising on your Web site because the ISP figures that you're already paying it for its service.

As a result, ISP Web site hosting gives you the benefits of experimenting with a free Web site without the drawbacks of unwanted advertisements.

However, your Web site address might contain something convoluted and non-intuitive, such as `http://www.ispname.net/joehutsko`.

Web sites hosted on free ISP Web sites are more often used for personal use rather than setting up on-line stores. Some ISPs might even restrict businesses from setting up sites because of the bandwidth problems that might occur if too many people visit the Web site every day.

Free Web site hosting services often limit the amount of storage space you can use. The less storage space available, the fewer Web pages, graphic images, and additional files (such as sound or video) you can put on your Web site.

Fee-based Web site hosts

If you want a Web site with no ads, more storage space, and a descriptive Web site address (called a *domain name*), you need to pay a fee-based Web site hosting service.

Many advertiser-supported Web hosts offer both a free and a subscription-based plan. These Web site hosting services give you the option of experimenting with designing a Web site under the free plan with a lengthy site address and later transferring the site to a registered domain name (like www.joehutsko.com) without having to change Web site hosting companies.

The first step to using a fee-based Web site hosting service is to compare prices and features. Prices vary from $1.99 per month to more than $19.99 per month depending on what additional options you might want. (What one Web site hosting service considers an option, another might throw in free as part of its basic package.) Some basic features to look for are

✦ **Storage space:** The more storage space, the more Web pages, pictures, videos, and animation you can post on your Web site. Typical storage space ranges from 10GB to 250GB or more.

✦ **File transfer limitation:** Defines how much data can flow from your Web site between the hosting service's servers and the computers visitors use to visit your Web site. A high transfer rate might be necessary if you offer files for people to download, such as pictures or music files.

✦ **Number of e-mail accounts:** Consider whether you need a few e-mail accounts for your family members or 50 accounts for your company.

✦ **E-mail storage space:** The more storage space, the more messages all your e-mail accounts can hold. If you don't have enough e-mail storage space, you have to move them to your local disk or erase them to make room for new messages.

✦ **Domain name registration:** You need to register your particular Web site domain name so no one else can use it. Many Web hosting services include domain name registration. Otherwise, you have to register the domain name yourself.

✦ **Number of domain names:** The price might include just one domain name or several domain names.

After you pick a Web hosting service, you need to pick a domain name for your Web site. Many domain names are already taken (such as www.white house.gov or www.dummies.com). After you decide on a descriptive domain name, you need to register it either through your Web site hosting service or through a separate domain name registration service.

To check whether a domain name is already taken, do a search on a site, such as Network Solutions (www.networksolutions.com).

Registration means picking a name that no one else is using, paying a one-time fee, and then paying periodic fees to maintain that domain name. If you don't continue paying to maintain your domain name, you lose it. Registration fees typically cost $5 to $25 per year, although some Web site hosting services will pay this fee for you as long as you keep using their services.

After you pick a Web site hosting service and register a domain name, you can always transfer your domain name (and all your Web page files) to a different Web site hosting service that offers lower rates or better service.

Uploading your Web pages

After you pick a Web hosting service and establish your Web address or register a domain, you're ready to *upload,* or publish, your Web pages.

iWeb has FTP capability built in, which makes uploading easy. FTP (File Transfer Protocol) is the most common way to transfer Web page files from your computer to a Web site server. Your Web hosting service provides the server address and username that are required for FTP uploads; the Web hosting service might also provide a password, and other parameters, such as a special directory, or a special communications protocol the Web site server requires to copy your Web pages to it. To upload your Web pages, follow these steps:

1. **In the sidebar of the iWeb window, click the name of the site you want to upload.**

   The Site Publishing Settings window appears, as shown in Figure 5-10.

2. **Choose FTP Server in the Publish To pop-up menu.**

3. **(Optional) Type a site name and contact e-mail in the first two fields.**

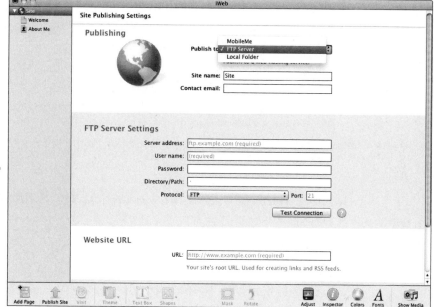

Figure 5-10:
Use the Site
Publishing
Settings to
choose how
to upload
your Web
pages.

4. **Type the FTP server settings provided by your Web site hosting service.**

5. **Type your Web site address in the Website URL field.**

6. **(Optional) If you have a Facebook account, select Update My Facebook Profile When I Publish This Site.**

7. **Click the Publish Site icon in the toolbar at the bottom of the iWeb window.**

Using MobileMe

Besides automatically keeping your contacts, calendar, and Safari bookmarks synchronized between multiple Mac and Windows computers (and your iPhone or iPod Touch if you have one), Apple's MobileMe service ($99 per year) can also take the trouble out of finding a Web site hosting service to host your iWeb-created Web pages.

To publish your Web site to MobileMe, follow these steps:

1. **In the sidebar of the iWeb window, click the name of the site you want to upload.**

   The Site Publishing Settings window appears (refer to Figure 5-10).

2. Choose MobileMe from the Publish To pop-up menu.

3. (Optional) Type your site name or iWeb creates one for you.

   This name is used in the Web site address.

4. (Optional) Choose Make My Published Site Private if you want to limit access to your Web site with a password.

5. (Optional) Select Update My Facebook Profile When I Publish This Site if you have a Facebook account.

6. Click the Publish Site icon in the toolbar at the bottom of the iWeb window.

Making changes to your uploaded Web pages

A Web site is a dynamic creature, and you'll probably want to change your Web pages to reflect changes in your business offerings or to show off pictures of your growing puppy. To upload revised Web pages, follow these steps:

1. In the sidebar of the iWeb window, select the Web page you changed.

2. Click the Publish Site icon in the toolbar at the bottom of the iWeb window.

If you made changes to many Web pages and would rather re-upload the entire Web site, choose File⇨Publish Entire Site.

Uploaded Web pages are blue in the iWeb sidebar; red Web pages haven't been uploaded.

Book VI

iWork

Contents at a Glance

Chapter 1: Creating Documents with Pages

In This Chapter

- ✔ Using document templates
- ✔ Creating text
- ✔ Formatting text
- ✔ Using text boxes
- ✔ Working with graphics
- ✔ Polishing a document

*P*ages is a combination word processor and desktop publishing program. As a word processor, Pages lets you type, edit, and format text quickly and easily. As a desktop publisher, Pages lets you arrange graphics and text boxes on a page to create business cards, menus, newsletters, or brochures.

Because Pages offers a dual personality as a word processor and a desktop publishing program, you can switch between the features you need in a single program. You can start writing and then decide to design your pages. Halfway through designing your pages, you might feel the urge to write again.

Pages is part of the iWork suite — and it ain't free. Your Mac might have a trial version of Pages that lets you play with the program to see whether it meets your needs. If your Mac doesn't have the trial version of Pages already installed, you can download it free from Apple's Web site (`www. apple.com/iwork`).

Working with Document Templates

To help you get started writing, Pages supplies a variety of document templates. By choosing a document template, you can just enter new text or customize the appearance of the template so you don't have to create everything from scratch.

Pages offers two types of templates: Word Processing and Page Layout. Word Processing templates are designed mostly for writing (relatively) plain and simple, while Page Layout templates are designed mostly for when you're mixing text and graphics. (You can always add pictures to a Word Processing template or write in a text box on a Page Layout template.)

To wax philosophical for a moment, the difference between word processing and page layout is that word processing is suited for "continuous" documents, such as letters, reports, contracts (yawn), novels, and so forth. Page layout targets "page-centric" documents where different types of content (text, photos, tables, advertisements, for example) and the various contents' positional considerations must all fit together nice and neat on the same proverbial page, such as flyers and brochures, newsletters, magazines, and catalogs, to name a few.

The main difference between Word Processing templates and Page Layout templates is that you can type directly on a page in a document created from a Word Processing template. If you want to type text on a document created from a Page Layout template, you have to create a text box and place that text box somewhere on your page.

A second difference is that you must manually add (or delete) pages in a Page Layout template (by choosing the Insert⇨Pages or Edit⇨Delete Page commands). With a Word Processing template, Pages automatically adds pages while you type and deletes pages while you delete text.

Generally, if you need a document that contains mostly text, such as letters or reports, start with a Word Processing template. If you need a document that consists mostly of pictures, or if you need to create newsletters, magazine pages, or Web pages, start with a Page Layout template.

After you create a document using a Word Processing (or Page Layout) template, you can't switch to a new template. If you want to use a different template, you have to create another document.

To choose a document template, follow these steps:

1. **Click the Pages icon in the Dock or double-click the Pages icon in the Applications folder (or choose File⇨New on the menu bar if Pages is already running).**

   A dialog appears, displaying different templates you can choose, as shown in Figure 1-1.

2. **Select a template category under the Word Processing or Page Layout headings in the listing on the left.**

   The templates for your selected category appear in the main pane of the dialog.

3. Select a template and then click the Choose button (or double-click the icon for the template you want to use).

Pages opens your chosen template as a new, untitled document.

If you want to start with a blank document, click the Blank template category under the Word Processing heading.

**Book VI
Chapter 1**

**Creating Documents
with Pages**

Figure 1-1:
Pages
provides a
variety of
templates
to help you
create a
document
quickly.

Replacing placeholder text

Nearly every template contains placeholder text that shows you gibberish that you have to replace with your own text. To change text in a template, follow these steps:

1. Double-click the placeholder text you want to change.

Pages selects the entire placeholder text, which can be as short as a single sentence or as large as several paragraphs, as shown in the newsletter title selection in Figure 1-2.

2. Type any new text you want to replace the placeholder text.

Replacing placeholder pictures

Many templates display placeholder pictures. Unless you happen to like the picture included with a template, you'll probably want to replace it with one of your own. The easiest way to add new pictures to your Pages document (or replace placeholder pictures) is to drag and drop your new pictures from a Finder folder window. You can also add or replace pictures in Pages documents by following these steps:

1. **Click the Media icon (the one displaying a musical note) on the toolbar or choose View⇨Show Media Browser on the menu bar.**

The Media Browser appears.

2. **Click the Photos tab in the Media Browser to view all the pictures stored in iPhoto.**

3. **Click and drag a picture from the Media Browser to any placeholder picture in your document.**

4. **Release the mouse button.**

Pages replaces the placeholder picture with the picture you choose from the Media Browser, as shown in Figure 1-3.

5. **Click the Close button on the Media Browser.**

Figure 1-2:
To replace placeholder text, double-click it and type new text.

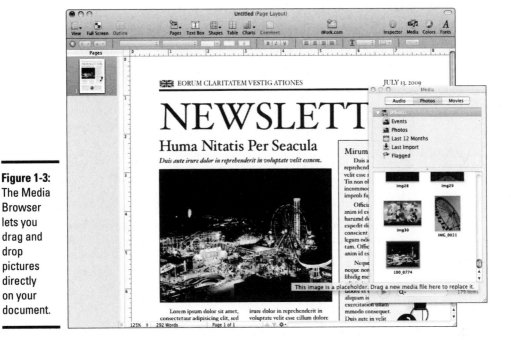

Figure 1-3:
The Media
Browser
lets you
drag and
drop
pictures
directly
on your
document.

Working with Text

Text can appear directly on a page or inside a text box. Word Processing templates let you type text directly on a page, but you can always add text boxes and type text inside those text boxes later. Page Layout templates allow you to type text only inside text boxes.

You can always tell what type of template your document is based on by peeking at the title bar of the document window, which identifies your document by name followed by either (Word Processing) or (Page Layout).

The advantage of typing text directly on a page is that you can keep typing and Pages automatically creates new pages while you type. The disadvantage of typing text directly on a page is that it's harder to define exactly where the text will appear on a page.

The advantage of using text boxes is that you can move them anywhere on a page (or to a different page). The disadvantage of typing text in a text box is that text boxes can display only a limited amount of text. (If you need to type a large amount of text, you might need to link text boxes so that when text overflows one text box, it automatically flows into another one.)

Editing text

Whether you're typing text directly on a page or inside a text box, you can edit text by adding, deleting, or rearranging it.

Adding text

Any new text you type appears wherever the cursor is located. To add text, just place the cursor where you want the new text to appear, click, and then type away.

Deleting text

You can delete text in two ways:

✦ **Move the cursor next to characters you want to erase and press Delete.** Press the big Delete key (the one that appears to the right of the +/= key) to backspace over characters to the left of the cursor.

✦ **Select text and then press Delete.** Select text by holding down the Shift key and moving the cursor with the arrow keys or by clicking and dragging the mouse over the text to select it, and then press the Delete key.

Rearranging text

After you've written some text, you might need to rearrange it by copying or moving chunks of text from one location to another. You can copy and move text between two text boxes or from one part of a text page to another part of the same page — or to another page all together.

To copy and move text, you can use the Cut, Copy, and Paste commands on the Edit menu, but you might find it quicker to select and drag text with the mouse. Here's how it's done:

1. **Select the text you want to copy or move.**

   If you want to copy text, hold down the Option key while doing Step 2. If you want to move text, you don't need to hold down any keys.

2. **Click and drag the selected text to a new location.**

3. **Release the mouse button to finish copying or moving your text.**

Formatting text

The text styles and images you choose for your document create the tone of what you want to communicate — businesslike, fun, weird, and so on. You can format text using fonts, styles, sizes, and colors. To give you fast access to the formatting options, Pages displays a Format bar (see Figure 1-4) near the top of the Pages window. To view (or hide) the Format bar, choose View⇨Show (or Hide) Format Bar.

Figure 1-4:
The Format bar lets you choose different fonts, sizes, and styles.

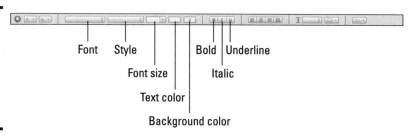

Font   Style   Bold Underline
       Font size   Italic
      Text color
      Background color

To format text, select the text you want to format and then do any of the following:

✦ **Click the Font pop-up menu** on the Format bar and then choose a font from the menu that appears.

✦ **Click the Style pop-up menu** on the Format bar and then choose a style, such as Regular or Heading 1. (Choosing Bold or Italic from the Style pop-up menu is identical to clicking the Bold or Italic icon on the Format bar.)

✦ **Click the Font Size pop-up menu** on the Format bar and then choose a size, such as 12 or 24.

✦ **Click the Text Color button** on the Format bar. A color menu appears, as shown in Figure 1-5. Click a color to change the color of your selected text.

✦ **Click the Background Color button** on the Format bar. A color menu appears, much like the one for the text color. Click a color to appear in the background of your selected text.

✦ **Click the Bold, Italic, or Underline icons** on the Format bar.

If you suddenly change your mind about any of the formatting changes you make, choose Edit⇨Undo on the menu bar or press ⌘+Z to reverse the last changes.

Figure 1-5:
Clicking the Text Color button displays a color menu.

Show Colors

Adjusting line spacing, justification, and margins

You can change how letters look by messing with the font, but you can also change the way a block of text looks by changing how it's spaced on the page. In concrete terms, this means changing:

✦ **Line spacing:** Defines how close together lines in a paragraph appear.

✦ **Text justification:** Defines how text aligns within the left and right margins.

✦ **Margins:** Defines the left and right boundaries that text can't go past.

Changing line spacing

Line spacing used for most purposes typically varies from 0.5 to 2.0. (A value of 1.0 is single spacing, and a value of 2.0 is double spacing.) To change line spacing, follow these steps:

1. **Select at least two lines of text you want to modify.**

2. **Click the Line Spacing pop-up menu on the Format bar and then choose a number, such as 1.5 or 2.0, as shown in Figure 1-6.**

Click Show More in the Line Spacing pop-up menu to choose spacing beyond the 0.5–2.0 range. Line spacing values less than 1.0, such as 0.5, can cause lines to overlap, which makes the text hard to read.

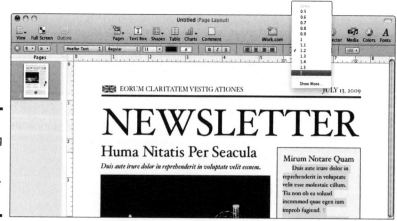

Figure 1-6:
Line spacing can make text appear squashed or far apart.

Changing justification

The four types of justification are

✦ **Align Left:** Text appears flush against the left margin but ragged along the right margin.

✦ **Center:** Each line of text is centered within the left and right margins, so text appears ragged on both left and right margins.

✦ **Align Right:** Text appears flush against the right margin but ragged along the left margin.

✦ **Justify:** Text appears flush against both the left and right margins, but extra space appears between words and characters.

Figure 1-7 shows four paragraphs. The first is aligned left, the second is centered, the third is aligned right, and the final paragraph is justified.

To set your text justification, follow these steps:

1. **Select the text you want to modify.**

2. **Click the Align Left, Center, Align Right, or Justify icons on the Format bar.**

**Book VI
Chapter 1**

**Creating Documents
with Pages**

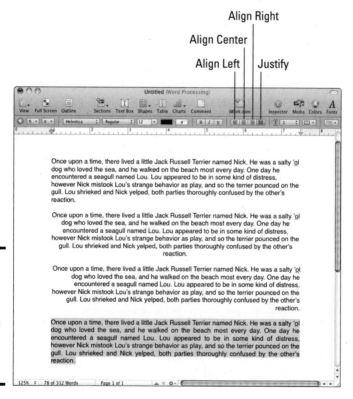

Figure 1-7:
Justifying text can make paragraphs appear in different ways.

Defining margins

The left and right margins only define text that appears on the page (Word Processing layout). The left and right margins of text boxes are defined by the text box size.

To define the left and right margins of text, you can use the ruler, which appears at the top of the Pages window. The ruler lets you define an exact location for your margins, such as placing the left margin exactly 1.5 inches from the left edge of the page.

To define the left and right margins of text, follow these steps:

1. **Select the text you want to modify.**

2. **Click and drag the Left Margin marker to a new position on the ruler and then release the mouse button.**

The Left Margin marker looks like an upside-down blue triangle that appears on the left side of the ruler, as shown in Figure 1-8.

If the ruler isn't visible, choose View➪Show Rulers.

3. **Click and drag the Indent marker to a new position on the ruler and then release the mouse button.**

The Indent marker looks like a thin blue rectangle that appears over the Left Margin marker.

4. **Click and drag the Right Margin marker to a new position on the ruler and then release the mouse button.**

The Right Margin marker looks like an upside-down blue marker that appears on the right side of the ruler.

Figure 1-8:
The ruler provides markers that you can drag to adjust paragraph margins.

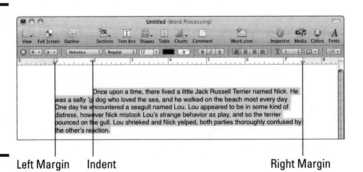

Left Margin   Indent   Right Margin

Dragging the Left Margin and Right Margin markers on the ruler is a fast way to adjust the margins, but for a more precise way, follow these steps:

1. **Select the text you want to modify.**

2. **Click the Inspector icon in the upper-right corner of the Pages window or choose View⇨Show Inspector from the menu bar.**

   The Inspector icon looks like a little "i" in a blue circle. When you click the icon, an Inspector window appears.

3. **Click the Text Inspector icon (the big T).**

4. **Click the Tabs tab, as shown in Figure 1-9.**

5. **Enter a value in the First Line, Left, or Right text box or click the up and down arrows to choose a value.**

6. **Click the Close button of the Text Inspector window.**

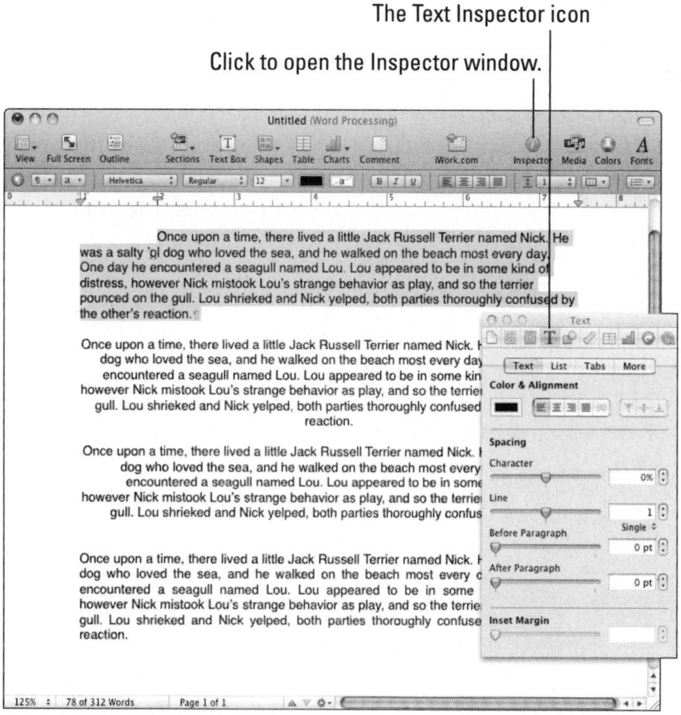

The Text Inspector icon

Click to open the Inspector window.

Figure 1-9: The Text Inspector lets you choose precise values for adjusting the margins of text.

Book VI
Chapter 1

Creating Documents
with Pages

Using Formatting Styles

You might have a favorite way to format text. Although you could manually change each formatting feature, you might find it faster and easier to use styles instead. *Formatting styles* store different types of formatting that you can apply to text. Pages' Word Processing and Page Layout templates have formatting styles stored already. When you create your own documents, you can create formatting styles, too. By using formatting styles, you can format text quickly and easily.

Applying styles

The following are the types of styles you can apply to text:

✦ **Paragraph styles** affect an entire paragraph where the end of a paragraph is defined by a line that ends where you press Return.

✦ **Character styles** affect characters or words.

✦ **List styles** affect multiple lines of text where each line of text ends where you press Return. (Think To-Do lists or bullet points.)

Using a paragraph style

To apply a paragraph style, follow these steps:

1. **Click the text (or move the cursor inside the text box) you want to modify.**

2. **Click the Paragraph Styles button.**

It's a gray button with a paragraph symbol and a downward pointing arrow on the far left of the Format bar. A menu of available paragraph styles appears, as shown in Figure 1-10.

If you can't see the Format bar, choose View➪Show Format Bar.

3. **Choose a style.**

Pages formats your entire paragraph.

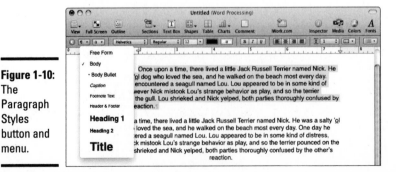

Figure 1-10: The Paragraph Styles button and menu.

Using a character style

To apply a character style, follow these steps:

1. **Select the text you want to modify.**

2. **Click the Character Styles button.**

   It's a gray button with a small letter "a" and a downward pointing arrow on the far left of the Format bar. A menu of available character styles appears, as shown in Figure 1-11.

3. **Choose a style.**

   Pages formats your selected text.

Some character styles, such as Emphasis and Italics, work identically as the Bold and Italics buttons on the far right of the Format bar.

Figure 1-11:
The Character Styles button and menu.

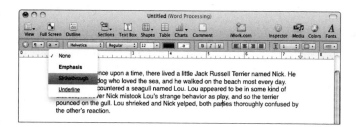

Using a list style

To apply a list style, follow these steps:

1. **Move the cursor where you want to start typing a list.**

2. **Click the List Styles button.**

   It's the last gray button on the far right of the Format bar. A menu appears, as shown in Figure 1-12.

3. **Choose a style, such as Harvard or Bullet.**

4. **Type some text and then press Return.**

   Pages displays your list in your chosen style, such as a numbered list or a bulleted list.

5. **Repeat Step 4 for each additional line of your list.**

6. **Turn off List mode by clicking the List Styles button and then choosing None.**

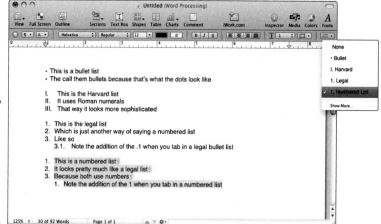

Figure 1-12:
The List
Styles menu
displays
the types of
lists you can
create.

Using the Styles Drawer

For a fast way to select paragraph, character, or list styles, use the Styles Drawer. The Styles Drawer slides out from the right or left of a Pages document (depending on where the Pages window is placed on your desktop) and displays different styles to use while showing how text appears in each style. By using the Styles Drawer, you can quickly pick a style to format text.

To use the Styles Drawer, follow these steps:

1. **Select the text you want to modify.**

2. **Click the View icon and then select Show Styles Drawer from the drop-down menu (or choose View⇨Show Styles Drawer from the menu bar).**

   The View icon is above the left corner of the Format bar. A drawer appears, listing all the available styles, as shown in Figure 1-13.

3. **Click a style in the Styles Drawer.**

   Your text takes the characteristics of your selected style.

4. **Click the View icon and then select Hide Styles Drawer from the drop-down menu to hide the Styles Drawer.**

Creating temporary styles

Pages provides paragraph, character, and list styles, but you might need to format text in a certain way that Pages doesn't offer. In that case, you can copy the style from existing text and paste that style to format other text automatically.

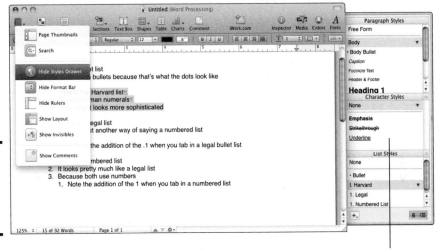

Figure 1-13:
The Styles
Drawer lists
all available
styles.

Styles Drawer

Copying and pasting formatting

To copy and paste formatting from existing text, follow these steps:

1. **Format text in a certain way, such as changing the fonts and font size.**

2. **Click (or move the cursor) inside the formatted text.**

3. **On the menu bar, choose Format⇨Copy Character Style (or Copy Paragraph Style).**

4. **Select text that you want to format the same way as the text you choose in Step 1.**

5. **On the menu bar, choose Format⇨Paste Character Style (or Paste Paragraph Style).**

Pages copies your style to the text you select in Step 4.

Saving a formatting style

If you format text a certain way repeatedly, you might want to save your formatting as a style that appears in the Styles Drawer. That way, you can choose that style later by clicking on the name of your saved style.

To save your own style in the Styles Drawer, follow these steps:

1. **Format text in a certain way, such as changing the fonts and font size.**

2. **Click (or move the cursor) inside the formatted text.**

3. **Click View⇨Show Styles Drawer to open the Styles Drawer.**

4. **Click the plus sign button in the bottom-left corner of the Styles Drawer.**

   A New Paragraph Style dialog appears.

5. **Type a descriptive name for your style and then click OK.**

   Your style name now appears in the Styles Drawer. The next time you need to use this style, select text and then click this style name in the Styles Drawer.

To delete a style from the Styles Drawer, Control-click the style and then choose Delete Style. When a dialog appears, click the pop-up menu to choose a style to format text currently formatted by the style you want to delete. Then click Replace.

Creating and Placing Text Boxes

Text boxes hold text that you can place anywhere on a page (even in the middle of other text). You can create and place text boxes on both word processing and page layout documents.

Creating a text box

To create a text box, follow these steps:

1. **Choose Insert⇨Text Box on the menu bar or click the Text Box icon.**

   Pages displays a text box, as shown in Figure 1-14.

2. **Type new text inside the text box.**

   Pages keeps your text within the boundaries of the text box.

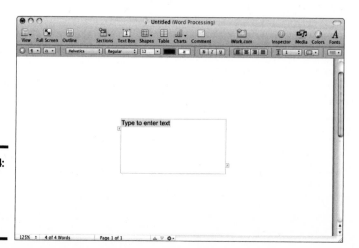

Figure 1-14:
A text box appears in the middle of a page.

Moving a text box

After you create a text box, you'll probably want to move it. To move a text box, follow these steps:

1. **Click a text box to select it.**

A border with handles appears around the text box, as shown in Figure 1-15.

2. **Click and hold down on the text box border and drag the text box to its new location.**

3. **Release the mouse button when you arrive at your destination.**

**Book VI
Chapter 1**

**Creating Documents
with Pages**

Figure 1-15:
A border with handles appears when you click a text box.

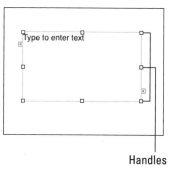

Handles

Resizing a text box

Sometimes a text box is too large or small for the text you type inside. To fix this problem, you can resize a text box by following these steps:

1. **Click anywhere inside the text box.**

2. **Move the pointer to a handle until the pointer turns into a two-way pointing arrow.**

3. **Click and drag a handle to resize the text box.**

4. **Release the mouse button when you're happy with the size of the text box.**

Creating linked text boxes

If you type more text than a text box can display, you see a *Clipping Indicator* icon — it appears as a plus sign inside a square at the bottom of the text box, as shown in Figure 1-16.

When you see the Clipping Indicator at the bottom of a text box, you have two choices. You can resize the text box so it can display more text, as described in the preceding section. This might not always be practical because you might not want to expand a text box.

Alternatively, you can link text boxes. Linked text boxes allow text from one text box to flow into another text box.

Figure 1-16:
The Clipping Indicator appears when a text box is too small to display all the text stored inside.

Clipping Indicator

Linking text boxes

To link text boxes, follow these steps:

1. **Click a text box that displays a Clipping Indicator at the bottom.**

Blue tabs appear on the sides of the text box.

2. **Click the blue tab on the right of the text box.**

A message appears, telling you to click an existing text box or anywhere on the page to create a new text box, as shown in Figure 1-17.

Figure 1-17:
To link a text box, you can click an existing text box or have Pages create a new text box for you automatically.

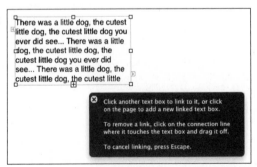

3. **Click an existing text box or click anywhere on the page to create a new text box.**

Pages displays a blue line linking your two text boxes and moves over-flowing text from the first text box to the linked second text box, as shown in Figure 1-18.

Depending on how much text you have, you can link multiple text boxes.

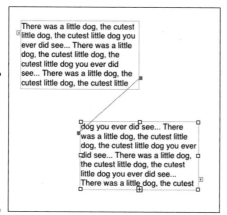

Figure 1-18:
Pages
identifies
linked text
boxes with
a blue
connecting
line.

Unlinking text boxes

After you link two or more text boxes, you might decide you don't want linked text boxes after all. To unlink text boxes, follow these steps:

1. **Click the text box that you want to unlink from another text box.**

2. **Do one of the following:**

- On the menu bar, choose Format⇨Text Box⇨Break Connection into Text Box.

- Move the pointer to the end of the connection line, hold down the mouse button, drag the mouse away from the text box, and then release the mouse button.

When you unlink text boxes, the text fills (and overflows) the first text box, leaving the unlinked text box empty.

Wrapping text around a text box

A new text box often appears near other text. To prevent a text box you add from covering other text, you need to wrap the (already present) text around the new text box. To define how to wrap text around a text box, follow these steps:

1. **Click a text box.**

2. **Click the Inspector icon or choose View⇨Show Inspector on the menu bar.**

   The Inspector icon looks like a little "i" in a blue circle in the upper-right corner of the Pages window. The Inspector window appears.

3. **Click the Wrap Inspector button.**

   It appears to the left of the big "T" button. The Wrap Inspector options appear, as shown in Figure 1-19.

4. **Select the Object Causes Wrap check box.**

5. **Click a text wrap button.**

   The five different text wrap buttons are

   - *Wrap Text on the Left*

   - *Wrap Text Around*

   - *Wrap Text on the Left or Right* (whichever has more space)

   - *Wrap Text Above and Below*

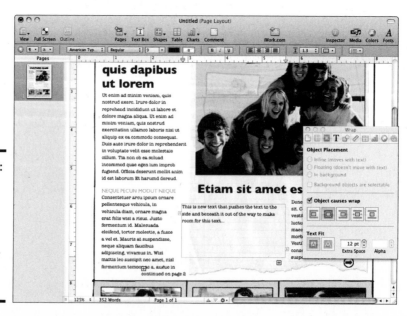

Figure 1-19:
The Wrap Inspector offers different ways text can appear around a text box.

Working with Digital Photographs

If you have digital photographs stored in iPhoto, you can place those pictures directly into a Pages document and manipulate those pictures as well.

Adding a picture

To add a picture from iPhoto into a document, follow these steps:

1. **Click the Media icon on the toolbar.**

   The Media Browser appears.

2. **Click the Photos tab, as shown in Figure 1-20.**

3. **Click and drag a picture from the Media Browser to your document.**

4. **Release the mouse button.**

   Pages displays your chosen image in the document.

**Book VI
Chapter 1**

**Creating Documents
with Pages**

Figure 1-20:
The Photos
tab in the
Media
Browser
lets you
browse
your iPhoto
library.

Moving and resizing a picture

After you place a picture in a document, you might need to resize or move it. To move a picture, follow these steps:

1. **Click and drag the picture to a new position.**

2. **Release the mouse button when you're happy with the new location of the picture.**

To resize a picture, follow these steps:

1. **Click the picture you want to resize.**

   Handles appear around your chosen picture.

2. **Move the pointer to a handle until the pointer turns into a two-way pointing arrow.**

3. **Click and drag the handle to resize your picture.**

4. **Release the mouse button when you're happy with the new size of the picture.**

Modifying a picture

Pages provides two ways to modify the appearance of a picture: Masking and Instant Alpha. *Masking* acts like a cookie cutter and displays only part of an image within a shape. *Instant Alpha* makes part of an image transparent so that you can remove parts of the image, such as the sky in the background.

Masking a picture

To apply a mask over a picture, follow these steps:

1. **Click the picture you want to mask.**

   Handles appear around your chosen picture.

2. **Choose Format⇨Mask (or Format⇨Mask with Shape) on the menu bar and then choose a shape, such as Right Triangle or Star.**

   Your chosen mask appears over your picture, as shown in Figure 1-21.

3. **Move the pointer to the mask handles and then click and drag the handles to resize the mask.**

4. **Move the pointer to the dimmed portion of the picture outside the mask and then click and drag the dimmed part to adjust which part of the picture appears within the mask.**

5. **Click Edit Mask.**

   Pages displays your completed masked picture, as shown in Figure 1-22.

If you drag the slider above the Edit Mask button, you can resize the picture to make it larger or smaller.

REMEMBER

You can apply only one mask to a picture at a time. If you want to apply a different mask to a picture, you must remove the first mask by clicking the masked picture and then choosing Format⇨Unmask from the menu bar.

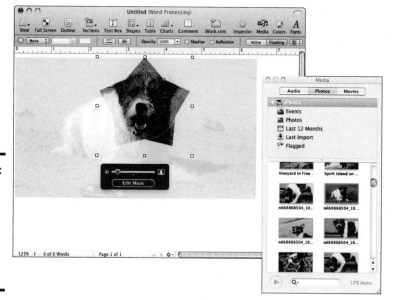

Figure 1-21:
The mask highlights the saved portion of a picture and dims the rest.

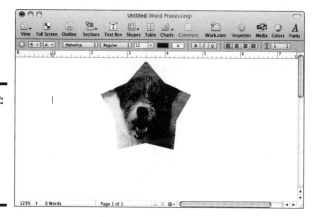

Figure 1-22:
A masked image can display pictures in unusual shapes.

Turning a picture transparent with Instant Alpha

The Instant Alpha feature lets you cut away parts of a picture. For example, if you have a picture of a person's face, you might want to trim away the background image of the wall so you see only the person's face and not the wall.

To use the Instant Alpha feature, follow these steps:

1. Click the picture you want to modify.

Handles appear around your chosen picture.

2. Choose Format⇨Instant Alpha on the menu bar.

A dialog appears over your picture, telling you how to use the Instant Alpha feature.

3. Click and drag your mouse over the portion of your picture that you want to make transparent (such as the sky).

Pages highlights all parts of your picture that are similar in color to the area that you originally pointed to, as shown in Figure 1-23.

4. Release the mouse button when you're happy with the portion of the picture that the Instant Alpha feature has highlighted and turned transparent.

You can use the Instant Alpha feature multiple times to remove different colors from the same picture.

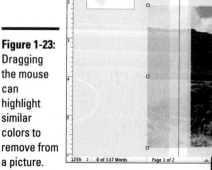

Figure 1-23: Dragging the mouse can highlight similar colors to remove from a picture.

Polishing Your Document

When you finish designing your document, you're ready to show it to the world. Of course, before you show your document to others, you should spell check your document. Fortunately, Pages is happy to help you check a document's spelling. Then you can choose to save your document in a variety of formats to ensure that others can read it.

Spell checking a document

Pages can spell check your entire document, including text trapped inside text boxes and shapes. To spell check an entire document, follow these steps:

1. **Choose Edit⇨Spelling⇨Spelling on the menu bar.**

(If you choose Edit⇨Spelling⇨Check Spelling, Pages highlights misspelled words but doesn't offer any suggestions.)

A dialog appears, highlighting misspelled words and offering possible corrections, as shown in Figure 1-24.

2. **Choose one of the following:**

- *Change:* Changes the misspelled word with the word selected in the list box.

- *Find Next:* Looks for the next misspelled word.

- *Ignore:* Skips the misspelled word.

- *Learn:* Stores the selected word in Pages' dictionary

- *Define:* Launches Mac's Dictionary program, then looks up and displays the word's definition in the Dictionary's main window.

- *Guess:* Offers best-guess word choices.

3. **Click the Close button of the Spelling dialog at any time to make it go away.**

Pages can check your spelling while you type. The moment Pages identifies a misspelled word, it underlines it with a red dotted line. If you Control-click any word underlined with a red dotted line, Pages displays a shortcut menu of correctly spelled words that you can choose. If you want to turn off spell checking while you type, choose Edit⇨Spelling⇨Check Spelling as You Type to clear the check mark in front of this command.

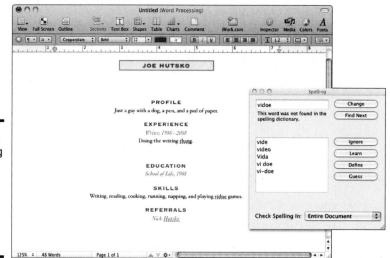

Figure 1-24:
The Spelling dialog lets you pick from a list of correctly spelled words.

It's a good idea to proofread your document even after spell-checking because the spell checker only makes sure the word is correctly spelled. If you type, "I have to dogs," when you really meant to type, "I have two dogs," no spell checker on earth is going to flag that.

Exporting a document

When you choose File⇨Save, Pages saves documents in its own proprietary file format. However, if you want to share your Pages documents with others who don't have the Pages program, you need to export your document into another file format, such as

✦ **PDF:** Saves your document as a series of static pages stored in the PDF Adobe Acrobat file format that can be viewed (but not necessarily edited) by any computer with a PDF viewing program.

✦ **Word:** Saves your document as a Microsoft Word file, which can be opened by any word processor that can read and edit Microsoft Word files.

✦ **RTF:** Saves your document as a Rich Text Format (RTF) file, which many programs can open and edit.

✦ **Plain Text:** Saves your document as text without any formatting or graphic effects.

The PDF file format preserves formatting 100 percent, but doesn't let anyone edit that file unless they use a separate PDF editing program, such as Acrobat Pro. If someone needs to edit your document, both the Word and RTF options preserve Pages documents well. The Plain Text option is useful only if you can't transfer your Pages document to another program as a Word or RTF file.

To export a Pages document, follow these steps:

1. **Choose File⇨Export on the menu bar.**

   A dialog appears, as shown in Figure 1-25.

2. **Select an option, such as Word or RTF, and then click Next.**

3. **In the new dialog that appears, enter a name for your exported document in the Save As text box.**

Figure 1-25:
The Export dialog lets you choose a format to save your Pages document.

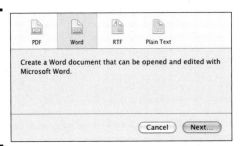

4. **Select the folder where you want to store your presentation.**

   You might need to switch drives or folders until you find where you want to save your file.

5. **Click Export.**

When you export a document, your original Pages document remains untouched in its original location.

Chapter 2: Presenting with Keynote

In This Chapter

- ✔ Creating a presentation
- ✔ Adding and deleting slides
- ✔ Manipulating text
- ✔ Working with graphics
- ✔ Modifying pictures and movies
- ✔ Using transitions and effects
- ✔ Giving a presentation

*I*f you need to inform or convince a group of people about a subject, you often need to make a presentation. Although you could give a presentation just by talking, sometimes it's hard to emphasize certain points and ideas through words alone. That's why you need the presentation program Keynote.

Keynote can take the hassle out of creating, organizing, and giving a presentation so you can concentrate more of your time on talking to an audience and less of your time fumbling around with jammed slide projectors, whiteboards, and felt markers that stain your fingertips.

Best of all, Keynote can spice up your presentation by including audio and visual effects, from playing music and movies to showing visually interesting effects — stuff like text sliding across the display or dissolving away into nothingness. Such effects help get your point across and hold an audience's attention.

Keynote comes as part of the iWork suite. Your Mac might come with a trial version of iWork, which lets you try Keynote to see whether you might find it useful before you lay out money to buy it.

Creating a Presentation

An entire Keynote presentation consists of one or more slides, where each slide displays information to make a single point. Each slide typically contains text, as shown in Figure 2-1, although graphics, video, and audio can make an appearance as well.

To make your slides more interesting to watch, you can also add *transition* effects that appear when you switch from one slide to another. To emphasize the information on a particular slide, you can add individual visual effects to specific items, such as making text rotate or making a graphic image glide across the screen and halt in place.

The basic steps to creating a presentation in Keynote involve

1. Picking a theme to use for your presentation.
2. Creating one or more slides.
3. Typing text or placing graphics on each slide.
4. (Optional) Adding an audio or video file to each slide.
5. (Optional) Adding visual effects to animate an entire slide or just the text or graphics that appear on that slide.

The rest of this chapter goes into detail about each of these steps.

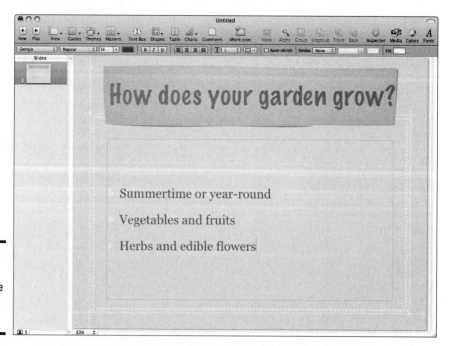

Figure 2-1:
The appearance of a typical slide.

Choosing a Theme for a New Presentation

A presentation consists of multiple slides. Although you could create a generic presentation where plain black text appears against a white background, this can be boring. To spice up your presentation, Keynote provides predesigned background graphics called *themes*, which provide a consistent appearance for your slides, such as the font, size, style, and background color.

To pick a theme, follow these steps:

1. **Double-click the Keynote icon in the Applications folder or click the Keynote icon in the Dock (or choose File⇨New on the menu bar if Keynote is already running).**

The Theme Chooser dialog opens, as shown in Figure 2-2.

2. **Click a theme and then click the Choose button or double-click a theme.**

Keynote creates the first slide of your presentation using your chosen theme. At this point, you can add text, graphics, audio, or video to the slide or you can add new slides.

If you want to change your theme after you open a new presentation, click the Themes icon on the Keynote toolbar and choose a different theme.

Figure 2-2:
Keynote
provides
a variety
of themes
for your
presen-
tations.

Changing Presentation Views

After you create a presentation, Keynote offers four ways to view a presentation:

+ **Navigator:** Useful for editing individual slides and manipulating all the slides in an entire presentation.

+ **Outline:** Useful for viewing and editing just the text that appears on slides, as shown in Figure 2-3.

    Note: In the Navigator and Outline views, the Slide Organizer appears to the left of the individual slide being viewed or edited.

+ **Slide Only:** Useful for editing the text and graphics of a single slide, as shown in Figure 2-4.

+ **Light Table:** Useful for manipulating a large number of slides in a presentation, as shown in Figure 2-5.

To switch to a different view, choose the View icon on the Keynote toolbar and then choose Navigator, Outline, Slide Only, or Light Table.

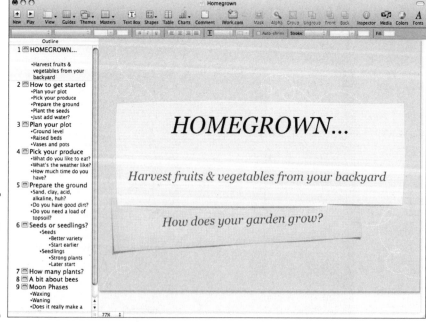

Figure 2-3:
Outline view helps you edit text without the distraction of graphics.

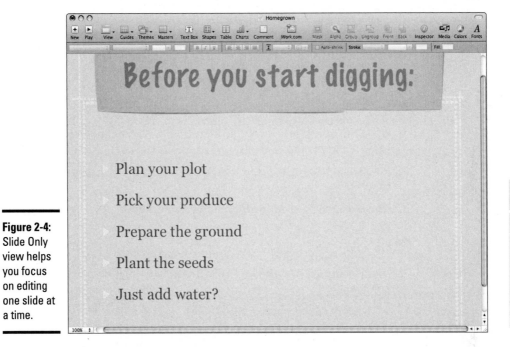

Figure 2-4:
Slide Only view helps you focus on editing one slide at a time.

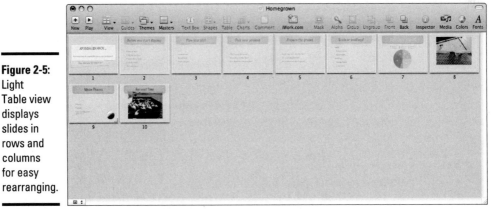

Figure 2-5:
Light Table view displays slides in rows and columns for easy rearranging.

Working with Slides

When you create a new presentation, that presentation contains just one slide. Because you usually need more than one slide to create a presentation, you probably want to add more slides. If you go overboard and add too many slides, you can always winnow a few.

When working with slides, you often need to select multiple slides in the Slide Organizer pane or the Light Table view. Hold down the ⌘ key to click and select multiple slides. Hold down the Shift key and click two different slides to select a range of slides.

Adding a slide

To add a slide to a presentation, follow these steps:

1. Click a slide in the Slide Organizer pane or the Light Table view.

Your new slide appears directly after the slide that you click and has the same theme.

2. Choose one of the following to add a new slide:

- Click the New (+) icon.

- Choose Slide⇨New Slide on the menu bar.

- Click a slide in the Slide Organizer pane or Light Table view and then press Return.

- Control-click a slide in the Slide Organizer pane and then choose New Slide.

Using Masters

Each Keynote theme has a selection of slide layouts, or Masters, already designed, which use the colors and style of the theme. To use Masters associated with a theme, follow these steps:

1. Click a slide in any of the views.

2. Click the Masters icon on the Keynote toolbar and then choose the template for the type of slide you want to create.

For example, you might choose Title & Bullets or Photo – Vertical.

Rearranging slides

Keynote displays slides in the order they appear in the Slide Organizer. The top slide appears first, followed by the slide directly beneath it, and so on. After you create two or more slides in a presentation, you might want to rearrange their positions.

To rearrange slides in a presentation, follow these steps:

1. Choose one of the following:

- View⇨Navigator (Displays slides vertically in the Slide Organizer pane.)

- View⇨Light Table (Displays slides in rows and columns.)

2. **Click and drag a slide in the Slide Organizer pane (or Light Table view) to its new position.**

   In Navigator view, Keynote displays a horizontal line with a downward-pointing arrow to show you where your slide will appear when you release the mouse button, as shown in Figure 2-6. In Light Table view, Keynote moves slide icons out of the way to show you where your new slide will appear.

3. **Release the mouse button when you're happy with the new position of the slide in your presentation.**

Deleting a slide

Eventually, you might find that you don't need a slide anymore. To delete a slide, go to the Slide Organizer pane or Light Table view, select the slide(s) that you want to delete, and then choose one of the following:

✦ Press Delete.

✦ Choose Edit⇨Delete on the menu bar.

✦ Control-click a slide in the Slide Organizer pane and then choose Delete.

If you delete a slide by mistake, choose Edit⇨Undo Delete on the menu bar (or press ⌘+Z).

**Book VI
Chapter 2**

**Presenting with
Keynote**

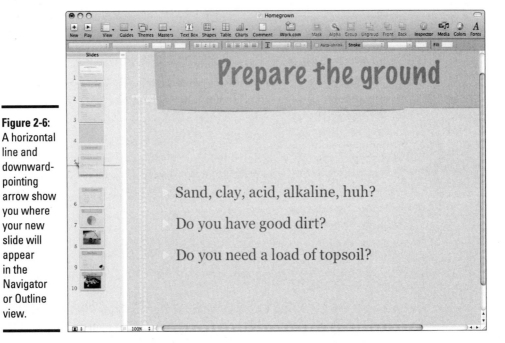

Figure 2-6:
A horizontal line and downward-pointing arrow show you where your new slide will appear in the Navigator or Outline view.

Manipulating Text

Text appears on a slide in a text box. Most slides contain two text boxes, where the top text box defines the title of a slide and the bottom text box displays the bullet points of a slide (refer to Figure 2-1).

The title of a slide typically defines the purpose of the slide, and the bullet points underneath provide supporting ideas. A slide can have only one Title text box and one Bullet Point text box, but each Bullet Point text box can contain multiple bullet points.

Editing text

Initially, every slide contains an empty Title text box and an empty Bullet Point text box, but you'll want to replace these items with your own words and bullets. To place text on a slide, follow these steps:

1. **Choose View⇨Navigator on the menu bar.**

2. **In the Slide Organizer pane, click the slide that you want to edit.**

   Your chosen slide appears.

3. **Double-click the placeholder text that appears in the Title or Bullet Point text box.**

4. **Type text or use the arrow keys and Delete key to edit existing text.**

To ensure you don't give a presentation filled with typos and misspelled words, check the spelling in your presentation by choosing Edit⇨Spelling⇨Spelling.

Formatting text

After you create text, you can format it by changing fonts, font size, or color. Formatting sets the tone of your presentation — upbeat, serious, fun, or businesslike.

Use fonts and colors sparingly. Using too many fonts or colors can make text harder to read. When choosing colors, make sure you use colors that contrast with the slide's background color. For instance, light yellow text against a white background is nearly impossible to read.

Changing fonts

To change the font of text, follow these steps:

1. **In the Slide Organizer pane, select the slide that contains the text you want to modify.**

2. **Double-click the text box that contains the text you want to modify.**

3. **Click and drag to highlight the text you want to format, or hold down the Shift key while pressing the arrow keys.**

4. **Click the Fonts icon on the Keynote toolbar.**

   The Fonts pane appears, as shown in Figure 2-7.

Figure 2-7:
The Fonts pane lets you choose a font to modify text.

Changing colors

To change the color of text, follow these steps:

1. **In the Slide Organizer pane, click the slide that contains the text you want to modify.**

2. **Double-click the text box that contains the text you want to color.**

3. **Click and drag to highlight the text you want to format or hold down the Shift key while pressing the arrow keys.**

4. **Click the Colors icon on the Keynote toolbar.**

   The Colors window appears, as shown in Figure 2-8.

Figure 2-8:
The Colors window lets you choose a text color.

5. **Click the desired color in the color wheel that appears in the Colors window.**

   Keynote immediately uses your selected color to color the text you select in Step 3.

The top of the Colors window provides a variety of different color pickers that display colors as sliders, color spectrums, or even crayons. So if you don't like the color wheel, click a different color picker and use that one.

Adding a chart

Sometimes presenting your information as a chart makes your information easier to understand. To add a chart to a presentation, follow these steps:

1. **Create a new slide or click an existing slide in the Slide Organizer or Light Table view.**

2. **Click Insert⇨Chart from the menu bar, or click the Charts icon on the Keynote toolbar, and then choose the type of chart you want to create — bar, pie, 2-D or 3-D, for example.**

   A chart appears and the Chart Inspector opens along with the Chart Data Editor, as shown in Figure 2-9.

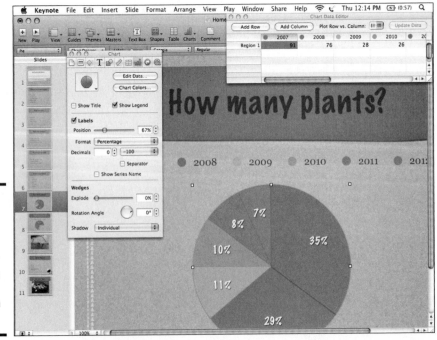

Figure 2-9: The Inspector and Chart Data Editor open when you insert a chart to a slide.

3. **Click the chart on the slide and the Inspector and Chart Data Editor become active.**

4. **Double-click the Row and Column field headers of the Chart Data Editor to select the placeholder text and enter the information you want on your chart.**

5. **Click the cells below the headers to enter the number values you want the chart to show.**

   The data entered appears in the chart and titles on the slide.

6. **Click the Format pop-up menu of the Chart Inspector to choose how you want the data to appear, such as a number or a percentage.**

   If you decide that you want to remove a chart, click it and press Delete.

**Book VI
Chapter 2**

Presenting with
Keynote

Adding Media Files

Text by itself can be as monotonous and confusing to read as the flight arrival and departure displays at an airport. To make your presentation more appealing and communicative, add sound, pictures, and movies. Sound can be an audio recording of a song stored in iTunes or edited in GarageBand; pictures can be digital photographs stored in iPhoto; and movies can be short video clips you've edited and stored in iMovie.

Adding sound

You can add any audio file stored in iTunes or GarageBand. To add sound to a slide, follow these steps:

1. **In the Slide Organizer pane, click the slide where you want to play an audio file.**

2. **Click the Media icon on the Keynote toolbar.**

   The Media Browser appears.

3. **Click the Audio tab.**

   The Media Browser displays the iTunes and GarageBand folders, as shown in Figure 2-10.

4. **Click the iTunes or GarageBand folder.**

   The bottom section of the Media Browser displays all the available files you can choose.

Figure 2-10:
The Audio
pane in
the Media
Browser
lets you
choose an
audio file
from iTunes
or Garage
Band.

5. **Click and drag an audio file from the Media Browser to your slide and then release the mouse button.**

   Keynote displays an audio icon directly on your slide to let you know that when this slide appears in your presentation, it will automatically play your chosen audio file.

6. **Click the Close button of the Media Browser.**

Although the audio icon appears when you edit a Keynote presentation, it won't appear when you show your presentation.

Adding iPhoto pictures

If you store digital pictures in iPhoto, you can paste those pictures on any slide in a Keynote presentation by following these steps:

1. **In the Slide Organizer pane, click the slide where you want to add a picture.**

2. **Click the Media icon on the Keynote toolbar.**

   The Media Browser appears.

3. **Click the Photos tab.**

   The Media Browser displays all the pictures stored in iPhoto, as shown in Figure 2-11.

Figure 2-11:
The Photos
pane in
the Media
Browser
lets you
choose a
picture from
iPhoto.

4. **Click and drag a picture from the Media Browser to your slide and then release the mouse.**

Your chosen picture appears on your slide.

5. **Click the Close button of the Media Browser.**

Adding iMovie videos

If you download, edit, and save digital videos, you can paste those movies on any slide. When you give your presentation, the movie will play automatically. To add a movie to a slide, follow these steps:

1. **In the Slide Organizer pane, click the slide where you want to play a video.**

2. **Click the Media icon on the Keynote toolbar.**

The Media Browser appears.

3. **Click the Movies tab.**

The Media Browser displays all the movies stored in your Movies folder, as shown in Figure 2-12.

4. **Click and drag a movie file from the Media Browser to your slide and then release the mouse.**

Your chosen movie appears on your slide.

5. **Click the Close button of the Media Browser.**

Figure 2-12:
The Movies
pane in
the Media
Browser
lets you add
a movie to a
slide.

Editing Pictures and Movies

After you paste a picture or movie to a slide, you can always move, resize, or modify that addition. Moving and resizing a picture or movie lets you place a picture or movie in the exact spot you want it to appear on a slide. Modifying the picture lets you correct an image and create unusual visual effects.

Moving and resizing a picture or movie

To move or resize a picture or movie, follow these steps:

1. **In the Slide Organizer pane, click the slide where you want to move or resize a picture or movie.**

2. **Click the picture or movie.**

   Handles appear around your chosen picture or movie.

3. **To move a picture or movie, place the cursor over the middle of the image, click and drag the picture or movie to a new location on the slide, and then release the mouse button.**

4. **To resize a picture or movie, click and drag a handle to resize the picture or movie and then release the mouse button.**

Holding down the Shift key while resizing a picture or movie retains the height and width proportions.

Modifying a picture

Keynote provides two ways to modify the appearance of a picture: Masking and Instant Alpha. *Masking* lets you display just a portion of an image, such as an oval or star-shaped area. *Instant Alpha* lets you make part of an image transparent so that the background of a slide can be seen through an image.

Masking a picture

A mask acts like a cookie cutter that you plop over a picture to save anything *inside* the cookie cutter shape but hide anything *outside* the shape. Keynote provides a rectangular mask and a variety of other shaped masks, such as ovals, stars, arrows, and triangles.

To apply a mask on a picture, follow these steps:

1. **In the Slide Organizer pane, click the slide that contains the picture you want to mask.**

2. **Click the picture you want to mask.**

   Handles appear around your chosen picture.

3. **Choose Format⇨Mask on the menu bar (or Format⇨Mask with Shape) and then choose a shape, such as Polygon or Diamond.**

   Your chosen mask appears over your picture, as shown in Figure 2-13.

Figure 2-13:
The mask highlights the saved portion of a picture and dims the rest.

4. **Click and drag a mask handle to resize the mask.**

   Holding down the Shift key while dragging a mask handle retains the height and width aspect ratio.

5. **Move the pointer to the dimmed portion of the picture outside the mask and then drag the dimmed portion to adjust which part of the picture appears within the mask.**

6. **Click the Edit Mask button.**

   Keynote masks your picture, as shown in Figure 2-14.

You can apply only one mask on a picture at a time. If you want to apply a different mask over a picture, you must remove the first mask by choosing Format⇨Unmask.

Making a picture transparent with Instant Alpha

Keynote's Instant Alpha feature lets you remove a portion of a picture. This can create unusual visual effects by stripping unwanted portions of a picture and keeping the parts you like.

Figure 2-14:
A masked image can create an unusual visual effect on a slide.

To use the Instant Alpha feature, follow these steps:

1. **In the Slide Organizer pane, click the slide that contains the picture you want to modify.**

2. **Click the picture you want to modify.**

   Handles appear around your chosen picture.

3. **Choose Format⇨Instant Alpha on the menu bar (or click the Alpha icon on the Keynote toolbar).**

   A dialog appears over your picture, telling you how to use the Instant Alpha feature.

4. **Place the pointer over the portion of your picture that you want to make transparent (such as the dirt) and then drag the mouse.**

   Keynote highlights all parts of your picture that are similar in color to the area that you originally pointed to, as shown in Figure 2-15.

5. **Release the mouse button when you're happy with the portion of the picture that the Instant Alpha feature has highlighted and made transparent.**

Figure 2-15:
Dragging
the mouse
highlights
similar
colors to
eliminate.

You can use the Instant Alpha feature multiple times to remove different colors from the same picture. If you make a mistake, choose Edit⇨Undo Instant Alpha on the menu bar or press ⌘+Z.

Creating Transitions and Effects

To make your presentations visually interesting to watch, you can add transitions and effects. Slide transitions define how a slide appears and disappears from the display. Text and graphic effects define how the text or graphic initially appears on or disappears from the slide and how it moves around a slide.

Creating a slide transition

To create a slide transition, follow these steps:

1. **Choose View⇨Navigator on the menu bar.**

2. **In the Slide Organizer pane, click the slide that you want to display with a transition.**

3. **On the menu bar, choose View⇨Show Inspector (or click the Inspector icon).**

An Inspector window appears.

4. **Click the Slide Inspector icon (shown in Figure 2-16) in the Inspector window and then click the Transition tab.**

Slide Inspector icon

Figure 2-16: The Transition tab in the Slide Inspector lets you define a transition.

5. **Click the Effect pop-up menu and then choose an effect, such as Shimmer or Confetti.**

    The Magic Move effect animates an object, moving it from its location on one slide to a new location on the next slide. The object must be the same on both slides. Place the object at the starting point on the first slide and then on the end point on the second slide. The Magic Move feature moves the object when the slide transitions from the first slide to the second slide.

    The Slide Inspector gives you a preview of what your transition will look like.

    Choose None in the Effect pop-up menu to remove a transition.

Book VI
Chapter 2

6. **(Optional) Depending on the transition effect you choose, you might need to define other options, such as the direction or duration of your transition.**

7. **Click the Close button of the Inspector window.**

Presenting with
Keynote

Creating text and graphic effects

Keynote offers three ways to create text and graphic effects:

+ **Build In:** Defines how text and graphics enter a slide. (If you choose the Build In transition, initially, the text and graphics won't appear on the slide.)

+ **Build Out:** Defines how text and graphics exit a slide.

+ **Action:** Defines how text and graphics move on a slide.

To define an effect for text or graphics, follow these steps:

1. **Choose View⇨Navigator on the menu bar.**

2. **In the Slide Organizer pane, click the slide that contains the text or graphic you want to display with a visual effect.**

3. **Click the text or graphic you want to modify.**

    Handles appear around your chosen text or graphic.

4. **Choose View⇨Show Inspector on the menu bar or click the Inspector icon.**

    An Inspector window appears.

5. **Click the Build Inspector tab in the Inspector window.**

    The Build Inspector appears, as shown in Figure 2-17.

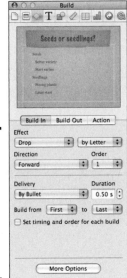

Figure 2-17:
The Build Inspector pane lets you choose an effect for text or graphics on a slide.

6. **Click the Build In, Build Out, or Action tab.**

7. **Choose an option from the Effect pop-up menu.**

   Rotate and Opacity are nice choices.

8. **(Optional) Depending on the effect you choose, you might be able to choose additional ways to modify that effect.**

9. **Click the Close button of the Inspector window.**

Making text and graphics move on a slide

If you choose the Action button for text or graphics, you can choose the Move Effect, which lets you define a line that the text or graphic follows as it moves across a slide. To define a line to move text or graphics on a slide, follow these steps:

1. **Choose View⇨Navigator on the menu bar.**

2. **In the Slide Organizer pane, click the slide that contains the text or graphic you want to display with a visual effect.**

3. **Click the text or graphic you want to modify.**

   Handles appear around your chosen text or graphic.

4. **Choose View⇨Show Inspector on the menu bar or click the Inspector icon.**

   An Inspector window appears.

5. **Click the Build Inspector tab.**

The Build Inspector appears (refer to Figure 2-17).

6. **Click the Action tab.**

7. **Choose Move from the Effect pop-up menu.**

Keynote displays a red line that shows how your chosen text or graphic will move, as shown in Figure 2-18.

8. **(Optional) Click and drag the handle at the beginning or end of the red line to move the line or change the line length.**

Moving the red line changes the direction your chosen text or graphic moves. Changing the line length determines how far your chosen text or graphic moves.

9. **(Optional) Click the Straight Line or Curved Line button under the Path heading in the Inspector window to change how your object moves.**

10. **Click the Close button of the Inspector window.**

The Action feature moves an object or text on a slide. The Magic Move feature animates objects or text from one slide to the next during the slide transition.

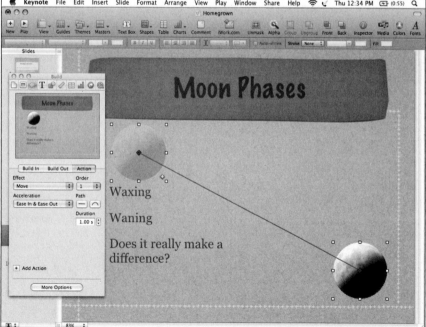

Figure 2-18:
Keynote displays the path connecting text or graphics on a slide.

Book VI
Chapter 2

Presenting with Keynote

Polishing Your Presentation

When you finish modifying the slides in your presentation, you'll need to show your presentation to others. You might give a presentation in person or just pass out your presentation to others so they can view it at their leisure.

Viewing a presentation

After you finish creating a presentation, you need to view it to see how it actually looks. The slide order or visual effects might have looked good when you put your presentation together, but when viewed in its entirety, you might suddenly notice gaps in your presentation. To view a presentation, follow these steps:

1. **In the Slide Organizer pane, click the first slide you want to view.**

If you click the first slide of your presentation, you'll view your entire presentation. If you click a slide in the middle of your presentation, your slideshow begins from that slide and proceeds until it reaches the last slide.

2. **Click the Play icon on the Keynote toolbar or choose Play⇨Play Slideshow on the menu bar.**

The slide you choose in Step 1 appears.

3. **Click the mouse button or press the spacebar to view each successive slide.**

If you're at the last slide of your presentation, clicking the mouse button or pressing the spacebar exits your presentation.

4. **(Optional) Press Esc if you want to stop viewing your presentation before reaching the last slide.**

Rehearsing a presentation

Viewing a presentation lets you make sure that all the slides are in the right order and that all effects and transitions work as you expect. Before giving your presentation, you might want to rehearse it and let Keynote approximate how much time you spend on each slide.

Rehearsing can give you only a guess of the time needed to give your presentation. In real life, the audience and conditions, for example an impatient audience sitting in a stuffy conference room where the air conditioning suddenly breaks down, might make you nervous or speed up your timing.

To rehearse a presentation, follow these steps:

1. **Choose View⇨Navigator on the menu bar.**

2. **In the Slide Organizer pane, click the first slide you want to view.**

3. **Choose Play⇨Rehearse Slideshow on the menu bar.**

   Keynote displays your slides with a timer underneath, as shown in Figure 2-19.

4. **Practice what you're going to say when presenting each slide and then press the spacebar or click the mouse button to advance to the next slide.**

Exporting a presentation

When you give a presentation, you'll probably do it directly from your Mac. However, there might come a time when you need to save your presentation to run on a different type of computer. Fortunately, Keynote lets you save (or *export*) a Keynote presentation in one of the following file formats:

✦ **QuickTime:** Saves your presentation as a movie that can play on a Windows PC or Mac computer that has the free QuickTime player. This movie preserves all transitions and visual effects.

✦ **PowerPoint:** Saves your presentation as a PowerPoint file that you can edit and run on any computer that runs PowerPoint. (Certain visual effects and transitions might not work in PowerPoint.)

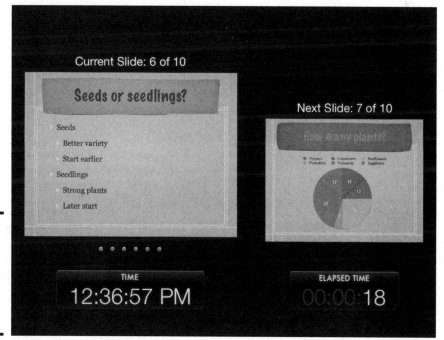

Figure 2-19:
Keynote tracks how much time you spend on each slide.

✦ **PDF:** Saves your presentation as a series of static images stored in the Adobe Acrobat portable document file format that can be viewed by any computer with a PDF viewing program. Any interesting visual or transition effects between slides will be lost.

✦ **Images:** Saves each slide as a separate graphic file.

✦ **HTML:** Saves each slide as a separate Web page. Any interesting visual or transition effects between slides will be lost.

✦ **iPod:** Saves your presentation as a movie specially designed to play on an iPod.

If you want to preserve your visual effects and transitions, save your presentation as a QuickTime or iPod movie. If you want to preserve and edit your presentation on a Windows PC running Microsoft PowerPoint, save your presentation as a PowerPoint file.

To export a Keynote presentation, follow these steps:

1. **Choose File⇨Export on the menu bar.**

   A dialog appears, as shown in Figure 2-20.

2. **Click an option, such as the QuickTime or PowerPoint icon.**

3. **(Optional) Depending on the option you choose in Step 2, you might see additional ways to customize your presentation.**

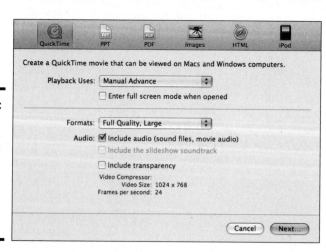

Figure 2-20: The Export dialog lets you choose a format to save your Keynote presentation.

4. Click Next.

Another dialog appears, showing all the drives and folders on your hard drive.

5. Click the folder where you want to store your presentation.

You might need to switch drives or folders until you find where you want to save your file.

6. Click the Export button.

When you export a presentation, your original Keynote presentation remains untouched in its original location.

Chapter 3: Crunching with Numbers

In This Chapter

✔ **Getting to know the Numbers spreadsheet**

✔ **Creating a spreadsheet**

✔ **Using sheets**

✔ **Working with tables**

✔ **Working with charts**

✔ **Polishing a spreadsheet**

✔ **Sharing your spreadsheet efforts**

*N*umbers is a spreadsheet program designed to help you manipulate and calculate numbers for a wide variety of tasks, such as balancing a budget, calculating a loan, and creating an invoice. The Numbers program also lets you create line, bar, and pie charts that graphically help you analyze and understand what your data means.

Understanding the Parts of a Numbers Spreadsheet

A Numbers spreadsheet consists of one or more *sheets,* which are completely blank like an empty sheet of lined paper made up of rows and columns. The intersection of a row and column is a *cell,* which is where you type and store numbers, text, and formulas, as shown in Figure 3-1.

Besides the mundane but fundamental cells that act as the backbone of any spreadsheet, you can also place the following eye-catching (and useful) items in your spreadsheets, as shown in Figure 3-2:

✦ Tables

✦ Charts

✦ Text boxes

✦ Pictures

A *table* consists of rows and columns that can contain words, numbers, calculated results, or a combination of all two or all three of these types of contents.

Cell

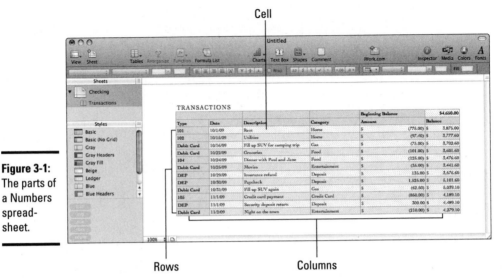

Figure 3-1:
The parts of a Numbers spreadsheet.

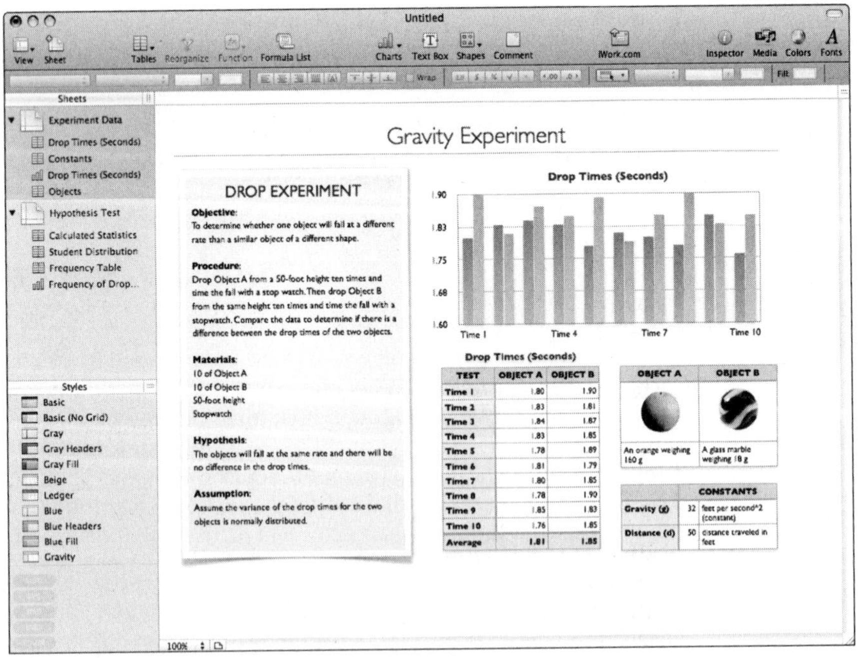

Figure 3-2:
The parts of a table.

A *chart* displays data stored in a table. Common types of charts are line, bar, pie, and column charts, as shown in Figure 3-3. With Numbers, you can build 2-axis and mixed charts, too.

Figure 3-3:
Numbers
can create
different
types of
charts to
help you
visualize the
meaning of
your data.

Text boxes and *pictures* serve mostly decorative functions. In a text box, you type and store text independent of the rows and columns in a table. With pictures, you add decorative images on a sheet, such as a company logo. Numbers helps you manipulate numbers and present your information in a visually appealing way.

Putting together a spreadsheet is a simple process. The following list points out the highlights:

✦ **Start with a sheet.** When you create a new Numbers file, either from scratch or by using a template, Numbers automatically creates one sheet with one table on it. Your job is to fill that table with data. Add more tables — yes, a sheet can hold multiple tables — or start spicing up your data presentation with charts or pictures. (More on that later.)

✦ **Fill a table with numbers and text.** After setting up at least one table on a sheet, you can move the table around on the sheet and/or resize it. When you're happy with the table's position on the sheet and the table's size, you can start typing numbers into the table's rows and columns. Don't forget to type titles for your rows and columns to identify what those numbers mean, such as "August Sales" or "Screwdrivers Sold."

✦ **Create formulas and use functions.** After you type numbers in a table along with titles, you'll want to manipulate one or more numbers in certain ways, such as adding a column of numbers. Numbers offers a slew of predefined functions to take your numbers and calculate a result, such as how much your company made in sales last month or how a salesperson's sales results have changed.

Formulas not only calculate useful results, but they also let you enter hypothetical numbers to see possible results. For example, if every salesperson improved his or her sales results by 5 percent every month, how much profit increase would that bring to the company? By typing in different values, you can ask, "What if?" questions with your data and formulas.

✦ **Visualizing data with charts.** Just glancing at a dozen numbers in a row or column might not show you much of anything. By turning numeric data into line, bar, or pie charts, Numbers can help you spot trends in your data.

✦ **Polish your sheets.** Most spreadsheets consist of rows and columns of numbers with a bit of descriptive text thrown in for good measure. Although functional, such spreadsheets are boring to look at. That's why Numbers gives you the chance to place text boxes and pictures on your sheets to make your information (tables and charts) compelling.

Creating a Numbers Spreadsheet

To help you create a spreadsheet, Numbers provides 30 templates that you can use as-is or modify. If you prefer, you can use the Blank template to create a spreadsheet (one sheet with one table) from scratch. If you design a particularly useful spreadsheet, you can even save it (by choosing File⇨Save as Template) as a template to use in the future.

To create a spreadsheet based on a template, follow these steps:

1. **Double-click the Numbers icon in the Applications folder or click the Numbers icon in the Dock (or choose File⇨New on the menu bar if Numbers is already running).**

The Template Chooser dialog opens, as shown in Figure 3-4.

2. **Click a template category in the list on the left, double-click the template that you want to use, or click a particular template displayed in the main pane, and then click Choose.**

Numbers opens your chosen template, which you can fill in with rows and columns of numbers you want to calculate, or text you want to associate with numbers that you want to sort by alphabetical order, or by highest to lowest number, or the other way around.

If you want to start with a blank spreadsheet, click the Blank template in the list on the left.

Figure 3-4: Numbers provides a variety of spreadsheet templates organized into categories, such as Personal or Business.

Working with Sheets

Every Numbers spreadsheet needs at least one sheet. A sheet acts like a limitless page that can hold any number of tables and charts. Ideally, you should use sheets to organize the information in your spreadsheet, such as using one sheet to hold January sales results, a second sheet to hold February sales results, and a third sheet to hold a line chart that shows each salesperson's results for the first two months.

To help organize your sheets, Numbers stores the names of all your sheets in the Sheets pane on the left. Indented underneath each sheet is a list of all tables and charts stored on that particular sheet.

To view the contents of a specific sheet, click that sheet name in the Sheets pane. To view a particular table or chart, find the sheet that contains that table or chart. Then click that specific table or chart.

Adding a sheet

You can always add another sheet if you need one. When you add a sheet, Numbers creates one table on that sheet automatically. To add a sheet, choose one of the following:

✦ Choose Insert⇨Sheet on the menu bar.

✦ Control-click anywhere inside the Sheets pane and choose New Sheet.

✦ Click the Sheet icon that appears above the Sheets pane.

Deleting a sheet

If you need a sheet to go away, clear out, disappear, whatever, you can delete it. When you delete a sheet, you also delete any tables or charts stored on that sheet. To delete a sheet, follow these steps:

1. **Click the sheet you want to delete in the Sheets pane.**

2. **Choose one of the following:**

- Press the Delete key.

- Control-click a sheet name and then choose Delete Sheet.

- Choose Edit⇨Delete on the menu bar.

A dialog appears, asking whether you really want to delete the sheet.

3. **Click Delete (or Cancel).**

Adding a table or chart

A sheet can hold one or more tables and charts. When you add a table or chart, the table or chart is blank. To add a table or chart, follow these steps:

1. **In the Sheets pane, click the sheet where you want to add a table or chart.**

2. **Choose one of the following and select an option:**

- Click the Tables icon (or choose Insert⇨Table on the menu bar). The Tables menu appears, as shown in Figure 3-5.

- Click the Charts icon (or choose Insert⇨Chart on the menu bar). The Charts menu appears, as shown in Figure 3-6.

Figure 3-5: The Tables menu lists different types of tables you can add.

Deleting a table or chart

When you create a table or chart, you don't have to keep it forever. Keep in mind, though, that when you delete a table, Numbers deletes all data (numbers, text, and formulas) stored on that table. If you created a chart that depends on those numbers you deleted, your chart will no longer display whatever information it displayed before you deleted the table.

Figure 3-6:
The Charts menu lists different types of charts you can add.

To delete a table or chart, follow these steps:

1. **In the Sheets pane, click the table or chart you want to delete.**

2. **Choose one of the following:**

  • Press the Delete key.

  • Control-click a table or chart and then choose Delete.

  • Choose Edit⇨Delete on the menu bar.

Naming sheets, tables, and charts

Numbers gives each sheet, table, and chart a generic name, such as Sheet 2, Table 1, or Chart 3. To help you better understand the type of information stored on each sheet, table, and chart, use more descriptive names, especially when you add multiple tables and charts (which you find out about later in this chapter).

To name a sheet, table, or chart in the Sheets pane, follow these steps:

1. **Choose one of the following:**

   • Double-click a sheet, table, or chart name.

   • Control-click a sheet, table, or chart name and then choose Rename.

2. **Type a new name or use the arrow keys and the Delete key to edit an existing name.**

Setting Up Tables

Just as you set the dinner table to accommodate the number and size of your guests — remember the children's table at Thanksgiving? — you set your Numbers table to accommodate your data. You define the number of rows and columns your table needs based on the quantity of data you have to enter. You set the row height and column width based on the kind of data you have as well as the font style and size you choose.

Adding rows and columns

When you add a table to a sheet, Numbers opens a table that's four columns by ten rows. This may be too small, or too big, for your data. If you know you want a bigger — or smaller — table, you use the Resize corner to add or subtract rows and columns. Just follow these steps:

1. **In the Sheets pane, click the table that you want to resize.**

   Numbers displays your selected table with handles around it.

2. **Click anywhere inside the table.**

   The table displays column and row headings, a Move corner (in the upper-left corner of the table), and a Resize corner (in the bottom-right corner of the table), as shown in Figure 3-7.

3. **Move the pointer to the Resize corner in the bottom-right corner of the table.**

4. **Click and drag the Resize corner to resize the table on the sheet.**

   While you drag the Resize corner, you add (or delete) rows or columns or both.

5. **Release the mouse button when you're happy with the table's number of rows and columns.**

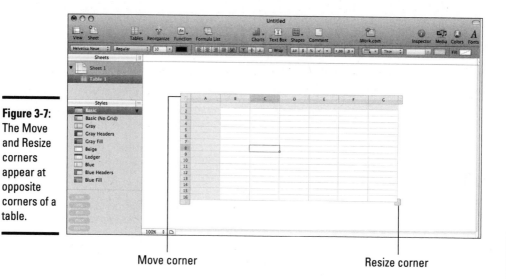

Figure 3-7:
The Move
and Resize
corners
appear at
opposite
corners of a
table.

Move corner   Resize corner

Inserting a row or column

You're entering your data and suddenly you realize you need to add a row or column in the middle of your table. No sweat.

To add a row or column in the middle of a table, click a cell where you want to insert another row or column, choose Table and then choose one of the following from the Table menu:

+ **Add Row Above:** Inserts a new row directly above the selected cell.

+ **Add Row Below:** Inserts a new row directly below the selected cell.

+ **Add Column Before:** Inserts a new column to the left of the selected cell.

+ **Add Column After:** Inserts a new column to the right of the selected cell.

To insert multiple columns or rows, highlight two or more column or row headings to equal the number of rows and columns you want to add, click the Table menu, and then choose Add Columns Before/After or Add Rows Above/Below.

If you move the pointer to a row or column heading (such as column D or row 5), a downward-pointing arrow appears, which you can click to display a menu. From this menu, you can choose any of the options in the preceding list.

Deleting a row or column

To delete a row or column, choose one of the following:

✦ Click a cell inside the row or column you want to delete and then choose Table⇨Delete Row (or Delete Column).

✦ Control-click a cell inside the row or column you want to delete, and then choose Delete Row (or Delete Column) from the shortcut menu.

✦ Move the pointer over the row or column heading (such as column A or row 3), click the downward-pointing arrow that appears, and then choose Delete Row (or Delete column).

You can delete multiple columns or rows by highlighting those column or row headings, clicking the Table menu, and then choosing Delete Columns or Delete Rows.

Resizing rows and columns

Just as a new table opens with ten rows and four columns, the cells in those rows and columns have preset widths and heights. However, a small cell might not show all the information stored in that cell. To fix this problem, you can resize rows and columns.

Resizing the fast way

To resize a row or column using the mouse, follow these steps:

1. **Move the pointer to the border between two row or column headings, such as between columns A and B.**

The pointer turns into a two-way pointing arrow around a vertical or horizontal line.

2. **Click and drag the mouse up/down or right/left to resize the row or column.**

3. **Release the mouse button when you're happy with the size of your row or column.**

If you have data stored inside a row or column, Numbers can automatically resize the row or column to fit the largest item stored in that row or column. To resize a row or column, click a cell inside the row or column you want to resize and choose Table⇨Resize Columns to Fit Content (or Resize Rows to Fit Content).

Resizing the precise way

If you want to resize a row or column to a specific height or width, follow these steps:

1. **Click a cell inside the row or column you want to resize.**

2. **Choose View⇨Inspector on the menu bar or click the Inspector icon on the toolbar.**

   An Inspector window appears.

3. **Click the Table Inspector icon on the Inspector toolbar, as shown in Figure 3-8.**

Table Inspector icon

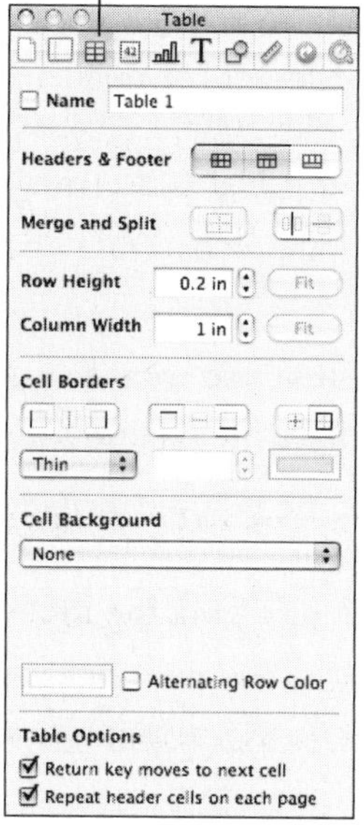

Figure 3-8: The Table Inspector pane displays text boxes to define a Row Height or Column Width precisely.

4. **Click the Row Height or Column Width text box and then type a value or click the up/down arrows in that text box to define a value.**

5. **Click the Close button of the Inspector window.**

Formatting a table

To make your table easier to read, you can format it with a style, which provides ways to color row and column headings of an entire table with one click of the mouse. To format a table, follow these steps:

1. **In the Sheets pane, click the table that you want to format.**

   Numbers displays your chosen table.

2. **Click a formatting style, such as Ledger or Blue Headers, in the Styles pane in the bottom-left corner of the Numbers window.**

   Numbers formats your table. If you don't like the way your table looks, choose another of the ten styles available.

Resizing a table

You might need to resize a table to fit it in a small space or to make it larger and easier to read. You can make a table larger (or smaller) while retaining the same number of rows and columns, which increases (or decreases) the height and width of rows and columns.

To stretch or shrink a table (without adding or subtracting rows or columns), follow these steps:

1. **In the Sheets pane, click the table that you want to resize.**

   Numbers displays your selected table with handles around it.

2. **Move the pointer to a handle until the pointer turns into a two-way pointing arrow.**

3. **Click and drag a handle to enlarge or shrink the table.**

   Notice that any data inside the table grows or shrinks as well.

4. **Release the mouse button when you're happy with the size of your table.**

Moving a table

After creating a table on a sheet, you can move it around to better highlight your data, especially if you have other tables, charts, or images on the sheet. To move a table, follow these steps:

1. **In the Sheets pane, click the table that you want to move.**

   Numbers displays your selected table.

2. **Click anywhere inside the table.**

3. **Move the pointer to the Move corner (refer to Figure 3-7) until the pointer turns into a four-way pointing arrow underneath.**

4. **Click and drag the table to a new location on the sheet.**

5. **Release the mouse button when you're happy with the table's new location.**

Typing Data into Tables

When you're ready to enter your data, you need to know about the three types of data you can store inside a table:

✦ Numbers

✦ Text

✦ Formulas

**Book VI
Chapter 3**

Crunching with
Numbers

You must type an equal sign "=" at the start of a formula you type into a cell so that Numbers recognizes the contents of the cell as a formula and not a number value or text item.

To type anything into a table, follow these steps:

1. **Select a cell by clicking it or by pressing the arrow keys.**

2. **Type a number, text, or formula (which must be preceded by an equal sign "=").**

3. **Press Return to select the cell below, press Tab to select the cell to the right, or click any cell where you want to type new data.**

4. **Repeat Steps 2 and 3 for each additional item you want to type into the table.**

Formatting numbers and text

When you type a number in a cell, the number will look plain, such as 45 or 60.3. To make your numbers more meaningful, you should format them. For example, the number 39 might mean nothing, but if you format it to appear as $39.00, your number now clearly represents a dollar amount.

To format numbers, follow these steps:

1. **Click to select one cell or click and drag to select multiple cells.**

Numbers draws a border around your selected cell(s).

If you select empty cells, Numbers automatically formats any numbers you type into those cells.

2. **Click one of the following icons on the Format bar, as shown in Figure 3-9:**

   - *Decimal:* Displays numbers with two decimal places, such as 3.19.

   - *Currency:* Displays numbers with a currency symbol, such as $3.19.

   - *Percentage:* Displays numbers as a percentage, such as 3.19%.

   - *Increase decimal places:* Displays numbers with an additional decimal place, such as 3.190.

   - *Decrease decimal places:* Displays numbers with one less decimal place, such as 3.2.

To customize the way formatting works, such as changing the currency format from displaying dollar symbols to Euros or Swiss francs, follow these steps:

1. **Select the cells that contain one or more numbers.**

2. **Click the Inspector icon or choose View⇨Show Inspector on the menu bar.**

   An Inspector window appears.

3. **Click the Cells Inspector icon on the Inspector toolbar, as shown in Figure 3-10.**

4. **Choose a format from the Cell Format pop-up menu.**

5. **Choose any options to customize your chosen format.**

   For example, if you chose the Currency format in Step 4, you can click a Symbol pop-up menu to define the type of symbol (dollar sign, Euro, and so on) that appears with each number.

6. **Click the Close button of the Inspector window.**

Figure 3-9:
The Format bar displays icons for quickly formatting numbers.

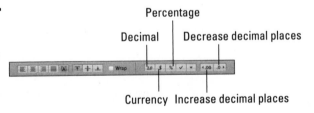

Cells Inspector icon

Figure 3-10:
The Cells
Inspector
lets you
customize
number
formats.

To make your text easier to read, you can choose different fonts and styles by following these steps:

1. **Select the cells that contain text.**

2. **Click one of the following on the Format bar, as shown in Figure 3-11:**

   - *Font:* Displays a variety of fonts.

   - *Style:* Displays different options, such as bold or italic.

   - *Font size:* Displays a range of sizes from 9 to 288.

   - *Text color:* Displays a color window for coloring numbers or text.

Figure 3-11:
The Format
bar displays
pop-up
menus for
changing
the font of
selected
cells.

Font   Font size

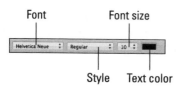

Style   Text color

Typing formulas

The main purpose of a table is to use the data (such as numbers, textual data, and dates and times) you store in cells to calculate a new result, such as adding a row or column of numbers. To calculate and display a result, you need to store a formula in the cell where you want the result to appear.

Numbers provides three ways to create formulas in a cell:

✦ Quick formulas

✦ Typed formulas

✦ Functions

Using Quick Formulas

To help you calculate numbers in a hurry, Numbers offers a variety of Quick Formulas that can calculate common results, such as

✦ **Sum:** Adds numbers.

✦ **Average:** Calculates the arithmetic mean.

✦ **Minimum:** Displays the smallest number.

✦ **Maximum:** Displays the largest number.

✦ **Count:** Displays how many cells you select.

✦ **Product:** Multiplies numbers.

To use a Quick Formula, follow these steps:

1. **Select two or more cells that contain numbers.**

2. **Click the Function icon, or choose Insert⇨Function on the menu bar, and then choose a Quick Formula (Sum, Average, Minimum, Maximum, Count, or Product).**

Numbers displays your calculated results.

If you highlight a row of numbers, the Quick Formula displays the result to the right. If you highlight a column of numbers, the Quick Formula displays the result at the bottom of the column. If you highlight both rows and columns of numbers, the Quick Formula displays the result at the bottom of each column.

Typing a formula

Quick Formulas are handy when they offer the formula you need, such as adding rows or columns of numbers with the Sum formula. However, most of the time, you need to create your own formulas.

Every formula consists of two parts:

✦ **Operators:** Perform calculations, such as addition (+), subtraction (–), multiplication (*), and division (/).

✦ **Cell references:** Define where to find the data to use for calculations.

A typical formula looks like this:

```
= A3 + A4
```

This formula tells Numbers to take the number stored in column A, row 3 and add it to the number stored in column A, row 4.

To type a formula, follow these steps:

1. **Click (or use the arrow keys to highlight) the cell where you want the formula results to appear.**

2. **Type =.**

   The Formula Editor appears, as shown in Figure 3-12.

   You can move the Formula Editor if you move the pointer to the left end of the Formula Editor. When the pointer turns into a hand, click and drag the Formula Editor to a new location.

3. **Click a cell that contains the data you want to include in your calculation.**

4. **Type an operator, such as * for multiplication or / for division.**

5. **Click another cell that contains the data you want to include in your calculation.**

Figure 3-12:
The Formula
Editor lets
you create
and edit
a formula
stored in a
cell.

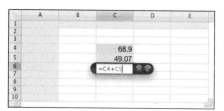

6. **Repeat Steps 4 and 5 as often as necessary.**

7. **Click the Accept (or Cancel) button on the Formula Editor when you're done.**

   Numbers displays the results of your formula. If you change the numbers in the cells you define in Step 3 and Step 5, Numbers calculates a new result instantly.

For a fast way to calculate values without having to type a formula in a cell, you can use Instant Calculations. Just select two or more cells that contain numbers and you can see the instant calculations in the bottom-left corner of the Numbers window, as shown in Figure 3-13.

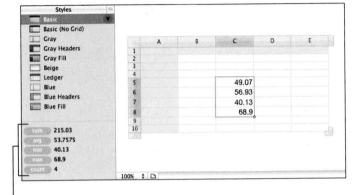

Figure 3-13:
Instant
calculations
can show
results
without
you typing
a formula
first.

Instant calculations

Using functions

Typing simple formulas that add or multiply is easy. However, many calculations can get more complicated, such as trying to calculate the amount of interest paid on a loan with a specific interest rate over a defined period.

To help you calculate commonly used formulas, Numbers provides a library of *functions* — prebuilt formulas that you can plug into your table and define what data to use without having to create the formula yourself.

To use a function, follow these steps:

1. **Click (or use the arrow keys to highlight) the cell where you want the function results to appear.**

2. **Click the Function icon.**

A pull-down menu appears.

3. **Choose Show Function Browser.**

A Functions Browser opens, as shown in Figure 3-14. It displays all the available functions along with a definition for each one.

4. **Click a function category in the left pane, such as Financial or Statistical.**

The right pane displays only those functions stored in that category.

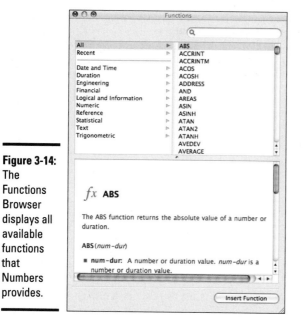

Figure 3-14:
The
Functions
Browser
displays all
available
functions
that
Numbers
provides.

5. **Click a function in the right pane and then click the Insert button.**

   The Formula Editor appears, containing your chosen function.

6. **Edit the formula by typing the cell names (such as C4) or clicking the cells that contain the data the function needs to calculate.**

7. **Click the Accept (or Cancel) button on the Formula Editor.**

   Numbers shows your result.

Formatting data entry cells

After you create formulas or functions in cells, you can type new data in the cells defined by a formula or function and watch Numbers calculate a new result instantly. Typing a new number in a cell is easy to do, but sometimes a formula or function requires a specific range of values. For example, if you have a formula that calculates sales tax, you might not want someone to enter a sales tax over 10% or less than 5%.

To limit the types of values someone can enter in a cell, you can use one of the following methods, as shown in Figure 3-15:

✦ **Sliders:** Lets the user drag a slider to choose a value within a fixed range.

✦ **Steppers:** Lets the user click up and down arrows to choose a value that increases or decreases in fixed increments.

✦ **Pop-up menus:** Lets the user choose from a limited range of choices.

Figure 3-15:
Sliders,
steppers,
and pop-up
menus
restrict the
types of
values a cell
can hold.

Formatting a cell with a slider or stepper

A *slider* or *stepper* is useful when you want to restrict a cell to a range of values, such as 1 to 45. The main difference between the two is that a slider appears next to a cell, whereas a stepper appears inside a cell.

To format a cell with a slider or stepper, follow these steps:

1. **Click a cell that you want to restrict to a range of values.**

2. **Click the Format button (it looks like a downward-pointing arrow) on the Format bar and then choose Slider or Stepper from the pull-down menu that appears, as shown in Figure 3-16.**

The Cells Inspector appears, as shown in Figure 3-17.

3. **Click the Minimum text box and type the minimum acceptable value.**

4. **Click the Maximum text box and type the maximum acceptable value.**

5. **Click the Increment text box and type a value to increase or decrease by when the user drags the slider or clicks the up and down arrows of the stepper.**

Figure 3-16:
Choosing
your
restraint.

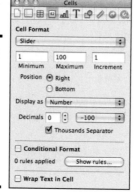

Figure 3-17:
The Cells
Inspector
lets you
define the
range of
values for
a slider or
stepper.

6. **Click the Close button of the Inspector window.**

Numbers displays a slider next to the cell. Users have a choice of typing
a value or using the slider to define a value. If you choose a value outside the minimum and maximum range defined in Steps 4 and 5, the cell
won't accept the invalid data.

Formatting a cell with a pop-up menu

A pop-up menu restricts a cell to a limited number of choices. To format a
cell with a pop-up menu, follow these steps:

1. **Click a cell that you want to restrict to a limited choice of values.**

2. **Click the Format button (it looks like a downward-pointing arrow) on
the Format bar.**

A pull-down menu appears (refer to Figure 3-16).

3. **Select Pop-up Menu from the pull-down menu.**

The Cells Inspector appears, as shown in Figure 3-18.

Figure 3-18:
The Cells
Inspector
window lets
you define
a list of
values.

4. **In the Cells Inspector, click the list box under the Cell Format pop-up menu and then click the plus (+) or minus (–) sign buttons to add or remove an item from the pop-up menu list.**

5. **Click the Close button of the Cells Inspector window.**

   Numbers displays a pop-up menu that lists choices when users click that cell.

Deleting data in cells

After you type data into a cell, you might later want to delete that data. Numbers provides two ways to delete data in cells:

+ Delete data but retain any formatting.

+ Delete data and formatting.

To delete data but retain any formatting, follow these steps:

1. **Select one or more cells that contain data you want to delete.**

2. **Press Delete or choose Edit⇨Delete on the menu bar.**

To delete both data and formatting in cells, follow these steps:

1. **Select one or more cells that contain data and formatting you want to delete.**

2. **Choose Edit⇨Clear All on the menu bar.**

Making Charts

Charts help make sense out of your numeric data by turning numbers into pictures that can show trends or help you spot patterns, such as identifying which salesperson is most consistent (and which ones are consistently the best and worst).

Creating a chart

Creating a chart is a three-step process. First, you have to decide what numeric data you want to turn into a chart. Second, you need to choose a specific type of chart to create, such as a mixed bar and line chart or pie chart. Finally, you have to decide whether you want to create a two-dimensional or three-dimensional chart.

A 3D chart might look cool, but it can often make understanding your data harder. You might need to experiment with different charts until you find one that displays your data the best.

To create a chart, follow these steps:

1. **Highlight the data you want to convert into a chart.**

You can highlight data by dragging the mouse or by holding down the Shift key and pressing the arrow keys.

2. **Click the Charts icon or choose Insert⇨Chart on the menu bar.**

A pull-down menu of different chart types appears.

3. **Click a chart type.**

Numbers creates your chart, along with a Chart Inspector window, as shown in Figure 3-19.

If you don't like the chart type you chose, click the Chart Type icon in the Chart Inspector and then choose a different chart type.

4. **Click the Close button of the Inspector window.**

Book VI Chapter 3

Crunching with Numbers

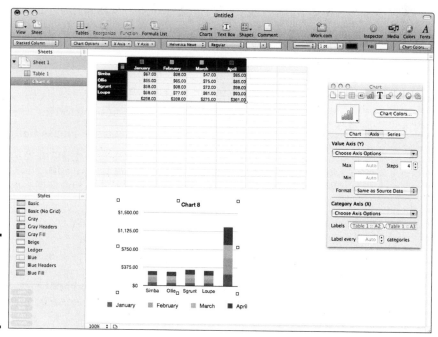

Figure 3-19: A chart appears directly on a sheet.

Editing a chart

After you create a chart, you might need to edit it later. To edit your chart, follow these steps:

1. **Click the chart name in the Sheets pane that you want to edit.**

   Numbers displays your chart with handles around its edges.

2. **Choose View⇨Show Inspector on the menu bar.**

   The Chart Inspector appears, giving you options you can modify.

3. **Choose any options in the Chart Inspector pane.**

   You might want to change the title of your chart or hide the legend that explains what each color represents.

4. **Click the Close button of the Inspector window.**

Manipulating a chart

A chart is just another object that you can move, resize, or delete.

Any time you resize, move, or delete a chart, you can always reverse your action by pressing ⌘+Z or choosing Edit⇨Undo.

Moving a chart on a sheet

To move a chart, follow these steps:

1. **Click a chart name in the Sheets pane.**

   Numbers displays your chart with handles around it.

2. **Click the middle of the chart, hold down the mouse button, and then drag the chart to a new location.**

3. **Release the mouse button when you're happy with your chart's new home.**

Moving a chart from one sheet to another sheet

To move a chart to a different sheet, hold down the Option key and drag the chart from one sheet to another sheet, or follow these steps:

1. **Click and drag the chart name underneath a Sheet icon of a different sheet in the Sheets pane.**

2. **Release the mouse button when you're happy with the location of your chart.**

   Numbers displays your chart on the other sheet. You might need to move the chart to a specific location on the sheet to make your chart look nicer.

Resizing a chart

To resize a chart, follow these steps:

1. **Click a chart name in the Sheets pane.**

   Numbers displays your chart with handles around it.

2. **Move the pointer to a handle until the pointer turns into a two-way pointing arrow.**

3. **Click and drag the handle to resize the chart.**

   Release the mouse button when you're happy with the size of your chart.

Deleting a chart

To delete a chart, choose one of the following:

+ Click a chart name in the Sheets pane and then choose Edit⇨Delete on the menu bar.

+ Control-click a chart name in the Sheets pane and then choose Delete.

Book VI Chapter 3

Crunching with Numbers

Making Your Spreadsheets Pretty

Tables and charts are the two most crucial objects you can place and arrange on a sheet. However, Numbers also lets you place text boxes, shapes, and pictures on a sheet. Text boxes can contain titles or short descriptions of the information displayed on the sheet; shapes can add color or indicate navigational cues, such as arrows; and pictures can make your entire sheet look more interesting.

Adding a text box

To add a text box to a sheet, follow these steps:

1. **In the Sheets pane, click the name of a sheet you want to add the text box to.**

   Numbers displays your chosen sheet and any additional objects that might already be on that sheet, such as tables or charts.

2. **Click the Text Box icon (or choose Insert⇨Text Box on the menu bar).**

   A text box appears on the sheet.

3. **Type any text that you want to appear in the text box. (Press Return to type text on a new line.)**

While you type, your text box becomes longer to accommodate your text. You can make the text box wider by clicking and dragging on the handles on the sides of the text box.

4. **(Optional) Select any text and choose any formatting options from the Format bar, such as different fonts or font sizes.**

Adding a picture

To add a picture from iPhoto into a document, follow these steps:

1. **In the Sheets pane, click the name of a sheet you want to add a picture to.**

   Numbers displays your chosen sheet and any additional objects that are already on that sheet, such as tables or charts.

2. **Click the Media icon.**

   The Media Browser appears.

3. **Click the Photos tab, as shown in Figure 3-20.**

4. **Click and drag a picture from the Media Browser to a blank area of your sheet.**

   If you drag a picture to a table, Numbers displays your picture as a tiny image inside a single cell, which probably isn't what you want.

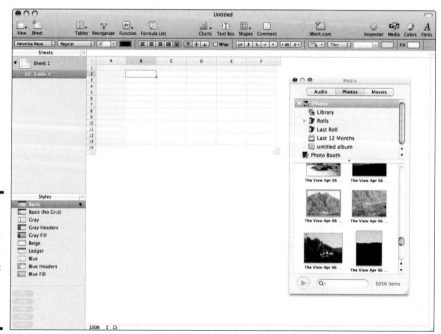

Figure 3-20: The Photos pane in the Media window lets you browse your iPhoto library.

5. **Release the mouse button.**

   Numbers displays your chosen image on the sheet.

6. **Click the Close button of the Media Browser.**

You can resize your photo by clicking on the photo and then using the handles to click and drag to the size you want. You can also edit your photo by choosing Format➪Mask, or Format➪Instant Alpha, as I explain in Book VI, Chapters 1 and 2.

Deleting text boxes, shapes, and pictures

When you want to remove an object, you can delete it by following these steps:

1. **In the Sheets pane, click the name of the sheet containing the object you want to delete.**

2. **Click the object (text box, shape, or picture) you want to delete.**

   Handles appear around your object.

3. **Press the Delete key.**

Sharing Your Spreadsheet

You've put a lot of effort into making your spreadsheet presentable. Now's the time to actually *present* it, which usually means sharing your spreadsheet with others by printing it or saving it as a file.

Printing a spreadsheet

In other spreadsheet programs, you can print your spreadsheet and chart — only to find that part of your chart or spreadsheet is cut off by the edge of the paper. To avoid this problem, Numbers displays a Content Slider, which lets you magnify or shrink an entire sheet so that it fits and prints perfectly on a page.

To shrink or magnify a sheet to print, follow these steps:

1. **In the Sheets pane, click the name of a sheet you want to print.**

2. **Choose File➪Show Print View (or View➪Show Print View).**

   Numbers displays a page and shows how the charts and tables on your sheet will print, as shown in Figure 3-21.

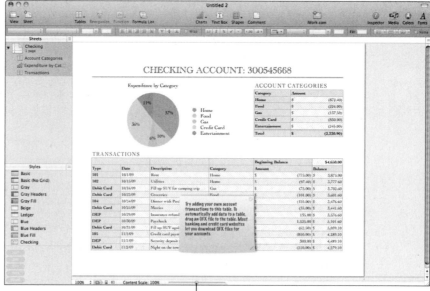

Figure 3-21:
The Print
view shows
you exactly
how your
sheet will
print on
paper.

Content slider

3. **Drag the Content Slider to magnify or shrink your data until it fits exactly the way you want on the page.**

 The Content Slider is located at the bottom center of the Print view.

4. **Choose File⇨Print on the menu bar (or press ⌘+P).**

 A dialog appears asking how many copies to print, which pages to print, and which printer to use.

5. **Choose the print options you want and then click Print.**

Exporting a spreadsheet

When you choose File⇨Save, Numbers saves your spreadsheet in its own proprietary file format. If you want to share your spreadsheets with others who don't have Numbers, you need to export your spreadsheet into another file format, such as:

✦ **PDF:** Saves your spreadsheet as a series of static pages stored in the Adobe Acrobat portable document format that can be viewed by any computer with a PDF viewing program.

✦ **Excel:** Saves your spreadsheet as a Microsoft Excel file, which can be opened and edited by any spreadsheet that can read and edit Microsoft Excel files.

+ **CSV:** Saves your spreadsheet in Comma-Separated Values format, a universal format that preserves only data, not any charts or pictures you have stored on your spreadsheet.

The PDF file format preserves formatting 100 percent, but you need extra software to edit it. Generally, if someone needs to edit your spreadsheet, choose File⇨Save As and save a copy as an Excel document. The CSV option is useful only for transferring your data to another program that can't read Excel files.

To export a spreadsheet, follow these steps:

1. **Choose File⇨Export on the menu bar.**

   A dialog appears, as shown in Figure 3-22.

2. **Click an icon, such as PDF or Excel.**

3. **(Optional) Click Security Options if you want to add a password to open, print, or copy the document.**

4. **Click Next.**

   A dialog appears, letting you choose a name and location to save your exported spreadsheet.

5. **Enter a name for your exported spreadsheet in the Save As text box.**

6. **Click the folder where you want to store your spreadsheet.**

   You might need to switch drives or folders until you find where you want to save your file.

7. **Click Export.**

   When you export a spreadsheet, your original Numbers spreadsheet remains untouched in its original location.

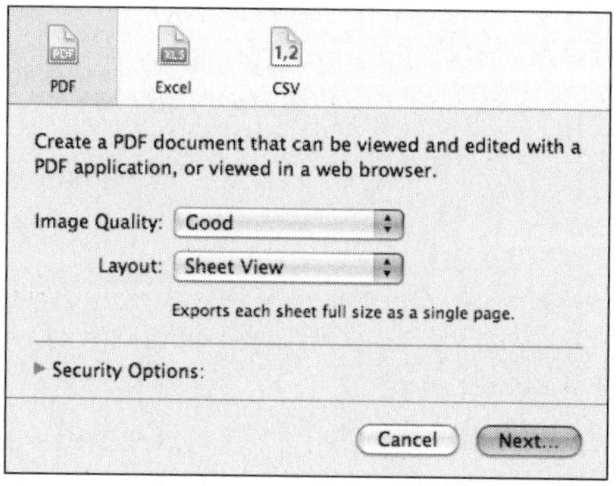

**Book VI
Chapter 3**

Crunching with Numbers

PDF	Excel	CSV

Create a PDF document that can be viewed and edited with a PDF application, or viewed in a web browser.

Image Quality: ☐ Good ▾

Layout: ☐ Sheet View ▾

Exports each sheet full size as a single page.

▸ Security Options:

(Cancel) (Next...)

Figure 3-22: The Export dialog lets you choose a format to save your spread sheets.

Book VII

Address Book, iCal, and Running Windows

Contents at a Glance

Chapter 1: Managing Contacts with Address Book

Most people write down important names and contact information in an address book, but your Mac comes with an electronic version called (surprise!) Address Book. Besides storing contact names and related contact information, the Address Book also connects with other programs so that you can click someone's e-mail address and immediately write and send a message to that person.

The Mac Address Book lets you search through stored contacts and print them as mailing labels or lists, which is impossible to do with a paper address book. Therefore, the next time you need to store contacts and contact information, you'll find it much easier to store this data in the Address Book on your Mac.

Setting Up Address Book

The Address Book acts like a giant Rolodex file that can hold contact cards and contact information including e-mail addresses, telephone numbers, and postal addresses in separate windows referred to as *contact cards*. When you save information about a person on a card, you can find that information again.

Designing a template

Each time you add a contact, the Address Book displays blank fields, with each field representing information to fill in about that person, such as company, first and last name, title, and e-mail address. You might not want or need to store all that information about everyone, so you can define the Address Book template to list only the fields you want to use, such as name and e-mail address. To modify the Address Book template, follow these steps:

1. **Click the Address Book icon in the Dock (or double-click the Address Book icon inside the Applications folder).**

2. **Choose Address Book⇨Preferences.**

    A Preferences window appears.

3. **Click the Template icon.**

    The Template pane appears, as shown in Figure 1-1.

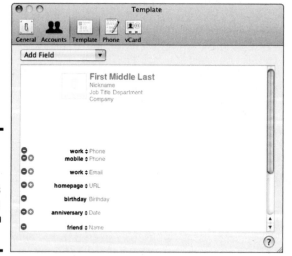

Figure 1-1:
The Template pane shows all the fields that you can store.

4. **Remove a field you don't want by clicking the minus sign to the left of the field and then repeating this for every field you want to remove.**

5. **Click the Add Field menu and choose a field to add, such as URL or Birthday (see Figure 1-2), repeating this for each field you want to add.**

6. **(Optional) Click the Phone icon to make the Phone pane appear, as shown in Figure 1-3.**

7. **Click the Formats pop-up menu and then choose the way you want your phone numbers to appear. You can also choose Custom and then type your custom format, or use the down-arrow and choose another preformatted telephone format.**

You can uncheck the Automatically Format Phone Numbers check box if you don't want Address Book to automatically format phone numbers.

8. **Click the Close button of the Address Book preferences window.**

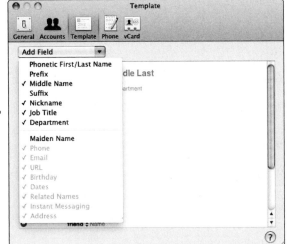

Figure 1-2: The Add Field menu provides additional fields you can add to a template.

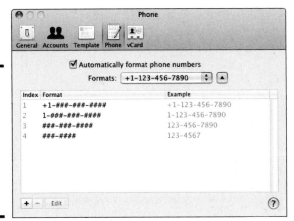

Figure 1-3: The Phone pane defines a specific format for displaying telephone numbers.

The template defines only the fields you know you want to use for storing contacts you'll save in the Address Book. You can always add fields to individual cards later. I show you how in the "Editing a card" section, later in this chapter.

Storing contacts

After you define a template for your Address Book, the next step is to store actual contact names and information, such as phone numbers and e-mail addresses, by creating contact cards, referred to as *contacts*.

I explain how to import existing contacts you might already have saved as a file or as contact cards near the end of the chapter, in the section "Importing data into your Address Book."

To add a new contact, follow these steps:

1. **Choose File⇨New Card.**

The Address Book window displays a blank card for you to fill in by clicking the fields that appear in this contact edit view, as shown in Figure 1-4.

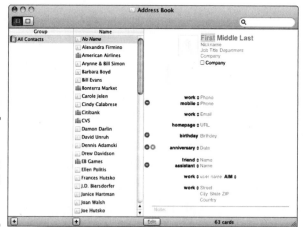

Figure 1-4: Adding a new contact means filling out a blank card.

2. **Click the text fields, such as First, Last, or Telephone Number, and then type the information you want to save for your contact.**

You don't need to fill every field.

3. **Click the Edit button at the bottom of the Address Book window (or press ⌘+S) to save your new card and return to the Address Book contact card view.**

Displaying companies and people

You have two ways to display your contact cards: by a person's name or by company name. To help you differentiate between company and people names, the Address Book displays different icons to the left of each contact card, as shown in Figure 1-5.

My Card icon

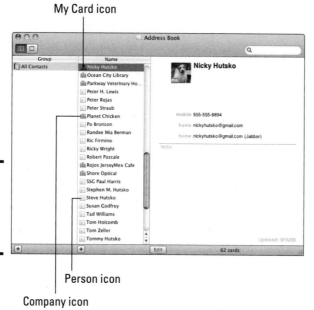

Figure 1-5: Icons identify companies and people.

Person icon

Company icon

Book VII Chapter 1

Managing Contacts with Address Book

One special contact card, identified by the My Card icon, always represents your own contact card and any information it contains, such as your e-mail address, phone number, and picture. To define a different card to represent you, click that card and choose Card➪Make This My Card. To view your card at any time, choose Card➪Go to My Card.

When you create a new contact card, the Address Book assumes that you want to display that card by a person's name. To make a card appear in the Address Book by company name instead, click the card and choose

Card⇨Mark as a Company (or check the Company check box when you're creating a new contact card; refer to Figure 1-4). Your chosen card now displays a company name and icon. To change a company back into a person's name, choose Card⇨Mark as a Person.

Editing a card

Information on cards will need to change whenever people change their address or company. To keep this information up-to-date, you can edit a card by following these steps:

1. **Click All Contacts under the Group category in the Address Book window and then click the card you want to edit.**

   You might need to scroll down if you have a long list of stored names.

2. **Click the Edit button at the bottom of the Address Book window.**

3. **Click the field in which you want to type or edit information, such as an e-mail address or phone number.**

4. **(Optional) Choose Card⇨Add Field to choose a field to add on a card, as shown in Figure 1-6.**

   After you add a field to a card, you need to type information into that field.

5. **Click the Edit button again.**

   Address Book saves your updated contact information.

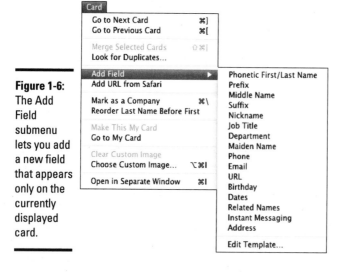

Figure 1-6: The Add Field submenu lets you add a new field that appears only on the currently displayed card.

Adding pictures to a name

To help yourself remember certain people or companies, you can include a picture, either a photograph of that person or a symbolic image that reminds you about that person. To add a picture to a card, follow these steps:

1. **Click the name for which you want to include a picture.**

2. **Choose Card⇨Choose Custom Image.**

   A dialog appears, as shown in Figure 1-7, allowing you to take a picture by using the built-in iSight camera (or optional external webcam), or to choose a picture file stored on your hard drive.

Figure 1-7: You can add a picture to a contact by choosing a picture file or snapping a picture with the iSight camera.

Camera button

3. **Click the Camera button to take a picture or click Choose to select a picture file.**

4. **Click Set when you're happy with your chosen image.**

Searching contacts

The more contact cards you store in your Address Book, the harder to find a particular contact you want. Rather than scrolling through every contact card to locate one you're looking for, you can search for specific contacts by following these steps:

1. **Click the Spotlight text box in the upper-right corner of the Address Book window.**

2. **Type a word or phrase that you want to find, such as a person's name or company that person works for.**

   The Address Book displays a list of contacts that match the text you typed.

3. **Click a contact to display all the information about that person or company.**

Deleting a contact

Periodically, you can browse through your Address Book and prune the contact cards of people you don't need to save any more. To delete a name from your Address Book, just click the contact and choose Edit⇨Delete Card. If you accidentally delete a contact, press ⌘+Z or choose Edit⇨Undo to restore it.

If you hold down the ⌘ key, you can click and choose multiple contacts to delete. If you hold down the Shift key, you can click two contact cards and select those two contacts and all contacts in between as well.

Creating Groups

To help you find all the contacts you've stored, the Address Book program lets you organize your list of contacts into groups, such as for your co-workers, friends, family members, restaurants, and so on. For greater convenience, you can even store the same contact in multiple groups. Although you don't have to use groups, this feature can help you manage your list of important contact cards.

Your Address Book initially contains one group: All Contacts. The All Contacts group automatically stores all contacts you've saved in the Address Book.

If your Mac is connected to a local area network, you may see a second group: Directories. The directories group contains a list of contacts of everyone connected to a local area network. If you're using a Mac at home without a local area network, you won't see the Directories group.

Creating a group

You can create as many groups as you want, but for groups to be useful you need to add contacts to that group. To create a new group, choose File⇨New Group. Replace Group Name with a more descriptive name in the Address Book window, and then press Return.

To add contacts to a group, follow these steps:

1. **Click All Contacts in the Group column to see all the contacts stored in your Address Book.**

2. **Move the cursor over a contact, hold down the mouse button, and then drag the cursor over the group name where you want to store your contact.**

   If you hold down the ⌘ key, you can click and choose multiple contacts. If you hold down the Shift key, you can click two noncontiguous contacts to select those two contacts and all contacts in between as well.

3. **Release the mouse button when the group name appears highlighted.**

   Your chosen contact now appears in your newly created group and in the All Contacts group.

Creating a group from a selection of contacts

If you already have a group of contacts selected that you want to organize, you can create a new group and store those contacts at the same time. To create a new group from a selection of contacts, follow these steps:

1. **Click All Contacts in the Group column to see all the names stored in your Address Book.**

2. **Hold down the ⌘ key and click each contact you want to store in a group.**

   You can select a range of contacts by holding down the Shift key and clicking two noncontiguous contacts. Doing so selects those two contacts and all contacts in between.

3. **Choose File⇨New Group from Selection.**

4. **Type a more descriptive contact for your group and then press Return.**

   Your group now contains the contacts you selected in Step 2.

Adding contacts automatically with Smart Groups

Adding contacts manually or selecting them for a group is fine, but what if you frequently add and delete contacts? Doing all this manually can get old. To keep your group's contacts accurate and up-to-date more easily, you can use the Smart Group feature.

With a Smart Group, you define the types of contacts you want to store, such as contacts for everyone who works at a certain company. Then the Smart Group automatically adds any contacts to the group from your Address Book.

To create a Smart Group, follow these steps:

1. **Choose File⇨New Smart Group.**

A dialog appears, asking for a contact and rule for storing contacts in the group, as shown in Figure 1-8. A *rule* lets you group contacts based on certain criteria. For example, you might want to group the contacts of all people who work for Apple and live in Texas.

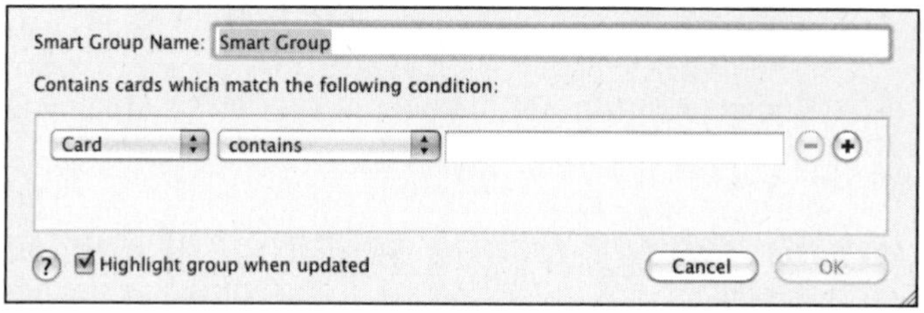

Figure 1-8:
A dialog
appears
for defining
a contact
and rule for
creating
a Smart
Group.

Smart Group Name: Smart Group

Contains cards which match the following condition:

Card ⇕ | contains ⇕ | ⊖ ⊕

(?) ☑ Highlight group when updated   Cancel   OK

2. **Click the Smart Group Name text box and type a descriptive name for your Smart Group.**

3. **Click the first pop-up menu and choose the criteria for including a contact in your Smart Group, such as Company or City, as shown in Figure 1-9.**

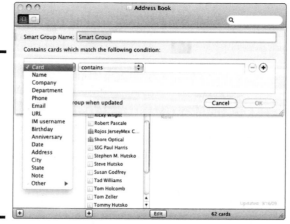

Figure 1-9:
The first
pop-up
menu
defines
the criteria
for storing
contacts in
your Smart
Group.

4. Click the second pop-up menu and then choose how to use the criteria you defined in Step 3, such as Contains or Was Updated After.

5. Click the text box and then type a word or phrase for your criteria to use.

For example, if you want to create a Smart Group that stores only contacts of people who work at Apple, your entire Smart Group rule might look like Company Contains Apple (refer to Figure 1-9).

6. (Optional) Click the plus sign to the right of the text box to create any additional rules.

If you create any additional rules and then decide you don't want them, you can always remove them by clicking the minus sign that appears next to the rule.

7. Click OK.

Creating a Smart Group from search results

Defining the criteria for automatically storing names into a Smart Group can be cumbersome when you aren't quite sure whether the defined criteria will work exactly the way you want. As an alternative, you can use Spotlight to search for the types of contacts you want to store and then create a Smart Group based on your Spotlight search results. By doing this, you can see exactly which types of contacts appear in your Smart Group.

To create a Smart Group from Spotlight search results, follow these steps:

1. Click the Spotlight text box in the upper-right corner of the Address Book window, type the text you want to find, such as the name of a company or part of an e-mail address, and then press Return.

The middle Address Book pane shows the contacts found by the text you typed into Spotlight.

2. Choose File➪New Smart Group from Current Search.

A Smart Group appears in the Group category, using the text you typed as the group name.

Deleting a Group

If you create a group and no longer need it, you can delete it. When you delete a group, you delete only the group folder; you do not delete any contact cards stored in that group. To delete a group, click the group and then choose Edit➪Delete Group.

Managing Your Address Book Files

Eventually, your Address Book can hold so many important contacts that you can't afford to risk losing this information. One way to preserve your contact information is to create an archive file of your Address Book, which you then store on a backup device other than your Mac, such as a USB drive or external hard drive. Another way is to print your entire Address Book (although this isn't a very *green* option, is it?). Either way, you always have access to your important contact information, even if your Mac's hard drive is wiped out.

Archiving your Address Book

There're few things worse than manually retyping all your contacts if you lose them in a computer disaster. You can create an archive file of your Address Book and then back it up to an external drive or write it to a CD for safekeeping. Follow these steps:

1. **Choose File⇨Export⇨Address Book Archive.**

A Save As dialog opens.

2. **Keep the default name or type a new name in the Save As text box.**

3. **Select the location for storing your file; this can be an external drive or another folder on your Mac that you regularly back up to an external backup device.**

4. **Click Save.**

For more details on backing up files, see Book II, Chapter 2.

Printing your Address Book

Besides printing a backup copy of your contacts, Address Book lets you print all or some of your contact information in different formats, such as mailing labels or cards that you can carry with you. To print your Address Book, follow these steps:

1. **Use one of the following methods to select the names you want to print:**

• Click a single contact card.

• Hold down the ⌘ key and click multiple contacts.

• Hold down the Shift key, click a contact, and then click another contact elsewhere in the list. Selecting these two contacts highlights them both and all contacts in between.

• To print all contact cards stored in a group, click the group name, and then choose Edit⇨Select All or press ⌘+A.

• Use Spotlight to find names that meet a certain criteria.

2. **Choose File⇨Print.**

   A Print dialog appears.

3. **Expand the Print dialog by clicking the down arrow that appears to the right of the Printer pop-up menu.**

   You see before you the expanded Print dialog, as shown in Figure 1-10.

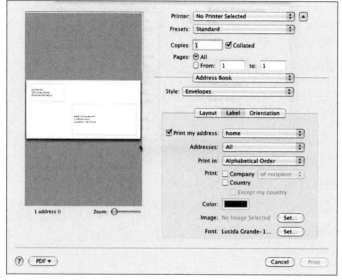

Figure 1-10:
The expanded Print dialog lets you choose how to print your selected contacts.

4. **Click the Printer pop-up menu and then choose a printer to use.**

5. **Click the Style pop-up menu and choose one of the following:**

   - *Mailing Labels:* Prints names and addresses on different types of mailing labels.

   - *Envelopes:* Prints names and addresses on envelopes fed into your printer.

   - *Lists:* Prints your Address Book as a long list.

   - *Pocket Address Book:* Prints your Address Book in a condensed form suitable for carrying with you.

   Depending on the style that you choose in this step, you might need to pick additional options, such as defining the specific size of your mailing labels or choosing whether to print names in alphabetical order. You can also adjust other setting and options, such as number of copies and the font you want to use for your printed output.

6. **Click Print.**

Exporting your Address Book

Sometimes you might need to share your contact information with others. To save one or more names from your Address Book into a file that other programs and people can use, you export your data to a vCard or archive format. A *vCard* is a standard format that many programs use to store contact information. By storing your data as a vCard, you can copy information to another program and computer, such as a Windows PC running Outlook.

If you need to share contact information with another Mac user, you can save your Address Book data as an archive file (as detailed in the earlier "Archiving your Address Book" section), or as a vCard file.

To export contacts from your Address Book, follow these steps:

1. **Select the names you want to export.**

2. **Choose File⇨Export.**

   A submenu appears.

3. **Choose Export vCard or Address Book Archive.**

   A Save As dialog appears.

4. **Type a descriptive name for your file in the Save As text box.**

5. **Choose the location to store your file.**

6. **Click Save.**

When exporting contacts for use in another program, the program you're importing might not recognize every detail for the contact, such as a person's picture or notes you've added to a person's contact card.

Importing data into your Address Book

You might already have your contacts in another program, or other people might have contact information that you want. Before you can import this information, you must export and save the data in one of four file formats:

✦ **vCards:** Standard file format that is used to store contact information; used by programs on different types of computers.

✦ **LDIF:** Standard data interchange file format; stands for LDAP Data Interchange Format.

✦ **Text File:** Tab-delimited or Comma-Separated Value (CSV) format; comes from database or spreadsheet programs, or contact programs.

✦ **Address Book Archive:** Standard Address Book file format useful for transferring data between Macs with Address Book.

To import a contact's data file into your Address Book, follow these steps:

1. **Choose File⇨Import.**

   A dialog appears.

2. **Select the file you want to import and then click Open. Leave Text Encoding on Automatic.**

   The Address Book displays your newly imported names.

3. **(Optional) If you're importing a text or CSV file, make sure the correct field labels are associated with the data being imported. You can change the field labels if necessary.**

In programs that use the vCard format, such as Outlook and Entourage, you can export the contents to a vCard file and then e-mail the file to you. Save the attached vCard file and then double-click it to import the contact into Address Book automatically without having to bother with the steps above.

Your newly imported contacts will appear in both the All Contacts group and the Last Import group in the Group column.

Syncing with other devices

You can synchronize your Address Book contacts with your iPhone or iPod when you connect it to your Mac and open iTunes. Follow these steps:

1. **Connect your iPhone or iPod to your Mac with a USB cable.**

2. **Click your iPhone or iPod in the Devices column, click the Info tab, and then choose Sync Address Book Contacts.**

   Your Address Book contacts transfer or update automatically on your iPhone or iPod.

If you have a MobileMe account, your Address Book contacts (and iCal events and other information) can stay up to date automatically between your Mac and one or more other Macs and/or Windows PCs, and your iPhone.

Chapter 2: Staying on Schedule with iCal

In This Chapter

✔ Understanding the iCal window

✔ Using calendars

✔ Creating and storing events

✔ Finding events

✔ Storing To-Do Lists

✔ Subscribing to calendars

✔ Printing, saving, and exporting calendars

The iCal program lets you track appointments you need to attend and tasks that you want to complete. To help juggle your appointments, such as personal and business appointments, you can create separate calendars so that you can see which days you're busy with work and which days you're busy with your personal schedule.

Calendars can be a powerful tool to organize your schedule, track your time, and help you plan your goals. The more efficiently you can use your time, the more you can accomplish and the faster you can reach your goals.

Understanding iCal

The iCal window displays the following items, as shown in Figure 2-1:

✦ **Calendar List:** Displays all calendars that contain related appointments, such as home or work-related events.

✦ **Mini-Month:** Displays the dates for an entire month so you can see which day a specific date falls on, such as Tuesday or Saturday.

✦ **Events:** Shows events scheduled in Day, Week, or Month views.

✦ **To Do List:** Displays tasks that you need to accomplish.

Calendar List   Events   To Do List

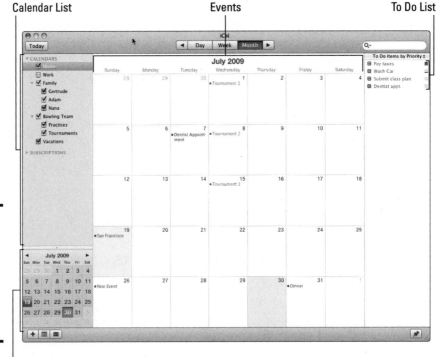

Figure 2-1:
The iCal
window
provides
different
ways to
view times
and dates.

Mini-Month

Any scheduled activity, such as a doctor's appointment, a business meeting, or your daughter's soccer practice, is an *event*.

Working with the Calendar List

The iCal program initially includes a Home and Work calendar, but you can always create or rename additional calendars. You might want an additional calendar for a specific work or home-related project, or you might need a separate calendar to keep track of your children's scheduled activities.

The Calendar List displays the calendars you've created, as well as the Home and Work calendars provided by iCal. The Calendar List has two uses:

✦ To select a calendar to view (which appears in the middle pane of the iCal window)

✦ To hide or display events stored on a particular calendar

When you want to store an event, you must first choose which calendar to use. The main reason to have separate calendars is to organize your events into calendar types. For example, the Home calendar is for storing personal events, and the Work calendar is for storing business-related events.

By selecting or deselecting the check box next to each calendar in the Calendar List, you can selectively view specific events, such as only business events. Or, you can view business and personal events together.

The following sections explain managing your calendars in iCal.

Creating a new calendar

Although iCal provides a Home and Work calendar, you might need to create additional calendars for other purposes. To create a new calendar, follow these steps:

1. **Click the iCal icon in the Dock (or double-click the iCal icon in the Applications folder).**

2. **Choose File⇨New Calendar, or Control-click the Calendar List and choose New Calendar from the pop-up menu.**

   An Untitled calendar appears in the Calendar List, as shown in Figure 2-2.

3. **Type a descriptive name for your calendar and then press Return.**

**Book VII
Chapter 2**

Staying on Schedule
with iCal

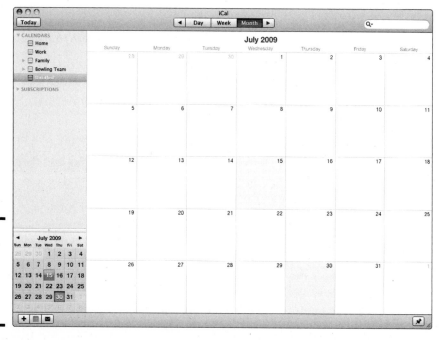

Figure 2-2:
A new calendar appears without a name.

Creating a new calendar group

Rather than create a bunch of separate calendars, you might want to organize multiple calendars in a group. For example, if you had a calendar to schedule events for your son and daughter, you could put both of those calendars into a Family group.

Grouping helps you to see the relationships between calendars, and it lets you hide grouped calendars to avoid cluttering the Calendar List. When you hide a calendar group, you hide all calendars stored within that group.

A calendar group can't store events; it simply stores one or more calendars.

To create a calendar group, follow these steps:

1. **Click the iCal icon in the Dock (or double-click the iCal icon in the Applications folder).**

2. **Choose File⇨New Calendar Group, or Control-click the Calendar List and choose New Group from the pop-up menu.**

A calendar group appears in the Calendar List with a triangle to its left, which you click to hide or show any grouped calendars.

3. **Type a descriptive name for your group and press Return.**

Adding a new calendar to a group

After you create a group, you can add new calendars to the group by following these steps:

1. **In the Calendar List, click the group name to which you want to add a new calendar.**

2. **Choose File⇨New Calendar.**

A new calendar appears indented under the group.

3. **Type a descriptive name for your new calendar and then press Return.**

Moving an existing calendar to a group

If you have an existing calendar that you want to move into a group, follow these steps:

1. **Move the cursor over a calendar in the Calendar List that you want to move into a group.**

2. **Hold down the mouse button, drag the mouse to the group you want to place the calendar in, and then release the mouse button.**

Your existing calendar now appears indented under the group.

Moving a calendar out of a group

In case you don't want a calendar in a group, you can move it out of a group by following these steps:

1. **Move the cursor over a calendar in the Calendar List that appears indented under a group.**

2. **Hold down the mouse button, drag the mouse to the CALENDARS title, and then release the mouse button.**

   Your existing calendar now appears outside any groups.

Moving a calendar or group

To help organize your calendars and groups, you might want to rearrange their order in the Calendar List by following these steps:

1. **Move the cursor to the calendar or group you want to move.**

2. **Hold down the mouse button and drag the mouse up or down.**

   A thick horizontal line appears where your calendar or group will appear in the Calendar List, as shown in Figure 2-3.

3. **Release the mouse button when you're happy with the new location of your calendar or group.**

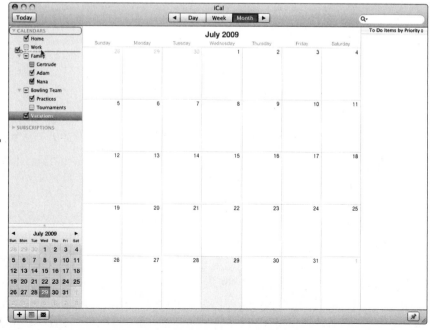

Figure 2-3: A horizontal line shows where your calendar or group will appear when you release the mouse button.

Renaming and deleting calendars and groups

At any time, you can rename a calendar or group. The name of a calendar or group is for your benefit and has no effect on the way iCal works. To rename a calendar or group, double-click a calendar or group name, which highlights that name. Type a new name and press Return.

If you find that you no longer need a particular calendar or group, click the one you want to delete and choose Edit⇨Delete. If you have any events stored on a calendar, a dialog appears, asking whether you really want to delete that calendar or group. Click Delete. If you delete a calendar or group by mistake, choose Edit⇨Undo or press ⌘+Z.

When you delete a calendar, you also delete any events stored on that calendar. When you delete a group, you delete all calendars stored in that group along with all events stored on those calendars. Make sure you really want to delete a calendar or group of calendars.

Using the Mini-Month

The Mini-Month is a miniature view of the current month that lets you see which days fall on specific dates. You can also use the Mini-Month display to switch to a different day or week within the Day or Week view displayed in the center pane of the iCal window. You can hide or show the Mini-Month by choosing View⇨Show/Hide Mini Months or by clicking the View/Hide Mini-Month icon in the bottom-left corner of the iCal window.

Creating and Modifying Events

An event is any occurrence that has a specific time and date associated with it. Some common types of events are meetings, appointments with clients, times when you need to pick someone up (such as at the airport), or recreational time, such as a two-week vacation. If you know a particular event will occur on a specific day and time, you can store that event in an iCal calendar so that you won't forget or schedule something else in that time.

Viewing events

iCal lets you display time frames by day, week, or month, and shows all the events you've scheduled for the day, week, or month you choose to view. To change the time frame of your displayed events, click the Day, Week, or Month button at the top of the iCal window. Figure 2-4 shows the day and week views (refer to Figure 2-1 for the month view).

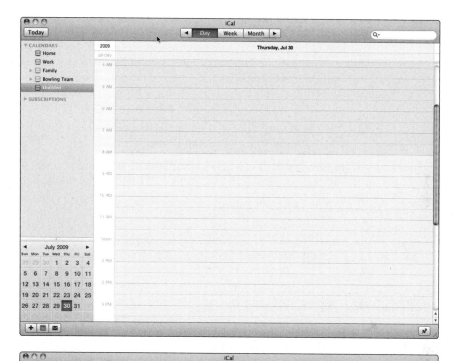

Figure 2-4:
The day and
week time
frames to
view events.

Creating an event

To store an event, you need to decide which calendar to store the event on, the date and time to schedule the event, and the event's duration. To create an event, follow these steps:

1. **In the Calendar List, click the calendar you want to store the event on.**

2. **Click the Day, Week, or Month button at the top of the iCal window, whichever you prefer to work with.**

3. **In the Day or Week view, double-click the time you want to place the event.**

A New Event color-coded box appears, as shown in Figure 2-5.

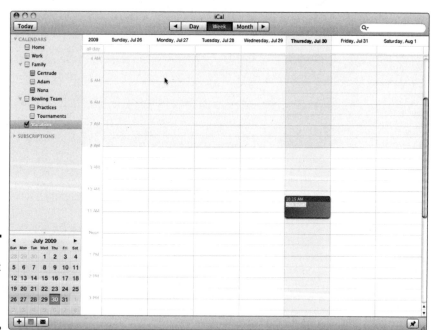

Figure 2-5:
A new event appears as a color-coded box.

4. **Type a description of your event and press Return.**

In the Day or Week view, iCal automatically sets your event for one hour. You can define the start and end time of an event by moving the mouse cursor to the top or bottom of an event until it turns into a two-way pointing arrow. Hold down the mouse button and move it up or down to define your start and end times in 15-minute increments.

5. **To create a new event in the Month view — which is the view I prefer to work in — double-click a day, and the Edit Event box appears, as shown in Figure 2-6.**

   In this box, you can define the details of your event, such as establishing the starting and ending dates and times, and also writing a location or setting the event to Repeat. Repeating events are handy to remind you of such events as weekly swimming lessons, monthly pet meds, or an anniversary. I explain details for each function of the Edit Event box in the next section.

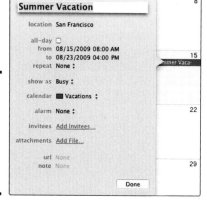

Figure 2-6:
The Edit
Event box
lets you
define the
details for
your event.

6. **When you finish defining your event, click Done.**

Editing an event

Sometimes you don't have all the details of an event when you create it, or the details change. Editing an event lets you change the time, the date, or the description of an event. You can also add features to an event, such as setting an alarm or automatically opening a file.

Changing the description of an event

Each time you create an event, you type in a description of that event. To modify this description, follow these steps:

1. **Click the event you want to modify and then choose Edit⇨Edit Event or press ⌘+E.**

2. **Click the event description (in Figure 2-6, this is Summer Vacation).**

   A text box appears around the event description.

3. **(Optional) Click the All Day check box to remove the From and To fields if you don't need to use those fields for the event.**

4. **Use the arrow and Delete keys to edit the event description and type any new text. Click Done when you finish.**

Click the Location field to type a location where the event takes place.

Creating a recurring event

For an event that occurs regularly, such as every Monday or every month, you can create an event one time and tell iCal to display that event on a recurring basis. To create a recurring event, follow these steps:

1. **Create a New Event and open the Edit Event dialog; or click an existing event and then choose Edit⇨Edit Event.**

An Edit Event dialog appears (refer to Figure 2-6).

2. **Click the Repeat pop-up menu and choose an option, such as Every Day or Every Month.**

3. **(Optional) In the Repeat pop-up menu, click Custom.**

A dialog appears, as shown in Figure 2-7, letting you define specific days for the recurring event, such as every Monday and Thursday or the first Wednesday of every month. Click OK when you finish creating your custom recurring event.

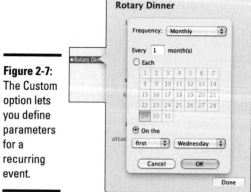

Figure 2-7:
The Custom option lets you define parameters for a recurring event.

4. **In the Edit Event dialog, click Done.**

iCal automatically displays your recurring event throughout the rest of the calendar until you modify the event.

Setting an alarm for an event

Scheduling an event is useless if you forget about it. That's why iCal gives you the option of setting an alarm that can notify you of upcoming events. To set an alarm, you need to decide how you want the alarm to notify you, such as displaying a message on the screen.

To set an alarm for an event, follow these steps:

1. **Click an event you want reminded about and then choose Edit⇨Edit Event or press ⌘+E.**

   An Edit dialog appears (refer to Figure 2-6).

2. **Click the Alarm pop-up menu.**

   You can choose the following options:

   • *None:* Removes any alarms you've already set for the event.

   • *Message:* Displays a message on the screen to alert you of an event.

   • *Message with Sound:* Displays a message on the screen and plays a sound to alert you of an event.

   • *Email:* Sends an e-mail message to you.

   • *Open File:* Loads and displays a file, such as a report that you can review for an upcoming meeting.

   • *Run Script:* Runs an AppleScript file that can control your Mac.

3. **Click the time pop-up menu to define when you want the alarm to trigger, such as 15 minutes or 1 hour before the event.**

4. **(Optional) Depending on the alarm type you choose, other pop-up menus might appear and let you choose how to use your alarm. Adjust the settings as desired.**

   You can add an additional alarm (or many additional alarms) to an event by clicking the Alarm pop-up menu that automatically appears beneath a new or existing alarm.

5. **Click Done.**

Moving an event to another calendar

You can always move an event from one calendar to another, such as from your Work calendar to your Home calendar. To move an event to another calendar, follow these steps:

1. **Click an event that you want to modify and then Choose Edit⇨Edit Event or press ⌘+E.**

Book VII
Chapter 2

Staying on Schedule
with iCal

2. **Click the Calendar pop-up menu and then choose the calendar name you want the event to appear in.**

3. **Click Done.**

Adding information to an event

To prepare for an event, you can also store information about that event's location, attendees, any important files related to the event (such as a presentation), a Web site URL, and any additional notes you want to jot down.

To add information to an event, follow these steps:

1. **Click an event that you want to modify and then Choose Edit⇨Edit Event or press ⌘+E.**

2. **Choose one or more of the following:**

   - *Location:* Remind yourself where the event will take place.

   - *Attendees:* Type the names of people associated with an event.

   - *Attachments:* Attach a file to an event, such as a business presentation that you need to give at the event.

   - *URL:* Type a Web site address that's relevant to your event, such as the restaurant's Web site for an upcoming dinner.

   - *Note:* Type any additional notes about your event.

3. **Click Done.**

Moving an event

In case you store an event at the wrong date or time, you can change the date and time in the Edit Event dialog, or move it to a new date and time by following these steps:

1. **Move the cursor to the middle of the event box.**

2. **Hold down the mouse button and drag the cursor to a new time or date.**

   The event moves with the cursor; the duration doesn't change.

3. **Release the mouse button when you're happy with the new date and time of the event.**

Duplicating an event

If a particular event occurs more than one time, you could type the event multiple times, but why spend all that effort? Instead, you can create an event, duplicate it, and then move the duplicate to another date. To duplicate an event, just click it and choose Edit⇨Duplicate or press ⌘+D (or hold down the Option key and then drag the event to the new time slot). When the duplicate appears, move the cursor to it, drag the event to a new date, and then release the mouse button.

If your event occurs at a regular interval — for example, once a month or every Tuesday and Thursday — you can make your event a recurring event in the Repeat pop-up menu of the Edit Event dialog.

Deleting an event

When you no longer need to remember an event, you can delete it. Just click it and choose Edit⇨Delete. If you delete an event by mistake, press ⌘+Z or choose Edit⇨Undo to retrieve your event.

Finding Events

Storing events is only useful if you can view upcoming events so you can prepare for them. To help you find and view events, iCal offers several different methods that include using colors to identify different types of events and letting you search for a specific event by name.

Color-coding events

To help identify which events belong to which calendars, you can assign a color to every calendar in your Calendar List. So if you assign the color blue to your Home calendar and the color red to your Work calendar, you can quickly identify which events on your calendar are home-related (blue) or work-related (red).

To assign a color to a calendar, click a calendar in the Calendar List and choose Edit⇨Get Info or press ⌘+I. In the Info dialog that appears (see Figure 2-8), click the color pop-up menu, choose a color, and then click OK. Events stored on that calendar now appear in the color you chose.

Use contrasting colors for multiple calendars to make it easy to tell which events belong to which calendar.

Selectively hiding events

Normally, iCal displays all events, color-coding them so that you can tell which events belong to which calendars. However, if you have too many events, you might find that mixing Home and Work events can seem too confusing. If you want to see only events stored on a specific calendar (such as Home or Work calendars), you can hide events stored on other calendars.

Figure 2-8:
The Info
dialog lets
you edit a
calendar's
name and
assign it a
color.

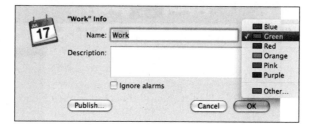

To hide events stored on other calendars, deselect the check box of any of
those calendars in the Calendar List. To view events stored on a calendar,
make sure a check mark appears in the check box of that calendar, as shown
in Figure 2-9.

Hidden calendar

Figure 2-9:
Hiding a
calendar
hides all
events
stored
on that
calendar.

Checking for today's events

Probably the most important events you need to worry about are the ones you've scheduled for today. To see all events scheduled for today, click the Day or Week button at the top of the iCal window and then choose View⇨Go to Today.

Another quick way to review any upcoming events for today is to use the Calendar widget in Dashboard. To display today's events in the Calendar widget, click the current date (which appears in the left pane) of the Calendar widget until the events pane appears. (For more information about Dashboard, see Book II, Chapter 1.)

Checking events for a specific date

Sometimes you might need to know whether you have any events scheduled on a certain date. To check a specific date, click the Day or Week button at the top of the iCal window and then choose View⇨Go to Date.

The Month view can show you the events scheduled for a particular date, but the Day and Week views can show you the specific times of your events for that day.

Searching for an event

If you scheduled an event several days ago, you might forget the exact date of that event. To help you find a specific event, iCal lets you search for it by typing all or part of the information stored in that event, such as the event name, the attendee names, or any notes you stored about the event.

To search for an event, follow these steps:

1. **Click the Spotlight text box in the upper-right corner of the iCal window.**

2. **Type as much text as you can remember about the event you want to find, such as an attendee's name or the location of the event.**

   The iCal program displays a list of events that match the text you type. The list appears below the calendar, as shown in Figure 2-10.

3. **Double-click an event that Spotlight found.**

   Your chosen event appears.

4. **Click the Clear button in the Spotlight text box to remove the list of matching events from the bottom of the iCal window (or choose View⇨Hide Search Results).**

Clear button

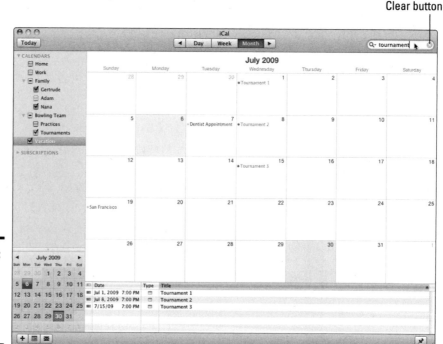

Figure 2-10: Spotlight can help you search and find events.

Making a To-Do List

A To-Do List typically contains goals or reminders of important tasks that you want to accomplish usually by a specific date or time. By reviewing your To-Do List every day, you can stay focused on achieving the goals that are most important to you so that you don't waste time accomplishing tasks that won't get you any closer to your goals.

Viewing and hiding the To-Do List

You can view your To-Do List and then hide it to make more room for viewing your events. To show the To-Do List, choose View⇨Show To Do List. The To-Do List appears on the right side of the iCal window.

To hide the To-Do List from view, choose View⇨Hide To Do List. This tucks the To-Do List out of sight once more. By default, iCal hides the To-Do List.

Another way to hide or display the To-Do List is to click the pushpin icon at the bottom-right corner of the iCal window.

Adding tasks to the To-Do List

When you add a task to your To-Do List, you must assign it to a calendar so that it appears color coded, like an event. By color-coding your To Do tasks, you can identify which tasks might be work-related and which might be related to any other calendars you've created.

To add a task to the To-Do List, follow these steps:

1. **Choose View⇨Show To Do List. (Skip this step if the To-Do List is already visible.)**

2. **Click a calendar that you want to assign a task to, such as the Work or Home calendar.**

3. **Double-click any blank space in the To-Do List.**

   A blank To-Do task appears, color-coded to match the calendar you chose in Step 2.

4. **Type a description of your task and press Return.**

   Your chosen task appears in the To-Do List.

Setting due dates for your To-Do List tasks

It's a good idea to place due dates on your To-Do List tasks so that you have a deadline, which can spur you into taking action to achieve your goal.

To assign a due date to a To-Do task, follow these steps:

1. **Double-click a task in the To-Do List or click a task in the To-Do List and Choose Edit⇨Edit To Do.**

   An Edit dialog appears, as shown in Figure 2-11.

2. **Select the Due Date check box.**

   When you select the Due Date check box, a date appears so that you can type a month, day, and year for the due date.

3. **Click Close.**

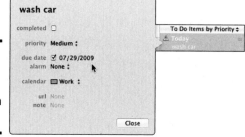

Figure 2-11:
The Edit dialog lets you modify a To-Do task.

Prioritizing your To-Do List

Not all tasks are equally important. To prioritize your tasks, click the Prioritize button that appears to the right of a task in the To-Do List. A pop-up menu appears, from which you can choose None, Low, Medium, or High, as shown in Figure 2-12. Click the To Do pop-up menu (the gray button at the top of the To Do window that contains the text "To Do Items by Priority") and then choose Sort by Priority. This option puts your High priority tasks at the top of your To-Do List.

Figure 2-12:
If you sort tasks by priority, you can see the most important tasks on your To-Do List.

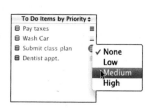

Completing, editing, and deleting To-Do tasks

Completing tasks can give you a sense of accomplishment. Rather than delete a completed task, you can mark it completed. To mark a task completed, select the check box that appears to the left of a task in the To-Do List.

After you create a task, you can always edit it later to correct any misspellings or make any modifications. To edit a To Do task, follow these steps:

1. **Double-click a task.**

An Edit dialog appears (refer to Figure 2-11).

2. **Click the top text box and type a new description of your task, or use the arrow and Delete key to edit the existing text.**

3. **Click Done.**

When you finish a task, you'll eventually want to delete it to avoid cluttering your To-Do List. To delete a task, click the task and choose Edit⇨Delete. If you accidentally delete a task, you can retrieve it by pressing ⌘+Z or choosing Edit⇨Undo.

Subscribing to Online Calendars

The iCal program allows you to subscribe to online calendars, such as a calendar of holidays, or a calendar of new DVD releases. Calendars you subscribe to appear under the Subscriptions category in the Calendars column. Events that appear in these calendars are added, deleted, and modified by the person or organization that maintains the online calendar.

You can also add *calendar accounts,* typically known as CalDAV or Exchange accounts, which can display one or more calendars you use at your workplace or a calendar you created and use with your Google or Yahoo! e-mail account. Events that you create or change at work using your company's calendar program, or events you create or change using your Google or Yahoo! account, are automatically added to your iCal calendar, and vice versa.

To subscribe to an online calendar:

♦ Choose Calendar⇨Subscribe to open the URL dialog, type the Internet URL for the calendar you want to subscribe to, such as the URL for a U.S. holidays online calendar (shown in Figure 2-13), and then click Subscribe. The name of your new online calendar appears in the Calendars column, and the online calendar's events appear in your iCal calendar window.

♦ Choose iCal⇨Preferences to open the iCal Preferences window, click the Accounts tab, and then add an online calendar account, as I describe in the next section.

Figure 2-13:
The URL
dialog is
where you
type the URL
of an online
calendar
you want to
subscribe
to.

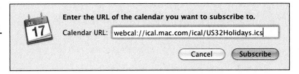

Enter the URL of the calendar you want to subscribe to.

Calendar URL: | webcal://ical.mac.com/ical/US32Holidays.ics |

Cancel   Subscribe

Two Web sites you can visit to find hundreds of useful (or just plain fun) online calendars to subscribe to are

+ **Apple iCal Calendars (`www.apple.com/downloads/macosx/calendars`)**

+ **iCalShare (`www.icalshare.com`)**

Adding an online calendar account

To add an online calendar:

1. **Choose iCal⇨Preferences to open the iCal preferences window and then click the Accounts tab to open the Accounts preferences window, as shown in Figure 2-14.**

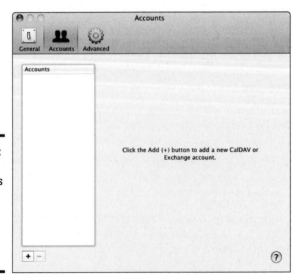

Accounts

General   Accounts   Advanced

Accounts

Click the Add (+) button to add a new CalDAV or
Exchange account.

+ −

Figure 2-14:
Accounts
preferences
let you add
and delete
online
calendar
accounts.

2. **Click the plus sign button in the lower-left corner to open the Add an Account dialog, as shown in Figure 2-15.**

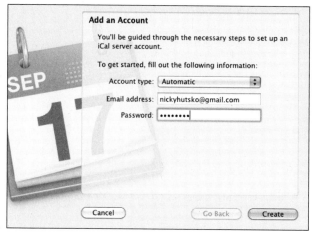

Figure 2-15:
The Add an
Account
dialog
prompts for
your online
calendar
account
information.

Add an Account

You'll be guided through the necessary steps to set up an iCal server account.

To get started, fill out the following information:

Account type: Automatic

Email address: nickyhutsko@gmail.com

Password: •••••••

Cancel   Go Back   Create

3. **Leave the Account Type pop-up menu set to Automatic, type your online account e-mail address and password into the appropriate fields, and then click Create.**

iCal determines and configures your online calendar's account settings, the name of your online calendar appears in the Calendars column, and your online calendar's events appear in your iCal calendar window.

If iCal is unable to configure your online calendar account, click the Account Type pop-up menu (refer to Figure 2-15), choose CalDAV, Exchange 2007, Google, or Yahoo!, fill the necessary fields, and then click Create.

Managing iCal Files

The iCal program stores files in a special file format called iCalendar (which uses the .ics file extension). Because the iCalendar file format is a standard for storing calendar information, you can share your calendar files with any program that recognizes the iCalendar format, including Microsoft Outlook.

Exporting iCal data

To share your calendars with other programs (even those running on other operating systems, such as Windows or Linux), you need to export your iCal file by following these steps:

1. **Choose File⇨Export.**

A dialog appears, giving you a chance to choose a filename and location to store your iCal data, as shown in Figure 2-16.

Figure 2-16:
To export your calendars, you need to specify a name for your exported file and a location to store it.

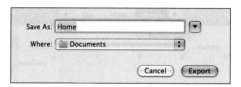

Save As: Home

Where: Documents

Cancel   Export

2. **Click the Save As text box and type a name for your file.**

3. **Choose the location to store your file from the Where pop-up menu.**

4. **Click Export.**

Importing iCal data

If you store calendar information in another program, you can export that data as an iCal file or a vCal file, and then import that file into iCal. If you're using Microsoft Entourage, you can save your Entourage calendar information as a separate file.

After you save calendar data from another program, you can import that file into iCal by following these steps:

1. **Choose File⇨Import and choose Import or Import from Entourage.**

If you choose Import from Entourage, iCal scans your Mac's hard drive for your existing Entourage calendar data and imports those calendar events into iCal, and you can skip the remaining steps.

2. **Click the drive and/or folder that contains the file you want to import.**

3. **Click the file you want to import and then click Import.**

iCal imports your chosen calendar file's data into iCal.

Backing up iCal data and restoring a backup file

Because iCal can store all your upcoming events (appointments, meetings, and so on), disaster could strike if your hard drive fails and wipes out your iCal data. For that reason, you should always keep a backup copy of your iCal data. To do so, follow these steps:

1. **Choose File⇨Export⇨iCal Archive.**

   The Save dialog appears.

2. **Click the Save As text box and type a descriptive name for your iCal backup file.**

3. **Choose the location for storing your file from the Where pop-up menu.**

4. **Click Save.**

It's a good idea to save your iCal backup file on a separate drive, such as an external hard drive. That way if your Mac hard drive fails, you won't lose both your original iCal data and your backup file at the same time. For more details on backing up files, see Book II, Chapter 2.

To retrieve your schedule from a backup file that you created earlier, choose File⇨Import⇨Import. In the Open dialog that appears, click the drive and folder where you saved your backup iCal file. Then click Import. iCal imports the backed-up file; any changes you made since the last backup will be lost.

Printing an iCal file

Even if you have a laptop, you can't always have your computer with you, so you might want to print your calendar in the Day, Week, or Month view. To print a calendar, follow these steps:

1. **Choose File⇨Print.**

   A Print dialog appears, as shown in Figure 2-17.

2. **Click the View pop-up menu and choose Day, Week, or Month.**

3. **(Optional) Change any other settings, such as the paper size or time range that you want to view.**

4. **Click Continue.**

   Another Print dialog appears.

5. **Click the Printer pop-up menu, choose a printer, and then click Print.**

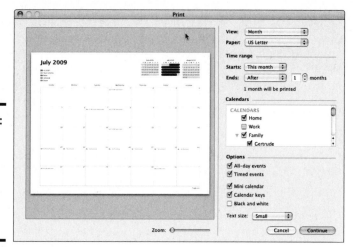

Figure 2-17:
The Print
dialog
shows you
how your
calendar
will appear
on paper.

Syncing with other devices

You can synchronize your iCal calendars with your iPhone or iPod when you
connect it to your Mac and open iTunes. Follow these steps:

1. **Connect your iPhone or iPod to your Mac with a USB cable.**

2. **Click the Info tab and then choose Sync iCal Calendars.**

3. **Choose to synchronize all your calendars or just selected ones.**

4. **Click Apply.**

   Your iCal calendars transfer or update automatically on your iPhone or
   iPod.

If you have a MobileMe account, you can keep your iPhone, Mac, and even
Windows computers all synchronized automatically.

Chapter 3: Running Windows on a Mac

In This Chapter

✔ Understanding why you might need Windows

✔ Giving your Mac a split personality with Boot Camp

✔ Running virtual machines

✔ Using CrossOver Mac

As much as you might enjoy using your Mac, sometimes you might need to run Windows because you need to use a program that runs only on Windows. Many programs are Windows-only, such as a number of astrology or stock picking programs, as are many custom applications developed by a company for in-house use. When faced with this dilemma, you have a choice:

✦ You can buy a Windows PC and use that computer just to run the Windows program you need.

✦ You can run Windows on your Mac. Ever since Apple started using Intel processors, you've been able to turn your Mac into a Windows PC.

Don't worry — you don't have to wipe out your hard drive and eliminate the Mac OS to run Windows. You have ways to run Windows on your Mac that still let you use all the features that made you want to use a Mac in the first place.

 If you need Windows to access Microsoft Exchange services like address lists, calendar events, and e-mail, Mac OS X 10.6 Snow Leopard gives you access to this information through Mail, iCal, and Address Book. Therefore, you might not need to install Windows after all.

Giving Your Mac a Split Personality with Boot Camp

To install Windows on a Mac, you can split your hard drive in two parts (the parts are *partitions*) and use one partition to install and run Windows and a second to keep using Mac OS X the way you've been using it. By storing two different operating systems on your hard drive, you can choose which operating system to use every time you turn on your computer. To divide your hard drive into partitions and install Windows, Apple provides a program called Boot Camp.

To use Boot Camp, you need the following:

✦ A Mac with an Intel processor

✦ Version 10.5 or later of the Mac OS X operating system

✦ (Optional) A printer for printing instructions for installing Boot Camp

✦ At least 10GB free space on your Mac's hard drive

✦ An optical disc drive, either internal or external

✦ The latest firmware updates

Firmware is software stored on your Mac's internal processor. Firmware tells your Mac how to turn itself on and work with all of its hardware components. If Apple has released new firmware for your Mac, you can find and retrieve it by clicking the Apple menu and choosing Software Update.

✦ A Mac OS X version 10.6 installation disc

✦ A legitimate copy of Windows XP Service Pack 2 (SP2) or any version of Vista (Basic, Home Premium, Business, or Ultimate editions) or Windows 7

You must use a full, 32-bit version of Windows XP, Vista, or Windows 7 that comes on a single CD or DVD. You can use a 64-bit version of Windows Vista or Windows XP Pro if your Mac Pro or MacBook Pro was built in 2008 or later.

Follow these basic steps to use Boot Camp:

1. **Make sure your Mac can run Boot Camp.**

2. **Create a partition on your hard drive and install Windows.**

The following sections give the details you need to complete these steps.

Making sure you can run Boot Camp

If you have a new Mac, chances are very good that you can run Boot Camp. However, the older your Mac is, the lower your chances of using this program.

Identifying the hardware capabilities of your Mac

To identify the processor, firmware version, and version number of the Mac OS X operating system running on your computer, follow these steps:

1. **Click the Apple menu and choose About This Mac.**

   An About This Mac window, shown in Figure 3-1, appears.

Figure 3-1:
The About
This Mac
window
identifies
the
processor
type and
version of
Mac OS X.

2. **Make sure the processor type contains the word *Intel,* such as Intel Core 2 Duo.**

   If the processor type contains the term *PowerPC,* you can't use Boot Camp.

3. **Make sure the version number is 10.5 or higher.**

   If the version number is lower, such as 10.3, you can't use Boot Camp until you acquire and install a newer version of Mac OS X.

4. **Click the Close button of the About This Mac window.**

Identifying the amount of free space on your hard drive

You need at least 10GB of free space on your hard drive to install both Boot Camp and Windows. To find out how much free space you have on your hard drive, click the Finder icon in the Dock and, in the Finder window that opens, click the Macintosh HD icon in the sidebar. If you look at the status bar at the bottom of the Finder window, you can see how much space is available on your hard drive.

Installing Windows

When you're certain your Mac can run Boot Camp, you need to go through two more steps before you can install Windows. First, you need to partition your hard drive. This reserves a chunk of your hard drive for Windows. Some good news here: Creating a partition and installing Windows on

**Book VII
Chapter 3**

**Running Windows
on a Mac**

your computer are tasks you have to do only once (unless your hard drive crashes and you have to reinstall everything).

Second, you need to install Windows on your newly created hard drive partition. Installing Windows can be time-consuming but isn't necessarily difficult. The two most technical parts of installing Windows on a Mac involve partitioning your hard drive and choosing that partition to install Windows on.

Partitioning divides your hard drive in two parts: one part for Mac OS X and the second part for Windows. Boot Camp uses nondestructive partitioning, which means you resize your hard drive without losing data. After you partition your hard drive, you must tell Windows which partition to install on, and you must specify the partition designated for Windows.

If you install Windows on the wrong partition, you'll wipe out everything on your Mac. If you don't feel comfortable partitioning a hard drive and choosing the right partition to install Windows on, get a more knowledgeable friend to help you.

Before installing Windows, it's a good idea to run the Disk Utility to verify and repair your Mac hard drive and then back up your files. You can read about backing up in Book II, Chapter 2 and about verifying a disk in Book II, Chapter 5.

To install Windows, follow these steps:

1. **Open the Finder window by clicking the Finder icon on the Dock.**

2. **Choose Go⇨Utilities.**

   The contents of the Utilities folder appear in the right pane.

3. **Double-click the Boot Camp Assistant icon.**

   A Boot Camp Assistant window appears, informing you of the process of using Boot Camp, as shown in Figure 3-2.

4. **Click the Print Installation & Setup Guide button.**

   A Print dialog appears.

5. **Change the default settings, such as changing the paper size, and click OK.**

   A second Print dialog appears, letting you choose a specific printer and number of copies to print.

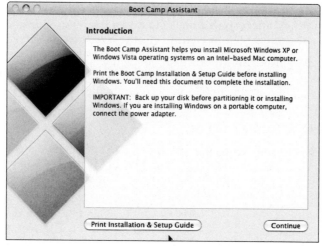

Figure 3-2:
The introductory Boot Camp Assistant window tells you what you need to run Boot Camp.

6. **Choose a printer and click the Print button.**

   The Installation & Setup Guide prints and then the Boot Camp Assistant window appears again (refer to Figure 3-2).

7. **Read the Installation & Setup Guide for the most current instructions for installing Boot Camp and then click the Continue button.**

   The Boot Camp Assistant window displays a Create a Partition for Windows box, as shown in Figure 3-3.

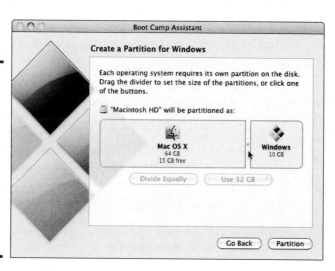

Figure 3-3:
The Create a Partition for Windows box lets you define how much hard drive space to allocate for Windows.

8. **Move the pointer over the divider between the Macintosh partition and the Windows partition, hold down the mouse button, and then drag the mouse left or right to choose a partition size.**

   If you're installing Windows XP, the minimum partition size should be 5GB. If you're installing Vista, the minimum partition size should be 8GB. You might want to choose an even larger partition size if you plan to install many Windows programs.

9. **Click the Partition button.**

   Boot Camp partitions your hard drive. (This process might take a little while.) When partitioning is complete, another Boot Camp Assistant window appears, asking you to insert your valid Windows installation disc in your Mac, as shown in Figure 3-4.

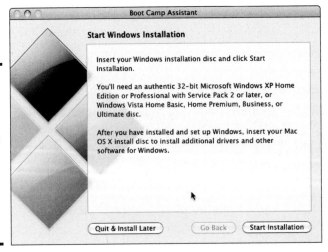

Figure 3-4: The Boot Camp Assistant window lets you know when to insert your Windows installation disc.

10. **Insert your Windows installation disc in your Macintosh and then click the Start Installation button.**

   When the Windows installation program asks you which partition to install on, look for the partition size you specified in Step 8 that displays BOOT CAMP. If you choose the wrong partition, Windows might install on your Mac's partition, which could wreck your files and bring your entire Mac crashing to its knees. Refer to your printed Installation & Setup Guide for specific XP, Vista, and Windows 7 help.

11. **Follow the Windows installation instructions on the screen, and when the installation is finished, eject the disc.**

   Be patient. Installing Windows can take time and Windows will reboot several times during installation, so don't panic if the screen suddenly goes blank.

12. **Insert the Mac OS X installation disc.**

13. **Follow the onscreen instructions to install the Boot Camp drivers.**

The Boot Camp drivers allow certain Mac components to work in the Windows environment, such as AirPort, the built-in iSight camera, the trackpad on a notebook MacBook, and the function keys on the Apple keyboard. Also, a Windows control panel installs from the Mac OS X installation disc.

Click Continue Anyway if you see a message that tells you the software you are installing has not passed Windows Logo testing. Do not click Cancel in any of the installer dialogs. Follow the instructions for any wizards that appear.

Choosing an operating system with Boot Camp

After you use Boot Camp to install Windows on your Mac, you can use Boot Camp to choose which operating system to run by following these steps:

1. **Restart your computer and hold down the Option key until two disk icons appear.**

One disk icon is labeled Windows and the other is labeled Macintosh HD. (If you changed the name of your Mac's hard disk, you'll see this name displayed instead.)

2. **Double-click the Windows or Macintosh Startup Disk icon.**

Your chosen operating system starts.

Holding down the X key after you power your Mac tells your Mac you want to load Mac OS X. You can let go of the X key as soon as you see the Mac OS X startup screen.

To switch to a different operating system, you have to shut down the current operating system and repeat the preceding steps to choose the other operating system.

If you start your Mac without holding down the Option key, your Mac starts the default operating system. You can define the default operating system in Mac OS X by following these steps:

1. **Within Mac OS X, click ⇨System Preferences to open the System Preferences window.**

2. **Click the Startup Disk icon under the System category.**

The Startup Disk window opens, as shown in Figure 3-5.

3. **Click the Mac OS X or Windows icon and click the Restart button.**

**Book VII
Chapter 3**

Running Windows on a Mac

Figure 3-5:
The Startup
Disk
window lets
you choose
which
partition
to make
the default
startup disk.

If you click the Target Disk Mode button, you can make your Mac appear like an external hard drive when connected to another computer with a FireWire cable.

Sharing Mac and Windows files

With Mac OS X version 10.6, whether you're running the Mac or Windows operating system, you can open and view files from the other operating system's hard drive partition. To modify files, copy the file from the partition where the file is stored to the operating system partition you're using. For example, if you're in Windows and want to modify a file saved on your Mac partition, copy the file from the Mac partition to the Windows partition, and then make the changes.

Removing Windows from your Mac

If you want to wipe out the partition on your hard drive that contains Windows, you can do so by following these steps:

1. **Double-click the Boot Camp Assistant icon in the Utilities folder.**

An Introduction dialog appears.

2. **Click the Continue button.**

A Select Task dialog appears.

3. **Click the Create or Remove a Windows Partition button and then click the Continue button.**

A Restore Disk to a Single Volume dialog appears.

Wiping out your Windows partition deletes all data stored on that partition that you created using Windows.

4. **Click the Restore button.**

Using Virtual Machines

Although you can share files between the Mac and Windows partitions as described previously in this chapter, you might still want to purchase a virtualization program, such as Parallels (www.parallels.com) or Fusion (www.vmware.com), to run Windows and Mac OS X at the same time and switch between the two. Another virtualization program that you can download and use free is VirtualBox (www.virtualbox.org).

Virtualization is a technology that lets you run multiple operating systems at the same time where each operating system time-shares the computer's hardware. Because the operating system isn't really controlling the computer's hardware completely, the operating system is called a *virtual machine* (as opposed to a real machine).

Parallels, Fusion, and Virtual Box work in similar ways by creating a single file on your Mac hard drive that represents a virtual PC hard drive that contains the actual Windows operating system plus any additional Windows programs you might install, such as Microsoft Office.

When you run Parallels, Fusion, or Virtual Box, the program boots up from this virtual hard drive while your original Mac OS X operating system continues to run. This lets you run another operating system, such as Windows, inside a separate Mac OS X window, as shown in Figure 3-6.

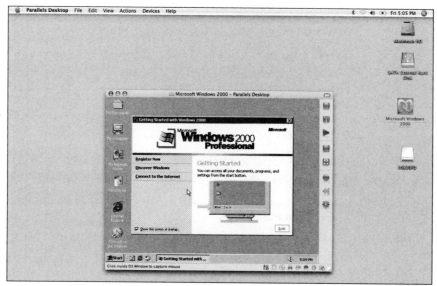

Figure 3-6:
A virtualization program lets you run Windows inside a separate Mac window.

Instead of forcing you to load Windows and then load a specific program within Windows, virtualization programs let you store a Windows program icon directly on the Desktop or in the Dock so that it behaves like a Mac program icon.

Clicking a Windows program icon loads Windows and the Windows program at the same time without showing the Windows desktop or the Windows Start menu.

Because the operating system stored on the virtual hard drive has to share the computer's processor and memory with Mac OS X, operating systems running on virtual machines tend to run slower than when you run Windows and Windows programs within Boot Camp. In Boot Camp, the program has total access to your computer's hardware, meaning the program runs as fast as it would on a standalone Windows PC.

To ease the migration from Windows to the Mac, virtualization programs can clone your existing Windows PC and duplicate it, with all your data and programs, on to the Mac. You can essentially use your old Windows PC as a virtual computer on your Mac.

Using CrossOver Mac

With Boot Camp, VirtualBox, Parallels, and Fusion, you need to buy a separate copy of Windows. CrossOver Mac lets you run Windows programs without out a copy of Windows. The program works by fooling Windows programs into thinking they're really running on a Windows PC.

CrossOver Mac lets you pop a Windows CD into your Mac and install the Windows program on a simulated PC that CrossOver Mac creates automatically on your Mac. After you install a Windows program, CrossOver Mac displays the normal Windows icons inside a Finder window. Double-clicking the Windows program icon runs that Windows program on your Mac, as shown in Figure 3-7.

Like Parallels, Fusion, and Virtual Box, CrossOver Mac runs only on Intel Macintosh computers. A more crucial limitation is that CrossOver Mac works with only a handful of Windows programs, so you can't run just any Windows program on a Mac with CrossOver Mac and expect it to run flawlessly.

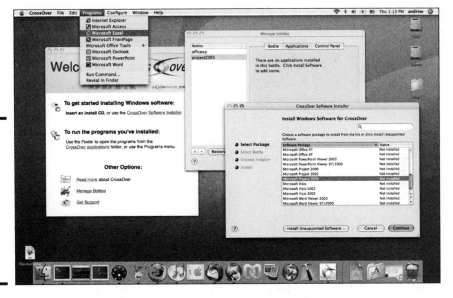

Figure 3-7:
CrossOver Mac lets you run a handful of Windows programs without running Windows.

To help you determine whether your favorite Windows program will work with CrossOver Mac, the product's Web site (www.codeweavers.com/compatibility/browse/name) lists all known programs that have been tested and verified to work correctly. If you need to run the latest Windows programs, a little-known Windows program, or a custom Windows program, CrossOver Mac probably won't let you run it. However, if you need to run only a handful of older or popular programs, CrossOver Mac might be the ideal solution.

Book VIII

Mac Networking

Contents at a Glance

Chapter 1: Networking Your Macs

In This Chapter

🗸 **Creating a wired network**

🗸 **Creating a wireless network**

*I*f you have multiple Macs in the same place, you might find it convenient to connect your Macs to a network. A *network* allows multiple computers to share files and other resources like printers or backup hard drives. Although you could copy a file on a USB flash drive, plug it into another computer, and copy the files onto the second computer or print using the second computer's printer, such an approach (dubbed *sneaker net*) is tedious and inconvenient. However, when multiple computers connect to a network, they can share files almost as quickly and easily as copying a file from one folder to another.

Creating a Wired Network

The simplest wired network just connects two computers together using either a FireWire cable or a cable that conforms to a networking cable standard called *Ethernet.* Only the MacBook Air and two short-lived MacBook models shipped without a FireWire port. Every Mac (except the MacBook Air, again) has an Ethernet port, so if you plug a FireWire cable or Ethernet cable into the FireWire or Ethernet ports of two Macs, you'll have a simple network, as shown in Figure 1-1.

Figure 1-1:
A simple network connects two Macs via a FireWire cable or an Ethernet cable.

Ethernet or FireWire cable

Ethernet cables are often identified by the speeds that they can send data. The earliest Ethernet cables were Category 3 (or Cat 3) cables and could transfer data at 10 megabits per second (Mbps). The next generation of Ethernet cables was Category 5 (Cat 5) cables, which could transfer data at 100 Mbps. Category 6 (Cat 6) cables transfer data at 1,000 Mbps or one gigabit per second (Gbit/s). With networking, speed is everything and Category 6a (Cat 6a) and Category 7 (Cat 7) transfer data at 10 Gbit/s. Category 7a reaches transfer speeds of 100 Gbit/s.

Connecting two computers can be convenient for sharing files, but most networks typically consist of multiple computers connected together. Such a large network of multiple computers allows different computers to share files with each other.

Because it's physically impossible to connect more than two computers together with a single cable, networks typically use something called a *hub*. Each computer connects to the hub, which indirectly connects each computer to every other computer also connected to the hub, as shown in Figure 1-2.

An improved variation of a hub is called a *switch*. Physically, a hub and a switch both connect multiple computers in a single point (as shown in Figure 1-2).

With a hub, a network acts like one massive hallway that every computer shares. If a bunch of computers transfers data at the same time, the shared network can get crowded with data flowing everywhere, slowing the transfer of data throughout the network.

With a switch, the switch directs data between two computers. As a result, a switch can ensure that data transfers quickly regardless of how much data the other computers on the network are transferring at the time.

A variation of a switch is a *router,* which often adds a firewall. Because routers cost nearly the same as ordinary hubs and switches, most wired networks rely on routers. So if you want to create a wired network of computers, you need

✦ Two or more computers

✦ A network switch or router

✦ Enough cables to connect each computer to the network switch or router

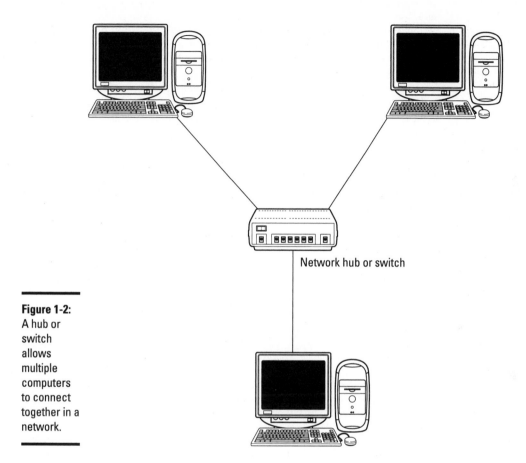

Network hub or switch

Figure 1-2:
A hub or
switch
allows
multiple
computers
to connect
together in a
network.

The speed of a wired network depends entirely on the slowest speed of the components used in your network. If you plan to use Cat 6 cables in your network, make sure your network switch is designed for Cat 6 cables. If not, you'll have the fastest Ethernet cables connected to a slow network switch, which will run only as fast as the slowest part of your network.

Creating a Wireless Network

Because wired networks can be inflexible, more people set up wireless networks instead. Essentially a wireless network is no different from a wired network, except (as the name implies) there are no wires. Wireless networks are generally a bit slower than wired networks.

Because of physical obstacles, wireless networks don't always reach certain parts of a room or building, resulting in "dead spots" where you can't connect wirelessly. Walls or furniture can disrupt the wireless signals.

All you need is a device called an *access point,* which can plug into your existing wired network. This access point broadcasts a signal that other computers can receive, creating a wireless connection to the network, as shown in Figure 1-3.

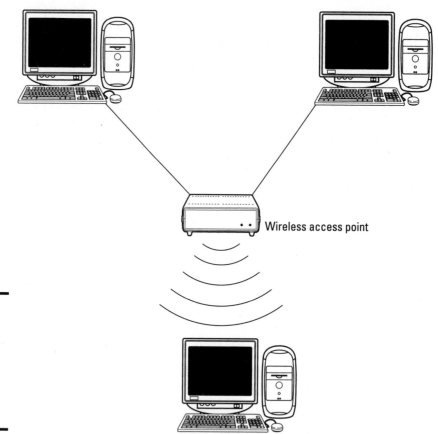

Wireless access point

Figure 1-3:
A wireless access point extends the reach of a wired network.

Your router may have wireless capabilities so you can connect the computer or printer that stays in one place to the router with an Ethernet cable but connect to the wireless network connection on your MacBook to work from your lawn chair in the garden, or from a desktop Mac located in another room in the house. Some cable and DSL modems come with built-in Wi-Fi transmitters, which means one device does the job of two if you choose to use a separate Wi-Fi router to connect to your cable or DSL modem.

The hazards of wireless networking

To access a wired network, someone must physically connect a computer to the network using a cable. However, connecting to a wireless network can be done from another room, outside a building, or even across the street. As a result, wireless networks can be much less secure because a wireless network essentially shoves dozens of virtual cables out the window, so anyone can walk by and connect into the network.

The practice of connecting to unsecured wireless networks with malicious intentions is *war driving* (also war flying, war walking, or war boating, depending on how you move around). The basic idea behind war driving is to drive around a city and keep track of which areas offer an unsecured wireless network. After getting connected to an unsecured wireless network, an intruder can wipe out files, capture personal information or interfere with the network's operation.

When creating a wireless network, you can make your network more secure by taking advantage of a variety of security measures and options. The simplest security measure is to use a password that locks out people who don't know the password. For further protection, you can also use encryption.

Encryption scrambles the data sent to and from the wireless network. Without encryption, anyone can intercept information sent through a wireless network (including passwords). Still another security measure involves configuring your wireless network to let only specific computers connect to the wireless network. By doing this, an intruder cannot gain access to the wireless network because his or her computer is not approved to access the network.

Ultimately, wireless networking requires more security measures simply because it offers potential intruders the ability to access the network without physically being in the same room, house, or building. Wireless networks can be as safe as wired networks — as long as you turn on security options that can make your wireless network as secure as possible.

The difference between an access point and a router is the router is at the center of the network, allowing the computers to share printers, Internet connections, and external hard drives. The access point is what allows the computers with wireless capabilities to connect to the network from across the room, from another room, or even outside on the porch, providing the wireless signal is strong enough to reach wherever you are with your Mac.

For more information about wireless networking, pick up a copy of *AirPort and Mac Wireless Networks For Dummies,* by Michael E. Cohen (Wiley).

Not all wireless networks are alike. The earliest wireless networks followed a technical specification called 802.11b or 802.11a. Newer wireless equipment followed a faster wireless standard called 802.11g, and the latest standard (at the time of this writing) is 802.11n.

When setting up a wireless network, make sure your router and/or wireless access point use the same wireless standard as the built-in wireless radio or wireless adapter plugged into each of your computers. All new and recent Macs connect to Wi-Fi routers that use one or up to all four types of the wireless network standards.

You can buy any brand of wireless access point or router to create a network, including Apple's Airport Extreme Base Station. Any router you choose will come with specific software and instructions for setting up your network. The basic steps are to

1. Name your network and base station so computers on the network can then find and connect to your Wi-Fi network.

2. Set up a password. (WPA2 provides the most security.)

3. Define how you connect to the Internet. (You may need information from your Internet Service Provider for this step.)

4. Add printers and/or external hard drives.

After you physically connect your wired network or configure your wireless network, you might still need to configure your Mac to work on your network if you want to share files and printers, which is the topic of Book VIII, Chapter 2.

Chapter 2: Sharing Files and Resources on a Network

In This Chapter

✔ **Sharing files**

✔ **Sharing printers**

✔ **Sharing an Internet connection**

*B*y sharing over a network, everyone can benefit, and the benefits can range from swapping files quickly and easily to sharing a single printer instead of having to buy a printer for every computer.

Although networks allow others to share your files, nobody on a network can rummage through your Mac without your permission. Ideally, a network allows you to share files and equipment without risking the loss or corruption of crucial files on your own computer.

Sharing Files

Sharing files makes it easy for different people to work on a project. Without a network, you could give someone a copy of a file, but then you might suddenly have three different versions of the same file, and nobody would know which file contains the most accurate information.

When your Mac is connected to a network, you have the option of sharing one or more folders with everyone else on the network. To share folders, you need to define different permission levels that allow or restrict what users can do with a folder and the files inside it:

✦ **Read & Write:** Other users have the ability to retrieve, delete, and modify files in the shared folder.

✦ **Read Only:** Other users can copy and open files, but they cannot modify or delete them.

✦ **Write Only (Drop Box):** Other users can only place files in the folder; they cannot copy, open, or even see any files stored in that folder.

✦ **No Access:** Specified users are blocked from accessing files on your Mac.

You decide which folder (or folders) to share, who can access that folder, and what access level you want others to have in accessing your shared folder.

You don't have to share folders. If you don't share folders, you can still use a network to access someone else's shared folders or use devices, such as printers, that are on the network.

Turning on file sharing

To turn on file sharing, follow these steps:

1. **Choose É⇨System Preferences to open the System Preferences window and then click the Sharing icon.**

The Sharing pane appears, as shown in Figure 2-1.

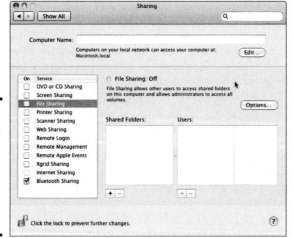

Figure 2-1: The Sharing pane lets you turn on file sharing and choose folders to share.

2. **Select the File Sharing check box in the leftmost Service column.**

3. **Click the plus sign button underneath the Shared Folders column.**

A dialog appears, displaying all the drives and folders on your Mac, as shown in Figure 2-2.

4. **Click a folder, such as the Public folder, which contains the Drop Box folder. The Public folder is in your Home folder.**

The Drop Box folder is a Write Only folder that allows others to drop files in, but it doesn't allow anyone (except you) to view and retrieve files.

Figure 2-2:
The Public
folder
contains a
special Drop
Box folder.

5. **Click Add.**

6. **Repeat Steps 4 through 6 for each additional folder you want to share via the network.**

7. **Click the Close button of the System Preferences window.**

Defining user access to shared folders

After you define one or more folders to share, you can also define the type of access people can have to your shared folders, such as giving certain people the ability to open and modify files and stopping other people from accessing your shared files.

The three types of network users are

+ **Yourself:** Gives you Read & Write access or else you won't be able to modify any files in your shared folders.

+ **Everyone:** Allows others to access your shared folders as guests without requiring a password.

+ **Names of specific network users:** Allows you to give individuals access to your shared folders with a name and password.

If you trust everyone on a network, you can give everyone Read & Write privileges to your shared folders. However, it's probably best to give everyone Read privileges and only certain people Read & Write privileges.

Defining access privileges for guests

To define access privileges for guests, follow these steps:

1. **Choose ⌂⇨System Preferences to open the System Preferences window.**

2. **Click the Sharing icon under the Internet & Wireless category to open the Sharing pane.**

3. **Click a folder in the Shared Folders list.**

   The Users list enumerates all the people allowed to access this particular shared folder, as shown in Figure 2-3. By default, every shared folder lists your name with Read & Write privileges.

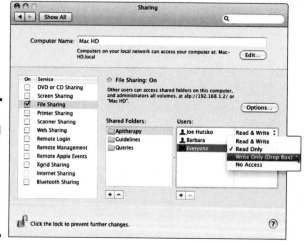

Figure 2-3: Each shared folder displays a list of users who can access that folder.

4. **Click Everyone (the guest account) to call up the access option pop-up menu and choose an access option, such as Read & Write, Read Only, Write Only (Drop Box), or No Access.**

5. **Repeat Steps 3 and 4 for each shared folder you want to configure.**

6. **Click the Close button of the System Preferences window.**

Giving individuals access to shared folders

The access level you give to the Everyone account for a shared folder means anyone on the network has that level of access to your files — Read & Write, Read Only, Write Only. You probably want to give Everyone the minimum access to a shared folder and give specific individuals higher levels of access.

To define a username and password to access a shared folder, follow these steps:

1. **Choose ⌘⇨System Preferences to open the System Preferences window and then click the Sharing icon to open the Sharing pane.**

2. **Click a folder in the Shared Folders list.**

   The Users list enumerates all the people allowed to access this particular shared folder (refer to Figure 2-3).

3. **Click the plus sign button under the Users list and then click the Address Book category in the left pane.**

   A dialog appears, as shown in Figure 2-4, where you can choose the name of a person stored in your Address Book or create a new user.

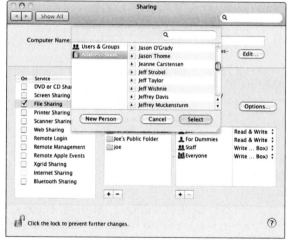

Figure 2-4:
A dialog lets you choose users in your Address book who can access shared folders.

4. **Click New Person.**

   A New Person dialog appears. Here you can type a username and password, as shown in Figure 2-5.

5. **Enter a name in the User Name text box.**

   The name can be an actual person or a made-up name, such as "Superman" or "John Doe." Don't forget to let the people who are going to use your folder know the username and password for that folder.

Figure 2-5:
The New
Person
dialog lets
you define
a new
user and
password
for
accessing
a shared
folder.

New Person

User Name: [   ]

Password: [   ]

Verify: [   ]

(?)   (Cancel)   (Create Account)

6. **Enter a password in the Password text box.**

7. **Reenter the password in the Verify text box.**

8. **Click the Create Account button.**

Your new account name appears in the Users & Group category, as shown in Figure 2-6.

Figure 2-6:
New
network
account
names
appear in
the Users
& Groups
category.

Users & Groups | Administrators
Address Book | Bo Katz
| Joey Harris
| Nuit

(New Person)   (Cancel)   (Select)

9. **Click the name of your new account, in the Users & Groups category, and click Select to return to the Sharing preferences pane (refer to Figure 2-3).**

Your chosen account name appears in the Users box.

10. **Click the pop-up menu that appears to the right of the name you just added to the Users box, and choose Read & Write, Read Only, or Write Only (Drop Box) to assign access privileges.**

11. **Click the Close button of the System Preferences window.**

Removing accounts from shared folders

If you create an account for others to use to access your shared folders, you might later want to change their access privileges (such as changing their access from Read & Write to Read Only) or delete their account altogether.

To delete an account from a shared folder, follow these steps:

1. **Choose ⬤⇨System Preferences to open the System Preferences window and then click the Sharing icon to open the Sharing pane.**

2. **Click a folder in the Shared Folders list.**

   The Users list enumerates all the people allowed to access this particular shared folder (refer to Figure 2-3).

3. **Click a name in the Users list that you want to delete.**

4. **Click the minus sign button under the Users list.**

   A dialog appears, asking whether you want to keep the account from accessing your shared folder.

5. **Click OK.**

6. **Click the Close button of the System Preferences window.**

File sharing in Sleep mode

With OS X Snow Leopard, your Mac can share files even if you set up your Mac to sleep when it's inactive for a certain time. (You can use this feature if your wireless network supports the 802.11n wireless protocol — see Book VIII, Chapter 1 for a brief explanation.) If you want your Mac to wake up when another user on the network wants to access your shared files, follow these steps:

1. **Choose ⬤⇨System Preferences to open the System Preferences window.**

2. **Click the Energy Saver icon in the Hardware category to open the Energy Saver pane.**

3. **Choose Power Adapter.**

4. **Click Wake for Network Access, as shown in Figure 2-7.**

5. **Click the Close button of the System Preferences window.**

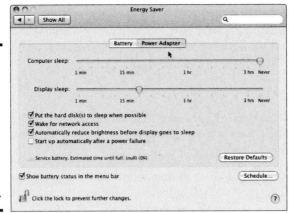

Figure 2-7:
Choose
Wake for
Network
Access
to allow
sharing
when your
Mac is in
Sleep mode.

Accessing shared folders

You can share your folders with others on a network, and likewise, others might want to share their folders with you. To access a shared folder on someone else's computer, follow these steps:

1. **Open the Finder by clicking the Finder icon in the Dock or clicking the white space on your Desktop.**

2. **Choose Go⇨Network.**

   A Network window appears, listing all the computers that offer shared folders as shown in Figure 2-8.

Figure 2-8:
The
Network
window lets
you connect
to other
computers.

3. **Double-click the computer you want to access.**

   Another Network window appears, listing all the shared folders you can access.

4. **Click the Connect As button to display the dialog shown in Figure 2-9.**

Figure 2-9:
The Connect As dialog lets you access a shared folder with an account name and password.

Enter your name and password for the server "Joe's MacBook 13'".

Connect as: ○ Guest
⦿ Registered User

Name: Joe

Password: ••••••

☑ Remember this password in my keychain

Cancel   Connect

5. **Select the Registered User (or Guest) radio button.**

   If you select the Guest radio button, skip to Step 8.

6. **Click the Name text box and type the account name to use for accessing that shared folder.**

   The account name is the name that the computer's user created in the earlier section, "Giving individuals access to shared folders."

7. **Click the Password text box and type the corresponding password.**

8. **Click Connect.**

   Depending on your access to the shared folder, you might be able to copy, open, modify, or delete files.

Another way to access a shared folder is to type a shared folder's AFP (Apple Filing Protocol) address into the Safari browser address text. To find a computer's AFP address, follow these steps:

1. **Choose ⇨System Preferences to open the System Preferences window and then click the Sharing icon to open the Sharing pane.**

2. **Click File Sharing in the Service list.**

   Directly underneath the File Sharing: On text is the AFP address of that particular Mac, such as afp://192.168.1.2, as shown in Figure 2-10.

3. **Click the Close button of the System Preferences window.**

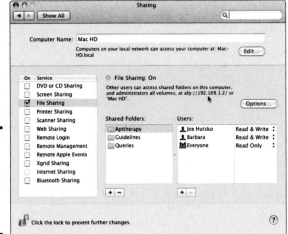

Figure 2-10:
The AFP
address
appears in
the Sharing
window.

Sharing Printers

You could buy a separate printer for each computer on your network. However, this solution would be expensive and space-consuming. An alternative is to connect a printer directly to one computer, and configure that one computer to share its printer with any computer connected to the same network. To share a printer, follow these steps:

1. **Choose ⬛⇨System Preferences to open the System Preferences window, and click the Sharing icon under the Internet & Wireless category to open the Sharing pane.**

2. **Select the Printer Sharing check box.**

   A list of printers physically connected to your Mac appears, as shown in Figure 2-11.

3. **Select the check boxes of the printers you want to share.**

   Note that Everyone Can Print is the default in the Users column.

4. **(Optional) Add individual users just as you would for sharing files by clicking the plus sign button beneath the Users column; choose No Access for Everyone and give selected users access to that printer.**

5. **Click the Close button of the Sharing window.**

When you choose File⇨Print in an application you're using and you want to print from, a Print dialog appears. If you click the Printer pop-up menu and choose Add Printer, a window appears (as shown in Figure 2-12), listing all the available printers connected directly to your Mac (USB) or shared over the network (Bonjour or Bonjour Shared).

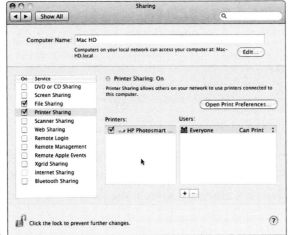

Figure 2-11: Each physically connected printer appears with a check box in the Sharing window.

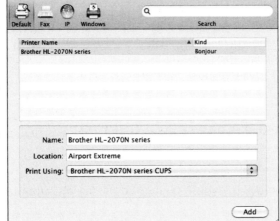

Figure 2-12: A Printer window lists all available printers you can use over a network.

Bonjour is a networking standard developed by Apple, which is used by most printers to connect to other computers through Ethernet cables (wired networks) or through wireless (Wi-Fi) connections (802.11a/b/g/n). Because Apple released Bonjour as an open source standard, printer companies have written software drivers to make their printers compatible with Bonjour, meaning Windows users can download the Bonjour for Windows program free so Windows PCs can access shared printers on a network.

Sharing an Internet Connection

Sharing an Internet connection lets one Mac access the Internet through another Mac. For example, one laptop Mac might have access to the Internet through a wireless connection, but a second, older laptop Mac might not have a wireless adapter and might lack access to the Internet. With Internet Sharing turned on, the second Mac can access the Internet through the first Mac.

To share an Internet connection, follow these steps:

1. **Choose ⌘⇨System Preferences to open the Systems Preferences window and then click the Sharing icon to open the Sharing pane.**

2. **Click the Internet Sharing option in the list box on the left.**

   Internet Sharing options appear, as shown in Figure 2-13.

3. **From the Share Your Connection From pop-up menu, choose how your Mac is connected to the Internet: Ethernet, AirPort, External Modem, or Bluetooth PAN.**

Figure 2-13: To turn on Internet Sharing, you must define how to share your Internet connection.

4. **In the To Computers Using list, check the box that indicates how the other computer is connected to your Mac: Ethernet, AirPort, or Bluetooth PAN.**

   To learn about the different connection options for connecting your Macs to create a network, see Book VIII, Chapter 1.

5. **Select the Internet Sharing check box.**

A dialog appears, asking whether you're sure that you want to turn on Internet Sharing.

6. **Click Start.**

7. **Click the Close button on the System Preferences window.**

The second computer, connected to your Mac through Ethernet, AirPort, or Bluetooth, can now access the Internet.

Book VIII
Chapter 2

Sharing Files and Resources on a Network

Chapter 3: Connecting to Bluetooth Wireless Devices and Networks

In This Chapter

✔ **Identifying Bluetooth capabilities**

✔ **Configuring Bluetooth**

✔ **Pairing devices**

✔ **Sharing through Bluetooth**

*B*luetooth is the name of a wireless technology standard designed primarily for connecting devices within a short distance of one another rather than through networks where one computer is in one room and another computer is in a room on another floor of the building — or on the other side of the globe.

Because of its short-range nature, Bluetooth is handy for connecting computers for short periods and for transferring small files, unlike faster wired or wireless (Wi-Fi) networks that connect computers on a more permanent basis.

Many handheld devices, such as mobile phones and personal digital assistants (PDAs), have built-in Bluetooth capabilities, which makes it easy to wirelessly sync calendars and address books between a handheld device and a computer (as explained in Book II, Chapter 3).

Common Bluetooth-enabled peripherals you can use with your Mac, such as wireless keyboards and mice, and headsets for chatting with iChat or using Internet phone services like Skype, can also connect to your Mac by using your Mac's built-in Bluetooth feature.

Bluetooth can connect devices up to 30 feet (10 meters) away, although any obstacles, such as walls, can limit the range of a Bluetooth device.

Identifying Bluetooth Capabilities

All new and recent Macs have Bluetooth capabilities. If you have a Mac that's more than a few years old, chances are, your Mac does not have Bluetooth capability built-in. In that case, you need to buy a Bluetooth adapter that plugs into a USB port or fits inside your Mac.

To determine if your Mac has Bluetooth capability, choose **⬢⇨System Preferences** to open the System Preferences window. Then look for the Bluetooth preferences icon like the one shown in the margin.

If you see a Bluetooth preferences icon, your Mac has Bluetooth capability. If you don't see a Bluetooth icon, your Mac doesn't have Bluetooth capability.

Configuring Bluetooth

After you determine that your Mac has Bluetooth capability (either built-in or added through a Bluetooth adapter that you bought separately), you can configure how Bluetooth works on your Mac. For example, you might not want to allow other computers to browse your hard drive through Bluetooth without your express permission. Otherwise, it's possible for someone to access your Mac and browse its hard disk from across the room, and you would never know it.

To configure how Bluetooth works on your Mac, follow these steps:

1. **Choose ⬢⇨System Preferences to open the System Preferences window and then click the Sharing icon to open the Sharing preferences pane.**

2. **Select the Bluetooth Sharing check box.**

A list of Bluetooth options appears, as shown in Figure 3-1.

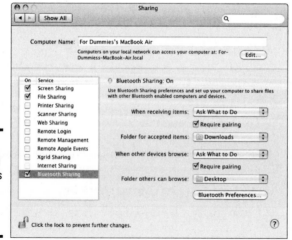

Figure 3-1:
The Sharing window lists options for Bluetooth sharing.

3. **Choose one of the following from the When Receiving Items pop-up menu:**

   - *Accept and Save:* Automatically saves any files sent to you through Bluetooth. (Not recommended because someone can send you a malicious program, such as a virus or Trojan Horse, which can wipe out your files when opened.)

   - *Accept and Open:* Automatically saves and opens any files sent to you through Bluetooth. (Not recommended because this — like the previous option — could automatically run a malicious program sent to your Mac through Bluetooth.)

   - *Ask What to Do:* Displays a dialog that gives you the option of accepting or rejecting a file sent to you through Bluetooth — probably your best choice.

   - *Never Allow:* Always blocks anyone from sending you files through Bluetooth.

4. **Select or deselect the Require Pairing check box.**

   If selected, this check box won't let anyone send files to you until you pair that other computer with your own. *Pairing* links another device specifically to your Mac, and is commonly used to link Bluetooth keyboards, mice, and the Apple Remote to a specific Mac. I explain that next.

5. **Choose either Documents or Other from the Folder for Accepted Items pop-up menu.**

   If you choose Other, an Open dialog appears, letting you click a folder where you want to store any files sent to you through Bluetooth.

6. **Choose one of the following from the When Other Devices Browse pop-up menu:**

   - *Always Allow:* Automatically gives another Bluetooth device full access to the contents of your Mac. (Not recommended — this allows others to mess up your files accidentally or deliberately.)

   - *Ask What to Do:* Displays a dialog that gives you the option of accepting or rejecting another device trying to access your Mac through Bluetooth.

   - *Never Allow:* Always blocks anyone from browsing through your Mac using Bluetooth.

7. **Select or deselect the Require Pairing check box.**

   Generally, you want pairing because pairing lets you selectively choose which devices can access your Mac through Bluetooth.

8. **Choose either Public or Other from the Folder Others Can Browse pop-up menu.**

If you choose Other, an Open dialog appears, letting you select a folder that you can share.

Choosing Desktop as the folder you want to share can make it easier to keep track of files you want to send (or those you receive) if you plan to share files this way only occasionally, on an as-needed basis.

9. **Click the Close button of the System Preferences window.**

Pairing a Device

Pairing allows you to predetermine which Bluetooth-enabled devices can connect to your Mac. By pairing, you can keep strangers from trying to access your Mac without your knowledge. For additional security, you can also require that paired devices use a password (also called a *passkey*) that further verifies that a specific device is allowed to connect to your Mac.

Pairing with your Mac

To pair a device with your Mac, follow these steps:

1. **Choose ⌘⇨System Preferences to open the System Preferences window and then click the Bluetooth icon.**

The Bluetooth preferences pane appears, as shown in Figure 3-2.

2. **Click the Set Up New Device button.**

The Bluetooth Setup Assistant window appears and immediately begins searching for Bluetooth devices.

Figure 3-2:
Bluetooth preferences let you pair a device with your Mac.

3. **While your Mac finds devices, such as mobile phones, headsets, or other computers, they appear in a list, as shown in Figure 3-3.**

4. **Select the device you want to pair with your Mac.**

5. **Click Continue.**

   Another Bluetooth Setup Assistant pane appears, displaying a passkey you can use to link with the other Bluetooth device, as shown in Figure 3-4.

Figure 3-3: The Bluetooth Setup Assistant searches for nearby Bluetooth-enabled devices automatically.

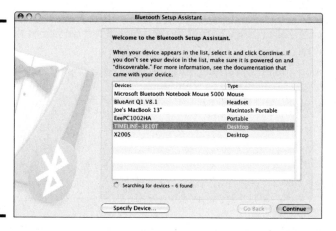

Figure 3-4: The Bluetooth dialog shows a passkey for linking another device to your Mac.

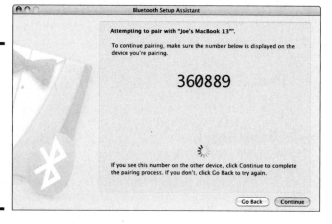

6. **Type the passkey on the other device that you want to pair with your Mac.**

   The Bluetooth Setup Assistant window informs you that the pairing has succeeded.

7. **Click Quit.**

Removing a paired device from your Mac

After you pair a device with your Mac, you might want to remove it later. To remove a paired device from your Mac, follow these steps:

1. **Choose ⛓⟹System Preferences to open the System Preferences window and then click the Bluetooth icon.**

   A Bluetooth preferences pane appears, as shown in Figure 3-5, listing all devices paired with your Mac.

2. **Click to select the device you want to unlink from your Mac and then click the minus sign button in the bottom-left corner of the Bluetooth window.**

   A dialog appears, warning you that if you disconnect this device, it will no longer be available to your Mac.

3. **Click Remove.**

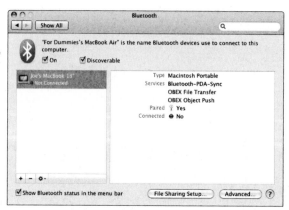

Figure 3-5:
The Bluetooth preferences pane shows you all paired devices on a Mac.

Sharing through Bluetooth

Because Bluetooth lets you create a simple, short-range network between Macs, you can use a Bluetooth network to share files or even an Internet connection with others. Such a simple network isn't meant to share massive numbers of files or an Internet connection for a long-term basis, but it is handy for quick file copying, browsing a Web page, or sending a photo or song to a mobile phone or iPod.

The speed of ordinary networks connected through Ethernet cables is 10, 100, or 1,000 megabits per second (Mbps), whereas the maximum speed of a Bluetooth network is only 1 Mbps.

Sharing files

When you want to copy a file from your Mac to another device, such as another Mac or a mobile phone, you can set up a Bluetooth connection. Sharing files through Bluetooth allows you to transfer files to another device without the hassle of using connecting cables or mutually compatible removable storage devices like portable hard drives or USB flash drives.

To share files through Bluetooth, follow these steps:

1. **Click the Finder icon in the Dock or click the white space of the Desktop.**

2. **Choose Go⇨Utilities in the Finder window that appears.**

The contents of the Utilities folder appear.

3. **Double-click the Bluetooth File Exchange icon.**

A Select File to Send window appears, as shown in Figure 3-6.

Figure 3-6: The Select File to Send window lets you choose a file to send over a Bluetooth connection.

4. **Select a file.**

To select multiple files, hold down the ⌘ key and click each file you want to send.

5. **Click Send.**

A Send File window appears, listing all Bluetooth-enabled devices near your Mac, as shown in Figure 3-7.

Figure 3-7:
The Send
File window
lets you
choose a
Bluetooth-
enabled
device to
receive your
file.

6. **Select a Bluetooth-enabled device and click Send.**

   If you choose another Mac or mobile phone to receive your files, a
   dialog might appear on the receiving device, asking the user to accept or
   decline the file transfer, as shown in Figure 3-8.

If the receiving device has been configured to Accept and Save or Accept
and Open (transferred files), you won't see the dialog in Figure 3-8. The
dialog in Figure 3-8 appears only if the user has selected Ask What to Do (the
default option) when configuring their Bluetooth settings.

Figure 3-8:
The
receiving
device can
accept or
decline a
file transfer.

Sharing an Internet connection

Sharing a Bluetooth Internet connection is great for letting someone do
simple things like browse Web sites or retrieve e-mail using your Mac's
Internet connection, but you can't use Bluetooth for video conferencing or
hosting a Web site because of slower Bluetooth data transfer speeds.

To share an Internet connection, follow these steps:

1. **Choose ⬧System Preferences to open the System Preferences window and then click the Sharing icon to open the Sharing pane.**

2. **Select the Bluetooth Sharing check box.**

   A list of options for configuring Bluetooth sharing appears (refer to Figure 3-1).

3. **Click the Bluetooth Preferences button.**

   A Bluetooth window appears (refer to Figure 3-2).

4. **Click the Advanced button.**

   A dialog appears, as shown in Figure 3-9.

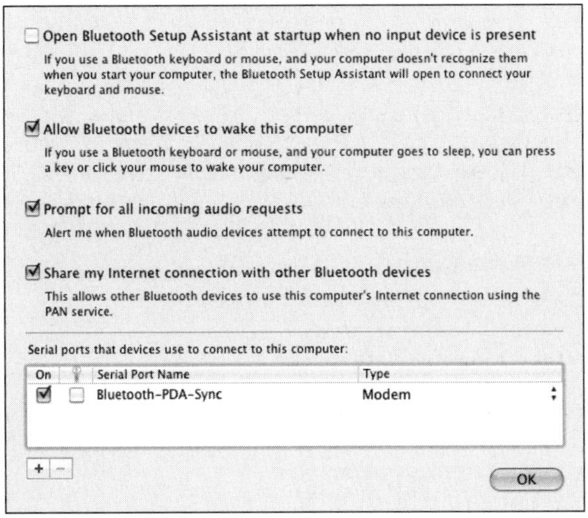

☐ Open Bluetooth Setup Assistant at startup when no input device is present
If you use a Bluetooth keyboard or mouse, and your computer doesn't recognize them when you start your computer, the Bluetooth Setup Assistant will open to connect your keyboard and mouse.

☑ Allow Bluetooth devices to wake this computer
If you use a Bluetooth keyboard or mouse, and your computer goes to sleep, you can press a key or click your mouse to wake your computer.

☑ Prompt for all incoming audio requests
Alert me when Bluetooth audio devices attempt to connect to this computer.

☑ Share my Internet connection with other Bluetooth devices
This allows other Bluetooth devices to use this computer's Internet connection using the PAN service.

Serial ports that devices use to connect to this computer:

On	▼	Serial Port Name	Type	
☑	☐	Bluetooth-PDA-Sync	Modem	⇕

[+] [−]   (OK)

Figure 3-9: Advanced options for sharing Bluetooth connections.

5. **Select the Share My Internet Connection with Other Bluetooth Devices check box.**

6. **Click OK.**

   At this point, follow the steps in the earlier "Pairing with your Mac" section to use the Bluetooth Assistant to link your Mac to a Bluetooth-enabled device. After you finish linking another device to your Mac, you'll be able to share your Internet connection. Pairing keeps other computers from trying to access the Internet through your Mac.

Appendix: Brushing Up on Painting and Drawing

In This Chapter

✔ Understanding painting versus drawing

✔ Working with common raster-editing features

✔ Using vector-editing features

✔ Choosing a painting and drawing program

✔ Understanding graphic file formats

*T*he Mac is best known for its graphics capabilities. Although many companies, such as Adobe, sell virtually identical graphics programs for both Mac and Windows computers, the majority of professional artists and graphic designers use the Mac.

One common way to play with graphics is to modify an existing image. Many people capture pictures with a digital camera and then touch up those pictures in a graphics-editing program.

Another way to use graphics is to create an image from scratch. Creating graphics from scratch isn't necessarily difficult, but it can be time-consuming. As a result, creating graphics is the realm of most professionals, whereas editing graphics is common to both amateurs and professionals.

Understanding Painting versus Drawing

Two types of graphics programs are painting and drawing programs. The main difference between the two is the way the programs create, edit, and display pictures.

A painting program draws pictures using individual dots called *pixels*. A single picture can consist of millions of individual pixels. By changing the color of these pixels, you can change the appearance of an image.

Pictures made of pixels are called *raster images*. When you take a picture with a digital camera, your camera stores that picture as a raster image.

If you capture a picture using a scanner, your scanner saves that picture as a raster image, too. The most popular raster-editing program is Adobe Photoshop.

The biggest disadvantage of raster images is that you can't resize them. The more you enlarge a raster image, the grainier and chunkier it gets, as shown in Figure A-1.

Figure A-1: Enlarged raster images appear chunky and grainy.

The alternative to a painting program is a drawing program. Drawing programs store pictures as *vector graphics*. Whereas a raster image physically draws an image on the screen, vector graphics store images as mathematical equations that define how to display an image on the screen.

A vector graphics picture consists of multiple items called *primitives*, such as points, lines, curves, and shapes. A mathematical equation tells the computer where to place the items and each item's width, length, height, and color. As a result, vector graphics generally don't display the subtle details that a raster image does, but vector graphics can be resized without losing resolution, as shown in Figure A-2.

Vector graphics typically consist of separate items that you can modify and manipulate individually. This gives vector graphics more of a cartoon look than a realistic image. Because the resolution of vector graphics remains sharp, no matter how large you make the picture or what resolution you use to display the image, vector graphics are used in many Web page advertisements and animated movies. One popular vector graphics program is Adobe Flash.

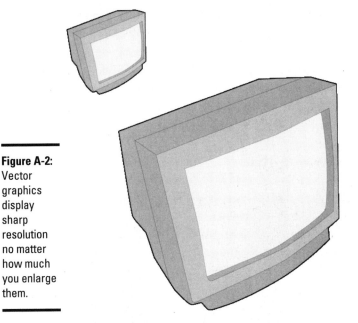

Figure A-2:
Vector
graphics
display
sharp
resolution
no matter
how much
you enlarge
them.

Many companies sell libraries of clip art images that you can use to spice up a document or desktop publishing file. Sometimes these clip art images are vector images, which let you resize them without degrading their appearance, but sometimes these clip art images are raster images, and resizing them can make them look grainy.

Common Raster-Editing Features

Editing involves a two-step process. First, you must select the item you want to modify. Second, you have to choose a command to modify your selected item.

In most programs, such as a word processor or a spreadsheet, you can easily select text by dragging the mouse. In a graphics program, selecting parts of a picture can be much harder because, in contrast to text, there isn't always a clear boundary of what to choose. When looking at a digital photograph of a man, how can you tell the computer to select just the man's face but not his mustache or hat? Computers see every raster image as just as series of colored pixels, so selecting which pixels you want to manipulate can be tricky.

To help you select all or part of an image, raster-editing programs offer tools that usually appear as icons in a group known as a *toolbox*, as shown in

Figure A-3. After selecting a tool, you can use the mouse to select and manipulate a picture in different ways.

Hand tool

Rectangular Selection tool | Rectangle Shape tool

Figure A-3:
Raster-
editing
programs
offer a
toolbox of
icons that
represent
different
ways to
manipulate
a picture.

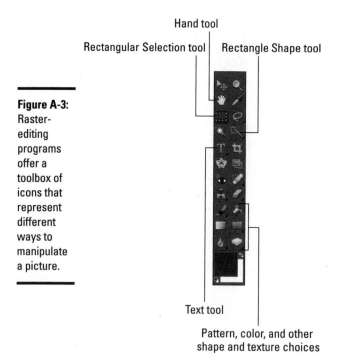

Text tool

Pattern, color, and other
shape and texture choices

In the following list, I briefly describe the tools called out in Figure A-3:

✦ **Hand tool:** Click and drag on your document to move it around on the screen.

✦ **Rectangular Selection tool:** Use this for clicking and dragging a rectangle marquee around a section you want to copy or cut.

✦ **Rectangle (or box) Shape tool:** Click to select and then drag on document and let go to draw a square. The tiny triangle in the lower-right corner indicates more options, such as line thickness and whether your box is see-through or filled with a pattern.

✦ **Paintbrush tool:** Use this for freehand painting with brush strokes.

✦ **Text tool:** Use this tool to add text to your document

✦ **Pattern, color and other shape and texture choices:** These tools enable you to create objects and to fill in objects you draw.

The toolbox shown in Figure A-3 comes from Photoshop Elements; other graphics programs likely display tool icons in different positions.

Selecting an entire picture

The simplest way to select a raster image is to select an entire image by pressing ⌘+A. (In some programs, you can also choose this command by choosing Edit➪Select All or just Select➪All.)

After you select an entire picture, you can modify that entire picture by rotating it, making it lighter or darker, increasing/decreasing its contrast, and converting a color picture to black and white.

Many raster-editing programs also offer a Select Invert command. When you want to select a large area of a picture except for a small region in the middle, it's actually easier to select the small region in the middle first. Then use the Select Invert command to select the opposite region, the large region that you actually want.

Selecting an area

Instead of selecting a whole picture, you can also select part of a picture. You can't select part of a picture until you choose a selection tool, which typically appears in a toolbox (refer to Figure A-3).

One of the simplest ways to select part of a picture is to select a rectangular or elliptical area. To select a rectangular or circular part of a picture, follow these steps:

1. **Click the rectangular or elliptical selection tool in the toolbox and move the pointer over the part of the picture you want to select.**

2. **Hold down the mouse button and drag the mouse.**

The selection tool draws a dotted line, called a *marquee,* around your selected item, as shown in Figure A-4.

Figure A-4: Dragging the mouse draws a marquee around your selection.

Variations of the Lasso tool

Although the Lasso tool can select irregular shapes, it can also be clumsy to use because it requires a steady hand to drag the mouse exactly where you want to select part of a picture. To compensate for this, some programs offer two varieties of the Lasso tool called the Polygonal Lasso tool and the Magnetic Lasso tool.

The Polygonal Lasso tool lets you point and click to draw straight lines. By letting you click the mouse around an area, the Polygonal Lasso tool makes it easy to select an irregularly shaped part of a picture.

The Magnetic Lasso tool lets you drag the mouse around an area, but it's smart enough to detect contrast differences between different parts of a picture. So rather than force you to drag the mouse exactly around a selected area in a picture, the Magnetic Lasso tool lets you drag the mouse approximately near an area you want to select, and the Magnetic Lasso tool automatically selects the boundary of an area.

Selecting an irregular shape

The problem with the rectangular and elliptical selection tools is that the part that you want to edit will almost never be perfectly rectangular or elliptical. Because images in a picture are often irregularly shaped (think of the shape of a puppy's face in a digital photograph), most raster-editing programs offer a special tool called a Lasso tool.

The Lasso tool lets you drag the mouse and draw the boundaries of the area you want to select, as shown in Figure A-5.

Figure A-5:
The Lasso tool can select an irregular shape.

Selecting with the Magic Wand tool

Dragging the mouse to select an area might still be difficult, especially if the item you want to select consists of multiple irregular shapes, such as a tree branch. In cases like this, it might be easier to select the color of a picture by using the Magic Wand tool.

The Magic Wand tool selects adjacent pixels based on color. Therefore, if you want to select the blue sky behind a tree, you can click the Magic Wand tool and then click the blue sky. The Magic Wand tool selects the blue pixels that you click, along with any adjacent blue pixels. By adjusting the sensitivity of the Magic Wand tool, you can make it select more or fewer pixels. Additionally, if you select the Magic Wand tool and then click the black portion of a picture, you select all adjacent black areas, as shown in Figure A-6.

Figure A-6:
The Magic Wand can select areas that contain similar colors.

Erasing pixels

One common way to modify a picture is to erase part of it, which you can do by using the Eraser tool. When you choose the Eraser tool, you can drag the mouse over a picture and wipe out the pixels underneath, as shown in Figure A-7.

Figure A-7:
The Eraser tool wipes out anything that you drag the mouse over.

By changing the shape and size of the Eraser tool, you can trim away parts of a picture without erasing the parts that you want to keep. For added flexibility, many raster-editing programs offer a Magic Eraser tool. Like the Magic Wand tool, which selects an area based on similar colors, the Magic Eraser tool erases adjacent pixels that contain similar colors.

Using the Paint Brush and Paint Bucket tools

Rather than erase part of your picture, you might want to color pixels. By changing the color of pixels, you can change the appearance of an image, such as creating a third eye on someone's forehead or coloring in a tear in a scanned photograph to make the tear disappear.

To color pixels, raster-editing programs offer a Paint Brush and Paint Bucket tool. The Paint Brush tool lets you use the pointer as a brush by clicking and dragging the mouse

If you need to paint a large area, dragging the mouse with the Paint Brush tool can get tedious, so raster-editing programs offer a Paint Bucket tool, which colors in any enclosed area. To use the Paint Bucket tool, just click it in the toolbox and then click the color that you want to use. Next, click the part of your picture that you want to color and your chosen color floods that part of your picture as if you spilled a bucket of paint over it.

As an alternative to clicking a color, many raster-editing programs offer a special Eyedropper tool. The purpose of the Eyedropper tool is to let you choose an existing color in your picture. After you click a color in your picture, the Paint Brush or Paint Bucket tool can use that color in another area.

Common Vector-Editing Features

Unlike raster-editing programs that modify individual pixels, vector graphics–editing programs modify objects. To create a picture, a vector graphics program gives you various tools for drawing different types of objects, called *primitives*. Some common primitive objects are lines, curves, and points.

After you create a picture using primitive objects, you can modify those primitives using a variety of tools that scale (enlarge or shrink) or reshape those primitives.

Moving and resizing objects with the Selection tool

Vector graphics consist of multiple objects. When you use the Selection tool, you can move or resize one or more objects by selecting them with a Selection tool and then dragging them with the mouse. To use the Selection tool, follow these steps:

1. **Click the Selection tool, which usually appears as a dark arrow in the toolbox.**
2. **Click an object you want to modify, such as a line.**

   Handles appear around your object, as shown in Figure A-8, which displays the EazyDraw program.
3. **(Optional) To move your selected object, move the pointer to your selected object, hold the mouse button, and drag the mouse.**

   Release the mouse button when you're happy with the new location of your object.
4. **(Optional) To resize your selected object, move the pointer to a handle, hold down the mouse button, and drag the mouse.**

   Release the mouse button when you're happy with the new size of your object.

After selecting an object with the Selection tool, you can press Delete if you want to remove that selected object.

Reshaping an object with the Direct Selection tool

Rather than move or change the size of an object, you might want to modify the shape of an object, which you can change by using the Direct Selection tool. This tool often appears as a white arrow pointer directly underneath the Selection tool icon in the toolbox.

Handles

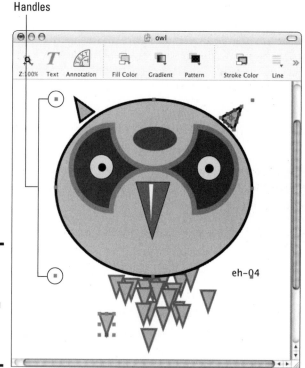

Figure A-8:
The
Selection
tool lets you
choose an
object to
modify.

When you click an object with the Direct Selection tool, that object displays anchor points and direction points. *Anchor points* appear as squares directly on an object. By dragging an anchor point, you can reshape an object. *Direction points* appear as lines with a circle or point on each end. By dragging a direction point, you can reshape the curve of an object. Figure A-9 shows an image displayed in the Intaglio drawing program.

Vector graphics programs sometimes use different terms to describe identical items. For example, Adobe Illustrator has a Direct Selection tool; however, another program might call the same tool a Point Selection tool. Just remember that the names might be different, but the functions remain the same.

To use the Direct Selection tool, follow these steps:

1. **Click the Direct Selection tool, which usually appears as a white arrow in the toolbox.**

Anchor points

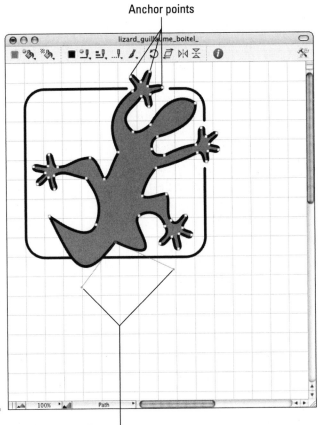

Figure A-9:
The Direct
Selection
tool lets you
reshape an
object.

Direction points

2. **Click an object you want to modify, such as a line.**

   Anchor points and direction points appear on your chosen object.

3. **(Optional) To reshape your chosen object, move the pointer to an anchor point, hold down the mouse button, and drag the mouse.**

   Release the mouse button when you're done.

4. **(Optional) To change the curve of an object, move the pointer to a direction point, hold down the mouse button, and drag the mouse.**

   Release the mouse button when you're done.

Drawing lines

To create lines, vector graphics programs typically offer a Pencil tool, a Line tool, a Pen tool, and different Shape tools, as shown in Figure A-10.

Pen Pencil

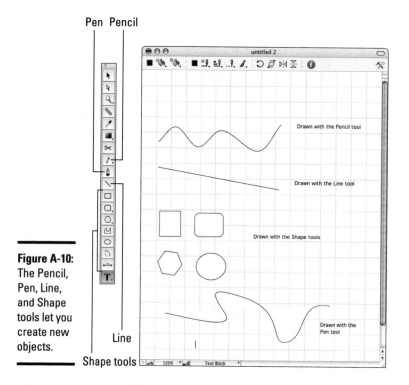

Figure A-10:
The Pencil, Pen, Line, and Shape tools let you create new objects.

Line

Shape tools

The Pencil tool lets you draw a line by dragging the mouse. Doing so creates lines of any shape along any path you select.

The Line tool lets you draw straight lines by dragging the mouse. After you draw a straight line, you can always reshape it, but if you need a perfectly straight line, the Line tool will meet your needs.

The Shape tools (Rectangle, Rounded Rectangle, Polygon, and Oval) let you draw specific shapes, which you also can reshape.

The Pen tool lets you draw a line by clicking define points. Each time you click another point, the drawing program draws a connecting straight line. To curve a line, you can drag the direction points that appear. Some drawing programs might also let you drag the Pen tool to create curved lines.

Choosing a Painting and Drawing Program

If you're a professional or aspiring graphic designer, your only real choices are Adobe Photoshop, Adobe Illustrator, and Adobe Flash (`www.adobe.com`). The graphic design industry heavily uses all three programs.

Although these programs are mandatory for graphic design professionals, most other people will likely find Photoshop, Illustrator, and Flash too expensive and complicated to use. As an alternative to these three professional-quality programs, you can find plenty of low-cost (or even free) programs that offer most of the features of these programs.

Photoshop alternatives

Perhaps the best alternative to Photoshop is a similar, less expensive program dubbed Photoshop Elements, which is also sold by Adobe. Adobe markets Photoshop to professionals and Photoshop Elements to digital photography hobbyists who want to touch up their digital photographs quickly and easily.

If you like the idea of an easy-to-use digital photography editor, consider these programs geared for beginners: PhotoStudio 6 (`www.arcsoft.com`), Color It! (`www.microfrontier.com`), GraphicsConverter (`www.lemkesoft.com`), and Pixelmator (`www.pixelmator.com`).

Specialized digital photography editors and organizers

Programs such as Photoshop can help you edit and modify digital photographs, but they do nothing to help you organize your digital photographs. If you work exclusively with digital photographs, you might want to skip Photoshop and consider Adobe Photoshop Lightroom 2 (`www.adobe.com`) or Apple Aperture 2 (`www.apple.com`), programs especially designed for professional photographers.

Lightroom 2 and Aperture 2 organize, sort, edit, and store your digital photographs. Both programs also offer nondestructive editing, which means your original digital image is never changed. This means that you can always return to your original image without having to make a separate copy of that image.

After you make changes to a digital photograph, you can organize and sort the photo in a library so that you can find it again. You can also create a slideshow of your favorite images or print your pictures in different ways (such as one big picture on a page or several smaller pictures on a page).

Think of Lightroom 2 and Aperture 2 as advanced versions of the iPhoto program. If you need only to organize your digital images occasionally, iPhoto should be sufficient. But if you're constantly storing, editing, and organizing digital images, consider Lightroom 2 or Aperture 2.

Although it's not much cheaper or easier to use than Photoshop, another alternative raster editor is Corel Painter 11 (www.corel.com). Whereas Photoshop specializes in editing digital photographs, Corel Painter specializes in mimicking the use of ordinary artist tools, such as drawing with charcoal or creating oil paintings on different types of paper and canvases where your ink or oil paints can drip and soak into the surface just like the real thing. If you're an aspiring artist and want a program specifically designed to mimic the handheld tools you're already familiar with, Corel Painter might actually be a better choice for you than Photoshop.

Before you buy any raster editor, grab a free copy of Paintbrush (http://paintbrush.sourceforge.net). If you have children, grab a free copy of TuxPaint (www.tuxpaint.org), a simple painting program designed to help kids learn the basics of painting with a computer.

Illustrator alternatives

Although designed mostly for editing raster images, Adobe Photoshop also includes some vector drawing capabilities. If you need to create vector drawings every now and then, you can use Photoshop and never bother with a separate vector graphics program at all. However, you might prefer using a simpler vector drawing program.

For a free vector graphics program, use the Draw program included in OpenOffice (www.openoffice.org) and NeoOffice (www.neooffice.org). If you need to draw diagrams, organizational charts, or flow charts, consider OmniGraffle (www.omnigroup.com).

In case you need a drawing program for creating technical illustrations, you could use any drawing program, but you might be better off using Canvas 11 (www.deneba.com). In addition to letting you create technical drawings, Canvas 11 also offers options for scientific imaging and geographical information systems (GIS), which can be handy if you need to draw molecular structures or create maps.

If you just want a simpler, less expensive version of Adobe Illustrator, consider Intaglio (www.purgatorydesign.com). Instead of attempting to offer as many features as possible, as Illustrator does, Intaglio offers the basic features that most people need 90 percent of the time. As a result, Intaglio lets you focus more on your work and less on trying to find the features you need.

Another low-cost drawing program for novices is Lineform (www.freeverse.com). One unique feature of Lineform is that of artistic strokes, which combines the visual appearance of brush strokes found in painting programs with the ability to edit and manipulate them as separate objects, as in a drawing program.

A third low-cost drawing program is EazyDraw (www.eazydraw.com). Although geared for beginners, EazyDraw actually offers some advanced features for mechanical drawings, printed circuit layouts, and electronic schematics.

If you want to create simple animated drawings, get iDraw (www.macpower user.com), which can save your drawings as animated GIF, Flash, or QuickTime movies. Despite its animation capabilities, iDraw offers a simplified user interface that won't overwhelm you with options.

Flash alternatives

Flash actually consists of two separate programs. First, there's the Flash development program, which lets you design and create Flash animation. Second, there's the free Flash player, which lets Safari or your preferred Web browser display Flash movies and animation. If you need to create Flash animation for different purposes, you can buy the Flash development program (www.adobe.com).

If you want to create cartoons in Flash but don't want to buy the Flash development program, alternatives are Toon Boom Studio (www.toonboom.com), and Anime Studio Debut 6 and Anime Studio Pro (www.e-frontier.com). Although all three programs use the Flash file format, they provide tools to help you create and animate cartoons much faster than the Flash development program.

All three programs specialize in helping you draw characters, animate them, and even synchronize audio with the movements of their mouths so that the characters appear to speak naturally. If you're just getting started with Flash animation, you might want to buy the less costly Anime Studio Debut 6. When you get familiar with creating Flash animation, you can move up to the costlier but more powerful Anime Studio Pro.

Graphic File Formats

Because Adobe Photoshop, Illustrator, and Flash lead the market in raster editing, vector graphics, and vector graphics animation, the three most important file formats are Photoshop's PSD format, Illustrator's AI format, and Flash's SWF format. Although these file formats are the most popular, most painting and drawing programs can use other file formats as well.

You can easily save a vector graphics file as a raster file, but then you lose the ability to manipulate the objects of that picture. If you save a raster picture as a vector graphics picture, you won't be able to modify its parts as though it were a true vector graphics picture. (Adobe Illustrator offers a raster-to-vector graphics conversion feature, but most drawing programs don't.) If you need to manipulate individual parts of a picture, create and save your picture as a vector graphics file. If you need to manipulate individual pixels, create and save your picture as a raster file.

Raster (painting) formats

In addition to Photoshop PSD files, another popular raster file format is TIFF (Tagged Image File Format). TIFF was designed as a universal graphics file format, so most graphics programs can save and open TIFF files.

TIFF files are, like Photoshop PSD files, often large, which makes them impractical for use on Web pages. To display graphics on a Web page, Web designers use three file formats that compress images yet retain much of the visual quality. The most popular of these raster compressed file formats is JPEG (Joint Photographic Experts Group), which is also used by many digital cameras.

JPEG files are great for storing photographic-quality images, but if you just need simple graphics, such as company logos or cartoons, then you'll find that the GIF (Graphics Interchange Format) file format is more popular. Because the GIF format was patented at one time, a free alternative appeared known as PNG (Portable Network Graphics).

PNG files offer better compression than GIF files and unlike JPEG files, PNG files can shrink files in size without tossing out data, thus preserving image quality.

One file format used exclusively with digital cameras is RAW, which stores images in a format that must be converted before you can edit or print. The advantage of the RAW format is its ability to store more data about an image, which can give you higher-quality digital photographs. Two big drawbacks with the RAW format is that these files tend to be much larger than equivalent JPEG files, and every digital camera manufacturer creates its own RAW format that is incompatible with RAW formats created by other digital cameras. If you can't convert your RAW formats into a universal file format, such as JPEG, you could trap your images in a particular RAW format forever.

Vector graphics (drawing) formats

Adobe Illustrator AI files are the most popular vector graphics formats, so many drawing programs can open and save AI files and save files in an open standard called SVG (Scalable Vector Graphics).

Another popular open standard format for vector graphics is EPS (Encapsulated PostScript). Much like SVG files, EPS files are often used as an intermediary file format to transfer files from one drawing program to another.

Although not an open standard, many vector graphics programs can also store pictures as PDF (Portable Document Format) files. PDF files are used to display the exact formatting and appearance of a picture so that others can view and print it on their own computers. To read PDF files, you can use the Preview program that comes with every Mac, or you can download a free copy of the Adobe Acrobat Reader.

If you run across a graphics file format that you can't open, try to convert it by using GraphicConverter (www.lemkesoft.com) or DeBabelizer Pro (www.equilibrium.com).

Index

E

N

U

viewing
  contacts in Address Book, 659–660
  folders, 97–104
  iCal events, 676–677
  iCal To-Do Lists, 686–687
  images, 451–453, 464–466
  Keynote presentations, 600–601, 618–621
virtual hard drive, 704
virtual machines, 703–704
VirtualBox program, 703, 704
virtualization, 703
viruses, 82
vision limitations, accessibility for,
    147–148
visual effects, adding to images, 471–472
VLC Media Player, 238, 239, 240
Voice icon, GarageBand, 531
voice recognition, 153–159
VoiceOver feature, Seeing tab, 147
volume, 134, 241
VRAM (Video RAM), 15

W

Wacky Mini Golf game, 316
Wake for Network Access, Energy Saver
    pane, 721–722
war driving, 713
Watch Me Do action, 216–218
WAV (Waveform audio format), 238
Weather widget, Dashboard, 31, 164, 169
Web. *See* Internet; Web page; Web site
Web archive, 352
Web Clips
  creating, 349–350
  searching for text on Web page, 350–351
Web page. *See also* iWeb program; web site
  adding to Web sites, 552
  capturing digital photos from, 271–272
  deleting from Web sites, 552
  deleting objects from, 557
  graphics, 548–549, 553–554, 560–561
  moving objects, 555
  overview, 547–548

printing, 353
publishing, 561–566
rearranging objects, 555–557
resizing objects, 555
saving as file, 352–353
sending by e-mail, 353–354
text, formatting, 558–559
text, hyperlinks, creating, 559–560
text, overview, 548
text, replacing placeholder, 552–553
text, text boxes, creating, 558
themes, 554–555
Web site. *See also* iWeb program; Web page
  adding Web pages, 552
  deleting Web pages, 552
  hosts, 561–564
  overview, 549–550
  themes, 550–551
Webcam, 269
Website Restrictions section, 433
WebStratego game, 313
WeCyclers group, 400
Weekday Time Limits category, Parental
    Controls preferences window, 435
Welcome to Mail dialog, Mail, 361
Welcome Web page, 551
When Other Devices Browse pop-up menu,
    Sharing preferences pane, 731
When Receiving Items pop-up menu,
    Sharing preferences pane, 731
widgets
  adding to Web pages, 560–561
  for Dashboard, 163–166
Wi-Fi. *See* wireless
window
  manipulating with Exposé, 47–49
  viewing data in, 40–47
window mode, in DVD Player, 280
Windows Media Audio (WMA), 239
Windows Media Player, 355
Windows Media Video, 276
Windows Mobile, synchronizing with, 202
Windows operating system, running on
    Macs. *See also* Boot Camp program
  CrossOver Mac, 704–705
  virtual machines, 703–704

Business/Accounting & Bookkeeping

Bookkeeping For Dummies
978-0-7645-9848-7

eBay Business
All-in-One For Dummies,
2nd Edition
978-0-470-38536-4

Job Interviews
For Dummies,
3rd Edition
978-0-470-17748-8

Resumes For Dummies,
5th Edition
978-0-470-08037-5

Stock Investing
For Dummies,
3rd Edition
978-0-470-40114-9

Successful Time
Management
For Dummies
978-0-470-29034-7

Computer Hardware

BlackBerry For Dummies,
3rd Edition
978-0-470-45762-7

Computers For Seniors
For Dummies
978-0-470-24055-7

iPhone For Dummies,
2nd Edition
978-0-470-42342-4

Laptops For Dummies,
3rd Edition
978-0-470-27759-1

Macs For Dummies,
10th Edition
978-0-470-27817-8

Cooking & Entertaining

Cooking Basics
For Dummies,
3rd Edition
978-0-7645-7206-7

Wine For Dummies,
4th Edition
978-0-470-04579-4

Diet & Nutrition

Dieting For Dummies,
2nd Edition
978-0-7645-4149-0

Nutrition For Dummies,
4th Edition
978-0-471-79868-2

Weight Training
For Dummies,
3rd Edition
978-0-471-76845-6

Digital Photography

Digital Photography
For Dummies,
6th Edition
978-0-470-25074-7

Photoshop Elements 7
For Dummies
978-0-470-39700-8

Gardening

Gardening Basics
For Dummies
978-0-470-03749-2

Organic Gardening
For Dummies,
2nd Edition
978-0-470-43067-5

Green/Sustainable

Green Building
& Remodeling
For Dummies
978-0-470-17559-0

Green Cleaning
For Dummies
978-0-470-39106-8

Green IT For Dummies
978-0-470-38688-0

Health

Diabetes For Dummies,
3rd Edition
978-0-470-27086-8

Food Allergies
For Dummies
978-0-470-09584-3

Living Gluten-Free
For Dummies
978-0-471-77383-2

Hobbies/General

Chess For Dummies,
2nd Edition
978-0-7645-8404-6

Drawing For Dummies
978-0-7645-5476-6

Knitting For Dummies,
2nd Edition
978-0-470-28747-7

Organizing For Dummies
978-0-7645-5300-4

SuDoku For Dummies
978-0-470-01892-7

Home Improvement

Energy Efficient Homes
For Dummies
978-0-470-37602-7

Home Theater
For Dummies,
3rd Edition
978-0-470-41189-6

Living the Country Lifestyle
All-in-One For Dummies
978-0-470-43061-3

Solar Power Your Home
For Dummies
978-0-470-17569-9

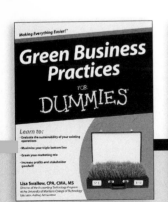

Internet
Blogging For Dummies,
2nd Edition
978-0-470-23017-6

eBay For Dummies,
6th Edition
978-0-470-49741-8

Facebook For Dummies
978-0-470-26273-3

Google Blogger
For Dummies
978-0-470-40742-4

Web Marketing
For Dummies,
2nd Edition
978-0-470-37181-7

WordPress For Dummies,
2nd Edition
978-0-470-40296-2

Language & Foreign Language
French For Dummies
978-0-7645-5193-2

Italian Phrases
For Dummies
978-0-7645-7203-6

Spanish For Dummies
978-0-7645-5194-9

Spanish For Dummies,
Audio Set
978-0-470-09585-0

Macintosh
Mac OS X Snow Leopard
For Dummies
978-0-470-43543-4

Math & Science
Algebra I For Dummies
978-0-7645-5325-7

Biology For Dummies
978-0-7645-5326-4

Calculus For Dummies
978-0-7645-2498-1

Chemistry For Dummies
978-0-7645-5430-8

Microsoft Office
Excel 2007 For Dummies
978-0-470-03737-9

Office 2007 All-in-One
Desk Reference
For Dummies
978-0-471-78279-7

Music
Guitar For Dummies,
2nd Edition
978-0-7645-9904-0

iPod & iTunes
For Dummies,
6th Edition
978-0-470-39062-7

Piano Exercises
For Dummies
978-0-470-38765-8

Parenting & Education
Parenting For Dummies,
2nd Edition
978-0-7645-5418-6

Type 1 Diabetes
For Dummies
978-0-470-17811-9

Pets
Cats For Dummies,
2nd Edition
978-0-7645-5275-5

Dog Training For Dummies,
2nd Edition
978-0-7645-8418-3

Puppies For Dummies,
2nd Edition
978-0-470-03717-1

Religion & Inspiration
The Bible For Dummies
978-0-7645-5296-0

Catholicism For Dummies
978-0-7645-5391-2

Women in the Bible
For Dummies
978-0-7645-8475-6

Self-Help & Relationship
Anger Management
For Dummies
978-0-470-03715-7

Overcoming Anxiety
For Dummies
978-0-7645-5447-6

Sports
Baseball For Dummies,
3rd Edition
978-0-7645-7537-2

Basketball For Dummies,
2nd Edition
978-0-7645-5248-9

Golf For Dummies,
3rd Edition
978-0-471-76871-5

Web Development
Web Design All-in-One
For Dummies
978-0-470-41796-6

Windows Vista
Windows Vista
For Dummies
978-0-471-75421-3

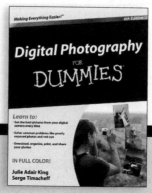

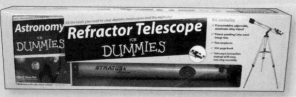
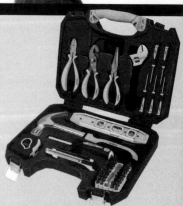